Lone Star Regiments in Gray

Ralph A. Wooster

EAKIN PRESS Austin, Texas

Cover illustration: "Charge of 9th Texas Cavalry at Pea Ridge" by Gary Zaboly

Maps by George Farrar

FIRST EDITION

Published in the United States of America
By Eakin Press
A Division of Sunbelt Media, Inc.
P.O. Drawer 90159 Austin, Texas 78709-0159
email: sales@eakinpress.com
website: www.eakinpress.com

1 2 3 4 5 6 7 8 9

1-57168-546-4

Library of Congress Cataloging-in-Publication Data

Wooster, Ralph A.
Lone Star regiments in gray / by Ralph A. Wooster. — 1st ed.
p. cm.
Includes bibliographical references and index.
ISBN 1-57168-546-4
1. Texas–History–Civil War, 1861-1865–Regimental histories. 2. United States–History–Civil War, 1861-1865–Regimental histories. I. Title
E580.4.T4 W66 2002
973.7'464–dc21 2001006256

Contents

Maps

Preface

As a student and teacher I have studied for fifty years the role that Texans played in the American Civil War. While it is perhaps understandable that today we might question both the necessity for war and the support for a socio-economic system that rested upon the institution of slavery, we cannot help but admire the courage and conviction that led thousands of Texans to leave their homes and families to fight for a cause in which they deeply believed.

In an effort to recount the contributions made by Texans in the struggle for southern independence, several years ago I wrote *Texas and Texans in the Civil War* (Eakin Press, 1995) in which I attempted to provide a synthesis of modern scholarship on the subject. Five years later I completed a study of Texas military leadership in the war entitled *Lone Star Generals in Gray* (Eakin Press, 2000). As I finished these works it appeared to me that a brief history of each of the military units from Texas in the Confederate army would be helpful in understanding the contributions Texans made in the war.

As Civil War students are well aware, the regiment, consisting theoretically of ten companies of one hundred men each, was the basic military unit around which Civil War armies were organized. Usually made up of individuals recruited in the same region of the state and commanded (in the early stages of the war, at least) by an individual elected by the men, it was the regiment with which most Civil War soldiers identified.

In the pages that follow I describe the organization, leadership, and combat experiences of each of the seventy-eight regiments from Texas that served in the Confederate army. As most artillery units were not organized in regiments but were attached to various infantry regiments and brigades I have also included a brief history of the thirty-five Confederate artillery batteries from Texas.

Many of the Texas regiments served in the same brigade or division for much of the war. I have grouped these together under a common brigade or division heading. For purposes of clarity the regiments and brigades are also grouped geographically and by arm of service (infantry, cavalry, dismounted cavalry, or artillery). In Chapter One I provide the reader with an overview of Texas unit organization, including a table which lists all the Confederate regiments and batteries from Texas, the names of their first commanders, areas in which they served, and the number of the chapter in which they are discussed. The three Texas infantry regiments that served in Hood's Brigade in Virginia are described in Chapter Two. In the third chapter I discuss the six Texas mounted cavalry units that served in the Confederate Heartland, the vast region stretching from the Carolinas to the Mississippi River. In the fourth chapter I describe the Texas infantry and dismounted cavalry regiments that served in the same region.

The thirty-one Texas cavalry regiments that spent the war west of the Mississippi River are discussed in Chapter Five, the longest chapter in the book. In the sixth chapter I describe the eight Texas dismounted cavalry regiments and the sixteen Texas infantry regiments assigned to the Trans Mississippi. The last chapter provides a description of the one artillery regiment, four artillery battalions, and thirty-five artillery batteries from Texas in the Confederate army. Information concerning the postwar activities of 159 individuals mentioned in the text is located in the appendix.

It should be noted that this is a study of units from Texas that served in the Confederate army. I have made no attempt to describe the four cavalry regiments, five cavalry battalions, and five infantry regiments recruited for state service during the war, nor have I included the two regiments of Texas cavalry that served in the Union army during the Civil War.

As is always true, many individuals contributed to the completion of this work, both directly and indirectly. Thanks are given to the many historians who have written accounts of individual regiments or brigades or have described the role these units played in Civil War battles and campaigns. All of their names are found in the bibiliographical essay at the end of the book. Space precludes mentioning them all here, but I would particularly like to thank Alwyn Barr, Anne J. Bailey, Norman Brown, Tom Cutrer, Donald S. Frazier, Richard Lowe, Richard McCaslin, Michael Parrish, the late Harold B. Simpson, Charles D. Spurlin, Jerry Thompson, and Kevin Young, whose works have provided so many insights into the role played by Texans in the war.

Again I wish to thank Ron Ellison, religious historian in Beaumont, for his assistance on a number of matters. W. D. "Bill" Quick, an authority on Sabine Pass and Texas coastal waters, was once again most helpful, especially on questions relating to the Davis Guards, Likens' Cavalry Battalion, Spaight's Infantry Battalion, and the Daly-Ragsdale Cavalry Battalion. Joseph V. Patterson of Camas, Washington, provided a copy of his expanded version of the *History of Debray's 26th Regiment of Texas Cavalry*, which was most helpful. Kevin Ladd, director of the Wallisville Historical Park, contributed numerous pieces of information from his own collection and Internet sources as well as enthusiasm for the project. Dr. Kevin Smith, associate vice president for academic affairs at Lamar University, provided a copy of the diary of his great-grandfather, who served in Waul's Legion. Robert Madden, emeritus professor of art at Lamar, furnished a photograph and information concerning his great-grandfather, who was a member of the Seventeenth Texas Cavalry (dismounted). My thanks to all of these individuals for their support and interest in the project.

Special thanks are extended to Peggy Fox, director of the Simpson Confederate Research Center at Hill College, Hillsboro, Texas. Peggy once again provided most of the photographs included in the book. She was also most helpful in assisting my wife and me in the use of the regimental files in the Center.

I especially wish to acknowledge the valuable contributions by Gary Zaboly, the distinguished military artist who once again provided the beautiful art work for the dust jacket of the book. Another artist, my friend George Farrar of Beaumont, designed the maps that illustrate the campaigns in which many of the Texas regiments participated. My thanks to him for his excellent work. As in my previous works on Civil War Texas, Melissa Locke Roberts, editor at Eakin Press, did another outstanding job in editing the manuscript.

Friends and family members provided encouragement and advice at times when both were badly needed. Among these I particularly wish to thank Valerie Majors Domingue and Terry Rioux, two young historians who were good listeners; Karen Farrar, as always a good friend; and son Robert Wooster and daughter-in-law Catherine Cox. And as always, my wife Edna was willing to offer support when I most needed it; without her life would have little meaning.

I wish to dedicate the work to Ed Eakin, longtime friend of Texas history and Texas historians. As the publisher of hundreds of books on Texas history, Ed has befriended many aspiring authors (young, old, and in-between) and offered them the encouragement and support needed to continue their work. We are all grateful to him for making our work available to the reading public.

RALPH A. WOOSTER

Chapter One

"Texans always move them ..."

ONE OF THE MOST DRAMATIC moments in the Southern War for Independence came on May 6, 1864. The massive Union Army of the Potomac, now under the command of U. S. Grant, was attempting to force its way through the densely forested area in northern Virginia known as the Wilderness. Veteran Northern troops in Winfield Scott Hancock's Second Corps overwhelmed Confederates in A. P. Hill's Corps and threatened a breakthrough in the Rebel defense line. Confederate army commander Robert E. Lee was on the scene as he watched Virginians, Carolinians, and Mississippians of Cadmus Wilcox's and Henry Heth's divisions give way to the onrushing Federal attackers.

Just as the hour looked the darkest for the beleaguered Confederates, a brigade of James Longstreet's Corps arrived on the scene. General Lee, not recognizing brigade commander John Gregg, who had previously commanded troops in Confederate western armies, inquired, "General, what brigade is this?"

"The Texas Brigade," replied Gregg.

"I am glad to see it," said Lee. "When you go in there, I wish you to give those [Northern] men the cold steel. They will stand and fight all day, and never move unless you charge them." As he watched the advancing Federal troops, Lee added, "The Texas Brigade always has driven the enemy, and I want them to do it now. And tell them, General, that they will fight today under my eye—I will watch their conduct."

Gregg, a seasoned veteran of the western campaigns but a relative newcomer to the Texas Brigade, called to his men: "Attention, Texas Brigade. The eyes of General Lee are upon you. Forward, march!"

General Lee was usually a calm man not given to displays of emotion, but on this occasion he could not contain himself. He raised himself in his stirrups, took off his hat, and waved it high. "Texans always move them," he shouted.

The Texans nearest to Lee began to cheer. Lee's words were passed down the line and a yell went up from others in the brigade as they showed support for their beloved commander. "I would charge hell itself for the old man," cried one of the brigade's veterans.

With that yell the Texans began their advance against the Federal line. Still caught up in the enthusiasm of the moment, Lee spurred his horse, Traveller, on and rode with the Texans as they advanced. At first the Texans did not notice, but when it became apparent that he meant to lead the charge himself, some of the veterans cried out: "Go back, General Lee, go back!" Soon others were calling, "Lee to the rear! ... Lee to the rear!"

Lee apparently wanted to go on, but other Texans shouted that they would not continue the advance if Lee exposed himself to the deadly enemy fire. Several soldiers seized Traveller's reins and insisted their commander retire to a place of safety.[1]

After Lee was conducted to the rear, the Texas Brigade continued its move forward, driving the enemy back in what historian Harold B. Simpson called "its finest hour."[2]

This moment of high drama was only one such incident in which the Texas Brigade demonstrated its fighting spirit. At Eltham's Landing, Gaines' Mill, Second Manassas, Sharpsburg, Gettysburg, and Chickamauga the brigade was called upon to perform similar feats of heroic valor. It is little wonder that Robert E. Lee considered the Texans his shock troops to be called upon at the most critical times.

While the Texas Brigade of the Army of Northern Virginia was perhaps the most famous military unit from the Lone Star State in the Civil War, it was by no means the only one to distinguish itself on the field of battle. Texas regiments in brigades commanded by Matthew D. Ector and Hiram Granbury were vital components in the Confederacy's other major force, the Army of Tennessee, playing significant roles in the battles of Chickamauga, Kennesaw Mountain, Atlanta, Franklin, and Nashville. Two other Texas regiments, the Second Infantry and Waul's Legion, held vital positions in the Confederate line at Vicksburg and helped beat off Federal attacks in May 1863. The Texas infantry and dismounted regiments that made up John G. Walker's Texas Division performed with similar bravery and gallantry in the Louisiana and Arkansas campaigns of 1864.

Texas provided more cavalry regiments for Confederate service than any other state. Mounted troops from the Lone Star State quickly gained recognition for their bravery and courage. In this respect none were more famous than the Eighth Texas Cavalry, better known as Terry's Texas Rangers. Armed primarily with shotguns and Colt revolvers, the Rangers established a reputation for their bold charges against the enemy. Along with a sister Lone Star regiment, the Eleventh Texas Cavalry, the Rangers served with distinction in a cavalry brigade commanded by Texan John A. Wharton, and later Tom Harrison, in the Kentucky-Tennessee-Georgia heartland. Similarly, the Third, Sixth, Ninth, and Twenty-seventh Texas cavalry regiments which made up a brigade commanded first by John Whitfield and later Sul Ross were recognized for their skill and prowess under fire.

In all, Texas furnished fifty-three cavalry regiments, twenty-four infantry regiments, an artillery regiment, four artillery battalions, and thirty-five artillery batteries for Confederate service. Texas regiments fought in New Mexico, Pennsylvania, Maryland, and every state of the Confederacy (including Kentucky and Missouri) except Florida. They participated in every major battle and campaign of the war with the exception of First Manassas and Chancellorsville.[3]

Some of the Texas regiments and battalions were organized late in the war and saw little action. Others, like the Eighth and Eleventh Texas cavalries mentioned above, were formed early in the conflict and continued to fight until the final surrender of the Confederate army.

In many instances Texas military regiments were grouped together in brigades, such as Hood's Texas Brigade in the Army of Northern Virginia, Granbury's and Ector's Brigades in the Army of Tennessee, and Polignac's Brigade in Richard Taylor's Louisiana army. In one instance, Walker's Texas Division, brigades consisting of Texas regiments made up an entire division. Often Texas regiments remained with the same brigade throughout the war. On the other hand, some units, such as the Second Texas Infantry and the Good-Douglas artillery battery, served with different brigades during the war.

In the chapters that follow, each of the Texas cavalry and infantry regiments and artillery batteries in Confederate service is discussed. These are grouped by geographical region and where possible described as a part of the brigade in which they gained their greatest recognition. The table that follows gives the numerical designation of each regiment, the name of its first commander, the states (or territories) in which the regiment served, and the number of the chapter in which the regiment or battery is discussed.

TABLE 1
TEXAS CONFEDERATE REGIMENTS
CAVALRY

Regiment	First Commander	Assignments	Chapter
First	Augustus Buchel	TX, LA	5
First, Ariz.Brig.	W. P. Hardeman	AR, IT*	5
First, Partisan R.	Walter P. Lane	AR, LA, MO	5
Second	John S. Ford	TX, NM, LA	5
Second, Ariz.Brig.	George W. Baylor	LA, TX	5
Second, Partisan R.	Barton W. Stone	LA, TX	5
Third	Elkanah Greer	IT, AR, MO, MS, GA, TN	3
Third, Ariz.Brig.	George T. Madison	LA	5
Fourth	James Reily	NM, TX, LA, AR	5
Fourth, Ariz.Brig.	Spruce M. Baird	TX	5
Fifth	Tom Green	NM, TX, LA, AR	5
Fifth, Partisan R.	L. M. Martin	IT, AR, TX	5
Sixth	Barton W. Stone	IT, AR, MS, GA, TN	3
Seventh	William Steele	NM, TX, LA, AR	5
Eighth	Benjamin F. Terry	KY, TN, MS, GA, SC, NC	3
Ninth	William B. Sims	IT, AR, MS, GA, TN	3
Tenth**	Matthew F. Locke	MS, KY, TN, GA, AL	4
Eleventh	William C. Young	IT, AK, MS, KY, TN, GA, SC, NC	3
Twelfth	William H. Parsons	AR, LA, TX	5

Thirteenth**	J. H. Burnett	AR, LA	6
Fourteenth**	M. T. Johnson	MO, KY, TN, GA, AL	4
Fifteenth**	George H. Sweet	AR, TN, GA, KY, SC, NC	4
Sixteenth**	William Fitzhugh	AR, LA, MS	6
Seventeenth**	George F. Moore	MS, AR, TN, GA, SC, NC	4
Seventeenth Cons.**	James R. Taylor	LA, AR	6
Eighteenth	Nicholas Darnell	AR, TN, GA, SC, NC	4
Nineteenth	Nathaniel Burford	AR, LA	5
Twentieth**	Thomas C. Bass	IT, AR	6
Twenty-first	George W. Carter	AR, LA	5
Twenty-second**	Robert Taylor	IT, AR, LA, MO	6
Twenty-third	Nicholas Gould	TX, LA	5
Twenty-fourth**	Francis Wilkes	AR, TN, GA, SC, NC	4
Twenty-fifth**	C. C. Gillespie	TX, AR, TN, GA, SC, NC	4
Twenty-sixth	Samuel B. Davis	TX, LA	5
Twenty-seventh	John W. Whitfield	MS, AL, GA, TN	3
Twenty-eighth**	Horace Randal	AR, LA	6
Twenty-ninth	Charles DeMorse	IT, AR	5
Thirtieth	Edward J. Gurley	AR, IT, TX	5
Thirty-first**	Trezevant C. Hawpe	AR, LA, MO	6
Thirty-second**	Julius Andrews	MS, KY, TN, GA, AL	4
Thirty-third	James Duff	TX, IT	5
Thirty-fourth	A. M. Alexander	IT, LA, MO	5
Thirty-fourth	A. W. Terrell	TX, LA	5
Thirty-fifth	Reuben R. Brown	TX	5
Thirty-fifth	James B. Likens	TX, LA	5
Thirty-sixth	Peter C. Woods	TX, LA	5
Anderson's	T. S. Anderson	TX	5
Benavides'	Santos Benavides	TX	5
Border	James Bourland	TX	5
Bradford's	Charles M. Bradford	TX	5
Frontier	James M. Norris	TX	5
Terry's	David S. Terry	TX	5
Wells'	John W. Wells	TX, LA	5

* Indian Territory
**Dismounted Cavalry

INFANTRY

Regiment	First Commander	Assignments	Chapter
First	Louis T. Wigfall	VA, TN, GA	2
Second	John C. Moore	TN, MS, TX	4
Third	Philip N. Luckett	TX, LA, AK	6
Fourth	Robert T. P. Allen	VA, TN, GA	2
Fifth	James J. Archer	VA, TN, GA	2
Sixth	Robert R. Garland	MS, AR, GA, TN, SC, NC	4
Seventh	John Gregg	TN, MS, GA, SC, NC	4
Eighth	Alfred M. Hobby	TX	6
Ninth	Samuel Bell Maxey	TN, MS, KY, GA, AL	4
Ninth (Nichols')	Ebenezer B. Nichols	TX	6
Tenth	Allison Nelson	AR, TN, GA, SC, NC	6
Eleventh	Oran M. Roberts	LA, AR	4
Twelfth	Overton Young	TX, LA, AR	6
Thirteenth	Joseph Bates	TX, LA	6
Fourteenth	Edward Clark	LA, AR	6
Fifteenth	Joseph W. Speight	LA, AR, IT	6
Sixteenth	George Flournoy	TX, LA, AR	6
Seventeenth	Robert T. P. Allen	TX, AR, LA	6
Eighteenth	W. B. Ochiltree	TX, AR, LA	6
Nineteenth	Richard Waterhouse	TX, AR, LA	6
Twentieth	Henry M. Elmore	TX	6
Twenty-first	Ashley W. Spaight	TX, LA	6
Twenty-second	Richard B. Hubbard	TX, AR, LA	6

WAUL'S LEGION

Thomas N. Waul, Commander

Unit	First Commander	Assignments	Chapter
First Infantry Bn	Bernard Timmons	MS, TX	4
Second Infantry Bn	James Wrigley	MS, TX	4
Cavalry Battalion	Leonidas Willis	MS, AL, TN	4
Artillery Battery	William Edgar	AR, LA	7

ARTILLERY

Regiment	First Commander	Assignments	Chapter
First Hvy Artillery	Joseph J. Cook	TX	All artillery units described in Chapter 7

Battalion	First Commander	Assignments
Third	Joseph J. Cook	TX
Fourth	Daniel D. Shea	TX
Seventh	Sidney T. Fontaine	TX
Willke's	H. Willke	TX

Battery	First Commander	Assignments
Abat-Dashiell	E. Abat	TX, LA, IT
Cayce-Allen	Henry P. Cayce	TX
Christmas	H. H. Christmas	TX
Creuzbaur-Welhausen	Edmund Creuzbaur	TX, LA
Daniel	James M. Daniel	AR, LA
Duke	W. H. Duke	VA
Edgar-Ransom	William M. Edgar	AR, LA
Galveston	H. Van Buren	TX
Gibson	William E. Gibson	TX, LA
Good-Douglas	John J. Good	AR, MS, TN, GA, AL
Greer Rocket	John S. Greer	TX
Howe	M. G. Howe	TX
Howell	Sylvanus Howell	IT, AR, MO
O. G. Jones	O. G. Jones	TX
W. R. Jones	W. R. Jones	TX
Keith	K. D. Keith	TX
Krumbhaar-Stafford	W. B. Krumbhaar	TX, IT, AR
Lee-Humphreys	Roswell W. Lee	IT
Maclin-Fox-Dege	R. B. Maclin	TX
McMahan	M. V. McMahan	TX, LA
Marmion	J. R. Marmion	TX

Mechling-Haldeman	W. T. Mechling	AR, LA
Moseley	W. G. Moseley	TX, LA
Neal-Maltby	Benj. F. Neal	TX
Nichols	W. H. Nichols	TX, LA
Perry	James S. Perry	TX
Pratt-Hynson	Joseph W. Pratt	AR, MO
Reily	John Reily	NM
Ruess	Joseph Ruess	TX
Shea-Vernon	Daniel D. Shea	TX
Teel	T. T. Teel	NM
Valverde	Joseph Sayers	NM, LA
Willke	H. Willke	TX
Wilson-Gonzales-Hughes	George R. Wilson	TX, LA
Wood	William S. Wood	NM

CHAPTER TWO

Texas Regiments in Virginia: Hood's Brigade

First Texas Infantry
Fourth Texas Infantry
Fifth Texas Infantry

THE FIRST, FOURTH, AND FIFTH Texas Infantry Regiments, which made up three-fourths of what came to be known as Hood's Texas Brigade, were the only military units from the Lone Star State to serve in Robert E. Lee's Army of Northern Virginia. Formed as a brigade in October 1861, the Texas regiments were initially commanded by Louis T. Wigfall, former U.S. senator from Texas and a leader in the secessionist movement.[1]

The three Texas regiments in Wigfall's Brigade were organized in the spring and summer of 1861. Eleven of the companies that made up the First Texas were raised under the April 1861 Confederate request for troops. The twelfth company of the First Texas was mustered into service in the spring of 1862. The ten companies of the Fourth Texas and the ten companies of the Fifth Texas were raised under a June 1861 levy on the state for 2,000 troops.

The majority of men recruited for the First Texas were East Texans; the majority of those in the Fourth Texas came from Central Texas. The Fifth Texas was fairly evenly divided between recruits from East and Central Texas.[2] The table on page 11 indicates the counties in which the companies of the regiments were organized. It should be noted, however, that not all the men in the company came from the county where the unit was organized.[3]

Initially there was little uniformity in weapons and clothing among the three regiments. County officials usually voted to issue funds to purchase uniforms and equipment, but procuring the needed items was difficult. As a result the Texans were dressed in a variety of uniforms and carried a wide assortment of weapons, including double-barreled shotguns, muskets, hunting rifles, dueling pistols, and Bowie knives. Val C. Giles, a private in the Tom Green Rifles of the Fourth Infantry, noted that no two companies of his regiment had similar uniforms. "We were a motley-looking set," he later wrote. "In my company we had about four different shades of gray, but the trimmings were all of black braid." The men of Company E in the Fourth Texas and Company K in the First Regiment wore gray uniforms trimmed in blue. Troops in Capt. W. H. "Howdy" Martin's Company K, Fourth Infantry, were issued blue coats and trousers when they reported to their staging area. The Reagan Guards, Company G of the First Infantry, wore dark uniforms trimmed with bright red stripes.[4]

Harold B. Simpson, author of the definitive four-volume history of the Texas Brigade, pointed out that the companies that eventually made up the First Texas Infantry journeyed to Virginia during late spring and summer of 1861 in small groups "without much order or planning." By midsummer the first eight companies had arrived in Richmond, where they were placed under the command of Louis T. Wigfall, the flamboyant South Carolinian who had moved to Texas in 1846 and had become a major political figure in the Lone Star State. Although he had only brief previous military experience as a college student, Wigfall, one of the Texas representatives in the Provisional Confederate Congress, was named commander of Texas troops in Virginia. At that time the Texas companies were only at battalion strength, so Wigfall had the rank of lieutenant colonel. When additional troops arrived in August, Wigfall was promoted to colonel in what became the First Texas Infantry. Hugh McLeod, a graduate of West Point and a former brigadier general in the army of the Texas Republic, was selected as lieutenant colonel of the regiment. Alexis T. Rainey, a lawyer and Texas legislator from Palestine who formerly commanded Company H, was chosen major.[5]

Meanwhile the twenty companies that were to form the Fourth and Fifth regiments were making the journey from Texas to Virginia. They followed a more organized plan than the companies of the

TEXAS REGIMENTS, ARMY OF NORTHERN VIRGINIA

First Texas Infantry, Col. Louis T. Wigfall, Lt. Col. Hugh McLeod

Co.	County	Local Name	Captain
A	Marion	Marion Rifles	Harvey H. Black
B	Polk	Livingston Guards	D. D. Moore
C	Harris	Palmer Guards	A. G. Dickinson
D	Marion	Star Rifles	A. G. Clopton
E	Harrison	Marshall Guards	Frederick S. Bass
F	Tyler	Woodville Rifles	Philip A. Work
G	Anderson	Reagan Guards	J. R. Woodward
H	Anderson	Texas Guards	Alexis T. Rainey
I	Houston	Crockett Southrons	Edward Currie
K	S.Augustine	Texas Invincibles	B. F. Benton
L	Galveston	Lone Star Rifles	Alfred C. McKeen
M	Trinity	Sumter Lt.Infantry	Howard Ballenger

Fourth Texas Infantry, Col. John B. Hood, Lt. Col. John Marshall

Co.	County	Local Name	Captain
A	Goliad	Hardeman Rifles	John C. G. Key
B	Travis	Tom Green Rifles	B. F. Carter
C	Robertson	Five Shooters	W. P. Townshend
D	Guadalupe	Guadalupe Rangers	John P. Bane
E	McLennan	Lone Star Guards	E. D. Ryan
F	Bexar	Montgomery Greys	E. B. Cunningham
G	Grimes	Grimes Co. Greys	J. W. Hutcheson
H	Walker	Porter Guards	P. P. Porter
I	Navarro	Navarro Rifles	C. M. Winkler
K	Henderson	Sandy Point Rifles	W. H. Martin

Fifth Infantry, Col. J.J. Archer, Lt. Col. J.B. Robertson

Co.	County	Local Name	Captain
A	Harris	Bayou City Guards	W. B. Botts
B	Colorado	——	John C. Upton
C	Leon	Leon Hunters	D. M. Whatley
D	Walker	Waverly Confederates	Robert M. Powell
E	Washington	Dixie Blues	John D. Rogers
F	Washington	Company Invincibles	King Bryan
G	Milam	Milam Co. Greys	Jeff C. Rogers
H	Polk	Texas Polk Rifles	John S. Cleveland
I	Washington	Texas Aides	J. B. Robertson
K	Polk	Flying Artillery	Ike N. M. Turner

First Texas. After they rendezvoused at Camp Van Dorn at Harrisburg on Buffalo Bayou, they traveled by rail to Beaumont, and then by river steamer to Niblett's Bluff on the Louisiana side of the Sabine. From there they marched to New Iberia, where they boarded another riverboat for travel to New Orleans. At New Orleans they boarded the cars of the New Orleans, Jackson, and Great Northern Railroad for the 1,200-mile ride to Richmond, Virginia.[6]

By the end of September all of the twenty companies that left Camp Van Dorn in mid-August were in Virginia. On September 30, 1861, they were formally organized as the Fourth and Fifth Texas Infantry regiments. Confederate authorities appointed Col. R.T.P. Allen, former superintendent of the Bastrop Military Institute, as the first commander of the Fourth Texas. Allen, a West Point graduate in the class of 1834, was a strict disciplinarian whose role as a drill instructor of the troops while in Texas made him unacceptable both to the officers and men of the regiment. A protest against the appointment signed by all the company commanders led to Allen's reassignment back to Texas.[7] The Confederate secretary of war appointed John Bell Hood to replace Allen as commander of the Fourth Texas. Hood, a native of Kentucky and a West Point graduate, was known by a number of men in the regiment. He had served as a junior officer in the U.S. Second Cavalry in Texas during the 1850s and had a good reputation as a fighter and leader. When Kentucky failed to secede from the Union, Hood declared Texas to be his adopted state and entered Confederate service as an officer from Texas. During the summer of 1861 he successfully demonstrated his leadership skills while serving under John B. Magruder on the York Peninsula. A big man, about six-foot-two in height, with a broad chest and a booming voice, Hood looked and acted like a soldier. Nicholas A. Davis, chaplain of the Fourth Texas, noted that "his commanding appearance, manly deportment, quick perception, courteous manners and decision of character, readily impressed the officers and men, that he was the man to govern them in the camp, and command them on the field."[8]

John Marshall, the fiery editor of the *Texas State Gazette* and a personal friend of President Davis from his days in Mississippi, was appointed lieutenant colonel of the Fourth Texas. Although a brave man who was admired as a champion of southern rights, Marshall had no previous military experience or background. According to

John Marshall, Colonel, Fifth Texas Infantry.
—Courtesy Harold B. Simpson Research Center, Hillsboro, Texas

Chaplain Davis his selection over others more qualified "was looked upon as savoring too much of a spirit of political favoritism."[9]

The appointment of twenty-two-year-old Bradfute Warwick as major of the regiment was equally unpopular with the men of the Fourth. The scion of a wealthy family of Richmond, Virginia, Warwick was unknown to the Texans who regarded his selection as "a direct stab at . . . State pride." Unlike Marshall, however, Warwick, who had been educated at the University of Virginia and the Medical College of New York, had previous military experience, first as a surgeon and later as a soldier in Garibaldi's Italian army. He proved to be a capable officer and soon won the respect of the Texans.[10]

The Fifth Texas, organized at the same time as the Fourth, shared some of the initial difficulties in appointment of officers. A Jewish colonel named Shaller was appointed as commander but quickly departed after the Texans made known their displeasure by cutting off his horse's tail. His successor, Col. James J. Archer of Maryland, was a professional soldier who had served in the Mexican War and on frontier duty. Although there was some resentment because he was not a Texan, Archer soon gained the respect of the men of the Fifth Texas.[11] Jerome Bonaparte Robertson, a Washington County physician and veteran of the army of the Texas Republic, was selected lieutenant colonel of the Fifth Texas. The

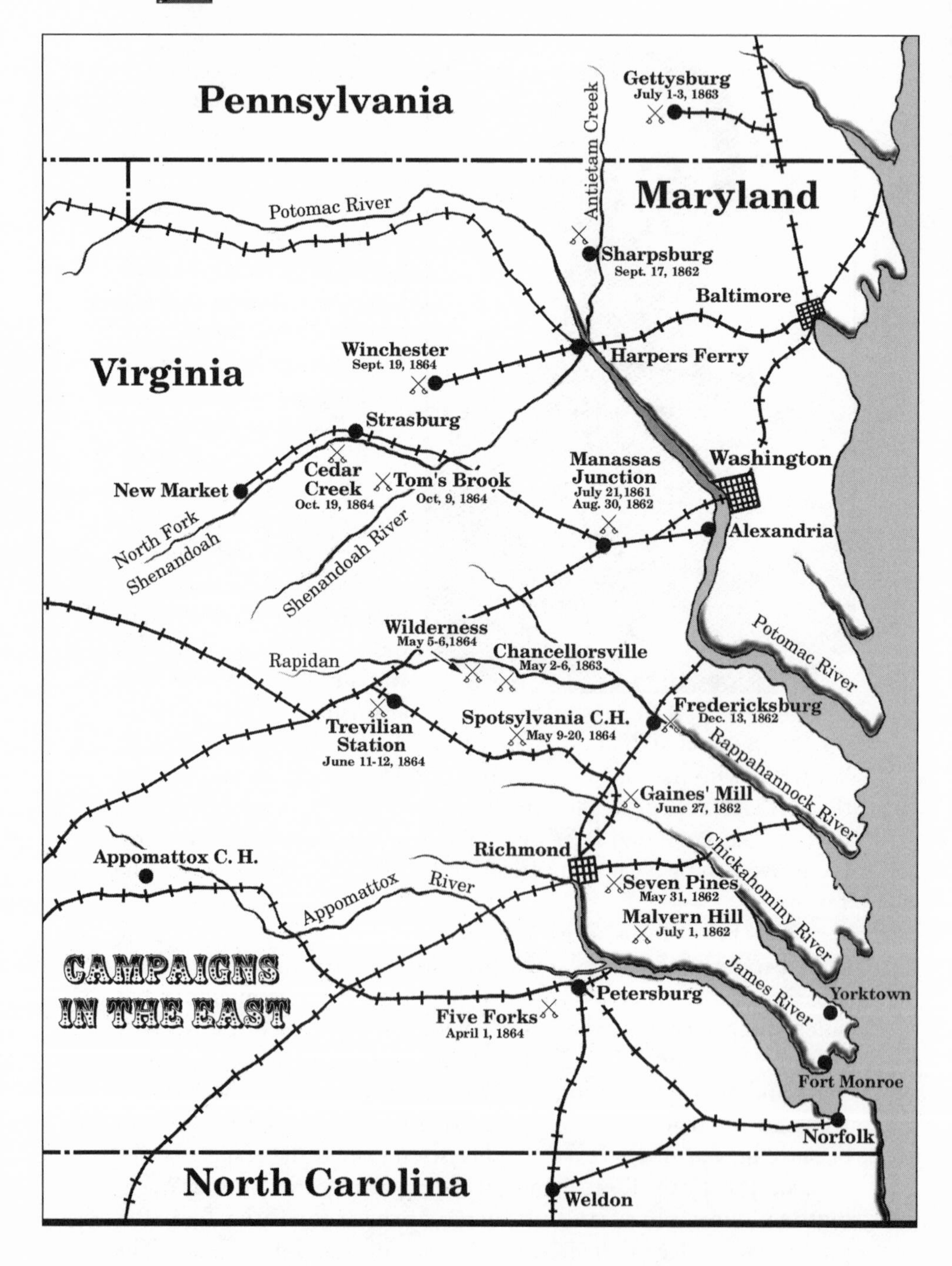

Pennsylvania
Gettysburg
July 1-3, 1863
Antietam Creek
Maryland
Potomac River
Sharpsburg
Sept. 17, 1862
Baltimore
Winchester
Sept. 19, 1864
Harpers Ferry
Virginia
Strasburg
Washington
Manassas
Junction
July 21, 1861
Aug. 30, 1862
Cedar
Creek
Oct. 19, 1864
Tom's Brook
Oct, 9, 1864
New Market
North Fork
Shenandoah
Shenandoah River
Alexandria
Wilderness
May 5-6, 1864
Chancellorsville
May 2-6, 1863
Rapidan
Potomac River
Fredericksburg
Dec. 13, 1862
Trevilian
Station
June 11-12, 1864
Spotsylvania C.H.
May 9-20, 1864
Rappahannock River
Gaines' Mill
June 27, 1862
Richmond
Appomattox C. H.
Chickahominy River
Appomattox
River
Seven Pines
May 31, 1862
Malvern Hill
July 1, 1862
CAMPAIGNS
IN THE EAST
James River
Yorktown
Petersburg
Five Forks
April 1, 1864
Fort Monroe
Norfolk
North Carolina
Weldon

Robertson appointment was popular with the men of the regiment. Robertson would succeed Archer as commander when the Marylander was later appointed commander of another brigade. Paul J. Quattlebaum, a graduate of West Point from South Carolina, was appointed major. Quattlebaum, not a popular choice with the Texans, soon departed from the regiment.[12]

With the completion of their organization the Fourth and Fifth regiments moved from their temporary camp along the York River Railroad to a bivouac four miles east of Richmond. On October 22, 1861, the Fourth and Fifth were officially grouped with the First Texas as a brigade. Louis T. Wigfall, commander of the First Texas, was promoted to brigadier general and given command of the new brigade. Hugh McLeod, promoted to colonel, replaced Wigfall as regimental commander. The initial orders called for the assignment of an undesignated Louisiana regiment to the brigade, but the Louisianans never joined the Texans.[13]

In mid-November the three Texas regiments were brought together for the first time near the vicinity of Dumfries, about three miles west of the junction of Quantico Creek with the Potomac. On November 20 the Eighteenth Georgia Infantry, which was camped nearby, was assigned as the fourth regiment in the brigade. The following year eight small companies of Wade Hampton's South Carolina Legion were attached to the brigade.[14]

Louis Wigfall, Colonel, First Texas Infantry, later commander of the Texas Brigade.
—Courtesy Harold B. Simpson Research Center, Hillsboro, Texas

The new brigade, referred to as the Texas Brigade even though not all of its regiments were from the Lone Star State, spent the winter months of 1861-62 guarding the west bank of the Potomac from Occoquan Creek to Quantico Creek. Although there was some skirmishing with the enemy during the period, the major concern was illness. Many of the men suffered from measles, diarrhea, and dysentery, but typhoid fever and pneumonia were the real killers. About 20 percent of the Texans died or were discharged for illness between September 1861 and March 1862. Among those who died was Col. Hugh McLeod, commander of the First Texas. Following McLeod's death from pneumonia on January 3, 1862, Palestine lawyer Alexis T. Rainey was promoted to colonel and given command of the regiment.[15]

In late February, Wigfall resigned his commission to take a seat in the Confederate Senate. Command of the brigade passed to the senior colonel, James J. Archer, but he held the post only briefly. On March 8, 1862, John Bell Hood was assigned to command the brigade. From that day forward the unit would be known as Hood's Texas Brigade.[16]

Hood's appointment came while the brigade was on march to Fredericksburg. Several days earlier Joseph E. Johnston, commander of Confederate forces in northern Virginia, ordered his troops to abandon the Potomac line and fall back to the Rappahannock. This move proved to be only temporary. When Union general George B. McClellan began moving the Army of the Potomac by water to the York Peninsula, Johnston ordered his troops southward to meet him. On April 8 Hood and his men began their march to Yorktown, where they were assigned to W. H. C. Whiting's Division.

Hood's Texans arrived just as the Confederates at Yorktown began withdrawing under pressure from McClellan's larger Federal army. When Federal troops commanded by Brig. Gen. William B. Franklin tried to outflank the Confederates near Eltham's Landing on the Pamunkey River, Whiting ordered Hood to drive the Federals back. John Marshall's Fourth Regiment (Hood's old command) opened the assault on the enemy but the First Texas and Fifth Texas were called upon to stop the Union counterattack and drive the enemy back to the river. At the cost of fifteen men killed and twenty-five wounded, mostly in the First Texas, the Texans captured forty Union troops and eighty-four abandoned wagons. An

John B. Hood, Colonel, Fourth Texas Infantry, later commander of the Texas Brigade.
—Courtesy Harold B. Simpson Research Center, Hillsboro, Texas

estimated 300 enemy soldiers were killed.[17]

The Texas Brigade was praised by President Davis and Generals Johnston, Whiting, and Gustavus W. Smith for its successful efforts at Eltham's Landing in protecting the left flank as the Confederates withdrew to defensive positions near Richmond. In the battle fought at Seven Pines and Fair Oaks on May 31–June 1 the Texas regiments that were there as part of the Confederate reserve saw little action. In the fighting Joe Johnston was wounded. President Davis, who was on the scene, named Robert E. Lee to take command of the Confederate forces in Virginia. For the next three years the Texas Brigade would serve under Lee's command.

More aggressive than his predecessor, Lee launched a series of major assaults on McClellan's army. In these battles, known as the Seven Days, the Texas Brigade was part of Stonewall Jackson's command. Lee's plan called for Jackson's troops, including the Texas Brigade, to join the divisions of A. P. Hill and James Longstreet in a massive assault on the Union right flank at Mechanicsville, north of the Chickahominy River. For a variety of reasons Jackson's troops arrived too late to play an effective part in the fighting on June 26. On the following day, the Confederates, including Jackson's men, attacked at Gaines' Mill. Early assaults against the strong Federal position along Boatswain's Swamp were unsuccessful. In the early afternoon General Lee requested that Hood, whom he knew from frontier service in Texas, lead his brigade in an assault against the enemy.[18]

Hood led the brigade into the attack with fixed bayonets. Although enemy fire was intense and Colonel Marshall, commander of the Fourth Texas, fell mortally wounded, the Texans charged to victory. The Federal lines were broken and the enemy forced to retreat. Historian Richard McMurry assessed that "one cannot overstate the importance of the battle or of Hood's attack." Victory at Gaines' Mill insured that McClellan would not take Richmond.[19]

The price of victory was high. Eighty-six men of the Texas Brigade were killed, 481 wounded, and four missing, for a total of 571 casualties, or a little over 25 percent. The Fourth Texas, which spearheaded the attack, had the highest casualties: 252 men killed or wounded, or about half the regiment. All three of the field-grade officers of the regiment were casualties: Colonel Marshall killed in the early fighting, Lieutenant Colonel Warwick mortally wounded in the chest, and Maj. John Key seriously wounded. Ten company-grade officers in the Fourth were killed and nine wounded.[20]

Losses in the other regiments of the brigade were not quite as high. The First Texas reported thirteen killed and sixty-five wounded. The Fifth Texas had thirteen killed and sixty-two wounded. Both regimental commanders were injured. Alexis T. Rainey of the First Texas was hit by a minie ball that badly cut his finger and lodged in his arm. Jerome B. Robertson, who succeeded James J. Archer as head of the Fifth Texas when the Marylander was transferred to command a Tennessee brigade, was wounded slightly in the shoulder. The Eighteenth Georgia, the fourth regiment in the brigade, had higher casualties, with fourteen killed, 128 wounded, and three missing. The companies of Hampton's South Carolina Legion, which joined the brigade at Seven Pines, had two killed and sixty-three wounded.[21]

Historian Stephen W. Sears noted that Gaines' Mill was the "largest and costliest battle of the entire Peninsula campaign." He wrote, "For concentrated fury, only Shiloh among the war's earlier battles even approached it; few later battles would exceed it." Lee's army sustained 7,993 casualties in the fighting. Union losses were 6,837.[22]

Following the Battle of Gaines' Mill, McClellan pulled his

army back toward the James River. Hood's Brigade saw little action in the fighting at Savage Station and Glendale. In the last battle of the Seven Days fought at Malvern Hill the Texans were exposed to Union artillery fire much of the day but did not take part in the costly frontal assault on the Federal lines.

After the end of the fighting on the Peninsula, the Texas Brigade moved into camp three miles northeast of Richmond. The Texans remained there for a month, resting, refitting, and receiving some replacements from home. On August 8 the brigade, now part of James Longstreet's command, was ordered northward as General Lee moved to bring his army together in an attack on John Pope's Union army. Division commander W.H.C. Whiting had taken medical leave from the army, so Hood, the senior brigade commander, temporarily led the division as well as the Texas Brigade.[23]

Longstreet's troops reached the Rapidan on August 15 and took their position to the right of Stonewall Jackson's divisions. Several days later the Confederates pushed Pope back toward the Rappahannock. As Pope withdrew, the Texas Brigade skirmished with the Federal rear guard at Kelly's Ford on August 21 and at Freeman's Ford on August 22. When Pope fell back toward Manassas, Lee split his army, with Jackson swinging through the Bull Run Mountains to attack Pope from the west. As the two armies maneuvered for position, the Texas Brigade was engaged in fierce fighting on the afternoon of August 29.[24]

The fighting on the 29th was only a preliminary to the main battle that took place on the old Manassas battlefield the following afternoon. Pope, not realizing that Longstreet was massing his entire command on the Union left flank, launched a series of assaults against Jackson's troops. When the bulk of Pope's army turned against Jackson, Longstreet's divisions attacked Pope's exposed flank.

Hood's Division led the Confederate assault. Moving out of the woods and across a wheat field, the Texas Brigade shattered two New York regiments. The Fourth Texas, in the center of the brigade's line, overran a Pennsylvania artillery battery, but heavy enemy crossfire forced the Texans to take cover in a ravine. Similarly, the First Texas, after an initial advance on the left, withdrew to cover in the valley of Young's Branch.

The Fifth Texas, on the brigade's left, moved out ahead of

other advancing Confederates. The Texans overran a New York Zouave regiment and pushed through several Federal lines. General Hood ordered the brigade to halt and hold the ground taken, but apparently officers of the Fifth Texas did not hear the order. The regiment continued to push forward across Chinn Ridge and by nightfall was far to the front of Longstreet's divisions in the vicinity of the Sudley Springs Road.[25]

That evening General Pope ordered his battered army to withdraw across Bull Run toward Centreville. The Texas regiments and their South Carolina and Georgia comrades in the brigade had played a major role in the assault that led to Pope's defeat. John J. Hennessy, whose *Return to Bull Run* is the most complete account of the battle, noted that "Lee and Longstreet could hardly have asked for more from the Texas Brigade than the success it had attained in the first thirty minutes of the attack."[26]

Again the Confederate victory was costly. Jackson lost nearly 4,000 men; Longstreet about 4,700. The Texas Brigade had slightly more than 600 casualties. The Fifth Texas, which advanced farther than any other regiment in the initial attack, sustained 261 casualties—approximately 43 percent of the brigade's losses. All three regimental officers were casualties. Colonel Robertson was hit in the groin while leading the attack. Lt. Col. J. C. Upton was killed, and Maj. King Bryan was wounded. During the last phase of the battle a captain commanded the regiment, and three of its companies were commanded by non-commissioned officers.[27]

Losses for the other regiments of the brigade were not as high. The Fourth Texas had ninety-nine casualties; of these, twenty-two were deaths. The First Texas, which saw less fighting than the other regiments, sustained twenty-eight casualties. The Eighteenth Georgia had 133 casualties. The South Carolina Legion, the brigade's smallest unit, had 74 casualties.[28]

The Texas Brigade got little rest after the heavy fighting at Second Manassas. Lee's army followed Pope's retreating Federals to Centreville, then turned north. On September 5 the army began crossing the Potomoc River while the regimental bands played "Maryland, My Maryland." Lee hoped that Marylanders would welcome his troops as liberators, but most of the residents greeted the Confederates either coolly or in disbelief at the ragged uniforms and bare feet of many of the Rebels.

Hood was not at the head of the division as it moved north. He had been placed under arrest following an incident that occurred at Manassas on the evening of August 30. In the battle some of Hood's Texans captured several new Federal ambulances. Brig. Gen. Nathan "Shanks" Evans, the Confederate commander of operations in the area, ordered the ambulances turned over to his brigade, but Hood refused to comply with the order. Evans placed Hood under arrest, and General Longstreet ordered him to remain at Culpepper until he could be brought before a military court. General Lee, unwilling to leave one of his best combat officers behind in the Maryland campaign, allowed Hood to accompany the army but not in command of his division. Hood was directed to the rear of the column.[29]

Lee divided his army as he crossed into Maryland. One wing of the army, commanded by Stonewall Jackson, was ordered to capture the Federal garrison at Harpers Ferry. The other wing, commanded by Longstreet and including the Texas Brigade, moved on to Boonsboro and Hagerstown. When a copy of Lee's orders was found by Federal troops, the Union commander George B. McClellan moved his army to crush Lee's divided command. Lee hurriedly took steps to bring his scattered forces together to avoid disaster. He ordered Jackson to complete his assignment at Harpers Ferry as quickly as possible and join him in Maryland. At the same time Lee suspended Hood's arrest and returned him to command of his division.[30]

Hood resumed command in time to lead the division in a delaying action against the Union army at South Mountain on September 14. The three Texas regiments sustained nineteen casualties in skirmishes with Federal troops before withdrawing under heavy enemy pressure.

Lee pulled his various units together at the small Maryland village of Sharpsburg. There he formed a line back of the small stream, Antietam Creek, which ran between the town and the approaching Federal army. Hood was ordered to move his division, consisting of the Texas Brigade (temporarily led by Georgian W. T. Wofford) and Evander Law's Brigade, to the left flank of the Confederate line near a small Dunker Church on the Hagerstown Pike. After skirmishing with two Pennsylvania regiments late in the afternoon on September 16, Hood's troops were allowed to fall back behind

Alexander R. Lawton's Division in order to cook their rations. General Jackson, who commanded that section of the Confederate line, alerted Hood to be prepared to move his troops to support Lawton in the event of a major Federal assault.[31]

In the early morning hours of the 17th the Union army began the major attack that Jackson had anticipated. Between 5:00 and 6:00 that morning the Union First Corps, commanded by Joe Hooker, launched an assault against Lawton's Division. Supported by an intense artillery barrage, Union troops drove across Miller's cornfield and down the Hagerstown Pike. Although Lawton's troops, mainly Georgians, Virginians, and Louisianians, fought gallantly, they fell back under the weight of the Union assault. Lawton himself was wounded and half of his troops were casualties. To hold the Confederate line Hood's Division was now ordered into the fray.

With Law's Brigade on the right and the Texas Brigade on the left, Hood's Division moved through the West Woods, across the Hagerstown Pike, and into the cornfield as the tide of battle ebbed and flowed. The First Texas, led by Lt. Col. Philip A. Work, took the lead in the fighting as it pushed the Federals back to the northern edge of the cornfield. Unfortunately, the aggressiveness of the Texans "was their undoing." As they pursued the retreating enemy the men of the First came under heavy fire from a Pennsylvania brigade that had been posted along the fence line. Nine colorbearers went down, and four of every five men in the regiment were killed or wounded.[32]

Momentarily the Confederates controlled the field, but the heavy casualties and a second enemy attack, this time by the Union Twelfth Corps, forced Hood's men to fall back toward the West Woods. With most of its ammunition gone and casualties high, Hood's Division held until relieved by Lafayette McLaws' Division.[33]

Hood's Division saw no major action after 10:00 that morning. The Union commander, McClellan, shifted his main assault first to the center and then to the south. The Confederates gave ground in both sectors but held their line. The battle, the bloodiest single day of the war, was over. Tactically, it was a draw, but strategically it was a Union victory as the Confederates withdrew back into Virginia after the battle.

Both sides lost heavily in the Battle of Sharpsburg, or Antietam as the Federals called it. McClellan's army suffered the most casualties, slightly over 12,000, compared to 10,000 Confederate casualties. However, the Confederates had a higher pecentage loss, 31 percent of those engaged compared to 25 percent for the Federals.

The Texas regiments had particularly heavy losses. The First Texas, nicknamed the "Ragged First" because of its threadbare appearance in clothing and discipline, had 186 killed, wounded, and missing, or 82.3 percent casualties—the highest rate for any regiment, North or South, for one day in the Civil War. The Fourth Texas sustained 154 casualties, or 53.5 percent. The Fifth Texas, already small because of losses at Second Manassas, had eighty-six casualties, or 49.6 percent of its effective strength. The other two regiments in the Texas Brigade had substantial losses as well. The South Carolina Legion, which entered the battle with only seventy-seven men, sustained 69.7 percent casualties. The Eighteenth Georgia had 57.3 percent casualties. Evander Law's command, the other brigade in Hood's Division, had 23.2 percent casualties.[34]

Fortunately for the men of the Texas Brigade there was little military action in the two months that followed the Battle of Sharpsburg. Both the Confederate and Union armies had been battered at Sharpsburg and needed time for resting and reorganizing before another major campaign.

In late September the Texas Brigade moved into camp near Winchester in the Shenandoah Valley, where it remained for five weeks. Historian Harold B. Simpson noted that "it was a well-earned rest for the depleted and exhausted Brigade." In the previous three months the Texans, Georgians, and South Carolinians had fought in three major battles and four minor ones. The brigade had marched over 500 miles and sustained more than 1,800 casualties.[35]

The Texas regiments were badly in need of new clothing and shoes. As the men farthest from home, where they might secure clothing, the Texans were the most poorly clad and shod troops in Lee's army. Some new uniforms and shoes were issued by the quartermaster at Winchester, but the number was inadequate. At a review of Longstreet's Corps on October 8, Col. Garnet Wolsley, a visitor from the British army, expressed his surprise at the frayed trousers of Hood's men. Although General Lee retorted "never mind the raggedness, Colonel, the enemy never see the backs of my

Texans," he, too, realized that additional clothing and shoes were sorely needed. In early November the army's inspector general, Col. Edwin J. Harvie, reported that two-thirds of all the regiments in the Texas Brigade were "badly clothed and shod." He found that 440 men, about one-third of the brigade, were barefooted.[36]

The shoe shortage was so serious that Rev. Nicholas Davis, the Presbyterian chaplain of the Fourth Texas, appealed to the citizens of Virginia by means of a letter to the *Richmond Whig* entitled "Texans Barefooted." In this appeal Davis pointed out that the Texans were too far from home to seek help in that quarter. "We are from the far South, and the cold is severe to us," he wrote. At least one hundred pairs of shoes and five hundred pairs of socks were needed.[37]

The response to Davis' request was immediate. The citizens of Richmond quickly provided the requested number of shoes and socks. In addition they contributed $443 in cash, 146 drawers, 109 shirts, 94 pairs of gloves, and a number of smaller packages which Chaplain Davis reported "warmed both the feet and hearts of our men."[38]

At the time of Davis' appeal in the *Richmond Whig* the Texas Brigade was camped near Cedar Mountain, six miles south of Culpepper. The Army of Northern Virginia was undergoing reorganization at the time. Both James Longstreet and Stonewall Jackson were promoted to lieutenant general and their commands were now designated as army corps. In November, John Bell Hood was promoted to major general and two new brigades joined his division. At the same time Jerome B. Robertson, commander of the Fifth Texas, who had recovered from his wounds at Second Manassas, was promoted to brigadier general and assigned command of the Texas Brigade. Robert M. Powell, who originally commanded Company D and led the regiment in Robertson's absence, was promoted to colonel and made commander of the Fifth Texas. King Bryan was promoted to lieutenant colonel, and Jefferson C. Rogers was promoted to major in the Fifth Texas. The First Texas, whose officers had been sharply criticized for "inexcusable neglect" in the inspector general's report, was still commanded by Tyler County lawyer Lt. Col. Philip A. Work. Lt. Col. Benjamin F. Carter, former mayor of Austin and a popular man with the troops, led the Fourth Texas while Col. John Key recovered after being wounded at Gaines' Mill.[39]

The Texas Brigade was reorganized in November when the Eighteenth Georgia and the South Carolina Legion were reassigned to brigades from their own states. To replace them the Third Arkansas, a large regiment and the only unit from the state serving in Lee's army, was assigned to the brigade. The Arkansans, who had performed well while assigned to John G. Walker's Division in the Maryland campaign, remained with the Texas Brigade throughout the rest of the war.

The period of resting and refitting came to an end in late November. Ambrose E. Burnside replaced George B. McClellan as commander of the Union Army of the Potomac. Burnside was appointed commander because the Lincoln administration wanted a more aggressive leader than the cautious McClellan. Realizing that quick victories were expected, Burnside began moving his massive army southward toward Fredericksburg. General Lee moved his army to meet this new threat.

As part of Longstreet's Corps, the Texas Brigade was assigned to a position south of the Rappahannock River on the heights overlooking Fredericksburg. Longstreet's five divisions occupied the left side of the Confederate line, with Jackson's Corps stretched out in the valley to the right. Richard Anderson's Division held the extreme left side of Longstreet's Corps with Hood's Division on the right side. Lafayette McLaws' Division of Longstreet's Corps was on Hood's left, and William B. Taliaferro's Division of Jackson's Corps was to Hood's right.

Hood's Division, in the center of the entire Confederate line, saw comparatively little action in the Battle of Fredericksburg. Burnside's main assaults were directed against McLaws' Division to Hood's left and at Jackson's Corps to Hood's right. Evander Law's Brigade, which held the right flank of Hood's Division, was engaged in fighting as it helped Jackson's troops drive the Federals back, but the Texas Brigade, occupying Hood's left flank, escaped the fury of the Federal assaults. One sergeant of the Fourth Texas was killed while on scouting duty after Burnside withdrew across the Rappahannock. Four men in the Fifth Texas were wounded by Union artillery. Neither the First Texas nor the Third Arkansas reported any casualties.[40]

After the costly and futile assaults on December 13, Burnside withdrew his army. Although he intended to resume the campaign a few miles above Fredericksburg, heavy rains soon turned the area into a quaqmire. Campaigning in Virginia came to an end until the spring of 1863.

The Texas Brigade spent the winter of 1862-63 in camp near the Massaponax River, a small tributary of the Rappahannock. Here the troops went into winter quarters, a series of semi-permanent shelters they constructed from timber cut in the pine forest and covered with tent covers. In his reminiscences published after the war, William A. Fletcher, a private from Beaumont in the Fifth Texas, described the construction of his hut. "The splitting of boards was rather hard, with the tools which we we had," he later wrote, "and as we had—with others—been instructed to build some sort of protection (as there was not a sufficient number of tents for all) my mess constructed our quarters by digging a pit about fourteen feet square and something over two feet deep, logging up the sides so roof would be above our heads. The roof was made of poles with the necessary support underneath to permit a good amount of earth to be thrown on in cone shape to make a very warm roof, and supposed to be waterproof." A heavy rain soon flooded their tent, however. Before the next rain Fletcher and his comrades stretched canvas over the dirt roof and the men "passed the balance of the winter comfortably."[41]

Except for foraging for food, picket duty, and some scouting there was little military activity in the winter months. Although fraternization with the enemy was offically prohibited, trade between the Confederates and Federals was opened across the rivers and streams separating the two sides. In his printed recollections, Val C. Giles, a non-commissioned officer in the Tom Green Rifles of the Fourth Texas, remembered that "sugar, coffee, tobacco, newspapers, and lies" were the chief items of exchange. "Some of the yarns exchanged there would have made old Baron Munchansen green with envy," Giles wrote.[42]

Giles noted that gambling was rampant among the Texans that winter. "There were a good many expert card players in the Texas Brigade," he wrote, "and they managed to keep the novices and greenhorns pretty well strapped." He described one instance where a captain in the First Texas lost $1,800 and a slave to two privates in the Fourth Texas who employed trickery and deception.[43]

The men in Hood's Brigade had a reputation for their skills in foraging and "requisitioning" foodstuffs. Rabbits, guinea hens, chickens, and hogs were targets for the Texans who sought to supplement their sparse rations with fresh meat. Bill Fletcher noted that rabbits had been plentiful in the area, but as the soldiers outnumbered them by great odds the supply was quickly exhausted. Guinea hens remained plentiful but were difficult to catch. According to Fletcher "the guinea was the only safe fowl in time of war."[44]

The Texans' success in appropriating chickens and hogs from local farmers and using fence rails for cooking and heating led to a mild rebuke from General Lee. In a conversation with Hood one evening, Lee complained that the army was guilty of "burning fence rails, killing pigs, and committing sundry delinquencies." Hood spoke up in defense of his division, declaring his men were not guilty of such offenses. Lee, who had high regard for Hood and his men, turned toward the tall Texan and laughingly said, "Ah, General Hood, when you Texans come about the chickens have to roost mighty high."[45]

In an attempt to overcome the boredom of long hours with little to do during the winter months, the Texans built a log theater in which they could see amateur theatrical productions and listen to musical concerts. Each of the regiments had small bands. The Fourth Texas brass band, consisting of eleven musicians, was the largest and most popular. Black-faced theatricals were a favorite with the Texans. A group from the brigade known as "Hood's Minstrels" took top billing. General Hood frequently attended the shows, and General Lee was in the audience on at least one occasion.[46]

Another favorite pastime of the Texans in Lee's army during the winter months was throwing snowballs. Most of the Texans had never before seen deep snows like those that covered the Virginia landscape that winter. Although they complained of the cold, the Texans enjoyed throwing snowballs at one another. Soon companies were organizing to challenge other units in snowball fights. This spread to regimental and brigade level—even division level on one occasion. Before the contest ended, more than 9,000 members of Longstreet's Corps were engaged in throwing snowballs in what Bill Fletcher called "the greatest snowball battle of the age." Unfortunately, some of the participants hid rocks in their snowballs, resulting in injuries to the participants. As a result, General Longstreet issued an order prohibiting snowball battles.[47]

In mid-February 1863 the Texans' tranquil life in the Fredericksburg area came to an end. Increased Federal activity in the Suffolk area of southern Virgnia caused the War Department to request that General Lee send additional troops to the region. Longstreet and two of his divisions, Pickett's and Hood's, were assigned to the area. On February 17, in the midst of a snowstorm, the Texas Brigade moved out of its winter quarters and began the march south. The Texans marched to a campsite south of the Confederate capital. They remained there for two weeks preparing for the farther move southward. In mid-March they were ordered back to the Fredericksburg area. Joe Hooker had been appointed to replace Ambrose Burnside as Union army commander. Confederate authorities feared an immediate resumption of hostilities. When it became apparent that Hooker was not ready to move, the Texas Brigade and other units of Longstreet's command were ordered to turn around and retrace their steps to the campsite south of Richmond.[48]

In early April, Longstreet's two divisions completed their move toward Suffolk. Because the Union defense lines around the city appeared too strong to assault, Longstreet determined to bottle up the enemy while his own troops drew provisions and forage from the area, which was rich in hogs, cattle, fish, and grain. For two weeks some of Longstreet's men held a line along the west bank of the Nansemond River while others were detailed in foraging operations. Although there was no heavy fighting, the Texas Brigade was under daily artillery and sharpshooter fire from Union gunboats on the river. Several Texans were killed by enemy fire. The death of Capt. Ike Turner, the youthful commander of Company K of the Fifth Texas, was a particularly painful loss. Turner, youngest company commander in the brigade, was an officer of great promise who had just been appointed commander of a special battalion of sharpshooters. General Hood referred to Turner's death as "a grave misfortune" and praised Turner as a man of "pre-eminent qualities."[49]

The foraging operations in southern Virginia were quite successful. Longstreet's biographer, Jeffrey D. Wert, pointed out that the area "yielded tens of thousands of bushels of corn and an estimated million pounds of bacon." Enough foodstuffs were gathered to feed Lee's army for two months. In addition, dozens of wagons,

Ike Turner, Captain, Fifth Texas Infantry.
—Courtesy Harold B. Simpson Research Center, Hillsboro, Texas

horses, and mules were appropriated for the Confederate army.[50]

The procurement program came to an end in late April. On April 29, Joe Hooker began his spring offensive. The following day Lee requested that Longstreet's two divisions return to the Army of Northern Virginia as quickly as possible. Secretary of War James Seddon ordered Longstreet to "move without delay" to join Lee's army. As many of the forage wagons were far below Suffolk gathering supplies, it was two days before the actual move began. Pickett's Division moved first, with Hood following the next day. The Texas Brigade served as the rear guard in the operation, skirmishing with the Federals as it withdrew.[51]

Before Longstreet's divisions joined Lee, the great Battle of Chancellorsville had been fought. Outnumbered more than two-to-one, Lee had outmaneuvered the enemy and won a major victory. The price was high. The Confederates suffered 12,000 casualties, including Stonewall Jackson, who later died from his wounds.

News of the Confederate victory reached Hood's troops while en route to join Lee. The brigade rejoined Lee's army in mid-May. For the next four weeks the Texans were camped near Raccoon Ford of the Rapidan. Both the Confederates and Federals needed time to recuperate from the fighting at Chancellorsville. Lee reorganized his army, creating a new corps and appointing Richard Ewell and A. P. Hill as lieutenant generals and corps commanders. Hood's Division remained in Longstreet's Corps. There was some thought given to mounting the Texans with horses acquired in the Suffolk interlude, but nothing came of the proposal. Even though a few new recruits arrived, the Texas regiments remained undersized due to the attrition of two years of campaigning. Hood's men did draw new clothes, arms, and equipment and were put through a series of drills, inspections, and reviews.[52]

In early June the Army of Northern Virginia began moving north. After serious discussions at a high governmental-military level, Lee had won approval for an invasion of Pennsylvania. He believed such a campaign would be the best means for relieving the growing Union threat to Vicksburg, the great Confederate bastion on the Mississippi. Such an offensive would have tremendous political, diplomatic, and psychological impact, the Confederate commander believed. Although corps chief James Longstreet, who favored a defensive mode of operations, was not supportive of the plan, division commander John Bell Hood entered the campaign with high hopes for success, a view he believed was shared by his men.[53]

Hood's Division, nearly 8,000 strong, crossed the Potomac near Williamsport on June 26. The river was swollen by recent rains. Artillery and wagon trains crossed the river on pontoon bridges, but most of the infantry waded across after removing shoes and socks. As the Texas Brigade forded the river, regimental bands played "Dixie."[54]

After crossing the Potomac the men were allowed to stack their arms and build fires to dry their clothing. Several barrels of whiskey had been confiscated near Hagerstown. General Hood authorized the distribution of one gill per man in his brigades, but some company commanders ignored the ration limitation. Those men who did not drink gave their ration to their comrades. As a result, many men in the brigade were intoxicated as they marched across the narrow neck of Maryland. By dusk the Texans had reached the vicinity of Greencastle, Pennsylvania.[55]

The next morning the brigade was on the march again, entering the town of Chambersburg in late afternoon of June 27. Lt. Col. Arthur Fremantle, the British observer in Lee's army, described

Hood's troops as "a queer lot to look at at. They carry less than any other troops; many of them have only got an old piece of carpet or rug as baggage; many have discarded their shoes in the mud; all are rugged and dirty, but full of good humor and confidence in themselves and in their general, Hood."[56]

Hood's troops camped near Chambersburg that night. They spent the next two days there—foraging, resting, and refitting. The valley around was rich with foodstuffs of all types, and the Texans and Arkansans took full advantage of the bounty. Chickens, turkeys, ducks, and geese all fell victim to the Confederates. In addition, bread, ham, bacon, jellies, pickles, preserves, butter, and fresh milk were purchased with Confederate money or appropriated from local civilians.[57]

The brief interlude at Chambersburg came to an end on June 30. Hood's brigades were ordered to swing east as Longstreet's Corps joined Ewell's and A. P. Hill's Corps north and west of the town of Gettysburg. At the time it was not clear as to the exact location of the Union army now commanded by George Meade. On July 1, Hood's troops were at Fayetteville (about five miles east of Chambersburg) when they received orders to march to Gettysburg, where fighting was under way. Hood's Division started in late afternoon and reached the Gettysburg area at 2:00 A.M. on July 2.

While his troops rested from the long march, Hood met with Generals Lee, Longstreet, and Hill to discuss the plan of operations. Confederate troops under Ewell and Hill had driven the enemy out of Gettysburg the previous day. Lee was determined to attack the Union position on Cemetery Ridge south of the town. The main assault would be by Longstreet's divisions up the Emmitsburg Pike against the Union left flank.

Longstreet did not like Lee's plan of attack. He believed the enemy too strong in its present position. He suggested that the Confederates swing wide to the right, secure a stronger defensive position between the enemy and Washington, and wait for an enemy attack (much as at Fredericksburg). Lee refused Longstreet's request but did agree to let Longstreet wait for the arrival of Evander Law's Brigade (which had been on detached duty) before making the attack. Since Pickett's Division of Longstreet's Corps could not reach the Gettysburg area until the next day, Lee assigned

Dick Anderson's Division of Hill's Corps to support Longstreet's two divisions in the attack.[58]

When Law's Brigade joined Hood around noon on July 2, Longstreet moved his troops into place. Hood's Division was on the extreme right of the Confederate line. Lafayette McLaws' Division was on Hood's left, and Anderson was on McLaws' left. Just as the attack formation was ready, Hood's scouts reported that the small hills, Round Top and Little Round Top, on the Union extreme left were unoccupied. Hood, believing he could turn the Union flank by swinging around the Round Tops, asked Longstreet for permission to change the direction of the attack, but Longstreet refused. Three times Hood appealed, but each time he was turned down.

By 3:30 the attack force was in position. Hood deployed his brigades in two lines: Robertson's Texas Brigade and Law's Alabama Brigade were in the front line; the two Georgia brigades of Henry L. Benning and George T. Anderson were behind them. An artillery battalion of eighteen guns was slightly in advance of Hood's line.[59]

After a brief artillery exchange, the attack began with the Texas and Alabama brigades advancing across the open field. As the Texas Brigade rushed forward the Third Arkansas was on the left and the First, Fourth, and Fifth Texas in succession to its right. Hood, on horseback, cheered his troops on; however, early in the attack he was dangerously wounded by a shell fragment which shattered his left arm. He was taken to a hospital in shock and great pain. Evander Law, the senior brigadier in the division, took command.

As the troops advanced there was a great deal of confusion. The Confederates encountered heavy enemy fire from Federal batteries in the rocky formation known as the Devil's Den. Col. J.C.G. Key, commander of the Fourth Texas, who had just recovered from his wounds at Gaines' Mill, went down again. Lt. Col. Benjamin F. Carter assumed command, but he was mortally wounded, leaving Maj. John P. Bane in command of the regiment. Col. R. M. Powell of the Fifth Texas was severely wounded and taken prisoner. Lt. Col. King Bryan, who assumed command of the Fifth Texas, was also wounded. Brig. Gen. Robertson was wounded in the right leg but continued to lead the brigade until the fighting ended that day.[60]

The Fourth and Fifth Texas, which found themselves intermingled with two Alabama regiments of Law's Brigade, fought their way through the area south of the Devil's Den to the base of Little Round Top but were unable to dislodge the enemy from the crest of the hill. The First Texas and Third Arkansas meanwhile reached the Rocky Ridge north of Devil's Den. They drove the Fourth Maine Infantry from the area and captured three guns from a New York battery. Heavy enemy resistance, however, checked the Confederate advance. As darkness fell, the fighting came to an end. The Confederates had advanced several hundred yards but had failed to break the enemy lines.[61]

The fighting resumed the next day when General Lee ordered a frontal assault against the center of the Union line. Except for some skirmishing between the First Texas and Union cavalry led by Judson Kilpatrick, the Texas Brigade saw little action that day. Hood's battered division was held in reserve as troops under George Pickett and James J. Pettigrew made an unsuccessful assault on the Federals on Cemetery Ridge. Lee's army began its withdrawal back into Virginia on the evening of July 4.

The Texas Brigade suffered heavy losses at Gettysburg. The brigade entered the battle with 1,100 men but sustained 597 casualties, or 54.3 percent of its total. Losses were fairly evenly distributed by regiment, with the Fifth Texas and Third Arkansas suffering the highest casualties. Only one brigade in Lee's army, G. T. Anderson's Brigade, had greater losses than the Texas Brigade. The army as a whole sustained between 25,000 and 28,000 casualties, or roughly a little more than one-third of its total strength.[62]

Following the Battle of Gettysburg, Lee's battered army recrossed the Potomac and headed into the Shenandoah Valley. The Texas Brigade arrived at its old campsite near Culpepper, Virginia, on July 24. The brigade was there for a week before moving on to the Fredericksburg vicinity, where it remained for a month guarding the Rappahannock fords. During this time some men received new uniforms and shoes, both desperately needed items. For many of the Texans these weeks in August 1863 were some of the most pleasant days of the war.[63]

In early September the restful days on the Rappahannock came to an end. The men of the Texas Brigade were ordered to march to Milford Station, where they boarded a train for Richmond. In Richmond they joined other units of Hood's Division on a long train ride that took them through the Carolinas and Georgia to join Braxton Bragg's Army of Tennessee. The movement to reinforce Bragg was part of a Confederate plan to deliver a surprise attack against the Union army of William S. Rosecrans, which had just forced the Confederates out of Chattanooga. Unfortunately, the troop movement, which took nine days, proceeded more slowly than planned. Only three brigades of Hood's Division, including the Texas Brigade, arrived in time to take part in the first day's fighting at Chickamauga Creek.[64]

The Texas Brigade was the first of Hood's troops to reach Ringgold, Georgia, the rendezvous point for the reinforcements coming to Bragg. Since General Hood, still recovering from the wounds suffered at Gettysburg, had not yet arrived, the Texans became part of Bushrod Johnson's provisional division as Bragg's army attempted to cross the Chickamauga on September 18. Skirmishing with the enemy was under way in the afternoon when Hood, his left arm in a sling, arrived. Hood took command of the provisional division, consisting of his own brigades and those from Joe Johnston's Army of Mississippi, and pushed across the Chickamauga. By nightfall, all Hood's units held a line over a mile long on the west side of Chickamauga.

Heavy fighting took place on the morning of September 19. Since Longstreet and his staff were still en route from Richmond, Bragg placed Hood in temporary command of the left wing of his army. Bragg hoped to roll back the Federals, but a delay by Leonidas Polk, commanding the Confederate right wing, allowed Rosecrans time to prevent a breakthrough. The three brigades of Hood's old division, temporarily commanded by Evander Law, were on the right flank of the Confederate left wing. The struggle for control of the La Fayette-Chattanooga road, which paralleled the Chickamauga, was particularly intense in the midafternoon. The Fourth Texas drove across the road near the Veniard farm house around 3:30 P.M., giving the Confederates a salient in the Union line, but enemy artillery fire forced the Texans to fall back.[65]

The fighting on the 19th resulted in heavy casualties for both sides but little change in position. Bragg was determined to renew the attack the next morning. His battle plan called for the attack to begin on the right and then be taken up by the divisions to the left. Longstreet arrived on the evening of the 19th and assumed command of the left wing. Hood was named commander of five divisions on the right side of Longstreet's wing.

Hood's divisions began their attack at 11:00 A.M. on the 20th. His old division, including the Texas Brigade, was in the center of the strike force. The Texas Brigade pushed ahead of the other brigades in the assault, but in the confusion drew heavy fire from the enemy as well as from fellow Confederates who mistook them for Union troops.[66]

Fortunately for the Texans and other Confederates, Union commander General Rosecrans, in the confusion of shifting troops to meet the attack, left a gap in his line near the point of Hood's assault. Hood's Division charged through the opening and rolled up the Union center. Only the gallant efforts of Maj. Gen. George H. Thomas halted the Confederate advance and prevented a complete Union disaster. Rosecrans and the Federal army fell back toward Chattanooga, leaving the Confederates in command of the field.

Hood did not get to see the success of Confederate arms at Chickamauga. At the height of the attack, while talking with General Robertson, Hood was struck in the upper right thigh by a minie ball that shattered the bone. He was taken to a field hospital, where his damaged limb was amputated at the thigh. Although Hood would recover and later command the Army of Tennessee, this was the last time he would lead troops of the Texas Brigade.[67]

Although the Confederates won the Battle of Chickamauga, their losses were high. Missing reports and contradictory estimates make it difficult to determine the exact number of Confederate casualties. One historian (Glenn Tucker) gives a total of 20,950 Confederates killed, wounded, and missing; another (Thomas Livermore), 18,454. Bragg himself said he lost two-fifths of his army, which numbered about 68,000.[68]

The losses in the Texas Brigade are equally confusing. In his book *Lee's Grenadier Guard,* historian Harold Simpson lists 570 killed, wounded, and missing in the brigade, but in his *Hood's Texas Brigade: A Compendium,* Simpson shows only 410 casualties. The brigade's loss of regimental officers was high: Lt. Col. John P. Bane, commanding the Fourth Texas, Maj. J. C. Rogers, commanding the Fifth Texas, and Maj. John W. Reedy, executive officer of the Third Arkansas, were all wounded.[69]

In the Battle of Chickamauga the men of Hood's Brigade fought alongside other Texans for the first time. The Eighth Texas Cavalry (better known as Terry's Texas Rangers), the Eleventh Texas Cavalry, the Seventh, Ninth, and Tenth Texas infantries, and several Texas dismounted cavalry regiments were in the fighting. Among the Texas casualties was John Gregg, an East Texas lawyer and judge who commanded a brigade of Texans and Tennesseans in Bushrod Johnson's Division. Gregg was shot in the neck in the fighting on the 19th. He fell from his horse and was near death when rescued from scavengers by men of the Texas Brigade. Little did the Texans realize at the time that Gregg would later command their brigade in the Army of Northern Virginia.[70]

After the victory at Chickamauga, Bragg lay siege to Rosecrans' army in Chattanooga. For the next six weeks Hood's Division, now commanded by Micah Jenkins, held the left flank of the Confederate line near Lookout Mountain. There was little military activity during this period. The Texas Brigade was involved in a small engagement on October 28 known as the Battle of Wauhatchie, or Raccoon Mountain. In an ill-conceived and poorly executed night operation the Confederates attacked a Union division which was part of the Federal forces sent to relieve Rosecrans. In the original plan two divisions, McLaws' and Hood's, were to make the attack but a mix-up in orders caused Hood's Division to make the attack alone. Further confusion and lack of coordination resulted in a complete failure. Fortunately for the Confederates, casualties were low, but the reputation of the Texas Brigade was slightly tarnished. In the confused fighting the Fourth Texas, believing itself outflanked, gave way and withdrew in what some called the "Raccoon Races."[71]

The siege around Chattanooga came to an end for the men of the Texas Brigade in early November. Longstreet and his corps were ordered to drive Gen. Ambrose Burnside out of the Knoxville area. The move was made partly by rail and partly by foot in bitterly cold and rainy weather in early November. Once in the area south of Knoxville Longstreet's troops pushed Burnside's Federals back to a defensive perimenter on the hills surrounding the city. By November 17 Longstreet had drawn a semicircle around Knoxville and lay siege to the enemy.

The Texas regiments were engaged in some skirmishing with the enemy during the Knoxville campaign but performed only a diversionary role in Longstreet's one major attempt to break through Burnside's lines. This assault, an attack on a Union strong point, Fort Sanders, was a complete failure. Several days later, Longstreet, having learned that Bragg had been defeated at Chattanooga, gave up the siege and moved his troops east toward Virginia.[72]

Longstreet's Corps went into winter quarters at Morristown, on the East Tennessee and French Broad Railroad in a valley about forty miles northeast of Knoxville. There continued to be some skirmishing with Union troops as both Federals and Confederates vied for control of the East Tennessee valley. Lack of food for the men and fodder for the animals was a major problem during the winter months. Foraging operations occupied much of the troops' time.

Shortages of footwear continued to be a major concern for the Texas regiments and other units in Longstreet's command. A makeshift factory was established, providing some shoes and boots. Longstreet encouraged his men to make moccasins from green hides. One Texan, Sgt. D. H. Hamilton of the First Texas, reported that the mocassins "were not gaudy footwear but many thousands in Longstreet's Corps blessed their good fortune when they were able to get them."[73]

The morale of the Texas Brigade continued to be high in spite of hardships endured. When the enlistment period for many of the men expired in December, most reenlisted for the duration of the war. Even so, the brigade remained uunderstrength due to the months of hard campaigning. General Robertson reported in December the brigade had only 784 men present for duty, the size of a small regiment. The Fourth Texas with 213 officers and men was the largest regiment, followed by the Third Arkansas, 202 officers and men. The Fifth Texas had 196 men; the "Ragged First" had only 173.[74]

To increase the number of men available for duty, Robertson recommended that the entire brigade be allowed to return to the Trans Mississippi for the purpose of conducting a recruitment drive. Once the unit was back to proper size the brigade would return to the Army of Northern Virginia. Robertson's plan had the support of the Texas congressional delegation and General Hood, now recuperating from his wounds at Chickamauga; however, the Confederate War Department refused to approve the plan.[75]

Meanwhile, General Robertson was at odds with new division commander Micah Jenkins and corps commander James Longstreet. Jenkins, who had only joined the division after the Chickamauga campaign, was a particular favorite of Longstreet, who placed him in temporary command when it appeared Hood would not return to the division. Robertson and most of the Texans supported Evander Law, who had been with the division since Gaines' Mill, for the position. Law had commanded the division both at Gettysburg and at Chickamauga, when Hood was wounded and had earned the respect of the Texans.

Jenkins quarreled with both Law and Robertson from the moment of his appointment. Law was accused of failure to support Jenkins in the fighting at Wauhatchie and was removed from command. However, Law had the support of President Davis and was returned to command of his old brigade.[76]

Robertson was also relieved in November by Jenkins, who charged the Texan was not fit to command. After an investigation, however, General Bragg restored Robertson to command of the Texas Brigade. On December 18 Jenkins preferred new charges against Robertson. These charges stemmed from Robertson's opposition to orders by Jenkins that entailed a long and harried march over rough terrain in extremely bad weather. Robertson, who believed the march would result in unnecessary suffering for the men in his command, advised his regimental commanders that he opposed the march and would obey only under protest.

Longstreet, who believed Robertson exercised "an injurious influence over the troops," ordered the Texan tried by a military court. The court, presided over by Maj. Gen. Simon Bolivar Buckner, convened in early February 1864. Although the court acquitted Robertson of "improper motives," it disapproved of his conduct. Robertson was reprimanded and relieved as commander of the Texas Brigade.[77]

The decision to remove Robertson, who commanded the brigade longer than any other general, was not popular with the Texans. Although they sometimes complained about his excessive "mothering," they supported Robertson, whom they referred to as "Aunt Polly." Several petitions protesting his removal were forwarded to Richmond, but to no avail. One soldier later wrote "this action [removal of Robertson] came very near destroying the efficiency of Hood's Texas Brigade. . . . The boys love Aunt Polly and would have fought for him to the last extremity."[78]

Robertson returned to Texas after his removal as commander of the Texas Brigade. His successor was John Gregg, the East Texas brigadier whom the Texans had rescued at Chickamauga. Gregg had now recovered from his wounds and was ready for reassignment. An experienced combat officer who had led troops in both the Army of Mississippi and the Army of Tennessee, Gregg was commanding a mixed brigade of Tennesseans and Texans when wounded. He had the reputation as a gallant and courageous officer. According to historian William C. Davis, Gregg was "a rugged and unrelentless fighter . . . personally without fear, even looking the role of a rugged frontiersman with his 'spade' beard, high forehead, and fierce gaze." But he was a no-nonsense leader, quite unlike the free, easygoing Robertson.[79]

Two weeks before Gregg assumed command, a new commander of Hood's old division was appointed. General Longstreet, the corps commander, supported Micah Jenkins for the post, but President Davis gave the appointment to Charles W. Field, a Kentuckian and West Point graduate. Like Gregg, Field was an experienced and highly competent officer who had been wounded and was now ready for reassignment. And like Gregg, Field was respected more than loved by the men of the Texas Brigade.[80]

Field and Gregg had been in command of their units for only a few weeks when orders were received for the return of Longstreet's Corps to Virginia. The Texans and Arkansans were the last of Longstreet's troops to leave Tennessee, boarding the train at Zollicoffer on April 20. They arrived at Charlottesville on the 22nd. From there they marched to Gordonsville, where they camped for several days. While there they received badly needed supplies including food, uniforms, and shoes. On April 29 the brigade participated in a corps review by General Lee in which the Confederate commander described the Texas Brigade as "the best fighting brigade in the corps."[81]

The Texas Brigade was soon tested again on the field of battle. U. S. Grant, now commanding all Union armies, began a major offensive against Lee's army in early May. The Union Army of the Potomac, over 100,000 men strong, crossed the Rapidan at Germanna and Ely's Fords in a new drive on Richmond. Lee moved his Confederate troops to meet Grant in the Wilderness area to the west of the old Chancellorsville battleground. Longstreet's Corps, which was forty miles to the southwest when the fighting began, was ordered to join the troops of A.P. Hill and Richard Ewell in the attempt to halt Grant's advance. Field's Division, with the Texas Brigade in the lead, arrived on May 6 at a critical time. Winfield Hancock's Union Corps was pushing the Confederates back and a breakthrough seemed imminent when the Texas Brigade, less than 800 men, came on the scene. There, in a dramatic moment (described in Chapter One of this book), General Lee called upon Gregg and his men to drive the enemy back. Under heavy enemy fire the Texans and Arkansans charged to the attack. The Third Arkansas, commanded by the veteran colonel Van H. Manning, formed the left of the brigade. The First Texas, led in battle by Lt. Col. Frederick S. Bass (who replaced Philip A. Work when Work returned to Texas due to poor health) was to the right of the Arkansans. The Fourth Texas, commanded by Col. John P. Bane, was to the right of the First Texas, while the Fifth Texas, led by Lt. Col. King Bryan, was on the extreme right of the brigade.

The Texans and Arkansans broke through the first line of Federals but were forced to fall back due to heavy fire from entrenched Union troops. After regrouping, Gregg's men charged again. For thirty minutes the fighting raged. Casualties mounted on both sides. Lt. Col. Bryan of the Fifth Texas was wounded in the arm. Colonel Manning of the Third Arkansas was wounded in the thigh and taken prisoner. Lt. Whit Randle of the Fifth Texas was shot through the body five times but survived. Willis Watts, a soldier in the First Texas, was wounded three times. General Gregg avoided injury himself but had three horses shot out from under him. Two-thirds of his men were casualties. Some companies were almost wiped out.[82]

With such losses the Texas Brigade finally withdrew, but Gregg and his men had accomplished their purpose. The Union advancing column had been halted and later gave ground when hit by other brigades in Field's Division. The fighting continued for the rest of the day, but Gregg's Brigade saw no additional action except for some skirmishing in the evening.[83]

After the failure to break the Confederate lines in the Wilderness, Grant swung his army around Lee's right and moved toward the crossroads town of Spotsylvania Court House. Lee moved his army to prevent the capture of the town. Field's and Kershaw's divisions were the first Confederate units to arrive. They quickly entrenched in anticipation of a Union attack. On May 10 Grant launched a series of major assaults at the sector held by the Texas Brigade. The first two attacks were beaten back, but in the third charge the Federals broke through the thinly held lines of the First Texas. The Federals were on the verge of victory when enfilading fire from the Third Arkansas on the left and the Fourth and Fifth Texas on the right drove them back.[84]

Fighting went on at Spotsylvania for nearly two weeks before Grant broke off and slid his army southward. The Texas Brigade saw little action in the engagements that took place along the North Anna River in late May. In the vicinity of Cold Harbor, near the old battlefield at Gaines' Mill, both armies dug long lines of trenches supported by strong breastworks. Longstreet's Corps was in the center of the Confederate line where Grant attacked on June 3. The Texas Brigade was slightly to the right of the opening assault but poured fire into the flank of the attacking Union troops. Sgt. D. H. Hamilton of the First Texas described the carnage: "The slaughter was fearful to look at. It was one of the most horrible sights of all that war of slaughter and suffering." The attack ended in thirty minutes with thousands of Union casualties.[85]

After his failure to break Lee's lines at Cold Harbor, Grant swung his army across the James River in an attempt to take Richmond from the south. Once again Lee moved his army to meet Grant. The Texas Brigade crossed the James River on June 16 and two days later moved into trenches east of Petersburg and south of the Appomattox River. For the next month the brigade was in the trenches exposed to enemy artillery fire. The brigade was in the vicinity of the area where Union troops were digging a tunnel in which they placed heavy explosives. Fortunately for the Texans and Arkansans, the brigade was ordered to move to a new position north of the James River just before the Federals exploded 8,000 pounds of gunpowder, creating a massive crater in the Confederate line.[86]

The Texas Brigade spent the next eight months in the defensive lines east of Richmond. During this period the brigade participated in six battles. Several, such as a skirmish at White Oak Swamp in August, were small engagements; others, such as the one at New Market Heights on September 29, were much larger affairs. In this battle the Federals attempted to capture two Confederate forts, Harrison and Gilmer. Although the Texas Brigade successfully defended the outer works north of Harrison from enemy assault, the fort itself was taken by other Union troops. The brigade did, however, assist a Georgia brigade in the successful defense of Fort Gilmer.[87]

Lee was determined to retake Fort Harrison. On October 7 he ordered Field's Division and Robert Hoke's Division to attack the enemy position between Darbytown and New Market roads while two other Confederate brigades outflanked the Federals and attacked from the rear. In the attack the Texas Brigade assaulted a strong enemy position on Darbytown Road. The Texans and Arkansans had a difficult time because they were not properly supported by other brigades of the division. Also, enemy troops were equipped with new Spencer repeating rifles, which allowed them to put up a massive wall of fire. Although some members of the brigade managed to get within a hundred yards of their objective, they were beaten back by enemy fire.

Casualties were high. General Gregg was killed almost instantly by a ball through the neck as he led the attack. His body lay in a pool of blood but was recovered by several Texans who crawled through enemy fire. Col. Frederick S. Bass, who assumed command when Gregg fell, was also wounded, requiring Lt. Col. Clinton Winkler of the Fourth Texas to direct the brigade in the final stages of the battle. Over one hundred members of the brigade, which entered the battle with only 450 men, were killed or wounded.[88]

After the failure to take Fort Harrison, the Texas Brigade took a position on the Richmond defense line about four miles southeast of the capital between the Williamsburg and Charles City roads, where it remained until the last month of the war. Skirmishing continued throughout the autumn and into the winter. On October 27, 1864, the brigade was in the center of a Union assault against the inner defenses of Richmond. The Texas Brigade, supported by two Georgia brigades, beat back the enemy attackers and captured more than a hundred Federal troops and several battle flags.[89]

The 1864 campaigns took a severe toll on the depleted ranks of the Texas regiments. Before his death on Darbytown Road, General Gregg, estimating that he had only about 430 men ready for duty, revived Jerome Robertson's plan to send the brigade back to the Trans Mississippi for recruitment duty. His plan had the support of the Texas legislature, General Field, and Gen. Dick Anderson, who was acting corps commander at the time. General Lee agreed that additional troops should be enrolled in the Trans Mississippi but was opposed to releasing men from the brigade for recruiting purposes.[90]

In December 1864 Col. Frederick S. Bass, commanding the Texas Brigade following Gregg's death, brought up the Robertson plan once again. He wrote to Secretary of War James Seddon requesting that the brigade be furloughed home for recruitment duty and return for the spring campaign. Seddon referred the request to Lee, who once again stated his opposition. Seddon thereupon denied the request.[91]

At President Davis' suggestion General Lee established committees to discuss the possibility of consolidating small units in the Confederate army. There was fear that the Texas Brigade might be consolidated with one or more other small brigades. To prevent such action the officers and men of the brigade drafted an appeal to the president. The appeal was delivered by Maj. William H. Martin of the Fourth Texas, a lawyer and former state legislator. Before Martin, a gregarious raconteur nicknamed "Howdy," could make his comments to the chief executive, General Lee, who was present, remarked to Davis that "I never ordered the [Texas] Brigade to hold a place they did not hold it." Davis, moved by the words of General Lee and "Howdy" Martin, then assured the Texan "as long as there is a man to carry that battle flag you shall remain a brigade."[92]

With these words, fears of consolidation evaporated. The men of the Texas Brigade spent the bitterly cold winter of 1864-65 in the trenches around Richmond, confident that their unit would remain intact.

The future of the Confederacy, however, appeared grim. Sherman completed his march through Georgia, Phil Sheridan drove Jubal Early and his army out of the Shenandoah Valley, and George H. Thomas shattered the Confederate Army of Tennessee at Nashville. Rations were scarce and the cause looked hopeless. Even so, the men of the Texas Brigade remained loyal to the cause. In late January 1865 the men of the brigade adopted resolutions expressing their desire to continue the struggle and to rid the country "of the hated and despised foe" or "die in the attempt."[93]

The odds against the success of the Confederate cause continued to grow. As the size of his army increased, Grant extended his lines around the Confederate defenses at Richmond. In late March, Lee made a desperate effort to prevent encirclement. On the night of March 24-25 he ordered Maj. Gen. John Gordon to attack the enemy just east of Petersburg. Gordon captured a Federal strong point, Fort Stedman, but a Union counterattack forced him to fall back to the Confederate lines. A week later, on April 1, Union troops commanded by Phil Sheridan defeated the Confederates at Five Forks to the west of Petersburg. The Southside Railroad, the last artery connecting Petersburg with the South, was now exposed to Union attack. On the morning of April 2, General Lee advised President Davis that he could no longer defend the Confederate capital. As Davis and the Confederate government evacuated the city, Lee ordered his troops to pull out of the Petersburg and Richmond lines. He hoped to withdraw his army to the west and join forces with Confederates retreating north from the Carolinas.

Field's Division, which included the Texas Brigade, was ordered to withdraw from its defensive lines east of Richmond and take a position along the Appomattox River near Petersburg. The Texas Brigade, now commanded by Col. Robert M. Powell, who had rejoined the army after his release from a Union prison, was ordered to delay the Federals as the Confederate army pulled out of its lines. The Texas Brigade formed the rear guard of Lee's army as it withdrew westward. For the next several days the Texans skirmished with the enemy as the army retreated.[94]

Although hungry and tired, the men of the Texas Brigade continued to beat off attacks by the enemy. As the brigade approached Appomattox Courthouse on April 8, they heard that General Lee had opened negotiations with Grant for the surrender of the army. When news of the surrender was confirmed, many Texans stood in disbelief. Some were angry and smashed their weapons against rocks rather than turn them over to the enemy. Others accepted the decision as recognition of the hopeless situation they faced in confronting overwhelming enemy numbers.

The formal surrender of the Army of Northern Virginia took place on April 12, 1865. Of the 5,300 men who had served in the three Texas and one Arkansas regiment that made up the brigade, only 617 were present at the day of the surrender: five in headquarters (Col. R. M. Powell), 149 in the First Texas (Col. Frederick S. Bass), 158 in the Fourth Texas (Lt. Col. Clinton M. Winkler), 161 in the Fifth Texas (Capt. W. T. Hill), and 144 in the Third Arkansas (Lt. Col. Robert Taylor).[95]

Under the terms of the surrender the men of Lee's army were given paroles and allowed to return home. A few of the Texans made their way to Yorktown, Virginia, where they took water transportation to New Orleans or Galveston. The majority of the brigade headed overland by the most direct route home. Most of the Arkansans took a route through Chattanooga, while the Texans went through the Carolinas, Georgia, and the Gulf states. By early June most of them were back in Texas. A large group of them led by Maj. W. H. Martin and Capt. W. T. Hill attended a final farewell dinner in Houston before heading to their home communities. Later many would join the Hood's Brigade Association and attend the various annual reunions, where they would commemorate the sacrifices, hardships, and great moments they shared together in one of the Confederacy's greatest fighting units.[96]

Chapter Three

Texas Cavalry in the Heartland

Eighth Texas Cavalry
Eleventh Texas Cavalry
Ross' Texas Cavalry Brigade
Third Texas Cavalry
Sixth Texas Cavalry
Ninth Texas Cavalry
Twenty-seventh Texas Cavalry

CAVALRY REGIMENTS FROM the Lone Star State played a significant role in military operations in the region between the Mississippi River and the Carolinas, referred to by historian Thomas L. Connelly as the Confederate Heartland. In this vast territory covering over 225,000 square miles Civil War armies moved great distances in a conflict that centered around rivers, roads, and railroads that were vital to the social and economic life of the area. Both sides used their mounted troops to gather information by reconnaissance, to screen infantry troop movements, to raid enemy military depots, and to attack supply lines. In these activities the Confederacy was fortunate to have several bold and energetic cavalry commanders. Best known of these were Nathan Bedford Forrest, John Hunt Morgan, and Joe Wheeler. In addition to these well-known cavalrymen there were a number of lesser known but highly capable subordinates, including Texans John A. Wharton, Tom Harrison, and Sul Ross.[1]

Six mounted regiments from Texas served in the Confederate

Heartland. One of these regiments, the Eighth Texas Cavalry, better known as Terry's Texas Rangers, spent the entire Civil War in the Heartland. The other regiments, the Third, Sixth, Ninth, Eleventh, and Twenty-seventh Texas cavalries, fought in the Trans Mississippi region the first year of the war, but spent the last three years in the Heartland. The Eleventh Texas, recruited in northeastern Texas, was sometimes brigaded with the Eighth Texas. The Third, Sixth, Ninth, and Twenty-seventh made up an all-Texas brigade commanded first by John W. Whitfield and later Lawrence Sullivan "Sul" Ross.

Since the Eighth and Eleventh cavalries were in brigades that included regiments from other states, each will be discussed individually. The other regiments, in the all-Texas brigade for much of the war, will be discussed together.

In addition to the mounted cavalry regiments described in this chapter there were eight Texas dismounted cavalry regiments that served in the Heartland. Although they continued to be called cavalry, these dismounted regiments fought as infantry. They will be discussed with Texas infantry regiments in the chapter that follows.

EIGHTH TEXAS CAVALRY (TERRY'S TEXAS RANGERS)

The Eighth Texas Cavalry was the most famous mounted regiment from the Lone Star State in the American Civil War. Organized by Benjamin F. Terry, a wealthy Fort Bend planter, and Tom Lubbock, Houston commission merchant and brother of Texas Civil War governor Francis R. Lubbock, Terry's Texas Rangers, as they came to be known, fought in many of the great battles in the West, including Shiloh, Perryville, Murfreesboro, Chickamauga, Atlanta, and Bentonville. In more than two hundred engagements with the enemy the Rangers established a reputation for their boldness and daring. Noted for their fearlessness in the attack, the Rangers preferred the six-shooter and the double-barreled shotgun to the saber. By the end of the war their reputation for courage and bravery was well established. With the possible exception of Hood's Texas Brigade they were the best known Texas unit in the Confederate army.[2]

The Eighth Texas was organized in late summer 1861. Terry

Benjamin F. Terry, Colonel, Eighth Texas Cavalry.
—Courtesy Harold B. Simpson Research Center, Hillsboro, Texas

and Lubbock, both ardent secessionists and supporters of states' rights, journeyed to Richmond, Virginia, shortly after Texas withdrew from the Union. There they received authorization for the creation of a mounted regiment. After serving as volunteer aides to Gen. James Longstreet at the first Battle of Manassas, they returned to Texas, where on August 12, 1861, Terry issued a call for volunteers. Each man was required to furnish his own weapons and equipment, including a shotgun or carbine, Colt revolver, Bowie knife, saddle, bridle, and blanket. Horses were to be provided by the army.[3]

There was little difficulty in obtaining Texas recruits for cavalry service. In a state where distances were great, most men preferred the cavalry rather than the infantry. The British observer Lt. Col. Arthur Fremantle of the Coldstream Guards, who came through Texas during the war, noted "it was very difficult to raise infantry in Texas, as no Texan walks a yard if he can help it." Texas Governor Edward Clark, who was responsible for providing troops for the Confederacy, noted that the "predelection of Texans for cavalry service, found as it is upon their peerless horsemanship, is so powerful that they are unwilling in many instances to engage in service of any other description unless required by actual necessity."[4]

Most of the recruits for Terry's regiment came from coastal

and Central Texas counties. In Houston on September 9, 1861, ten companies consisting of approximately one hundred men each were formed and mustered into Confederate service. Shown below are names of the captains of each company and the counties from which most of the volunteers came.[5]

Company	Captain	County or Counties
A	Thomas Harrison	McLennan & Adjoining
B	John A. Wharton	Brazoria, Matagorda
C	Mark Evans	Gonzales & Adjoining
D	Stephen C. Ferrell	Bastrop & Adjoining
E	L. N. Rayburn	Gonzales & Adjoining
F	Louis M. Strobel	Fayette
G	W. Y. Houston	Bexar, Goliad
H	John T. Holt	Fort Bend
I	Isham G. Jones	Gonzales & Adjoining
K	John G. Walker	Harris, Montgomery

The regiment was originally organized for service in Virginia. In late September the recruits boarded trains in Houston and headed east. From Beaumont they proceeded across the bayou country of Louisiana by a combination of foot, horseback, rail, and steamboat. Upon arriving in New Orleans they learned that they were being diverted to Kentucky for service in the army commanded by Albert Sidney Johnston. Although this was a disappointment because Virginia was considered the pivotal area of the war, the men were pleased to serve under Johnston, who had been a brigadier general in the army of the Texas Republic, had owned a plantation in Brazoria County, and was well known to Terry and others in the regiment.

The Texans traveled by rail, first to Nashville and then to Bowling Green, Kentucky, where Johnston made his headquarters. Final organization of the regiment, officially the Eighth Texas Cavalry but referred to by the men as Terry's Texas Rangers, was completed with the election of Terry as colonel, Lubbock as lieutenant colonel, and Tom Harrison (captain of Company A) as major.[6]

The first weeks in Kentucky were frustrating. Although assurances had been given that horses would be readily available, it was several weeks before sufficient mounts for all the men were acquired. An additional setback occurred when an outbreak of measles sent many of the Texans to the hospital. In their weakened condition a number of the men contracted pneumonia and died.[7]

Their numbers reduced considerably by illness and death, the Texans first saw action against the enemy in mid-December. Colonel Terry and 250 Rangers were part of a reconnaissance expedition led by Brig. Gen. Thomas C. Hindman in the Green River country on December 17. Near the town of Woodsonville, Kentucky, the Rangers encountered Union infantry concealed behind some haystacks and a fence. Hindman wanted the Texans to wait until his infantry and artillery were in place, but Terry favored a more aggressive course of action. After a brief exchange of fire, he led seventy-five Rangers in a bold attack against the enemy. Although the Union troops outnumbered the Texans nearly four to one, the surprise of the sudden cavalry charge caused the Federals to fall back in panic and confusion. More than fifty of the Federals were killed or captured. The Texas losses were minimal—four killed and ten wounded. One of those killed was Colonel Terry, hit in the jaw by a bullet which traveled up through the brain.[8]

Historian Tom Cutrer noted that the fighting at Woodsonville "resulted in a Confederate victory achieved with much elan and gallantry but bought at too high a price." Terry's sacrifice accomplished little. Additional Union troops arrived on the scene, and Hindman withdrew the Confederates from the area.[9]

The Rangers saw little action in late December and early January. After Terry's death at Woodsonville, Tom Lubbock became commander of the regiment. Because of illness, however, he remained in the hospital at Nashville. In his absence Tom Harrison, the ranking regimental officer, directed the Rangers. After Lubbock died in January, elections were held for new regimental officers. John A. Wharton, wealthy planter and lawyer from Brazoria County, was chosen colonel and commander of the regiment.[10]

The new commander was a member of a distinguished Texas family. His father, William H. Wharton, was a leader in the Texas struggle for independence from Mexico. Two uncles, John Wharton and Leonard W. Groce, were officers in the Texas revolutionary army. Although he was only in his early thirties, John A. Wharton played a prominent role in the Texas secession convention. He accompanied Terry and Lubbock in their journey to Richmond but

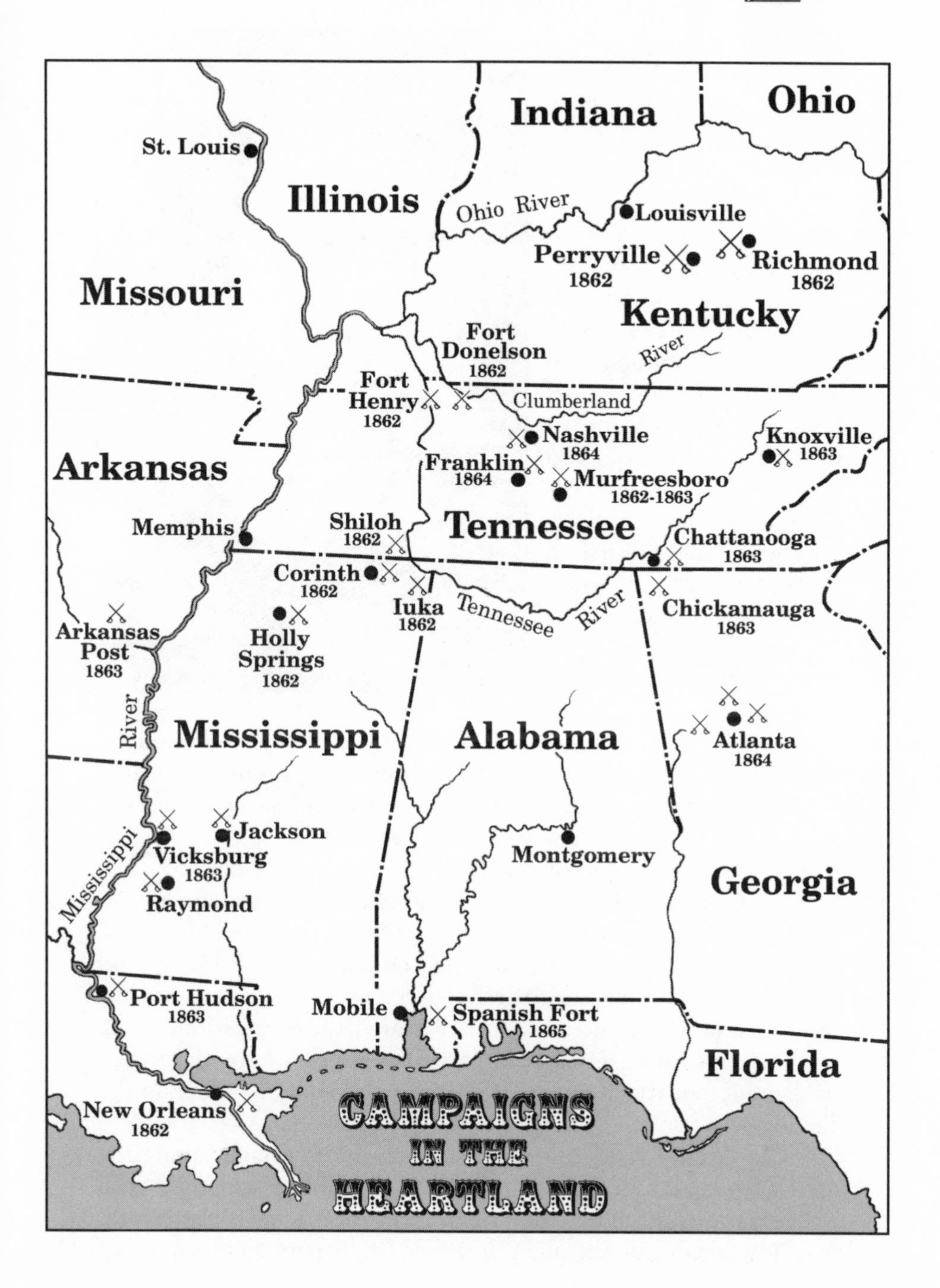
Indiana
Ohio
St. Louis
Illinois
Ohio River
Louisville
Perryville
1862
Richmond
1862
Missouri
Kentucky
Fort
Donelson
1862
River
Fort
Henry
1862
Clumberland
Nashville
1864
Knoxville
1863
Arkansas
Franklin
1864
Murfreesboro
1862-1863
Memphis
Shiloh
1862
Tennessee
Chattanooga
1863
Corinth
1862
Iuka
1862
Tennessee
River
Chickamauga
1863
Arkansas
Post
1863
Holly
Springs
1862
River
Mississippi
Alabama
Atlanta
1864
Jackson
Vicksburg
1863
Raymond
Mississippi
Montgomery
Georgia
Port Hudson
1863
Mobile
Spanish Fort
1865
Florida
New Orleans
1862
CAMPAIGNS
IN THE
HEARTLAND

John A. Wharton, Colonel, Eighth Texas Cavalry.
—Courtesy Harold B. Simpson Research Center, Hillsboro, Texas

missed the Battle of Manassas due to illness. He returned to Texas with Terry and Lubbock and was elected captain of Company B, made up of men from Brazoria and Matagorda counties. Although his prior military experience was limited to the cadet corps at South Carolina College, Wharton was well thought of by the men in the regiment. L. B. Giles, a member of Company D, later recalled that Wharton was a "captivating public speaker" who was enterprising and politically ambitious. According to Giles, Wharton "never forgot during a wakeful moment that the soldier who survived the war would be a voter."[11]

Under Wharton's command the Rangers carried out scouting, picketing, and patrolling duties in Kentucky during late January and February 1862. When Albert Sidney Johnston ordered the withdrawal of his army southward after the fall of Forts Henry and Donelson in late February, the Rangers served as a rear guard for the retreating Confederates. In late March the Texans joined the rest of Johnston's army at Corinth, Mississippi, where plans were finalized for an attack on Grant's army at Pittsburg Landing on the Tennessee River.[12]

On April 3 Johnston ordered his army to advance along the narrow roads leading from Corinth to the Tennessee River. The Rangers rode on the left wing of the army as it moved northward. A steady rain during the night drenched the Texans. In the morning the men convinced Wharton to allow them to test their weapons to see that they were still working. The firing set off such a commotion that Wharton was reprimanded by General Johnston for this violation of security which might warn the enemy of the Confederate approach.[13]

Apparently, the indiscretion of the Rangers caused no harm. When the Confederates attacked the Union army in its camps near the little church named Shiloh on April 6, the enemy was taken by surprise. Assigned to the Confederate army's left flank, the Rangers were in the thick of the fighting. As the Federals fell back toward the Tennessee River the Rangers fought both as mounted and dismounted troops. In the afternoon the Texans came under heavy fire from the enemy; five men were killed and twenty-six wounded, including Colonel Wharton, who was hit in the leg. Although Wharton refused to leave the field, the Rangers were forced to fall back.

On the next day, Gen. P. G. T. Beauregard, who succeeded to command when Albert Sidney Johnston was killed the previous afternoon, ordered the Rangers to ride around the Federal right flank. Although the Texans once again charged the enemy, heavy Federal fire forced them to give ground. They soon reformed their ranks and spent the rest of the day fighting as dismounted troops. The Rangers and other Confederates fought stubbornly but continued to give ground throughout the day. That night General Beauregard ordered a retreat to Corinth. The Rangers and other Rebel cavalry helped cover the Confederate withdrawal.[14]

For the next three weeks the Rangers, along with other troops in Beauregard's army, rested and recuperated from their losses at Shiloh. Dunbar Affleck, a seventeen-year-old private and son of well-known agricultural reformer Thomas Affleck of Washington County, was a new recruit who joined Company B during this period. Young Affleck wrote his parents that the Rangers were camped about two miles from Corinth in a beautiful grove of trees. He reported that other recruits were coming in each day but that the regiment had "not more than seven or eight hundred efective [*sic*] men, and most of them were poorly mounted." Affleck experienced some difficulty in finding a horse. In a letter written a week after he joined the regiment he complained that he still did not have a mount. He reported that the Rangers were well provided with food,

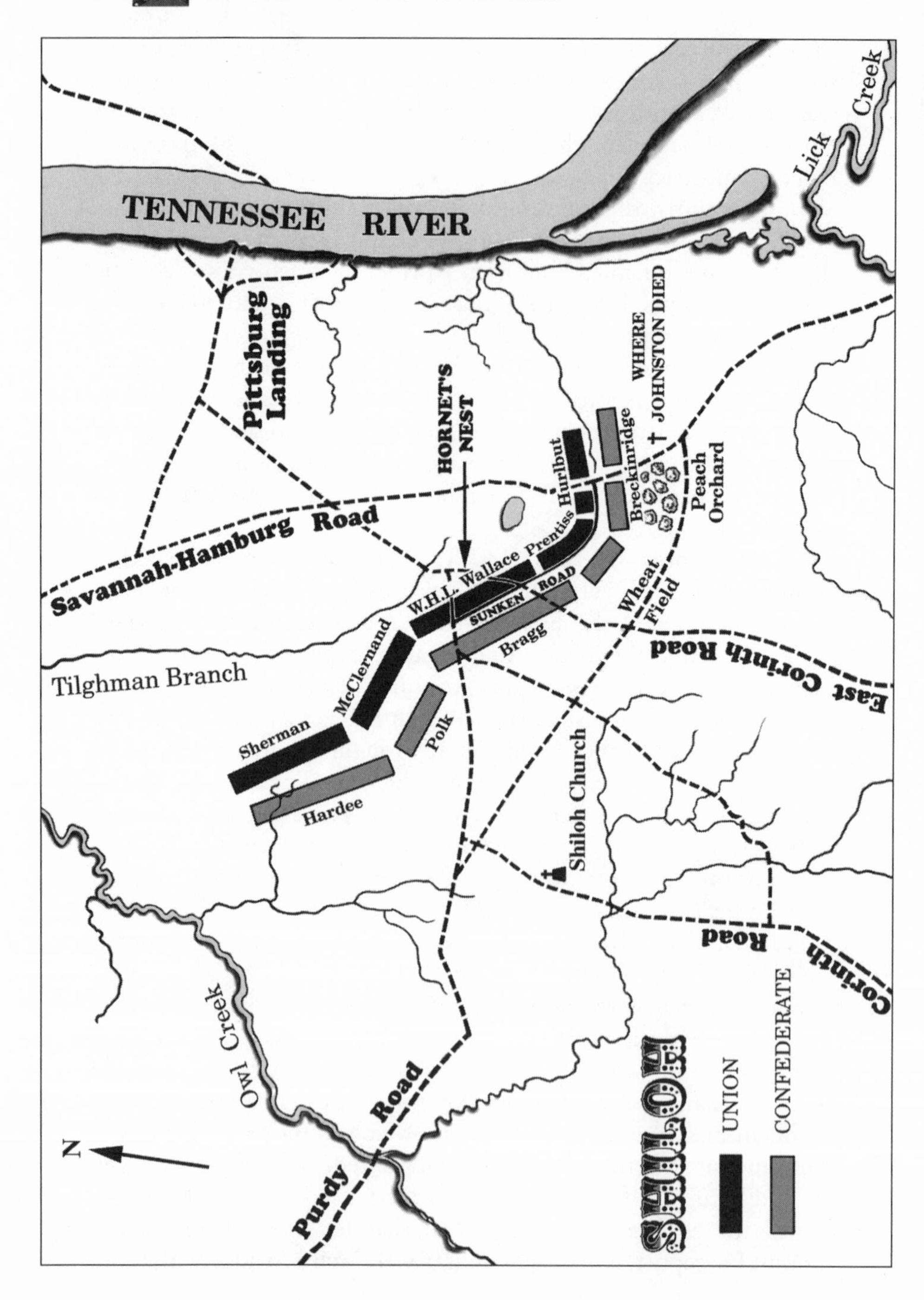
TENNESSEE RIVER
Lick Creek
Pittsburg Landing
HORNET'S NEST
WHERE JOHNSTON DIED
Hurlbut
Breckinridge
Peach Orchard
Savannah-Hamburg Road
Prentiss
W.H.L. Wallace
SUNKEN ROAD
Wheat Field
Bragg
McClernand
Tilghman Branch
East Corinth Road
Sherman
Polk
Hardee
Shiloh Church
Corinth Road
Owl Creek
Purdy Road
N
SHILOH
UNION
CONFEDERATE

having plenty of coffee, sugar, flour, meal, bacon, beef, chickens, and eggs. His own health was good, but apparently many others were ill. L. B. Giles of Company F remembered that there "was much sickness, caused by bad water."[15]

In May the Rangers were ordered to East Tennessee, where they engaged in scouting and patrolling. In the summer they were assigned to Nathan Bedford Forrest's cavalry brigade. After some skirmishes with the enemy at Bethel and Morrison's Depot, the Rangers took part in Forrest's raid on the Union supply depot at Murfreesboro, Tennessee. In this campaign the Rangers led the attack on the camp of the Ninth Michigan Infantry and the Seventh Pennsylvania Cavalry. In a fearless charge against the enemy several Texans went down, including Colonel Wharton, who was severely wounded in the arm. Fighting raged for several hours before the Federals surrendered. Twelve hundred enemy troops were taken prisoner, the railroad was dismantled, and the depot burned. When the Confederates withdrew they carried off several wagons loaded with military stores and supplies. In his report of the battle Forrest praised Wharton and his regiment for their boldness in the attack.[16]

In autumn the Rangers were part of Braxton Bragg's army in the attempt to free Kentucky from Union control. Nathan Bedford Forrest had been promoted to brigadier general and given a new command in Middle Tennessee. John A. Wharton was named commander of Forrest's old cavalry brigade consisting of the Eighth Texas, the Fourth Tennessee, and the First Kentucky. Lt. Col. Tom Harrison, the next senior officer in the regiment, succeeded Wharton as commander of Terry's Rangers.

Fighting occurred almost daily as Wharton's cavalry, including the Eighth Texas, covered the right wing of Bragg's army as it marched north. In the Battle of Perryville, fought on October 8, the Rangers drove the Federals back in a wild charge against the enemy's left flank. Although the results of the battle were inconclusive, the Confederates withdrew back into Tennessee after the encounter.[17]

Wharton's cavalry won the praise of both Generals Bragg and Leonidas Polk for its part in the Kentucky campaign. Shortly thereafter, Wharton was promoted to brigadier general and Harrison to colonel.

The new commander of the Rangers, Tom Harrison, lacked

the polish and personal skills of his predecessor. Described by one of his soldiers as "a small, nervous, irascible man," Harrison was personally courageous and once in battle knew no fear. He grew up in Mississippi but lived in Brazoria County during the early 1840s. He returned to Mississippi to serve in Jefferson Davis' regiment in the Mexican War but returned to Texas after the war. Harrison practiced law briefly in Houston and Marlin, before moving to Waco. He helped raise the company of volunteers in the Waco area that became Company A of Terry's Rangers. When the regiment was formally organized, he was chosen major.

After the deaths of Terry and Lubbock, Harrison led the Rangers briefly and became lieutenant colonel when Wharton was chosen as regimental commander. Although he was frequently ill, he avoided injury during the first year of fighting, leading the Texans to give him the nickname "Old Ironsides." His good fortune ended when be became regimental commander; in the next two years he was wounded three times and had five horses killed under him.[18]

The Rangers' first battle under their new commander was at Murfreesboro, Tennessee, in late December 1862. In this battle, called Stones River by the Federals, Braxton Bragg launched a major assault against the Union army led by William S. Rosecrans. In the initial attack on the morning of December 31, Wharton's Brigade, including Harrison and the Eighth Texas, slashed away at the Federal right wing and rear, capturing 1,500 prisoners, a four-gun battery, and several hundred wagons. Wharton's cavalry drove the Federals back to the Nashville Pike but was not strong enough to cut Rosecrans' supply line back to Nashville. The fighting continued throughout the day with heavy casualties on both sides. After a pause in fighting on January 1, the contest resumed in earnest on January 2 with the Confederates once again attempting to break the Union line. In this second day of battle Colonel Harrison, who had eluded injury so far, was wounded in the hip. Nevertheless, he remained with the Rangers throughout the day.[19]

Although Wharton's cavalry fought well on both days, the results of the fighting at Murfreesboro were indecisive. Having lost one-third of his men in casualties and receiving information that the enemy was stronger than he initially believed, Bragg ordered his army to retreat to Tullahoma, twenty miles to the south.[20]

Wharton's Brigade, including the Eighth Texas, was in Joe Wheeler's Cavalry Division throughout most of 1863. In late January, Wheeler, who was not highly regarded by the Texans, led the brigades commanded by Wharton and Nathan Bedford Forrest on an ill-conceived attempt to recapture Fort Donelson on the Tennessee River. Neither Wharton nor Forrest believed the operation had much chance of success. The Federals were well entrenched and supplied, the weather was bitterly cold, and the Confederates were low on ammunition. Pvt. L. B. Giles of the Rangers' Company D remembered the whole affair as "a wild-goose chase" exceeded only by Napoleon's Russian campaign in terms of "suffering, hardships, and barrenness of results." Although the Confederates captured the enemy's outer works, they were forced to abandon the campaign after they exhausted their limited supply of ammunition.[21]

The retreat from Donelson back to their camp north of the Duck River was made across icy streams and rivers. Private Giles noted that "it was so cold that if we touched a gun-barrel or bridle bit our hands stuck to the metal." Later, he added, "For a long time when the men wanted to reach the superlative of suffering they spoke of the Donelson trip."[22]

The Rangers took part in several skirmishes and raids during the spring and summer of 1863 but were not involved in any major battles. During this period the Texans had some opportunity to relax and recuperate from the hard campaigning. Pvt. Ephraim S. Dodd, like Giles a member of Company D, noted in his journal that on April 4 General Wharton and Colonel Harrison had a horse race, which many of the Rangers watched. Another Ranger, Dunbar Affleck of Company B, in a letter to his parents in early May, reported that "Wharton was badly hurt a few days earlier when his horse ran into a tree during a race"; whether this was in the race with Colonel Harrison or not Affleck does not state.[23]

Although forage for the mounts and finding replacements for lame or injured horses remained problems, food for the men was readily available during the summer months. Private Giles observed that "roasting ears were in season, fruit was beginning to ripen, and so we feasted on good things." Frank Batchelor, a lieutenant on Harrison's staff, wrote his father "we fare sumptuously every day," and listed blackberry and peach cobbler, beans, cabbage, cucumbers, onions, tomatoes, potatoes, beets, squash, fruits, and melons readily available. Private Dodd noted in his journal that "we are living high on peach pie." He recorded that in August the Rangers had a barbecue in which a new horse, purchased with money contributed by the men, was presented to General Wharton.[24]

The spiritual needs of the Rangers were attended to by Rev. Robert F. Bunting, a Presbyterian minister from Central Texas who served as chaplain. Nightly religious meetings were held throughout July. Thirty troopers made professions of faith and many others renewed previous commitments.[25]

The lull in military action for the Rangers ended in early autumn. Rosecrans' Union army outmaneuvered Bragg and the Confederates, leading to the evacuation of Chattanooga. The situation was so desperate that the Richmond government sent reinforcements to Bragg, who launched an attack on Rosecrans' army at Chickamauga Creek, just south of Chattanooga. The Rangers went into this campaign under a new commander, Gustave Cook. In August Wharton had been appointed commander of a cavalry division, consisting of two brigades. Tom Harrison, who had led the Rangers since the previous autumn, was named commander of one of the brigades. Cook, who was executive officer of the Rangers under Harrison, took command of the regiment.

A former county judge from Fort Bend, Cook was a veteran Ranger. He joined the Eighth Texas as a private in 1861 and gradually worked his way up through the ranks. He was elected major when Harrison replaced Wharton as regimental commander. When Stephen Ferrell, the regiment's lieutenant colonel, was forced to resign because of poor health, Cook replaced him as lieutenant colonel and second in command of the Rangers.[26]

In the Battle of Chickamauga Wharton's cavalry, now in the brigade commanded by Tom Harrison that included the Eleventh Texas Cavalry, was assigned to the left wing of the Confederate army. Since the heaviest fighting was in the center of the line, the Rangers escaped much of the carnage of the battle. The Rangers were engaged twice during the battle, in both instances beating off attempts by Ohio cavalry to attack the rear of Bragg's infantry.[27]

The Rangers rode with Joe Wheeler's Cavalry Corps in the raid against Rosecrans' supply line in October 1863. Although the Confederates destroyed 800 enemy wagons in the Sequatchie Valley and swept almost to Nashville, they failed to destroy the Federal supply line and suffered severe losses in men and horses. At Farmington in Marshall County, Tennessee, the Rangers charged Federals who held a strong position in a cedar thicket. The first assault scattered the enemy, but Union reinforcements armed with Spencer repeating rifles drove the Texans back. Twenty Rangers were killed or wounded. Capt. J.K.P. Blackburn of Company E and Maj. Samuel F. Christian were among those wounded. Blackburn, whose memoirs provide one of the most informative accounts of the regiment, was captured and remained a prisoner until the closing months of the war.[28]

In late 1863 Wharton's Cavalry Division, including the Rangers, served under James Longstreet in the futile effort to drive Union forces out of the Knoxville area (described in the previous chapter). In this campaign the Rangers were in several skirmishes, but little was achieved. Bad weather and superior enemy strength led Longstreet to abort the campaign and go into winter quarters.[29]

The Knoxville campaign was the last one in which the Rangers served under John A. Wharton. Wharton never had confidence in the leadership abilities of corps commander Joe Wheeler. The Wharton-Wheeler relationship gradually deteriorated, and in early 1864 Wharton requested and was granted transfer to the Trans Mississippi Department.[30]

The Rangers remained in eastern Tennessee during the winter months of 1863–1864. In early 1864 Harrison's Brigade, which included the Rangers, was tranferred to William C. Y. Humes' Division stationed near Dalton, Georgia. The Rangers saw considerable action during late spring and early summer as part of Joe Johnston's efforts to block Sherman's move toward Atlanta. General Wheeler, the corps commander, praised Harrison and his cavalry for their role in battles at Resaca, Dug Gap, and Varnell's Station. The encounter at Dug Gap was particularly satisfying for the Rangers, who routed Indiana cavalry and captured one hundred prisoners, including regimental commander Col. Oscar H. La Grange. At Big Shanty and New Hope Church the Rangers fought as dismounted cavalry, but were less effective than as cavalrymen. Of their performance as infantrymen, one historian of the Rangers said "in this last capacity, they do not appear to have done anything to brag about."[31]

Tom Harrison, Colonel, Eighth Texas Cavalry.
—Courtesy Harold B. Simpson Research Center, Hillsboro, Texas

Harrison's Brigade was on the east side of Atlanta in the battles for control of the city. Although the main fighting was between infantry, the Rangers saw some action, again as dismounted cavalry, in the battle for Atlanta on July 22. Later that month they were part of cavalry operations south of Atlanta in defending railroad lines from attacks by Federal cavalry led by Edward McCook and George Stoneman.[32]

In mid-August John Bell Hood, who had replaced Joe Johnston in command of Confederate forces at Atlanta, ordered Wheeler to take his cavalry, including the Eighth and Eleventh Texas, on a massive sweep into north Georgia. Hood believed that such a raid against Sherman's supply line would force the Union army to abandon its attempts to take Atlanta. Wheeler's mission was to destroy the Western & Atlantic Railroad to Chattanooga, but the ambitious Wheeler exceeded his orders and launched what historian Tom Connelly called "a haphazard dash into East Tennessee." Wheeler's cavalry destroyed some enemy property, but in the process suffered heavy losses in running engagements with the Federals.[33]

The Rangers were more fortunate than much of Wheeler's cavalry in the Tennessee raid. Although they traveled over 800 miles and destroyed immense quantities of Federal property, their own losses in the campaign were minimal; by rounding up deserters they returned with more men than they started with.[34]

Most of Wheeler's cavalry was not so fortunate. While historian Connelly perhaps overstated the case when he wrote "Wheeler had destroyed Hood's cavalry," the raid was costly and did not accomplish its purpose of stopping Sherman's encirclement of Atlanta. One Ranger, Henry W. Graber, wrote that "it did not take one with much intellect to see that one of the greatest cavalry raids of the war was a failure."[35]

Wheeler's cavalry rejoined Hood's army after the fall of Atlanta. Hood had not given up his belief that Sherman's supply line in north Georgia was vulnerable. In late September he swung his army northwest to attack the railroad lines leading into Atlanta. A series of attacks were launched, but the Confederates again failed to achieve their objective. In one such engagement, later referred to as the "Rome Races," the Rangers suffered one of their most embarrassing moments in the war. While skirmishing with the enemy near Rome, the Rangers were attacked on the flank by Union cavalry. Surprised and confused, the Texans panicked and fled from the scene. In the melee the Rangers lost two cannon, several men, and a beautiful blue silk flag that had been given them a month earlier by the women of Nashville. After running five miles the Rangers finally regrouped and held their ground.[36]

When Hood moved his army northward toward Nashville in the autumn of 1864, he left Wheeler's cavalry to harass Sherman's army on its march to the sea. The Rangers and other regiments of Harrison's Brigade took part in several actions as the outnumbered Confederates fell back to Savannah. When the Confederates were forced to evacuate that city just before Christmas, Harrison's Brigade helped screen William J. Hardee's Confederate troops as they withdrew into the Carolinas. The Rangers continued to serve with Hardee's army as Sherman headed into the Carolinas. Continuing skirmishes with the larger Union cavalry took their toll on the brigade. Harrison was disabled from a wound received on March 10, 1865, when the brigade attacked the enemy at Fayetteville, North Carolina.[37]

At Bentonville, the Confederates, under the command of Joe Johnston again, made a surprise attack on the left wing of

Sherman's army. The initial attack, in which Colonel Cook and Maj. William R. Jarman of the Rangers were wounded, almost succeeded before Union reinforcements turned the tide against the Confederates. In the closing stages of the battle an assault by Joseph Mower's Union Corps endangered the Confederates' route of retreat across Mill Creek Bridge. General Hardee, who was nearby, realized the bridge must be held. He asked John F. "Doc" Matthews, captain of Company K and now the senior officer of the Rangers on the field, if he and his men could hold the enemy until the Confederates brought up artillery and infantry. Matthews responded that the Rangers would try. With no hesitation he ordered the Texans, now reduced to 200 troops, to attack. With a charge "rarely equaled and never surpassed in impetuosity and daring," according to one Ranger, the Texans with their customary yell and with pistols blazing rode into the enemy. The shock of the attack drove the Federals back and gave Hardee time to bring up infantry and artillery to hold the bridge so that the Confederate army could withdraw.[38]

Although the Rangers' charge was successful, there were numerous casualties. Among them was the sixteen-year-old son of General Hardee, Willie. Young Hardee had joined Company D of the Rangers only that morning after overcoming his father's objections that he was too young for military service. In the attack Hardee was shot through the chest. He was held in the saddle by another Ranger and brought to the rear, then was taken in a wagon to the home of a cousin, where he died several days later.[39]

Bentonville was the Rangers' last battle. On April 16, 1865, General Johnston surrendered what remained of his army at Durham Station, North Carolina. Cavalry commander Joe Wheeler personally urged his troopers to accept their parole and return to their homes. "You have done all that human exertion could accomplish," he told his men. "You fought your fight. Your task is done."[40]

Only ninety-eight Rangers showed up for the surrender ceremonies. The others slipped away and attempted to make their way across Georgia and Alabama to join Richard Taylor at Mobile or Kirby Smith at Shreveport. Before they could reach them the war had ended. A few Rangers joined veterans of Hood's Brigade making their way home. Others made their journey back to Texas by ones and twos.

ELEVENTH TEXAS CAVALRY

During the last two years of the Civil War, the Eleventh Texas Cavalry was often in the same brigade as Terry's Rangers and fought in many of the same battles. The Eleventh Texas, however, seldom received the same attention or public praise as the Rangers. Harold B. Simpson, who devoted many years studying the role of Texas military units in the Civil War, believed the regiment "never received the acclaim due it." This is probably due to several factors: the Eleventh was a small regiment, particularly after early 1862, when many of the original members went home; it served the first year of the war in the less publicized Trans Mississippi region; and it had fewer veterans who later published their memories and reminiscences than units such as Terry's Rangers or Hood's Brigade. Also, the Eleventh was never identified with the name of a commander such as Benjamin Terry, John Bell Hood, or Sul Ross.[41]

Historian Richard B. McCaslin, who has written about the people and the area from which the Eleventh Cavalry was formed, referred to the original members of the regiment as "conditional Confederates." Many of the men, recruited mainly in the Red River counties of northeast Texas, were opposed to secession but enlisted to protect their homes from hostile Indian attacks. They were willing to serve the Confederacy, but only if they remained in Texas or Indian Territory.[42]

Their organizer and colonel, William Cocke Young, was the largest slaveholder in Cooke County; however, like most of his troops, he opposed secession. Young was concerned that once Texas withdrew from the Union, Federal troops would be pulled out of Indian Territory, leaving North Texas exposed to raids by tribes north of the Red River. A former sheriff, Mexican War veteran, and U.S. marshal, Young accepted Governor Clark's request that he raise a regiment for frontier defense. One company of local volunteers had already been formed by James and John Diamond, friends of Young but unlike Young ardent secessionists. Young used this company as the starting point for recruitment. He published calls for volunteers in various North Texas newspapers and rode through Grayson, Fannin, Hunt, and Collin counties seeking recruits. By early May he had raised ten companies with about 550 men. Elections were held confirming Young as colonel, James W. Throckmorton of Collin County, another opponent of secession, as lieutenant colonel, and Hugh F. Young, former chief justice of Grayson County, as major.[43]

Young lost little time in committing his new recruits to action. On May 3 he sent a detachment across the Red River to occupy nearby Fort Washita, recently abandoned by the Federals. The next day the rest of his command occupied Fort Arbuckle, fifty miles to the northwest of Washita. During the second week of May, Young's troops rode farther north to take control of Fort Cobb, also abandoned by the Federals. This was followed by agreements between state authorities and Native American leaders assuring support for the Confederacy.[44]

In early June, Young returned to Sherman and established his headquarters there. Governor Clark appointed him commissioner of the Texas Eighth Military District with broad powers for recruitment. Additional volunteers, mainly from Cooke and Grayson counties, were mustered into service and sent to join Young's troops in Indian Territory. By the end of July about 800 troopers were occupying the former Federal forts.[45]

In late summer Young learned that his regiment would soon be transferred to Confederate service. He made visits to Austin and Richmond seeking some assurance that he and his men would continue to remain on frontier duty, but with no success. On October 2, 1861, the regiment was formally mustered into the Confederate army as the Eleventh Texas Cavalry. The regiment was ordered to report to Brig. Gen. Ben McCulloch for service in Arkansas and Missouri.[46]

Young's regiment joined McCulloch's army in northwestern Arkansas in late autumn. McCulloch had planned a move into Kansas, but supply problems, illnesses, and renewed enemy activity in Missouri caused him to abandon the idea. In December he went to Richmond to consult with Confederate authorities. While he was away, dissident Creek Indians led by Opothleyahola threatened pro-Confederate Indians. Col. James McIntosh, commanding in McCulloch's absence, led 1,300 cavalrymen, including Colonel Young and seven companies of his regiment, in an attack on the Creeks at their stronghold at Chustenahlah. In fighting on December 16, 1861, Young and his troops were on the left side of the Confederate line in the attack that shattered the Indian defenders. In his report of the battle Young claimed that his companies killed 211 Indians while suffering only six casualties themselves. He also reported that his men took many women, children, and black prisoners.[47]

After the battle at Chustenahlah, McIntosh's cavalry, including the Eleventh Texas, went into winter quarters in northwestern Arkansas. In February McCulloch returned from Richmond and assumed command of the various units that made up his army.

In early 1862 Maj. Gen. Earl Van Dorn, a highly regarded former officer in the U.S. Army, was appointed commander of Confederate forces in the Trans Mississippi. McCulloch's command became a division in Van Dorn's Army of the West. The Eleventh Cavalry was originally assigned to a brigade in McCulloch's Division commanded by Louis Hebert, but in February was transferred to James McIntosh's Brigade.[48]

The Eleventh Texas was in McIntosh's Brigade during the Battle of Pea Ridge in early March 1862. In this campaign Van Dorn divided his forces for an attack on the Union army camped near Little Sugar Creek. McCulloch was to lead his division in an assault on the Union left flank near Leetown while Sterling Price and his Missouri division attacked the Union right near Elkhorn Tavern.

The opening phases of the battle went well for the Confederates. McCulloch sent McIntosh and his brigade, consisting of four Texas cavalry regiments (including the Eleventh Texas) and an Arkansas and Texas battalion, on a charge that drove the enemy back several hundred yards. When Federal resistance stiffened, McCulloch attempted to reconnoiter the enemy position but was killed by a volley of fire. McIntosh, who assumed command, ordered a new attack but was killed a few moments later. From that time on, confusion prevailed in the division. Louis Hebert, the next senior officer, was captured while leading his brigade against the enemy. Albert Pike, commanding the third brigade, pulled his troops from the battle, leaving Col. Elkanah Greer of the Third Texas Cavalry the ranking officer on the scene.[49]

During the evening of March 7, Greer led McCulloch's Division on an all-night march around Big Mountain to join Van Dorn and Price in the Battle at Elkhorn Tavern. Unfortunately, the troops in Greer's command, which included the Eleventh Texas, were too exhausted to be of much value in the fighting the next morning. Around midday on the 8th, Van Dorn, convinced the enemy was too strong, broke off the engagement and ordered a retreat.

The Confederate troops suffered hardships in the retreat from Pea Ridge. The men were exhausted, the weather extremely cold, and the army's commissary department had difficulty in finding provisions in the sparsely populated countryside. Tom Coleman, a soldier in the Eleventh Texas, later wrote his parents: "I never knew what it was to want for something to eat until the last fifteen days." When Van Dorn's army finally reached Van Buren, Arkansas, all were in poor condition.[50]

Morale in the Eleventh and other Texas regiments gradually improved as the troops rested and received better food. The Texans were made unhappy, however, when they learned that Van Dorn's army was being transferred east of the Mississippi. This particularly displeased Colonel Young and his men, who had joined the army initially to protect their homes in northeast Texas. Their displeasure was increased when they learned that Van Dorn's mounted regiments were to leave their horses behind and become dismounted cavalry.[51]

Van Dorn's army, including the Eleventh Texas, reached Corinth in late April. Conditions in the area were deplorable. Fifty thousand soldiers, many of them wounded at Shiloh or Pea Ridge, crowded into the small town. Dysentery and typhoid fever raged through the camps, and hundreds of Confederates died. The poor physical conditions, news from home of Union plots and Jayhawker raids, and general dissatification over the transfer east of the Mississippi led many men of the Eleventh Texas to go home when their twelve months' enlistment expired. Colonel Young, in poor health, resigned his commission and returned home in late April. His son, James, left the regiment in May. Lt. Col. James J. Diamond went home after he failed to be elected commander of the regiment. By early May the Eleventh Cavalry listed only 472 troops present for duty.[52]

John C. Burks, a Clarksville lawyer and politician, was chosen commander of the regiment after Young's departure. When Burks took command, the Eleventh, along with three other recently dismounted Texas regiments, was in Joseph L. Hogg's Brigade. Following Hogg's death in May, William L. Cabell became brigade commander, but by midsummer Col. T. H. McCray of Arkansas was leading the brigade.[53]

McCray's Brigade was transferred from the Army of Tennessee to the East Tennessee Department commanded by Edmund Kirby Smith in late summer. The brigade crossed into Kentucky in August as part of the combined efforts by Smith and Braxton Bragg to free the Blue Grass state from Federal control. On August 30 the Eleventh Texas was in the attack that broke the Federal defense line at Richmond, Kentucky, and gave the Confederates the victory.[54]

The success at Richmond enabled the Confederates to occupy Lexington and Frankfort, Kentucky. The campaign itself was a failure, however, as Bragg and Smith, facing supply problems and fearing superior enemy numbers, withdrew back into Tennessee in mid-October.

Matthew D. Ector, East Texas lawyer and commander of the Fourteenth Texas Cavalry (dismounted), was given command of the brigade in late October. The veterans of the Eleventh Texas were pleased to be under the command of a fellow Texan. Ector had been with the brigade since the early days in the Trans Mississippi and was generally popular with the men in the ranks.

Ector's Brigade, which now included the Tenth, Eleventh, Fourteenth, and Fifteenth Texas cavalries (all dismounted) and Douglas' Texas artillery battery, was transferred back to the Army of Tennessee in late autumn and participated in Bragg's attempt to drive William S. Rosecrans' Union army out of Middle Tennessee. In the bloody battle at Murfreesboro, Ector's Brigade and another brigade from J. P. McCown's Division made the initial assault against the Union right flank on the morning of December 31, 1862. In the attack the Texans drove the enemy back two miles before Federal artillery stopped the advance. The fighting raged all day. Casualties mounted on both sides. The Eleventh Texas was particularly hit hard. Colonel Burks and nine of his men were killed and more than eighty others were wounded. Burks was leading the regiment in the assault when he received a fatal wound in the chest. He attempted to cover the wound with his hand and continued to lead his men until, from loss of blood, he could go on no further. Among his last words to his troops was the admonition "charge them, my boys, charge them."[55]

The death of Burks was a bitter blow to men of the Eleventh Texas. He was highly popular and esteemed by all—from his brigade commander, who eulogized him by saying that "a better friend, a warmer heart, a more gallant leader than he was never drew the breath of life," to the lowest private in the ranks.[56]

Lt. Col. Joseph M. Bounds, Mexican War veteran and former hotelkeeper in McKinney, took command of the regiment following Burks' death. The fighting at Murfreesboro resumed on January 2. Fortunately for the troops in Ector's Brigade, the major action shifted to the Confederate right, relieving the Texans from heavy fighting. On the evening of January 3, 1863, the Confederates retreated toward Shelbyville and Tullahoma.[57]

In late January the men of the Eleventh Texas received word that the regiment was being remounted and transferred to John A. Wharton's cavalry brigade. This was good news to the Texans, who were still unhappy about losing their mounts when they crossed the Mississippi. Although they regretted leaving an all-Texas brigade, they were pleased to be serving as mounted cavalry in a brigade commanded by a Texan.[58]

Once remounted, the Eleventh Texas took part in several raids that spring, including one in April against railroads in the Nashville area. As noted earlier, Tom Harrison, formerly commander of the Eighth Texas, became brigade commander in the summer of 1863 when John A. Wharton was given command of the division. Like Wharton, Harrison was a Texan generally respected by his men, although he ran a slighly more disciplined brigade than did Wharton.

The Eleventh Texas was in the Chickamauga campaign in September, but like their fellow Texans in the Eighth Cavalry, they saw comparatively little action. Later the Eleventh Texas and Harrison's Brigade served in the early stages of Bragg's Chattanooga siege and with Longstreet in the futile attempt to capture Knoxville.[59]

In the midst of the Chattanooga siege Lt. Col. Joseph Bounds, who had succeeded Colonel Burks as regimental commander, was murdered. Bounds was shot by an enlisted man, Pvt. William Dulaney of Company E. Dulaney, a farmer from the Clarksville area, had been in the regiment for over a year. Although the reason for his action is not clear, some believe it related to Bounds' succession to regimental command. Dulaney fled from the regiment after the killing but was arrested in Arkansas. He later secured his release from prison by informing upon and testifying against a Confederate who had been working as a Union agent.[60]

George R. Reeves, former sheriff and state legislator from Grayson County, was the new colonel and commander of the Eleventh Texas. Reeves, the senior company commander among the Texans, had been with the regiment since the beginning of the war. Highly popular with the men, Reeves would command the regiment for the remainder of the war.[61]

In 1864 Harrison's Cavalry Brigade, which included the Eighth and Eleventh Texas, the Third Arkansas, and the Fourth Tennessee, served with Joe Johnston's Army of Tennessee in efforts to stop William T. Sherman's drive toward Atlanta. The brigade was on the east side of Atlanta, in the thick of fighting on July 22, when John B. Hood, who had succeeded Johnston as army commander, made an unsuccessful assault on the Union left flank. The Eleventh Texas later took part in the cavalry operations to defend the railroads south of the city on July 26 and in Wheeler's raid into eastern Tennessee in August. When Hood evacuated Atlanta and made his swing toward Nashville in autumn, the Eleventh Texas, along with other units in Wheeler's Cavalry Corps, was left behind to harass Sherman in his march to the sea. The heavily outnumbered cavalry could do little to stop Sherman; they could only delay him.[62]

After the fall of Savannah in December, the Eleventh Texas was part of Wade Hampton's command as the Confederates withdrew into the Carolinas. The Texans fought in the last major battle of the Army of Tennessee at Bentonville, North Carolina, on March 19-21. When Joe Johnston surrendered his army at Durham Station in April, the men of the Eleventh Texas accepted their paroles and headed home. After four years of fighting that had taken them from Indian Territory through Arkansas, Mississippi, Tennessee, Kentucky, Georgia, and the Carolinas, the men of the Eleventh Texas returned to northeast Texas.[63]

ROSS' TEXAS CAVALRY BRIGADE

Third Texas Cavalry
Sixth Texas Cavalry
Ninth Texas Cavalry
Twenty-seventh Texas Cavalry

In the early days of the war the Eleventh Texas Cavalry served in Arkansas and Indian Territory with several mounted regiments that became part of a cavalry brigade commanded first by John W. Whitfield and later by Lawrence S. "Sul" Ross. Since its greatest success came under Ross, the brigade is usually referred to as Ross' Texas Cavalry Brigade.

The brigade was formed in October 1862, when Whitfield, commander of the Twenty-seventh Texas (which was sometimes referred to as "Whitfield's Legion"), was appointed commander of the four regiments which at the time were dismounted. Each of these regiments had previously served in the Trans Mississippi under Earl Van Dorn. In the battle at Pea Ridge the Third, Sixth, and Ninth regiments were in the cavalry brigade commanded by James McIntosh. Five companies of Whitfield's Regiment served as the Fourth Texas Cavalry Battalion (dismounted) under Louis Hebert's com-

Sul Ross, Colonel, Sixth Texas Cavalry.
—Courtesy Harold B. Simpson Research Center, Hillsboro, Texas

mand in the same battle. When seven additional companies joined Whitfield in April 1862, the Fourth Battalion became the Twenty-seventh Regiment.[64]

The Third Texas was with Ben McCulloch's army in the battle at Wilson's Creek in August 1861. Its commander, Elkanah Greer, was an ardent southern expansionist and former grand commander of the Texas Knights of the Golden Circle. When Texas seceded from the Union, Greer traveled to Montgomery, Alabama, where he received one of the first colonelcies from the new Confederate government. He returned to Texas, where he and his friends recruited and organized a cavalry regiment. The regiment was orginally called the South Kansas-Texas Cavalry as Greer intended the unit to be used in liberating Kansas from abolitionist control. When it was mustered into Confederate service at Dallas in June 1861, however, it officially became the Third Texas Cavalry.[65]

The ten companies that made up the Third Texas came from northeastern Texas, much like the Eleventh Texas. In his history of the regiment, Douglas Hale pointed out that more than half of the original 1,097 volunteers (53 percent) were from slaveholding households; 106 were from families owning twenty or more slaves. Hale noted that while one-half of the regiment were planters and farmers, almost one-fifth of the recruits were from the white-collar, commercial, or professional class. The regiment included two dozen lawyers, twenty-three schoolteachers, and sixteen physicians. Many of the volunteers were officeholders or sons of officeholders. Three had served in the secession convention and seven were sons of convention delegates.[66]

The volunteers were sworn into Confederate service on June 13 and proceeded to elect their regimental and company officers. Greer became commander of the regiment. Walter Paye Lane, an Irish adventurer, veteran of the Battle of San Jacinto and the Mexican War, and a legend in his own time, was chosen lieutenant colonel. George W. Chilton of Tyler, lawyer, politician, and Knight of the Golden Circle, became major. Matthew D. Ector, a future Confederate general, was regimental adjutant. Company commanders chosen were Thomas W. Winston of Harrison (A), Robert H. Cumby of Rusk (B), Francis M. Taylor of Cherokee (C), Stephen M. Hale of Hunt (D), Daniel M. Short of Shelby (E), Isham Chisum of Kaufman (F), Hinche P. Mabry of Marion (G),

Jonathan L. Russell of Upshur (H), John A. Bryan of Cass (I), and David Y. Gaines of Smith (K).[67]

The Third Texas, first of the Texas cavalry regiments organized for out-of-state duty, was ordered to join Ben McCulloch's army in Arkansas. After a march across Indian Territory, the Texans reached McCulloch's army near the Arkansas-Missouri state line on August 1. The Texans received their baptism of fire ten days later in the Battle of Wilson's Creek. There, as part of McCulloch's small army, they saw limited action as the combined forces of McCulloch and Sterling Price defeated the Union forces of Nathaniel Lyon and Franz Sigel.

The East Texans, approximately 800 strong, were involved in two cavalry charges at Wilson's Creek. In the first of these the Texans and a Missouri battalion drove the enemy back with heavy casualties. The second, an attack against a Federal artillery position, was less successful as heavy enemy fire led Colonel Greer to withdraw his men into the protection of the sheltering woods. Six Texans were killed, twenty-three wounded, and six missing in the day's fighting.[68]

The Third Texas saw little action during the next four months. Although his fellow Confederate general, Sterling Price, favored an aggressive campaign against the enemy, Ben McCulloch, realizing the inadequacy of his own small army, favored a more cautious approach until he had more troops. After briefly occupying Springfield, Missouri, McCulloch withdrew his army back into northwestern Arkansas. The infantry made camp near Bentonville while the cavalry camped along the Arkansas River east of Van Buren. For the next several weeks McCulloch was content to drill his forces and build up supplies while seeking additional volunteers.[69]

McCulloch's army was strengthened in October by the arrival of several new Texas cavalry regiments. One of these, the Eleventh Texas Cavalry commanded by Col. William C. Young, served alongside the Third Texas during the next several months, but as we have seen earlier in this chapter was later transferred to another brigade. Three other units that arrived in October, the Sixth and Ninth Regiments and John W. Whitfield's Battalion (which later became the Twenty-sixth Regiment), remained with the Third Cavalry in what later became Ross' Texas Cavalry Brigade.

The companies that made up Whitfield's Cavalry Battalion

were the first to join McCulloch's army. Whitfield, political activist and former Kansas territorial delegate to the U.S. Congress, had organized a cavalry company in Lavaca County. A staunch defender of southern rights, he was anxious to take part in any effort to free Kansas from the abolitionists. When he and his company, known as the Whitfield Rifles, joined McCulloch, Whitfield was promoted to major and made commanding officer of a battalion that consisted of his own company, three East Texas independent companies (Capt. E. R. Hawkins' Hunt County company, Capt. John H. Broock's San Augustine County company, and B. H. Norsworth's Jasper County company), and a company from Arkansas.[70]

The Sixth Texas Cavalry reported to McCulloch on October 20, 1861. Organized by Barton Warren Stone, a Dallas lawyer and judge, the Sixth Texas was made up of recruits from Central and Northeast Texas. Like his friend Sam Houston, Stone opposed secession but with the coming of war obtained authorization to raise a regiment of volunteers. Ten companies, numbering 1,150 men, were mustered into Confederate service in early September. Stone was named colonel; John S. Griffith, a prosperous merchant and cotton grower from Kaufman County, was elected lieutenant colonel; and Lawrence S. "Sul" Ross from McLennan County was chosen major. Although he was only twenty-one years old, Ross already had established a reputation as a bold Indian fighter and Texas Ranger captain.[71]

The Ninth Texas Cavalry was the last mounted unit from Texas to report to McCulloch. Organized by William B. Sims, a wealthy Clarksville merchant, the regiment was originally intended for state service but was mustered into the Confederate army on October 14, 1861. Like the Third and Eleventh Texas, most of the volunteers came from North Texas, especially Fannin, Hopkins, Red River, Tarrant, and Titus counties. In addition to Sims, who as colonel commanded the regiment, other officers were Lt. Col. William Quayle, a district judge from Grapevine, and Maj. Nathan Towns, a thirty-four-year-old lawyer from Lamar County. Dudley W. Jones, a nineteen-year-old student from Titus County, was named regimental adjutant. Company commanders selected were T. G. Berry (A, Tarrant), Sidney Smith (B, Fannin), J. E. McCool (C, Grayson), M. J. Brinson (D, Tarrant), J. C. Hart (E, Red River), M. E. Duncan (F, Titus), L. D. King (G, Hopkins),

J. D. Wright (H, Lamar), Charles Stewart (I, Titus), and J. H. Williams (K, Hunt and Hopkins).[72]

The Ninth Texas was ordered to join McCulloch in October but was delayed en route. At Northford Village on the Canadian River in Indian Territory Sims received orders from McCulloch to assist Brig. Gen. Douglas Cooper, the Confederate commander in Indian Territory, in efforts to control dissident Creeks led by Chief Opothleyahola. Sims turned his troops north into the Creek Nation. On November 19 and December 9 the regiment fought with the Indians, first at Round Mountain and later at Bird's Creek. In both instances the Texans drove the Creeks from the field but Opothleyahola and most of his followers remained at large. Sims was then ordered to proceed to Fort Gibson, where Cooper was bringing together cavalry for a campaign against the Creeks. In the third week of December, Cooper's command, which included the Ninth Texas and Whitfield's Texas Battalion, marched north to attack Opothleyahola. Before Cooper's column reached the Indians, however, Col. James McIntosh and troops from Ben McCulloch's army (including the Third, Sixth, and Eleventh Texas Cavalry regiments), defeated Opothleyahola at Chustenahlah.[73]

All of the units that later made up Ross' Texas Cavalry Brigade were with Ben McCulloch's Division in the Battle of Pea Ridge. Whitfield's Battalion served as dismounted cavalry in Louis Hebert's Infantry Brigade. The Third, Ninth, and Sixth Texas, along with the Eleventh Texas, were in McIntosh's Cavalry Brigade. As noted earlier, McCulloch commanded one division of the Confederate army led by Maj. Gen. Earl Van Dorn, and Sterling Price commanded another division.

The original Confederate plan called for McCulloch and Price to bring their forces together in one assault, but early detection by Union troops on McCulloch's front resulted in two separate battles going on at the same time, with McCulloch attacking the Union flank at Leetown while Sterling Price, accompanied by Van Dorn, fought the enemy at Elkhorn Tavern.

At midmorning on March 7, the Sixth and Ninth Texas, along with the Eleventh Texas and two cavalry battalions, made what historians William L. Shea and Earl J. Hess describe "as one of the Civil War's most colorful cavalry charges." Shouting, yelling, and brandishing sabers, pistols, shotguns, and carbines, the Texans charged across an open wheat field to attack the enemy. They overran the Union position, capturing three artillery pieces and killing or wounding nearly sixty Federals before halting when they encountered Union reinforcements. Confederate losses in the charge were light, but among the casualties was Col. William Sims, who suffered a crippling wound when his right arm was shattered by grapeshot.[74]

The Third Texas did not participate in the cavalry charge that morning. Just as the attack was to commence, General McCulloch ordered the Third Texas to stay behind and cover Capt. John J. Good's artillery battery pending further orders. Colonel Greer and his regiment remained in a belt of trees awaiting orders from McCulloch. The orders never came. McCulloch was killed while attempting to reconnoiter the enemy position.

When Colonel McIntosh, the next senior officer, was informed of McCulloch's demise, he gave his cavalry commanders instructions to wait for further orders while he rode off to join his old regiment, the Second Arkansas Mounted Rifles, which had been fighting as dismounted cavalry with Hebert's Brigade. Within minutes McIntosh was killed. Louis Hebert, the next ranking Confederate officer, who was leading the Confederates in the fighting on the right, was missing and presumed dead. Albert Pike, who commanded a small Indian brigade, led his troops away from the battle site. In the confusion the Confederate cavalry stood idle for much of the afternoon awaiting orders.[75]

When Colonel Greer, the senior Confederate cavalry officer on the field, finally learned what had happened he did what he could to bring some order to the situation. He gathered together the various scattered Confederate units in the area and fell back to the previous night's camp. Late that night Greer received orders from Van Dorn to march his troops to join Van Dorn and Price near Elkhorn Tavern. As noted earlier, the weary Texans played little part in the fighting on March 8. After a Union counterattack at midday, Van Dorn broke off the engagement and ordered a retreat.

Failure to defeat the Union forces at Pea Ridge disappointed the Texans. Many blamed the Confederate commander, Earl Van Dorn. Newton Keen, a young private in the Sixth Texas, believed that the Confederates should have continued the battle on the second day. "General Van Dorn was perhaps the only man in the army

Elkanah Greer, Colonel, Third Texas Cavalry.
—Courtesy Harold B. Simpson Research Center, Hillsboro, Texas

that was whiped [*sic*]," Keen later wrote. "He was a poor general and the men had no confidence in him." Douglas Cater, a member of the Third Texas, thought that Van Dorn "had given up the fight." W. P. Lane, veteran of the Battle of San Jacinto and the Mexican War, found it difficult to believe Van Dorn broke off the fighting. "I was never so astonished in my life," he later recalled. Sul Ross, the young major in the Sixth Cavalry who would later command the brigade, was convinced "we whipped ourselves." Historians William L. Shea and Earl J. Hess believed that "Van Dorn failed as an army commander in almost every respect."[76]

Morale was extremely low in the Texas cavalry regiments following the failure at Pea Ridge. This was compounded when the men learned their units were being dismounted and ordered to cross the Mississippi River and join Beauregard's army at Corinth. The poor physical conditions and illnesses in the camps did little to improve their spirits after the men arrived at Corinth. When general reorganization of the army, as required by the Conscription Act of April 1862, took place in early May, a number of changes in leadership were made. Colonel Greer, commander of the Third Texas, unhappy with Van Dorn and ambitious for a generalship, returned to Texas. Lane, dissatisfied that the regiment was dismounted, made plans to return home to organize a regiment of Partisan Rangers.

John Whitfield, Colonel, Twenty-seventh Texas Cavalry.
—Courtesy Harold B. Simpson Research Center, Hillsboro, Texas

Capt. Robert H. Cumby of Company B was elected colonel of the Third Texas and Capt. Hinche P. Mabry of Company G was chosen major, but as both men were in poor health, Lane agreed to stay on temporarily as regimental commander.[77]

The men of the Sixth Texas, unhappy with their commander, Col. B. Warren Stone, elevated Sul Ross to colonel. Stone returned to Texas, where he organized and commanded another regiment, the Second Texas Partisan Rangers. Lt. Col. John S. Griffith, in poor health at the time, was reelected executive officer of the regiment.

The Ninth Texas also had new leaders. Col. William B. Sims, seriously wounded at Pea Ridge, and Lt. Col. William Quayle, who was in poor health, returned home. Maj. Nathan W. Townes was chosen colonel and the young adjutant, Dudley W. Jones, was elected lieutenant colonel. When Townes was injured in an accident two weeks later, Jones assumed command of the Ninth Texas. All but one of the regiment's companies elected new captains. The Fourth Cavalry Battalion, strengthened by the addition of seven companies, became the Twenty-seventh Cavalry Regiment. Maj. John W. Whitfield was elected colonel, Capt. Edwin R. Hawkins lieutenant colonel, and Pvt. Cyrus K. Holman major.[78]

During the late spring and summer of 1862, the four Texas cavalry regiments, now dismounted, were in two different brigades.

The Sixth and Ninth cavalries were in a brigade in Dabney Maury's Division first commanded by former Arkansas governor John Seldon Roane and later by Brig. Gen. Charles W. Phifer of North Carolina. The Third and Twenty-seventh cavalries were in a brigade commanded by Brig. Gen. Louis Hebert (who had been exchanged after his capture at Pea Ridge). At the time, Hebert's Brigade was assigned to the Army of the West, commanded by Sterling Price.

Hebert's Brigade played a major role in the battle at Iuka, Mississippi, on September 19. Price's army had occupied the town and was preparing to withdraw when attacked by Union troops commanded by William S. Rosecrans. In the fighting that followed, casualties for the two Texas regiments were high. The Third Texas lost one of every four men that day: twenty-two killed and seventy-four wounded. Whitfield's Twenty-seventh Texas suffered 106 casualties. Colonel Whitfield was shot in the shoulder and would be on inactive duty for several weeks.

Hinche P. Mabry, who commanded the Third Texas in the battle, was wounded three times and captured. He was soon exchanged, but his injuries were so serious that he did not return to the army for several months.[79]

All four of the regiments that became part of Ross' Brigade were in Van Dorn's army when the Confederates attempted to retake Corinth, Mississippi, in early October. The Third Texas, led by Lt. Col. Jiles Boggess in place of Hinche Mabry, and the Twenty-seventh Texas, commanded by Lt. Col. Edwin R. Hawkins in place of John Whitfield, were now part of the Second Brigade, which was held in reserve on the first day of the battle. On the second day the brigade was ordered to support Dabney Maury's Division in the attack upon the Union Battery Robinett, but because of the distance and rough terrain they never reached the enemy entrenchments and were thus spared the heavy fighting.[80]

The Sixth and Ninth Texas cavalries were not so fortunate. As part of Phifer's Brigade in Maury's Division they helped drive the Federals back on October 3 and made a frontal assault against the well-entrenched Federal Battery Robinett the next day. In the attack Phifer's Brigade and John C. Moore's Brigade (which included the Second Texas Infantry) suffered heavy losses before being forced to retire under murderous enemy artillery and musket fire. At one point the Texans went hand-to-hand in fighting the

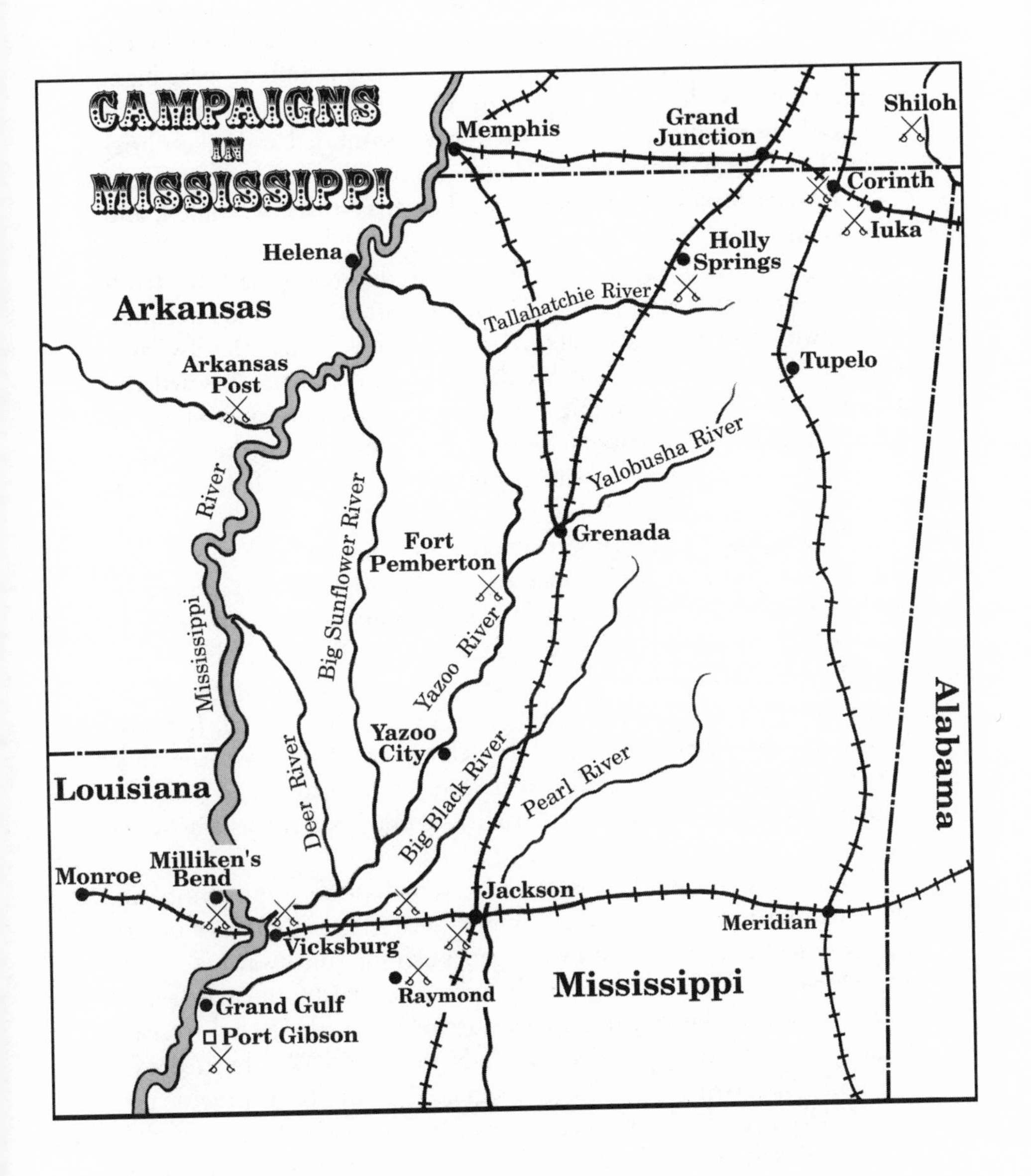
CAMPAIGNS IN MISSISSIPPI
Memphis
Grand Junction
Shiloh
Corinth
Iuka
Helena
Holly Springs
Arkansas
Tallahatchie River
Arkansas Post
Tupelo
Yalobusha River
Mississippi River
Big Sunflower River
Fort Pemberton
Grenada
Yazoo River
Yazoo City
Deer River
Big Black River
Pearl River
Alabama
Louisiana
Monroe
Milliken's Bend
Jackson
Meridian
Vicksburg
Raymond
Mississippi
Grand Gulf
Port Gibson

enemy. In the confusion Sul Ross, commanding the Sixth Texas, was thrown from his horse, giving rise to fear that he had been killed. He was not seriously injured, but losses in the regiment were high. Capt. James A. Jones of Company C and six other members of the Sixth were killed; sixteen others were wounded and taken prisoner. The Ninth Texas, which fought alongside the Sixth, suffered even heavier losses, with nineteen killed, fifty-three wounded, and twenty missing.[81]

Casualties mounted as the Confederates retreated from Corinth on October 5. As Van Dorn attempted to pull his defeated army away, the Federals pursued aggressively. When the Twenty-seventh Texas attempted to block the enemy advance toward the Davis bridge on the Hatchie River, the Texans were overwhelmed by superior enemy numbers. Seventy-five members of the Twenty-seventh were captured in the confusion as the Confederates fell back across the bridge.[82]

The last of Van Dorn's army crossed the Hatchie River during the predawn hours of October 6. The Confederates retreated to Holly Springs, a railroad town fifty miles southwest of Corinth. It was there that the four Texas regiments (the Third, Sixth, Ninth, and Twenty-seventh) were remounted and brought together to form a brigade under the command of the senior colonel, John W. Whitfield. As Whitfield was still on sick leave and Sul Ross, the only other colonel presently active, had received a furlough to visit his wife in Texas, Lt. Col. John S. Griffith of the Sixth Texas was temporarily in charge of the brigade.[83]

The new Texas cavalry brigade soon had an opportunity to show its merit. The Union army in northern Mississippi, now under the command of U. S. Grant, began pushing southward, forcing Van Dorn to withdraw from Holly Springs toward Grenada, seventy-five miles to the south. In an effort to block the Rebel retreat, Union cavalry led by Brig. Gen. Cadwallader C. Washburn drove deep into Mississippi. Van Dorn assigned the new Texas brigade the task of driving off the Federal horsemen. For four days Griffith's cavalry chased the Federals, finally catching them at the town of Oakland, twenty miles north of Grenada. There, on December 3, 1862, a brief but fierce battle between the two cavalries took place. The following day Washburn withdrew toward the Mississippi River, allowing Van Dorn's army to continue on to Grenada.[84]

John S. Griffith, Lieutenant Colonel, Twenty-seventh Texas Cavalry.
—Courtesy Harold B. Simpson Research Center, Hillsboro, Texas

Once in Grenada the Confederates could rest, at least for the moment. Lieutenant Colonel Griffith, the acting commander of the Texas cavalry, was concerned, however, about the buildup of enemy strength in northern Mississippi. Through scouts he learned that Grant was accumulating tons of supplies in Holly Springs to support a drive toward Vicksburg. Griffith was convinced that a bold cavalry sweep could destroy the supplies and disrupt Grant's plans. Unlike some Texans who had lost confidence in Van Dorn, Griffith believed that the Mississippian should lead such a raid.

On December 5 Griffith forwarded his suggestions, endorsed by all his regimental commanders, to Lt. Gen. John C. Pemberton, who commanded all Confederate forces in Mississippi. Pemberton, intrigued by the prospect of disrupting Grant's campaign, approved the plan after interviewing Griffith.[85]

Pemberton notified Van Dorn of the mission and assigned him three brigades to carry it out: William H. "Red" Jackson's Tennessee brigade of 1,200 men, Robert McCulloch's Missouri-Mississippi brigade of 800 men, and Griffith's Texas brigade of 1,500 men. On December 15 Van Dorn and the cavalry left their camps and headed north. To conceal his intentions, Van Dorn took a circuitous route to Holly Springs. When the raiders rode into town on the morning of December 20, they completely surprised the enemy.

During the next ten hours the Confederates burned and destroyed Federal supplies that Van Dorn estimated at $1.5 million in value. At 4:00 P.M., the Confederates remounted, many on captured horses with new weapons, and headed into southern Tennessee to destroy railroad tracks and bridges before swinging back into Mississippi. On December 27 the weary riders were back in Grenada after one of the most successful cavalry raids of the war.[86]

In early January 1863 the Texas cavalry brigade was on the move again. Van Dorn and his cavalry were ordered to Tennessee to aid Braxton Bragg in his efforts to prevent Rosecrans' Union army from capturing Chattanooga. Van Dorn divided his cavalry into two brigades, one commanded by Brig. Gen. William H. "Red" Jackson and the other by Col. John W. Whitfield, who had recovered sufficiently from his wounds to assume command of the Texas cavalry brigade.

During the winter and spring, Van Dorn's cavalry engaged in several scouting expeditions and some skirmishes with the enemy. At Thompson's Station, between Spring Hill and Franklin, Tennessee, on March 5, the Texans made three assaults on a strong enemy position, forcing the Federals to surrender. In mid-May the brigade, now part of a division commanded by "Red" Jackson, was ordered back to Mississippi to assist in the defense of Vicksburg. On June 3 Whitfield's troopers arrived at Canton, where they reported to Joseph E. Johnston, who was attempting to put together a force large enough to break Grant's hold on Vicksburg. The Confederate effort was too little and too late. On July 4, 1863, John C. Pemberton surrendered the Vicksburg garrison.[87]

For the next six months Whitfield's Brigade was involved in a futile series of skirmishes and delaying actions as the Confederates struggled to hold eastern Mississippi. Both Jackson, the division commander, and Stephen D. Lee, commander of all cavalry in Mississippi, were convinced that because of age and poor health Whitfield should be replaced as brigade commander by the younger, more energetic Sul Ross. Whitfield, who had strong political allies in Richmond, fought the move, but in late October returned to Texas on medical leave. Since Ross and the Sixth Texas were on detached duty in Tennesssee at the time, Col. Hinche Mabry, who had returned to the Third Texas after recovering from his wounds, commanded the brigade briefly. Ross, promoted to brigadier general, formally assumed command of the brigade in mid-December.[88]

Only twenty-five years of age, Sul Ross was one of the youngest generals in the Confederate army. At the time Ross was not in good health, suffering from malaria. Nevertheless, he brought a new vigor and enthusiasm to the post. Dashing and aggressive, Ross was already a military celebrity, well liked by his superiors and the men under his command. From this time forward the men of the Third, Sixth, Ninth, and Twenty-sixth Texas cavalries would proudly refer to themselves as members of Ross' Texas Cavalry Brigade.[89]

When Ross assumed command the brigade was camped near Vernon on the Big Black River, thirty miles northeast of Jackson, Mississippi. For the next four months the brigade engaged in skirmishes with Union cavalry. When William T. Sherman made a massive raid across central Mississippi to destroy the Confederate facilties at Meridian, Ross could do little more than harass the larger Union army. In March the brigade, supported by a Tennessee regiment, was involved in a bitter fight at Yazoo City against both Union infantry and river gunboats. Although Federal reinforcements forced the Confederates to break off the attack, the enemy eventually evacuated the city.[90]

In April, "Red" Jackson, the division commander, received orders to take his cavalry, including Ross' Brigade, to Tuscaloosa, Alabama. Lt. Gen. Leonidas Polk, now commanding the Department of Alabama, Mississippi, and East Louisiana, was fearful of a Union drive from Tennessee into the coal and iron regions of central Alabama. He wanted Jackson's cavalry for scouting and patrol duty. In addition, the cavalry could be used to round up deserters, draft evaders, and suspected unionists. For the next several weeks Ross' Texans were involved in this unpleasant duty.[91]

The Alabama sojurn came to an end in early May. Sherman had begun his campaign to capture Atlanta. Jackson's cavalry, including Ross' Brigade, was ordered to join Joseph E. Johnston's army in the defense of northern Georgia. For the first time in months the men of Ross' Brigade would be fighting alongside other Texans in brigades commanded by Matthew D. Ector, Hiram Granbury, and Tom Harrison.

Ross' Texans arrived at Rome, Georgia, on May 14 and went

into battle the next day. The brigade was under fire for the next 112 days and participated in eighty-six separate clashes with the enemy. Many of these were small affairs with few casualties; others, such as the Battle of New Hope Church on May 15, 1864, were bloody engagements with heavy casualties. Of the encounter at New Hope Church, Pvt. Newton Keen of the Sixth Texas later recalled that "the cannon balls and minnie [*sic*] balls rattled like hail among the oaks and the bark and splinters flew from the trees in every direction while the limbs of trees came sweeping to the ground constantly."[92]

Ross' Brigade was on the extreme left side of Johnston's army as the Union forces drew closer to Atlanta in June. Although the Texans and other Confederates fought tenaciously, they were forced to fall back south of the Chattahooche River. Most of the Texans were still convinced that Johnston could stop Sherman. They were disappointed when Johnston was replaced by John Bell Hood as commander of the army. Although Hood was a Texan and was widely regarded as a bold fighter, most men in Ross' Brigade believed he lacked Johnston's maturity, experience, and defensive skills.[93]

The brigade was not involved in the Battle of Peachtree Creek on July 20, when Hood launched a major attack on Sherman's army. While the battle raged around Atlanta, Ross and his Texans were south of the city attempting to block Edward McCook's Union cavalry from cutting the railroads into the city. Ross' Brigade overtook McCook near Lovejoy's Station. Although heavily outnumbered, the Texans delayed McCook's troops until additional Confederate cavalry arrived. When the Union cavalry attempted to break out of the Confederate encirclement, Ross' Brigade was attacked by the Eighth Iowa Cavalry. In the confusion Ross himself was temporarily a prisoner but was soon liberated by his own men. McCook was able to pull away, but left behind his artillery, wagons, and hundreds of men and horses. The Texas brigade lost five killed and twenty-seven wounded.[94]

In mid-August Ross' Texans were involved in a battle with Judson Kilpatrick's Union cavalry near Lovejoy's Station. In this affair Ross' heavily outnumbered command suffered fifty casualties but helped prevent Kilpatrick from cutting the Confederate supply line.[95]

The Atlanta campaign came to an end on the first day of September when Hood, fearing entrapment by Sherman's army, evacuated the city. The attrition in Ross' Brigade in the four months of campaigning in Georgia was high. Ross had entered Georgia with a little over 1,000 men; he now had just over 700. As the brigade rode to Tennessee with Hood's army in November, morale was low. Many of the Texans had not seen home in more than two years, and the prospects for victory were not high. Although the brigade did not participate in the major battles at Franklin and Nashville, the Texans, now in Nathan Bedford Forrest's command, were in several skirmishes with the enemy. When Hood's defeated army retreated into Alabama in December, Ross' troopers were part of the rear guard beating off attacks by pursuing Union cavalry.[96]

In January 1865 Ross and his brigade were assigned picket duty in Mississippi. In late February about 180 members of the brigade, tired and weary, mounted their horses and headed home. "Not a harsh word was said to them, nor was [any] effort made to stop them," wrote Sam Barron of the Third Texas. A few days later Richard Taylor, who now commanded the department, gave Ross permission to grant furloughs to one-half of his remaining men. On March 13, Ross, whose own health was poor, took a ninety-day leave himself. Dudley W. Jones, "the boy colonel" of the Ninth Texas, was left in command. A month later Robert E. Lee surrendered at Appomattox. Other capitulations took place during the following month. Then, on May 4, General Taylor surrendered his department, and the war came to an end for the men of Ross' Brigade. There was briefly some talk of continuing a guerrilla war, but the idea quickly evaporated. After receiving paroles on May 15, the men lowered their flag for the last time and headed home.[97]

Chapter Four

Texas Infantry and Dismounted Cavalry in the Heartland

Second Texas Infantry

Waul's Texas Legion

Ector's Infantry Brigade
- **Ninth Texas Infantry**
- **Tenth Texas Cavalry (dismounted)**
- **Fourteenth Texas Cavalry (dismounted)**
- **Thirty-second Texas Cavalry (dismounted)**

Granbury's Infantry Brigade
- **Sixth Texas Infantry**
- **Seventh Texas Infantry**
- **Tenth Texas Infantry**
- **Fifteenth Texas Cavalry (dismounted)**
- **Seventeenth Texas Cavalry (dismounted)**
- **Eighteenth Texas Cavalry (dismounted)**
- **Twenty-fourth Texas Cavalry (dismounted)**
- **Twenty-fifth Texas Cavalry (dismounted)**

IN ADDITION TO THE TEXAS mounted cavalry regiments described in the previous chapter, five infantry regiments, eight dismounted cavalry regiments, and a legion (consisting of artillery, cavalry, and infantry) from Texas fought in the Confederate Heartland during the Civil War. One infantry regiment (the Ninth) and three dismounted cavalry regiments (the Tenth, Fourteenth, and Thirty-second Texas) spent much of the time in the brigade commanded by Texas lawyer Matthew D. Ector. Under his leadership the brigade, which later also included two North Carolina infantry regiments, distinguished itself in the battles of Murfreesboro, Chickamauga, Kennesaw Mountain, Atlanta, Allatoona, and Nashville.

Another Texas brigade, commanded by Hiram B. Granbury, fought in many of the same battles as did Ector's brigade. Consisting of the Sixth, Seventh, and Tenth Texas infantries and the Fifteenth, Seventeenth, Eighteenth, Twenty-fourth, and Twenty-fifth Texas dismounted cavalries, this all-Texas brigade was in the center of the Confederate assault at Franklin, where its popular commander, Hiram Granbury, was killed.

The Second Texas Infantry regiment, commanded originally by John C. Moore and including among its officers such well-known individuals as Xavier Debray, William P. Rogers, and Ashbel Smith, spent seventeen months (February 1862–July 1863) in Tennessee and Mississippi. During this time the regiment played a prominent role in the fighting at Shiloh, Corinth, and Vicksburg. Unlike the previously mentioned regiments, the Second Texas was never in a brigade with other Texans during this period, but served with Alabamans, Mississippians, and Arkansans.

After a brief peiod of training in Texas, the infantry and cavalry battalions of Waul's Legion were sent to Mississippi in October 1862 and fought in the battles for the defense of that state. Like the men of the Second Texas, the infantrymen of Waul's Legion were paroled after the surrender of Vicksburg and spent the rest of the war protecting the Texas coastline. The Legion's cavalry battalion was not in the siege of Vicksburg and thus avoided capture. The cavalry remained in Mississippi the last two years of the war.

In this chapter the Texas infantry and dismounted cavalry units serving in the Heartland will be discussed. Since neither the Second Infantry nor most of Waul's Legion served with other Texas units, each of these will be described separately. The regiments of Ector's and Granbury's brigades will then be discussed under the brigade subheading.

THE SECOND TEXAS INFANTRY

The Second Texas Infantry was made up of ten volunteer militia companies from coastal and Central Texas. The companies were brought together as a regiment under the command of Col. John Creed Moore. A West Point graduate and former artillery officer in the U.S. Army, Moore was teaching at Shelby College in Kentucky when the states of the lower South seceded. An ardent supporter of southern rights, Moore resigned his teaching position immediately to accept a commission in the Confederate army. He was sent to Texas in late spring 1861 to construct defensive fortifications for the state. When it became obvious that additional troops were needed, Moore was ordered to organize an infantry regiment from local militia.[1]

The men in the ten companies that made up the new regiment were primarily from the Houston-Galveston-lower Brazos River area. Joseph E. Chance, who has written the most complete modern account of the Second Texas, points out that the ranks of the regiment were filled "by proud, young volunteers imbued with a spirit of adventure and eager to serve." Among those in the regiment were the sons of former Texas presidents Sam Houston and Dr. Anson Jones. The older Houston initially opposed his son's enlistment but eventually came to take an interest in the unit and later claimed to be a private in Company C, the Bayland Guards.[2]

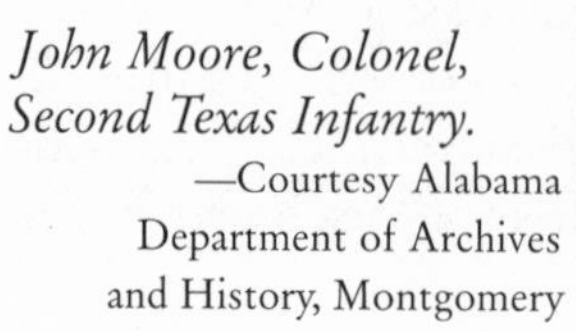

John Moore, Colonel, Second Texas Infantry.
—Courtesy Alabama Department of Archives and History, Montgomery

Co.	County	Local Name	Captain
A	Harris	San Jacinto Guards	Hal G. Runnels
B	Harris	Confederate Guards	William C. Timmons
C	Harris-Chambers	Bayland Guards	Ashbel Smith
D	Harris	Confederate Grays	Edward F. Williams
E	Robertson-Brazos	———	Belvedere Brooks
F	Galveston	———	John Muller
G	Burleson	Burleson Guards	John W. Hood
H	Burleson-Lee	Lexington Grays	Noble L. McGinnis
I	Gonzales	Gonzales Invincibles	George W. L. Fly
K	Jackson	Texana Guards	Clark L. Owen

Companies of the Second Texas Infantry[3]

Moore's regiment was mustered into Confederate service in September 1861 as the First Texas Infantry. However, Louis T. Wigfall, former U.S. senator and now Confederate senator, claimed that the Texans who had gathered in the Richmond, Virginia, area were entitled to the honor of being "first." Due to Wigfall's political influence the Confederate War Department agreed that the Texans in Virginia should be designated as the First Texas Infantry. Moore's regiment thus became the Second Texas Infantry.[4]

The Second Texas was quartered in a cotton warehouse in Galveston while organization of the unit was completed. Well-known Texas lawyer and Mexican War veteran William P. Rogers was chosen lieutenant colonel of the regiment. Rogers, who had served with distinction in Jefferson Davis' Mississippi Rifles in the Mexican conflict, was a cousin of Sam Houston's wife and a long-time friend of Houston. Like Houston, Rogers initially opposed secession but with Lincoln's election came to believe separation from the Union was necessary if southern rights were to be protected. After Texas seceded, Rogers was offered command of the First Texas in Virginia by Jefferson Davis, but at his wife's insistence he accepted the lieutenant colonelcy of the Second Texas instead. Hal Runnels, captain of Company A, was chosen major of the regiment. His place as captain of Company A was filled by William Christian.[5]

The men of the Second Texas were put through a rigorous training pace by their new officers. Colonel Moore had the reputation of being a strict disciplinarian, a reputation which seemed fully merited. In December the regiment moved to Camp Bee in Houston, where the training continued as the commander sought uniforms and equipment for the men. The routine of drill was occasionally interrupted by social activities provided by the local townfolk. Ralph Smith, a private in Company K from Jackson County, noted in his memoirs that the young Texans were supremely confident of victory when they met the enemy. "The possibility of such a thing as defeat never for a moment entered the minds of a member of our inexperienced corps," he wrote. "Day after day we were dined, wined, and flattered. Night after night we floated on a sea of glory. The ladies petted and lionized us; preachers prayed with and for us, declaring the lord was on our side, so we need have no fears." Even the admonitions of Sam Houston, who occasionally visited the drills, had little effect upon their self-confidence. When the old warrior cautioned the young Texans that the resources of the North were almost limitless and would wear them down, Smith observed "he might as well had been giving advice to the inmates of a lunatic asylum. We knew no such word as fail."[6]

The regiment had been formed to provide protection for the Texas coastline, but in March Colonel Moore received orders to report to Corinth, Mississippi, where Albert Sidney Johnston was concentrating all available troops for an attack on the Union army at Pittsburg Landing on the Tennessee River.

The Second Texas departed from Houston on March 18, 1862. The regiment traveled by rail to Beaumont, then by steamboat up the Neches River to Wiess' Bluff, and then overland by foot to Alexandria, Louisiana. From there they proceeded by steamboat on the Red and Mississippi rivers to Memphis, and from there by overland march to Corinth, arriving on April 1.[7]

Moore's regiment, nearly 1,300 men strong, reached Corinth as Johnston was completing his concentration of troops for the attack on Grant's army on the Tennessee River. Already two other Texas regiments, the Eighth Texas Cavalry and the Ninth Texas Infantry, were with the army as it completed preparations for the twenty-mile march to Pittsburg Landing. Supplies of the Second Texas were virtually exhausted after the long journey from Houston, but the Confederate commissary at Corinth could provide Moore with rations for only two and a half days.

After only a day's rest, the regiment moved with Johnston's army on April 3 as it headed toward Pittsburg Landing. The march took three days rather than two as Johnston had hoped. Many of the men in the Second Texas had consumed their rations and others had worn out their shoes on the march from Texas and were barefoot. To make matters worse, the Texans were wearing ill-fitting, undyed white cotton uniforms that were issued to them at Corinth.[8]

In the great battle that took place near the small country church named Shiloh on April 6-7, 1862, the Second Texas was in the thick of the fighting. As a part of John K. Jackson's brigade in Jones Withers' division, the Texans were on the right flank of Johnston's army during the attack. They overran the outlying Federal camps as the Union cooks were preparing breakfast. Young Sam Houston, Jr., a member of Capt. Ashbel Smith's Bayland Guards, scalded his hand as he took a large piece of beef from a boiling pot. Other Texans paused to pick various mementos from the Federal tents.

By midday the Union troops had formed a defense line along a sunken road flanked by open fields on both sides. Here Union General Benjamin Prentiss rallied his troops to make a stand. The rifle and musket fire was so severe that the embattled soldiers were soon referring to the area as the "Hornet's Nest." The fighting went on until late afternoon, when Prentiss finally surrendered to the Second Texas.

As the other Federal troops fell back toward the Tennessee River, the advancing Confederates, including the Second Texas, came under artillery fire from Union gunboats. When evening came the exhausted Confederates bedded down for the night. They had only partially achieved success that day. Although they had driven the enemy back several miles, the cost had been high. Albert Sidney Johnston, the highest-ranking field officer in the Confederate army, had been killed while trying to rally Confederate troops on the right flank in the early afternoon. Hundreds of Confederates were killed and wounded. The Second Texas sustained more than one hundred casualties that day, including Capt. Belvedere Brooks of Company E, who was mortally wounded in the opening attack. Capt. Ashbel Smith was shot in the right arm and was later sent to a hospital in Memphis.[9]

When fighting resumed on the morning of April 7, the Confederate forces found themselves outnumbered by Grant's Union army, which had received reinforcements during the night. Throughout the day the Confederates slowly gave ground, retreating back past the spot of their initial assault. In the confusion of the day's activities the Second Texas became the center of controversy between Col. John C. Moore and corps commander William J. Hardee. The Texans had performed so well under Moore's leadership in the first day's fighting that division commander Jones M. Withers appointed Moore as temporary brigade commander, replacing Brig. Gen. John Jackson, who had become separated from the brigade. About 11:00 that morning the Second Texas, now commanded by Lieutenant Colonel Rogers, was ordered to advance against the enemy without proper reconnaissance. When they encountered unexpected heavy enemy fire, they gave ground and fell back. General Hardee, who was on the scene, blamed the Texans for breaking and fleeing "disgracefully from the field."[10]

In his report of the battle, Hardee was highly critical of both officers and men of the Second Texas. In the instance "of the Second Texas Regiment, commanded by Col. Moore, the men seemed appalled, fled from the field without apparent cause, and were so dismayed that my efforts to rally them were unavailing," he reported.[11]

Moore, who was proud of the regiment and sensitive to any personal criticism, replied angrily to Hardee's charges. In a special attachment submitted with his regular report of the battle, Moore noted that Hardee's staff had not followed the proper chain of command. Staff officers had shouted orders to the Texans, adding to the confusion of the battle. Several men in the regiment, Moore contended, had heard orders to fall back. And, finally, Moore pointed out that Rogers was actually commanding the regiment that day, not Moore (who headed the brigade), as Hardee reported. Historian Joseph Chance, who studied the issue carefully, agreed that numerous errors were made by Hardee and his staff, but pointed out the Second Texas Infantry and General Moore "made a powerful enemy in General Hardee," a highly respected officer with considerable influence in Confederate affairs. Another historian, Kevin R. Young, was more critical of Hardee, writing that "it is highly possible that Hardee was using Moore and the regiment as a scapegoat for his own military blundering."[12]

Following the second day of fighting at Shiloh, the defeated Confederates, now commanded by Gen. P.G.T. Beauregard, retreated. The Second Texas formed part of the rear guard as the army made its way back to Corinth. The Confederate losses were heavy: 1,728 killed, 8,012 wounded, and 959 missing. The exact number of casualties in the Second Texas is not clear, as Moore's summary of losses was not found by the compilers of the *Official Records*; however, muster rolls indicate slighty over 30 percent casualties for the regiment. William P. Rogers, who commanded the Second Texas during the fighting on April 7, was injured by a limb that was snapped off by a cannon ball. Captains Edward F. Williams of Company D, Belvedere Brooks of Company E, Clark Owen of Company K, and Lt. John H. Fenney of Company E were all killed. Captains J. W. Hood of Company G and George W. L. Fly of Company I were seriously wounded. Ashbel Smith, wounded himself, had to report to his old friend Sam Houston that his son, Pvt. Sam Houston, Jr., was among the missing. Young Houston fortunately survived. He was found wounded on the battlefield by a Union chaplain, given medical attention, and taken as a prisoner to Camp Douglas, Illinois. After several months of imprisonment he was released and allowed to return home.[13]

For the next several weeks the Second Texas was camped near Corinth. The regiment took part in a small battle at Farmington, Mississippi, on May 9 in which it helped drive back Federal troops commanded by John Pope. Later that month several organizational changes took place as Colonel Moore was promoted to brigadier general and given command of a brigade consisting of the Second Texas, Fifteenth Arkansas, Twenty-third Arkansas, and Thirty-fifth Mississippi regiments. At the same time William P. Rogers was promoted to colonel, Ashbel Smith to lieutenant colonel, and William Simmons to major.[14]

In late May the Confederate army, under heavy enemy pressure, evacuated Corinth and fell back to Tupelo, fifty miles to the south. There the army rested and reorganized. Moore's brigade was now part of Sterling Price's Army of the West.

In June the Second Texas received a citation from division commander Dabney A. Maury for its service at Shiloh. The citation allowed the Texans to place the word "Shiloh" on their battle flag. At the same time the Second Texas was designated as the "sharpshooters" regiment in Moore's brigade. This designation meant that the regiment, from now on often referred to as the Second Texas Sharpshooters, would lead the brigade in the attack. Colonel Rogers and the men of the Second were pleased with this recognition, but as historian Joseph Chance pointed out, it was "an honor which . . . cost the Texans dearly in casualties."[15]

The Second Texas saw little action during the summer months of 1862. Because the regiment now had only slightly more than 500 present for duty, Lt. Col. Ashbel Smith was sent back to Texas to enroll a group of conscripted troops, a move not altogether popular with the volunteers.

While Smith was back in Texas, Sterling Price's army was ordered north to prevent a linkup of the armies of William S. Rosecrans and U. S. Grant in northern Mississippi. Price moved his army, including the Second Texas, to the small town of Iuka, thirty miles east of Corinth on the Memphis-Charleston Railroad. Although the Confederates occupied the town with little difficulty, they were attacked by Rosecrans' army on September 19. In the fierce fighting that took place, the Texas Third and Twenty-seventh cavalries were heavily involved, but the Second Texas saw only limited action.[16]

The Confederates held their own in the fighting on the 19th, but having suffered heavy casualties and fearing Union encirclement, Price reluctantly abandoned Iuka the following day. As the Confederates retreated, Rosecrans, now joined by Edward O. C. Ord's Corps from Grant's army, attempted to cut off the withdrawal. During this action the Second Texas, supported by a Missouri artillery battery, played a major role in driving off an attack by the Iowa Cavalry that threatened the Confederate withdrawal.[17]

Price's battered army made its way southward to Baldwyn, Mississippi, a town thirty miles south of Corinth. From there Price moved northwest to Ripley, where he joined other Confederates commanded by Earl Van Dorn. In late September their combined forces, numbering around 22,000 troops, marched north in an attempt to recapture Corinth, a key railroad juncture.

Sterling Price, shaken by his failure at Iuka, was opposed to the attack on Corinth. The city was garrisoned by only 15,000 Union troops, but Rosecrans, the area commander, could quickly bring up an additional 10,000 men. More importantly, the Federals were well entrenched in defense lines previously built by the Confederates and strengthened during the Union occupation. In spite of Price's objections, Van Dorn, who was senior in command, was determined to capture the city.[18]

Van Dorn hoped to surprise the enemy at Corinth by first moving his army north as if driving into southern Tennessee, then swinging back in a southeasterly direction toward the city. Unfortunately for the Confederates, Rosecrans, though puzzled somewhat by the Rebel movement, was prepared when the Confederates made their attack on the morning of October 3.[19]

Dabney Maury's Division, which included Moore's Brigade and the Second Texas, was on the Confederate right during the initial attack. Throughout the day Moore's Confederates battled with Federal troops from Illinois, Michigan, Missouri, and Wisconsin. The tide of battle ebbed and flowed, and casualties were heavy. Maj. William Timmons, leading the Texans in the assault, was seriously wounded, but Capt. John Muller of Company F took his place as the battle went on. Successive bayonet attacks by the Second Texas helped force the enemy slowly back so that by darkness the Confederates occupied the outer defenses of the city.[20]

The Confederate attack resumed the next morning. Due to some confusion by Gen. Mansfield Lovell on the Rebel right and the illness of Gen. Louis Hebert, who commanded the division on the left, Maury's Division carried the brunt of the assault. Moore's Brigade led the attack that broke through the Union lines. When heavy enemy artillery and musket fire threatened to halt the advance, Colonel Rogers, who was probably the most capable regimental commander in Van Dorn's army, rallied the Confederates as they continued to drive into the center of the town. At the head of his troops Rogers led a handful of Texans against the breastworks of Battery Robinett, the key post in the Federal defense line. For a brief moment the flag of the Second Texas fluttered over the battery, but a powerful enemy counterattack swept the Confederates back. Colonel Rogers, possibly trying to surrender in face of the overwhelming odds, was killed along with several of his men. Those who could do so fell back toward the Confederate lines. The desperate fighting continued for another hour before Van Dorn conceded failure. Around noon he called off the attack. The next day the Confederates withdrew across the Hatchie River under heavy enemy fire.[21]

Confederate losses at Corinth were high. Dabney Maury suffered the heaviest division losses, with nearly 2,500 casualties out of 3,800 men who took part in the battle. John C. Moore's brigade was particularly hard hit, losing 1,295 of 1,895 men engaged. The Second Texas, in the center of the fighting, sustained 116 casualties out of 314 troops who were in the battle. Among the casualties, in addition to Colonel Rogers, was Maj. John Muller (promoted when Major Timmons was wounded the first day). Muller was killed within twenty paces of Battery Robinett while leading his men. Capt. George W. L. Fly of Company I and Capt. W. F. Goff of Company K were both captured but later paroled.[22]

The Confederate army retreated to Holly Springs, Mississippi, after the battle at Corinth. The Second Texas was temporarily commanded by Capt. Noble L. McGinnis of Company H, the senior officer with the regiment following the deaths of Colonel Rogers and Major Muller and the wounding of Major Timmons at Corinth. In late November the advance of the Union army forced the Confederates to move to Grenada, seventy miles to the south. While there, promotions were announced. Ashbel Smith, still in Texas enrolling conscripts, was appointed colonel. William Timmons, returned to duty from medical leave, was made lieutenant colonel and temporary commander in Smith's absence. Noble McGinnis, commander of H Company, was promoted to major.[23]

In late December the Second Texas was ordered to Vicksburg to assist in the defense of that city. Union general William T. Sherman had attempted an amphibious landing at Chickasaw Bluffs, seven miles north of Vicksburg. The Second Texas joined Brig. Gen. Stephen D. Lee's Confederate forces there just as Sherman was trying to withdraw his troops by transport vessels. The Texans, led by Lieutenant Colonel Timmons, launched an immediate attack on the enemy, pouring deadly rifle fire on the Union transports. Although Sherman was able to withdraw his troops, the fire from the Second Texas resulted in many enemy casualties. In his report of the affair, Lee praised the Texans: "this most gallant regiment with a dash rushed almost up to the boats delivering their fire with terrible effect on their crowded transports." His superior, Lt.

Gen. John C. Pemberton, also praised "the noble Second Texas" for its performance.[24]

Lieutenant Colonel Timmons, who was wounded in the ankle while leading the regiment in the encounter at Chickasaw Bluffs, died later when surgeons attempted to amputate his foot. To fill his position Noble L. McGinnis was promoted to lieutenant colonel. Capt. George W. L. Fly was promoted to major.

The regiment remained in camp at Chickasaw Bayou for the next two months. In January, Colonel Smith returned from Texas with 150 conscripted soldiers. Although there was some resentment among the veterans, the new infantrymen slowly won acceptance by members of the regiment.

Confederate authorities learned in late February that Union general Grant was attempting to bring troops down the Yazoo River by transport vessels. Under the command of Maj. Gen. W. W. Loring, the Confederates hurriedly constructed Fort Pemberton at the confluence of the Tallahatchee and Yalobusha rivers as a defensive barrier to the move. In early March the Second Texas was moved by steamboat up the Yazoo to join Loring's command. Soon after the Texans arrived, they helped other Confederates in driving back the enemy in what some called the Battle of Tallahatchee. For their part in the successful Confederate defense Colonel Smith and the Texans won the praise and commendation of General Loring.[25]

When it became apparent that Grant was abandoning the Yazoo River approach, the Second Texas returned to its camp at Chickasaw Bayou. The regiment remained there until early May, when it was ordered to Warrenton, twelve miles south of Vicksburg. Grant's army had crossed the Mississippi at Bruinsburg to the south. The Second Texas was assigned to guard the road coming north from Grand Gulf.

On March 17 the Texans were ordered to fall back to the defensive lines around Vicksburg. Confederate efforts to block Grant's advance had failed, and the city was rapidly being encircled.

The Second Texas was assigned a fort in the center of the Confederate defense line commanding the Baldwin Ferry Road and the Southern Mississippi Railroad. Under Colonel Smith's direction the Texans immediately set to work improving the fort and the adjacent area. Because the fortification was designed in a half-moon shape, the position quickly became known as the Second Texas Lunette.

Smith's troops had barely finished improvements to their defensive position when Grant's army opened fire. Shelling began on May 19, but the main assault on the Texas position came on May 22, when five Union regiments attacked the Texas Lunette. Throughout the day wave after wave of Federal troops charged the Confederate line while the Texans poured lethal fire through the embrasures. During one of the heaviest attacks, fires were started in the cotton bales that were used inside the fort for protective cover. The fires were quickly put out. Some Federal troops attempted to scale the parapet but were driven back. A brief lull in hostilities took place around 3:00 P.M., but Union reinforcements resumed the assault soon after. The firing went on until nightfall. The ground in front of the lunette was covered with the bodies of dead Union soldiers.[26]

Union attacks on other Confederate positions were also unsuccessful and costly in casualties that day. As a result Grant decided that Vicksburg could not be taken by assault without prohibitive losses. With his troops encircling the city and the Union navy controlling the Mississippi River, Grant ordered a siege. For the next six weeks the Confederate defenders suffered from daily artillery bombardment, enemy probing efforts, sickness, hunger, and exposure. Joseph E. Johnston, who had been appointed overall Confederate commander of the Mississippi-Tennessee Department, attempted to raise sufficient forces to break the siege but was unsuccessful. On July 4, 1863, Lieutenant General Pemberton, commanding the besieged garrison, surrendered to General Grant.[27]

Under the terms of surrender the Confederate troops at Vicksburg were given paroles on condition they not perform military duties against the United States until properly exchanged. The Confederates were sent to a camp near Brandon, Mississippi, to await exchange, but many of the men, particularly from those from the Trans Mississippi, began leaving for home. General Pemberton, recognizing the futility of keeping men against their will, agreed to permit furloughs for many of his troops. On July 17, 1863, Colonel Smith received orders furloughing his men until exchanged.

The men of the Second Texas made their way home as best they could in late July and early August. Although the journey was difficult, they found assistance from their fellow Southerners. Ralph Smith, the private who had been wounded and captured at

Shiloh but exchanged in time to suffer through the Vicksburg siege, reported "we found the people along our route, though illy provided themselves, willing to divide their last morsel with us. . . ." By late August most of the men of the Second Texas were home for the first time in more than a year.[28]

The Second Texas was declared exchanged in October 1863 and ordered to report to Houston for reorganization. The regiment, now reduced in numbers to little more than 200 men, was reassigned to the District of Texas, Arizona, and New Mexico under the command of Maj. Gen. John B. Magruder. The Second Texas was ordered to Velasco near the mouth of the Brazos and then to Fort Caney at the mouth of the Caney River to help defend the Texas coast against an anticipated enemy invasion. The regiment remained there during the winter of 1863-1864 under the command of Maj. George W. L. Fly, who assumed command when Ashbel Smith was assigned other duty in Houston.[29]

In late spring the Second Texas joined other Texas units guarding Galveston Island. Colonel Smith rejoined the regiment in August. When Brig. Gen. James M. Hawes, commander of the Galveston defenses, contracted yellow fever, Smith assumed command of all troops on the island.

The Second Texas remained on Galveston Island for the last months of the war. Although Colonel Smith attempted to keep discipline and order, morale in all the Confederate units was low. Yellow fever, inadequate rations, and lack of pay contributed to a general deterioration. On one occasion the Second Texas was called upon to quell a riot by disgruntled soldiers. When word was received that Robert E. Lee had surrendered in Virginia, many of the men decided the war was lost and headed home. At the urging of Colonel Smith a few remained on the island until the final surrender by Kirby Smith on June 2.[30]

WAUL'S TEXAS LEGION

Serving alongside the men of the Second Texas Infantry on Galveston Island during the closing days of the war were the veteran infantrymen of Waul's Texas Legion. Like the men of the Second, the two battalions of infantry in the Legion spent the last

Thomas N. Waul, Colonel, Waul's Legion.
—Courtesy Harold B. Simpson Research Center, Hillsboro, Texas

eighteen months stationed on the Texas coast but had gained recognition in combat during the Vicksburg campaign east of the Mississippi River.

Waul's was the only true legion to be formed in Civil War Texas. Military units known as legions existed in the early American army but were generally considered obsolete by the time of the American Civil War. Usually consisting of two battalions of infantry, one battalion of cavalry, and one battalion or battery of artillery, such units were unwieldly and difficult to command. Even so, the concept remained popular in some quarters. Wade Hampton's South Carolina Legion was perhaps the best known in Confederate service. John W. Whitfield's Twenty-seventh Texas Cavalry, consisting of twelve rather than the usual ten mounted companies, was often referred to as "Whitfield's Legion," even though it had neither artillery nor infantry.[31]

Waul's Legion, a true legion with infantry, artillery, and cavalry, was formed in late spring 1862 by wealthy lawyer-planter Thomas N. Waul of Gonzales. A native of South Carolina, Waul was active in Texas public affairs in the late antebellum period. He supported secession and was chosen as one of the Texas delegates to the Montgomery convention that drafted the Confederate constitution. Waul sought a seat in the regular Confederate Senate during the November 1861 elections but was defeated by Williamson S. Oldham.

His hopes for a political career dashed, Waul began recruiting troops for Confederate service. His legion was organized at Brenham in May 1862 with Waul as colonel, Bernard Timmons of La Grange as lieutenant colonel commanding the first infantry battalion of six companies, and James Wrigley of Liberty as lieutenant colonel commanding the second infantry battalion of six companies. A cavalry battalion of six companies was headed by Maj. Leonidas Willis and a six-gun artillery battery was led by Capt. William Edgar.[32]

By late summer nearly 2,000 Texans were members of Waul's Legion. Many of the men had already served in Texas state units but were mustered out when their six-month enlistments ended. The majority of the men came from Central and coastal Texas, especially Fayette, Washington, Gonzales, DeWitt, Galveston, Harris, and Liberty counties. More than 200 of the recruits were born in Germany. Many of the younger members of the legion were native Texans.[33]

The legion spent several weeks in training at Camp Waul, seven miles north of Brenham. The camp was located along New Year's Creek near the rural community of Gay Hill and next to agricultural reformer Thomas Affleck's Glenblythe plantation. In letters to his wife Waul reported that the legion was well supplied with food but had shortages of weapons and uniforms. An outbreak of measles sent many of the recruits to bed, and several men died.[34]

In August 1862 Waul received orders to join Earl Van Dorn's army in Mississippi. The legion began the march toward Mississippi in three echelons with the cavalry in the lead. While marching through Louisiana the artillery and cavalry components were detached from the legion and assigned elsewhere. The twelve infantry companies, organized in two battaltions, reached Vicksburg on October 1. They joined Van Dorn's army at Holly Springs on October 10.

The legion infantry joined Van Dorn's army, which included the Second Texas Infantry previously discussed, as it was smarting from the defeat at Corinth earlier in the month. In late November the advance of Grant's army southward forced the Confederates to fall back to Grenada, seventy-five miles to the south. The legion remained in camp near Grenada for the rest of the year.[35]

As pointed out earlier, the Second Texas Infantry, also at

Grenada, was ordered to join Maj. Gen. W. W. Loring's Division on the Yazoo River in December. The following month Waul's Legion was also ordered to report to General Loring.

The legion reached Snyder's Mill northeast of Vicksburg on February 15, 1863. From there Waul and his infantry were ordered north to the confluence of the Tallahatchee and Yalobusha rivers, where the Confederates were hurriedly constructing Fort Pemberton to block a Union movement down the Yazoo River.

Waul and 600 infantrymen arrived at Fort Pemberton on February 22. The defensive works were not yet completed and the weather was bitterly cold, but Waul reported to General Pemberton that his men were in good spirits. They were joined a week later by other Texans with the arrival of Col. Ashbel Smith and his Second Texas Infantry. On March 13 the two Texas regiments helped drive off a Union naval flotilla carrying several regiments of enemy troops. This action won the praise of General Loring for both the legion and the Second Texas Infantry.[36]

After the repulse of the Union flotilla in early March, the Second Texas was ordered to the Vicksburg area. Waul's Legion remained at Fort Pemberton to guard against a surprise enemy movement along the Yazoo. In early May, when it was apparent that Grant had crossed the river south of Vicksburg, Waul was ordered to leave a battalion at Fort Pemberton and take the rest of his command to Vicksburg. There the legion, rejoined by a detachment of cavalry, was assigned to a brigade commanded by Brig. Gen. Stephen D. Lee in Carter L. Stevenson's Division. On May 16 Waul and his troops were with Stevenson's Division when the Confederates made an unsuccessful attempt to halt Grant's movement toward Vicksburg in a battle at Champion's Hill, or Baker's Creek as some Confederates called it. The Confederates made another attempt to stop Grant from crossing the Big Black River, but following this failure they fell back into the defense lines surrounding Vicksburg.[37]

In the initial stages of the fighting for Vicksburg, Waul's Legion was assigned as a reserve in Maj. Gen. John Forney's Division, which held the central section of the Confederate line. On the evening of May 19 the legion was transferred back to Stephen D. Lee's Brigade in Stevenson's Division on the Confederate right. When the enemy made a major assault on

May 22 the legion was in the rear of the brigade but was brought to the front line to support the Thirtieth Alabama defending the so-called Railroad Redoubt just south of the Southern Mississippi Railroad.[38]

The most critical moment of the fighting on May 22 occurred when Iowa and Illniois troops of Michael Lawler's Brigade pushed the Alabama infantry back and captured the Railroad Redoubt. Along with the Second Texas Lunette, just to the left, the Railroad Redoubt was critical to the entire Confederate defense line. Initial efforts by the Alabamans to retake the redoubt failed. After Lt. Col. E. W. Pettus of the Thirtieth Alabama was unable to convince his troops to make another effort, Brig. Gen. Stephen Lee asked Waul if the Texans could retake the vital outpost. Two companies of Texans immediately volunteered to undertake the assignment. To avoid unnecessary exposure of a large force to enemy fire, Waul assigned thirty-five men to the task. Lieutenant Colonel Pettus of the Thirtieth Alabama asked for permission to lead the attack. Three privates from the Alabama regiment also joined Waul's volunteers.

The attack force rushed forward with a wild Rebel yell, fixed bayonets, and blazing rifles. The Union defenders, stunned by the suddenness and ferocity of the charge, were overwhelmed. Fifty enemy troops and a stand of colors were captured. The other defenders fell back to the outer ditch of the redoublt with the Texans directing a steady fire at them. The fighting went on as the enemy without success attempted to regain the redoubt. When darkness fell the Federals slipped back toward their own lines.[39]

The heavy losses suffered on May 22 (slightly over 3,000 Union casualties) convinced Grant that Vicksburg could not be taken by frontal assault. For the next six weeks the Union army lay siege to the city. Like other Confederate troops the Texans in Waul's Legion (and the Second Texas Infantry) endured the hardships of daily artillery bombardment coupled with increasing shortages of food. When beef and bacon were exhausted in late June the army began slaughtering its mules. Teamsters attached to the legion assisted in drying and jerking the mule meat to make it resemble beef jerky.[40]

Frequent rain, damp fog, and hot and humid days added to the misery. Illness was commonplace. In June, Waul reported eighty-nine of his troops and fourteen civilians attached to the legion were ill.[41]

For some time the besieged Confederates held some expectations of relief. On June 8 Henry McCulloch's troops in John G. Walker's Texas Division attacked the Union garrison at Milliken's Bend above Vicksburg on the west side of the Mississippi in an attempt to break the Union stranglehold but were unsuccessful. Some hope remained that Joseph E. Johnston could raise sufficient forces in central Mississippi to hit Grant from the east, but by late June it was evident this was not possible.[42]

On July 4, 1863, General Pemberton surrendered the Vicksburg garrison to General Grant. As noted earlier, all Confederate troops were paroled on condition they not take part in any military action against the United States until properly exchanged.

In his report of the Vicksburg campaign brigade commander Stephen D. Lee praised Waul for his role in the fighting and long siege that preceded surrender. "Col. T. N. Waul," Lee wrote, "by his dashing gallantry and coolness, inspired every one around him with confidence, and handled his Legion with skill." In his own report Waul praised his officers and men for their steadfastness in the long ordeal. He noted that forty-seven of his troops were killed in the campaign, 190 were wounded, and eight were missing. Among those killed were Maj. Allen Cameron and Captains Samuel Carter and J. A. Ledbetter.[43]

Waul reported that thirty-two officers and 554 men of the legion as well as a signal company and escort company were among his troops being paroled. Although a small detachment of cavalry scouts commanded by Lt. Thomas Cleveland remained with the infantry, most of the legion's cavalry was not with Waul's men during the siege.

The bulk of the legion's cavalry, commanded by Lt. Col. Leonidas Willis, had been assigned to Robert McCulloch's brigade in James R. Chalmers' cavalry division before the siege of Vicksburg was under way. At the time of the Vicksburg surrender Chalmers' division was in central Mississippi serving with Nathan Bedford Forrest. During the last two years of the war, Willis' cavalry battalion, as it was now designated, took part in numerous cavalry raids and engagements in Mississippi, Tennessee, and Alabama, usually in Forrest's command. In all, the battalion, consisting of 200-300 men, fought in more than a hundred battles, including Tupelo, Fort Pillow, Brice's Cross Roads, and Nashville. The battalion was attached to Sul Ross' Brigade when the surrender came at Citronelle, Alabama, on May 4, 1865.[44]

One of Waul's infantry companies was not captured at Vicksburg. This unit, Company C of the First Battalion, commanded by Capt. Robert Voight, was part of the force Waul had been ordered to leave at Fort Pemberton. Voight's company was transferred later to Yazoo City to support Confederate forces there under the command of Lt. Col. William B. Creasman of the Twenty-ninth North Carolina Infantry. A week after the fall of Vicksburg a large Union combined army-navy expedition, numbering 5,000 men and commanded by Maj. Gen. Francis Herron, was sent to drive the Confederates out of the area. After a brief exchange of fire the heavily outnumbered Confederates abandoned the town and withdrew. Voight and his company failed to evacuate and were captured. Unlike the Vicksburg prisoners they were not paroled but were sent to Camp Morton, Indiana, where they remained until the end of the war.[45]

While the men of Company C of Waul's Legion were on their way to Union prison, the infantry companies that had been part of the Vicksburg garrison were camped at Brandon, Mississippi, with other units of Pemberton's army. Pemberton hoped to keep his army together until the men were exchanged, but the men in Waul's Legion, like those in the Second Texas Infantry, began heading home. By late August most of Waul's infantrymen, like those in the Second Texas, were back in the Lone Star State.

Colonel Waul remained at army headquarters near Brandon. On September 11, 1863, word was received that the Vicksburg parolees had been exchanged and could be reassigned military duty. A week later Waul was promoted to brigadier general and ordered to report to Edmund Kirby Smith, commanding the Trans Mississippi Department at Shreveport, Louisiana. Although Waul had no difficulty crossing the Mississippi River, which was now under Union control, he did not report to Kirby Smith at Shreveport until November 18. Meanwhile, orders had been issued to the infantrymen of the legion, along with those in the Second Texas, to report for duty at General Magruder's headquarters at Houston. There they would be resupplied with new uniforms, rifles, and other equipment.[46]

After reporting to Kirby Smith, General Waul was ordered to

proceed to Houston to take command of a new brigade consisting of the legion's infantry, the Second Texas, the Third Texas Infantry, and J. R. Likens' cavalry. Under orders from General Magruder, the new brigade was sent to Velasco as part of the buildup of troops to meet an expected Union invasion of the upper Texas coast. Although the invasion never took place, the brigade, including Waul's infantrymen, remained near the mouth of the Brazos during the winter months of 1863-1864.

In January 1864 Waul himself was reassigned to Louisiana, where he was given command of a brigade in John G. Walker's Texas Division. The men of the legion, without Waul, were now under the command of Bernard Timmons, formerly commander of the First Battalion, who was promoted to colonel. The infantry companies of Waul's Legion, now designated as Timmons' Regiment, spent the last seventeen months of the war on duty in Texas. They were stationed briefly at Anderson, Texas, in April 1864, but later that month were sent to Galveston. On May 5 they received orders to move to Louisiana, but the directive was quickly countermanded and the regiment stayed in Galveston.[47]

The last year of the war the regiment was on duty in Galveston as part of the Second Brigade, Second Texas Division, commanded by Brig. Gen. J. M. Hawes. Field reports show that regimental strength throughout the year was rather constant: fifteen officers and 302 men present for duty in May 1864, sixteen officers and 315 men in September, eighteen officers and 337 men in January, twenty officers and 322 men in April 1865.[48]

In spite of the growing pessimism as the South suffered military defeats in Tennessee, Georgia, and Virginia, the men of the legion remained steadfast in their support for the Confederacy. When 400 troops on Galveston Island tried to desert their posts in May 1865, Timmons' Regiment (the old Waul's Legion) helped Ashbel Smith, who had replaced General Hawes as commander, put down the mutiny. Only when it was clear that Kirby Smith was surrendering the Trans Mississippi Department did the men of the old legion head for home. They were now joined by cavalrymen of the legion who were returning from Alabama following the surrender there. It would be several months before the infantrymen of the legion held prisoner at Camp Morton, Indiana, made their way home.[49]

ECTOR'S BRIGADE

Ninth Texas Infantry
Tenth Texas Cavalry (dismounted)
Fourteenth Texas Cavalry (dismounted)
Thirty-second Texas Cavalry (dismounted)

Unlike the infantrymen of the Second Texas and Waul's Legion, the Texas regiments in Ector's Brigade were still east of the Mississippi River when the Civil War ended. The brigade, commanded by Brig. Gen. Matthew D. Ector of Henderson, Texas, was previously commanded by Joseph L. Hogg, William L. Cabell, and Thomas H. McCray. It became known as Ector's Brigade in September 1862 when Ector, who had led one of the regiments (the Fourteenth Texas Cavalry), was promoted to brigadier general and given command. At the time the brigade consisted of the Tenth, Eleventh, Fourteenth, and Fifteenth Texas cavalries (all dismounted) plus Capt. James Douglas' artillery battery. Several months later the Eleventh Texas was replaced by the Ninth Texas Infantry, the Twenty-ninth and Thirty-ninth North Carolina infantries were added, and the Fifteenth Texas was redesignated as the Thirty-second Texas Cavalry.[50]

The Eleventh Texas Cavalry was the only one of the four original regiments in Ector's Brigade to have seen combat before the brigade was formed. As noted in the previous chapter, this regiment, commanded by Col. William C. Young, fought at Chustenahlah and Pea Ridge. When Earl Van Dorn received orders transferring his army to Corinth, Mississippi, the Eleventh Cavalry was required to leave its horses behind.

Like the Eleventh Texas, the other cavalry regiments in Van Dorn's army left their horses when they crossed the Mississippi. This included three new cavalry regiments, the Tenth, Fourteenth, and Fifteenth Texas, that joined Van Dorn after the battle at Pea Ridge.

The first of these new regiments was the Tenth Texas Cavalry. The Tenth Texas was mustered into Confederate service in October 1861. Matthew F. Locke of Gilmer, a small slaveholder and delegate to the Texas secession convention, was largely responsible for raising the regiment and was named its colonel. The men were recruited from a tier of counties in East Texas including Panola,

Matthew D. Ector, Colonel, Fourteenth Texas Cavalry (dismounted), later brigade commander.
—Courtesy Harold B. Simpson Research Center, Hillsboro, Texas

Harrison, Rusk, Smith, Wood, Upshur, and Van Zandt. As was true of many of the regiments formed at this time, the men were largely responsible for furnishing their own horses, weapons, and equipment. Initially most of the men carried doubled-barreled shotguns and pistols. Many were also armed with Bowie knives.[51]

In early February 1862 the Tenth Texas was ordered to join Confederate forces in Arkansas, but did not reach Van Dorn's army until after the battle at Pea Ridge. As part of Van Dorn's command the regiment was ordered to Corinth, where the Confederate army was recovering from the defeat at Shiloh. Like the other cavalry outfits in Van Dorn's army the Tenth Texas was required to leave its horses before crossing the Mississippi.

The Fourteenth Texas was also with Van Dorn's army as it left Arkansas. Organized in summer 1861 and mustered into Confederate service at Dallas in early fall, the Fourteenth Texas, with 1,024 men, was the largest of the Texas cavalry regiments to cross the Mississippi in spring 1862. Col. Middleton T. Johnson, the first commander of the Fourteenth Cavalry, was a former Alabama legislator, Republic of Texas congressman, Mexican War veteran, Texas Ranger, and co-founder of Fort Worth. The men under his command came largely from north central and eastern Texas. Shortly after arriving at Corinth, Matthew D. Ector, who had served with the Third Cavalry in Arkansas and Missouri, was elected colonel of the regiment, replacing Johnson when he returned to Texas.[52]

The Fifteenth Texas grew out of the First Texas Cavalry Battalion organized by R. P. Crump in northeast Texas in November 1861. When additional recruits increased the battalion to regimental size in spring 1862, the unit was designated as the Fifteenth Texas Cavalry Regiment. It remained known as the Fifteenth through 1862, but when it was learned that another Texas regiment had the same number, the regiment, then commanded by Col. Julius A. Andrews, officially became the Thirty-second Texas Cavalry. As a regiment it was dismounted throughout its entire wartime service.[53]

The inexperienced Tenth, Fourteenth, and Fifteenth cavalries, all dismounted, the battle-tested Eleventh Cavalry (also temporarily dismounted), and Col. T. H. McCray's Thirty-first Arkansas Infantry were part of a new brigade commanded by Joseph L. Hogg. Following Hogg's death in May the brigade was commanded by Virginian William L. Cabell. After Cabell's transfer the brigade, part of Brig. Gen. Thomas J. Churchill's Division, was temporarily commanded by Colonel McCray.

While under McCray's command the brigade was assigned to Edmund Kirby Smith's department of East Tennessee in summer 1862. McCray's troops were in the vanguard of Smith's army when it crossed into Kentucky in late August as part of the combined effort with Braxton Bragg's army to liberate the state. At the battle of Richmond, Kentucky, on August 30, 1862, the brigade charged through a corn field and ravine to break the enemy line in what Kirby Smith described as "a well-timed and dashing charge."[54]

Although the Confederates were victorious at Richmond, they withdrew from Kentucky after an indecisive battle at Perryville in early October. The brigade in which the Texas regiments were assigned became part of J. P. McCown's Division in Bragg's Army of Tennessee. When Colonel McCray and his Arkansas regiment were assigned to another brigade, Matthew D. Ector was promoted to brigadier general and placed in command of the brigade consisting of the four Texas dismounted cavalry regiments. John L. Camp, a successful lawyer and planter from Grimes County who had been serving as a company commander, was promoted to colonel and replaced Ector as commander of the Fourteenth Texas.[55]

The new brigade commander, Matthew D. Ector, had risen from the ranks, having enlisted first as a private soldier in the Third Texas Cavalry. A native of Georgia, Ector came to Texas after having studied law and serving one term in the Georgia legislature. He opened his law practice in Henderson, Texas, served in the Texas legislature, and became editor of the Henderson *Democrat.* When the Civil War began, he joined the Third Texas, was soon promoted to lieutenant, and made regimental adjutant. Ector participated in the battles of Wilson's Creek, Chustenahlah, and Pea Ridge, gaining the praise of his regimental commander for his "gallant bearing and conduct." When the regiment moved to Corinth in April 1862, he became adjutant for brigade commander Joseph L. Hogg. In May he was chosen as colonel of the Fourteenth Texas. He was commended by brigade commander T. H. McCray for his conduct in the Kentucky campaign.[56]

The brigade received its first test of fire under its new commander at Murfreesboro, Tennessee, in late 1862. Along with Evander McNair's Brigade, Ector's troops made the opening assault against Rosecrans' Union army on the morning of December 31. In the attack Ector led the Texans against the Union right flank, driving the enemy back over two miles before Federal artillery stopped the advance. Col. Matthew Locke's Tenth Texas, which was next to McNair's Brigade in the assault, captured three stands of colors belonging to the Thirty-fourth Illinois and six brass cannon in the attack. The fighting raged through the day with casualties mounting on both sides.

Although the Confederates held the upper hand in the fighting on December 31, the Union lines did not break. When the battle resumed on January 2, the heaviest fighting was on the Union left. As a result Ector's Brigade, which was on the Confederate left, escaped major casualties that day. Even so, the brigade suffered 352 casualties, or approximately one-third of its effective strength, in the campaign. The Tenth Texas (118 casualties) and the Eleventh Texas (115) had the heaviest losses in the brigade. Among the twenty-eight killed or mortally wounded were Lieutenants M. V. Curry, L. G. Hefner, and J. M. Hopson of the Tenth Texas, and Col. John C. Burks, commander of the Eleventh Texas.[57]

After the battle at Murfreesboro the Confederate Army of Tennessee fell back to Tullahoma. Like other units in the army

Ector's Brigade needed time to recover from the heavy losses. Changes in the brigade's organization took place in late January, when the Eleventh Texas received orders remounting the regiment and transferring it to Tom Harrison's Cavalry Brigade. The Ninth Texas Infantry was assigned to Ector's Brigade as a replacement for the Eleventh Texas.[58]

The Ninth Texas was a veteran regiment that had fought at Shiloh, Perryville, and Murfreesboro before joining Ector's Brigade. The regiment had been organized at Camp Benjamin, near Paris, Texas, in October 1961. Made up of men from the Red River counties of North Texas, the Ninth was first commanded by West Point graduate and classmate of Stonewall Jackson, Samuel Bell Maxey. The regiment was originally scheduled for duty along the Texas coast, but in December 1861 Maxey was ordered to take his troops to Memphis, Tennessee, where he reported by letter to Albert Sidney Johnston, commanding Confederate Department No. 2 at Bowling Green, Kentucky.[59]

Maxey and his regiment reached Memphis in early February. Although Maxey expected to march north to join Johnston's army at Bowling Green, he received orders to move to Iuka in northeastern Mississippi to protect the vital railroad line supplying Johnston's army. For the next several weeks the regiment remained near Iuka. Confederate reversals at Forts Henry and Donelson soon caused Johnston to pull his army back into Mississippi. At the same time, defeat of Van Dorn's army in Arkansas caused the men of the Ninth Texas to be increasingly concerned over the possible threat to their families and homes in northeast Texas. A petition signed by the officers and men of the Ninth requesting transfer back to Texas was prepared and carried to Richmond by Colonel Maxey.[60]

Upon arrival in Richmond, Maxey found orders promoting him to brigadier general and transferring him from the Ninth Texas to duty at Chattanooga. The Ninth Texas was ordered to join Albert Sidney Johnston's army at Corinth, Mississippi. Maj. Wright A. Stanley was promoted to colonel and commander of the regiment, which was assigned to Brig. Gen. Patton Anderson's Brigade, Daniel Ruggles' Division, Braxton Bragg's Second Army Corps.[61]

As part of Anderson's Brigade the Ninth Texas was in the initial assault of Johnston's army against Sherman's Division near Shiloh Church on the morning of April 6. In the confused fighting that

Sam Maxey, Colonel, Ninth Texas Infantry.
—Courtesy Harold B. Simpson Research Center, Hillsboro, Texas

morning as brigades, divisions, and corps intermingled, Anderson's Brigade moved past the church on the Confederate left. As the fighting went on the brigade shifted more to the right, advancing against Illinois and Iowa regiments that retreated to the area known as the Hornet's Nest. In late afternoon the Ninth Texas continued a slow advance. When dusk fell, the regiment was near the center of the Confederate line south of Dill Creek.[62]

As noted earlier, the Confederates were forced to fall back in fighting on April 7 as Grant received reinforcements. That evening General Beauregard ordered a retreat back to Corinth.

Shiloh had taken a heavy toll on the Ninth Texas. Colonel Stanley reported 67 men killed, wounded, and missing, or approximately 30 percent of the 226 men he led into battle. Among those killed were Capt. J. J. Dickson of Company I and Lt. Samuel Hamil of Company F.[63]

The Ninth Texas remained at Corinth for a month. When the regiment was reorganized under the Conscription Act of April 1862 the men elected William H. Young of Grayson County, one of the company commanders, as colonel of the regiment. Although only twenty-four years old at the time, Young had already impressed his fellow North Texans as a highly capable leader. He would command the regiment for the next two years and eventually become a brigadier general.[64]

In late May 1862 the Confederates abandoned Corinth and retreated to Tupelo, Mississippi. In the army reorganization that took place when Braxton Bragg replaced P. G. T. Beauregard as commander, the Ninth Texas was assigned to Benjamin Frank Cheatham's Division in Leonidas Polk's Corps. For a brief period the Ninth, itself a small regiment, was in a small brigade commanded by its old colonel, Samuel Bell Maxey; however, in late July, Maxey was assigned elsewhere and the Ninth was placed in a brigade commanded by Tennessean Preston Smith. As part of Smith's Brigade the regiment took part in the Kentucky campaign of September–October 1862, but saw only limited action in the Battle of Perryville.[65]

The Ninth Texas remained in Cheatham's Division through the late fall. For two months there was little military action as the Confederate army recuperated from the arduous Kentucky campaigns. The arrival of a few fresh recruits from Texas, slighly better food, and the improved health of personnel allowed the Ninth to increase its strength to slightly more than 300 men.

At the Battle of Murfreesboro, Cheatham's Division was in the center of the Confederate line with McCown's Division (which included Ector's Brigade) on its left. Smith's Brigade (which included the Ninth Texas) was not in the opening attack on the morning of December 31 but entered the battle as heavy enemy fire caused the initial Confederate assault to falter. When a Union artillery barrage forced the brigade to fall back, Colonel Young and the men of the Ninth did not hear the order to withdraw. The Texans continued to battle the enemy and eventually worked their way around the Union flank to deliver enfilading fire on the Federals.

The fighting at Murfreesboro went on throughout the day and resumed on January 2. As was the case of the regiments in Ector's Brigade the Ninth Texas saw little action in the latter stages of the battle. Even so, losses were high. Out of 323 men in the Ninth who entered the battle, 132 were casualties. Among the eighteen Texans killed were Lts. R. F. Luckett and E. B. Parham. Colonel Young, hit by a minie ball in the right shoulder, was among those wounded.[66]

The Ninth Texas was assigned to Ector's Brigade three weeks after the Battle of Murfreesboro. The Confederate Army of Tennessee was then at Tullahoma, Tennessee. There was little military activity at the time as Bragg's army and Rosecrans' Union army recovered from the devastating losses suffered at Murfreesboro.

In late 1863 Ector was ordered to move the brigade to Mississippi to join Joseph E. Johnston in his efforts to relieve the Confederate garrison at Vicksburg. The brigade remained in Mississippi throughout the summer as Johnston attempted unsuccessfully to bring sufficient forces together to challenge Grant's army. The temporary addition of two battalions of Alabama and Mississippi sharpshooters brought the strength of the brigade up to 1,357 men present for duty. The brigade, part of W. H. T. Walker's Dvision, moved several times that summer but saw little fighting.[67]

In August the brigade was joined by the Twenty-ninth North Carolina Infantry. Like the men in the Ninth Texas, the North Carolinians were veteran troops who served in the same division as Ector's Brigade at Murfreesboro. Col. Robert B. Vance, the older brother of North Carolina Governor Zebulon Vance, commanded the regiment at Murfreesboro but was promoted to brigadier general shortly thereafter. William B. Cressman, formerly executive officer of the regiment, now commanded the North Carolinians.[68]

In early September Walker's Division, including Ector's Brigade, rejoined the Army of Tennessee near Chattanooga. The division returned in time to take part in the bloody battle at Chickamauga Creek on September 19-20, 1863. Walker's Division was assigned to Bragg's Reserve Corps on the eve of battle. As part of the reserve the Texans expected to escape much of the heavy fighting. However, when Union troops under George H. Thomas attacked the Confederate right flank defended by Nathan Bedford Forrest's cavalry on the morning of September 19, Ector's Brigade and another brigade from the Reserve Corps commanded by Col. Claudius Wilson were called upon to support Forrest. With the efforts of these two infantry brigades, Forrest was able to stabilize his line and launch a counterattack. The advancing Confederates soon ran into a reinforced Union brigade that drove them back with heavy losses. Ector and Wilson pulled their brigades back into the woods to count their losses and regroup.[69]

In the early afternoon Walker's brigades were reinforced by Frank Cheatham's Division, which allowed the Confederates to hold their position on the right. Although the battle continued throughout the afternoon, the major fighting shifted toward the center and away from the right flank held by Forrest and Walker. When darkness fell, Walker's brigades were holding their position on the Confederate right near Jay's Mill.

Fighting resumed on the morning of September 20. John C. Breckinridge's Division opened the attack against the Union left. The brigades of Ector and Wilson, having suffered heavy casualties the previous day, were again held in reserve. When Breckinridge, who was several hours late in getting the attack under way, encountered stubborn enemy resistance, the reserve brigades were again called into action. By midday the Confederates had pushed the enemy's left wing back to the La Fayette Road. Meanwhile, the Confederates broke through the enemy's lines near the center of the battlefield, threatening a complete route of the Union army. Only the determined resistance of Thomas' Fourteenth Corps permitted the Federals to withdraw to Chattanooga.

Losses were high for both armies. Bragg's army suffered more than 18,000 casualties and Rosecrans' Federals lost slightly over 16,000 men. Walker's Division lost nearly 1,500 men; Ector's Brigade lost 536 of nearly 1,300 combatants, or slightly over 40 percent casualties. Ector himself was hit four times but did not leave the field.[70]

After the Battle of Chickamauga, Ector's Brigade was ordered back to Mississippi to rejoin Joseph E. Johnston's army. In October the brigade was assigned to Maj. Gen. Sam French's Division near Brandon, Mississippi. The division remained there until late January 1864, when William T. Sherman moved his army from Vicksburg across the state, forcing the Confederates, now under the command of Leonidas Polk, to withdraw into Alabama. When it appeared Sherman would turn south toward Mobile, part of French's Division was moved there by rail. Ector's Brigade was alerted to make the move, but when Sherman pulled back toward the Mississippi, Polk retained Ector and another brigade.

In late February 1864 Ector's Brigade was camped near Meridian, Mississippi, but in March the Texans moved to Demopolis, Alabama. Morale was low. One soldier, Andrew J. Fogle of the Ninth Infantry, writing to his girlfriend in Texas, noted that he had no word from her or his family in almost a year and expressed the view that the war was growing more and more hopeless.[71]

In May 1864 French's Division, including Ector's Brigade, was ordered to rejoin the Army of Tennessee, now commanded by

Joseph E. Johnston, in north Georgia. Before leaving Alabama, another regiment, the Thirty-ninth North Carolina Infantry, commanded by Col. David Coleman, joined the brigade. Formed in May 1862, when Coleman's Infantry Battalion was increased in size, the Thirty-ninth North Carolina had already seen its share of combat. Like the other regiments in Ector's Brigade, the Thirty-ninth had been in the battles at both Murfreesboro and Chickamauga.[72]

French's Division joined Joseph E. Johnston's army as the Confederates were falling back from Dalton, Georgia, under heavy pressure from Sherman's Union army. In the next three and one-half months the division, and Ector's Brigade, took part in several battles as the Confederates retreated toward Atlanta. In the fighting at New Hope Church in late May the brigade sustained thirty-one casualties, including General Ector, who was wounded. Heavier losses occurred at Latimer House on June 18 as French's Division held the Confederate line south of Pine Mountain. In this battle Ector's Brigade suffered 134 casualties while beating off a fierce enemy attack. Nine days later, the brigade was on the front line in a larger battle at Kennesaw Mountain. Although the enemy made repeated attacks, the strong defensive position enabled the brigade to drive back the enemy while sustaining only light losses (three killed and three wounded).[73]

Although the Confederates were victorious at Kennesaw Mountain, Sherman continued to slide toward Atlanta. On July 4

Regimental Losses, Ector's Brigade
May 18–September 5, 1864

Regiment	Killed	Wounded	Missing	Total
Ninth Texas	16	39	1	56
Tenth Texas	7	69	5	81
Fourteenth Texas	8	55	11	74
Thirty-second Texas	11	35		46
Twenty-ninth N. C.	6	58	87	151
Thirty-ninth N. C.	16	57	10	83
Total	64	313*	114	491*

* Does not include General Ector.
Source: *Official Records*, 38, Pt. 3: 908.

he forced Johnston to fall back from a defensive position at Smyrna Camp Ground after heavy fighting in which Ector's Brigade sustained sixty-five casualties. On July 9 Sherman pushed across the Chattahoochee River, the last major natural barrier standing in his way to Atlanta.[74]

French's Division, which included Ector's Brigade, was on the west side of the Confederate line during the first two battles for Atlanta at Peachtree Creek (July 20) and Bald Hill (July 22) and escaped the bloodiest fighting. When Sherman's army swung west of Atlanta, Ector's Brigade was heavily engaged in the fighting. The brigade suffered over one hundred casualties, including a severe injury to its commander, Matthew D. Ector. Ector was wounded when a fragment from an exploding shell ripped into his left leg above the knee. That evening surgeons removed the damaged limb by amputation.[75]

Col. William H. Young, commander of the Ninth Texas Infantry, assumed command of the brigade following Ector's injury and directed the brigade during the remainder of the Atlanta campaign. He was promoted brigadier general on August 16, one of the youngest Confederate general officers.

After the surrender of Atlanta in early September, General Hood, now commanding the Army of Tennessee, moved northward in an attempt to draw Sherman after him. French's Division, including Ector's Brigade (now led by Brigadier General Young), was ordered to attack a major Federal supply depot at Allatoona, Georgia. In the assault on the Union garrison on the morning of October 5, Ector's Brigade was in the middle of the Confederate line with Frances M. Cockrell's Missouri Brigade on the right and Claudius W. Sears' Mississippi Brigade on the left. The Confederates broke through the first and second line of the enemy's defense and drove within a few yards of the enemy's main fortification. By noon the Confederates had nearly exhausted their ammunition. When it appeared the Union defenders were receiving reinforcements, French ordered the withdrawal of his troops. Casualties were high on both sides. The Union commander, Maj. Gen. John M. Corse, reported 706 men killed, wounded, and missing out of 1,994 effectives. The Confederates lost 779 men, or about 30 percent of those engaged, in the four-and-one-half-hour battle.[76]

Brig. Gen. William Young was among the Confederate wounded.

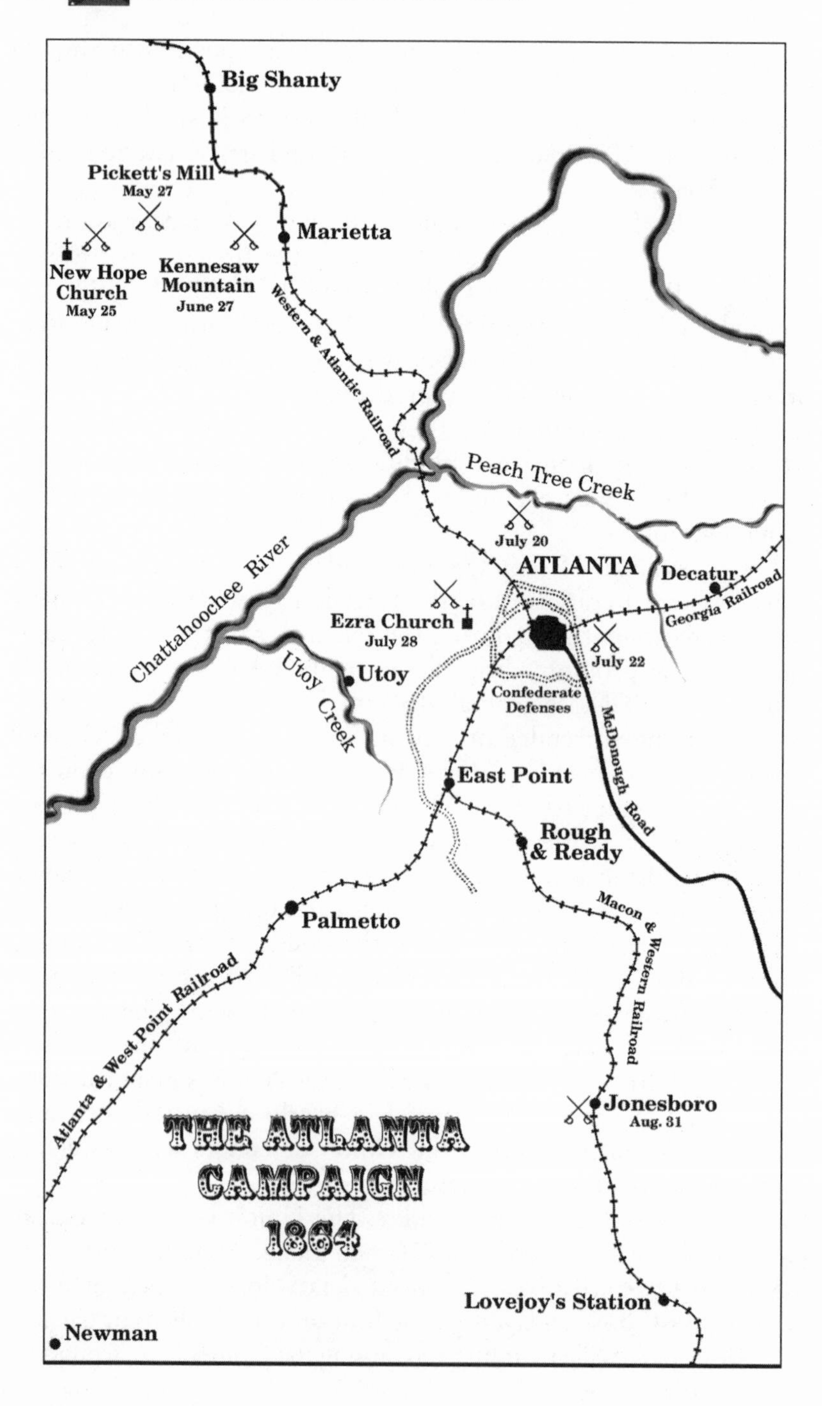
Big Shanty
Pickett's Mill
May 27
Marietta
New Hope Church
May 25
Kennesaw Mountain
June 27
Western & Atlantic Railroad
Peach Tree Creek
July 20
ATLANTA
Decatur
Georgia Railroad
Chattahoochee River
Ezra Church
July 28
July 22
Utoy
Utoy Creek
Confederate Defenses
McDonough Road
East Point
Rough & Ready
Macon & Western Railroad
Palmetto
Atlanta & West Point Railroad
Jonesboro
Aug. 31
THE ATLANTA CAMPAIGN 1864
Lovejoy's Station
Newman

William H. Young, Colonel, Ninth Texas Infantry.
—Courtesy Harold B. Simpson Research Center, Hillsboro, Texas

His horse was shot out from under him in the initial attack, but he continued to lead the brigade on foot until he was severely wounded in the left leg by enemy artillery. He was taken to the rear in an ambulance, but when the vehicle made a wrong turn he was captured. His wound became infected before he received medical treatment. Young recovered only after a painful operation and four months in a Federal hospital. He was sent to Johnson's Island, where he remained a prisoner until the war ended.[77]

Ector's Brigade sustained 200 casualties at Allatoona: 43 killed, 146 wounded, and 11 missing. Among the wounded (in addition to General Young) were Col. John L. Camp and Maj. Samuel Purdy of the Fourteenth Texas and Maj. J. H. McReynolds, commanding Young's old Ninth Texas Infantry.[78]

French's Division rejoined Hood's main army after the battle of Allatoona. Col. David Coleman, formerly commander of the Thirty-ninth North Carolina, was now commanding Ector's Brigade. Lt. Col. Abraham Harris was now commanding the Fourteenth Texas Cavalry, and Maj. William E. Harris was commanding the Thirty-second Texas Cavalry. As a result of the losses at Allatoona the brigade numbered less than 600 effectives.[79]

French's Division, now part of A. P. Stewart's Corps, marched north with Hood's army in the ill-fated Tennessee campaign. Two brigades of the division took part in the bloody Battle of Franklin on November 30, 1864. Ector's Brigade, however, was assigned duty protecting the army's supply train and did not take part in the battle.[80]

In the Battle of Nashville, the brigade was on the Confederate extreme left flank December 15-16 when George H. Thomas opened his attack aimed at breaking the Confederate siege of the city. The fighting began with a Union feint against the Confederate right, but the main blow of Thomas' army was aimed at the Confederate left held by Stewart's Corps. Ector's Brigade, which received the full fury of the Union attack, fell back under the heavy blow. As the Texans and Carolinians struggled to occupy an elevation later known as Shy's Hill, General Hood moved troops from the right and center to support Stewart's Corps. Until these reinforcements could reach the area, it was vital that the brigade hold the hill. Making his way to Ector's Brigade, Hood told Coleman's troops, "Texans, I want you to hold this hill regardless of what transpires around you."

"We will do it, General," was the response.[81]

Fortunately for the men of the brigade additional troops from Frank Cheatham's Corps soon arrived to assist the Texans and North Carolinians. When darkness fell, the Confederates still controlled the hill.

The next morning, Thomas resumed the attack. Although Union artillery pounded away at the Confederates on Shy's Hill, the Confederate lines remained intact. At midmorning, General Hood, convinced the main threat was on his right flank, sent some of Cheatham's troops to that sector. Then when Union cavalry threatened to break through on the extreme left flank, Hood moved Ector's Brigade south to reinforce the Confederate cavalry. The left center of the Confederate line was so weakened by these moves that Federal troops swarmed over Shy's Hill around 3:30 P.M., sending the Confederates fleeing in confusion. Once the line broke there was complete chaos as panic conditions prevailed. Only with great difficulty were the Confederates able to pull away and withdraw southward in the rain and darkness.[82]

As Hood's troops retreated into Alabama, Ector's Brigade and Sul Ross' cavalry served as part of the army's rear guard. Ector's Brigade had only 341 effectives on December 21, but this number increased when troops who had separated from their companies during the early stages of the retreat returned to their regiments.[83]

Following the disastrous Tennessee campaign, French's Division, including Ector's Brigade, was assigned to assist Maj. Gen. Dabney H. Maury in the defense of Mobile. Ector's Brigade was ordered to join the Confederates defending Spanish Fort at the mouth of the Apalachie River, where it empties into Mobile Bay east of the city.

In early April 1865 Union troops began a massive assault on Spanish Fort. Although the fort was a strong defensive position, the badly outnumbered Confederates were eventually overwhelmed. Ector's Brigade fought stubbornly in the defense of the left flank but to no avail. Many of the Texans and Carolinians were killed or captured before orders were received to withdraw. Some made it to Mobile, but the losses at Spanish Fort and nearby Fort Blakely forced Maury to evacuate the city on April 12.[84]

Spanish Fort was the last battle for the men of Ector's Brigade. After the fall of Mobile, General Maury marched the remnants of his command to Meridian, Mississippi. There, on May 8, Maury informed his troops that four days earlier Richard Taylor, commander of the Department of Alabama, Mississippi, and East Louisiana, had surrendered at Citronelle, Alabama, bringing the war to a close for his command. In a final address, Maury praised his troops for their courage and devotion. A band of Louisiana musicians played "Dixie," and the men headed home.[85]

GRANBURY'S BRIGADE

Sixth Texas Infantry
Seventh Texas Infantry
Tenth Texas Infantry
Fifteenth Texas Cavalry (dismounted)
Seventeenth Texas Cavalry (dismounted)
Eighteenth Texas Cavalry (dismounted)
Twenty-fourth Texas Cavalry (dismounted)
Twenty-fifth Texas Cavalry (dismounted)

Serving with the Confederate Army of Tennessee in many of

Hiram Granbury, Colonel, later brigade commander, Seventh Texas Infantry.
—Courtesy Harold B. Simpson Research Center, Hillsboro, Texas

the same battles as Ector's Brigade were the Texas regiments in what came to be Granbury's Brigade. James M. McCaffrey, who wrote a history of the brigade, pointed out that there were other commanders before and after Hiram B. Granbury, but Granbury was so highly regarded by the Texans that after he assumed command they always used his name in referring to their brigade.[86]

Eight Texas regiments served in Granbury's Brigade. Three of these, the Sixth, Seventh, and Tenth Texas, were infantry regiments. The other five, the Fifteenth, Seventeenth, Eighteenth, Twenty-fourth, and Twenty-fifth, were cavalry regiments that were dismounted and fought as infantry. At various times independent cavalry companies and Arkansas and Tennessee infantry were assigned to the brigade, but Texans always made up the bulk of the troops.[87]

All of the Texas regiments in the brigade except the Seventh Infantry first fought together in the unsuccessful defense of Arkansas Post in January 1863. In this campaign three of the regiments, the Sixth Infantry, the Twenty-fourth Cavalry, and the Twenty-fifth Cavalry, were part of Robert R. Garland's Brigade; the other four, the Tenth Infantry, the Fifteeenth Cavalry, the Seventeenth Cavalry, and the Eighteenth Cavalry, were in James Deshler's Brigade.

The two Texas infantry regiments at Arkansas Post were organized in the autumn of 1861; the cavalry regiments were not organized until spring 1862. The Sixth Texas, composed of volunteers from Central and South Texas, was mustered into Confederate service at Camp Henry McCulloch, about four miles from Victoria in autumn 1861 (although not all companies were formed until March of the following year). Col. Robert R. Garland, a Virginian with thirteen years of experience as an officer in the U.S. Army, was named commander of the regiment. Thomas S. Anderson, an Austin attorney and former Texas secretary of state, was lieutenant colonel, and Alexander M. Haskell was major. Company commanders chosen by the volunteers and the county from which the recruits came are shown in the following table.[88]

Sixth Texas Infantry

Company	Captain	County
A	A. H. Phillips, Jr.	Calhoun
B	James A. Rupley	Victoria
C	Alonso T. Bass	Gonzales
D	E. A. Peareson	Matagorda
E	John P. White	Guadalupe
F	Henry E. Bradford	Bell
G	Rhoads Fisher	Travis
H	George Finley	Calhoun, Lavaca, Victoria
I	C. P. Naunheim	DeWitt
K	Sam. H. McAllister	Bexar

The Sixth Texas (or at least those companies organized in the fall) spent the winter months of 1861-1862 training at Camp McCulloch. Colonel Garland, a veteran soldier, believed in discipline and drill. Jim Turner, a private in Company G, the Travis Rifles, declared that the colonel was "a perfect martinet and everything had to be done in strict accordance with military rules." Another member of the same company, William J. Oliphant, noted that Garland "kept us hard at work drilling until he converted the regiment into a regular machine which would move on the drill ground with clock-like precision."[89]

In March 1862 Garland received orders to join Van Dorn's Army of the West in Arkansas. On March 22 the regiment was under way, proceeding through Hallettsville, Eagle Lake, Houston, and Tyler. The regiment reached Camp Holmes, ten miles from Pine Bluff, in late July and remained there several weeks to wait for ailing troops to join their companies.[90]

While at Camp Holmes the Texans were joined by the Twenty-fourth and Twenty-fifth Texas cavalries. The men in these two regiments had initially been part of the Twenty-first Texas Cavalry organized by Rev. George W. Carter, a Methodist minister who had come to Texas from Virginia in May 1860 to become president of the newly created Soule University at Chappell Hill. An ardent Southerner, Carter rushed to Richmond, Virginia, after secession to obtain a commission authorizing creation of a regiment of lancers.

By late spring 1862, Carter had recruited enough volunteers to form three regiments: the First, Second, and Third Texas Lancers. It was soon apparent, however, that the use of the lance was not practical and the units were redesignated as the Twenty-first, Twenty-fourth, and Twenty-fifth Texas Cavalry. Carter became commander of the Twenty-first and fellow Methodist ministers Franklin C. Wilkes and Clayton C. Gillespie commanders of the Twenty-fourth and Twenty-fifth cavalries. The majority of the recruits for these regiments were residents of Central and South Texas counties, although some volunteers came from Jefferson and Orange counties of southeast Texas and Calcasieu Parish in Louisiana.[91]

The new regiments, organized temporarily into a brigade commanded by Colonel Carter, spent several weeks in camp on Clear Creek, three to four miles southeast of Hempstead. In May, Carter was ordered to lead the three regiments to Arkansas. Upon reaching Pine Bluff they received orders from Maj. Gen. Theophilus H. Holmes, the department commander, dismounting Wilkes' and Gillespie's regiments. The Twenty-first Texas, commanded by Colonel Carter, retained its mounts and was assigned to William H. Parsons' Cavalry Brigade.[92]

The Twenty-fourth and Twenty-fifth regiments, now dismounted cavalry, were ordered to join the Sixth Texas Infantry in a new brigade, commanded by Colonel Garland. Thomas S. Anderson, executive officer of the Sixth Texas, now promoted to colonel, replaced Garland as regimental commander. Late that summer the brigade was ordered to Arkansas Post, twenty-five miles from the mouth of the Arkansas River, where a new Confederate fort was being constructed.[93]

Allison Nelson, Colonel, Tenth Texas Infantry.
—Courtesy Harold B. Simpson Research Center, Hillsboro, Texas

Garland's Brigade reached Arkansas Post in mid-September. Work on the fortification, built at the site of an old French trading post to keep enemy naval vessels from steaming up the Arkansas River to Little Rock, was being completed by slave labor supervised by Confederate engineers. Named Fort Hindman in honor of Maj. Gen. Thomas C. Hindman, Confederate commander in Arkansas, the fortification was built in the shape of a square, each side measuring about 300 feet, with a moat outside the thick, earthen walls. Three large pieces of artillery were mounted on the eastern side of the fort facing the river. Outlying works were being constructed to accommodate smaller artillery and supporting infantry.[94]

Garland's Texans were soon joined at Arkansas Post by other Texans in a brigade commanded by Col. James Deshler. These were members of the Tenth Texas Infantry and the Fifteenth, Seventeenth, and Eighteenth Texas Dismounted Cavalry regiments. They had first been brigaded together under the command of Col. George H. Sweet of the Fifteenth Texas, then placed under the command of Col. Allison Nelson; following Nelson's death, Colonel Deshler took over. Each of the regiments had already seen some action against the enemy along the White River.

The Tenth Texas Infantry, one of the regiments in Deshler's Brigade, was organized in autumn 1861 by Allison Nelson of Bosque County. A native Georgian, Nelson was a veteran of the

Mexican War and a former brigadier general under Narcisco Lopez in the Cuban struggle for independence. He was a member of the Georgia legislature and mayor of Atlanta before moving to Texas in 1856. A staunch defender of slavery and states' rights, Nelson served in the Texas legislature in 1859 and the secession convention in 1861.[95]

The companies of the Tenth Texas, recruited primarily in Central Texas, assembled at Virginia Point, on the Texas coast across from Galveston, in October 1861. The unit was formally organized as an undersized regiment of eight companies—A through H. Companies I and K were added in January 1862. Nelson was chosen colonel, Roger Q. Mills (later a powerful figure in the U.S. Congress) was lieutenant colonel, and Robert B. Young major.[96]

The Tenth Texas spent the winter months of 1861-1862 training at Virginia Point. In late March the regiment was ordered to join Major General Hindman in Arkansas. The men were apparently well drilled and equipped. When they reached Camp Texas near Little Rock in June, General Hindman reported that Colonel Nelson and "his well armed and finely disciplined regiment of infantry" had arrived.[97]

Almost immediately Nelson and his regiment were sent to DeVall's Bluff on the White River, where they spent several weeks preparing for an enemy attack that never came. In mid-July they were ordered back to Camp Texas and brigaded there with several dismounted cavalry regiments, including the Fifteenth, Seventeenth, and Eighteenth Texas. Little did they know it at the time, but these Texas regiments would be together until the end of the war.[98]

The Texas cavalry regiments in Deshler's Brigade were raised as part of a major recruiting effort by Middleton T. Johnson, the prominent Tarrant County planter and rancher who became commander of the Fourteenth Texas Cavalry discussed in the previous section on Ector's Brigade. The Fifteenth Texas Cavalry, one of the regiments raised, was organized at McKinney, Texas, in early March 1862. New York-born George H. Sweet, a Mexican War veteran, former editor of the *San Antonio Herald*, and orginally captain of Company A, was elected colonel; William K. Masten, lieutenant colonel; and George B. Pickett, major.

The Seventeenth Texas Cavalry, recruited primarily in East Texas, was mustered into Confederate service at Dallas several days later. Nacogdoches lawyer George P. Moore was named colonel; Sterling B. Hendricks of Harrison County, lieutenant colonel; and John McClarty, major. The Eighteenth Texas Cavalry, commanded by Nicholas H. Darnell, former congressman of the Texas Republic, state legislator, and candidate for lieutenant governor, was organized at Dallas the same day. Jonathan T. Coit and Charles Morgan were chosen as lieutenant colonel and major.[99]

Like the Tenth Infantry, the three cavalry regiments received orders in late spring 1862 to report to Arkansas. Originally they were scheduled to join Confederate forces in Mississippi, but they were reassigned to serve with three other Texas regiments (the Twelfth, Fourteenth, and Sixteenth) under Brig. Gen. Albert Rust in northern Arkansas. In early July these regiments saw their first action against the enemy in a series of skirmishes near the White River. In the largest engagement—at Cotton Plant, near the Cache River—the Texans rode into an ambush and retreated in disarray, an action that historian James McCaffrey pointed out "did little to enhance the image of the dashing Texas cavalry soldier."[100]

Soon after the debacle at Cotton Plant the Fifteenth, Seventeenth, and Eighteenth regiments returned to Camp Texas, where in mid-July they were dismounted, much like the Twenty-fourth and Twenty-fifth Cavalry regiments. It was here that the three regiments were brigaded together with Allison Nelson's Tenth Texas Infantry. Colonel Sweet, commander of the Fifteenth Texas and the senior officer in the group, was named temporary commander of the brigade.[101]

In August the brigade moved to Camp Hope, near Austin, Arkansas. The Texans remained there for several weeks learning the fundamentals of infantry tactics. In late September Colonel Nelson, commander of the Tenth Infantry, was promoted to brigadier general and given command of the brigade. Nelson, an experienced soldier, was a popular choice with the men of the brigade, and expectations for his success were high. Unfortunately, he contracted typhoid fever three days after his promotion and died at Camp Hope on October 7. "He was the most talented of all our Texas generals," editorialized the Austin *Texas State Gazette.*

Theophilus Holmes, the departmental commander, lamented his death as an "irreparable loss."[102]

General Holmes appointed Col. James Deshler to replace Nelson as brigade commander. Deshler, an Alabama graduate of West Point, former officer of the U.S. Army, and an artillery officer, had served with Holmes in the Peninsula campaign earlier in the year and more recently had been on his staff in Arkansas. Soon after his appointment Deshler received orders to take his brigade (consisting of the Tenth Texas Infantry, and the Fifteenth, Seventeenth, and Eighteenth dismounted cavalries) to Arkansas Post. The brigade left Camp Hope on November 22, boarded steamboats at Little Rock on November 25, and reached Arkansas Post on November 28.[103]

When Deshler's Brigade arrived at Arkansas Post, the Confederates had completed work on the inner defensive positions but were still working on winter quarters, trenches, and rifle pits. With the addition of Deshler's regiments, Brig. Gen. Thomas J. Churchill, the commander at Fort Hindman, had nearly 5,000 men under his command. Supplies for the troops were adequate but medical conditions were poor. Letters from troops home refer almost constantly to sickness and death. Jim Turner of the Sixth Texas noted that the post was "a very unhealthy place and the hospitals soon became crowded with sick men." Flavius W. Perry, a lieutenant in the Seventeenth Texas, believed "this country was never made I don't think for white people to live in, nothing but frogs and craw fish can live here long. . . ."[104]

There were rumors of a Federal attack from the moment Fort Hindman was occupied. On January 9, 1863, these became reality when the Union fleet commanded by Rear Adm. David D. Porter began disembarking nearly 30,000 troops commanded by Maj. Gen. John McClernand. The following day, Union gunboats opened massive fire on the Confederate defenders. On January 11 McClernand's infantry and artillery, which had maneuvered around the fort, began firing on one side while the Union navy continued fire from the river. Federal infantry assaults were driven back by the steady fire of Garland's and Deshler's brigades. The fort itself, however, was battered to pieces by Union artillery. By 3:00 P.M. all the guns of the fort, except one, had been silenced by enemy fire. Still the Confederate infantry held out until several white flags appeared in the area occupied by the Twenty-fourth Texas. Confusion soon reigned among other Confederate units as to whether or not a surrender had occurred. Federal troops, taking advantage of the situation, breached the Confederate lines. General Churchill could do little but surrender.[105]

Confederate casualties in the fighting at Arkansas Post were comparatively light. General Churchill's incomplete report listed sixty killed and seventy-five to eighty Confederates wounded. In his report Colonel Deshler did not list casualties for his brigade. Colonel Garland reported twenty-five killed, sixty-four wounded, and sixty-eight missing in his regiments. The Twenty-fourth Texas, where white flags first appeared, had the heaviest losses in the brigade: twelve killed, seventeen wounded, and twenty-five missing. Although some Confederates, including some Texans, managed to escape, the majority of defenders, 4,791 men, became prisoners.[106]

Confederate commander Thomas J. Churchill placed the blame for the Arkansas Post surrender upon Col. Franklin Wilkes of the Twenty-fourth Texas and his brigade commander, Col. Robert R. Garland. Garland struggled for years to clear his name but without success. He requested a court of inquiry to look into the affair, but his appeal was denied. Historian Charles Spurlin pointed out that "whenever vacancies occurred for regimental commanders, he [Garland] was passed over, and the positions filled by officers junior to him."[107]

The Confederates who surrendered at Arkansas Post were taken by steamboat and rail to Northern prisoner of war camps. Officers were confined at Camp Chase, near Columbus, Ohio, while enlisted men were sent either to Camp Butler, near Springfield, Ohio, or Camp Douglas in Chicago. Treatment of the prisoners varied. Some, like Jim Turner of the Sixth Texas, reported they were treated well. Others, like Capt. Samuel T. Foster of the Twenty-fourth Texas, who lamented "we are treated like so many beasts," considered their captors to be harsh. Many died in prison from disease, poor medical care, and extremes of weather. Others, including Lt. Flavius W. Perry of the Seventeenth Texas, survived imprisonment only to die from disease or malnourishment several weeks after they were released.[108]

In April 1863 an exchange was arranged for the Arkansas prisoners. By early May most of the men were back in the South. The

Texans were assigned to a brigade commanded by Brig. Gen. Thomas J. Churchill. The Sixth and Tenth infantries and the Fifteenth Texas Cavalry were consolidated into one regiment commanded by Col. Roger Q. Mills. The Seventeenth, Eighteenth, Twenty-fourth, and Twenty-fifth Texas cavalries were brought together as one regiment. Even though his men had raised the white flag at Arkansas Post, Col. Franklin C. Wilkes, the senior officer in the new regiment, was placed in command. A third consolidated regiment consisting of men from the Nineteenth and Twenty-fourth Arkansas infantries made up the brigade.[109]

Churchill's Brigade joined Braxton Bragg's Army of Tennessee, at Tullahoma, Tennessee. The brigade was assigned to Patrick Cleburne's Division in William J. Hardee's Corps. As former prisoners of war, the Texans and Arkansans were the objects of curiosity and derision. Veterans of the Army of Tennessee were not enthused about serving with men who had surrendered. Derogatory remarks and critical comments were directed toward the former prisoners. Capt. Samuel T. Foster of the Twenty-fourth Texas later noted "we could never get out of the hearing of some fool making fun of us about that fight at Ark. Post."[110]

Bragg's Confederates, under pressure from Rosecrans' Union army, withdrew from Tullahoma in late June and pulled back to Chattanooga. The next month a new brigade commander, James Deshler, recently promoted to brigadier general, was appointed to replace Thomas J. Churchill, who returned to Arkansas. This move was popular with the men, especially those who had previously served under Deshler. Jim Turner of the Sixth Texas was pleased to see the change as Churchill, who blamed the Texans in Garland's Brigade for the surrender at Arkansas Post, was very unpopular. Deshler, on the other hand, was "an eloquent gentleman and everybody in the brigade liked him."[111]

In early September, Bragg evacuated Chattanooga and fell back into northern Georgia. With reinforcements received from the Army of Northern Virginia, he launched an assault against Rosecrans' army along Chickamauga Creek. In this battle Cleburne's Division (which included Deshler's Brigade) was on the Confederate right supporting the attack by Breckinridge's Division. Deshler's troops were inactive in the fighting on September 19 until midafternoon, when they were ordered forward. In fighting late that day the Texans and Arkansans captured over a hundred enemy troops and several regimental battle flags.[112]

The next morning the Confederates opened the attack again on the right. Initially, Deshler's Brigade was in reserve while other brigades in the division joined Breckinridge's Division in the assault against the enemy. At 9:30 A.M. Deshler's troops were ordered forward. When the brigade was within 200 yards of the Federal line, the Texans and Arkansans encountered heavy enemy fire. As the division was forced to fall back, Deshler was ordered to occupy and hold the crest of a small nearby hill.

The brigade was under steady fire for over an hour but held its position. Around noon Brigadier General Deshler was hit in the chest by an enemy artillery projectile and killed instantly. Roger Q. Mills, colonel of the consolidated Sixth-Tenth-Fifteenth Regiment, assumed command and directed the brigade as the fighting continued. The firing in the brigade's sector gradually died down in the afternoon as Confederate toops to the left broke through the center of the enemy line, forcing a Union retreat back toward Chattanooga.[113]

The brigade lost 52 men killed and 366 wounded, a casualty rate of about 23 percent. Among the wounded was Franklin C. Wilkes, colonel of the consolidated Texas Seventeenth/Eighteenth/ Twenty-fourth/Twenty-fifth Regi-

Franklin C. Wilkes, Colonel, Twenty-fourth Texas Cavalry.
—Courtesy Harold B. Simpson Research Center, Hillsboro, Texas

ment. He would not return to command the regiment until spring of the following year.[114]

The leadership and composition of the brigade changed after the Battle of Chickamauga. James A. Smith, a West Point graduate from Tennessee who had recently been promoted to brigadier general, was given command of the brigade. The brigade remained part of Cleburne's Division but was now in William J. Hardee's Corps. The Arkansas regiment was transferred to another brigade. The Seventh Texas Infantry, commanded by Col. Hiram B. Granbury, was assigned to the brigade in its place.[115]

The Seventh Texas Infantry already had established a reputation as a solid fighting unit. The regiment had been organized in the autumn of 1861 with John Gregg, former district judge from Freestone County and member of the Provisional Confederate Congress, as its commander. J. M. Clough, district attorney in Harrison County, was lieutenant colonel, and Hiram B. Granbury, Waco lawyer and judge, was major. The 746 volunteers came from fifteen East Texas counties. Nine in every ten men in the regiment were born in the South, but only one of every ten recruits owned slaves.[116]

The Seventh Texas left Marshall, Texas, for duty with Albert Sidney Johnston's army in October 1861. The regiment arrived in Hopkinsville, Kentucky, in early November and remained there for three months. During their stay at Hopkinsville the East Texans suffered severely from pneumonia, diarrhea, dysentery, typhoid, and measles. One hundred sixty-six men died from disease and another twenty-five were discharged from the army because of illness.[117]

Even though the regiment had lost one-fourth of its men, the Seventh was ordered to join Confederate forces at Fort Donelson on the Cumberland River in early February 1862. The Texans arrived just before the fort was surrounded by Union troops commanded by U. S. Grant. Assigned to T. J. Davidson's Brigade, Gregg's men were soon under enemy fire. The Seventh took part in the attempted Confederate breakout on February 15. In the fighting the regiment lost more than sixty men, including Lieutenant Colonel Clough. Although the Confederates were able to open an escape route, Rebel commander John B. Floyd mistakenly recalled the troops; escape for most Confederates became impossi-

John Gregg, Colonel, Seventh Texas Infantry, later brigade commander.
—Courtesy Harold B. Simpson Research Center, Hillsboro, Texas

ble. Colonel Gregg and most of the regiment were among the 16,000-17,000 Southerners who became prisoners of war.[118]

Enlisted men and company officers of the Confederates captured at Donelson were taken to prison camps in Ohio and Illinois, but senior personnel, including Gregg and Granbury, were sent to Fort Warren in Boston harbor. In late August the Donelson prisoners were exchanged. Gregg, promoted to brigadier general, was given command of his own brigade. Since the number of men in the Seventh Texas was too small to form a regiment, they were temporarily consolidated with other undersized units in a regiment commanded by Col. James E. Bailey. They remained there until January 1862, when sufficient recruits arrived to reform the regiment. Hiram Granbury, who had been promoted to colonel, was given command of the reformed regiment. W. L. Moody, the future Galveston cotton and banking tycoon who had commanded Company G, was promoted to lieutenant colonel, and K. M. Van Zandt, Harrison County lawyer and captain of Company D, became major of the regiment.[119]

Granbury's Regiment was assigned to Gregg's Brigade and ordered to Port Hudson, Louisiana. In March the regiment took part in the defense of that post when Union Admiral David Farragut attempted to pass the batteries with his fleet. In late April the Seventh was sent on detached duty to Woodville, Mississippi, in an unsuccessful attempt to intercept Ben Grierson's Union raiders.[120]

The Seventh Texas rejoined Gregg's Brigade near Jackson, Mississippi, after the failure to capture Grierson and his raiders. On May 12 Gregg's Brigade attempted to block Grant's army as it advanced toward Jackson. In heavy fighting at Raymond the Seventh Texas held its position against a much larger enemy force until its ammunition was exhausted. After sustaining 158 casualties, the regiment fell back to Jackson with the rest of the brigade.[121]

The Seventh Texas spent the next two months near Enterprise, Mississippi, recuperating from their losses and preparing for future campaigns. In early September Gregg's Brigade, which included the Seventh Texas, joined Bragg's army in northern Georgia. In the battle at Chickamauga the brigade was on the Confederate left flank. As part of Bushrod Johnson's Division, the brigade was in the thick of fighting on September 19-20. Both Gregg, the brigade commander, and Granbury, the regimental commander, were wounded on the 19th. Colonel Cyrus Sugg of the Fifteenth Tennessee assumed command of the brigade when Gregg fell. Major Van Zandt directed the Seventh Texas in the fighting on the 20th.[122]

Granbury was not seriously injured at Chickamauga and soon returned to duty. Gregg, on the other hand, was nearly killed and took weeks to recover. The regiments in his brigade were transferred to other commands.

K. M. Van Zandt, Major, Seventh Texas Infantry.
—Courtesy Harold B. Simpson Research Center, Hillsboro, Texas

Granbury's Seventh Texas now became part of James A. Smith's Brigade along with the two consolidated Texas regiments commanded by Col. Roger Q. Mills and Lt. Col. William A. Taylor (serving in place of Col. Franklin Wilkes, who had not yet recovered from injuries at Chickamauga).

In the siege of Chattanooga that followed the battle at Chickamauga, Smith's Brigade (part of Cleburne's Division) was posted on the Confederate right flank on Missionary Ridge near a point called Tunnel Hill. There was little activity for two months, but in late November, Grant, who had replaced Rosecrans, opened a major assault against Bragg's army. On the morning of November 25 nearly 30,000 Union troops commanded by William T. Sherman attacked Cleburne's brigades, numbering about 4,000 men. In the bitter fighting Brigadier General Smith was wounded, and Granbury, the senior colonel, assumed command. Cleburne's Division stood its ground; however, Union troops broke through the Confederate line to the south, necessitating a withdrawal of Bragg's army back into Georgia.[123]

Cleburne's troops served as the army's rear guard during the retreat. Granbury and his brigade played a major role in the Confederate defense when troops under Joe Hooker attempted to capture Rebel wagons and artillery near Ringgold, Georgia. In the fighting the Texans sustained more than sixty casualties but were able to hold the line, allowing the Confederates to complete their withdrawal to Dalton, Georgia, where they went into winter quarters.[124]

On March 5, 1864, Granbury was promoted to brigadier general and given permanent command of the brigade that would bear his name throughout the remaining months of the war. One of his first acts as brigadier was to make some organizational changes in his command. The Tenth Infantry, led by Col. Roger Q. Mills, was given a separate identity again. The Sixth Infantry and Fifteenth Cavalry remained as a consolidated regiment under the temporary command of Capt. Rhoads Fisher. The combined Seventeenth/Eighteenth/Twenty-fourth/Twenty-fifth was split into two regiments with Capt. George D. Manion temporarily commanding the Seventeenth/Eighteenth and Col. Franklin C. Wilkes returning to duty as commander of the Twenty-fourth/Twenty-fifth Regiment. The Seventh Infantry, Granbury's old regiment, was commanded by Capt. J. H. Collett.[125]

Except for a brief sojurn in Mississippi in mid-February to meet an expected Federal movement, Granbury's Brigade remained in Georgia for seven months as Joseph E. Johnston attempted to stop the southward movement of Sherman's army. At Dug Gap, near Dalton, on May 8 Granbury's Brigade assisted Lucius Polk's Brigade in holding a key defensive position. Three weeks later Granbury and his regiments carried out a night attack against the enemy near Pickett's Mill. In this action the Texans captured more than 200 Union troops. Division commander Pat Cleburne praised Granbury and his men for "the brilliancy" of their attack. Unfortunately, the affair cost the Texans: 33 men killed and 114 wounded.[126]

The defeat at Pickett's Mill did not stop Sherman from moving closer and closer to Atlanta. On July 17 President Davis, exasperated by Johnston's constant retreating, removed him from command and replaced him with John B. Hood. Although Hood had a reputation as a bold fighter, most members of Granbury's Brigade considered the removal of Johnston a mistake. Capt. Samuel Foster of the Twenty-fourth Cavalry believed "Genl Joe Johnston has more military sense in one day than Hood ever did or ever will have." Samuel Alonza Cooke of the Seventeenth Cavalry declared that Johnston's removal "threw a damper on our army and most of us felt it was a death stroke to our entire army."[127]

Hood went on the attack almost immediately. Granbury's Brigade saw little action in the fighting at Peachtree Creek, but on July 21 they were under heavy enemy fire near Bald Hill. Gen. James A. Smith, a veteran of all the western fighting who temporarily commanded the brigade again while Granbury was on sick leave, declared he had never before "witnessed such accurate and destructive cannonading" by the enemy. Within a few minutes forty Texans were killed and more than a hundred wounded by Union artillery. Seventeen of eighteen men in one small company of the Eighteenth Texas Cavalry were killed by one artillery shell.[128]

The fighting continued the following day as Hardee's Corps was sent on a sweeping flank attack on the Union right, held by Maj. Gen. James McPherson. For several hours Hardee pounded away at the Union troops. In the fighting McPherson was killed, probably by a member of Granbury's Brigade. The Texas Brigade and Daniel Govan's Arkansas Brigade led the attack that drove the enemy back. Union resistance stiffened, however, and the Confederates were forced to give ground.

Brigadier Smith, commanding the Texans, was wounded and many of the men in the Seventeenth-Eighteenth Consolidated Regiment were captured in a Federal counterattack. The fighting continued until dusk, but the Confederate effort to break the Union line had failed. The battle for Atlanta was over, with 5,500 Confederate and 4,000 Union casualties. Granbury's Brigade had 311 casualties, including 19 killed, 107 wounded, 160 captured, and 25 missing.[129]

Granbury returned from sick leave as the fighting north and east of Atlanta came to an end. Sherman now shifted his army west of Atlanta and moved southward to cut the railroads bringing necessary supplies to the city. In the Battle of Jonesboro, fought south of Atlanta in late August, Granbury's Texans were on the extreme left side of the line as the Confederates attempted to drive the enemy back. Granbury's Brigade led off the attack; however, instead of swinging to the right against the flank of the Federal infantry the Texans moved straight ahead against the Union cavalry. Granbury forced the Northern horsemen back across the river but failed to attack the entrenched Union infantry to his right. This resulted in a mild rebuke from Brig. Gen. Mark Lowrey, who was temporarily commanding the division, but Granbury defended the brigade's action, reporting that his orders "were to drive all opposing forces beyond the Flint River."[130]

When Confederate efforts to stop Sherman from cutting the railroads were unsuccessful, Hood evacuated Atlanta to escape encirclement. Granbury's Brigade accompanied the army when Hood moved into Tennessee in the autumn. When Hood made his ill-fated attack on John Schofield's army at Franklin on November 30, the Texas Brigade was in the center of the Confederate line. Although the initial assault drove the Federals back, the Union center rallied and held. In the bitter fighting division commander Pat Cleburne, Granbury, and four other Confederate generals were killed. Lt. Col. Robert B. Young of the Tenth Infantry was killed, and regimental commanders Maj. William A. Taylor of the Twenty-fourth/Twenty-fifth Cavalry, Capt. J. W. Brown of the Seventh Infantry, and Capt. Rhoades Fisher of the Sixth/Fifteenth Cavalry were missing. In all, the

Confederates suffered nearly 7,000 men killed, wounded, missing, and captured.[131]

Schofield withdrew his army under the cover of darkness and continued on to Nashville, where he joined Union forces commanded by George H. Thomas. Hood's crippled army followed behind. Brig. Gen. James A. Smith, former commander of the Texas Brigade, replaced Cleburne as division commander. Capt. Edward T. Broughton of the Seventh Infantry, senior officer present at the time, assumed command of the brigade.

For nearly two weeks Hood's army camped outside Nashville. The weather was extremely cold, resulting in much suffering by the Confederates. On December 15 Thomas' large, well-equipped army struck a heavy blow at the Confederates. Granbury's Brigade, now reduced to 500 men, was in Frank Cheatham's Corps on the Confederate right flank and helped ward off the initial enemy attack. When Thomas made his major assault on the Confederate left, Cleburne's Division, including the Texas Brigade, was moved to the left to support the beleaguered defenders (including Ector's Brigade). For nearly two days the Confederates held—but they gave way on the afternoon of December 16. First Cheatham's Corps, then Stewart's, retreated in wild disarray. Stephen D. Lee's Corps maintained some order as the army withdrew southward.[132]

The retreating Confederates reached Tupelo, Mississippi, in early January 1865. After a brief rest many of the troops, including Granbury's Brigade, boarded railroad cars that took them to Milledgeville, Georgia. From there they marched to North Carolina, where they joined Joseph E. Johnston's army, made up of remnants of various commands. The Texas Brigade reached Johnston's army just as the Battle of Bentonville was ending. They marched with Johnston's weary troops (which included Tom Harrison's cavalry discussed earlier) as the Confederates continued to retreat before Sherman's larger army. In early April the regiments of the brigade were brought together in one unit, called the First Consolidated Texas Regiment. Lt. Col. William A. Ryan of the Eighteenth Texas, senior officer in the former brigade, became commander of the regiment, which was assigned to Daniel C. Govan's Brigade in Hardee's Corps.[133]

A week after the final reorganization, Joseph E. Johnston opened surrender negotiations with William T. Sherman. Terms of the surrender were finalized on April 26. In a farewell address to his troops Johnston praised his men for their courage and devotion and urged them to discharge their obligations of good and peaceful citizens as well as they had performed their duties as soldiers. On May 2 paroles were issued to the 440 members of Granbury's Brigade. These were all who remained of the over 11,000 men who had served in the regiments comprising the brigade.[134]

The end of the war was a bittersweet moment for the proud veterans. After hearing of the surrender, Capt. Samuel T. Foster of the Twenty-fourth Texas stated that "if crying would have done any good, we could have cried all night." After getting his parole, however, he concluded: "it is all over and we are going home. HOME after an absence of four years from our families and friends."[135]

Chapter Five

Texas Cavalry in the Trans Mississippi

THIRTY-NINE OF THE fifty-three Texas cavalry regiments in the Confederate army served the entire Civil War west of the Mississippi River. Eight of these regiments (the Thirteenth, Sixteenth, Seventeenth Consolidated, Twentieth, Twenty-second, Twenty-eighth, Thirty-first, and Thirty-fourth) were dismounted early in the conflict and fought as infantry in Arkansas, Louisiana, and Indian Territory. They will be discussed in the following chapter devoted to infantry and dismounted cavalry in the Trans Mississippi. The other thirty-one Texas Trans Mississippi regiments that remained mounted will be described in this chapter. Those cavalry regiments usually identified with a brigade will be discussed as a part of the brigade in which they were assigned in their most significant battle or campaign. Regiments that operated independently most of the time will be described separately.

SIBLEY-GREEN-BAGBY BRIGADE

Fourth Texas Cavalry
Fifth Texas Cavalry
Seventh Texas Cavalry

The three Texas regiments that made up the old Sibley Brigade took part in extensive campaigning in both New Mexico and Louisiana. These three regiments, known originally as the Fourth,

Fifth, and Seventh Texas Mounted Volunteers, were recruited in the late summer of 1861 by Brig. Gen. Henry Hopkins Sibley. A native of Louisiana, Sibley was a West Point graduate and veteran soldier, having served in the Seminole and Mexican wars, on the Kansas frontier, and more recently in campaigns against the Navajo in New Mexico. He resigned his commission as an officer in the U.S. Army in May 1861 and accepted service with the Confederates.[1]

In late June 1861 Sibley journeyed to Richmond, Virginia, where he outlined his plans for securing New Mexico for the Confederacy. On July 5 he was commissioned brigadier general with instructions to proceed to Texas, where he would recruit troops for the purpose of driving Federal forces from New Mexico.[2]

Sibley returned to San Antonio and immediately set about raising troops. Already several companies of the Second Texas Mounted Rifles under the command of Lt. Col. John R. Baylor had occupied the southern portion of New Mexico. After capturing the Union garrison at Fort Fillmore, Baylor issued a proclamation creating the Confederate Territory of Arizona, assumed power as civil governor, and established his capital at Mesilla.[3]

By early October, Sibley had recruited thirty companies which were organized into three cavalry regiments. The Fourth Texas Mounted Volunteers, or Fourth Texas Cavalry as it was officially known, was commanded by Col. James Reily, a native of Ohio who had set-

James Reily, Colonel, Fourth Texas Cavalry.
—Courtesy Harold B. Simpson Research Center, Hillsboro, Texas

tled in Texas shortly after independence. Reily had experience as a soldier, diplomat, and politician. Sibley would later send Reily on a diplomatic mission to the Mexican states of Chihuahua and Sonora. As a result, direction of the regiment in the New Mexico campaign fell upon Reily's second-in-command, Lt. Col. William R. Scurry, a Texas lawyer-soldier-poet, who had served in the Army of the Texas Republic and the Mexican War. A colorful orator, Scurry earned the sobriquet "Dirty Shirt" because of the grimy garments he wore while touring the state speaking for secession in 1861. Henry W. Raguet, a thirty-five-year-old native of Nacogdoches, was named major of the regiment.[4]

Tom Green, a veteran of San Jacinto, Indian wars, and the Mexican War, was appointed colonel of the Fifth Texas Cavalry. Historian Donald Frazier noted that "of all the officers in the brigade, Green had the greatest reputation." Modest and unassuming, with a boyish personal appearance, Green was immensely popular and affectionately called "Daddy" by his troops. Henry C. McNeill, a native Mississippian and graduate of the U.S. Military Academy at West Point, was named lieutenant colonel of the Fifth Texas. McNeill, who served with the U.S. Army in New Mexico in the late 1850s, accompanied Sibley to Richmond in 1861. Samuel "Nicaragua" Lockridge, a filibuster, soldier of fortune, and Knight of the Golden Circle, was appointed major.[5]

The Seventh Texas

Tom Green, Colonel, Fifth Texas Cavalry.
—Courtesy Harold B. Simpson Research Center, Hillsboro, Texas

Cavalry, last of the Sibley regiments to be organized, was commanded by New York native and West Point graduate William Steele. A professional soldier and veteran with twenty years of service with the U.S. Army in Florida, Mexico, and the Southwest, Steele was one of the most experienced officers in the Confederate army. His second-in-command, John Schuyler Sutton, was also a native New Yorker who moved to Texas in the closing days of the Texas Revolution. An officer in the Army of the Republic, he took part in the Santa Fe Expedition and spent several months in a Mexican prison. Arthur Pendleton Bagby, Jr., an 1852 graduate of West Point and lawyer from Gonzales, was named major of the Seventh Texas.

Each company of the regiment was supposed to consist of one hundred men, but muster rolls reveal that most companies had between seventy and eighty men. The majority of the recruits came from South Central and East Texas, but a few volunteers were from frontier counties such as Palo Pinto, Parker, and Tarrant. Donald Frazier pointed out that most of the troopers were young men who had not yet established themselves in a fixed occupation. Few owned real estate or slaves, and only one-fourth of them were married. The average age of the volunteers was twenty-four.[6]

After a brief period of training along Salado Creek, Sibley's Brigade began its march to New Mexico. Because of the shortages of water and grass along the route, Sibley started his regiments at different dates. Each regiment was divided into smaller groups which departed on different days. Reily's Fourth Texas was the first to be under way, followed a week later by the Fifth Regiment. The first of Steele's Seventh Texas did not depart until November 18, and the last company moved out of San Antonio on December 15.[7]

The march to El Paso was difficult. Bad weather, disease, Indian raids, and poor rations made the journey unpleasant for most of the Texans. Sibley, who traveled light, reached El Paso ahead of his troops on December 13. He immediately assumed command of all Confederate forces in El Paso, New Mexico, and Arizona. John R. Baylor continued to function as governor of Arizona Territory, but the troops formerly under his command were placed under Sibley. Several days later Sibley issued a proclamation addressed to the people of New Mexico in which he declared that he and his army (now designated as the Army of New Mexico) came not as conquerors but as liberators.[8]

Sibley moved his army into New Mexico in early January and occupied the Confederate capital at Mesilla. After dispatching Col. James Reily on a diplomatic mission to northern Mexico and leaving Colonel Steele and several companies of the Seventh Texas behind, Sibley moved the Army of New Mexico north toward Fort Craig, a Union outpost on the west side of the Rio Grande defended by Col. Edward R. S. Canby and more than 3,000 Union troops. Canby, a classmate of Sibley at West Point, was a steady, veteran officer who carefully prepared Fort Craig to withstand an enemy attack.[9]

Sibley hoped to draw Canby and his soldiers into the open, where the mobile Confederates might have an advantage. When this failed, Sibley ordered his troops to cross to the east bank of the Rio Grande, move north, and then swing back across the river at Valverde (Green Valley) ford five miles north of Fort Craig.

When the Texans attempted to cross on the morning of February 21, they encountered heavy enemy opposition. Fighting went on throughout the day. About 1:00 in the afternoon, Sibley, who had kidney problems and was drinking heavily to ease the pain, became so ill that he relinquished command to Tom Green and retired to an ambulance in the rear. The fighting, highlighted by a futile attack by two lancer companies of the Fifth Texas, continued through the afternoon. Union artillery commanded by Capt. Alexander McRae took a heavy toll on the Texans, but a charge by Confederates on the right broke through the Federal lines, overran and captured McRae's battery, and drove the enemy back toward Fort Craig. Exhaustion, confusion over a Union flag of truce, and darkness prevented the Confederates from capturing the fort.[10]

Historian Frazier noted that Valverde, "while impressive in its intensity, had been a hollow conquest." The Confederates had driven the enemy from the field, but Canby still held Fort Craig and the Texans were runnning low on commissary supplies. Nearly 200 of the 1,750 Confederates in the battle were casualties. Thirty-six Texans were killed, including Lt. Col. John Sutton of the Seventh Texas and Maj. Sam Lockridge of the Fifth Texas. Losses were heaviest in the Fifth Texas: twenty killed and sixty-seven wounded. Scurry's Fourth Texas had eight killed and thirty-six wounded.[11]

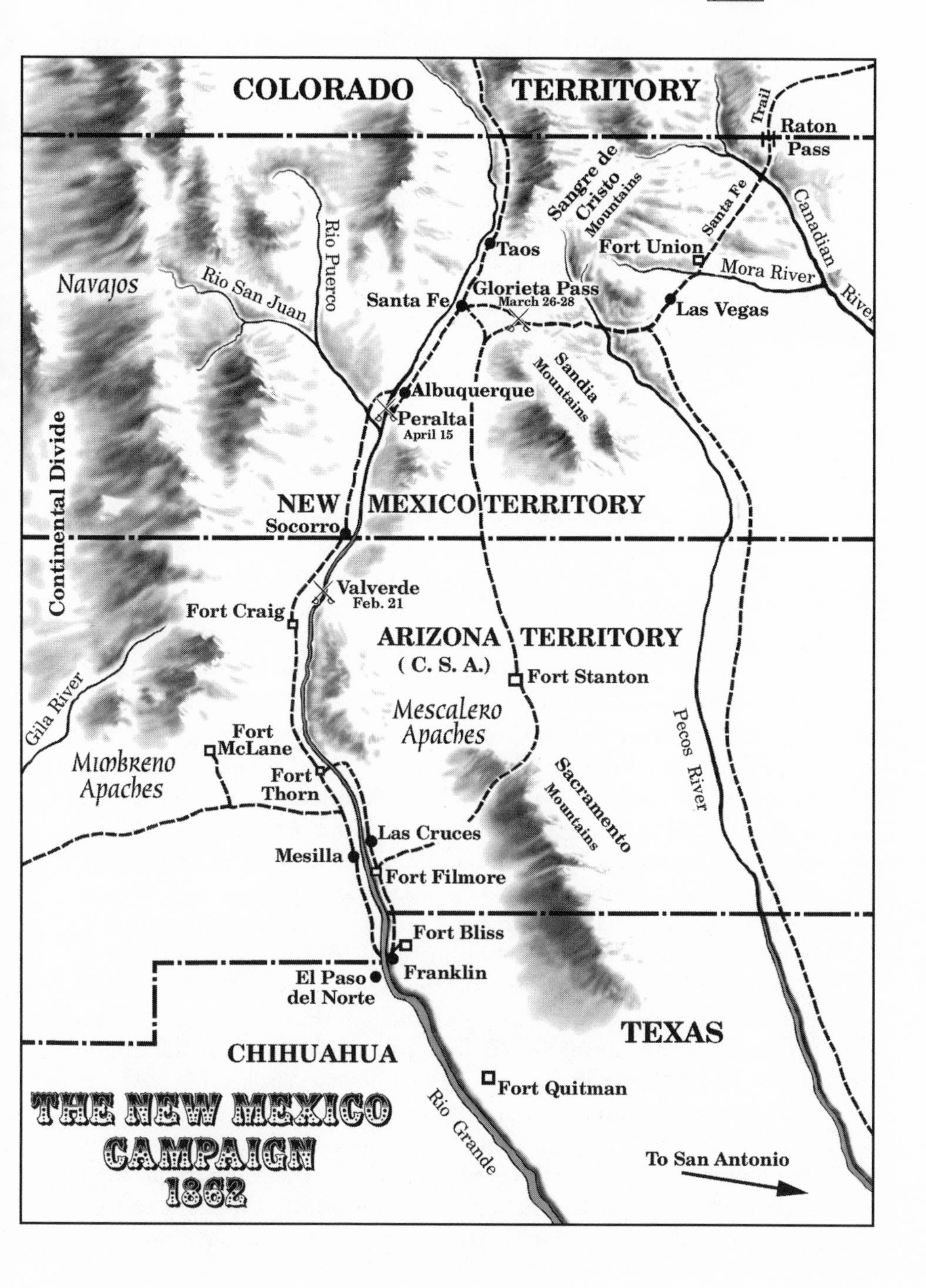
COLORADO TERRITORY
Trail
Raton Pass
Sangre de Cristo Mountains
Santa Fe
Canadian River
Rio Puerco
Taos
Fort Union
Mora River
Navajos
Rio San Juan
Santa Fe
Glorieta Pass
March 26-28
Las Vegas
Sandia Mountains
Albuquerque
Peralta
April 15
Continental Divide
NEW MEXICO TERRITORY
Socorro
Valverde
Feb. 21
Fort Craig
ARIZONA TERRITORY
(C. S. A.)
Fort Stanton
Gila River
Mescalero Apaches
Pecos River
Fort McLane
Mimbreno Apaches
Fort Thorn
Sacramento Mountains
Las Cruces
Mesilla
Fort Filmore
Fort Bliss
Franklin
El Paso del Norte
TEXAS
CHIHUAHUA
Fort Quitman
THE NEW MEXICO CAMPAIGN 1862
Rio Grande
To San Antonio

Sibley resumed command after the battle. Since Canby still held Fort Craig, Sibley decided to push north toward Albuquerque and Santa Fe, where he hoped to find supplies. The march was slow as there was a shortage of horses and mules. In an effort to increase efficiency of the brigade, Scurry convinced the men of the Fourth Texas who still had horses to turn them over to the quartermaster for redistribution as replacements for the two better mounted regiments. The men complied, but not without a good bit of grumbling and complaining. The capture of supplies near Socorro improved morale but only temporarily.

Arrival in Albuquerque brought some relief, and after a brief pause Sibley's men continued on to Santa Fe. When they entered the city, however, they found that most of the stores had been destroyed or taken to Fort Union, about eighty-five miles to the northeast.[12]

In the belief that the capture of Fort Union, an important supply depot on the Santa Fe Trail, would force Canby to surrender Fort Craig, Sibley sent a battalion of the Second Mounted Volunteers (previously under John R. Baylor's command), four companies of the Fifth Texas, a battalion of the Seventh Texas, and the Fourth Texas Regiment toward Fort Union. When the advanced elements of the Confederate force (consisting of the battalion from the Second Texas and the four companies from the Fifth Texas) moved through Apache Canyon at the western end of Glorieta Pass, they encountered a column of Colorado volunteers led by Maj. John M. Chivington, a Methodist minister. Although the opposing forces, each with about 400 men, were equal in size, the Confederates, commanded by Maj. Charles Pyron of the Second Texas, were driven back in bitter fighting. Casualties in killed and wounded were light, but seventy-one Texans were captured. Chivington, however, unsure of the size of the Confederate force, pulled his troops back to Pigeon's Ranch on the eastern slope of the mountains. The Texans fell back to Johnson's Ranch at the opposite end of the canyon.[13]

Late that afternoon Major Pyron sent a message to Lieutenant Colonel Scurry, who was with his Fourth Texas Regiment and the battalion of the Seventh Texas fifteen miles to the south, requesting support. Scurry quickly moved his troops during the night to join Pyron at Johnson's Ranch. After resting his men on March 27,

Scurry, now in command of the combined Confederate forces, moved troops through Apache Canyon to attack the Union forces, which had also been reinforced by troops commanded by Col. John P. Slough, at Pigeon's Ranch. In the battle for control of Glorieta Pass, Scurry's Texans drove Slough's troops away from Pigeon's Ranch. Although forty-eight Texans, including Maj. Henry Raguet of the Fourth Texas, Maj. John S. Shropshire of the Fifth Texas, and Capt. Charles Buckholts of the Fourth Texas, were killed or mortally wounded, the Confederates won a tactical victory.

Unfortunately for the Confederates, while the battle raged at Pigeon's Ranch, Major Chivington and 400 Union troops moved through the mountains and swung around the Rebel lines. They drove away the small force that Scurry had left at Johnston's Ranch to guard the supply train and destroyed eighty wagons containing the Confederate food, forage, ammunition, and medical supplies.[14]

The loss of the Confederate supply train was a major blow. Short of food and ammunition, Scurry withdrew to Santa Fe to join the rest of the brigade. At first, General Sibley believed he could continue the campaign; however, reports that additional Union troops were coming from California convinced him that a retreat was necessary.[15]

The Confederates began their withdrawal from Santa Fe on April 8. After a brief pause at Albuquerque, the retreat resumed on April 12. Scurry's Fourth Cavalry and men of the Seventh Texas forded the Rio Grande to the west side. Green's Fifth Texas and Pyron's Second Cavalry Battalion, acting as the army's rear guard, followed on the east side of the river. After a clash at Peralta with part of Canby's troops from Fort Craig, Sibley decided to bypass Craig by moving west of the Rio Grande through the mountains and returning to the river south of the fort. The detour took the Texans through a wilderness of mountains, brush, and undergrowth. The lack of adequate food, water, and medicine, the difficult terrain, and the cold weather decimated the Texans. When the brigade reached El Paso in May, morale was completely shattered.

The troops in Pyron's Second Battalion, whose one-year enlistments had expired, headed back to San Antonio in late May. The next month Sibley's regiments left El Paso for the long journey across West Texas. The Fourth Texas led the retreat, followed several days later by the Fifth Texas and four companies of the Seventh

Texas. Col. William Steele and the rest of the Seventh Texas brought up the rear. The march across West Texas was, according to historian Jerry D. Thompson, "a monumental ordeal." Lack of water, attacks by Apaches, poor roads, and extreme heat made the journey almost unbearable. In July the lead units of the Fourth Texas began arriving in San Antonio. The dream of conquest of New Mexico and Arizona had come to an end.[16]

The exact number of casualties in the Texas regiments during this campaign is not known. Historian Martin H. Hall, who wrote two books and several articles describing the New Mexico campaign, estimated that 400 Texans lost their lives because of battle or disease and that another 500 men were stragglers, deserters, or prisoners by the time the brigade reached El Paso. Others died or were killed on the retreat through West Texas. By the time the last units reached San Antonio in late summer, only half of the members of the brigade that marched into New Mexico were still with their regiments.[17]

As Sibley brought his weary troops back to Texas, he found himself facing criticism for his conduct. Much of this derived from soldiers' complaints that he had drunk excessively or had not demonstrated bravery at Valverde. More serious were charges preferred against Sibley by Capt. Alfred S. Thurmond, a veteran soldier in the Seventh Cavalry. Thurmond charged that Sibley was drunk on three occasions, had abandoned sick and wounded soldiers, had exhibited cowardice, and had misappropriated items for his personal benefit. In order to answer the charges Sibley proceeded to Richmond, Virginia. Although President Davis, who still had confidence in Sibley, dismissed the charges against him, Sibley's reputation as a soldier had been seriously damaged.[18]

While Sibley was in Richmond the brigade was under the temporary command of Col. James Reily of the Fourth Texas. Reily sent the men on furlough pending further instructions. On two different occasions orders were issued transferring the brigade out of Texas, but on both occasions the orders were canceled due to threats of Union operations against Texas. In December the brigade members were ordered to report back to their regiments at camp near Hempstead.[19]

Once back on duty the veterans of the New Mexico campaign, along with new recruits in the regiments, soon found themselves involved in Confederate efforts to recapture Galveston. The island had been under Union control since October 8, when a Union naval force commanded by Commodore William Renshaw seized the city. The newly appointed Confederate commander of Texas, Maj. Gen. John B. Magruder, was determined to retake Galveston. In early December he began assembling troops for the reconquest. The three regiments of the Sibley Brigade were moved by train to Houston in anticipation of the attack. Tom Green, commander of the Fifth Cavalry, and Arthur P. Bagby, now commanding the Seventh Cavalry, volunteered to provide troops from their regiments to serve as marksmen on the two small cotton-clad gunboats, *Bayou City* and *Neptune,* that Magruder planned to use in the assault on Galveston.[20]

The Confederate effort to retake Galveston began in the early morning hours of January 1, 1863. While Federal troops on the island slept after an evening of celebration, Magruder and William R. Scurry, who had been promoted to brigadier general as a result of his New Mexico service, led Confederate troops from Virginia Point on the mainland across the railroad bridge to the island. Among the Confederates were men of the Fourth Texas Cavalry commanded by Col. James Reily and companies of the Fifth and Seventh cavalries led by Lt. Col. Henry C. McNeill and Maj. Gustavus Hoffman. Under the cover of darkness the Confederates moved quietly down Broadway to the center of town. Scurry divided his forces: one group would attack Union troops quartered on Kuhn's Wharf; another took positions along the Strand; and men of the Sibley Brigade, serving as the reserve, assembled near the U.S. customshouse at Twentieth and Post Office streets.[21]

Shortly before dawn, Confederate artillery opened fire upon the Union troops along the waterfront. Union gunboats moored in the harbor returned the fire in a heavy artillery exchange. Meanwhile, about 500 Confederate troops led by Col. Joseph J. Cook attempted to storm Union positions at Kuhn's Wharf. Fire from the Union gunboats was so intense, however, that Cook was forced to withdraw his troops to the safety of nearby buildings.[22]

Just as the Confederate attack at Kuhn's Wharf was failing, the two Confederate vessels *Bayou City* and *Neptune* came steaming into the harbor. One hundred fifty volunteers from the Fifth Texas commanded by Tom Green were on board *Bayou City*, and one hundred men of the Seventh Texas commanded by Arthur P. Bagby were on *Neptune.* As the two Confederate gunboats closed quickly with the enemy warship *Harriet Lane,* Green's and Bagby's cavalrymen, now playing the role of sharpshooters, leveled a steady fire, forcing Union seamen below deck. When *Bayou City* managed to ram the *Lane*, locking the vessels together, Green's men, now acting as marines, stormed aboard the enemy vessel. In a few minutes the crew of *Harriet Lane* surrendered.

Another Union gunboat, *Owasco,* attempted to aid the *Lane*, but fire from Green's sharpshooters forced *Owasco* to pull away. Meanwhile, another Union vessel, *Westfield,* ran aground and was scuttled by her captain, who was killed in the explosion. The ranking Union naval officer in the area, believing the Confederates were much stronger than they actually were, ordered other Union warships to withdraw from the harbor. Without naval gunfire to support them, the Union troops along the waterfront quickly surrendered to General Scurry. Galveston was once again in Confederate hands.[23]

The recapture of Galveston was hailed as a great Confederate victory. President Davis praised General Magruder for his achievement. Magruder, in turn, commended both Tom Green and Arthur P. Bagby for their roles in the victory. There was some criticism of Colonel Reily's handling of his regiment in the battle, but on the whole the men of the Sibley

A. P. Bagby, Colonel, Seventh Texas Cavalry.
—Courtesy Harold B. Simpson Research Center, Hillsboro, Texas

Brigade came out of the affair with their enhanced reputations as soldiers.[24]

The troops of the Sibley Brigade had only a brief respite. In mid-January they were ordered to join General Sibley in New Iberia, Louisiana. Richard Taylor, the Confederate commander in that state, was opening a campaign along Bayou Teche and Bayou Lafourche. With Alfred Mouton's Louisiana infantry and Sibley's Texas cavalry, Taylor hoped to force Nathaniel P. Banks, Union commander in the area, to direct troops away from efforts to capture the Confederate garrison at Port Hudson, north of Baton Rouge.

In battles fought at Bisland and Irish Bend in April, Taylor's troops were defeated and driven from the field. Tom Green, whose Fifth Texas Cavalry anchored the Confederate right flank, handled his troops well, earning the praise of Taylor for his performance under fire. Sibley, on the other hand, made a number of errors and incurred the wrath of Taylor. Soon after the battles were over, Taylor removed Sibley from command of the brigade and named Green, promoted to brigadier general, as his successor.[25]

Although unsuccessful at Bisland and Irish Bend, Taylor continued his campaign in the bayou country. Green's Brigade played an active part in the campaign. The brigade now consisted of Green's old Fifth Texas (commanded by Col. Henry C. McNeill), the Fourth Texas (led by William P. "Gotch" Hardeman, who succeeded James Reily, killed at Irish Bend), the Seventh Texas (commanded by Arthur P. Bagby), and Edwin Waller's Thirteenth Texas Cavalry Battalion, which had recently joined the brigade. Along with Mouton's Infantry Brigade and another Texas cavalry brigade commanded by James P. Major, Green's Brigade took part in the capture of Brashear City, a Union stronghold on Bayou Teche. In late June, however, Green, commanding his own and Major's Brigade, failed in an attack upon an enemy earthwork, Fort Butler, near Donaldsonville. Although the Texans outnumbered the Federal defenders, poor coordination and communication by the Confederates plus the firepower of several Union gunboats resulted in a costly failure. Confederate losses in the affair were high: 262 casualties of 1,000 troops involved. Most of the losses were in the Fifth and Seventh Texas cavalries, each of which had 100 men killed and wounded.[26]

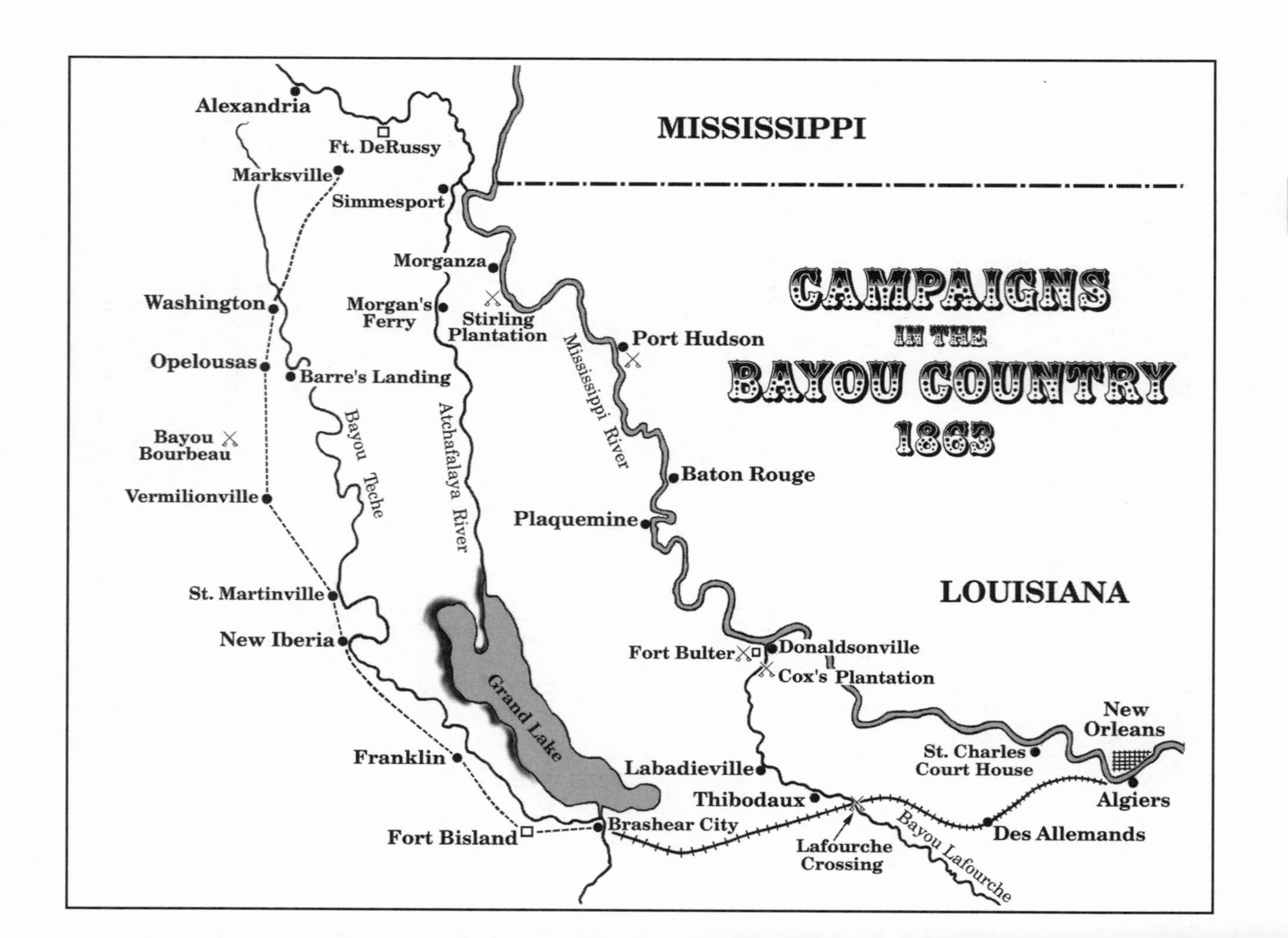
CAMPAIGNS
IN THE
BAYOU COUNTRY
1863
MISSISSIPPI
LOUISIANA
Alexandria
Ft. DeRussy
Marksville
Simmesport
Morganza
Washington
Morgan's Ferry
Stirling Plantation
Port Hudson
Mississippi River
Opelousas
Barre's Landing
Bayou Teche
Atchafalaya River
Bayou Bourbeau
Vermilionville
Baton Rouge
Plaquemine
St. Martinville
New Iberia
Fort Bulter
Donaldsonville
Cox's Plantation
Grand Lake
New Orleans
St. Charles Court House
Franklin
Labadieville
Thibodaux
Algiers
Fort Bisland
Brashear City
Lafourche Crossing
Bayou Lafourche
Des Allemands

Even though Taylor's troops had some success in the Lafourche region, they were unable to force Banks to abandon the siege of Port Hudson. When that Confederate outpost fell in early July, Banks turned his army against Taylor. Heavily outnumbered, Taylor was forced to fall back toward Bayou Teche. Green's Brigade fought a skillful delaying action at Cox's plantation near Donaldsonville, taking 200 prisoners and several enemy artillery pieces before retiring.[27]

Green's Brigade saw little action during August and early September. Part of Banks' army was embarked on a mission to invade Texas by way of Sabine Pass; fighting in Louisiana was almost at a standstill. Morale in the brigade was low and desertion high as many Texans saw little reason to remain in Louisiana. Those who stayed were restless. So serious was the situation that in mid-August Mouton's infantry was required to put down a possible mutiny among the Texans.[28]

The lull in operations ended in late September. Embarrassed by their failure at Sabine Pass on September 8, the Federals remained determined to move against Texas. General Banks decided that an advance up Bayou Teche toward Alexandria and the Red River offered the best prospect for success. He ordered Maj. Gen. William B. Franklin and 20,000 troops from the Thirteenth and Nineteenth Army Corps to move up the Teche.[29]

To oppose Franklin, General Taylor was equipped with 8,000 men from John G. Walker's Texas infantry, Alfred Mouton's Louisiana infantry, Tom Green's cavalry, and James P. Major's cavalry. To provide better coordination of his mounted troops Taylor brought his two cavalry brigades together in a division commanded by Green. Arthur P. Bagby of the Seventh Texas, who had performed well in the bayou campaigns, was named to succeed Green as commander of the old Sibley Brigade.[30]

Green's cavalry played a major role in impeding Franklin's move through the Teche country. On September 29, in a blinding rainstorm, Green's cavalry and Mouton's infantry surprised an enemy outpost at Stirling's plantation on Bayou Fordoche. They captured 450 Federal troops. Two weeks later the Texans attacked Franklin's army in a clearing near Opelousas known as Buzzard's Prairie. Although the outnumbered Texans were forced to give ground, they gave a good account of themselves before withdrawing.[31]

In spite of the harassing activities of the Texas cavalry, the Union army slowly moved north. By late October, Franklin's troops had reached the small town of Washington, several miles north of Opelousas. An attack by Walker's infantry and Major's cavalry convinced Franklin to pull back to Opelousas. While there he learned that his superior, General Banks, had taken a large force by water to invade South Texas. Although Franklin was instructed to keep up the pressure on the enemy, he decided to withdraw to winter quarters in New Iberia.

As Franklin's army began its withdrawal, Tom Green determined to strike the enemy with a powerful blow. Requesting and receiving the support of three of Walker's infantry regiments, Green struck the rear guard of the Union army at Bayou Bourbeau, several miles south of Opelousas. In a brilliant maneuver Green's Texans hit the enemy from all directions. In a three-hour battle the Union army lost 716 men, including over 500 captured. The Confederates lost 180 men, mainly in the infantry regiments.[32]

The victory at Bayou Bourbeau ended the fighting in Louisiana for the year. Green and his cavalry returned to Texas in December. Banks' army had landed at the mouth of the Rio Grande and occupied Brownsville. John B. Magruder, Confederate commander in Texas, believed that other Union landings would soon be attempted on the middle and upper Texas coast. He requested that Green's cavalry be returned to aid in the defense of Galveston.

In January 1864 the old Sibley Brigade was stationed at Virginia Point, on the mainland across from Galveston. A month later the brigade was located near Columbia in Brazoria County. The Fourth Texas listed 383 men present for duty, the Fifth Texas 325 men, and the Seventh Texas, 241. Waller's Thirteenth Texas Cavalry Battalion, attached to the brigade, had 156 men present for duty.[33]

The anticipated attack on the upper Texas coast never materialized as the Union command decided to stage a major offensive up the Red River in early spring 1864. To meet this threat Confederate commander Richard Taylor was concentrating his forces in northern Louisiana. In March various Texas cavalry units, including those under Tom Green's command, were ordered to join Taylor in Louisiana.

By the middle of March several Texas cavalry regiments were

on their way to Louisiana. Arthur P. Bagby's Brigade was the first to join Taylor's army. Col. Henry C. McNeill and 250 men of the Fifth Texas reached Taylor at Natchitoches on the night of March 30. Col. Philemon T. Herbert and 350 men of the Seventh Texas arrived the next morning. Col. William P. Hardeman and his Fourth Texas arrived on April 1. On the following day Bagby's Brigade and Col. Xavier Debray's Twenty-sixth Texas Cavalry (which had just arrived) were attacked by advanced units of Banks' army near Crump's plantation but were able to drive the enemy from the field.[34]

During the next several days other Texas cavalry units joined Taylor's army as it fell back to Mansfield, Louisiana. Now with nearly 9,000 troops under his command, Taylor launched an assault on the advanced divisions of Banks' army near Mansfield. In the battle fought on April 8, Bagby's regiments, fighting as dismounted cavalry, were on the Confederate left flank with W. P. Lane's Texas cavalry on one side and William G. Vincent's Louisianians on the other. The Confederate attack began at 4:00 P.M. with Rebel infantry and cavalry, including Bagby's Brigade, charging the Union right flank. Once the attack was under way, Taylor ordered Walker's infantry and Hamilton P. Bee's cavalry on the Confederate right to move forward. In spite of heavy enemy artillery and rifle fire the Confederates drove the Federals back to a second line of defense. When this line finally gave way the Union forces broke and ran with the Southerners in pursuit. Darkness and the arrival of fresh Union troops stopped the Confederate advance at a small orchard known as Pleasant Grove.[35]

The Battle of Mansfield, or Sabine Cross Roads as the Federals called it, was a major Confederate victory. Losses were heavy on both sides: approximately 2,230 Federal and 1,000 Confederate casualties. Losses in Bagby's Brigade included twelve killed and thirty-seven wounded. Among the casualties was Col. Philemon Herbert, commander of the Seventh Texas, who died from wounds received in the fighting.[36]

Banks withdrew his army from Pleasant Grove during the night of April 8. The next day Taylor attacked Banks again at Pleasant Hill. In this battle Bagby's troops were once more on the left of the Confederate line. The heaviest fighting in the battle took place on the Confederate right. Here the Confederates initially drove the Union troops back, but a determined Federal counterattack forced the Southerners to give ground. Late in the afternoon Taylor ordered a general withdrawal from the field. The exhausted Federals made no attempt to pursue.[37]

Although the Union army had the upper hand at Pleasant Hill, General Banks decided he would continue his withdrawal back toward the Union fleet on the Red River. Richard Taylor remained determined to prevent Banks' escape even though his superior, Edmund Kirby Smith, ordered two of the Confederate infantry divisions to Arkansas to deal with a Union threat there.

Taylor hoped to cut off some of the Union gunboats near Grand Bayou. He sent Bagby with his cavalry brigade and a battery of artillery to intercept the enemy. Unfortunately the lack of pontoons delayed Bagby at Bayou Pierre. By the time he arrived, the Union gunboats had passed. "The want of a pontoon alone prevented him [Bagby] from inflicting heavy damage upon the enemy," lamented Taylor.[38]

Bagby then attempted to block the Union fleet at Blair's Landing, a few miles down the river. When he arrived there, however, he found that the Union boats had passed after a fierce battle with Confederate cavalry in which the popular Tom Green was killed.[39]

Taylor still hoped to defeat Banks' army as it attempted to cross the Cane River at Monett's Ferry. He ordered Hamilton P. Bee with his own and Green's cavalry to move downstream past Banks' army and occupy the bluffs on the south side of the river overlooking the crossing at Monett's Ferry. With cavalry brigades commanded by Bagby, James P. Major, and Xavier Debray, Bee was to delay the enemy while Taylor brought up the rest of his army to attack Banks from the rear.

Bagby's Brigade, consisting of the Fourth, Fifth, and Seventh regiments and Waller's Battalion, was on the Confederate right at Monett's Ferry, with Major in the center and Debray on the left. When the Union army made an attack on the left flank, Bee, supported by Bagby and Major, ordered a withdrawal, allowing Banks' army to continue its move toward Alexandria.[40]

Confederate army commander Richard Taylor blamed Bee for the escape of the Union army. In early May he relieved Bee of his command as division commander and appointed Bagby, who had

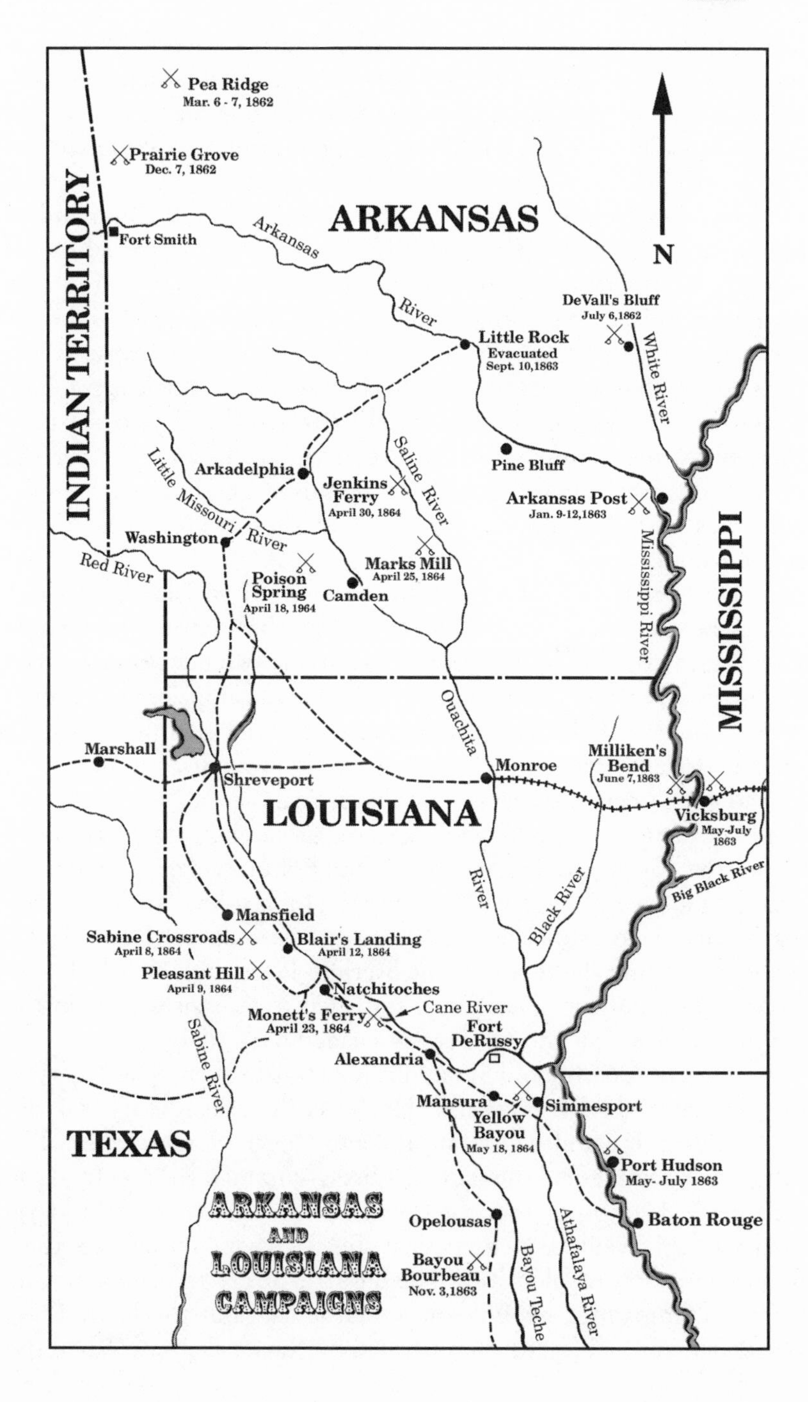
Pea Ridge
Mar. 6 - 7, 1862
Prairie Grove
Dec. 7, 1862
INDIAN TERRITORY
ARKANSAS
N
Fort Smith
Arkansas River
DeVall's Bluff
July 6,1862
Little Rock
Evacuated
Sept. 10,1863
White River
Pine Bluff
Arkadelphia
Jenkins Ferry
April 30, 1864
Saline River
Arkansas Post
Jan. 9-12,1863
Little Missouri River
Washington
Red River
Marks Mill
April 25, 1864
Poison Spring
April 18, 1964
Camden
Mississippi River
MISSISSIPPI
Ouachita River
Marshall
Shreveport
Monroe
Milliken's Bend
June 7,1863
Vicksburg
May-July 1863
LOUISIANA
Big Black River
Black River
Mansfield
Sabine Crossroads
April 8, 1864
Blair's Landing
April 12, 1864
Pleasant Hill
April 9, 1864
Natchitoches
Monett's Ferry
April 23, 1864
Cane River
Fort DeRussy
Alexandria
Sabine River
Mansura
Simmesport
Yellow Bayou
May 18, 1864
TEXAS
Port Hudson
May- July 1863
ARKANSAS AND LOUISIANA CAMPAIGNS
Opelousas
Baton Rouge
Bayou Bourbeau
Nov. 3,1863
Bayou Teche
Athafalaya River

been named brigadier general by Kirby Smith on April 13, to succeed Bee. The veteran Col. William P. "Gotch" Hardeman, commander of the Fourth Texas, was placed in command of the old Sibley Brigade, and Lt. Col. George J. Hampton took command of the Fourth Texas.[41]

The Confederate cavalry, now under the overall command of Maj. Gen. John A. Wharton, who succeeded Tom Green as head of Taylor's mounted arm, continued to harass Banks' army as it moved southward. Most of the engagements were small skirmishes, but as the Union army neared Simmesport on the Atchafalaya River, Wharton ordered a major assault. In the fierce battle at Yellow Bayou both sides lost heavily as Wharton ordered two separate charges by his infantry and cavalry in an unsuccessful effort to break the enemy's lines. The Confederates suffered more than 600 casualties at Yellow Bayou; fifty-four of these were in the Sibley Brigade commanded by Hardeman.[42]

The Battle of Yellow Bayou proved to be the last major engagement for the Sibley Brigade. While the fighting continued, Banks' army began crossing the Atchafalaya. Two days later the last of his army crossed, bringing the Red River campaign to an end. While the Confederates had prevented Banks from capturing Shreveport and invading East Texas, Taylor was disappointed that he had been unable to destroy Banks' army.

Hardeman's troops spent the rest of summer on patrol duty along the Black River in northeastern Louisiana, occasionally engaging in an exchange with the enemy. In late August the brigade was ordered to Monticello, Arkansas, to support Confederate forces defending the region while Sterling Price took his cavalry on a raid into Missouri. Once Price returned to Arkansas later in the autumn, Hardeman and his cavalry headed back to Texas.[43]

In early 1865 the old Sibley Brigade was broken up as a part of ongoing general reorganization. The Seventh Texas was sent to join its former commander, Arthur P. Bagby, near Natchitoches. The other two regiments, the Fourth Texas commanded by Lt. Col. George J. Hampton and the Fifth Texas commanded by Col. Henry C. McNeill, stayed in East Texas, where forage for their mounts was more plentiful. The Fourth Texas remained in the brigade commanded by William P. Hardeman, but the Fifth Texas was assigned to a brigade commanded by Xavier Debray. When the

Xavier Debray, Colonel, Twenty-sixth Texas Cavalry.
—Courtesy Harold B. Simpson Research Center, Hillsboro, Texas

Trans Mississippi Department was surrendered by Kirby Smith in June 1865, members of the old Sibley Brigade returned to their homes after a long journey that had taken them from the mountains and deserts of New Mexico to the bayous and forests of Louisiana and Arkansas. According to the calculation of one of its members, Theophilus Noel, the brigade had covered more than 7,000 miles.[44]

HAMILTON P. BEE'S DIVISION

First Texas Cavalry
Twenty-third Texas Cavalry
Twenty-sixth Texas Cavalry
Thirty-fourth Texas Cavalry
Thirty-fifth Texas Cavalry
Thirty-sixth [Thirty-second] Texas Cavalry

Six Texas mounted regiments in a cavalry division commanded by Brig. Gen. Hamilton P. Bee fought in many of the same campaigns in Louisiana as the men of the old Sibley Brigade. These regiments were on duty along the upper Texas coast when they were ordered to join Taylor's army in Louisiana under the immediate command of Hamilton P. Bee.

When Bee reported to Tom Green, commander of Taylor's

cavalry, his units were designated as the First Division of Green's Cavalry Corps. When the battles at Mansfield and Pleasant Hill were fought several days later, only three of Bee's six regiments—the First commanded by Augustus Buchel, the Twenty-sixth commanded by Xavier Debray, and the Thirty-fourth commanded by A. W. Terrell—had arrived. The other three—Nicholas Gould's Twenty-third Texas, James B. Likens' Thirty-fifth Texas, and Peter C. Woods' Thirty-sixth Texas (sometimes reported as the Thirty-second Texas)—joined Bee's command for the later battles in the Red River campaign. At various times during the next year, three of Bee's regiments, the First, Thirty-fourth, and Thirty-fifth, were brigaded under the command of Augustus Buchel (and following his death, William O. Yager). The Twenty-third, Twenty-sixth, and Thirty-sixth were brigaded under the command of Xavier Debray.[45]

The Texas regiments that came to Louisiana under Bee's command had limited previous combat experience. The First Texas Cavalry was an outgrowth of the old First Regiment of Texas Mounted Rifles. The Mounted Rifles had been formed in spring 1861 from ten companies of volunteers raised in three areas: the region around Austin and San Antonio, the frontier counties of Central Texas, and northeast Texas. Under the command of Col. Henry McCulloch, the Mounted Rifles occupied the Federal frontier posts evacuated by Union troops in the early days of the war. During summer and autumn of 1861, units of the Mounted Rifles led by Thomas C. Frost, Buck Barry, and Edward Burleson, Jr., engaged in a series of clashes with nomadic Indians who were raiding frontier settlements.[46]

The First Texas Mounted Rifles were officially designated the First Texas Cavalry Regiment by order of the Confederate Secretary of War on December 10, 1861. When Henry McCulloch became commander of the Western Sub-district of Texas, Lt. Col. Thomas C. Frost, a young lawyer from Comanche County who had previous service with the Texas Rangers, assumed leadership of the regiment. Under Frost's command the regiment continued to carry out patrol duties during the winter of 1861 but disbanded in April 1862, when the one-year enlistments of the men expired. Some of the men remained on active duty in the Third Texas Cavalry Battalion under Maj. William O. Yager and the Eighth Texas Cavalry Battalion under Maj. Joseph Taylor.[47]

In May 1863 Maj. Gen. John B. Magruder, commander of the Texas Military District, combined Yager's Battalion, Taylor's Battalion, and Capt. James A. Ware's company of Partisan Rangers to reform the First Texas Cavalry. Col. Augustus Buchel was named regimental commander, Maj. William Yager lieutenant colonel, and Robert A. Myers major. The initial headquarters of the regiment was near Carricitas Lake on the Rio Grande, twenty-five miles from Brownsville.[48]

The commander of the reorganized regiment, Augustus Buchel, was an experienced soldier. Born in the German province of Hesse in 1813, Buchel was a graduate of the Ecole Militaire of Paris and a veteran of the French Foreign Legion and the Turkish army. He came to Texas with his brother and other German colonists in 1845. After settling in Indianola, where he engaged in the lumber business, he led a small company of German volunteers during the Mexican War and later during a campaign against Juan Cortina. Prior to his appointment as commander of the First Texas, Buchel served as lieutenant colonel of the Third Texas Infantry at Brownsville.[49]

The First Texas remained along the Rio Grande only briefly. In June the regiment was moved up the Texas coast to Goliad, where it was positioned to meet possible enemy attacks at Corpus Christi and Matagorda. The regiment was ordered to Sabine Pass in late August 1863 when General Magruder became concerned about a Union invasion from Louisiana. Traveling much of the way by rail, lead elements of the regiment reached Sabine Pass two days after the Confederate victory over the Union invasion force on September 8. Fearful that the Union invaders might return, Magruder ordered additional troops to join Buchel, who was named brigade commander of Confederate forces in the area. As Yager was on detached duty in Brownsville, Maj. Robert A. Myers commanded the First Texas while Buchel led the brigade.[50]

During October and November 1863, Buchel's troops maintained a vigilant patrol of the region around Sabine Pass, occasionally crossing into southwestern Louisiana on reconnaissance missions. In December, Buchel was ordered to move his regiments, including the First Texas, A. W. Terrell's Thirty-fourth Texas Cavalry, Reuben R. Brown's Thirty-fifth Texas Cavalry, and two artillery batteries, to the San Bernard River, where General

Magruder believed Union landings might occur. The brigade was at first a part of Brig. Gen. James E. Slaughter's Brigade, but was soon transferred to Hamilton P. Bee's Brigade.[51]

For the next several weeks Buchel's troops, including the First Texas, were engaged in patrolling the upper Texas coast. During this time several skirmishes with the enemy occurred. In one such affair several companies of the First Texas and a detachment of Reuben Brown's cavalry attempted unsuccessfully to drive a Union landing party off Matagorda Island. In another engagement Capt. James Ware's Company F of the First Texas joined Confederate cavalry commanded by Maj. Matthew Nolan in defeating Union cavalry in San Patricio County.[52]

In carrying out its duties along the Texas coast in 1863 the First Texas Cavalry often served with other regiments that were later part of Bee's Division in the Red River campaign. Of these only the Twenty-sixth Texas Cavalry had participated in a signficant military engagement, the Battle of Galveston. And like the First Texas, the Twenty-sixth was commanded by a graduate of European military schools, Xavier B. Debray.

The Twenty-sixth Texas Cavalry was created on March 17, 1862, when the Seventh Cavalry Battalion, consisting of seven companies of volunteers from Harrison, Galveston, Liberty, Fort Bend, Montgomery, Washington, Grimes, and Leon counties, was expanded to regimental strength (ten companies). The original companies were organized under the command of Maj. Samuel B. Davis, the assistant adjutant general for the Military District of Texas. When Davis resigned his linial rank, Major Debray, at that time serving in the Second Texas Infantry, was promoted to lieutenant colonel and given command of the battalion. When the battalion reached regimental strength Debray was elected colonel, John J. Myers lieutenant colonel, and Medard Menard major.[53]

Debray's Regiment spent the late spring and early summer months in camp near the San Bernard River. Debray insisted that his regiment be drilled both on horseback and on foot with frequent inspections and parades. These activities attracted considerable interest from local citizens, who enjoyed viewing the activities as one would a circus. This led members of the regiment to give the Twenty-sixth Texas the sobriquet "the Menagerie."[54]

In July 1863 Colonel Debray was appointed commander of

the Eastern Sub-district of Texas with headquarters at Houston. His regiment remained along the San Bernard River for the time, continuing its training and patrolling under the executive officer, Lieutenant Colonel Myers. When Union forces occupied Galveston in early October, the regiment was ordered to Virginia Point. For the next two months the men of the Twenty-sixth Texas conducted day and night patrols to prevent Federal landings on the mainland.[55]

Colonel Debray developed plans for the recapture of Galveston, but these were rejected by his superior officer, Brig. Gen. Paul O. Hebert, who believed such an operation was too ambitious. The appointment of John B. Magruder to replace the cautious Hebert in November changed the situation. Magruder, who would respond more boldly than his predecessor, almost immediately began planning the recapture of Galveston.[56]

In the battle for Galveston, January 1, 1863, Debray and his Twenty-sixth Cavalry supported Confederate infantry and artillery in the attack on Union troops on Kuhn's Wharf. Although Debray and his men played a secondary role in the battle, they received the praise of General Magruder for their efforts.[57]

After the recapture of Galveston, Debray, who was recommended for promotion by General Magruder, was assigned command of the island. The Twenty-sixth Texas, the Third Texas Infantry, the Twentieth Texas Infantry, and several batteries of the First Texas Heavy Artillery were placed under Debray's command. Debray and the Twenty-sixth Texas remained at Galveston for the next ten months. Other than occasional alerts when reports of possible Union attacks were received, there was little serious threat to the island. A small disturbance occurred in August, when some of the troops of the Third Infantry refused to drill in the hot summer heat, but the matter was soon resolved.[58]

Garrison duty for Debray and his cavalry on Galveston Island came to an end in late November. Magruder, fearful of a Union invasion of the Texas coast west of Galveston, began concentrating troops along the San Bernard River. Debray and the Twenty-sixth Texas were ordered to join other Confederate forces being assembled in the area.

Upon arriving in Brazoria County, Debray was assigned command of a small brigade consisting of his own Twenty-sixth Cavalry, Nicholas Gould's Twenty-third Cavalry, A. W. Terrell's Thirty-

Nicholas Gould, Colonel, Twenty-third Texas Cavalry.
—Courtesy Harold B. Simpson Research Center, Hillsboro, Texas

fourth Cavalry, and M. V. McMahan's artillery battery. The brigade made its camp on Jones Creek, east of Churchill's Ferry in what was then called Camp Wharton No. 1. The brigade consisted of slightly more than 1,000 men present for duty.[59]

The two other cavalry regiments, the Twenty-third and Thirty-fourth Texas, brigaded with Debray's Regiment at Camp Wharton, were later part of Bee's Division in the Red River campaign. The Twenty-third Texas Regiment had been organized in northeast Texas in early 1862 with Nicholas Gould as colonel. Gould had just returned to Texas from Tennessee, where he had commanded Company D in Nathan Bedford Forrest's cavalry battalion. Gould and his company of ninety Texans had ridden with Forrest on some his early raids against enemy troops. Recruits for Gould's new regiment came primarily from Bowie, Denton, Hopkins, Lamar, Leon, and Red River counties.[60]

The Twenty-third Texas, with Gould as colonel, Isaac A. Grant as lieutenant colonel and John A. Corley as major, was stationed near Clarksville, Texas, in late 1862 but was ordered to report to Columbus on the Colorado River in early 1863 as part of the Confederate response to a threatened Union invasion. When Confederate concerns turned to southeast Texas in spring, Gould's Regiment was ordered to Niblett's Bluff. When this threat failed to materialize, the Twenty-third was sent back to the Texas coast west of Galveston. The regiment was stationed at Velasco at the mouth of the Brazos in late June 1863.[61]

In late August the Twenty-third was ordered to join Henry McCulloch's command at Bonham, Texas. The relationship between McCulloch, then commanding the Northern Sub-district of Texas, and Gould was difficult. Gould, a veteran of campaigns with Forrest in Tennessee, was apparently contemptuous of Texas officers whose experience was limited to the Trans Mississippi. McCulloch considered Gould arrogant and boastful. On October 21, 1863, McCulloch wrote district commander John B. Magruder that "our man Gould, who drinks, swaggers, and brags, has said many things which have had bad effect; he has neither brains nor prudence enough for a county lawyer, when sober, and none when he is not."[62]

Gould's Regiment returned to the lower Brazos River in December as part of the concentration ordered by General Magruder to meet another threatened invasion. Along with A.W. Terrell's Thirty-fourth Texas Cavalry, Gould's Regiment was assigned to Debray's Brigade biouvacked at Camp Wharton. In early January the regiment reported 33 officers and 451 men present for duty.[63]

The Thirty-fourth Texas Cavalry, the other regiment in Debray's Brigade, was often referred to as "Terrell's Texas Cavalry." John W. Spencer, who has traced the history of the Thirty-fourth Texas in his book *Terrell's Texas Cavalry,* has pointed out that there was another Texas cavalry regiment with the same numerical designation but this regiment (commanded by A. M. Alexander) was dismounted permanently in late 1862 and fought as infantry for the rest of the war.[64]

Terrell's Thirty-fourth Texas was officially organized on June 20, 1863, when the battalion commanded by A.W. Terrell was increased to regimental size. A.W. Terrell was well known in Texas. A lawyer, former district judge in Austin, and a friend of Sam Houston, he opposed secession. He originally turned down a military commission but accepted appointment as a volunteer aide to Brig. Gen. Henry McCulloch. Terrell accompanied McCulloch to Arkansas in 1862, but when McCulloch was replaced as division commander Terrell returned to Texas. In March 1863 he was commissioned lieutenant colonel with instructions to take command of a battalion being formed for frontier service. When the battalion was increased to regimental size, Terrell, promoted to colonel, became commander.[65]

John C. Robertson of Tyler, who had served as chairman of the powerful Committee of Public Safety of the Texas secession convention, was chosen lieutenant colonel of Terrell's Regiment. Hiram S. Morgan was named major. Most of the recruits for the regiment came from East Texas, although the men of one company (I) were from the Bastrop-Columbus area of Central Texas.[66]

After a brief period of training at Camp Groce near Hempstead, Terrell's Regiment was ordered to the mouth of the Brazos to defend against a possible enemy attack. From there the regiment moved to Colorado County in late August. While Colonel Terrell was in Houston discussing a proposal by Kirby Smith that he (Terrell) head the Texas Cotton Bureau, Lieutenant Colonel Robertson received orders that the regiment be dismounted and assigned duty at Galveston. Capt. C. G. Murray of I Company spoke out against the proposed dismounting. Robertson attempted to placate the unhappy troops, but Murray and several dozen men rode out of camp. When Terrell returned, he ordered Robertson and a detachment to pursue and arrest the mutineers. Robertson was unable to round up all the deserters but did bring back Murray, another officer, and twenty-three men. After a military trial Murray and the other officer were imprisoned and the men returned to duty. The orders for dismounting the troops were eventually rescinded and peace in the regiment restored.[67]

On Galveston Island Terrell's Regiment was assigned to Xavier Debray's command. The regiment remained on the island until late November, when it was ordered to Camp Wharton near the mouth of the Brazos, along with the regiments under Debray and Gould. In early January 1864 twenty-five officers and 402 enlisted men were listed as present for duty.[68]

Terrell's Regiment remained at Camp Wharton only briefly. In February the regiment was sent back to Galveston. The regiment was on duty there when ordered to join Confederate forces in northwestern Louisiana.[69]

The other two regiments in the brigade that accompanied Hamilton P. Bee to Louisiana in April 1864 were James B. Likens' Thirty-fifth Texas Cavalry and Peter C. Woods' Thirty-sixth Texas

Cavalry. Although it had a higher numerical designation than Likens' Regiment, the Thirty-sixth Texas was organized a year earlier than the Thirty-fifth. The higher number was a result of confusion in the Confederate War Department as another Texas cavalry regiment commanded by Col. Julius Andrews was formed the same month as Woods' cavalry. For several months both regiments were designated as the Thirty-second Texas. When the mistake was corrected, Woods' Regiment was given the higher number.[70]

Woods' Thirty-sixth Texas was recruited within a fifty-mile radius of San Antonio with companies formed in Atascosa, Bexar, Caldwell, DeWitt, Gonzales, Guadalupe, Hays, Live Oak, McMullen, and Wilson counties. The commander of the regiment, Peter C. Woods, was a native of Tennessee who had lived in Texas since 1851. A physician and planter, Woods raised the cavalry company in Hays County that later became Company A of the Thirty-sixth Texas. When the regiment was organized in late spring of 1862, Woods was elected colonel. Nathaniel Benton, a brother-in-law of Ben and Henry McCulloch, was lieutenant colonel, and William O. Hutchinson of San Marcos, major.[71]

The Thirty-sixth Texas spent the early summer months of 1862 training at Camp Clark near San Marcos. In the fall the regiment was assigned patrol duties in a triangle between Corpus Christi,

Peter C. Woods, Colonel, Thirty-sixth Texas Cavalry.
—Courtesy Harold B. Simpson Research Center, Hillsboro, Texas

Brownsville, and Eagle Pass with headquaters at Ringgold Barracks near Rio Grande City. During the next eight months, companies of the regiment carried out a variety of responsibilities in maintaining order in that vast stretch of land.

In June 1863 several companies of Woods' Regiment were moved up the coast to assist in the defense of Indianola. In September, Colonel Woods and six companies were ordered to southeast Texas as part of the Confederate buildup to meet a suspected Union invasion. When this threat passed, Woods and his men were ordered back to the lower Brazos with other Texas cavalry. In January 1864 the regiment was camped near the San Bernard River with the Second and Thirty-fifth Texas cavalries. An attempt to dismount Woods' Regiment led to widespread desertion, but when the dismount order was suspended most of the men returned to their unit.[72]

James B. Likens' Thirty-fifth Texas Cavalry, also camped on the San Bernard River in January 1864, had only been organized as a regiment in October 1863 by the consolidation of battalions commanded by Likens and James R. Burns. Likens, an attorney from Sabine Pass who had earlier commanded the post there, was named colonel of the new regiment. Burns became lieutenant colonel and William A. Wortham, major. When the regiment was first formed the various companies were scattered throughout East Texas. Muster rolls indicate the regiment was small in size, with most companies numbering approximately twenty men.[73]

Likens' Regiment was attached to Philip Luckett's Brigade in early December 1863 and ordered to Velasco. It remained there only briefly, moving on to the mouth of the Caney to become part of Buchel's Brigade. After taking part in some scouting expeditions there, the regiment moved on to the camp on the San Bernard River.[74]

The Union invasion of the Brazoria area that General Magruder feared in the winter months of 1863-1864 did not occur. Although the Union army occupied Brownsville and made some threats to the middle Texas coast, major attention shifted to Louisiana. When Nathaniel P. Banks began to move up the Red River, Confederate authorities ordered reinforcements from Texas be sent to join Richard Taylor's army.

On March 12, 1864, Brig. Gen. Hamilton P. Bee, commanding

the Western Sub-district of Texas, was ordered to proceed to Louisiana without delay with all his available cavalry. Leaving behind only sufficient force to safeguard the Texas coast, Bee headed to Louisiana with the six regiments that made up his brigade—the First, Twenty-third, Twenty-sixth, Thirty-fourth, Thirty-fifth, and Thirty-sixth Texas cavalries. The regiments traveled separately and were soon strung out along the roads leading to Louisiana. Bee reported to Taylor at Mansfield on April 5 with three of his regiments, Buchel's First, Debray's Twenty-sixth, and Terrell's Thirty-fourth. The other regiments did not reach Mansfield until several days later.[75]

Tom Green, commander of Taylor's cavalry, designated Bee's regiments as the First Division of his cavalry corps. The new division was quickly given its baptism under fire as Bee was ordered to delay the advanced elements of Banks' army moving toward Mansfield. On April 7 Bee's cavalry engaged the enemy at Wilson's Farm near Pleasant Hill. This series of clashes gave Taylor time to prepare his battle lines for a major assault against Banks' army as it approached Mansfield during the afternoon of April 8.[76]

In the battle fought at Mansfield, Terrell's and Buchel's regiments were initially placed on the extreme right of the Confederate line near Walker's Texas Infantry Division, with Debray's Regiment held in reserve on the road behind the main Confederate lines. As the lines shifted in the opening skirmishing, Taylor moved Terrell's Regiment to the Confederate left to serve with James P. Major's Cavalry Division; Debray was ordered to join Buchel on the Confederate right.

Taylor opened the main Confederate attack against Banks' army with the infantry regiments in Alfred Mouton's Division driving against the Union right. After the initial assault, Walker's Division on the Confederate right moved forward while Rebel cavalry under Major on the left and Bee on the right attempted to swing around the enemy flanks. The fighting was intense, and both sides sustained heavy casualties. Terrell's men and Major's cavalry on the Confederate left fought on foot as infantry; Buchel's and Debray's men remained on their horses but had difficulty advancing in the thickly wooded area on the right. The Union regiments eventually gave way and fell back. Darkness and the arrival of fresh Federal troops finally halted the Confederate attack.[77]

The Battle of Mansfield, or Sabine Cross Roads as the Federals called it, was a major Confederate victory. That night Banks began pulling his army back toward the Red River. Taylor ordered his troops to pursue the retreating enemy, with Bee's cavalry leading the pursuit. On the morning of April 9, Bee's horsemen encountered the Federals in a line of defense near Pleasant Hill. Reconnaissance indicated that this was the main Union army, so Bee awaited the arrival of the rest of Taylor's army.[78]

Taylor's infantry and artillery reached Pleasant Hill by noon, but the Confederate commander allowed his exhausted troops several hours of rest before ordering an attack. In the assault that afternoon the Confederates initially pushed the enemy back with heavy losses. In this battle Terrell's Regiment was on the Confederate far right. When the Confederates fell back under a Union counterattack, Terrell and some of his men were cut off from the rest of the army. They spent the night making their way back to the Confederate lines.[79]

In the fighting at Pleasant Hill, Buchel's and Debray's regiments were on the Confederate left near the Mansfield road. Tom Green, the Confederate cavalry chief, planned to use these regiments as shock troops to drive through the town after Confederate infantry on the right opened the assault. Once the Confederate infantry began to push the Federals back, Green ordered Buchel and Debray to attack. Buchel, believing such a move was folly, protested to Green. Convinced the enemy was reeling from losses on the Confederate right, Green refused to halt the attack. Buchel and Debray thereupon ordered their men forward.[80]

The two Texas regiments moved across the open field at a gallop but were stopped by what General Taylor described as "close and deadly fire of musketry from the dense woods on either side of the road." Bee and Debray were both injured from falls when their horses were shot out from under them. Buchel was mortally wounded and Lt. Col. William O. Yager took over direction of the First Texas as the fighting went on. Bee's regiments, now dismounted, joined Major's Division as it attempted to force the enemy back. As dusk fell the fighting was even more confusing, with Confederate units frequently firing upon fellow Southerners.[81]

The Confederate cavalry on the left held its own at Pleasant Hill, but Union success on the right forced Taylor to pull his troops back and abandon efforts to drive the enemy from Pleasant Hill. General Banks, believing Taylor's army much stronger than it was, withdrew his troops that evening and continued his retreat southward.

Even though part of his army was sent to Arkansas to stop a Union advance there, Taylor remained determined to pursue Banks. He sent General Bee with Buchel's (now Yager's) and Debray's regiments toward Grand Ecore. General Green, with the recently arrived regiments of Peter Woods, Nicholas Gould, and William H. Parsons, headed to Blair's Landing, where Green hoped to cut off the Union fleet as it attempted to withdraw down the Red River. There, on April 12, Green's cavalrymen, most of them fighting dismounted, charged two Union gunboats. For an hour firing went on between the Texans and the enemy. In the exchange General Green was killed when a Union shell tore away half of his skull. The firing continued until nearly dark, when Colonel Parsons ordered the Confederates to retire from the riverbank.[82]

With Green's death Hamilton P. Bee was temporarily in command of all Taylor's cavalry. Debray now commanded a brigade consisting of his own Twenty-sixth Texas, Gould's Twenty-third Texas, and Peter Woods' Thirty-sixth Texas. Terrell's Thirty-fourth Texas, Yager's First Texas, and James Likens' Thirty-fifth Texas, which had just arrived from Texas, remained directly under Bee's command. With these units and the cavalry commanded by A. P. Bagby and James P. Major, Bee was ordered by Taylor to stop the Union army from crossing the Cane River at Monett's Ferry; as noted earlier, however, Bee failed to do so.[83]

Although the Confederates did not stop Banks' army at Monett's Ferry, they continued to harass the Federals as they moved southward. On April 26 Bee's cavalry attacked Federal outposts along Bayou Rapides, twelve miles from Alexandria. That same day Likens' Thirty-fifth Texas exchanged fire with Union gunboats on the Red River near Montgomery. In the battle the enemy gunboat *Eastport* was sunk.[84]

General Taylor, who was unhappy with Bee for his conduct at Monett's Ferry, relieved him from command on May 14 and appointed Arthur P. Bagby as division commander. The Texas regiments in the division were on the Confederate right flank in the Battle of Yellow Bayou, fought on May 18. Although the

Confederates suffered heavy casualties overall in a futile attack, the regiments of Bee's old division suffered only slight losses.[85]

The Red River campaign ended with the Battle of Yellow Bayou. Using anchored transports and riverboats of the Union navy, Banks' army crossed the Atchafalaya River. Without boats or pontoons the Confederates could not continue the pursuit.

Both Confederates and Federals were exhausted from the strenuous campaigning. There was little fighting in Louisiana during the hot, humid summer months. The Confederates established patrols along the Atchafalaya from Simmesport to Morgan's Ferry. During late summer and early autumn, the First, Thirty-fourth, and Thirty-fifth Texas regiments, now in a brigade commanded by A. W. Terrell, helped patrol the region. In mid-September Federal forces at Morganza moved against Terrell's Brigade, first in a probing action on the 17th and then in a major attack on the 20th. Heavily outnumbered, Terrell fell back toward Simmesport. In December the brigade went into winter quarters at Alexandria.[86]

Debray's Brigade, consisting of the Twenty-sixth Texas commanded by Lt. Col. John J. Myers, Nicholas Gould's Twenty-third Texas, and Peter Woods' Thirty-sixth Texas, spent the summer in western Louisiana. After engagements at Opelousas, Natchitoches, and Alexandria, the brigade took its turn patrolling the Atchafalaya. "There," according to Debray, "bad rations, scanty forage, malarial fevers and camp diseases, the absence of medical stores, and worn out clothing and blankets caused much suffering and misery, nearly destroying the efficiency of the brigade."[87]

At the end of November, Debray's Brigade was ordered back to Texas. The brigade traveled through San Augustine, Carthage, and Crockett by slow march so that their horses could find forage. By the end of March 1865 the brigade reached Pittsville, near Richmond on the Brazos River. Although many Texas cavalry regiments were dismounted in the closing days of the war, Debray's Brigade retained its horses. Gould's Twenty-third Regiment was dismounted and transferred, however, to Sam Maxey's Infantry Division.[88]

Terrell's Brigade remained in Louisiana during the winter of 1864-1865. James Likens' Thirty-fifth Texas, which was returned to Texas as dismounted cavalry, was replaced by the Seventh Texas

Cavalry. The brigade did not return to Texas until late April. The First Texas, the first Lone Star unit in Confederate service, disbanded on April 30 at Wildcat Bluff on the Trinity River. Terrell's Thirty-fourth Regiment was camped at the same site as the First Cavalry but did not disband until May 14, 1865, when Lieutenant Colonel Robertson sent the men home. Terrell himself had remained behind at Marshall to attend a conference of military and political leaders. When he arrived at Wildcat Bluff on the 15th, he found his regiment gone.[89]

Debray's and Woods' regiments were ordered in early May to Houston, where Generals Magruder and Smith hoped to mount a strong defensive force. James Likens' Thirty-fifth Texas was in Galveston at the same time. When it became apparent the war had ended, these regiments were also disbanded and the men returned home.[90]

JAMES P. MAJOR'S BRIGADE

First Texas Cavalry, Partisan Rangers
Second Texas Cavalry, Partisan Rangers
Second Texas Cavalry, Arizona Brigade
Third Texas Cavalry, Arizona Brigade

A Texas cavalry brigade consisting of two Partisan Ranger regiments and two Arizona brigade regiments fought alongside the Sibley and Bee brigades in the 1864 Louisiana campaigns. The brigade was commanded by Brig. Gen. James P. Major, a native of Missouri and graduate of West Point. Major served with the U.S. Second Cavalry in Texas in the late 1850s and married a sister-in-law of Tom Green. When the Civil War began, Major resigned from the American army and accepted a commission in Confederate service. He served briefly on Van Dorn's staff in Texas before joining fellow Missourians under Sterling Price. He commanded a Missouri battalion in the battle at Wilson's Creek, gaining praise for his action. After the battle he rejoined Van Dorn's staff and served as chief engineer in planning the Vicksburg defenses. A close friend of Van Dorn, Major testified in defense of his commander in the court of inquiry held after the Corinth campaign.[91]

Major was transferred to the Trans Mississippi Department in early 1863. After temporary duty at Niblett's Bluff collecting stragglers and deserters, he was assigned command of a newly formed brigade of Texas cavalry under Richard Taylor in Louisiana. The brigade consisted of the First Texas Partisan Rangers commanded by Walter P. Lane, the Second Texas Partisan Rangers led by Barton W. Stone, the Second Texas Cavalry Regiment, Arizona Brigade, commanded by George W. Baylor, and the Third Texas Cavalry Regiment, Arizona Brigade, headed by George T. Madison.[92]

The regiments that made up the brigade were initially formed as Partisan Rangers. Such units were designed primarily for raiding and scouting and operated more or less independently, often near Federal lines. In his classic study of the Confederate soldier, *The Life of Johnny Reb*, Bell Wiley noted that such outfits were notorious for theft and destruction, so much so that the Confederate War Department eventually did away with such designations. In most cases the units continued to refer to themselves as "Partisan Rangers" or "Partisan Scouts," but they were considered regular cavalry by Confederate authorities.[93]

The First Texas Partisan Rangers, the first fully organized regiment in Major's Brigade, were led by Walter Paye Lane, who served earlier as an officer in the Third Texas Cavalry. A native of Ireland, Lane came to America with his parents as a lad. He fought in the Battle of San Jacinto while still in his teens and later served as a Texas Ranger and an officer in the Mexican War. After participating in mining activities in California, Nevada, Arizona, and Peru, he returned to Marshall, Texas, to operate a mercantile business. When the Civil War began, Lane was elected lieutenant colonel of the Third Texas Cavalry. Historian Douglas Hale described Lane "as a colorful fellow, full of blarney and bombast," but noted that Lane's "courage and resourcefulness under fire would vindicate his own high regard for himself."[94]

Lane was with the Third Texas in the battles at Wilson's Creek and Pea Ridge. He distinguished himself while leading the Third Texas in a battle at Farmington, Mississippi, in May 1862, but when the regiment was dismounted Lane returned to Texas to organize a mounted regiment.[95]

Recruiting for Lane's new regiment, advertised as a Partisan Ranger corps, took place during the summer of 1862. The regiment was officially organized in October and assigned duty in Arkansas. Lane was chosen colonel and R. Phillip Crump of Jefferson, who had commanded a cavalry battalion at Pea Ridge and Corinth, was elected lieutenant colonel. A. D. Burns of Marshall and William P. Saufley of Jefferson were majors in the regiment.[96]

The structure of the First Partisan Rangers was slightly different from the typical regiment. Instead of the customary ten companies, each with one hundred men, Lane's Rangers had fourteen companies, each with fifty to sixty recruits. The majority of volunteers came from Harrison, San Augustine, Marion, Upshur, Cass, Cherokee, and Rusk counties. More than 60 percent of the Rangers were married and most had children. There were few slaveholders in the regiment, but one volunteer, Royal Francis Lockett, owned fifty-five slaves and was accompanied by a servant.[97]

Lane's Rangers left for duty in Arkansas in November 1862. Many of the men were poorly clothed and suffered from the cold weather. Illness was common. Lane himself contracted a fever and returned to Marshall to recuperate. The regiment continued on to Arkansas under Lieutenant Colonel Crump. Under his command the Rangers fought in the battle at Prairie Grove on December 7, 1862. Although the Rangers performed well in driving the enemy back, Confederate commander Maj. Gen. Thomas Hindman, realizing he was low on ammunition and outnumbered, withdrew from the field under the cover of darkness.[98]

After the battle at Prairie Grove, the Rangers, supported by two Arkansas companies, were assigned to capturing pro-Union guerrillas, including the notorious Martin D. Hart.[99] Soon thereafter the Rangers, defending an advanced Confederate outpost north of Van Buren, Arkansas, were overwhelmed by a larger Union force commanded by Brig. Gen. James Blunt. The Texans were routed, leading many of them to leave their command and head for home. Brig. Gen. William Steele, newly arrived Confederate commander for Indian Territory, ordered the Texans to regroup in Indian Territory on the Red River, but Lieutenant Colonel Crump and what was left of the regiment continued on to Jefferson, Texas. There they were joined by Colonel Lane, who attempted to reassemble and reequip his shattered command. Some troops returned to duty; others did not. In his history of the brigade James T. Matthews pointed out that Lane's Regiment "never numbered much more than 300 men for the remainder of the war."[100]

In April and May 1863, General Steele wrote plaintively to Lane, urging him to return with his regiment to Indian Territory. Lane, who blamed Hindman for many of the difficulties the regiment encountered in Arkansas, had no desire to return to that area. He sought and secured transfer of the regiment to Louisiana, where in the summer of 1863 the Rangers were assigned to the newly formed brigade commanded by James P. Major.[101]

The Second Partisan Rangers, also assigned to Major's Brigade, were organized a few months later than Lane's Regiment. The Second Regiment was formed by Col. Barton Warren Stone, the Dallas lawyer who had earlier commanded the Sixth Texas Cavalry in Arkansas. Stone's two senior officers, Lt. Col. Isham Chisum of Kaufman County and Maj. James W. Throckmorton of Collin County, also had previous Civil War experience. Chisum had been a company commander in the Third Texas Cavalry in Missouri and Arkansas, while Throckmorton held a similar position in Stone's Sixth Texas Cavalry.[102]

The men of the Second Partisan Rangers were recruited from a cluster of counties around Dallas and the four-county area of Hopkins, Titus, Wood, and Upshur. Made up largely of farmers and ranchers, the regiment consisted of ten companies, each with approximately sixty volunteers. Like the men in Lane's Regiment, the majority of Texans in Stone's Regiment were married with families.[103]

The Second Rangers were mustered into service in November 1862 but spent the winter months in the Dallas area. In March 1863 the regiment moved into camp, first at Columbus and then later on the San Bernard River. Soon thereafter the Rangers were ordered to report to Arkansas, but new orders on April 24 assigned the regiment to Richard Taylor's army in Louisiana.[104]

While at Camp Bernard, Stone's Rangers were biouvacked with two regiments of what was known as the Arizona Brigade. These regiments evolved from the Confederate attempts to control the southwestern territories of New Mexico and Arizona. After the failure of the Sibley New Mexico expedition in early 1862, John R. Baylor, who had served briefly as governor of the Confederate Territory of Arizona, received permission to raise several battalions of Partisan Rangers for the purpose of regaining control of the area. With this authority Baylor established a recruiting camp at Columbus, Texas, for what he called his Arizona Brigade.[105]

Baylor was busy recruiting and organizing the units of his new brigade during late summer and autumn 1862. Although the response to his call for volunteers was less than he had hoped, he began forming battalions from the small companies of enrolled recruits and named his brother George Wythe Baylor, Peter Hardeman, and George T. Madison as battalion commanders. Before organization of the brigade was complete, however, Baylor was removed from command as a result of statements which seemed to support a war of extermination against the Apaches.

The removal of John R. Baylor left Texas district commander John B. Magruder the task of completing organization of the brigade. On February 21, 1863, Magruder ordered that three regiments be formed from the small, incomplete battalions. He authorized Spruce M. Baird, the leading Confederate sympathizer in New Mexico, to organize a fourth regiment from among New Mexico-Arizona residents.[106]

The First Regiment of the Arizona Brigade, commanded by Col. Peter Hardeman, who had served with John R. Baylor in the Second Texas Mounted Rifles, was ordered to North Texas to assist in the defense of that area. Hardeman's Regiment was later assigned to Richard Gano's Brigade and will be described more fully as a part of that brigade later in this chapter.

The Second and Third regiments of the so-called Arizona Brigade, both of which were later assigned to Major's Brigade, were ordered to Camp Bernard, where they would complete their organization.[107]

The Second Regiment, commanded by George W. Baylor, was made up primarily of recruits from Bexar, Harris, and Central Texas counties. Joining Baylor as regimental officers were Lt. Col. John W. Mullen, a Mexican War veteran from Williamson County, and Maj. Sherod Hunter, a Tennessean who had previous experience as an officer in New Mexico and Arizona.[108]

Members of the Third Regiment came largely from Harris, Brazoria, and Galveston counties and a line of Central Texas counties stretching from Grimes and Madison to San Saba. Joseph Phillips, a Virginian who had served on Magruder's staff, was named colonel of the regiment. George T. Madison, a Mexican War veteran and former Tucson deputy sheriff, was lieutenant colonel. Alonzo Ridley, former Indian agent and peace officer in Los Angeles, was appointed major. Both Madison and Ridley had previous service in scout companies: Madison in the New Mexico campaign and Ridley in the Shiloh campaign.[109]

The Second and Third regiments, Arizona Brigade, received orders in mid-April 1863 to report for service in Arkansas at the same time Barton W. Stone's Rangers received similar instructions. The three regiments began their march north but in late April were redirected to Richard Taylor's army. Once in Louisiana they joined Lane's Partisan Rangers in making up the brigade commanded by James P. Major.[110]

Major's Brigade joined Taylor near Alexandria. The brigade accompanied Taylor as he moved southward in his offensive aimed at relieving Union pressure on Port Hudson. In mid-June 1863 the brigade conducted a series of raids along Bayou Teche and Bayou Lafourche. On June 18 Joseph Phillips and his Third Cavalry, Arizona Brigade, captured 87 Federals, burned five steamboats, and destroyed 100 bales of cotton at Plaquemine on the Mississippi. Several days later Maj. Sherod Hunter of the Second Regiment led 300 volunteers from Major's and Green's brigades in a daring night attack upon Brashear City by means of flatboats. Approaching the town from the rear by water, Hunter took the Federals by surprise. After a brief skirmish, the enemy surrendered, turning over 1,000 prisoners, dozens of heavy cannon, thousands of small arms, and vast quantities of supplies to the Confederates. Two days later, Major's horsemen captured another Union outpost on Bayou Boeuf, adding another 275 Union troops, 3,000 slaves, four cannon, and various small arms and stores to their bounty. Joining Tom Green's Cavalry Brigade, which was nearby, Major's cavalrymen occupied the town of Thibodaux the following day.[111]

On June 26 Tom Green received orders to bring his own brigade and Major's Brigade to Donaldsonville, where they were to attack Fort Butler, an earthwork just above the town where Bayou Lafourche joins the Mississippi. As noted earlier in the chapter, the assault on Fort Butler was a failure due to poor coordination and communication among the Confederates and the unexpected firepower of the enemy's guns both from the fort and boats on the river. In the attack, made on the evening of June 27, Stone's Second Partisan Rangers made a diversionary raid on the town of Donaldsonville to take attention from the main efforts by other regiments from Major's and Green's brigades against the fort itself. Unfortunately for the Confederates neither Lane's First Partisan Rangers nor William P. Hardeman's Fourth Texas Cavalry (Green's Brigade) participated in the attack. Lane never received the promised guide to lead him to the battle site in the darkness, and Hardeman's guide failed to get his regiment to the fort in time to take part in the initial assault. The Texas regiments that did make the attack, the Fifth and Seventh Cavalry from Green's Brigade and Phillips' Third Texas, Arizona Brigade, encountered heavy enemy fire from the fort and three Union gunboats on the river. Colonel Phillips was mortally wounded while attempting to rally his men. Colonel Major and Lieutenant Colonel Madison were wounded, and Maj. Alonzo Ridley and several other officers from the two Texas brigades were captured.[112]

At dawn on June 28 the Confederate effort to take Fort Butler came to an end as Green pulled his battered command away. Losses for the Confederates were high: twenty-eight killed, sixty wounded, and over one hundred missing.[113]

During the next several weeks Major's Brigade, temporarily commanded by W. P. Lane while Major recovered from his wounds, operated along the Mississippi south of Donaldsonville. Here the brigade established artillery batteries which maintained fire upon enemy shipping on the river. In late July the brigade took part in an encounter with Union cavalry at Cox's plantation, approximately six miles below Fort Butler. In this engagement Tom Green's cavalry routed Union forces on the east side of Bayou Lafourche, while Major and 400 of his troops drove Union troops from the field on the west side of the bayou. Even so, increased Union numbers forced the Confederates to withdraw from the Lafourche region and fall back to Bayou Teche.[114]

A lull in Louisiana operations in late August led Kirby Smith, commander of the Trans Mississippi Department, to order Major and his brigade to North Texas. Before the order could be carried out, however, a new Federal offensive up Bayou Teche resulted in the brigade remaining with Taylor's army.[115]

During autumn of 1863, Major's Brigade played an active part in the Confederate efforts to stop the Union advance toward Opelousas. In September Major's Texans supported Tom Green's successful attack on Union troops at Stirling's plantation on Bayou Fordoche. In this affair the brigade served as the Confederate reserve and as a buffer against Union troops attempting to cross the Atchafalaya River. In November the brigade was on the Confederate right in the attack on Union troops at Bayou Bourbeau. In the fighting Major's troops pushed back the Federal left flank in what Tom Green called "the most brilliant charge on record."[116]

The battle at Bayou Bourbeau was the last major action for Major's Brigade in 1863. In December both Green's and Major's troops were ordered back to Texas to meet a threatened Union invasion. Major's cavalrymen spent late December and early January camped near Houston. On January 21 Major received orders to move the brigade to Virginia Point. The brigade spent the next two months there. Except for scouting and patrolling, there were few military duties to perform. Some new recruits joined the brigade and several staffing changes were made. Isham Chisum was elevated to the rank of colonel in command of the Second Partisan Rangers, replacing Barton W. Stone, who went home due to poor health. George T. Madison, recovered from wounds received at Fort Butler, replaced the deceased Joseph Phillips as commander of the Third Regiment, Arizona Brigade. In late February, Colonel Major received his promotion to brigadier general, with effective date of rank July 21, 1863.[117]

In March 1864 Major's Brigade was ordered to return to Louisiana to join Richard Taylor's army in its efforts to stop Nathaniel P. Banks' move into northern Louisiana. The brigade reached Mansfield on April 5. Major and his horsemen were sent on to Pleasant Hill, where they skirmished with enemy cavalry before falling back to Mansfield. In preparations for the impending battle, Taylor appointed Tom Green commander of his cavalry corps and gave Major command of what had been Green's Division.[118]

Major's Division, consisting of his old brigade, now commanded by W. P. Lane, A. P. Bagby's Brigade (the old Sibley Brigade), and William G. Vincent's Louisiana Cavalry Brigade, was posted on the Confederate left in the Battle of Mansfield. Fighting dismounted, Major's cavalrymen moved alongside Mouton's

Infantry Division in the assault on the enemy. While leading his troops across the open field, W. P. Lane was shot through the thigh and George W. Baylor assumed command of the brigade.[119]

In the battle at Pleasant Hill the next day, Major's Division was again on the Confederate left. Heavy enemy fire forced the Texans to dismount and continue their assault on foot. In the confused fighting some members of the brigade on the extreme left fired upon their own troops. The Union lines held firm, and a counterattack against the Confederate right drove the Rebels back. As dusk fell, the fighting came to an end.[120]

During the next several weeks Major's Brigade, commanded by George W. Baylor while Lane recovered from his wounds, rode with other Confederate cavalry as they continued to attack Banks' retreating army. At Monett's Ferry on April 23 the brigade, on the left wing of Hamilton P. Bee's combined cavalry brigades, received the brunt of the enemy assault when the Federals attempted to outflank Bee's command. When Baylor called for reinforcements to counter the heavy enemy numbers, he was advised by General Bee to withdraw as best he could.[121]

After the withdrawal from Monett's Ferry, Major's Brigade cooperated with other Confederates as they harassed the Union army and navy. On April 28, Baylor's troops joined with W. P. Hardeman's Brigade in a successful attack at Bayou Rapides. The brigade shelled the

W. P. Lane, Colonel, First Partisan Rangers, later brigade commander.
—Courtesy Harold B. Simpson Research Center, Hillsboro, Texas

enemy transport *City Belle* on May 3 and captured more than 200 enemy troops who had jumped overboard.

The brigade took part in the unsuccessful Confederate attack at Yellow Bayou on May 18. In this last effort to prevent the Union army from crossing the Atchafalaya, Baylor's troops were on the left side of the Confederate attack line between Rebel cavalry led by William P. Hardeman and Arthur P. Bagby. Although the initial Confederate attack drove the enemy back, Union artillery and infantry stopped the advance and forced the attackers back with heavy losses.[122]

The Battle of Yellow Bayou brought an end to the Red River campaign. Major's Brigade, which took part in all the principal engagements, had 34 men killed, 144 wounded, and 55 missing, or a total of 233 casualties, approximately one-fifth of brigade strength.[123]

After the Battle of Yellow Bayou there was relative calm in Louisiana during the summer of 1864. After Banks retreated across the Atchafalaya, the Confederates maintained patrols along the river to ensure that the Federals did not resume their efforts in northwestern Louisiana. In August, Major's Brigade, now known as Lane's Brigade, moved northeast to block Union movements along the Black and Tensas rivers. The following month the brigade was ordered to Arkansas.[124]

Lane's Brigade joined John B. Magruder's forces in Arkansas in the second week of September. For the next three months the brigade operated in the Monticello region, occasionally skirmishing with the enemy. Illness and bad weather took a toll on the troops during the late fall and early winter. An engagement between the Second Partisan Rangers, now led by Lt. Col. Crill Miller, and Union troops at Hurricane Creek, near Benton, Arkansas, on October 23, 1864, was the last battle fought by regiments of the brigade.[125]

The brigade returned to Texas in December 1864. In February, reorganization of the Trans Mississippi Department led to the dissolution of the old brigade. Facing severe shortages of all types and needing additional infantry, Kirby Smith ordered cavalry corps commander John A. Wharton to dismount nine cavalry regiments. Among those dismounted were Crill Miller's Second Partisan Rangers and George W. Baylor's Second Cavalry, Arizona Brigade. The other two regiments in the brigade, Phillip Crump's First Partisan Rangers and George T. Madison's Third Cavalry, were assigned to mounted brigades commanded by W. P. Lane and William P. Hardeman.[126]

The news that they were to be dismounted did not set well with the men of the Second Rangers and Second Texas, Arizona Brigade. George W. Baylor, commander of the Second Texas, was particularly incensed when he learned that his regiment was to report to Col. David S. Terry, an officer less experienced than he. Already diasppointed that he had not been appointed brigadier general, Baylor blamed cavalry commander John A. Wharton. He traveled to Houston to discuss the matter with Wharton. There the two men had a bitter exchange of words that led to a scuffle in which Baylor shot and killed Wharton.

Baylor was arrested and taken to jail. Before he could be tried by military court, the war ended. He was eventually tried by civil court and acquitted.[127]

Baylor's old regiment and the other three regiments that made up Major's Brigade spent the last months of the war in Texas. They were disbanded in late May 1865 and the men mustered out of service. A few of the veterans refused to admit defeat and crossed into Mexico, but the majority returned home. Losses in the brigade had been heavy. James T. Matthews, who wrote a thorough history of the brigade, estimated that the four regiments had 109 men killed, 307 wounded, and 192 missing, or approximately 30 percent of those who served in the brigade.[128]

WILLIAM H. PARSONS' BRIGADE

Twelfth Texas Cavalry
Nineteenth Texas Cavalry
Twenty-first Texas Cavalry
Morgan's Cavalry Battalion

A fourth Texas cavalry brigade participated in the Red River campaign. This brigade, commanded by William H. Parsons (and frequently George W. Carter), consisted of the Twelfth, Nineteenth, and Twenty-first Cavalry regiments and Charles L. Morgan's Cavalry Battalion. Although the brigade did not reach Richard Taylor's army in time to take part in the battles at

Mansfield and Pleasant Hill, Parsons' horsemen played a significant role in the latter stages of the Red River campaign.

William H. Parsons, commander of the brigade for much of the war, was a native of New Jersey who settled in Texas after service in the Mexican War. He became owner and editor of two Texas newspapers, first the *Tyler Telegraph* and later the *Waco South West*. When the Civil War began, Parsons was authorized by Governor Edward Clark to raise a regiment of mounted troops. First known as the Fourth Texas Mounted Dragoons, Parsons' Regiment was mustered into Confederate service as the Twelfth Texas Cavalry.[129]

Most of the men in the Twelfth Texas were recruited in North Texas, but two companies came from Bastrop, Travis, and Williamson counties of Central Texas. In addition to Parsons, who held the rank of colonel, other field-grade officers in the regiment were Lt. Col. John W. Mullen of Williamson County and Maj. Emory W. Rogers, hotel proprietor from Ellis County. Mullen remained with the regiment only until June 1862, when he returned home. As noted earlier, he later served as lieutenant colonel of the Second Cavalry, Arizona Brigade. Andrew Bell Burleson, nephew of famed Texas Ranger and Vice President of the Republic Edward Burleson, was chosen to succeed Mullen as lieutenant colonel in Parsons' Regiment.[130]

After organizing at Camp Beauregard near Waxahachie, Parsons' Regiment marched to Hempstead, where the unit was officially mustered into Confederate service in October 1861. The recruits remained there longer than a month, learning the rudiments of military life. In late November the regiment was ordered to Houston in anticipation of a Union threat to the Galveston-Houston area. The men made their camp on Sims Bayou, about eight miles south of Houston, and spent the winter of 1861-1862 in this locale.[131]

In late February, Parsons received orders to move his regiment to Arkansas. The regiment was scheduled to join Earl Van Dorn's army in northwestern Arkansas, but en route Parsons received conflicting orders—first directing him to Little Rock, then to Memphis, and finally back to Little Rock. In mid-May most of the regiment reached the Arkansas capital, although Parsons and two companies went to Memphis and did not join the regiment until later in the month.[132]

Before Parsons rejoined his regiment, Major Rogers and 400 men of the Twelfth Texas defeated a Union foraging party at Whitney's Lane near Searcy, Arkansas. This was the first of a series of clashes in which the regiment was involved as Union general Samuel R. Curtis attempted to move down the White and Cache rivers. In July the Twelfth Texas and other Confederates under the command of Brig. Gen. Albert Rust took part in an unsuccessful attack against the enemy at Cotton Plant, Arkansas. Later that summer Parsons avenged this defeat in a brilliant raid on a Union encampment near the L'Anguille River in eastern Arkansas. Driving the Federals from their camp, Parsons' men seized a dozen enemy wagons and captured or burned property valued at half a million dollars. The success of the raid not only enhanced Parsons' reputation but also helped restore sagging Confederate morale in Arkansas.[133]

In autumn 1862 Parsons was given command of a cavalry brigade that included his own Twelfth Texas, the Twenty-first Texas Cavalry, the Nineteenth Texas Cavalry, and independent companies commanded by Charles Morgan. The brigade was assigned to Allison Nelson's Second Division of the Army of the West, commanded by Thomas Hindman.[134]

Almost immediately there was controversy over Parsons' appointment as brigade commander. Col. George W. Carter, commander of the Twenty-first Texas, believed his commission gave him seniority over Parsons. As noted in the previous chapter, Carter, a Methodist minister and president of Soule University at Chappell Hill, Texas, had recruited three regiments known originally as the First, Second, and Third Texas Lancers. When it became apparent that the idea of equipping the men with lances was not practical, these became the Twenty-first, Twenty-fourth, and Twenty-fifth Texas cavalries. Carter became commander of the Twenty-first Texas, with DeWitt Clinton Giddings, a Brenham lawyer, as lieutenant colonel, and Benjamin D. Chenoweth, major.[135]

The three regiments formed by Carter were ordered to Arkansas in May 1862. When they arrived at Pine Bluff the Twenty-fourth and Twenty-fifth were dismounted and assigned to an infantry brigade. To avoid the possibility of the Twenty-first also being dismounted, Lieutenant Colonel Giddings, in command while Colonel Carter was absent, requested that the regiment be joined with a cavalry brigade commanded by Parsons. After this occurred, Carter argued that he, not Parsons, should command the brigade as his commission to recruit a regiment pre-dated that of Parsons. Carter appealed to Richmond for recognition of his claim, but the issue was not settled for two years. In the meanwhile Parsons commanded the brigade.[136]

The Nineteenth Texas, which joined Parsons' Twelfth and Carter's Twenty-first cavalries in the brigade, was led by Col. Nathaniel Macon Burford, a Dallas judge and law partner of John H. Reagan. Burford originally enlisted as a private in Good's Texas Artillery, but in early 1862 he received a commission to raise a mounted regiment in Dallas, Ellis, Kaufman, Hill, Navarro, Parker, and McLennan counties. Benjamin W. Watson of Ellis County was chosen lieutenant colonel and Joel T. Davis, a young Methodist minister, was elected major. Davis soon resigned his commission and was replaced by John B. Williams, a highly respected Hillsboro merchant.[137]

For a brief time an Arkansas cavalry battalion commanded by Francis M. Chrisman was assigned to Parsons' Brigade. This battalion was later replaced by companies led by Maj. Charles Morgan, a former member of Terry's Texas Rangers. Morgan's cavalry began as a squadron, increased to a battalion of three companies by March 1863, added several companies during 1864, and was at regimental strength by March 1865. In her history of the brigade, Anne Bailey pointed out that "Morgan's command was a hodgepodge of companies under him in name only, and the men displayed a stronger loyalty to their particular companies than to the regiment." She noted also that the companies were recruited from all over the state, never displayed unit pride, and seldom fought together.[138]

The new brigade spent the autumn months of 1862 carrying out patrol duties in eastern Arkansas. Occasionally, the Texans clashed with Union troops conducting patrols from Helena, Arkansas. In some instances the Texans killed or captured enemy troops; at other times the Federals had the upper hand. On one such occasion Lieutenant Colonel Giddings and a small patrol from the Twenty-first Texas were captured. Giddings and his men spent two months as prisoners before an exchange for their release was arranged.[139]

Parsons' first tenure as brigade commander was brief. In December 1862 he was replaced as brigade commander by Brig. Gen. James M. Hawes, a West Point graduate and former U.S. Regular Army officer from Kentucky. Hawes had only recently been transferred to the Trans Mississippi Department. Theophilus Holmes, Confederate commander of the Department, believed the appointment of the Kentuckian, who had previously commanded cavalry in the Army of the Mississippi, would bring needed experience and discipline to the brigade. Although some members of the brigade found Hawes acceptable as commander, the majority of Texans wanted the popular Parsons returned as brigade commander. Several of the officers petitioned Holmes to allow them to return to Texas, where Parsons was visiting relatives, but the request was denied. A new threat to Arkansas Post led Holmes to order all available units there.[140]

The order to the brigade came too late. By the time Parsons' Brigade (now Hawes') reached the Arkansas River, the Confederates at Arkansas Post had surrendered. The Texans remained in the area for the rest of the winter, monitoring Union troop movements along the Mississippi.

Another change in brigade leadership took place in late January 1863. Brigadier General Hawes, in poor health, resigned as commander. Colonel Carter assumed brigade command until Parsons returned from Texas.[141]

When Parsons returned, he found himself without much of his brigade. In March, General Holmes detached the Nineteenth and Twenty-first cavalries and Morgan's Battalion for service under Brig. Gen. John S. Marmaduke in a massive cavalry raid into Missouri. The units from Parsons' Brigade assigned to Marmaduke were brigaded together under Parsons' old rival, George W. Carter.

Marmaduke was assigned approximately 5,000 horsemen for the raid. This was Marmaduke's second such venture, his first raid taking place in January 1863. Marmaduke hoped the raiders could drive deep into Missouri, giving encouragement to the pro-Confederate elements in the state and at the same time relieving pressure upon Arkansas, Louisiana, and Mississippi. Initially he planned to strike toward Rolla in central Missouri, but scarcity of forage in the region casued him to move into southeastern Missouri instead. Under the plan of operations, Marmaduke divided his command: one column under Missourian Jo Shelby would move through Van Buren, Missouri, and a second column under George W. Carter would move through Doniphan, several miles to the south.[142]

The opening stages of Marmaduke's raid went fairly well, but heavy rain, flooded rivers and streams, and poor coordination between the various Confederate units impeded the operation. The Confederates reached the Mississippi but withdrew after failing to capture Cape Giradeau. By early May the weary raiders were back in Arkansas. Many of the men were convinced the raid accomplished its purpose, but historian Stephen B. Oates believed that in strategic terms the Missouri raid "was a complete failure." The Federal supply depot at Cape Giradeau had not been taken, Union armies were advancing on all fronts, and pro-Confederate elements in the state received little encouragement.[143]

While Colonel Carter and two-thirds of Parsons' Brigade rode with Marmaduke into Missouri, Parsons and the Twelfth Texas remained in the Little Rock area. When the Missouri raid was over, Carter and his men did not immediately rejoin Parsons but remained in eastern Arkansas, where they patrolled the St. Francis and L'Anguille rivers.

In June 1863 Parsons and the Twelfth Texas were ordered to join John G. Walker and his infantry division in operations against the enemy near Lake Providence and Milliken's Bend in the northeastern corner of Louisiana. It was hoped that their activities might relieve pressure being placed upon Vicksburg by Grant's army. The Nineteenth Texas Cavalry and a section of artillery were ordered to join Parsons, but Carter's Twenty-first Texas and Morgan's cavalry companies remained in Arkansas.

During late June and early July, Parsons and his Texas cavalrymen did their part in the Confederate effort to save Vicksburg. In what came to be known as "Parsons' Cavalry Raid," the Texans swept through the region between Milliken's Bend and Lake Providence, forcing the surrender of a fortified Union outpost, driving the enemy out of the village of Lake Providence, and capturing more than 1,000 slaves who were working for the Federals. Even so, efforts for relieving Vicksburg were unsuccessful. The city was surrendered to the enemy on July 4.[144]

Parsons and the Twelfth and Nineteenth cavalries remained in Louisiana throughout the summer and early autumn of 1863, carrying out patrols in the Monroe area. The rest of the brigade was in Arkansas performing picket duty along the lower Arkansas River. Morgan's cavalry and sections of Joseph Pratt's artillery (assigned to Parsons' Brigade) were in the Battle of Little Rock in early September. Both these units and the Twenty-first Cavalry took part in Marmaduke's unsuccessful attempt to recapture Pine Bluff in October.[145]

Most of the brigade was reunited in November 1863, when Parsons and his troops from Louisiana (with the exception of Burleson and five companies of the Twelfth Texas, who were on duty rounding up deserters in North Texas) rejoined the Twenty-first Texas and Morgan's Cavalry at Camden, Arkansas. For the next several weeks there was limited military activity as both Union and Confederate armies sought some relief from the extremely cold weather. This calm was broken in late December, when General Holmes attempted to place Brig. Gen. Thomas J. Churchill in command of the brigade. While the Texans of the Nineteenth and Twenty-first regiments seemed willing to accept the Arkansan as commander, the men of Parsons' own Twelfth Texas were not. Their protests led to Churchill's transfer to an Arkansas division.[146]

Shortages of forage in Arkansas and the threat of a Union invasion of the upper Texas coast led Confederate authorites to return most of Parsons' cavalry to Texas in early 1864. The men welcomed the opportunity to see relatives and visit friends, but their stay in Texas was brief; in March, Parsons was ordered to return his brigade to Louisiana. Banks' movement into northern Louisiana was under way, and Richard Taylor needed all the horsemen available.[147]

Although Parsons gathered his scattered troops together as quickly as he could, his brigade did not reach Taylor in time to take part in the battles at Mansfield and Pleasant Hill. The brigade arrived shortly after the battle at Pleasant Hill and rode with Tom Green toward Blair's Landing, where the Texans attempted to keep the Union fleet from escaping. Green placed Parsons in command of the attack on the Union transports and gunboats. In the opening attack the Confederates, most of whom were fighting dismounted, had the upper hand; however, the firepower of the Federal gunboats eventually forced the Texans to seek cover. In one of the final salvos Tom Green, who was observing the firing from an exposed position, was killed. As darkness fell, Parsons ordered his men to back away from the river. The Union fleet then continued on down the river toward Alexandria.[148]

For the next month Parsons' Cavalry was constantly on the move as the Confederates harassed Banks' retreating army. Brig. Gen. William Steele, a veteran professional soldier who had joined Taylor's army, was given command of a cavalry division consisting of Parsons' Brigade and a Louisiana cavalry brigade. The Louisiana brigade assigned to him never reported, however, so his command consisted only of Parsons' Brigade. Parsons himself was ill in early May, leaving direction of the brigade to Colonel Carter on several occasions.[149]

Fighting between the Confederates and Banks' army went on almost every day in late April and early May. At the Battle of Yellow Bayou, Parsons' Brigade was divided. Colonel Parsons and the Twelfth Texas Cavalry were on the Confederate extreme left flank while General Steele and the Nineteenth Texas, the Twenty-first Texas, and Morgan's Battalion were on the extreme right.[150]

After some skirmishing in the morning, Maj. Gen. John A. Wharton, commanding the Confederate forces, ordered Parsons to charge the Union troops on the left. Parsons, who had reconnoitered the Federal position, advised Wharton such an attack would result in heavy losses, but Wharton insisted his orders be carried out. With that admonition Parsons led his dismounted troops forward. The result was much as Parsons feared. After an initial advance, Parsons' men were forced to withdraw under heavy enemy fire that resulted in many casualties. Meanwhile, other Confederate brigades, including those from Polignac's Infantry Division, entered the attack but with similar results. Fighting went on throughout the afternoon, but as dusk fell the Confederates retreated from the scene.[151]

The battle at Yellow Bayou was costly to the Confederates, who reported more than 600 casualties. Parsons' Brigade suffered its heaviest losses of the war: eighty-one men killed, wounded, and captured. Seventy-three of the casualties were in the Twelfth Texas Cavalry.[152]

Yellow Bayou was the last major battle fought by Parsons' Brigade. The Texans remained in Louisiana for most of the summer, patrolling the region between the Red and Mississippi rivers. In June the brigade headed back to Texas, under orders to report to

General Magruder. But just after Parsons' troops crossed the Sabine, the order was countermanded and the Texans returned to Louisiana.[153]

In September 1864 the brigade was ordered to southeastern Arkansas. Sterling Price had taken most of the cavalry in the state in a sweeping raid into Missouri. Additional troops were needed to maintain Confederate control of southern Arkansas while Price was gone. General Steele was now listed as brigade commander. Parsons resumed direct command of the Twelfth Texas. Nat Burford had returned home because of poor health, leaving command of the Nineteenth Texas in the hands of Lt. Col. Benjamin W. Watson. Col. George W. Carter, also in poor health, was in Texas; his regiment, the Twenty-first Texas, was led by Lt. Col. DeWitt Giddings.[154]

The brigade spent the autumn of 1864 patrolling the Arkansas, Saline, Ouachita, and Mississippi rivers. Shortage of forage for the horses became an increasingly serious matter, requiring the brigade to move almost constantly. To alleviate this problem as well as to move more troops to a centralized location, Kirby Smith, the Trans Mississippi departmental commander, ordered several cavalry regiments including Parsons' Brigade back to Texas. At the same time he ordered General Wharton, commanding the department's cavalry corps, to dismount nine regiments for infantry duty. Those regiments keeping their mounts would be formed into two cavalry divisions commanded by Hamilton P. Bee and William Steele.[155]

Parsons' troops were pleased that their regiments were among those allowed to retain their horses. In the first suggested reorganization, Steele would command not only the division but also the brigade in which Parsons' regiments were assigned. This was soon modified to allow Parsons to command a brigade consisting of his old Twelfth Texas, Ben Watson's Nineteenth Texas, and Morgan's Cavalry (which was now at regimental size in numbers of companies). Edward Gurley's Thirtieth Texas Cavalry, previously in Richard Gano's Brigade, joined Parsons' Brigade, replacing the Twenty-first Texas, which was assigned to a brigade commanded by Walter P. Lane.[156]

Parsons' Brigade spent the last three months of the war in Grimes County camped near the Brazos River. Although there was no military action, Colonel Parsons continued to drill the men several hours a day. It became increasingly obvious, however, that the end of the war was near. The brigade was at Hempstead when news of Lee's surrender at Appomattox was received. Many of Parsons' veterans still seemed determined to carry on the struggle, but others began drifting home. In late May, Parsons addressed his men for the last time, declaring the brigade disbanded. He also expressed his intention to immigrate to Sonora, Mexico, and told his men that those who wished to come with him should join him at the falls of the Brazos within sixty days. With those final words, Parsons bade his men farewell. The proud veterans of the brigade headed home.[157]

RICHARD GANO'S BRIGADE

First Texas Cavalry, Arizona Brigade
Fifth Texas Cavalry, Partisan Rangers
Twenty-ninth Texas Cavalry
Thirtieth Texas Cavalry
Thirty-third Texas Cavalry

While the activities of the Texas cavalry brigades and regiments fighting in Louisiana during the Civil War have been described in various accounts, those of the Lone Star horsemen serving in Indian Territory are less well known. Four Texas cavalry regiments, the First Texas Cavalry (Arizona Brigade), the Fifth Texas Partisan Rangers, the Twenty-ninth Texas Cavalry, and the Thirtieth Texas Cavalry, spent much of the war patrolling, scouting, and raiding in the Territory. Three of these regiments served first in a brigade commanded by Mississippian Douglas Cooper, but they achieved their greatest recognition later in Richard Gano's Brigade. The fourth regiment, the First Texas Cavalry, Arizona Brigade, was not in Cooper's Brigade but served in the Territory before joining Gano's Brigade in April 1864. A fifth Texas regiment, James Duff's Thirty-third Texas Cavalry organized in 1863, spent eighteen months in South Texas before joining Gano's Brigade in September 1864.[158]

The Twenty-ninth Texas Cavalry was the first of the regiments within Gano's Brigade to be organized. Charles DeMorse, colonel of the regiment, was publisher and editor of one of the state's most influential newspapers, the Clarksville *Northern Standard.* A native of Massachusetts, DeMorse had arrived in Texas as a volunteer during the Texas Revolution. After brief service in both the Texas navy and army, DeMorse practiced law prior to founding the *Northern Standard* in 1842. Active in both newspaper circles and the Democratic Party, DeMorse is often referred to as "the father of Texas journalism." Although he had earlier hoped that separation from the Union would be unnecessary, the election of Abraham Lincoln convinced DeMorse that southern rights could be protected only by secession. He originally believed the war would be of short duration. When events convinced him otherwise, he secured permission to raise a regiment of mounted troops.[159]

DeMorse's Regiment was recruited during late spring of 1862. The volunteers were primarily from North Texas, particularly Bowie, Collin, Denton, Grayson, Lamar, Red River, and Titus counties. Most of the recruits had little prior military experience, but the men in one company led by Otis G. Welch, a prominent Denton lawyer, had served as one-year volunteers in Indian Territory and Arkansas and had seen action at the Battle of Pea Ridge. When their one-year enlistment expired, Welch's men joined DeMorse's Regiment.[160]

DeMorse's recruits were mustered into Confederate service at Clarksville on July 5, 1862 as the Twenty-ninth Texas Cavalry. DeMorse was chosen colonel, Otis Welch was lieutenant colonel, and Joseph A. Carroll, another Denton lawyer who had

Charles DeMorse, Colonel, Twenty-ninth Texas Cavalry.
—Courtesy Harold B. Simpson Research Center, Hillsboro, Texas

served as an officer in Welch's company, major. The lack of adequate weapons and other equipment convinced DeMorse that these needs had to be met before the regiment was ready for military service. He furloughed his troops and traveled east, where he spent the next three months acquiring the necessary materials of war. With this mission accomplished, DeMorse ordered his troops to assemble at Camp Jeff Davis near Clarksville on November 1. There they received their equipment and spent the next several months training.[161]

In February 1863 DeMorse received orders to move his regiment to Indian Territory. The regiment reached Fort Arbuckle in the south central part of present-day Oklahoma in March. For the next two months the Twenty-ninth Texas was on garrison duty there. In early May the regiment was ordered northeast to join Douglas H. Cooper's Brigade near Fort Gibson, at the confluence of the Neosobo and Arkansas rivers. Union troops occupied the fort in late 1862 after driving away pro-Confederate Indians led by the Cherokee Stand Watie. Cooper and his brigade, consisting primarily of Cherokees, Creeks, and Choctaws, were attempting to force Union troops out of Gibson. In mid-July, DeMorse's Texans saw their first real action in a skirmish with enemy troops near Fort Gibson.[162]

A month later the Twenty-ninth Texas was involved in what historian Alvin M. Josephy, Jr., has described as "the biggest and most decisive of any [battle] fought in Indian Territory." In this engagement the Union commander at Fort Gibson, Maj. Gen. James Blunt, led 4,000 Federal troops in an attack upon the Confederate supply depot at Honey Springs on Elk Creek, about eighteen miles south of the Arkansas River. Blunt's army, consisting of Union Indians, Kansas black troops, and Colorado infantry, launched a frontal assault on the Confederates. DeMorse's cavalry was in the center of the Confederate line, along with the Twentieth Texas Cavalry (dismounted) commanded by Col. Thomas C. Bass and the Fifth Texas Partisan Rangers commanded by Col. Leonidas M. Martin. Two Cherokee regiments, led by Col. Stand Watie, were on the Confederate right, and two Creek regiments under Col. D. N. McIntosh were on the Confederate left.[163]

The Texans and Confederate Indians held their ground under heavy enemy fire for nearly two hours, but Union artillery and a

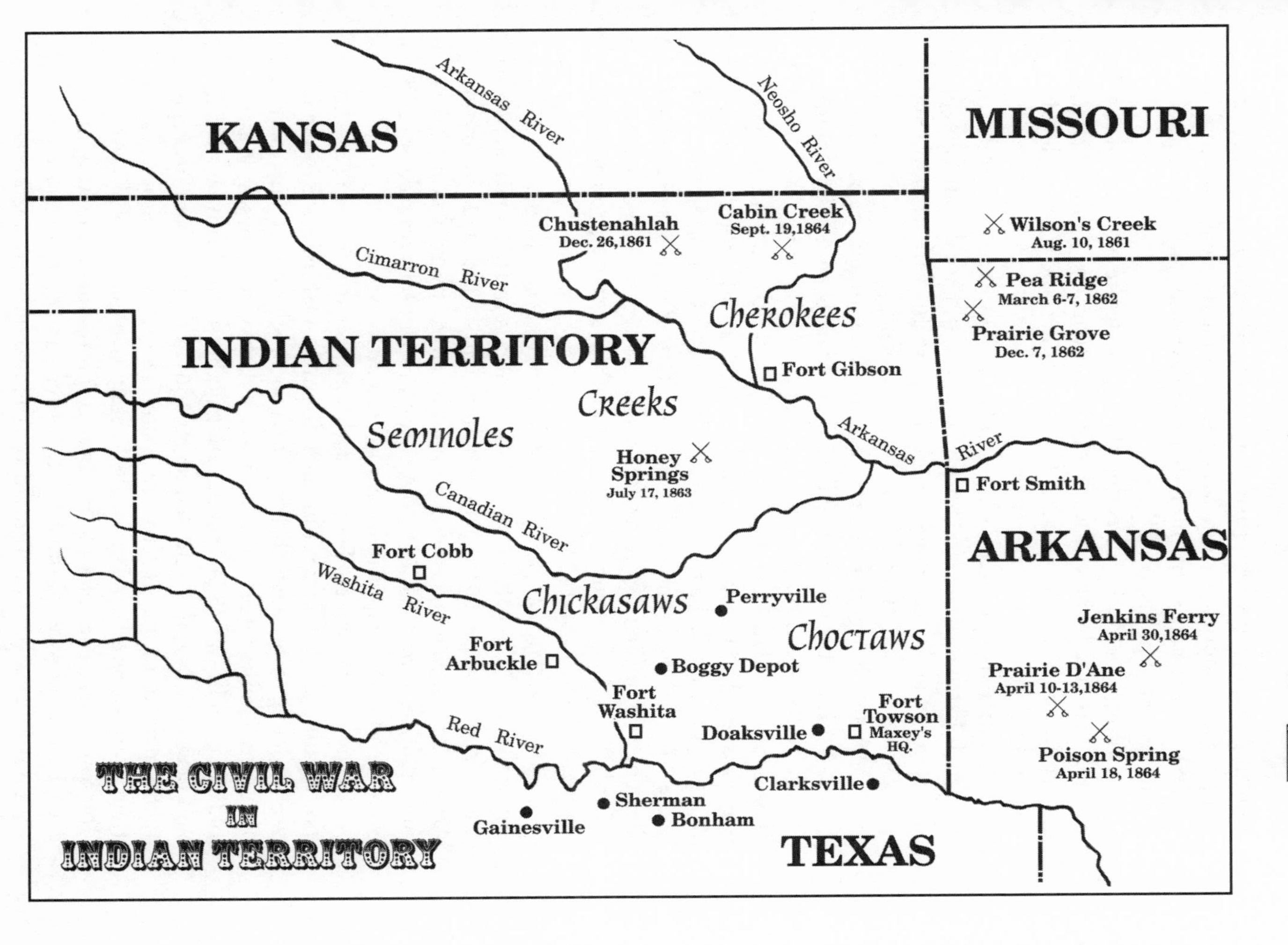
KANSAS
Arkansas River
Neosho River
MISSOURI
Chustenahlah
Dec. 26,1861
Cabin Creek
Sept. 19,1864
Wilson's Creek
Aug. 10, 1861
Pea Ridge
March 6-7, 1862
Prairie Grove
Dec. 7, 1862
Cimarron River
Cherokees
INDIAN TERRITORY
Fort Gibson
Creeks
Seminoles
Honey Springs
July 17, 1863
Arkansas River
Fort Smith
Canadian River
ARKANSAS
Fort Cobb
Washita River
Chickasaws
Perryville
Choctaws
Jenkins Ferry
April 30,1864
Fort Arbuckle
Boggy Depot
Prairie D'Ane
April 10-13,1864
Fort Washita
Fort Towson
Maxey's HQ.
Doaksville
Red River
Poison Spring
April 18, 1864
Clarksville
Sherman
Bonham
Gainesville
TEXAS
THE CIVIL WAR
IN
INDIAN TERRITORY

morning rainstorm which turned much of the inferior Confederate gunpowder (imported from Mexico) into paste eventually took a heavy toll. The center of the Rebel line gave way, and the Confederates retreated in disarray.[164]

Colonel DeMorse, directing the Confederate withdrawal, was severely wounded when he was hit in the left arm by a minie ball. In his report of the battle, General Cooper lauded the Clarksville editor for his bravery under fire.[165]

Cooper also praised Col. Leonidas Martin, the commander of the Fifth Partisan Rangers, "for his coolness and good management of his command, deceiving the enemy as to his real strength, and preventing our left [flank] from being turned . . ."[166]

Martin's Rangers had only recently been organized as a regiment. Formed by the consolidation of Maj. John L. Randolph's Ninth Texas Battalion, Partisan Rangers, and Martin's own Tenth Texas Cavalry Battalion in early 1863, the Fifth Partisan Rangers were assigned to Cooper's Brigade in April. In addition to Colonel Martin, Lt. Col. William M. Weaver and Maj. William N. Mayrant were the other regimental officers. The Rangers were often detached from the brigade to deal with deserters and jayhawkers in North Texas, but whenever called upon always gave a good account of themselves in combat.[167]

After the defeat at Elk Creek (or Honey Springs, as the Federals called the battle), the Confederates retreated south across the Canadian River, leaving the northern half of Indian Territory in Union hands. When General Blunt turned eastward toward Fort Smith in late summer 1863, Cooper took most of his brigade northward in a futile attempt to save northern Arkansas.

The Twenty-ninth Texas and the Fifth Partisan Rangers did not accompany Cooper on his march north. DeMorse's Regiment was ordered to proceed to Fort Towson on the north side of the Red River, only a few miles north of Clarksville. Towson was an old fort, built in 1824, evacuated by the U.S. Army in 1854, and occupied by the Confederates in 1861. DeMorse and his regiment arrived in late October, spent several weeks there, and then were ordered to Doaksville, about two miles southwest of Towson. There the men of the Twenty-ninth spent a cold winter. DeMorse requested permission to move his regiment across the river into Texas but was refused on the ground that such a move might cause the pro-southern Indians to lose faith in the Confederacy.[168]

Leonidas Martin's Fifth Partisan Rangers were sent back to Texas during the winter of 1863-1864 on detached service with Brig. Gen. Henry McCulloch, the Confederate commander of the Northern Sub-district of Texas. McCulloch needed military support in dealing with the deserters, draft dodgers, jayhawkers, and bushwhackers prevalent in the district. Compounding McCulloch's problems were the lawless operations of William Clarke Quantrill's guerrillas, who had established a winter camp northwest of Sherman. Due to the activities of the guerrillas, McCulloch ordered Martin to arrest Quantrill. The wily Quantrill learned of the plan, however, and made his escape from Texas. Martin and about one hundred cavalrymen pursued Quantrill but gave up the chase when the guerrilla chief and his men crossed the Red River.[169]

Meanwhile, the newly appointed Confederate commander of Indian Territory, Samuel Bell Maxey, was trying to bring Martin and his regiment back to the Territory. Shortly after assuming command, Maxey wrote Trans Mississippi Department commander Kirby Smith requesting the return of Martin and his cavalrymen. When this did not occur, Maxey repeated his pleas in March 1864. This time his request was approved; on March 21 Maxey received assurances that the Fifth Texas would be assigned to Indian Territory. It was actually late summer, however, before the reassigment was effected.[170]

At the time he was requesting the return of Martin's Regiment, Maxey was taking steps to find weapons, clothing, and other equipment for a small Texas brigade that arrived in Indian Territory in autumn of 1863. This brigade, consisting of the Thirtieth Texas Cavalry, commanded by Col. Edward J. Gurley, the First Texas Cavalry, Arizona Brigade, commanded by Col. Peter Hardeman, and an artillery battery commanded by Capt. William B. Krumbhaar, was originally under the direction of Col. Smith P. Bankhead. A Virginian and first cousin of Texas District commander John B. Magruder, Bankhead was not popular with the Texans. Discontent within the regiments threatened the brigade's effectiveness. Just prior to the brigade's assignment to Indian Territory, Bankhead was replaced by Col. Richard M. Gano.[171]

Gano, a native Kentuckian who practiced medicine in Texas in

Edward Gurley, Colonel, Thirtieth Texas Cavalry.

the late 1850s, had served as a regimental commander under John Hunt Morgan earlier in the war, but poor health caused him to return to Texas. He recovered sufficiently from his illness that he returned to active duty in July 1863 as commander of all state cavalry. When an experienced officer was needed to replace Bankhead, Gano was named commander of the brigade with orders to report to Indian Territory.

When Gano assumed command, conditions in the brigade were deplorable. Many of the men were unarmed and poorly fed and clothed. Morale was low and discipline lax. An inspector general's report noted that the two regiments and artillery battery were "in poor condition as a brigade." The Thirtieth Texas Cavalry, commanded by a senior captain in Gurley's absence, "presented a very poor appearance," according to the inspector general. The First Texas Cavalry, Arizona Brigade, was "very deficient in all things.... The drill was poor, discipline poor, arms badly kept, and military appearance not good."[172]

Neither cavalry regiment in the brigade had seen military action prior to assignment in Indian Territory, although a few of the men and the commander of the First Texas, Col. Peter Hardeman, had served under John R. Baylor in New Mexico. Hardeman's prominent Tennessee family had been supporters of Andrew Jackson. The Hardemans moved to Texas in 1835. Bailey Hardeman, an uncle of Peter, fought in the Texas Revolution, and William Polk Hardeman, an older cousin of Peter, temporarily commanded the First Cavalry, Arizona Brigade. After serving as an officer in the

Second Cavalry in New Mexico, Peter Hardeman joined his cousin William in organizing the Arizona Brigade in February 1863. When it became apparent the regiments of the Arizona Brigade would not be used in a campaign to bring Arizona under Confederate control, William Hardeman returned to his old regiment, the Fourth Cavalry, in Louisiana. Peter Hardeman was promoted to colonel and regimental commander. Edward Riordan was made lieutenant colonel, and Michael Looscan became major.[173]

The Thirtieth Texas, the other cavalry regiment in Gano's Brigade, was organized in summer 1862 by successful Waco lawyer Edward J. Gurley, who became colonel. Nicholas W. Battle, district judge from Waco, was chosen lieutenant colonel, and John H. Davenport became major. Most of the men in the regiment were recruited in the Central Texas counties around Waco.[174]

Gurley's Regiment remained in Texas in 1862 and the first half of 1863. The regiment was alerted for a move to Vicksburg in December 1862, but district commander John B. Magruder convinced Confederate authorities to allow the regiment to remain stationed near Columbus to protect the frontier and supply lines. In April 1863 Gurley was ordered to march to Louisiana, but these orders were soon rescinded. In June 1863 the regiment was ordered to join Hardeman's First Cavalry in marching to Bonham, Texas, for assignment in Indian Territory.[175]

Shortly after arriving in Indian Territory, Gano's Brigade was strengthened by the addition of Charles DeMorse's Twenty-ninth Texas Cavalry. The transfer of DeMorse's Regiment from Douglas Cooper's command was not popular with Cooper or the men in the Twenty-ninth Texas. Cooper, who had hoped to become commander of Indian Territory when Maxey was appointed, protested the move as an attempt to reduce his role by leaving him only Indian brigades. The veterans of the Twenty-ninth Texas, opposed to joining inexperienced and untested regiments in Gano's Brigade, supported Cooper, but to no avail. Maxey was convinced that Gano's Brigade, which had fewer than 1,000 men present for duty, had to be enlarged. He also believed that Cooper's command had to be organized into a more effective fighting unit.[176]

Maxey planned to add Leonidas Martin's Fifth Texas Partisan Rangers to Gano's Brigade. As noted earlier, Maxey was assured in March 1864 that Martin's Regiment would be returned to Indian

Territory. Before Martin's Regiment reached the Territory, however, Maxey and Gano's Brigade were on their way to Arkansas. Nathaniel P. Banks was moving up the Red River in Louisiana; at the same time, Frederick Steele and 10,000 Union troops were marching south from Little Rock. Kirby Smith, the Confederate commander of the Trans Mississippi, was determined to prevent a linkup between the two Federal armies. He reinforced Richard Taylor with additional regiments from Texas and ordered Maxey to move with some of his troops to assist Sterling Price in Arkansas.[177]

Maxey, with Tandy Walker's Choctaw Brigade and Gano's Texas Brigade, joined Sterling Price at Prairie D'Ane in south central Arkansas on April 12. At the time Price's forces were engaged in an artillery duel with Steele's Federals. After a brief skirmish in which Gano's regiments captured a Union outpost, the Union army broke off the battle and moved east to occupy Camden, an important military center. The Confederates followed after Steele. On April 13 Gano's Brigade defeated an enemy regiment near Munn's Mill on the Camden road. In the fighting Colonel Gano was severely wounded in the left arm, leaving DeMorse in temporary command of the brigade.[178]

Although Steele's army occupied Camden, the Federals needed supplies for both men and animals. Steele sent Col. James M. Williams and more than 1,000 troops, many of them from the First Kansas Colored Infantry, on a foraging expedition west of Camden. Williams and his troops obtained large quantities of corn and were heading back to Camden when they were intercepted at Poison Spring fourteen miles west of Camden by Confederate cavalry commanded by John Marmaduke. Believing himself outnumbered, Marmaduke requested reinforcements from Sterling Price, who ordered Maxey and his command to Poison Spring.[179]

Upon arriving at Poison Spring, Maxey found Marmaduke prepared to attack the Union forage train. Although senior in rank, Maxey deferred command to Marmaduke, who was more familiar with the terrain and troop dispositions. Marmaduke placed Maxey's troops on the left, with Tandy Walker's Indian Brigade on the extreme flank and Gano's Brigade, commanded by DeMorse in place of the injured Gano, between Walker's Brigade and Marmaduke's cavalry.[180]

The Confederates opened the attack at 10:00 A.M. In less than an hour the Union defenders were routed and the supply train of 170 wagons was captured. Dozens of black troops were slain while attempting to surrender; others were killed while trying to flee. The carnage may have been worse, but Maxey, who now assumed command, ordered the pursuit of the defeated foe ended.[181]

In all, Union losses were greater than 300; Confederate casualties, 111. In his report of the campaign, Maxey listed thirty-one killed and wounded in Gano's Brigade, sixteen of whom were in the Thirtieth Texas commanded in battle by Lt. Col. Nicholas Battle. Only three of the casualties in the brigade were fatalities.[182]

The defeat at Poison Spring, followed by the Confederate capture of a Union supply train at Mark's Mill on April 25, convinced Steele to abandon Camden and retreat to Little Rock. With the Union threat to Arkansas checked, Maxey and his two brigades returned to Indian Territory. Gano's Brigade made its way back to Fort Towson, where it remained during much of the summer. Colonel Gano, having recovered from his wound, resumed command of the brigade, and Colonel DeMorse returned to his regiment.[183]

The brigade was strengthened in June by the addition of Leonidas Martin's Fifth Partisan Rangers, who returned from detached service in Texas. The following month Gano led a picked squadron of men from all four regiments in a raid on Federal outposts near Fort Smith, Arkansas. In this operation Gano's troopers captured more than one hundred enemy soldiers at Diamond Grove on Massard Prairie, and then rescued a party of southern refugees who were being detained just outside Fort Smith. Brigadier General Cooper, Confederate commander in the area, described this raid as "a brilliant and dashing affair not unworthy of General Gano's reputation as one of [John Hunt] Morgan's best officers."[184]

In September 1864 Gano's entire brigade took part in a major raid in northeastern Indian Territory. In this operation Gano commanded a large cavalry force consisting of his own brigade and Stand Watie's and Daniel McIntosh's Indian brigades. After crossing the Canadian and Arkansas rivers, Gano's troops destroyed tons of hay being cut and stacked for Federal livestock near Fort Gibson. Then Gano led his horsemen some fifty miles north of Fort Gibson, where they quietly encircled a large Federal wagon train camped for the night at Cabin Creek. On the early morning of

September 19, the Confederates attacked the surprised Federals. One hundred thirty Union wagons loaded with supplies valued at more than a million dollars were captured; more than a hundred other wagons were burned. More than three hundred Union troops were killed, wounded, or captured. Confederate losses were minimal, with seven killed and thirty-eight wounded in Gano's Brigade.[185]

The Cabin Creek raid was the last large operation of Gano's Brigade in the war. Colonel Gano, whose left arm was shattered by an enemy bullet at Cabin Creek, left the brigade for assignment elsewhere. Command of the unit, which continued to be known as Gano's Brigade, passed to Edward J. Gurley of the Thirtieth Texas, who was the senior colonel. When Gurley received a leave of absence due to the serious illness of his wife, Peter Hardeman assumed temporary command.[186]

The brigade went into winter quarters at Laynesport, Arkansas, several miles from Indian Territory. The brigade now included not only the First Texas (Arizona Brigade), the Fifth Partisan Rangers, the Twenty-ninth Texas, and the Thirtieth Texas, but also the Thirty-third Texas Cavalry, which reached Indian Territory just after Gano and his troops had left on the Cabin Creek raid.

The Thirty-third Texas, commanded by Col. James Duff, had spent the last year in South Texas. The regiment was an outgrowth of the Fourteenth Texas Cavalry Battalion formed by Duff, a native of Scotland and merchant from San Antonio, in early 1862. As commander of two partisan ranger companies, Duff gained a bad reputation among Texas Unionists for conducting what they considered a reign of terror while enforcing martial law in the Texas Hill Country in 1862. Texas Confederates, on the other hand, praised Duff for his efficiency in dealing with opponents of the government.[187]

In 1863 Duff's Battalion was increased to regimental size by the addition of several companies of Anglo frontiersmen and South Texas Tejanos. James R. Sweet, former mayor of San Antonio, was lieutenant colonel of the new regiment, and Santos Benavides, former mayor of Laredo, was major. When Benavides later became commander of his own regiment, John L. Robinson succeeded him as major of the Thirty-third Texas.

The Thirty-third Texas made its headquarters at Ringgold Barracks near Rio Grande City during the early part of 1863. Later in the year the regiment was spread out: Duff and five companies were at Corpus Christi, one company was at San Antonio, and the other companies were patrolling the lower Rio Grande. In early December, Duff and seven companies were camped at Victoria. Because of shortages in forage, however, they were forced to move up the coast in early 1864. Duff and 330 men were ordered to Bonham in North Texas in April 1864, but two companies remained in San Antonio. In late summer the regiment joined Maxey's command in Indian Territory.[188]

The arrival of Duff's Regiment, along with a cavalry battalion commanded by Chaplin Good, pleased General Maxey, who believed morale among his troops had greatly improved. After visiting the camp of Gano's Brigade in early December, Maxey wrote to Kirby Smith, praising the spirit and confidence of the Texans. Much of this improvement Maxey attributed to Colonel Duff "for his valuable assistance to the brigade commander." The addition of "Duff's excellent regiment and Good's battalion to this brigade has greatly improved it," wrote Maxey.[189]

Maxey's enthusiasm was not shared by all. Tandy Walker's Choctaw Brigade was also camped at Laynesport. Although the Texans and Native Americans had been together in battle, this was the first time they camped together. Many of the Texans resented Confederate policy that treated the two races equally. Some white officers, particuarly Colonels DeMorse and Martin, refused to accept orders from higher ranking Indian officers. Weeks of idleness increased tension between the Texans and Native Americans. Discipline was lax, drinking increased, and occasionally fights broke out. Colonel DeMorse believed the only solution was the separation of whites and Indians. To this end he published a protest in which he described Native Americans "as an inferior race" and expressed his refusal to "subordinate myself to an individual of an inferior race."[190]

Immediately after his protest was published, DeMorse was placed under military arrest. He was brought before a court-martial board chaired by Colonel Duff on charges of "conduct prejudicial to good order and military discipline." The court found DeMorse guilty and sentenced him to suspension of rank and pay for six months. DeMorse appealed the court's action to the Confederate secretary of war and returned to Clarksville to await a decision. The war ended before a decision was made.[191]

In late January 1865 Gano's Brigade was transferred, over Maxey's protest, from Indian Territory and placed under the command of Hamilton P. Bee at Rusk, Texas. The brigade was sent to Natchitoches, Louisiana, but then ordered back to Texas. When Kirby Smith ordered the dismounting of nine Texas regiments in February, the First Texas Cavalry (Arizona Brigade), Fifth Partisan Rangers, and Twenty-ninth Texas Cavalry were among those dismounted and reassigned to infantry brigades. Edward Gurley's Thirtieth Texas and James Duff's Thirty-third Texas were among regiments keeping their horses. The Thirty-third was placed in William P. Hardeman's Brigade and the Thirtieth joined William Parsons' Brigade. By then the war was nearly over. In May 1865 most members of the old Gano Brigade returned to their homes. A few, including Col. Peter Hardeman of the Partisan Rangers and Lt. Col. James R. Sweet of Duff's Thirty-third Texas, went south of the Rio Grande.[192]

JAMES E. SLAUGHTER'S BRIGADE

Second Texas Cavalry
Fourth Texas Cavalry, Arizona Brigade
Anderson's - Border's Texas Cavalry
Benavides' Texas Cavalry

Several Texas regiments, like James Duff's Thirty-third Texas Cavalry described above, spent much of the war operating independently. Although these regiments were often brigaded with other regiments in tables of organization, there was little attachment or feeling of loyalty to the parent brigade. Indeed, they seldom had contact with other regiments in the brigade. Such was the case of the regiments in two brigades formed in Maj. Gen. John G. Walker's Third Corps in September 1864: the Seventh and Eighth Cavalry Brigades. The story of each of these two brigades is largely that of four separate regiments.

The Seventh Cavalry Brigade brought together (on paper at least) for organizational and reporting purposes the Second Texas Cavalry, the Fourth Texas Cavalry (Arizona Brigade), Anderson's-Border's Texas Cavalry, and Benavides' Texas Cavalry. Commander of the brigade was Brig. Gen. James E. Slaughter, a Virginia nephew of James Madison. Slaughter, who attended but did not graduate from Virginia Military Institute, was a professional soldier who had served in the Mexican War and in the regular U.S. Army. In 1861-1862 he was a member of Albert Sidney Johnston's staff and later took part in Braxton Bragg's Kentucky campaign. He was assigned to duty in Texas in early 1863. After serving briefly as chief of staff for John B. Magruder, Slaughter was appointed commander of the Western Sub-district of Texas, a post he held until the end of the war.[193]

The Second Texas Cavalry was the only one of the four regiments assigned to Slaughter's Brigade that was organized prior to 1863. It was also the only one to see extensive service outside the state. Formed in spring 1861, the regiment was originally known as the Second Texas Mounted Rifles. The Committee of Public Safety of the Texas secession convention authorized two veteran Texas Rangers, Henry E. McCulloch and John S. "Rip" Ford, to raise two regiments of volunteer cavalry for the purpose of securing Federal property in the state. McCulloch's Regiment became the First Texas Mounted Rifles, and Ford's the Second Texas Mounted Rifles.[194]

"Rip" Ford, already a legend for his exploits in the Mexican War, Indian campaigns, and frontier exploration, recruited his troops in the Houston area. Volunteers came largely from Houston and East Texas, but some were from San Antonio and Lavaca County as well. In February, Ford and 500 recruits sailed from Galveston to Brownsville, where Ford negotiated an agreement with the Union commander to surrender all the Federal forts from Brownsville to El Paso. In the next two months Ford's troops occupied the forts along the Rio Grande.[195]

On May 23, 1861, Ford's Mounted Rifles, numbering 1,200 men, was sworn into Confederate service as the Second Texas Cavalry. Ford was appointed colonel of the regiment; John R. Baylor, an experienced frontiersman, Indian agent, and adventurer, was named lieutenant colonel; and Edwin Waller, Jr., son of a signer of the Texas Declaration of Independence, was named major.[196]

Events moved rapidly. Earl Van Dorn, who had been appointed Confederate commander of Texas, was anxious to secure Federal forts in the trans Pecos area and at the same time prevent Federal incursion into West Texas from New Mexico. While Ford with four companies remained in South Texas, Baylor and six companies moved from San Antonio into West Texas. Leaving F Company under Capt. Sam Richardson at the Llano River to protect settlers against Indian raids and H Company commanded by Capt. James M. Roark to garrison Fort Clark, Baylor with four companies pushed on to El Paso to occupy Fort Bliss.[197]

Baylor was not content merely to occupy Fort Bliss. A firm believer in southern expansionism, Baylor was determined to liberate southern New Mexico, or Arizona as it was called, from Union control. With 300 men of the Second Cavalry he moved into New Mexico in late July and occupied Mesilla, the largest town in the region. Maj. Isaac Lynde, commanding Union troops at nearby Fort Fillmore, made a half-hearted effort to drive Baylor out, but after a skirmish fell back. Lynde then attempted to withdraw to Fort Stanton, 140 miles to the northeast. The aggressive Baylor pursued and overtook Lynde's troops, who were suffering from a shortage of water. Lynde surrendered his entire command of nearly 500 men to Baylor.[198]

Following the capture of the Fillmore garrison, Baylor issued a proclamation creating the Confederate Territory of Arizona with himself as civil governor. During the next few months, Baylor took steps to consolidate Confederate control of the region. His battalion of Second Cavalry was active during this time, skirmishing with New Mexico volunteers at Alamosa and attempting to track down raiding Apaches.[199]

Baylor's role in New Mexico was eclipsed in late December with the arrival of Brig. Gen. Henry Hopkins Sibley and his three regiments of Confederate cavalry. Sibley assumed command of all Confederate forces in the area, including the companies of the Second Texas Cavalry. He allowed Baylor to remain as governor but stripped him of military command. Maj. Edwin Waller, the second-ranking officer of the Second Cavalry in New Mexico, was sent back to Texas to recruit additional volunteers. The troops formerly under Baylor's command were now led by Maj. Charles L. Pyron, a Bexar County rancher who had formerly commanded B Company.[200]

Pyron and the companies of the Second Cavalry served as the advance guard of Sibley's army as it moved into New Mexico. In the battle fought at Valverde on February 21, 1862, Pyron's cavalry was on the Confederate left, which received most of the enemy's opening artillery fire. The battalion was fortunate to suffer only slight losses in what otherwise was a bloody engagement as the Confederates drove the Federals back to Fort Craig.[201]

Although the Confederates were victorious at Valverde, the battle accomplished little. As noted earlier in the discussion of Sibley's Brigade, Union troops still held Fort Craig. Sibley, low on supplies, decided to push north toward Albuquerque and Santa Fe. Pyron's Cavalry Battalion led the advance, reaching Albuquerque on March 2, only to find most of the supplies had been removed or destroyed. Sibley arrived several days later and sent Pyron and the Second Cavalry on ahead to Santa Fe. Units of Pyron's command reached the New Mexico capital on March 10. Pyron himself arrived with the rest of his cavalry on March 13. Once again the Texans found the enemy and many of the supplies gone.[202]

While occupying Santa Fe, Pyron learned that Federal troops from Fort Union, some forty miles to the northeast on the Santa Fe Trail, were marching toward the city. Pyron, who had been joined by four companies of Sibley's Fifth Cavalry commanded by Maj. John S. Shropshire, decided to move quickly to meet the enemy.[203]

With B and E companies of his own Second Texas Cavalry, four companies of the Fifth Texas Cavalry, a local irregular company known as the "Brigands," and a section of artillery, Pyron set out from Santa Fe on March 25. The next morning, while moving through Apache Canyon at the west end of Glorieta Pass, Pyron's troops unexpectedly ran into a column of Colorado volunteers led by Maj. John M. Chivington. In the fighting that lasted throughout the day the Confederates were outflanked, forcing Pyron to withdraw toward Johnson's Ranch at the lower end of Apache Canyon. Chivington meanwhile fell back through Glorieta Pass, first to Pigeon's Ranch on the eastern slope of the mountains and then to Kozlowski's Ranch, four miles to the southwest.[204]

Casualties in killed and wounded were surprisingly light given the nature of the fighting: five Federals killed and fourteen wounded, four Confederates killed and twenty wounded. Seventy-one Confederates, however (nearly one-fifth of Pyron's command), were taken prisoner. As historian Don E. Alberts noted, the Battle of Apache Canyon was "the greatest loss the Texans would experience during the New Mexico campaign."[205]

There was no fighting the next day. The Union commander,

Major Chivington, waited at Kozlowski's Ranch for the arrival of Col. John P. Slough and the main body of Colorado volunteers. Pryon meanwhile sent a message to Col. William R. Scurry, who was twenty miles to the south with his Fourth Texas Cavalry and a battalion of the Seventh Texas Cavalry. That evening Scurry and his troops joined Pyron at Johnson's Ranch. Later that same night Slough and the rest of his "Pike's Peakers" arrived at Kozlowski's Ranch.

The next day, March 28, 1862, the two reinforced commands clashed at Glorieta Pass in what some have called the "Gettysburg of the West." When the battle began, Pyron and eighty men of the Second Cavalry were on the Confederate right but were shifted to the left in the early afternoon to assist Maj. Henry Raguet and his battalion of the Fourth Texas. In the fighting Pyron's horse was shot out from under him and his cheek grazed by enemy fire, but he and his cavalry helped push the enemy back. By later afternoon the Confederates had the upper hand at Pigeon's Ranch, though the loss of their supply train forced them to fall back toward Santa Fe.[206]

Glorieta Pass was the last major engagement in New Mexico for most of the Confederates. After pulling back to Santa Fe, Sibley's army, including the companies of the Second Texas, began a long retreat back to Texas, reaching Fort Bliss in early May. Following a brief period for rest and resupply, the Confederates departed from El Paso on the journey back to San Antonio. The men of the Second Texas, whose terms of enlistment were expiring, led the way. In early July, Pyron's troops reached San Antonio, where their New Mexico adventure had begun over a year ago.[207]

The companies of the Second Texas returned at the time Col. John S. Ford, who had remained in South Texas with the other four companies of the regiment, accepted appointment as head of the Conscript Bureau of Texas. As the initial twelve-month enlistment period for the men of the Second had ended, some of the veterans chose to join one of the new regiments being formed as part of the Arizona Brigade.

The Second Texas was reorganized in summer 1862 with Pryon, promoted to colonel, now the commanding officer. James H. Walker was named lieutenant colonel and William A. Spencer, major. During late summer and autumn, the regiment, considerably reduced in numbers, was assigned to the Rio Grande

Sub-district. In December the regiment was transferred to the Houston area, where plans were being readied for the recapture of Galveston.[208]

The Second Cavalry was part of the Confederate forces that crossed the old railroad bridge leading into Galveston during the early morning hours of January 1, 1863. Once again under the direction of William R. Scurry, now a brigadier general, Pryon's men took part in the attack on Union troops quartered on Kuhn's Wharf. With other Confederates they celebrated when the Federal commander surrendered the city back to Generals Magruder and Scurry.[209]

The Second Cavalry remained in the Galveston area until late spring, when Pyron was ordered to take his regiment to Louisiana. The regiment was assigned to a new brigade commanded by James P. Major being organized to assist Richard Taylor in his efforts to relieve pressure upon Port Hudson. During early summer, the regiment served with Major's cavalry as it moved into the bayou country of southern Louisiana. Major and the other regiments of the brigade moved along the west bank of Bayou Lafourche while the Second Cavalry advanced along the east bank. In late June, Pyron made what proved to be a suicidal attack on a Federal fort at Lafourche Crossing. With only 206 men, he ordered an assault against a position defended by 800 troops. In the initial charge the Texans captured four guns and a number of Federal troops before being forced to retire from what Colonel Major described as "a position won by a daring assault, unequaled, I think in this war."[210]

The gallant but ill-conceived attack at Lafourche Crossing almost destroyed Pryon's small regiment. Pryon himself and Lt. Col. James Walker were both seriously wounded; more than fifty men (or 25 percent of the effective strength) were killed or wounded.[211]

Although the battered regiment took part with other regiments in Major's Brigade in the capture of Bayou Boeuf several days later, morale in the Second Texas was shattered. When both Colonel Pyron and Lieutenant Colonel Walker returned to Texas on injury leave, desertion increased appreciably, so much that General Taylor directed the remaining men of the regiment back to Texas.[212]

The Second Cavalry was reorganized at Austin in late summer 1863 with a blend of new recruits and old veterans under the command of Colonel Pyron. When enemy forces caused the abandonment of Fort Esperanza on Matagorda Island in late November, the regiment was sent to Victoria. The regiment was ordered to secure all rolling stock of the railroad and destroy the track should the Federals attempt to move inland. When the Federal threat to the region passed, the regiment was ordered to Caney Creek as part of the Confederate buildup there. Morning reports show the Second Cavalry with 26 officers and 325 enlisted men present for duty at a camp on the Old Caney on December 31, 1863. A month later the regiment was camped with the Thirty-fifth and Thirty-sixth Texas cavalries near San Bernard.[213]

In the spring of 1864 many of the Texas cavalry regiments were ordered to Louisiana to assist Richard Taylor in blocking Nathaniel P. Banks' movement up the Red River. Pyron's Regiment remained in Texas, as rumors of possible Union invasion along the Texas coast convinced Confederate authorities to keep some cavalry regiments in the state. As one of these regiments the Second Cavalry was moved from one locale to another. In June the Second Texas was at Clear Creek; in July the regiment was listed as part of the Galveston defenses.[214]

By the summer of 1864 the other three regiments that would join Pyron's Second Cavalry (on paper at least) in Brig. Gen. Slaughter's Seventh Texas Cavalry Brigade were all organized. One of these regiments, the Fourth Texas Cavalry, Arizona Brigade, never reached the regulation ten-company size. The regiment was authorized by the special orders issued in February creating the so-called Arizona Brigade. The organizer and colonel of the Fourth Texas, Spruce M. Baird, was well known to Pyron and the veterans of the Second Texas who had camped on his large estate near Albuquerque in the New Mexico campaign. A native of Kentucky, Baird was practicing law in Nacogdoches in 1848 when Governor George T. Wood appointed him judge of the newly created Santa Fe County. Although Baird was unsuccessful in his efforts to convince New Mexicans to accept Texas authority, he remained in New Mexico after congressional measures created a territory in 1850. Baird was active in pro-Southern affairs and welcomed Sibley's army when it occupied Albuquerque. When the Confederates withdrew from New Mexico in May 1862, Baird returned to Texas. He remained anxious to return to New Mexico. When John R. Baylor began organizing the Arizona Brigade for the purpose of reentering New Mexico, Baird was authorized to raise a regiment.[215]

As noted earlier, Baylor's dream of reoccupying New Mexico and Arizona never materialized. The first regiment of the Arizona Brigade was later assigned to Gano's Brigade in Indian Territory; the second and third regiments to Major's Brigade in Louisiana. Baird's Regiment, designated the Fourth Texas, Arizona Brigade, was the last to complete its organization. While the other three were already in the field by summer 1863, the Fourth Texas was still being recruited in San Antonio. Despite all his efforts, Baird had only eight companies formed by December when he was ordered to report to Brig. Gen. Hamilton P. Bee, Western Sub-district commander in San Antonio.[216]

In early 1864 the Fourth Texas was assigned to a cavalry force being assembled by John S. Ford to drive Union troops from the lower Rio Grande Valley. Federal troops, including two regiments of Texans recruited for the Union army, occupied the Brownsville area in late 1863. John B. Magruder, Confederate commander in Texas, ordered Ford to lead Confederate cavalry, including Baird's Fourth Texas, in driving them out. Almost immediately Baird challenged Ford on the question of rank. When the issue was decided against him, Baird withdrew and left the regiment under the command of Lt. Col. Dan Showalter.[217]

Under Showalter's command the Fourth Texas rode south with Ford's cavalry in March 1864. While camped near King Ranch south of Corpus Christi, Ford received a report from Col. Santos Benavides describing a Federal attack on Laredo on the afternoon of March 18. Approximately 200 Union troops, attached to John L. Haynes' Second Texas Union Cavalry, avoided Benavides' scouts by crossing into Mexico and then recrossing the Rio Grande near Laredo. With only a few hours' notice of the impending attack, Benavides, who was ill at the time, and seventy-two defenders beat off three Union assaults before darkness ended the fighting.[218]

Santos Benavides, the highest-ranking Mexican American to serve the Confederacy, was commander of one of the four regiments that later made up Slaughter's Brigade. A member of the distinguished family that founded Laredo, Benavides was a successful merchant, rancher, and public servant. When the war came he and his brothers, Cristobal and Refugio, raised companies for the

Confederate army which later became part of James Duff's Thirty-third Texas Cavalry. With the formation of Duff's Regiment, Santos was promoted to major. After steady service along the Rio Grande with the Thirty-third Texas, Benavides was promoted to colonel in November 1863 and authorized to form his own regiment of partisan rangers. This unit came to be known as Benavides' Texas Cavalry.[219]

Upon learning of the Union attack on Benavides' command, Ford and his cavalry headed for the Rio Grande, reaching Laredo on April 15. With Benavides' Regiment commanded by Refugio Benavides in place of an ailing Santos, Ford left Laredo and headed down the Rio Grande toward Brownsville. His column reached Rio Grande City a week later. Due to supply problems, it remained there several weeks before resuming its march. In late June, Ford and several hundred men from Showalter's Fourth Texas, Benavides' Regiment, and Lt. Col. George H. Giddings' Battalion overwhelmed a Union outpost at Los Rucias that was defended by companies of the First Texas Union Cavalry under Capt. Philip G. Temple.[220]

With nearly 2,000 troops under his command, Ford moved cautiously toward Brownsville, which had been occupied by more than 6,000 enemy troops. On July 30 the Confederate advance guard rode into Brownsville and found the enemy gone. The Union commander, Maj. Gen. Francis

Santos Benavides, Colonel, Benavides Cavalry.
—Courtesy Harold B. Simpson Research Center, Hillsboro, Texas

J. Herron, had been ordered to withdraw most of his troops to Louisiana. Ford's scouts reported, however, that a sizable Federal force was nearby. Ford, who was ill, ordered Lieutenant Colonel Showalter to pursue them. Refugio Benavides was sent ahead of Showalter's main body. When he sighted the Federals, Benavides attacked the enemy. Showalter, however, failed to follow up with the larger body of Confederates, allowing the Federals to escape to Brazos Island at the mouth of the Rio Grande.[221]

The Confederate reoccupation of Brownsville did not bring immediate peace to South Texas. Juan Cortina, the Mexican folk hero who gave Anglo Texans and John S. Ford much difficulty in the 1850s, was now military governor of Tamaulipas, the Mexican state across from Brownsville. On September 6 he opened artillery fire on Showalter's command at Palmito Ranch. This, followed by an attack by Federal troops from Brazos Island, caused Showalter and the Confederates to retreat in confusion back to Brownsville. For the moment there were fears that the Federals might retake the city, but Giddings and troops from his battalion, along with the Fourth Texas (now led by Maj. F. E. Kavanaugh), drove the enemy back with heavy losses.[222]

The Fourth Texas (Arizona Brigade) remained in the Brownsville area the rest of the year. Although under John Ford's immediate command, the Fourth was now officially part of Brig. Gen. James Slaughter's Seventh Texas Brigade in the Third Texas Cavalry Division, Third Army Corps.

The new brigade remained widely scattered. While the Fourth Texas was near the mouth of the Rio Grande, Benavides' Regiment patrolled the area from Laredo to Rio Grande City, and Charles Pyron's Second Cavalry was on the upper coast near Galveston. The fourth regiment in the brigade, Col. Thomas S. Anderson's Cavalry, was on duty near Tyler.[223]

Anderson's Regiment was formed in April 1864 by the consolidation of Philip Fulcord's small battalion with the larger battalion of John P. Border. Thomas S. Anderson, a prominent lawyer, former Texas secretary of state, and member of the secession convention, was chosen commander of the regiment. Border, a native of Lincolnshire, England, and veteran of San Jacinto, was selected as lieutenant colonel, and Fulcord as major.

In May 1864 Anderson's Regiment was assigned to the Tyler

area. Anderson was made commander of the Confederate prison Camp Ford but apparently devoted himself primarily to administering the post of Tyler and left management of the prison in the hands of Border. Anderson and his regiment were relieved of their duties in the Tyler area in early autumn and were assigned to the Houston-Hempstead area.[224]

Like most regiments late in the war, Anderson's cavalry had the effective strength of a battalion. Unit reports for the brigade in December 1864 show Anderson with twenty-four officers and 321 men present for duty, numbers comparable to Benavides' 17 officers and 266 men, Pyron's 59 officers and 313 men, and Showalter's 20 officers and 332 men.[225]

In the spring months of 1865, Slaughter's Brigade was scattered even more as the Confederate command attempted to defend the state with dwindling resources. Anderson's Regiment, which was commanded in the last days of the war by Lt. Col. John Border, was dismounted and ordered to Galveston. Companies of the veteran Second Cavalry were sent in various directions. One company was at Fort Duncan, another at Fort Clark, two at San Antonio where Colonel Pyron made his headquarters, and the others at Galveston. Companies of Benavides' Regiment were at Brownsville, Fort Duncan, and Laredo. The Fourth Texas left Brownsville in March 1865 with orders to proceed to Galveston, but was later reassigned to Central Texas. Discipline in the regiment virtually disappeared. In April, General Magruder reported to Kirby Smith that "great outrages are being perpetrated on citizens in McLennan and Williamson counties by Baird's [Showalter's] command and others," and proposed that other cavalry be used to arrest the offenders.[226]

For the men who served in the four regiments that made up Slaughter's Brigade, the war came to an end when Kirby Smith surrendered the Trans Mississippi Department in late May 1865. Like their fellow Confederates, most of the men in the brigade returned to their homes and resumed their prewar activities. A few, including brigade commander James E. Slaughter and John S. Ford, went to Mexico, but like Slaughter and Ford most returned to Texas after a brief time. For the majority, their loyalties and memories of the war were with their old regiments. Few probably remembered, or realized, that they had been in Slaughter's Brigade.[227]

HENRY McCULLOCH'S BRIGADE

Border Regiment
Frontier Regiment
Bradford's-Mann's Regiment
Thirty-fifth (Brown's) Regiment

The composition of the cavalry brigade formed under the command of Brig. Gen. Henry E. McCulloch in the autumn of 1864 was much like that of Slaughter's Brigade. Only one of the four regiments in the brigade, Reuben R. Brown's Thirty-fifth Texas Cavalry, was organized as a Confederate regiment prior to 1864, although the Frontier Regiment, also in the brigade, existed earlier as a state organization. Like Slaughter's Brigade, in which only one regiment served outside the state, only one of the regiments in McCulloch's Brigade (James G. Bourland's Border Regiment) saw duty outside Texas.[228]

The Thirty-fifth Cavalry, oldest of McCulloch's regiments in terms of Confederate service, was organized in late summer 1863, when Reuben R. Brown's Twelfth Cavalry Battalion was consolidated with Lee Rountree's Cavalry Battalion. Brown, who became commander of the new regiment, was a native of Georgia who went to Texas in November 1835 to serve in the revolutionary army. After harrowing experiences in the War for Texas Independence, in which he was captured and later escaped from the Mexican army, Brown operated a plantation at the mouth of the Brazos River. When the Civil War began, Brown organized a company and then a battalion of cavalry for service on the Texas coast.[229]

Brown's Battalion was shifted along the Texas coast as military needs changed. In June 1863 the battalion was camped near Velasco with Nicholas Gould's Twenty-third Texas Cavalry. When General Magruder decided to strengthen Confederate defenses in southeast Texas following the Union invasion attempt at Sabine Pass in September, Brown's Battalion, consisting of five companies, was sent to Sabine Pass, where with other Texas cavalry it was under the overall command of Augustus Buchel. When the threat to this area eased in November, Brown's troops, now consolidated with Rountree's Battalion as a regiment, returned to the lower Brazos. In late 1863 the regiment exchanged fire with a Union raiding party near the mouth of Caney Creek. Unit strength for the regiment in January 1864 was twenty-nine officers (including Colonel Brown, Lt. Col. Samuel W. Perkins, and Maj. Lee C. Rountree) and 409 enlisted men present for duty out of an aggregrate present and absent of 626.[230]

In early spring 1864 it appeared that Brown's Regiment would be sent to Louisiana as part of the cavalry reinforcements for Richard Taylor. On March 11 Brown received orders to make the move. Two days later the orders were changed as Brig. Gen. Hamilton P. Bee decided to leave Brown's Regiment on the Texas coast for scouting purposes, much to the delight of area commander Joseph Bates, who had earlier protested when it appeared the regiment would be moved.[231]

Brown's Regiment was moved up the coast to the Houston-Galveston area in early summer 1864 and remained there for the next six months. Strength of the regiment remained rather constant: approximately 400 officers and men present for duty (out of an aggregate strength of present and absent of slightly over 800).[232]

In late summer, Brown's Thirty-fifth Texas was joined in the defense of Galveston by Charles M. Bradford's Cavalry. This regiment, which also became part of McCulloch's Brigade, was formed in July by the consolidation of three small battalions and an independent cavalry command. Charles Bradford, commander of the new regiment, was a Pennsylvanian who moved to Louisiana on the eve of the Civil War. He served as a lieutenant colonel in the Third Battalion of Louisiana Infantry early in the war, but resigned in January 1862, apparently the result of a court-martial offense for disrespect to a superior officer. Bradford moved to Central Texas, where he became commander of a battalion assigned to round up deserters and disloyalists in the Austin-Bastrop area. When the battalion was combined with others to form a regiment, Bradford was chosen colonel.[233]

Bradford's Regiment was one of the military units created late in the war that was not given a numerical designation. Since Bradford himself left the regiment sometime in early 1865, some accounts refer to the unit as Mann's Regiment, so named for Col. Walter L. Mann, who commanded the regiment in the last months of the war. Muster rolls indicate the regiment had only nine companies, some of which were quite small. Only 243 officers and men were present for duty at Galveston in September 1864, but the number rose to 388 by late December. The regiment remained in Galveston until the war's conclusion; returns for May 10, 1865, list 26 officers and 369 men present for duty.[234]

Although Brown's Thirty-fifth Texas and Bradford's Regiment were part of McCulloch's Brigade from September 1864 through March 1865, when a general reorganization of Confederate units in Texas occurred, neither regiment had direct contact with the brigade commander. The North Texas Sub-district commander's headquarters were located at Bonham, several hundred miles from the coast.

The other two regiments in McCulloch's Brigade, James Bourland's Border Regiment and James E. McCord's Frontier Regiment, operated within McCulloch's Northern Sub-district at least part of the time. The history of these two regiments is closely related as both grew out of state and Confederate concerns for protection of northern and western Texas from Indian raiders, Union invaders, jayhawkers, and bushwhackers. In his study entitled *Frontier Defense in the Civil War*, historian David Paul Smith discussed in some detail the complex relationship between Confederate, state, and local officials as they struggled to meet the challenge of defending hundreds of miles of territory with comparatively few men and limited resources.[235]

The Frontier Regiment was created by an act of the state legislature in December 1861. Under this act ten cavalry companies would be raised from specified frontier counties for a twelve-month enlistment with the men furnishing their own weapons, horses, and accoutrements. The initial hope was that the new regiment would soon be in Confederate service, thus releasing the state from a financial burden. However, a state stipulation that the regiment could not be removed beyond the limits of Texas was unacceptable to the Confederate president, delaying the transfer for two years.[236]

Meanwhile, the Frontier Regiment was organized under state authority in early 1862. Governor Lubbock appointed James M. Norris, a successful Coryell County lawyer and former member of the secession convention, as colonel. Alfred T. Obenchain, a Parker County lawyer who had also been a delegate to the secession convention, was appointed lieutenant colonel, and James E. McCord, a frontier surveyor and former Texas Ranger, was named major.[237]

Norris was not successful as commander of the Frontier Regiment. With little previous experience in frontier service, he failed to win the respect of the men under his command. Lack of discipline became a serious problem. When he resorted to extensive use of courts-martial, he became even more unpopular. Historian David Paul Smith noted that the discipline problem extended to the officers as well as enlisted personnel. Lieutenant Colonel Obenchain became involved in a quarrel with one of the company commanders that led to Obenchain's death. Major McCord replaced Obenchain as lieutenant colonel, and James "Buck" Barry, a former Texas Ranger and Mexican War veteran, became major.[238]

In the hope that Richmond authorities would finally approve the transfer of the regiment to Confederate service, Governor Lubbock reorganized the regiment in February 1863 with the requirement that the men serve three years as provided by Confederate army regulations. Norris resigned as colonel, and the men elected McCord as his replacement. "Buck" Barry was chosen lieutenant colonel and W. J. Alexander, major, in the reorganized regiment.[239]

With McCord the regiment had an officer with practical frontier experience as commander. Under his leadership the Frontier Regiment, still under state control, established a defense line running from Red River Station to Eagle Pass on the Rio Grande. Lieutenant Colonel Barry and six companies covered the line from the Red River to Camp Colorado near Brady. Major Alexander, with four companies, was responsible for the line running south from Camp Colorado to the Rio Grande.[240]

At the same time the Frontier Regiment was being reorganized, Confederate authorities were creating a new cavalry battalion to assist in the protection of the northwestern frontier of Texas. This battalion, increased to regimental size late in 1863, was commanded by James Bourland, a seasoned veteran of Indian campaigns and the Mexican War. A native of South Carolina, Bourland moved to Lamar County in 1837 and later to Cooke County. In addition to his military service, Bourland was active in North Texas political affairs, serving as a senator in the first and second state legislatures. A wealthy slaveholder and staunch supporter of states' rights, Bourland was a leader in the "great hangings" at Gainesville in the autumn of 1862. Quick-tempered and volatile, Bourland was a controversial leader who believed in immediate action when dealing with deserters, disloyalists, or Indians. Assisting him in command of his new Border Regiment were Lt. Col. John R. Diamond, a Grayson County slaveholder, secessionist, and participant in the "great hangings" who had earlier served in the Eleventh Texas Cavalry, and Maj. Charles L. Roff, a recent arrival in Texas from Virginia and former captain of a local militia company.[241]

Bourland's Regiment was initially under the jurisdiction of Brig. Gen. William Steele, commander of Indian Territory. In autumn 1863 the regiment, which had more than 700 men on its muster rolls but seldom had 400 men present for duty, had troops located on both sides of the Red River. Bourland made his headquarters at Fort Arbuckle in Indian Territory. In January 1864 the Border Regiment was transferred to Henry E. McCulloch's Northern Sub-district of Texas, and Bourland moved his headquarters to Gainesville. Two of his companies remained on detached duty in Indian Territory for several months.[242]

Bourland's Border Regiment and McCord's Frontier Regiment, which was finally transferred to Confederate service in early 1864, shared the task of defending the Texas frontier with state troops of a newly created Frontier Organization during the last year of the war. This involved dealing with not only Indian raiders but also increasing numbers of deserters, draft dodgers, disloyalists, and marauders in the Northern Sub-district. The task was made even more difficult when McCord and six companies of the Frontier Regiment were transferred to the interior of Texas to replace cavalry sent to join Richard Taylor in northern Louisiana in spring 1864. The vast distances to cover allowed Indians to make successful raids and return to Indian Territory before the Texans could mount a successful defense. Such incursions took place in December 1863, when Comanches made a raid into Cooke County, and in October 1864, when they swept as far south as Elm Creek, a tributary of the Brazos. On another occasion excessive zeal by frontier commanders led to the unfortunate attack on a wandering band of Kickapoos at Dove Creek in January 1865, resulting in the unnecessary death of a number of Indians as well as troops from Capt. Henry Fossett's Company of the Frontier Regiment and Capt. Silas Totten's state militia.[243]

Although there were some failures, historian David Paul Smith believes the Frontier Regiment, the Border Regiment, and the state Frontier Organization did a satisfactory job in defending the Texas frontier during the Civil War. And when the end of the war came in late spring of 1865, there was "no laying down of arms and going home" as occurred elsewhere in the Confederacy. The men were already home, and many kept their weapons to defend their homes from the same threats they faced during the war.[244]

UNATTACHED/INDEPEDENT CAVALRY REGIMENTS/BATTALIONS

Terry's Texas Cavalry
Wells' Texas Cavalry (Thirty-fourth Texas Cavalry)
Giddings' Texas Battalion
Daly's/Ragsdale's Battalion

Two Texas regiments, Terry's Cavalry and Wells' Cavalry, operated independently of any brigade organization throughout most of their brief existence, although battalions of what became Wells' Regiment did campaign earlier with Richard Gano's Brigade in Indian Territory.

Terry's Regiment was organized in early 1864 by the colorful and volatile David S. Terry, the younger brother of Benjamin F. Terry, the first commander of Terry's Texas Rangers. Because of the similarity of names, Terry's Regiment is often confused with the more famous regiment of older brother Benjamin. David Terry, like his brother, was born in Kentucky and moved to Texas at an early age. After practicing law briefly, the younger Terry served in Jack Hays' First Texas Regiment in the Mexican War. The gold rush led him to California in 1849. Although unsuccessful as a miner, he prospered as a lawyer and was elected to the California Supreme Court. He became involved in a controversy with San Francisco vigilantes and later killed U.S. Senator David C. Broderick in a duel. He returned to Texas in 1863, enlisted in the Confederate army, and fought in the Battle of Chickamauga. After being wounded in that engagement, he returned home. In 1864 he raised the regiment that bore his name.[245]

The new regiment, with Terry as colonel, S. H. Brooks as lieutenant colonel, and J. M. Evans as major, consisted of ten undersized companies recruited in South Central Texas. Muster rolls show that only one company ("A" with 83 officers and men) had more than 60 men. Average size of the companies was between 40 and 50 men, with a total of 487 for the entire regiment. Organized late in the war, the regiment apparently never left Texas, even though John B. Magruder desperately wanted Terry's troops in Arkansas in late 1864.

Terry's Regiment was in northeast Texas in spring of 1865. In the general reorganization in April the regiment was dismounted and assigned to Hamilton P. Bee's Brigade, Maxey's Infantry Division. The *Official Records* show that on May 20, 1865, the regiment was ordered to move by rail from Richmond, Texas, to Navasota, where it disbanded when Kirby Smith surrendered the Trans Mississippi Department in May 1865.[246]

The record of John W. Wells' Regiment is even more sketchy than that of Terry's Regiment. The regiment was formed in spring 1865 by the consolidation of three independent cavalry battalions commanded by Wells, Chaplin Good, and L. E. Gillett. Wells became colonel; Good, lieutenant colonel; and Gillett, major, in the new regiment. All three of the battalions had served previously in Indian Territory. Wells' and Good's battalions had distinguished themselves in fighting while attached to Gano's Brigade. The new regiment, with 594 men on its muster rolls, was slightly larger than Terry's.[247]

Wells' Regiment had been formed only briefly when it was among the nine cavalry regiments ordered dismounted by Kirby Smith. The regiment joined Walker's Texas Division (now commanded by Maj. Gen. John Forney) camped near Mansfield, Louisiana, in late February 1865. Soon thereafter the division, including Wells' Regiment, headed back to Texas, arriving at Hempstead in mid-April. According to Forney's biographer, the division disbanded in Texas on May 19-20 after learning of Kirby Smith's impending surrender.[248]

Stewart Sifakis, in *Compendium of the Confederate Armies: Texas,* lists thirty-three battalions of Texas cavalry that served in the Confederate army at one time or another. Most of these battalions were either expanded or consolidated with other battalions to form regiments. One battalion that maintained its independent status and saw considerable military action was George H. Giddings' Cavalry. Organized with six companies in spring 1864, Giddings' Battalion with 571 men on its muster rolls was larger than many Confederate regiments at that stage of the war. The commander of the battalion, George H. Giddings, was a well-known and highly respected Texas lawyer, soldier, and businessman whose San Antonio-San Diego Mail Line provided a vital link between Texas and California in the late 1850s. His younger brother, DeWitt Clinton Giddings, was lieutenant colonel of the Twenty-first Texas Cavalry in Parsons' Brigade.[249]

Giddings' Battalion played a major role in John S. Ford's campaigns in the lower Rio Grande Valley. It was Giddings and his battalion who pushed Union troops back to Brazos Island when they launched a drive toward Brownsville in September 1864. Companies from the battalion defeated Union troops at Palmito Ranch, May 12-13, 1865, in the last battle of the Civil War.[250]

A battalion commanded first by Lt. Col. Andrew Daly and later by Lt. Col. Samuel G. Ragsdale also maintained its separate identity throughout the last year of the war. Created with four companies under Daly's command in January 1864, the battalion eventually listed nine companies with more than 900 men on its muster rolls. The battalion had a distinctly Latin flavor. The personnel of First Company A (there were two companies A, two companies C, and two companies F in addition to single companies B, D, and E) and of First Company C were almost entirely Mexican Texans, and at least half of Company B were Mexicans. Also, a considerable number of French Acadian names appear on the muster rolls of several companies.[251]

The Daly-Ragsdale Battalion spent the Civil War in southeast Texas. Morning reports for the post of Sabine Pass show the battalion, or at least a part of it, stationed at Sabine Pass in the early months of 1864. Some of Daly's troopers accompanied Lt. Col. William H. Griffin in a surprise attack on two Union gunboats at Calcasieu Pass, Louisiana, on May 6, 1864. In a spirited battle the Texans forced the surrender of the gunboats, easing a potential threat of an attack on southeast Texas. Texas losses in the affair were eight killed and fourteen wounded; two of those killed and two of the wounded were from Daly's Battalion.[252]

The battalion was listed as an unattached unit assigned to Brig. Gen. Thomas F. Drayton's Cavalry Division in the latter part of 1864. Daly left the battalion during the winter; reports for Sabine Pass in January 1865 show the battalion, with approximately 200 men, stationed there under the command of Ragsdale. On April 20 five companies of the battalion were at Beaumont. Reports for May 10 list only forty-eight men of A Company of the battalion at Sabine Pass. Any record of what happened to the other companies of the battalion has not been found. In all probability the battalion was transferred elsewhere before being disbanded.[253]

CHAPTER SIX

Texas Infantry and Dismounted Cavalry in the Trans Mississippi

FIFTEEN TEXAS INFANTRY REGIMENTS and seven dismounted cavalry regiments spent the Civil War years west of the Mississippi River. Eight of these infantry regiments and three of the dismounted cavalry regiments (as well as a dismounted cavalry battalion) served in the infantry division commanded first by Henry McCulloch but made more famous under John G. Walker. One infantry regiment and four dismounted cavalry regiments served in what became Polignac's Brigade. The other six infantry regiments in the Trans Mississippi served primarily in independent units assigned to departmental sub-districts of Texas rather than in divisions or brigades, although one of this number, the Third Texas Infantry, was attached to Walker's Division for several months during 1864.

Each of the Texas Trans Mississippi infantry and dismounted cavalry regiments will be discussed in this chapter either under the heading of Walker's Texas Division, Polignac's Texas Brigade, or Independent Regiments.

WALKER'S TEXAS DIVISION

First Brigade

Twelfth Texas Infantry

Eighteenth Texas Infantry
Twenty-second Texas Infantry
Thirteenth Texas Cavalry (dismounted)

Second Brigade
Eleventh Texas Infantry
Fourteenth Texas Infantry
Twenty-eighth Texas Cavalry (dismounted)
Sixth Texas Cavalry Battalion (dismounted)

Third Brigade
Sixteenth Texas Infantry
Seventeenth Texas Infantry
Nineteenth Texas Infantry
Sixteenth Texas Cavalry (dismounted)

What came to be known as Walker's Texas Division was first organized in Arkansas in autumn 1862. Because of the threat to Little Rock and the fertile Arkansas valley, large numbers of Texas troops were rushed to the state in late summer 1862. By early fall more than 20,000 Texans were in Arkansas. In late September these troops in the Little Rock area were organized into two divisions, each composed of two brigades. Brig. Gen. Henry E. McCulloch, former Texas Ranger and brother of the celebrated Ben McCulloch, who was killed at Pea Ridge earlier in the year, was appointed commander of the First Division. Col. Overton Young, a wealthy Brazoria County planter, commanded the First Brigade, and Col. Horace Randal, one of the state's first West Point graduates, commanded the Second Brigade. The Second Division was commanded by recently promoted Brig. Gen. Allison Nelson, a Bosque County Indian agent and veteran of the Mexican War and the Cuban War for Independence. Nelson also commanded the First Brigade in his division. Col. George Flournoy, former Texas attorney general and secessionist leader, headed the Second Brigade in Nelson's Division.[1]

Ten days after the organization of the two divisions, Nelson died from typhoid fever, which was prevalent in the Arkansas camps. Soon thereafter, Lt. Gen. Theophilus Holmes, commander of the Trans Mississippi Department, combined the two Texas divisions into one under McCulloch's command. The new division was soon reduced to three brigades. The brigade previously led by Nelson and now under the command of Col. James Deshler was detached from McCulloch's Division and assigned duty at Arkansas Post, leaving the division with three brigades.[2]

Col. Overton Young, commander of the First Brigade of McCulloch's Division, also remained as the commander of the Twelfth Texas Infantry, one of the four regiments in the First Brigade. His executive officer, Lt. Col. Benjamin A. Philpott, directed the regiment when Young had brigade duties. The other regiments in the First Brigade were the Eighteenth Texas Infantry, commanded by well-known East Texas lawyer and political leader William Beck Ochiltree; the Twenty-second Texas Infantry, commanded by Tyler lawyer, state legislator, and future governor Richard Bennett Hubbard; and the Thirteenth Texas Cavalry (dismounted), commanded by Mexican War veteran, farmer, and merchant John H. Burnett of Crockett.[3]

The First Brigade was made up primarily of men recruited in East Texas and the Brazos River valley. The regiments in the brigade were all large, each listing greater than 1,000 men on their muster rolls. The Twelfth and Eighteenth infantries had eleven companies; the Thirteenth Cavalry and the Twenty-second Infantry had the traditional ten companies.[4]

Horace Randal, commander of the Second Brigade, had been the commander of the Twenty-eighth Texas Cavalry (dismounted), one of the regiments in the brigade. When Randal assumed his duties as brigade commander, Lt. Col. Eli Baxter, Jr., a Marshall lawyer and state legislator, was promoted to colonel and commander of the regiment.[5]

The Twenty-eighth Texas was originally a mounted unit; however, like several other cavalry regiments in Arkansas, it was ordered on September 18, 1862, to give up its horses because infantry troops were needed. M. Jane Johansson, author of a history of the Twenty-eighth Texas, noted that "it is not known how the men of the 28th reacted to the news of dismounting." Men in other cavalry regiments forced to give up their horses reacted with bitterness and anger, threatening to desert if they were not remounted, so it may be assumed the men of the Twenty-eighth reacted similarly. Like other cavalrymen who lost their mounts, the men of the Twenty-eighth, wrote Johansson, "refused to call themselves infantry, pre-

Horace Randal, Colonel, Twenty-eighth Texas Cavalry.
—Courtesy Harold B. Simpson Research Center, Hillsboro, Texas

ferring the label 'dismounted cavalry' as though it were a temporary condition."[6]

Oran M. Roberts, a justice on the Texas Supreme Court, president of the Texas secession convention, and future governor, commanded the Eleventh Infantry, one of the regiments in Randal's Brigade. Although he lacked the military training of Randal, Roberts (who was nearly twenty years older than Randal) believed his commission made him senior in rank. He appealed the matter to Generals McCulloch and Holmes, who in turn referred the issue to Richmond. The issue was closed when the secretary of war ruled in Randal's favor.[7]

Former Texas governor Edward Clark commanded the Fourteenth Infantry, the third regiment in Randal's Brigade. A Marshall lawyer, state legislator, and Mexican War veteran, Clark was serving as lieutenant governor when the secession convention declared the chief executive's office vacant after Sam Houston failed to take the oath to support the Confederacy, thus elevating Clark to the position. As governor in the early months of the Civil War, Clark worked closely with Confederate officials in raising and equipping troops for military service. Although he performed credibly as chief executive, Clark was narrowly defeated when he sought election as governor in autumn 1861. He accepted his defeat gracefully and almost immediately received a commission to raise and organize an infantry regiment. His regiment was recruited primarily in East Texas, like the others in Randal's Brigade.[8]

The six companies of Robert S. Gould's Sixth Texas Cavalry Battalion made up the other unit in Randal's Brigade. The commanding officer, Lieutenant Colonel Gould, was a native of North Carolina and graduate of the University of Alabama. He migrated to Texas in 1850 and settled in Centerville, governmental seat of Leon County. After serving in the secession convention, Gould organized the six companies that made up the battalion. Although the unit was organized as cavalry, it was dismounted before leaving Texas and ordered to Arkansas. The battalion was originally assigned to Allison Nelson's Brigade but following his death was transferred to Randal's Brigade.[9]

George Flournoy's Third Brigade consisted of one dismounted cavalry and three infantry regiments. Unlike the other two brigades in the division, which were made up almost entirely of East Texans, Flournoy's Brigade was a mixture of recruits from both East and Central Texas. The men of Flournoy's own Sixteenth Infantry came largely from Central Texas and included among its ranks an Irish private, Joseph P. Blessington, who later wrote the classic account of the division entitled *The Campaigns of Walker's Texas Division.* Lt. Col. James E. Shepard, a Washington County attorney and, like Flournoy, a member of the secession convention, was executive officer of the Sixteenth Texas. He directed the regiment while Flournoy handled brigade duties.[10]

The second regiment in Flournoy's Third Brigade, the Seventeenth Texas Infantry, was also recruited primarily in Central Texas. Commander of the regiment was the experienced and capable, but sometimes unpopular, Col. R. T. P. Allen. An 1834 graduate of the U.S. Military Academy, Allen served in the Seminole Wars before resigning from the army to pursue a career that included civil engineering, the Methodist ministry, and education. He moved to Texas from California in 1857 to serve as superintendent of the newly created Bastrop Military Institute. With the outbreak of war he was named commander of the Fourth Texas Infantry, which after brief training in Texas was assigned to duty in Virginia. As noted previously, Allen was highly competent, but his strict training regime made him unacceptable to the officers and men of the Fourth. A protest against his appointment led him to return to

R.T.P. Allen, Colonel, Seventeenth Texas Infantry.
—Courtesy Harold B. Simpson Research Center, Hillsboro, Texas

Texas. He resumed leadership of the Bastrop Military Institute, but following a call by Governor Lubbock for additional regiments he raised what became the Seventeenth Texas Infantry.[11]

Although Allen continued to be a strict disciplinarian, he was generally considered fair by the men of the regiment. He commanded the Seventeenth Texas until November 1863, when he was appointed commandant of the Confederate prison at Camp Ford, near Tyler, Texas. He was succeeded as regimental commander by Lt. Col. George W. Jones, a popular lawyer and district attorney from Bastrop. Jones commanded the regiment for the remainder of the war.[12]

One of the company officers of the Seventeenth Infantry, Capt. Elijah P. Petty of Company F, was a law partner of Lieutenant Colonel Jones. When he volunteered for Confederate service, Petty promised his wife, Margaret, that he would write to her at every opportunity to keep her informed of his activities. His letters, covering the period from his enlistment in the Bastrop Lubbock Guards in October 1861 to his death at Pleasant Hill in April 1864, have been edited by historian Norman D. Brown and published as *Journey to Pleasant Hill.* They form a rich and complete account of the Seventeenth Infantry and Walker's Division for much of the war.[13]

Richard Waterhouse, Colonel, Nineteenth Texas Infantry.
—Courtesy Harold B. Simpson Research Center, Hillsboro, Texas

Thirty-year-old Richard Waterhouse was the commander of the Third Infantry Regiment in Flournoy's Brigade, the Nineteenth Texas. A native of Tennessee, Waterhouse had run away from home as a teenager to take part in the Mexican War. He rejoined his family after the war and moved with them to San Augustine, Texas, in 1849. There he went into the mercantile business with his father. When the war began, he helped organize the Nineteenth Texas with recruits from East Texas. Robert H. Graham was lieutenant colonel and Ennis W. Taylor major of the regiment.[14]

The Sixteenth Texas Cavalry (dismounted), the fourth regiment in Flournoy's Brigade, joined McCulloch's Division after brief service with Van Dorn's army in Mississippi. Commanded by Seminole and Mexican War veteran William F. Fitzhugh of Collin County, the Sixteenth Texas was organized at Dallas in early 1862, dismounted almost immediately, and rushed to Corinth, Mississippi, as part of the Confederate buildup following the Battle of Shiloh. After the evacuation of Corinth, the Sixteenth was ordered to Arkansas, where it was assigned to Flournoy's Brigade.[15]

McCulloch's Division spent the autumn months of 1862 in Camp Nelson, two miles north of Little Rock. Extremely cold weather, impure drinking water, lack of proper clothing, dysentery, diarrhea, and various fevers led to much suffering. Hundreds of troops died that autumn and winter, and others were discharged because of illness. Almost every company saw its ranks diminished by illness. Capt. Elijah Petty of the Sixteenth Texas reported that men "are dying around us fast.... At almost all hours of the day, you can hear guns firing the salute over some soldier gone to his long home far away from friends & home."[16]

In December, Lieutenant General Holmes ordered the division to move to Arkansas Post. After a march of eighteen miles, however, the order was countermanded and the men marched back to the Little Rock area. While camped there the Texans were informed that Maj. Gen. John G. Walker was being assigned as the new division commander. Brig. Gen. Henry McCulloch was reassigned as commander of the Third Brigade, and Colonel Flournoy resumed his duties as commander of the Sixteenth Infantry.[17]

General Walker assumed his duties as division commander on January 1, 1863. The new commander came to the Trans Mississippi from Virginia, where he had the reputation as a highly capable officer. Although he was not a West Point graduate, the Missouri-born Walker had served as an officer in the U.S. Army before resigning to accept a commission with the Confederates. As a brigade and later division commander he served with Lee's army in the Virginia and Maryland campaigns of 1862. Because of his performance at Sharpsburg in September 1862, he was promoted to major general and assigned to the Trans Mississippi Department. A small man, weighing 140 pounds, Walker was a quiet, dignified, professional soldier who demanded, and expected, the best from his men. Although an outsider with the reputation of being a strict disciplinarian, Walker quickly won the respect and admiration of the Texans who became proud to say they served in "Walker's Texas Division."[18]

The week after Walker assumed command, the division received orders to march to the relief of Arkansas Post, which was under attack from Union forces commanded by John McClernand. The Texans, who had marched to Pine Bluff the previous week, marched twenty-five miles in the direction of Arkansas Post when they learned that the Confederate garrison of nearly 5,000 troops had surrendered. The division marched back to its encampment a few miles north of Pine Bluff, where it remained until ordered in late April to move to northern Louisiana as part of the effort to relieve Union pressure on Vicksburg.[19]

As the division headed toward Monroe, Louisiana, the First Brigade marched under a new commander. Brig. Gen. James M. Hawes, a West Point graduate and Mexican War veteran from Kentucky who had served with Bragg's Army of Tennessee, was reassigned to the Trans Mississippi Department and appointed commander of Walker's First Brigade, replacing Col. Overton Young, who resumed command of the Twelfth Infantry.[20]

When Walker's troops reached Monroe on May 10, the military situation in Louisiana was unsettled. In the northern corner of the state U. S. Grant was marching his army southward for a move across the Mississippi so that he could approach Vicksburg from the east. At the same time Nathaniel P. Banks in southern Louisiana was showing signs that he might move his army up the Red River. Edmund Kirby Smith, who succeeded Theophilus H. Holmes as commander of the Trans Mississippi Department, ordered Walker's Division to join Richard Taylor, the Confederate commander of Louisiana, near Natchitoches. By the time the Texans reached Natchitoches, however, the situation was changed. Banks was encircling Port Hudson, and Grant had crossed the Mississippi and was approaching Vicksburg from the east. The Texans, who would soon acquire the sobriquet "Walker's Greyhounds" because of their long and rapid marches, were now ordered to swing back to northeastern Louisiana to attack Union supply lines believed to extend from Milliken's Bend south through Young's Point and on to Warrenton on the eastern side of the Mississippi below Vicksburg.[21]

Walker's Texans attacked the enemy in northeastern Louisiana on June 7. Under the plan developed by General Taylor, three points were to be attacked simultaneously. McCulloch's Brigade was to assault Union forces at Milliken's Bend at the same time three regiments from Hawes' Brigade assailed the enemy at Young's Point, ten miles to the south. Meanwhile, the Thirteenth Louisiana Cavalry Battalion and the Thirteenth Dismounted Texas Cavalry were to raid Union-held cotton plantations near Lake Providence to the north of Milliken's Bend.

McCulloch's troops began the assault at Milliken's Bend near dawn. Waterhouse's Nineteenth Infantry, which was on the Confederate right, opened the attack, followed by the Seventeenth Infantry in the center and the Sixteenth Cavalry on the left. Flournoy's Sixteenth Infantry supported all three regiments making the main assault. The initial charge drove the enemy, consisting of troops from four black regiments supported by Iowa and Illinois cavalry, from the outer defense lines. Resistance stiffened as the battle continued, with the Federals receiving artillery support from two gunboats on the river. In hand-to-hand fighting some of McCulloch's men gave no quarter to Union black troops, killing dozens who attempted to surrender.[22]

Around 10:00 in the morning McCulloch concluded the Federal position was too well defended and withdrew his troops from enemy fire. General Walker meanwhile ordered Randal's Brigade to the scene but found that McCulloch had already pulled his brigade away from the site. The weather was extremely warm, drinking water was scarce, and the men exhausted. Later that day Walker moved the two brigades to the village of Richmond, several miles to the east.[23]

Losses in the battle at Milliken's Bend were high. Federal casualties were 652 killed, wounded, captured, and missing. McCulloch reported forty-four men killed, 131 wounded, and ten missing, or 12.2 percent of those engaged. Half of the Confederate casualties were in Colonel Allen's Seventeenth Texas: twenty-one killed, sixty-eight wounded, and three missing. The Sixteenth Texas Cavalry, led in the battle by Lt. Col. Edward P. Gregg, had nineteen killed, forty-seven wounded, and one missing. Surprisingly, Waterhouse's Nineteenth Texas, which opened the assault, had only two killed, eleven wounded, and six missing. Flournoy's Sixteenth Infantry, which supported the other regiments making the attack, reported two killed and five wounded.[24]

McCulloch, while praising his men for their courage in the fighting, blamed the Confederate failure on poor information he had received from a local guide concerning the rugged terrain. His immediate superior, General Walker, agreed that the Texans had shown gallantry in the attack, and attributed the setback to want of local knowledge and strength of the enemy defenses. General Taylor, the overall commander, was more critical, reporting to Kirby Smith that "much greater loss ought to have been inflicted upon the enemy." He also noted that "General McCulloch appears to have shown great personal bravery, but no capacity for handling men."[25]

The other Confederate efforts in Taylor's three-pronged

attack accomplished little. General Hawes moved his brigade to Young's Point as ordered, but concluded the enemy strength there was too great. He withdrew his troops after a brief skirmish. The raid on the Lake Providence cotton plantations by the Louisiana and Texas cavalry also achieved little.[26]

General Taylor had always believed that efforts to relieve Vicksburg by attacks in northeastern Louisiana were futile. The failure at Milliken's Bend strengthened that belief. Departmental commander Kirby Smith remained unconvinced, however, and instructed General Walker to continue his activities in the area. In late June, supported by James C. Tappan's Arkansas Brigade and William H. Parsons' Texas Cavalry, Walker's Division destroyed dozens of Union-controlled cotton plantations and captured more than 2,000 African Americans working at the plantations. Near Goodrich Landing, Randal's Brigade assisted Parsons' cavalrymen in the capture of a small Union post defended by black troops. Apparently, a dozen or more of the blacks were killed by Randal's men as they were being escorted back to camp as prisoners.[27]

Despite Confederate efforts, the Vicksburg garrison surrendered on July 4, 1863. The loss was a tremendous blow to the Texans of Walker's Division. Joseph Blessington, the Irish private in the Sixteenth Texas, later wrote "as soon as it became known for certain, in camp, that Vicksburg had surrendered, a perfect storm of indignation burst forth among the troops." Edward Cade, a surgeon in the Twenty-eighth Cavalry, wrote his wife that "the army in consequence of the sad news is despondent and gloomy." He noted, however, there was "no feeling on the part of anyone to abandon the struggle. . . ."[28]

With the loss of Vicksburg, and Port Hudson a week later, the need for Confederate troops in northeastern Louisiana diminished. In mid-July Kirby Smith ordered Walker to move his division to Alexandria to join other Confederate troops commanded by Richard Taylor. While on the march Brig. Gen. Henry McCulloch was relieved from command of the Third Brigade and resigned to duty in Texas. Flournoy resumed temporary command of the brigade pending the arrival of the new brigade commander, William R. Scurry.[29]

The division remained in the vicinity of Alexandria throughout the latter part of August and most of September. Except for a march by Randal's Brigade north to the Ouachita River in early

September, there was little military activity for the division. The Texans battled boredom, heat, and the disappointment of not receiving furloughs to visit home.[30]

In late September Walker's Greyhounds were on the move again. A large Union army under the command of Maj. Gen. William B. Franklin was moving up the Bayou Teche country in southern Louisiana. Walker's Division joined other Confederate forces that Richard Taylor was bringing together to block the Federal advance.

The division left Alexandria on September 27, and after a thirty-mile march it reached the village of Washington, about five miles north of Opelousas, two days later. Taylor, who was concerned about a possible Union movement from Natchez as well, then ordered the Texans to march back to Simmesport, near the confluence of the Atchafalya and Red rivers. The division remained there briefly and then returned to the vicinity of Washington.[31]

Walker's troops arrived back in the Washington area in time to help Taylor block Franklin's forward movement. On October 24 three regiments of Walker's Division—the Eleventh, Fifteenth (which had been temporarily attached to Flournoy's Brigade), and Eighteenth infantries—and James P. Major's cavalry attacked and drove back lead units of Franklin's army near Washington. The attack was delivered with such fury that Franklin pulled his army below Opelousas while he reconsidered the whole campaign.[32]

After the fighting on the 24th, Walker's Division fell back to a new campground at Holmesville. While there the division was joined by the new commander of the Third Brigade, Brig. Gen. William R. Scurry. Skilled orator, poet, and born fighter, Scurry had acquired a reputation as one of the state's premier soldiers. His arrival was greeted with considerable enthusiasm by his fellow Texans. J. P. Blessington of the Sixteenth Infantry observed that "General Scurry was generally known by all the troops in the division" due to his service at Valverde, Glorieta Pass, and Galveston. Capt. Elijah P. Petty of the Seventeenth Texas wrote to his wife: "I am pleased with him. I knew him well in Texas. He is a fighter and those who follow him will go to the Cannon's Mouth."[33]

While the Texans in Walker's Division were celebrating the arrival of General Scurry, Franklin was still considering what action he should take. Because of logistical problems his troops were scattered from Opelousas back to New Iberia. General Taylor determined to strike quickly while Franklin hesitated. He ordered Tom Green's cavalry and three regiments of Walker's Division (the Eleventh, Fifteenth, and Eighteenth, now serving temporarily as a separate brigade under the command of Col. O. M. Roberts) to attack a small, isolated Union division of two brigades near Bayou Bourbeau several miles south of Opelousas.

In the attack on November 3, Roberts' infantry, numbering 950 men, was on the Confederate left. Green's cavalry, 2,000 troopers, was on the right. In the fighting that lasted approximately three hours the Confederates overwhelmed the outnumbered Union defenders, driving them back through the woods and across the bayou. When the fighting ended, 25 Federals were dead, 129 wounded, and 562 captured, or almost 40 percent of the 1,800 Union troops engaged. Confederate losses totaled 180. The majority of these were in Roberts' infantry: 21 killed, 82 wounded, and 38 missing, or a total of 141 men.[34]

Walker's Division moved north to the Simmesport area several days after the battle at Bayou Bourbeau. The division, which listed 375 officers and 3,878 men present for duty at the end of November, marched toward Plaquemine, twelve miles south of Baton Rouge, on December 1. They turned back when General Walker received reports that the enemy had reinforced the garrison there. The division returned to the Simmesport area and went into winter quarters near Marksville, halfway between Alexandria and Simmesport.[35]

During the winter months of 1863-1864, the men of Walker's Division spent much of the time drilling and constructing fortifications. The appearance of enemy gunboats on the river led to an occasional exchange of fire, but there was no major military activity. In late February the Texans bade farewell to Brig. Gen. James Hawes, who was relieved of his command of the First Brigade and assigned to duty in Texas. Although Hawes had disappointed his superiors by failing to attack at Young's Point, he apparently had the affection of his men. Before he departed, members of the brigade held a farewell meeting at which they adopted resolutions praising him for his "mild, but firm, discipline, his unflinching pursuit of the dictates of duty, coupled with a paternal solicitude for the safety and comfort of his troops...."[36]

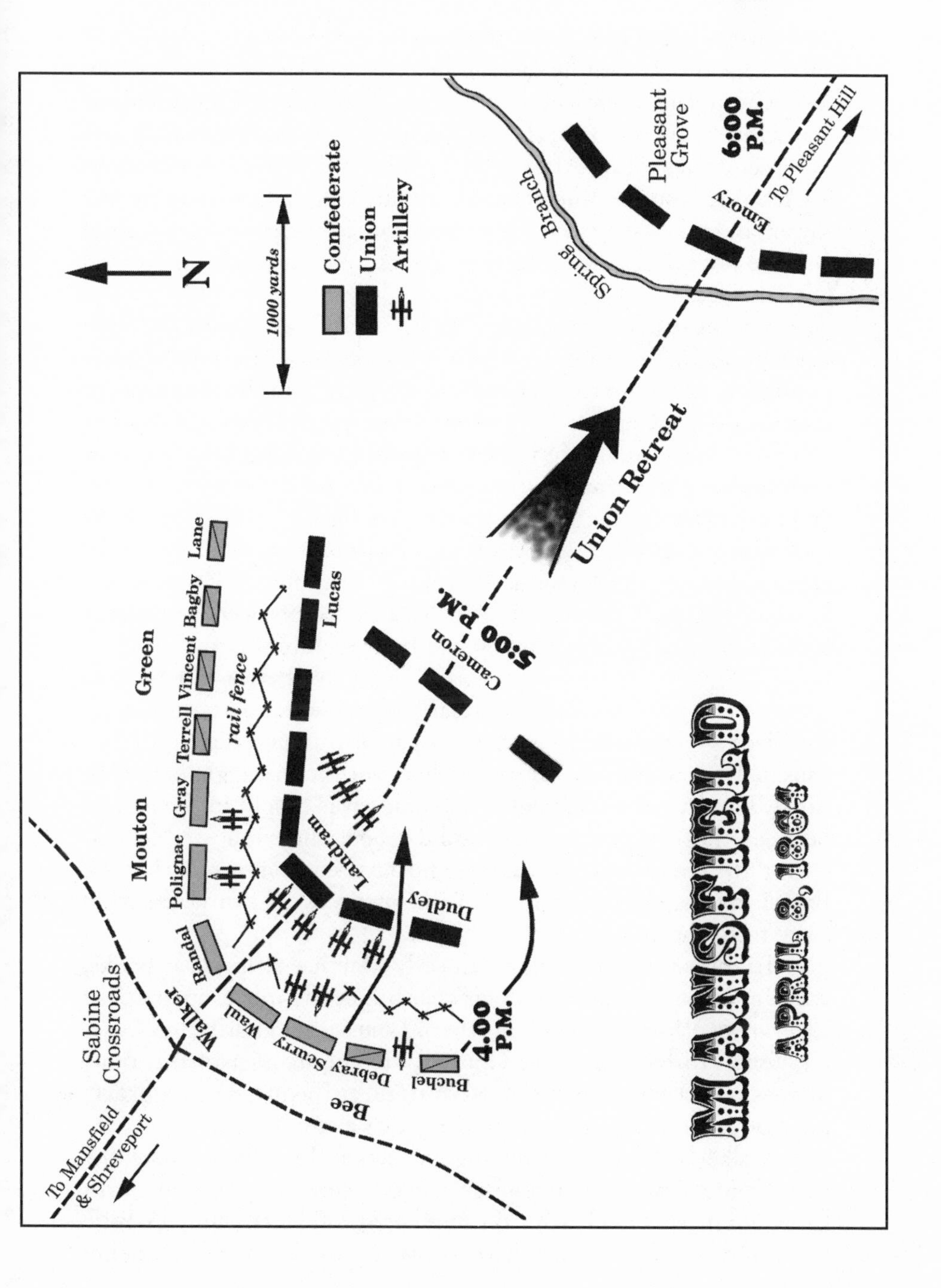
N
1000 yards
Confederate
Union
Artillery
Pleasant Grove
6:00 P.M.
Spring Branch
Emory
To Pleasant Hill
Union Retreat
Lucas
Cameron
5:00 P.M.
Green
Mouton
Polignac
Gray
Terrell
Vincent
Bagby
Lane
rail fence
Landram
Dudley
Randal
Walker
Waul
Scurry
Debray
Buchel
Bee
4:00 P.M.
Sabine Crossroads
To Mansfield & Shreveport
MANSFIELD
APRIL 8, 1864

Brig. Gen. Thomas N. Waul was the new commander of the First Brigade. A wealthy lawyer and cotton planter from Central Texas, Waul had raised and commanded Waul's Legion earlier in the war. Under his command the Legion played a prominent role in the defense of Vicksburg. After the surrender and prisoner exchange at Vicksburg, Waul commanded an infantry brigade defending the lower Brazos Valley. His appointment to command the First Brigade provided Walker's Division with a mature and experienced combat officer.[37]

The morale of the men in Walker's Division appears to have been good in the winter months of 1863-1864. Furloughs were granted a little more freely, food was adequate, and the health of the men improved. Captain Petty of the Seventeenth Infantry wrote his daughter "our army here is in fine health and spirits. I never saw men looking better and more cheerful. We are in better condition and humor for fighting than we ever have been. . . ."[38]

Unfortunately, there was some discontent, particularly in the cavalry units of the division. Men in the dismounted cavalry regiments were angry that additional mounted units were still being formed in Texas even after they had been required to give up their horses. This unhappiness was exacerbated by the lower pay scale received for infantry service. In early March several companies of the Twenty-eighth Texas refused to perform their assigned duties. This led to arrests and bitter feeling within the regiment. Col. Eli H. Baxter, the regimental commander, was caught in the middle between those in the regiment and division who supported leniency for the mutineers and those who favored severe punishment. Baxter believed only a fight with the enemy would turn attention away from the affair.[39]

Baxter soon got his fight. In early March, Nathaniel P. Banks, the Union commander in Louisiana, began his move up the Red River in an effort to occupy northern Louisiana and drive into eastern Texas. Kirby Smith, the Confederate commander of the Trans Mississippi Department, took steps to meet the invaders by ordering troops from Texas to support Taylor's army.[40]

Walker's Texans, occupying the lower Red River, were the first Confederates to encounter Banks' army as it moved north from Simmesport. Heavily outnumbered, Walker could do little to stop the Union advance. After some skirmishing with the enemy on March 14, Walker pulled his division back to Bayou du Lac. There he received word from General Taylor to withdraw toward Natchitoches. On the 16th the division began a march that would take it northwest toward Natchitoches. On the march, which covered more than 160 miles, Walker's Greyhounds were joined by Taylor and infantry brigades commanded by Alfred A. Mouton and the Prince de Polignac. As they approached Pleasant Hill, a small town west of Natchitoches, the Confederates were joined by the first of the cavalry reinforcements from Texas. While the Texas cavalry remained in the Pleasant Hill area to scout out the approaching Union army, Taylor and the other Confederates moved on to Mansfield, a crossroads town fifteen miles to the north. There the Confederates, including Walker's three brigades, camped for three days while waiting for additional reinforcements.[41]

Taylor was joined at Mansfield by departmental commander Edmund Kirby Smith. Smith suggested either falling back to Shreveport or withdrawing into Texas. Taylor, who had grown weary of constant retreating, was determined to fight. Although the reinforcements from Arkansas had not arrived, Taylor believed the enemy should be attacked while the Union army was scattered along a single road from Grand Ecore to Pleasant Hill and Mansfield. On April 7 he ordered Walker, Mouton (now commanding a two-brigade division), and his cavalry commander, Tom Green, to prepare for battle the next day.[42]

On the morning of April 8 the Confederates left Mansfield and marched three miles down the Pleasant Hill road to the site Taylor had chosen to make his stand. By 2:00 in the afternoon Confederate troop dispositions were complete. Taylor placed Waul's Brigade and Scurry's Brigade on the right side of the road, with Hamilton P. Bee's cavalry on their right. Randal's Brigade was immediately to the left of the road, with Mouton's two brigades to Randal's left. James P. Major's cavalry division anchored the left side of the Confederate line. Two artillery batteries were posted on the Confederate right and two on the left. Taylor's army numbered 8,800 men: 5,300 infantry, 3,000 cavalry, and 500 artillery.[43]

The lead units of Banks' army approached the battle site in the early afternoon. Although he had only 4,800 troops in the immediate area, Banks, who arrived around 3:00, seemed determined to push past the Confederates. When his subordinates argued that such action would be unwise with the number of troops available, Banks agreed to postpone the advance until additional infantry could be brought up.[44]

While Banks waited, Taylor ordered his troops to attack. Since the fighting was on Louisiana soil, Taylor gave the honor of opening the assault to Henry Gray's Louisiana Brigade in Mouton's Division, followed by the Prince de Polignac's Texas Brigade. Once the attack was under way, Taylor ordered Randal's Brigade forward, then Waul and Scurry. In the initial assault losses were high as the Confederates, "yelling like Indians," rushed across the open field. After being initially repulsed, Scurry's Texans broke through the Union line on the left. At the same time Confederate horsemen were moving around the enemy on both flanks. Brig. Gen. Thomas E. G. Ransom, the Union commander on the front, ordered his troops to fall back to a second line of defense. The arrival of Union reinforcements halted the Confederates for about an hour before the second line gave way. The Federal troops broke and ran, with the Confederates in pursuit through the woods. "Urged on by the excitement of victory, we pursue[d] the flying foe," wrote Pvt. Joseph Blessington of the Sixteenth Texas, "killing where they dare[d] resist, and capturing them by the hundreds." Darkness and the arrival of additional Union troops stopped the Confederates in spirited fighting at a small orchard known as Pleasant Grove.[45]

Banks withdrew the Union army from Pleasant Grove during the night. He fell back to Pleasant Hill, some eleven miles to the southeast. The Confederates, now joined by Thomas J. Churchill and the Arkansas and Missouri divisions from Sterling Price's army, followed the next morning. As the Confederates neared Pleasant Hill, they found Banks' army, reinforced by A. J. Smith's Corps, in battle line stretching from an elevated area on the left known as College Hill to a wooded height on the north side of the Mansfield road.[46]

Taylor allowed his army a few hours to rest before beginning the attack. Churchill's two divisions were placed on the Confederate right, or south, side of the line. Walker's Division occupied the center of the line with Scurry's Brigade next to the Arkansas division, Waul's Brigade to Scurry's left, and Randal's Brigade to Waul's left. Tom Green's cavalry was on the extreme left.

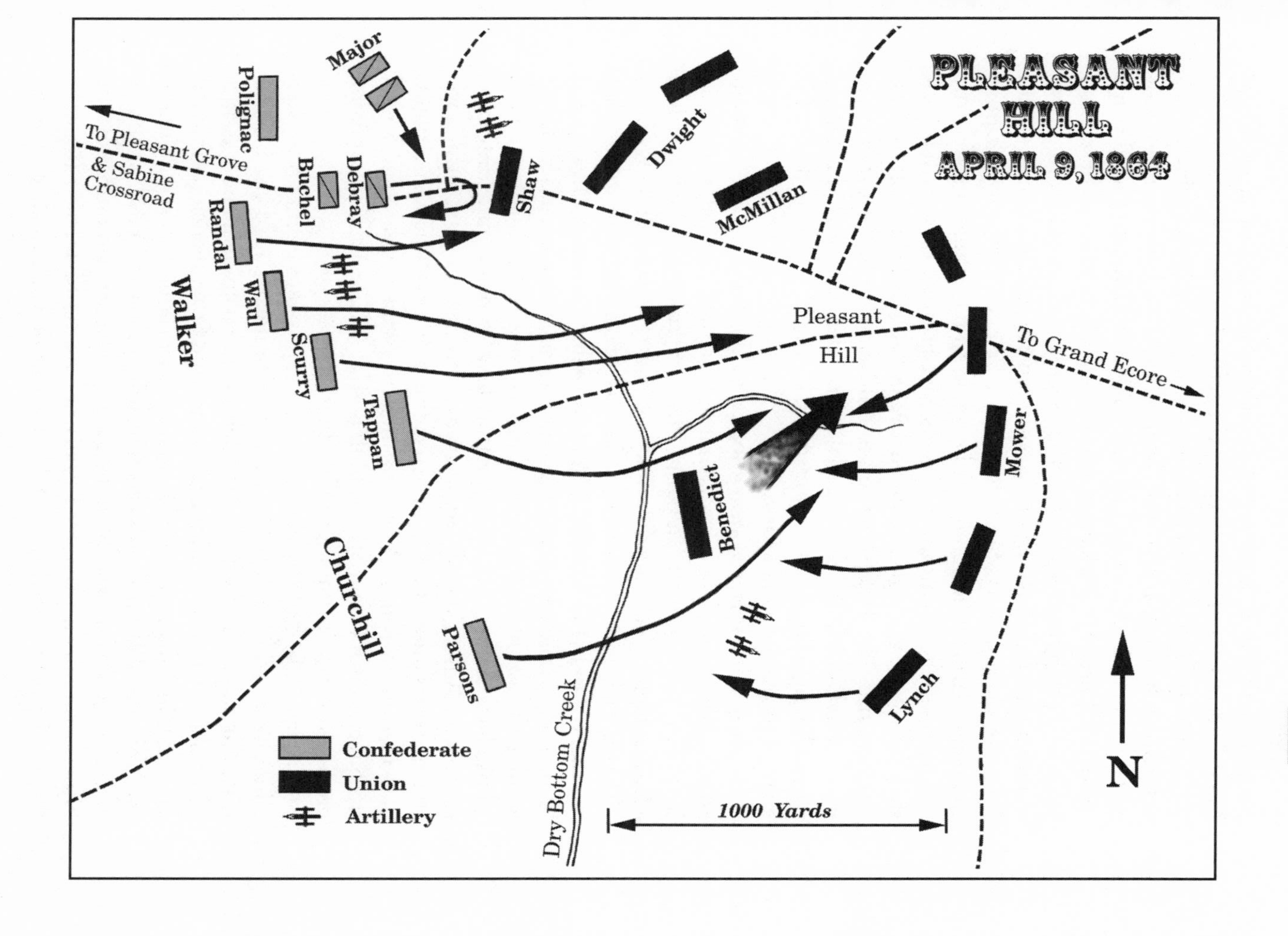

PLEASANT HILL
APRIL 9, 1864
To Pleasant Grove & Sabine Crossroad
Polignac
Major
Buchel
Debray
Shaw
Dwight
McMillan
Randal
Waul
Walker
Scurry
Tappan
Pleasant Hill
To Grand Ecore
Mower
Benedict
Churchill
Parsons
Lynch
Dry Bottom Creek
Confederate
Union
Artillery
1000 Yards
N

Mouton's Division, which had suffered the heaviest casualties at Mansfield, was held in reserve on the left.

Slightly after 4:00 in the afternoon, Taylor ordered his troops forward. Churchill's divisions opened the attack on the Confederate right, followed soon after by Walker's Division and Green's cavalry. Churchill's Arkansans and Missourians drove the enemy back on the south, exposing the enemy's right wing to heavy Confederate fire. Just when it appeared the Confederates would rout the enemy, A. J. Smith's troops, veterans of the Vicksburg campaign, struck Churchill's right flank. In bitter fighting first the Missourians and then the Arkansans gave ground. As they fell back they left Walker's right, manned by Scurry's Brigade, exposed to flanking fire. The Texans battled to hold their ground but were giving way when Waul's and Randal's Brigades stemmed the Union tide. The fighting went on until dusk, when Taylor ordered his exhausted troops to fall back.[47]

Both sides suffered heavy losses in the fighting at Mansfield and Pleasant Hill. The Confederates sustained 1,000 casualties at Mansfield and another 1,200 at Pleasant Hill. The Federals had 2,200 casualties at Mansfield and 1,400 at Pleasant Hill. Walker's Division had 614 casualties in the two days; 69 men killed, 404 wounded, and 141 missing (and presumed captured). General Walker, hit in the groin while rallying his men at Pleasant Hill, was among the wounded. Among the dead was Capt. Elijah P. Petty, whose letters to his family in Central Texas provide much information about Walker's Division. Petty was hit in the breast with grape shot at Pleasant Hill. He survived the battle but died that night. Col. George W. Jones, Petty's former law partner who commanded the Seventeenth Infantry after Col. R. T. P. Allen returned home the previous year, was among the captured.[48]

Scurry's Brigade, which was badly exposed to enemy fire when Churchill's troops fell back at Pleasant Hill, sustained the highest losses in Walker's Division: 250 men killed, wounded, and missing. The bulk of these were in the Sixteenth and Seventeenth regiments, each of which had over 100 casualties. The other two regiments in the brigade, Waterhouse's Nineteenth Infantry and Fitzhugh's Sixteenth Cavalry, had few casualties: sixteen wounded in the Nineteenth and no reported casualties in the Sixteenth. Randal's Brigade had 188 casualties and Waul's Brigade 176 casualties. Of the regiments in these two brigades, Randal's old Twenty-eighth Cavalry, now commanded by Eli H. Baxter, had the highest losses, with twelve killed, sixty-two wounded, and two missing in the two days' fighting.[49]

Although he won a tactical victory at Pleasant Hill, Banks continued his withdrawal toward Grand Ecore on the Red River. Richard Taylor favored aggressive pursuit with his full army but was overruled by his superior Kirby Smith, who was more concerned about the Union advance from Little Rock by Frederick Steele. In spite of Taylor's pleas, Smith ordered Walker's and Churchill's divisions to Arkansas to support Sterling Price in his efforts to stop Steele from moving south to join Banks.

Smith left Taylor with Polignac's infantry and Green's cavalry to deal with Banks while he rode north to direct operations in Arkansas.[50]

Walker's veterans began their march to Arkansas three days after the battle at Pleasant Hill. They were joined near Shreveport by Col. Philip N. Luckett and his Third Texas Infantry. This regiment, whose previous service was exclusively in Texas, had been ordered to join William R. Scurry's Brigade as replacement for the losses at Mansfield and Pleasant Hill.[51]

On April 24 Walker's Texans crossed the Arkansas state line. Two days later they camped twelve miles south of Camden. On that day General Steele, learning that Banks was retreating, decided to abandon Camden and withdraw to Little Rock. Kirby Smith, who assumed direct command of Confederate forces in Arkansas, ordered his troops to pursue Steele. Heavy rain, deep mud, and poor roads made movement difficult for both armies. The Confederate cavalry overtook the rear guard of Steele's army as it neared Jenkins' Ferry on the Saline River. Steele's troops fought off the Confederate attackers while Federal engineers threw pontoon bridges across the flooded river. Sterling Price's Arkansans and Missourians, who were in the lead of the Confederate column, made a series of uncoordinated attacks but failed to stop the enemy withdrawal. Walker's Division reached Jenkins' Ferry just as the earlier Confederate efforts were failing. In a last effort to crush the enemy, Kirby Smith ordered the Texans to attack the enemy's left flank. In the assault Scurry's Brigade was on the Confederate extreme right, Randal's Brigade to Scurry's left and in the center, and Waul's Brigade to

Randal's left. Although Walker's exhausted troops attacked with fury, they were unable to prevent the Federal withdrawal.[52]

In the savage fighting at Jenkins' Ferry all three brigade commanders in Walker's Division were wounded; two of them, William R. Scurry and Horace Randal, mortally. Scurry, the fierce warrior who had proved himself at Valverde, Glorieta, Galveston, Mansfield, and Pleasant Hill, refused to leave the field when he was wounded and bled to death on the battlefield. Horace Randal, wounded about the same time, did not die until May 2, an hour after Scurry's funeral. Thomas Waul, who was also wounded, remained on the field until the fighting ended. He spent the summer recovering from his wounds.[53]

Walker's Division sustained 341 of the nearly 1,000 Confederate casualties. Randal's Brigade, which was in the center of the attack, had the heaviest loss: forty-five killed and 111 wounded. Once again Randal's old regiment, the Twenty-eighth Cavalry, had the highest losses in the brigade, with twenty killed and forty wounded. Waul's Brigade suffered one hundred casualties in the fighting. Most of these were in Overton Young's Twelfth Infantry, which had eight killed and sixty-eight wounded. Scurry's Brigade, on the extreme right, sustained the smallest number of casualties in the division, eighty-six. Two-thirds of these were in the newly assigned Third Texas Infantry, which had twelve men killed and thirty-eight wounded.[54]

On May 4, four days after the battle at Jenkins' Ferry, Walker's Division left its camp and returned to Camden. After a brief rest there the division headed south to rejoin Richard Taylor in his continuing efforts to crush Banks' Union army. En route Robert P. Maclay, an officer on Walker's staff, was placed in command of Randal's Brigade by Kirby Smith. A West Point graduate and veteran of the Seminole and Mexican wars, Maclay had been assigned duty as a brigadier general by Kirby Smith and placed in temporary command of Waul's Brigade immediately after the Battle of Jenkins' Ferry. He was now reassigned as commander of Randal's Brigade. At the same time Col. Richard Waterhouse, the youthful commander of the Nineteenth Texas, was given command of Scurry's Brigade.[55]

The elevation of Waterhouse, who had been with the division since its inception, was a popular move. The appointment of Maclay, a native Pennsylvanian who previously had been only a major and had not held field command, caused considerable dissatisfaction. Historian M. Jane Johansson noted that Maclay's appointment "increasingly rankled the men who believed that one of the brigade's unit commanders should have been promoted."[56]

Walker's Texans reached the Alexandria area on May 22, too late to be of value to Taylor in his efforts to prevent the withdrawal of Banks' army. While camped there the Texans learned that men of the division taken prisoner at Pleasant Hill had been exchanged and were performing guard duty at Natchitoches. This was, according to the division's chronicler Joseph Blessington, "glad tidings to their old comrades in arms."[57]

A month later, while still camped in the Alexandria region, the Texans received what many considered bad news. General Walker was leaving the division. He had been named commander of the West Louisiana District, replacing Richard Taylor, who had requested to be relieved. Although a demanding officer, Walker was extremely popular with the men; they virtually idolized him. Wilburn H. King, a young Texan who had served as lieutenant colonel in the Eighteenth Infantry prior to being wounded at Mansfield, was named temporary commander of the division. King, who had shown bravery and courage as a regimental officer, was acceptable to the men as a leader. They were soon disappointed, however, when they learned that Maj. Gen. John Forney, a North

W. H. King, Colonel, Eighteenth Texas Infantry.
—Courtesy Harold B. Simpson Research Center, Hillsboro, Texas

Carolinian who had commanded a small division at Vicksburg, was to be the regular commander of the division. Forney, referred to by Blessington as "an old United States army officer," was a strict disciplinarian, regarded by many as a martinet.[58]

In late July, before Forney actually assumed command, Walker's Division and Polignac's Division were ordered to cross the Mississippi River and join Richard Taylor, who had been appointed commander of the Alabama, Mississippi, and Eastern Louisiana District. The order was unpopular with the Texans. The constant campaigning of the spring, failure to pay the troops for a year, the absence of many field-grade officers due to illness and injury, the dislike of being even farther from home, and, in the case of Walker's Division, the appointment of an unpopular commander resulted in low morale and opposition to the proposed move. As the two divisions neared the Mississippi, hundreds of Texans deserted. The problem was so acute that Kirby Smith ordered cavalry posted along the Red River to intercept deserters heading for Texas. A possible mutiny was averted when Confederate authorities suspended the movement across the river.[59]

Soon after the decision was made not to send the Texans across the Mississippi, Walker's Division, now joined by its new commander Major General Forney, was ordered to Arkansas once again. A major Confederate cavalry raid into Missouri under the command of Sterling Price was under way. Divisions under Walker and Polignac were to be used to keep Union general Frederick Steele from moving into southern Arkansas while Price was in Missouri.[60]

During the march north, Forney did little to endear himself to the men in his division. To prevent straggling the new commander had roll call at every stop, thereby reducing the actual rest time. Once in Arkansas, Forney further antagonized the division veterans by a series of inspections and drills.[61]

The division remained near Monticello, Arkansas, from September 20 until October 2 then marched to Camden, where the Texans worked on completing fortifications. In mid-November the division was ordered back to Louisiana. After a brief stop at Camp Sumter near Shreveport, the Greyhounds marched to Camp Magruder near Minden, where they went into winter quarters.[62]

Near the end of January 1865 the division moved to a site near Shreveport, where the Texans remained until February 21. At

Shreveport the division had its last grand review before a large crowd that included Generals Forney, Magruder, and Smith. In late February the division marched to Natchitoches and camped there for several days. While there the division was joined by four Texas cavalry regiments which had recently been dismounted: the Second Partisan Rangers, the Twenty-ninth Texas, the Thirty-fourth Texas, and Wells' Regiment. A fourth brigade was formed consisting of a regiment from each of the three old brigades and two of the new regiments. This new brigade, which included the Sixteenth Infantry, Eighteenth Infantry, Twenty-eighth Cavalry, Thirty-fourth Cavalry, and Wells' Regiment, was placed under the command of Brig. Gen. Wilburn H. King.[63]

In early March 1865 Kirby Smith received reports that a huge Federal invasion force had sailed from New Orleans heading for Texas. To meet what proved to be an unfounded threat, Smith ordered Forney's Division to Texas. Marching through Mansfield, Rusk, and Crockett, the division reached Camp Groce near Hempstead on April 15 and remained there during the last month of the war.

As word of Confederate surrenders in Virginia and North Carolina reached Texas, it became difficult to keep the men at their posts. In hopes of keeping as many men in arms as possible, Kirby Smith relieved General Forney on May 12 and reappointed General Walker as division commander. But even the popular Walker could do little to maintain discipline and order. On May 19 he informed Smith that troops in the division had mutinied, seized supplies, horses, and wagons, and left for home. Walker tried to persuade those officers and men who remained to follow him into Mexico, but he had little success. On May 20 goodbyes were said and the last of the men of Walker's proud division headed home. Memories of Mansfield, Pleasant Hill, Jenkins' Ferry, and hundreds of miles of marching would remain with them in the difficult days ahead.[64]

POLIGNAC'S TEXAS BRIGADE

Twenty-second Texas Cavalry (dismounted)
Thirty-first Texas Cavalry (dismounted)
Thirty-fourth Texas Cavalry (dismounted)
Seventeenth Texas Consolidated Cavalry (dismounted)
Fifteenth Texas Infantry

Fighting alongside Walker's Texas Division in the Louisiana campaigns was a Texas infantry brigade commanded by a French aristocrat, Camille Armand Jules Marie, Prince de Polignac. Made up of four Texas dismounted cavalry regiments and one infantry regiment, Polignac's Brigade was composed of men recruited primarily in North Texas, many of whom had not supported secession. As historian Alwyn Barr observed in his book *Polignac's Texas Brigade*, the brigade was an "oddly assorted unit" which served under ten different commanders and fought in ten major engagements in Missouri, Arkansas, Louisiana, and Indian Territory.[65]

Three of the regiments in what became Polignac's Brigade—the Twenty-second Cavalry, Thirty-first Cavalry, and Thirty-fourth Cavalry—were brigaded together for the first time in late summer 1862 near Fort Smith, Arkansas. All three of the regiments had only recently been formed, and none had yet been in combat.

The Twenty-second Texas Cavalry was recruited in northeast Texas during the winter months of 1861-1862. Formal organization of the regiment took place at Fort Washita in Indian Territory in January 1862. Robert Taylor of Bonham, a successful lawyer, state legislator, and Mexican War veteran, was chosen as colonel of the regiment. A friend and supporter of Sam Houston, Taylor was a Unionist who signed the anti-secessionist "Address to the People of Texas" in spring 1861. Once Texas seceded, however, Taylor gave his support to the Confederacy and helped raise troops for the new regiment.[66]

William H. Johnson of Paris, a lawyer and former state legislator, was chosen lieutenant colonel of the Twenty-second. Like Taylor, Johnson opposed separation from the Union. As a member of the state convention he was one of eight delegates who voted against the secession ordinance. James G. Stevens, Hunt County judge and trader, was elected major of the regiment.[67]

In April 1862 the Twenty-second Texas was joined at Fort Washita by another regiment recruited primarily in northeast Texas, the Thirty-fourth Texas Cavalry. Almerine M. Alexander, Kentucky-born merchant from Sherman, was colonel of the regiment. George H. Wooten and John H. Russell were lieutenant colonel and major. Unlike the Twenty-second Texas, which carried more than 1,000 names on its muster roll, the Thirty-fourth was an undersized regiment, listing only 752 men on its rolls.[68]

The Twenty-second and Thirty-fourth regiments spent late spring and early summer at Fort Washita and Fort McCulloch completing their organization and constructing fortifications. In early July they received orders to proceed to Fort Smith in northwestern Arkansas. There they were joined by the Thirty-first Texas Cavalry, which originally had been sent to Little Rock. The Thirty-first had been recruited mainly in the Dallas County area, although two companies came from Bexar and Travis counties in Central Texas. Trezevant C. Hawpe, Dallas businessman, county official, and staunch secessionist, was the organizer and colonel of the regiment. George W. Guess, Dallas attorney and alderman, was named lieutenant colonel, and Frederick J. Malone, Mexican War veteran and Goliad County cattleman, was chosen major. The regiment had only nine companies instead of the usual ten. None of these were at full strength at the time of organization, but recruitment was continuing.[69]

At Fort Smith the three Texas cavalry regiments were brigaded with Indian regiments under the command of Col. Douglas Cooper, former Indian agent and an officer in the Mexican War in Jefferson Davis' Mississippi Regiment. Cooper, who commanded all Confederate troops in Indian Territory north of the Canadian River, was an extremely ambitious officer anxious to impress Confederate authorities. During the next several months the Texans and Indians under his command took part in several forays into Arkansas and Missouri.

In late September Cooper's regiments attacked the Union garrison at Newtonia in southwestern Missouri. In this engagement the Twenty-second Texas, commanded by recently promoted Col. James G. Stevens, took the lead in driving Federal troops from the field. In this encounter the Texans sustained thirty-three casualties: one killed, thirty-one wounded, and one missing.[70]

The Confederate victory at Newtonia led Maj. Gen. John Schofield, commanding Union forces in southwestern Missouri, to send additional troops to the area. Faced with large Union numbers, the Confederates retreated back into northwestern Arkansas. Here the Texans were separated from Cooper, who withdrew into Indian Territory.

The Texans were joined in Arkansas by an additional regiment from the Lone Star State, the Twentieth Texas commanded by Col. Thomas C. Bass.[71]

Morale and discipline declined in the Texas regiments during the retreat from Missouri. Increased illness, lack of pay, poor food, inadequate clothing, and bad weather took its toll among the Texans. In an effort to improve discipline and order in the Texas regiments, Maj. Gen. Thomas Hindman, commanding Confederate troops in northwest Arkansas, brought the four regiments together as a brigade and named Col. William R. Bradfute, an experienced officer on his staff, as brigade commander. Hindman, a volatile and impatient officer who was under pressure to turn defeat into victory, was convinced the Texans were "worthless as cavalry," and ordered them dismounted.[72]

The four Texas regiments, now dismounted, were with Hindman's army in the battle at Prairie Grove in December 1862. In this battle the Texans were part of Brig. Gen. John S. Roane's command, which formed the left wing of Hindman's army. On three separate occasions the Texans beat off enemy attempts to turn the Confederate flank. Although the Confederates held their position throughout the day, shortage of ammunition and other supplies led Hindman to withdraw his army from the field that evening. The battle was tactically a draw, but a strategic defeat for the Confederates who had hoped to prevent Union forces from controlling northwest Arkansas.[73]

After the Battle of Prairie Grove, the Texas

Joseph W. Speight, Colonel, Fifteenth Texas Infantry.
—Courtesy Harold B. Simpson Research Center, Hillsboro, Texas

regiments, once again under the command of William R. Bradfute, retreated back to the Arkansas River near Fort Smith. In early January, the Fifteenth Texas Infantry, which had previously been in McCulloch's Division, was added to the brigade. Joseph W. Speight, a Waco lawyer-planter and former grandmaster of the Masonic Lodges of Mississippi, was organizer and colonel of the regiment. James E. Harrison of Waco, a former state senator in Mississippi and Indian commissioner for Texas, was lieutenant colonel, and John W. Daniel of Smith County, major.[74]

The Fifteenth Texas included recruits from a wide occupational background. The majority were farmers, but there were also teachers, carpenters, clerks, blacksmiths, stockmen, miller, merchants, and teamsters. Several of the officers either had or would have distinguished careers. John B. Jones, the regimental adjutant, would later achieve fame as a major of a Texas Ranger battalion. David R. Wallace, the regimental surgeon, was a pioneer in psychiatric medicine who became president of the Texas Medical Association. Austrian-born George B. Erath, captain of I Company, had already achieved recognition for his service in the Battle of San Jacinto, the Somervell and Mier expeditions, and the Texas Rangers. Capt. Richard Coke of K Company later would become governor of Texas and U.S. senator.[75]

The Fifteenth Texas joined the brigade east of Van Buren, Arkansas, on January 1, 1863. The condition of the troops in the other regiments at the time was poor. Illness, poor food, and weariness from the constant retreating demoralized the Texans. Desertions, particularly in the Twenty-second and Thirty-fourth regiments, were increasing daily. In an effort to restore some order and stability, Confederate authorities relieved an ailing Bradfute from command and placed Colonel Speight of the Fifteenth Texas in charge of the brigade.

Several days after Speight's appointment as brigade commander, the Texas regiments were ordered to report to Brig. Gen. William Steele, newly appointed commander of Indian Territory, at Fort Smith. The brigade reached Fort Smith on January 15. Marching through rain and snow and with few provisions, the Texans were exhausted and half-starved. Steele, seeing the demoralized state of the regiments and having few provisions to give them, ordered four of the regiments to march south to Doaksville near the Red River. Here he believed they could find food, clothing, and shelter for the winter. Colonel Bass' Twentieth Cavalry, which had joined the brigade the previous autumn, remained at Fort Smith for garrison duty and would no longer be in the brigade.[76]

Speight's weary troops reached Camp Kiamichi near Doaksville in mid-February after a march through snow several inches deep. In an effort to improve morale, Speight granted a number of furloughs to his men, many of whom were now close to their homes across the Red River. Speight himself returned to Waco for a visit, leaving Col. A. M. Alexander in charge of the brigade. Because of the bad weather there was little campaigning during the next two months. As the weather improved, General Steele attempted to move the brigade north in anticipation of the coming spring campaign. Alexander delayed responding as long as possible, but in April the brigade made ready for the march north.[77]

Just when it appeared the Texans would join Steele for the spring campaign, Speight's Brigade was ordered to join Richard Taylor's army in Louisiana. Taylor needed additional troops in his attempt to relieve Union pressure upon Port Hudson. As discussed earlier, Walker's Division was already on its way to join Taylor. Despite protests from General Steele that Speight's regiments were needed in Indian Territory, Kirby Smith sent Speight's troops south.

In early May the brigade moved across the Red River through Clarksville and Mount Pleasant to Jefferson, where the troops boarded steamers that took them to Shreveport. When they arrived at Shreveport they were detained by General Smith, who was appalled at their condition. Smith decided that two of the regiments, the Twenty-second and the Thirty-fourth, were so poorly equipped and trained that they would remain in Shreveport for retraining. He sent the Fifteenth Infantry and the Thirty-first Cavalry (dismounted) on to Taylor.[78]

Speight, with the Fifteenth Texas commanded by Lt. Col. James Harrison and the Thirty-second Texas commanded by Guess (in place of Colonel Hawpe, who had returned to Dallas), moved down the Red River to Alexandria. From there the small brigade traveled along the Atchafalaya River to join Taylor's army in the Bayou Lafourche region. While in the bayou country Lieutenant Colonel Harrison became acting commander of the brigade when

James Harrison, Colonel, Fifteenth Texas Infantry.
—Courtesy Harold B. Simpson Research Center, Hillsboro, Texas

Colonel Speight was arrested after a controversy with Col. Joseph Bates of the Thirteenth Texas Infantry. Under Harrison's command the brigade fought alongside Tom Green's Cavalry during Taylor's efforts to block the enemy advance in southern Louisiana.[79]

The Federal capture of Port Hudson in mid-July allowed Nathaniel P. Banks to put additional troops in the field against the Confederates in the bayou country. To strengthen his badly outnumbered forces Taylor called upon Kirby Smith for the release of the regiments being retrained at Shreveport. The two Texas regiments there had been joined by other Texans who had escaped capture when Arkansas Post surrendered. These men were brought together as the Seventeenth Texas Consolidated Cavalry (dismounted) under twenty-five-year-old James R. Taylor, the former commander of the Seventeenth Cavalry, as colonel.[80]

Smith organized the Seventeenth Consolidated, the Twenty-second Cavalry, and the Thirty-fourth Cavalry into a new brigade commanded by a French aristocrat, Brig. Gen. Camille Armand Jules Marie, Prince de Polignac. The son of Charles X's chief minister, Polignac had served as an officer in the Crimean War. He was studying plant life in Central America when the Civil War began. Offering his services to the Confederacy, he was commissioned lieutenant colonel. He served with P.G.T. Beauregard and later Braxton Bragg in Tennessee and Kentucky. In the Battle of

Richmond (Kentucky) he distinguished himself, leading to his promotion to brigadier general in January 1863. After brief additional service with the Army of Tennessee he was transferred to the Trans Mississippi Department in March 1863.[81]

Taylor was hopeful that the new brigade would join him immediately, but Kirby Smith held Polignac's troops in the Alexandria as a reserve, allowing the new commander to settle lingering discipline and morale problems.[82]

Meanwhile, Taylor's army, under increased Union pressure, withdrew up Bayou Teche to a camp near Vermilionville. Lieutenant Colonel Harrison was still acting commander of Speight's Brigade. Colonel Speight had been cleared of the arrest charges but remained in Texas due to illness. In August Companies C, D, and E of Lt. Col. Ashley W. Spaight's Eleventh Texas Infantry Battalion from the Beaumont area were assigned to the brigade. Prior to service in Louisiana, the battalion, which included infantry, artillery, and cavalry, had been engaged in the defense of the upper Texas coast. In May 1863 the infantry and cavalry companies were ordered to Louisiana. After brief service with Tom Green's command in the bayou country the three infantry companies of the battalion (C, D, and E) were assigned to Speight's Brigade; the two cavalry companies (A and F) were attached to Major's cavalry brigade.[83]

In early September, Taylor learned that Federal

Ashley Spaight, Lieutenant Colonel, Eleventh Infantry Battalion, later colonel, Twenty-First Texas Infantry.
—Courtesy Harold B. Simpson Research Center, Hillsboro, Texas

troops had landed at Morganza, near the mouth of the Red River. Fearing an enemy movement against Alexandria, Taylor sent Confederate cavalry and infantry (including Speight's Brigade) under the overall command of Tom Green to the upper Atchafalaya River. When the Confederates reached the area, Green decided to attack a Union outpost at Stirling's plantation on Bayou Fordoche. Dividing his force, Green sent his infantry, consisting of Speight's Texas Brigade and Henry Gray's Louisiana Brigade, on a wide swing around the enemy's right flank while his cavalry attacked the left flank. When in position the Confederate infantrymen swept across an open field and overwhelmed the Federal defenders. More than 400 Union troops were captured, sixteen killed, and forty-four wounded in the Confederate victory. Total Confederate casualties numbered 121; of these, 104 were in Speight's Brigade. The Fifteenth Texas Infantry, led into battle by Maj. John W. Daniel, sustained the heaviest losses, with fifteen killed, fifty-two wounded (including Daniel), and one missing. The Thirty-first Texas had one killed, twelve wounded, and four missing including Lt. Col. George W. Guess, who was captured while attending to the wounded. Spaight's Battalion had six killed, ten wounded, and three missing.[84]

Following the victory at Stirling's plantation, Speight's Brigade headed back toward Washington, the small village on the upper Teche where Taylor was concentrating his forces to meet the advance of William B. Franklin's Union army.[85]

On October 12 Colonel Speight returned from Texas and assumed command of the brigade. His tenure was brief, however. Polignac and his brigade, consisting of the Twenty-second Cavalry, Thirty-fourth Cavalry, and Seventeenth Consolidated Cavalry (all dismounted), joined Taylor's army on October 18. Almost immediately Polignac's Brigade and Speight's Brigade were merged into one brigade. By virtue of his rank Polignac became commander of the consolidated brigade. Colonel Speight, who was still in poor health, returned home.[86]

In his memoirs Richard Taylor noted that the appointment of Polignac as brigade commander was not popular with the Texans, who "swore that a Frenchman whose very name they could not pronounce, should never command them, and mutiny was threatened." Taylor held a meeting with the officers in which he reminded them of their duty but promised he would remove Polignac if they remained dissatisfied after he led them into battle. The Texans agreed to give the new commander a try. Tension gradually eased after Polignac showed his courage under fire. The Texans were soon referring with affection to their commander as their "General Polecat."[87]

The brigade remained in the region north of Washington during early autumn of 1863. There was little fighting as the Texans grew accustomed to their new commander. Several regiments experienced changes in leadership during this period. Col. A. M. Alexander of the Thirty-fourth Texas returned home because of poor health. John H. Caudle, a merchant from Red River County who had been with the regiment since its formation, replaced Alexander as commander. Col. James G. Stevens, who commanded the Twenty-second Texas, citing his inability to control his men, resigned his commission and went home. Lt. Col. Robert D. Stone replaced Stevens as regimental commander. Maj. Frederick J. Malone, a veteran of the Mexican War, commanded the Thirty-first Texas in place of Lieutenant Colonel Guess, who was captured at Stirling's plantation.[88]

While most of the brigade performed few military tasks other than patrol and picket duty during the autumn, James Harrison's Fifteenth Infantry participated in the Confederate attack at Bayou Bourbeau described earlier in the chapter. Assigned detached duty with Tom Green's command, the Fifteenth was on the right flank in the Confederate assault that drove the enemy back a mile and half. Harrison's infantry sustained thirty-three casualties in the battle: nine killed, twenty-one wounded (including future governor Capt. Richard Coke), and three missing.[89]

Harrison's Regiment rejoined Polignac's Brigade after the battle at Bayou Bourbeau. Renewed concerns about Union activity on the Red River caused General Taylor to order the brigade to march east toward Bayou Fordoche in early December. When it became apparent there was no major threat there, the brigade returned to the Alexandria region. After a brief rest the brigade was ordered to northeastern Louisiana. Spaight's Battalion, which had been attached to the brigade since August, left at that time and headed back to Texas.[90]

Polignac's Texans spent the first month of 1864 in the vicinity of Harrisonburg on the Ouachita River. In February the brigade carried out a raid against a small Union outpost at Vidalia on the Mississippi River. Unfortunately for the Texans, Federal infantry reinforcements and fire from three Union gunboats made the raid a costly one. Although several hundred cattle, horses, and mules were captured, the brigade had six men killed, ten wounded, and eight captured in the affair.[91]

In early March Polignac received orders to join Richard Taylor at Alexandria. Nathaniel P. Banks and the Union army had begun a major move up the Red River. Taylor was concentrating his widely scattered forces to meet the new threat. Polignac's Texas Brigade joined Henry Gray's Louisiana Brigade in a new infantry division commanded by Alfred Mouton, son of former Louisiana governor Alexander Mouton. With Walker's Texas Division and Mouton's Division, Taylor fell back to Mansfield, a crossroads town to the northwest, to await cavalry reinforcements from Texas.[92]

With the arrival of Texas cavalry during the first week of April, Taylor was ready to strike the advanced wing of Banks' army as it approached Sabine Crossroads, three miles south of Mansfield. Taylor placed Walker's Division to the right of the Pleasant Hill road and Mouton's Division on the left. Polignac's Brigade was on the right side of Mouton's Division next to Randal's Brigade of Walker's Division. Gray's Louisiana Brigade was on Polignac's left, next to Major's cavalry.[93]

At 4:00 P.M. on the afternoon of April 8 Taylor ordered Mouton's Division to open the attack. Gray's and Polignac's brigades rushed forward with a Rebel yell. Volleys from the Federal defenders cut down many of the onrushing Rebels as they swept across the open field. General Mouton went down, and Lt. Col. Sebron M. Noble of the Seventeenth Texas Consolidated Regiment fell soon after. Polignac assumed command of the division, with Col. James R. Taylor of the Seventeenth taking over leadership of the brigade. The fighting raged for over an hour as Polignac's troops on the Confederate left and Walker's Texans on the right pushed forward. The first Union line gave way, forcing the defenders back to a second line. After continued fighting, this line, too, was broken. Union troops fell back in confusion as the Rebels continued to advance. In one of the last volleys fired before darkness James R. Taylor, the young colonel commanding the brigade, was killed.[94]

Fighting resumed the next afternoon at Pleasant Hill. Walker's

Division was on the Confederate left with Thomas Churchill's Arkansas and Missouri divisions (which had just arrived) on the right. Polignac's Division was held in reserve because of the heavy casualties suffered at Mansfield. The initial Confederate assault against the Union left was successful, but Union reinforcements forced the Confederates back. As the Rebel line was pushed in, Taylor called upon Polignac's Division to enter the battle. With the admonition "My boys, follow your Polignac," the dapper Frenchman led his troops forward. The Texans and Louisianans in the two brigades pushed back the Federal attackers and recovered some lost ground before darkness ended the fighting.[95]

Losses were high in the two days of fighting. Polignac's Texas Brigade suffered 212 casualties. Two-thirds of these were in two regiments: eighty-five in the Thirty-fourth Cavalry and sixty-eight in the Seventeenth Consolidated Cavalry. Losses were smaller in the other regiments: thirty-four in the Twenty-second Cavalry, twenty-nine in the Thirty-first Cavalry, and sixteen in the Fifteenth Infantry. In all, the brigade had thirty-eight men killed (twenty-three of them in the Seventeenth Texas), 173 wounded, and one missing.[96]

After the fighting at Pleasant Hill, Polignac's troops went back to their camps near Mansfield. Several days later, after refitting and reequipping from captured Federal stores, the division, now under the permanent command of Polignac, moved south as part of Taylor's continuing attempt to prevent Banks' army from escaping. Departmental commander Kirby Smith ordered the divisions of John G. Walker and Thomas Churchill to assist Sterling Price in Arkansas, so Taylor's army now consisted of Polignac's two brigades and Tom Green's cavalry. Newly promoted Col. James Harrison, who had been in Texas when the battles at Mansfield and Pleasant Hill were fought, was acting commander of the Texas Brigade for a brief time. Most of the Texans hoped Harrison would be named permanent brigade commander, but Confederate authorities appointed Wilburn H. King, a colonel in the Eighteenth Infantry in Walker's Division, to command the brigade. However, King had received serious injuries at Mansfield and could not assume command at the time. Robert D. Stone of the Twenty-second Texas, the senior colonel in the brigade, was named acting commander in King's absence.[97]

During the next six weeks Polignac's Division, including his old brigade, was constantly on the move as Taylor attempted to block the withdrawal of Banks' army and its naval support on the Red River. At Grand Ecore sharpshooters from Harrison's Fifteenth Infantry prevented the enemy from refloating the grounded ironclad *Eastport*. To avoid her capture by the Confederates, Adm. David Porter ordered the vessel blown up. A day later Confederate artillery and sharpshooters from John Caudle's Thirty-fourth Cavalry forced two Union transports aground near the mouth of the Cane River. In spite of these and other Confederate efforts, however, the Union fleet managed to withdraw down the river.[98]

Similarly, Taylor was unable to block the retreat of Banks' army. The Confederate commander planned to attack the Union army as it attempted to cross the Cane River at Monett's Ferry, but Hamilton P. Bee's cavalry failed to delay the enemy until Polignac's infantry could attack from the rear.[99]

The last opportunity for the Confederates to hit the enemy came when Federal troops crossed the Atchafalaya River near Yellow Bayou. On the morning of May 18 Gen. John A. Wharton, the senior Confederate officer in the area, ordered the cavalry divisions of James P. Major, Hamilton P. Bee, and William Steele to attack. At midday Polignac's infantry, which had marched nine miles that morning, entered the battle. The Texas Brigade, commanded by Col. Robert Stone, was on the Confederate left with Col. Henry Gray's Louisiana Brigade on Stone's right near the center of the Confederate line. The Thirty-fourth Texas Cavalry was on the extreme left of the Texas Brigade, the Fifteenth Infantry in the center of the brigade, and the Twenty-second Texas (now reduced to battalion size) on the brigade's right next to Gray's Louisianans. The Seventeenth Consolidated Cavalry and the Thirty-first Cavalry were held in reserve and saw little action. In bitter fighting that lasted four hours, neither side gained much ground. A flanking movement by enemy reinforcements on the Confederate left in late afternoon forced the Thirty-fourth Texas to fall back, exposing Harrison's Fifteenth Infantry to enfilading fire, but support from Confederate cavalry allowed Harrison's troops to withdraw in some order. Losses were heavy on both sides and the heat and humidity exacerbated the suffering of the wounded and dying. As dusk fell, the Confederates pulled back and the fighting ended.[100]

Yellow Bayou was a costly battle, especially for the Confederates, who reported 608 casualties. Four-fifths of these (491) were Texans. The Texas Brigade had especially high losses: thirty-two men including brigade commander Col. Robert Stone killed, eighty-eight wounded, and eighty-eight missing or captured. The highest losses were in the Thirty-fourth Texas (sixteen killed, forty-two wounded, sixty-two missing, or a total of 120) and the Fifteenth Texas (twelve killed, thirty-seven wounded, and twenty-four missing, or a total of seventy-three). The Twenty-second Cavalry, smallest of the Texas units, had fourteen casualties. The Seventeenth Consolidated had one man wounded. The Thirty-first Cavalry, like the Seventeenth held in reserve, had no casualties.[101]

The Battle of Yellow Bayou brought an end to the Red River campaign. Banks' troops crossed the Atchafalaya, using anchored transports and riverboats side by side. Further pursuit by the Confederates was not undertaken.

The Texas Brigade, with Colonel Harrison again in temporary command, spent June and most of July 1864 along the Red River. In late July both Polignac's and Walker's divisions marched to the Ouachita River in northeastern Louisiana as Confederate authorities considered ordering them across the Mississippi River to join Richard Taylor, who had been appointed commander of Mississippi and Alabama.[102]

The possibility of a move across the Mississippi was no more popular with Polignac's troops than with those in Walker's Division. During August nearly 200 men in Polignac's Division deserted, many of them Texans. In late August the move was suspended. The two divisions were ordered to join John B. Magruder, district commander in Arkansas at the time. Polignac's Division was soon under way, reaching Magruder's headquarters at Monticello, Arkansas, on September 18. The division remained there briefly and was then ordered to Camden to meet a potential Union move from Pine Bluff.[103]

In the march to Camden, Brig. Gen. Wilburn Hill King, who had recovered from his wounds, joined the Texas Brigade as commander. King, who had served in Walker's Division in the Louisiana campaigns, was well known and respected by men of the brigade.

There was disappointment, however, that Col. James Harrison, who had been with the brigade since its inception and had twice served as acting commander, was not appointed. Polignac, Wharton, and Walker all supported Harrison, and Kirby Smith recommended his promotion and appointment to brigade command. Harrison himself was disappointed and went to Richmond, ostensibly to discuss Indian affairs but probably to seek promotion.[104]

The Texas Brigade, now under King's command, did not remain in Arkansas long. In late November, when the threat to Camden failed to materialize, Kirby Smith ordered Polignac's and Walker's divisions back to Louisiana, where supplies were more plentiful. The Texas Brigade spent December camped near Minden, Louisiana. In early January 1865 the brigade moved to Grand Ecore, where it established winter camp. Morale had improved somewhat. On the whole, members of the brigade were pleased with their new commander, Wilburn Hill King, possibly because of improvements in rations and health after the return to Louisiana.[105]

In February there was a general reshuffling of regiments and brigades when Kirby Smith was forced to dismount nine Texas cavalry regiments because of shortages of forage for the mounts. As a part of this reorganization several of the Texas regiments, including all of those in the old Polignac Brigade, were ordered to Texas. Col. John Caudle's Thirty-fourth Texas Cavalry (dismounted) joined Brigadier General King in a new brigade which also included the Sixteenth and Eighteenth Texas Infantries, the Twenty-eighth Cavalry (dismounted), and Wells' Cavalry Regiment (dismounted). James E. Harrison, who was promoted to brigadier general while in Richmond, was named commander of a brigade consisting of his old Fifteenth Texas Infantry, Thomas F. Tucker's Seventeenth Consolidated Cavalry (dismounted), James Likens' Thirty-fifth Cavalry (dismounted), and Peter Hardeman's Cavalry Battalion (dismounted). The other two regiments of the old Polignac Brigade, the Twenty-second Cavalry (now battalion size and commanded by Lt. Col. George W. Merrick) and the Thirty-first Cavalry (dismounted) commanded by Col. Frederick J. Malone, were placed in an infantry brigade commanded by Brig. Gen. Hamilton P. Bee.[106]

These organizational changes in the spring of 1865 had little impact upon the course of the war but represented futile bureaucratic efforts to preserve some order and stability. The regiments of the old Polignac Brigade, now separated in three different brigades, were in camps at Richmond, Hempstead, and Navasota when it became obvious even to the most die-hard Confederate that the Southern bid for independence had failed. As in the case of other Texas units in the Trans Mississippi, there was no mass surrender. The men simply left their regiments and went home.[107]

INDEPENDENT INFANTRY AND DISMOUNTED CAVALRY REGIMENTS

Third Texas Infantry
Eighth Texas Infantry
Ninth Texas Infantry (Nichols' Regiment)
Thirteenth Texas Infantry
Twentieth Texas Infantry
Twenty-first Texas Infantry
Twentieth Texas Cavalry (dismounted)

As was true of Texas cavalry regiments in the Trans Mississippi that cannot be identified with a single brigade or division in the Civil War, six Texas infantry regiments and one regiment of dismounted cavalry in the department either operated independently of brigade organization or were in several different brigades during the course of the war.

Third Texas Infantry. The Third Texas Infantry spent the first three years of the war along the Rio Grande and the Texas coast. In the spring of 1864 the Third Texas was ordered to join Walker's Texas Division in Louisiana. The regiment arrived in Louisiana too late to take part in the battles at Mansfield and Pleasant Hill but joined the division in time to participate in the Arkansas campaign. After serving with William R. Scurry's Brigade in the battle at Jenkins' Ferry, the Third Texas was with the brigade when Walker's Division returned to Louisiana late that spring. The regiment remained with the division until the closing months of the war.[108]

The men of the Third Texas were recruited in the San Antonio-Austin area during the summer of 1861. Muster rolls list slightly more than 800 men divided into ten companies of uneven size. Many of the volunteers, especially in C and F companies, were

Mexican Americans. The recruits in Companies B, H, and K were German Americans. The other five companies were ethnically more diverse, with Mexican, German, Anglo, and Celtic names appearing on their rosters.[109]

Philip Noland Luckett, a Corpus Christi physician, was commander of the Third Texas throughout the war. A Virginian by birth, Luckett briefly attended the U.S. Military Academy at West Point. After studying medicine, he migrated to Texas in 1847. He practiced medicine in the Corpus Christi area throughout the 1850s. During this time he also served as a surgeon with the Texas Rangers. In 1861 he was elected to the secession convention. There he was chosen as one of the three commissioners to negotiate with U.S. authorities over the surrender of Federal forces in the state. After brief service as quartermaster and commissary general of Texas, he helped organize the Third Texas Infantry.[110]

Luckett was appointed colonel of the new regiment. Augustus Buchel, the professional soldier described earlier in the chapter, was named lieutenant colonel but left the regiment later to command his own regiment. Edward Gray of Houston was appointed major and later lieutenant colonel, succeeding Buchel. Charles Schreiner, later a highly successful rancher and banker, was a non-commissioned officer in the regiment.

The Third Infantry spent the year 1862 on duty in South Texas. Colonel Luckett, who replaced John S. Ford as the senior Confederate in the area, made his headquarters at Fort Brown. Although the men spent most of their time patrolling the lower Rio Grande, there was no contact with the enemy. As was true of many regiments, desertion and absence without leave was a constant problem. In January 1862 the regiment reported 769 men present for duty. That number was reduced to 648 men by November.[111]

In early summer 1863 the Third Infantry was ordered to Galveston Island to serve as part of the garrison commanded by Col. Xavier Debray. At the same time Colonel Luckett was made acting brigadier general by district commander John B. Magruder and assigned temporary command of the Eastern Sub-district of Texas with headquarters at Houston.[112]

Service on Galveston Island during the summer of 1863 was unpleasant. In spite of the heat and humidity, Colonel Debray, an officer trained in French military schools, ordered daily drill for the

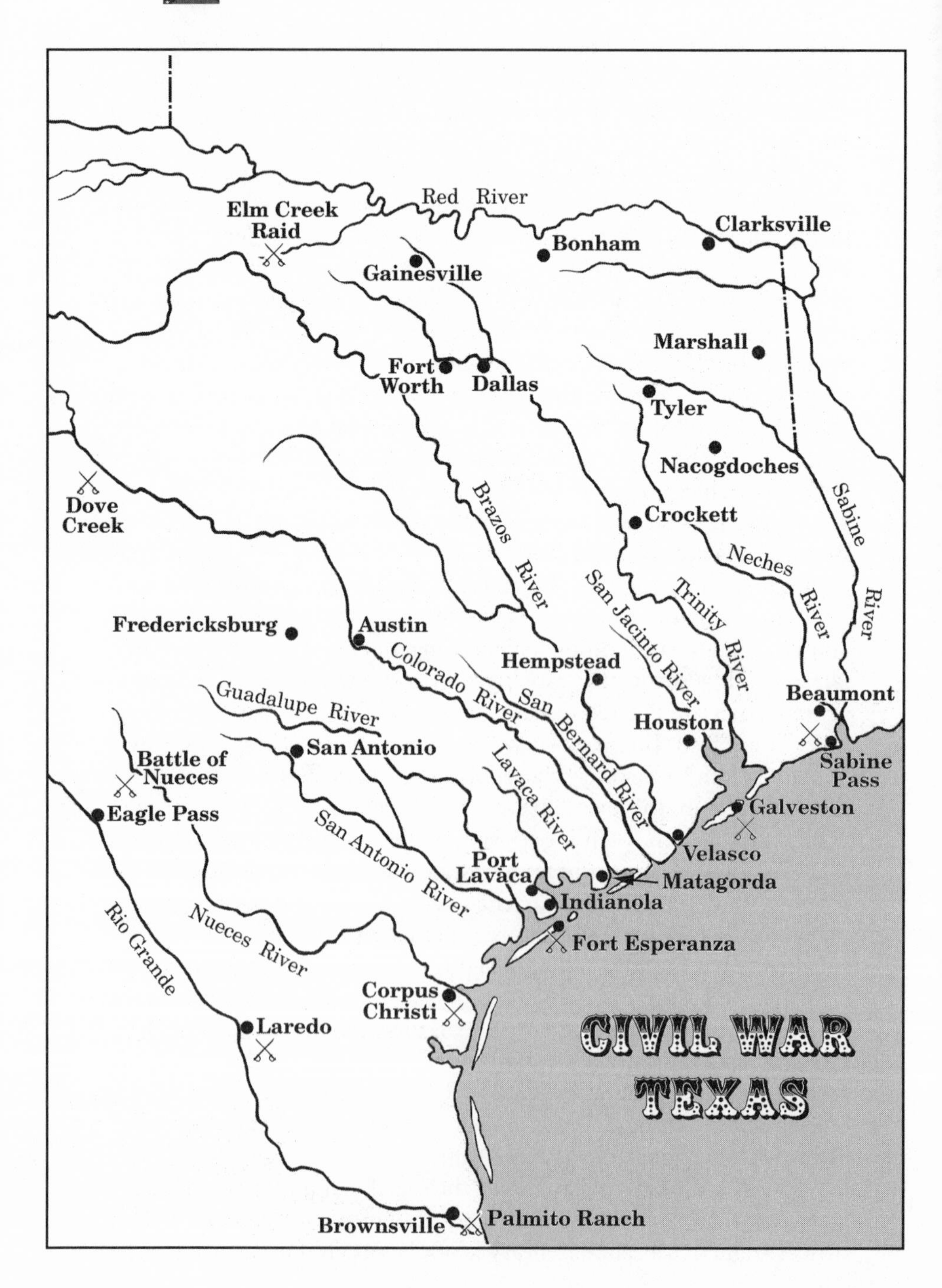
Red River
Elm Creek Raid
Clarksville
Bonham
Gainesville
Marshall
Fort Worth
Dallas
Tyler
Nacogdoches
Dove Creek
Crockett
Brazos River
Sabine River
Neches River
San Jacinto River
Trinity River
Fredericksburg
Austin
Hempstead
Colorado River
San Bernard River
Beaumont
Guadalupe River
Houston
San Antonio
Sabine Pass
Battle of Nueces
Lavaca River
Eagle Pass
Galveston
San Antonio River
Velasco
Port Lavaca
Matagorda
Indianola
Rio Grande
Nueces River
Fort Esperanza
Corpus Christi
Laredo
CIVIL WAR TEXAS
Brownsville
Palmito Ranch

troops under his command. At the same time rations for the men grew progressively bad. On August 4, Lt. Col. Edward F. Gray, commanding the Third Texas in Luckett's absence, warned that the men were complaining of eating sour, weevil-infested meal while abundant supplies of wholesome flour were stored in nearby warehouses at Harrisburg and Columbus.[113]

When no improvements in their rations were forthcoming the men of the Third Infantry refused to drill. Colonel Debray, angry at what he considered mutiny, ordered the men disarmed and sent to their quarters under arrest. The next day, August 11, several companies of Joseph Cook's First Heavy Artillery Regiment also refused to drill. Debray, who had only the men of his own regiment and those of Henry Elmore's Twentieth Infantry to support him, feared the worst.[114]

Galveston historian Edward T. Cotham, Jr., pointed out that at this critical moment Colonel Luckett, "a more practical and sensible officer, appeared on the scene and acted as a peacemaker." After talking with the men, he determined that they were not disloyal but simply saw no reason to drill in the sun while being provided inadequate rations. Luckett suspended all drill and promised improved rations as soon as possible. The men accepted this approach, better rations did gradually appear, and conditions returned to normal.[115]

The threat of a Union invasion of the upper Texas coast soon turned thoughts away from rations to the war itself. On August 17, 1863, Luckett was charged with the defense of the Sabine River and the Texas coast from Sabine Pass to the western end of Matagorda Peninsula. He ordered companies of his own Third Infantry dispersed from Niblett's Bluff back to Houston. Lieutenant Colonel Gray and four companies of the Third Texas were assigned to Sabine Pass. Before these orders could be fully implemented, however, the Union attempt to take Sabine Pass was defeated by Dick Dowling and his artillerymen of the Davis Guard.[116]

Even though Dowling and his men were victorious at Sabine Pass, district commander John B. Magruder was fearful of another Federal attack. He appointed Col. Augustus Buchel as commander of the area and ordered several regiments, including the Third Texas, to Sabine Pass. By the end of the month more than 3,000 Confederates were in Jefferson County.[117]

The Third Infantry, considerably reduced in numbers by illness, furloughs, and desertion, spent October and November 1863 at Sabine Pass. In early October the inspector general for the Trans Mississippi Department visiting the area reported only 265 men present for duty in the Third Texas. Lieutenant Colonel Gray and Maj. John F. Kampmann were both absent on sick leave. S. G. Newton, the senior captain in the regiment, was in command. The inspector general found clothing, equipment, and arms in good supply and condition. He noted the unit "has the reputation of being the best drilled regiment in the State," but concluded "this was, perhaps, the case when Colonel Buchel was lieutenant colonel but it [the Third Texas] is now in need of officers." He pointed out that it was unfortunate that Colonel Luckett was on detached duty and had seen little service with the regiment.[118]

In late November General Magruder decided the threat to the Texas coast south of Houston was greater than that to Sabine Pass. Accordingly, he ordered the Third Texas and several other units at Sabine Pass transferred to the mouth of the Brazos. In early December the Third Texas arrived at Velasco, where it remained for the next three months. Colonel Luckett, relieved of his duties in Houston, was again with the regiment. Both morale and discipline improved under his direction. An inspector general's report in early February noted the spirit of the troops was high and praised the general efficiency of the regiment.[119]

On March 13, 1864, the Third Infantry received orders to join Confederate forces in northern Louisiana. The Third Texas joined Walker's Texas Division near Shreveport as it headed toward Arkansas under orders to prevent Frederick Steele's Union troops from occupying southern Arkansas. The Third Texas was assigned to W. R. Scurry's Brigade as replacement for heavy losses suffered at Mansfield and Pleasant Hill.[120]

The Third Texas saw its first combat at Jenkins' Ferry in late 1864. In this engagement, described more fully earlier in the chapter, the regiment was on the Confederate right flank. Although Scurry's Brigade had the lowest casualties in the division, the Third Texas, perhaps eager to show its courage to the veteran regiments in the brigade, sustained fifty casualties, including twelve killed and thirty-eight wounded.[121]

Soon after the battle at Jenkins' Ferry, Walker's Division returned to Louisiana. The Third Texas remained with the division through the remaining months of the war. The division saw little fighting during these months but did a great deal of marching in northern Louisiana and Arkansas. Colonel Luckett was on detached duty much of the time, leaving command of the regiment to Gray.[122]

The Third Texas returned to Texas in late March 1865. The regiment was at Camp Groce near Hempstead when the dissolution of Walker's Division occurred in late May and the men went home.

Eighth Texas Infantry. Unlike the Third Texas, Alfred M. Hobby's Eighth Texas Infantry never left the state during the Civil War.[123]

The regiment was organized in February 1863 by the consolidation of the Eighth Infantry Battalion and the Fourth Artillery Battalion. Alfred M. Hobby, who had headed the Eighth Battalion, was promoted to colonel and became commander of the new regiment. A native of Georgia, Hobby moved to Texas with his widowed mother while still a teenager. He became a successful merchant in Refugio County and, although only twenty-two years old at the time, was elected to the Texas legislature in 1859. A member of the Knights of the Golden Circle, Hobby was a delegate to the secession convention. With the outbreak of war he recruited a local company which became part of the Eighth Battalion in 1862. Under Hobby's command the battalion successfully defended Corpus Christi from enemy attack in August 1862.[124]

A. M. Hobby, Colonel, Eighth Texas Infantry.
—Courtesy Harold B. Simpson Research Center, Hillsboro, Texas

Daniel D. Shea, commander of the Fourth Artillery Battalion, became lieutenant colonel of the newly consolidated regiment. Like Hobby and his battalion, Shea and his artillery companies had prevented the enemy from capturing a Texas coastal port. In October 1862 Shea and his gunners drove off two enemy warships that attempted to seize Port Lavaca.[125]

John Ireland, lawyer and former mayor of Seguin, was chosen major of the new regiment. He had served with Hobby in the Texas secession convention and was a captain in the Eighth Infantry Battalion. A future governor of Texas, Ireland played a prominent part in the battalion's successful defense of Corpus Christi.[126]

The men who served in the Eighth Infantry were drawn largely from South Central and South Texas. As was true of the Third Texas, Anglo, Celtic, German, and Mexican names were listed on the muster rolls of the regiment. Two companies, C Company commanded by Capt. Joseph M. Penaloza and H Company commanded by Capt. Sexto B. Navarro, were made up almost entirely of Tejanos. The men of B Company, commanded by Capt. Otto L. Schaubert, were almost all Germans.[127]

The Eighth Texas spent most of 1863 along the coastal bend trying to prevent the Union navy from occupying Texas ports. In May, E Company, commanded by Capt. Edwin M. Hobby (younger brother of Col. Alfred M. Hobby and father of future governor William P. Hobby), drove a Federal landing party off St. Joseph's Island near Aransas Pass, earning the praise of General Magruder for its efforts. The regiment was less successful in efforts to save Fort Esperanza on Matagorda Island. When Union forces landed on the island, Major Ireland and two companies rushed to the defense of the fort but after two days' fighting abandoned the fort after spiking their guns and setting fire to the installation.[128]

The men of the Eighth Texas were not happy when they were ordered to leave South Texas in December 1863 and report to Galveston Island. Shortly after their arrival, sixty men of the regiment deserted en masse, taking their arms with them and heading for Victoria. Confederate authorities ordered a pursuit. Some of the men were brought back under arrest, but others eluded capture and returned home.[129]

The Eighth Texas remained in the Galveston area for the rest of the war. Companies were occasionally detached for duty elsewhere along the coast, but Colonel Hobby, John Ireland (promoted to lieutenant colonel), and most of the regiment remained as part of the island garrison. The number of men present for duty dropped slightly during the last half of the year, as the table below indicates.[130]

Month (1864)	Officers	Enlisted Men
June	22	371
July	18	350
September	18	340
November	19	334
December	15	313

Although the contest between Confederate blockade runners and the Union navy continued in the waters around Galveston, there was little military action on the island itself during the last eighteen months of the war. Like other troops garrisoned on the island, the men of the Eighth Texas battled a combination of poor food, yellow fever, and boredom. Rations grew increasingly bad and complaints from the troops increased. Yellow fever took the lives of more than a hundred soldiers in 1864. Many others, including Brig. Gen. James M. Hawes, commander of the island, were seriously ill.[131]

Fear of a possible Union invasion created a flurry of excitement on the island in early 1865, but the threat soon passed. It was increasingly obvious that the end of the southern struggle for independence was near. Desertions increased as troops were convinced the war was lost. Troop strength of the Third Texas dropped to fifteen officers and 224 enlisted men in March. Col. Ashbel Smith, who succeeded General Hawes as island commander on April 12, 1865, urged his troops to remain at their posts; however, news of Lee's surrender in Virginia doomed his efforts to maintain stability and order. The final terms for the surrender of Texas were signed by Generals Smith and Magruder in Galveston harbor on June 2, 1865. By that time most of the island's troops, including those in the Third Texas Infantry, had gone home.[132]

Ninth Texas Infantry (Nichols' Regiment). One of the Texas soldiers who remained on the island after the surrender of the city was Col. Ebenezer B. Nichols. Nichols, who had recently served on the staff of General Magurder, had earlier organized and commanded a Texas infantry regiment. This regiment, which carried the same numerical designation, Ninth Texas Infantry, as a regiment formed in northeast Texas by Sam Maxey, was organized in autumn 1861 with Nichols as colonel, Josiah C. Massie as lieutenant colonel, and Frederick Tate as major.[133]

Colonel Nichols was one of Galveston's most prominent citizens. A native of New York, he moved to Texas in 1838. After brief experience with the Texas militia fighting Indians and Mexicans, Nichols settled in Houston. There he formed a successful merchandising partnership with William Marsh Rice. In 1850 he moved to Galveston, where he formed his own cotton export company. By 1860 he was one of the state's wealthiest citizens with over $100,000 in property. Although he initially opposed secession, he voted for secession as a member of the state convention called to consider the issue. When war came he was appointed financial agent and commissioner for the state and was instrumental in securing arms and munitions for Texas troops. A general in the state militia, Nichols accompanied John S. Ford to Brownsville and was instrumental in securing the surrender of Federal troops in the area.[134]

After returning to Galveston in late spring 1861, Nichols began recruiting troops in the Galveston-Houston-Central Texas area. In early autumn the unit, designated as the Ninth Texas Infantry, was officially organized. Muster rolls show eleven companies (the traditional A-K, plus a small additional company commanded by Capt. David D. Atchison) with 1,100 men. An abstract of field returns for Galveston dated February 28, 1862, lists the regiment, part of the First Brigade of Texas Volunteers, also commanded by Colonel Nichols, with forty officers and 523 enlisted men present for duty.[135]

The lifespan of Nichols' Ninth Texas Infantry was brief. In late spring 1862 the regiment dissolved. The exact cause for dissolution is unknown, but it may be speculated that this was a result of the reorganization of Confederate military units required by the Conscription Act of April 1862.[136]

Many of the men joined other regiments, particularly Waul's Legion, which was being organized at the time. Nichols himself later served on Governor Pendleton Murrah's staff and represented the state in transactions involving the exchange of cotton for weapons and ammunition. As previously noted, he was on General Magruder's staff when the war ended.[137]

Thirteenth Texas Infantry. The Thirteenth Texas Infantry had its origin in September 1861, when Brig. Gen. Paul O. Hebert, the district commander of Texas, appointed Joseph Bates of Brazoria County as colonel of a regiment to consist of six companies of infantry, two companies of artillery, and two companies of cavalry. Under Hebert's orders, the regiment was to be stationed at or near the coast between San Luis Pass and the Caney River.[138]

Although Bates' Regiment, consisting of volunteers primarily from Texas coastal counties, was designated as the Fourth Texas Volunteers in Hebert's orders, the number was later changed to the Thirteenth Regiment in deference to the Fourth Texas Infantry in Hood's Brigade. Joseph Bates, the commander of the regiment, was a native of Alabama who served four terms in that state's legislature and fought in the Seminole Wars before going to Texas in 1845. Locating first in Galveston, he was elected mayor of the isle city in 1848 and was later appointed Federal marshal by President Fillmore. In 1854 he moved to Brazoria County, where he established a large plantation on the west side of the San Bernard River. Like Colonel Nichols mentioned earlier, Bates was one of the state's wealthiest citizens in 1860, possessing $55,900 in real and $47,000 in personal property (including thirty-three slaves).[139]

Because of his seniority and prior military service, Bates temporarily commanded a brigade of Texas volunteers, including his own regiment, with headquarters in Galveston in early 1862. During this period units of the Thirteenth Infantry were involved in two small clashes with the enemy. The first occurred near San Luis Pass on April 5-6, 1862. A detachment from B Company led by Lt. O. W. Edwards attempted unsuccessfully to prevent the Union navy from destroying the cotton-laden schooner *Columbia.* Not only did the Confederates fail, but Lieutenant Edwards and seven of his men were captured. On the other occasion in early July Capt. William Sanders and men from A Company were unable to protect a Confederate schooner from destruction but did prevent the Union navy from establishing a beachhead on the lower Brazos.[140]

In the summer of 1862 Bates' Regiment was reduced in size when two companies were transferred to Maj. Lee Rountree's Cavalry Battalion. Soon thereafter another two companies and the regiment's second-ranking officer, Lt. Col. Reuben R. Brown, left to form their own cavalry battalion. The remaining companies in Bates' Regiment were reformed into a battalion, commanded by Bates, who reverted to the rank of lieutenant colonel.[141]

Bates' Battalion remained along the lower Brazos throughout autumn and winter of 1862-1863. Correspondence published in the *Official Records* shows Bates was very concerned about adequate defense in the area. His efforts to rebuild the regiment by recruitment were eventually successful. By early spring 1863 sufficient numbers of recruits made possible the reorganization of the regiment, with Bates again as colonel. Henry P. Cayce from Wharton, a veteran of the Texas Revolution and Mexican War, became lieutenant colonel. Robert L. Foard, Princeton-educated lawyer from Columbus, was selected as major.[142]

The reorganized regiment was ordered to join two other Texas regiments at Niblett's Bluff in Louisiana in May 1863. Several sources, including John D. Winters' *The Civil War in Louisiana* and Henry M. Henderson's *Texas in the Confederacy,* indicate the Thirteenth Texas was with Richard Taylor's army in the summer and autumn of 1863. However, the *Official Records* contain no reference to the regiment during this period. The companies formerly with the regiment and now in Rountree's Battalion did play a prominent role in the battle at Stirling's plantation in late September, but none of the published reports mention Bates' Regiment.[143]

All sources agree that the Thirteenth Infantry spent 1864 stationed near Velasco. Abstract returns for the Texas District in April show the strength of the regiment at eighteen officers and 334 men. The number increased to twenty-four officers and 387 men present for duty in June, but dropped slightly to twenty-one officers and 379 men by October. Although an infantry regiment, the Thirteenth Texas was listed with six pieces of heavy artillery.[144]

There was little military activity for the Thirteenth Texas in the last eighteen months of the war. The Red River and Arkansas campaigns drained both Union and Confederate commands in the Trans Mississippi. Although there was a skirmish between Confederates and Federal troops near the mouth of the Rio Grande in September 1864, peaceful conditions prevailed along the lower Brazos where the Thirteenth Texas was stationed. Although most Confederate units showed a decline in numbers during the winter months, the Thirteenth Infantry had more men present for duty in December 1864 than in the previous summer and autumn months. Abstract returns for the month show thirty-four offices and 560 enlisted men present for duty.[145]

During the last months of the war, the regiment was occasionally called upon to send detachments to other Confederate outposts. While Colonel Bates and most of the regiment remained near Velasco, two companies of the regiment with four officers and eighty-five men were stationed at Fort Griffin near Sabine Pass in April 1865. They were there when the war came to an end a few weeks later.[146]

Twentieth Texas Infantry. The Twentieth Texas Infantry, organized in Walker County in the spring of 1862, spent most of the Civil War stationed in or near Galveston. Made up of recruits primarily from the Trinity valley counties north of Houston, the Twentieth Infantry was one of the largest regiments formed in Texas, listing more than 1,800 men on its muster rolls. Even late in the war, when most Texas regiments had fewer than 300 men, the Twentieth Texas reported more than 600 men present for duty. The regiment consisted for the most part of middle-aged men, heads of families, and prominent citizens. Because it was stationed in Texas throughout the war and had comparatively light duty, it was sometimes referred to as "the Feather-bed Regiment."[147]

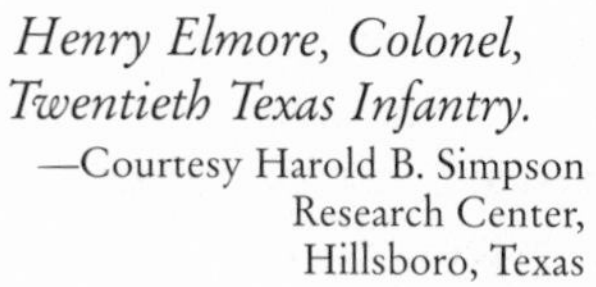

Henry Elmore, Colonel, Twentieth Texas Infantry.
—Courtesy Harold B. Simpson Research Center, Hillsboro, Texas

Henry M. Elmore, native of South Carolina, resident of Waverly, and Walker County representative in the Ninth Texas Legislature, was colonel and commanding officer of the Twentieth Texas. Leonard A. Abercrombie, twenty-nine-year-old prosecuting attorney from Huntsville and member of the Texas secession convention, was lieutenant colonel. Robert E. Bell was major.[148]

The regiment spent the summer of 1862 at Camp Groce near Hempstead. Training went smoothly, although illness and lack of weapons reduced the numbers and effectiveness of the troops. In late September the regiment was ordered to move to Sabine Pass. Maj. Josephus Irvine, Confederate commander at Sabine Pass, reported that a Federal landing party had come ashore, destroyed the fort and barracks, and burned the railroad bridge at Taylor's Bayou and the railroad depot near the town. Col. Xavier Debray, commanding the Houston Sub-district, feared this might be a major invasion. He ordered Elmore and his regiment to move by train to Houston and then on to Sabine Pass.[149]

By the time the Twentieth Texas reached Sabine Pass the Federal raiders had returned to their ships. Debray, who accompanied Elmore's men to Sabine Pass, ordered the regiment back to Houston. In his report of the affair to Gen. Paul O. Hebert, commander of the Texas District, Debray complained that while the Twentieth Texas had "an excellent composition of men," it was poorly officered. "In fact," he wrote, "they have no notion of discipline or military instruction." He went on to point out that the men were terrified by the threat of yellow fever in the region. "I was so harassed by the objections and remonstrances of the lieutenant-colonel in command at my taking them so close to an infected place that I was compelled to forbid him to mention the word[s] yellow fever before me," concluded Debray.[150]

The Twentieth Texas remained in the Houston area after the excursion to Sabine Pass. Following the Union occupation of Galveston in early October, the regiment was stationed at Virginia Point near the old railroad bridge connecting the island with the mainland. When General Magruder ordered the attack on the island on January 1, men from Pyron's Regiment, Griffin's Battalion, and Companies A and B of Elmore's Regiment made up the storming party that attempted unsuccessfully to drive Union troops off Kuhn's Wharf. The remainder of the regiment led by Lieutenant

Colonel Abercrombie served with Scurry in the Confederate forces that moved into the center of town. In his report of the battle, General Magruder praised Abercrombie and men of the Twentieth Texas for their part in the liberation of Galveston.[151]

After the Confederate reoccupation of the city, the Twentieth Texas remained as part of the Galveston garrison. In later September 1863 four companies of the regiment led by Abercrombie were sent to Sabine Pass. Colonel Elmore and the rest of the regiment stayed in Galveston. Drills and military appearance in the Sabine companies of the regiment were apparently lax, due perhaps in part to Lieutenant Colonel Abercrombie's illness. When the inspector general visited Sabine Pass in September, he found Capt. Jesse C. Dickie of Company H in command. The inspector reported the clothing of the men was good but their Springfield and Enfield rifles not in good order. He also noted that the officers and men of the regiment were deficient in drill and military appearance.[152]

As the threat of Union attack at Sabine Pass eased, the companies of the Twentieth Texas returned to Galveston. Apparently, the deficiencies found in the October inspection were corrected. While the inspector general was critical of many of the regiments in the Texas District in February 1863, he praised Elmore's Regiment and four other regiments in the Galveston area for their spirit, discipline, and drill.[153]

The regiment spent a rather uneventful spring and summer of 1864 garrisoning various fortifications on and around Galveston Island. While there was little threat from the enemy, the men of the Twentieth shared the same frustrations that caused unrest in the Third and Eighth infantries on the island. Although the men of the Twentieth did not take part in the refusal to drill, there was unhappiness with the food, the heat, and the drilling. In mid-September Capt. D. H. Lewis, in command at Fort Magruder, reported that a dozen men in G Company considered joining a larger group from Fort Point who threatened to leave their posts. Cooler heads prevailed, however, and the men were talked out of leaving.[154]

Although there were some absences due to illness and desertion, the Twentieth Texas maintained a roster of 600 or more men present for duty throughout 1864 and early 1865. From time to time there were organizational changes for reporting purposes, but these had little effect upon the men. The regiment was part of James

M. Hawes' Brigade from May 1864 until April 1865, when it was assigned to a new brigade commanded by Brig. Gen. James E. Harrison, the former commander of the Fifteenth Texas Infantry.[155]

In the closing days of the war the Twentieth Texas was moved from Galveston to the Houston area. In late April 1865 the regiment was at Richmond when it received orders to report to Navasota. The regiment was there on May 24, 1865, when Harrison ordered his regimental commanders to discharge their men from service. For most of the men it was only a short trip home.[156]

Twenty-first Texas Infantry. The Twenty-first Texas Infantry was created in November 1864 by the consolidation of William H. Griffin's Twenty-first Battalion and Ashley W. Spaight's Eleventh Battalion. Since the consolidation came so late in the war the new regiment, with Spaight as colonel and Griffin as lieutenant colonel, was never committed to battle. It spent its brief existence on garrison duty at Sabine Pass, Galveston, and Houston.[157]

The two battalions that formed the Twenty-first Infantry had previous combat experience. Griffin's Battalion, made up of volunteers from the Fort Worth area, was organized in early 1862. The battalion received its baptism under fire in the Battle of Galveston on January 1, 1863. Although inexperienced, the battalion was selected to be part of the Confederate force that attempted to drive Union troops off Kuhn's Wharf. Joining men from Pyron's Second Texas and Elmore's Twentieth, Griffin's men waded into the water carrying ladders with which they hoped to reach the top of the wharf. Unfortunately for the Confederates, their ladders were too short and enemy fire from gunboats so intense that the attackers were driven back. The appearance of two Confederate river steamers, however, soon turned the tide of battle, and Galveston was liberated. Griffin and his men received the thanks of General Magruder for their gallant action.[158]

At the time of the Battle of Galveston, Spaight's Battalion, consisting of infantry, artillery, and cavalry, was stationed at Sabine Pass. The battalion was an outgrowth of a local militia company commanded by James B. Likens, a Sabine Pass attorney. Likens' Battalion was mustered into Confederate service as the Eleventh Cavalry and Infantry Battalion in March 1862. Shortly thereafter, Likens was promoted to colonel and authorized to raise his own cavalry regiment (described as part of Bee's Division in Chapter

Five). Ashley W. Spaight, a Liberty County lawyer and planter who commanded one of the cavalry companies (the Moss Bluff Rifles), was promoted to lieutenant colonel and commander of the battalion. Josephus S. Irvine, a San Jacinto veteran and commander of Company C from Newton County, was promoted to major of the battalion.[159]

During 1862 Spaight's Battalion, made up of men from southeast Texas, was charged with defending the upper Texas coast from Galveston Bay to Louisiana. Although there were no major threats to the area at the time, yellow fever and Union raiding parties caused difficulties for Spaight's command. The yellow fever epidemic of late summer took the lives of forty or more soldiers, left others ill, and caused many civilians to evacuate. The weakened defenders put up little resistance when Union naval forces entered the narrow passageway on the Sabine in late September and opened fire upon Fort Sabine, a fortification built the previous year to guard Sabine Pass. Major Irvine, commanding the fort, ordered the guns spiked and buried and the fort evacuated. A Union landing party came ashore, burned the fort and a railway bridge, and did other damage before withdrawing. As noted earlier, additional Confederate forces, including Elmore's Twentieth Texas, were rushed to the area but remained only briefly. Several weeks later another enemy landing party from the gunboat *Dan* came ashore and burned sawmills, stacked lumber, barracks, and stables near Sabine City.[160]

The men of Spaight's Battalion attained satisfaction when volunteers from A Company rowed up to the *Dan* on the night of January 8 and set her afire with blazing pine knots. According to historian W. T. Block, the Confederates "watched gleefully as the hated gunboat burned to the waterline and sank at its anchorage at the Sabine lighthouse."[161]

Two weeks later the men of Spaight's Battalion enjoyed even greater success when, serving as artillerymen and sharpshooters on two river steamers, the *Uncle Ben* and *Josiah H. Bell*, converted as gunboats, they captured two Union blockaders, *Morning Light* and *Velocity*. With no losses themselves, the Confederates took 109 prisoners and for the moment broke the Union naval blockade. Prize crews brought the two captured vessels to Sabine Pass; however, after two unsuccessful attempts to float *Morning Light* over the bar, the ship was scuttled and burned when Union warships appeared.[162]

In spring 1863 Griffin's Battalion was transferred to Sabine Pass, relieving Spaight's Battalion. With the exception of the artillery company (B) which remained assigned to the *Uncle Ben*, Spaight's Battalion was sent to Louisiana to help in the defense of that state. As pointed out earlier the three infantry companies (C, D, E) were assigned to Joseph W. Speight's Texas Brigade. The two cavalry companies (A and F) were attached to James P. Major's Cavalry Brigade. During the summer and early fall, companies of the battalion took part in more than twenty engagements with the enemy. The infantry companies played a prominent role in the battle at Stirling's plantation in late September. In this clash the battalion suffered nineteen casualties, including six men killed.[163]

In late autumn Spaight's Battalion returned to southeast Texas. While the battalion had been away, the Confederates defeated the Union navy in its attempt to destroy the new fort named for Lieutenant Colonel Griffin, who commanded defenses in the area. This was followed by a massive buildup of Confederate forces. However, once the threat of another Union invasion passed, these troops were sent elsewhere. Only Andrew Daly's Cavalry Battalion, Griffin's Infantry Battalion, state troops, and some artillerymen remained in the area.[164]

After furloughs to visit relatives and friends, Spaight's troops were back on duty in the Sabine Pass area. The threat of a Union overland invasion in early April resulted in the battalion being ordered to Niblett's Bluff, Louisiana. The battalion remained there only briefly. In late April, Lieutenant Colonel Spaight and F Company rode to Lake Charles to protect Confederate cotton and blockade runners. The other four companies of the battalion joined Griffin in an attack on two Union gunboats at Calcasieu Pass. During this engagement, in which companies of Griffin's and Spaight's battalions fought side by side, the Confederates wrecked two Union gunboats and captured sixteen guns and 166 prisoners. Fourteen Confederates were killed in the battle.[165]

The Battle of Calcasieu Pass was the last for either of the two battalions which were consolidated into one regiment, the Twenty-first Texas Infantry, in November. As noted earlier the new regiment spent the last months of the war on garrison duty. The abstract returns for the Second Texas Infantry Division to which the regiment was assigned showed twenty-nine officers and 610 men present for duty in December 1864. The regiment was in Houston in January 1865, transferred to Galveston in late April, and in late May was back in Beaumont, where the companies were discharged as the war came to an end.[166]

Twentieth Texas Cavalry (dismounted). Unlike the Texas independent regiments which spent most of the war within the state boundaries, the Twentieth Texas Cavalry (dismounted) served outside the state most of the war. Organized with recruits from North Texas in summer 1862, the regiment was ordered to Arkansas in autumn 1862 and spent the next two years in Arkansas and Indian Territory. In 1863 the regiment served in three different brigades; in 1864 it was not attached to any brigade.[167]

Thomas C. Bass, commander of the regiment, was a native of Mississippi who moved to Sherman, Texas, in 1858. Thirty-one years old when the war began, Bass was a lawyer by profession and an avid secessionist. He raised recruits from Cooke and Grayson counties for the new regiment. His executive officer, Lt. Col. Andrew Jackson Fowler, was fifteen years Bass' senior, a longtime resident of the state, and a veteran of Indian campaigns. Also a lawyer, Fowler had years of public service as a district attorney, judge, and college professor. Because of his age Fowler was later excused from military service and replaced by Thomas D. Taliaferro.[168]

The Twentieth Texas Cavalry was ordered to Arkansas soon after it was mustered into Confederate service. It joined three other Texas cavalry regiments, the Twenty-second, Thirty-first, and Thirty-fourth, in northern Arkansas as they retreated from southwestern Missouri after the battle at Newtonia. As mentioned earlier in the chapter, morale was extremely low due to poor food, inadequate clothing, lack of pay, and bad weather. Thomas Hindman, the Confederate commander in northwest Arkansas, believed the Texas regiments were worthless as cavalry. He ordered the four regiments, including the Twentieth Texas, to be dismounted and appointed William R. Bradfute, an experienced officer, as brigade commander.[169]

The Twentieth Texas and the other Texas regiments (now all dismounted) took part in the Battle of Prairie Grove on December 7, 1862. By all accounts the men of the regiment fought well, as did the other Texans, but shortages of ammunition led the Confederates to withdraw from the field after a hard day of fighting.[170]

The Twentieth Texas remained with the other Texas dismounted cavalry, now commanded by Col. Joseph W. Speight, as they moved to join Brig. Gen. William Steele at Fort Smith. Whey they reached Steele's headquarters on January 15, the Texans were in pitiful condition. Steele ordered the other regiments to march south in Indian Territory to Doaksville, where they might find food, clothing, and shelter. The Twentieth Cavalry, however, was held at Fort Smith for garrison duty.[171]

Bass' Regiment remained at Fort Smith during the early months of 1863 as part of an Arkansas brigade commanded by Brig. Gen. W. L. Cabell. In late June the regiment was ordered to join Brig. Gen. Douglas Cooper in Indian Territory. The Twentieth Texas arrived in time to take part in the battle at Elk Creek, or Honey Springs, on July 17, 1863. Although Cooper's Brigade, consisting of Indian and Texas regiments, was defeated, the Confederate commander praised Bass' Texans for supporting a Texas artillery battery while under heavy enemy fire. When the Confederates were forced to withdraw, the Twentieth fell back in good order. "Their steady conduct . . . enabled us to save the train and many valuable lives," reported General Cooper.[172]

After the defeat at Elk Creek, the Confederates retreated south of the Canadian River. Later in autumn Cooper took most of his brigade northward again, but the Twentieth Texas remained on garrison duty; half of the companies were stationed at Fort Washita and the other half at Boggy Depot. Continued logistical problems, bad weather, and boredom took their toll on Bass' troopers. Discipline was lax and morale low. The Trans Mississippi Department's inspector general reported in late October that Washita was "in a dilapadated and broken-up condition." The post was "badly policed, companies poorly drilled, and men not in soldierly appearance." The inspector general added that "Lt. Col T. D. Taliaferro, commanding, is an officer of no energy."[173]

The post at Boggy Depot, commanded by Colonel Bass, fared no better. Conditions were about the same as at Washita: no drill, lack of discipline, and poor military appearance. "Colonel Bass, if one judges from the fruit of his labors, is an officer of no competency," the inspector general's report concluded.[174]

The Twentieth Texas remained in Indian Territory throughout 1864. Samuel Bell Maxey, who became commander of the Territory in late 1863, attempted to improve conditions but with only limited success. Over the protests of Brigadier General Cooper, Maxey removed the Texans from Cooper's Brigade, placing them in Richard Gano's Brigade or, as was the case of the Twentieth Texas, leaving them unattached. Maxey requested that Bass' Regiment be remounted, but because of lack of forage his request was not approved. Desertion became an increasing problem in the regiment; in March 1864 Maxey noted that Bass' Regiment was reduced to battalion size in numbers.[175]

The Twentieth Texas Cavalry returned to Texas in early 1865. As a part of general reorganization in the closing days of the war, the unit was listed as the Twentieth Texas Cavalry Battalion (dismounted), commanded by Maj. J. R. Johnson in Hamilton P. Bee's Brigade, Maxey's Division. The battalion was stationed at Richmond in May. A general order of May 26 provided that as soon as Elmore's Regiment left Richmond other units, including Johnson's Battalion, would move by rail from Richmond via Houston to Navasota. There the war ended for men of the Twentieth Texas Cavalry.[176]

CHAPTER SEVEN

Artillery Regiments, Battalions, and Batteries

TEXAS PROVIDED AN ARTILLERY regiment, four artillery battlions, and thirty-five artillery batteries for Confederate service. Most of these units were field batteries assigned to support infantry brigades operating in the Trans Mississippi Department. Although one small Texas battery, Duke's Battery (or the Jefferson Guards), served briefly in Virginia before it was dissolved, the only Texas battery to see extensive service east of the Mississippi was the Dallas Light Artillery, better known as the Good-Douglas Battery for its two commanders, John J. Good of Dallas and James P. Douglas of Tyler.

Although the artillery units of the Trans Mississippi Department were grouped into battalion organizations under Special Orders No. 290, on November 19, 1864, this was purely for administrative purposes. Individual batteries continued to be moved where needed. These individual batteries as well as the one artillery regiment and four functioning battalions will be descibed in this chapter.[1]

FIRST TEXAS HEAVY ARTILLERY REGIMENT

The First Texas Heavy Artillery Regiment was created when the Third Texas Artillery Battalion was increased to regimental size on April 18, 1862. The Third Battalion had been organized in the summer and fall of 1861. The first company of the battalion was formed in Fayette County in June 1861 by Joseph J. Cook, a native of Alabama and graduate of the U.S. Naval Academy at Annapolis.

During the autumn and winter months, six additional companies were formed by men from the Houston and Galveston area. When the companies were organized as a battalion, Cook became lieutenant colonel and commander. Augustin S. Labuzan, who had raised B Company in Galveston, became major of the battalion. The battalion was assigned duty on Galveston Island in late 1861 and early 1862, during which time it occasionally exchanged fire with enemy warships testing the defenses of the city.[2]

Four additional companies were recruited in spring 1862, increasing the battalion to regimental size. When the regiment was organized in late April, Cook was promoted to colonel and commander. John H. Manly, Harris County lawyer and railroad builder who had commanded C Company, the Houston Artillery, became lieutenant colonel; Edward Von Harten, captain of E Company, rose to the rank of regimental major. An additional company (L, later designated as Second Company A) was added in June 1862.[3]

Although more than 1,700 men served in the First Texas Heavy Artillery Regiment during the course of the war, the regiment normally had fewer than 600 men present for duty. The table that follows lists the name of each company's first commander, the total number of men on the muster rolls during the war, and date of initial organization.

COMPANIES OF FIRST TEXAS HEAVY ARTILLERY[4]

Company	Commander	Number on Roster	Date Organized
1st A	J. J. Cook	105	June 1861
2nd A*	N. J. King	88	June 1862
B	A. S. Labuzan	199	December 1861
C	E. B. H. Schneider	238	June 1861
D	Charles M. Mason	248	October 1861
E	Edward Von Harten	174	October 1861
F	Frederick Odlum	184	December 1861
G	John H. Manly	199	April 1862
H	Thomas J. Catching	200	April 1862
I	D. M. Jackson	150	May 1862
K	David G. Adams	180	May 1862

*Originally Company L; designated 2nd Company A on April 30, 1863

The new regiment spent the summer and early autumn of 1862 manning the defenses of Galveston Island. Although artillery batteries were established on Bolivar Point, Pelican Spit, Fort Point, and San Luis Pass, Brig. Gen. Paul O. Hebert, the Confederate commander for Texas, thought these were inadequate for the defense of the city. Believing that the city could not be defended with the resources available, he ordered the removal of most of the island's artillery to the mainland to avoid its capture. When a Union naval vessel arrived at the entrance to Galveston Bay in October 1862, there was little the Confederates could do but surrender the city. Colonel Cook, commanding the Galveston garrison, withdrew to Virginia Point on the mainland, taking with him what military materials he could.[5]

For the next two months Cook's artillerymen helped man the defenses at Virginia Point overlooking Galveston Bay. When John B. Magruder, who replaced Hebert as district commander, determined to recapture Galveston, he placed Cook in charge of the force assigned to attack the Union troops on Kuhn's Wharf. Many of Cook's artillerymen joined Confederate infantry and dismounted cavalry in the opening phases of the battle for Galveston. The men of B Company served as gunners aboard the Confederate steamer *Bayou City;* men from C Company served the guns on *Neptune.* Other members of the regiment manned artillery in fighting along the Strand. Among the casualties in the Confederate victory was Lt. Sidney Sherman, Jr., of A Company, son of one of the Texas infantry commanders at San Jacinto, Sidney Sherman.[6]

After the recapture of Galveston, most of Cook's Regiment remained on the island. Unlike his predecessor, General Magruder was determined to hold the island at all costs. Several new artillery positions were established and companies of the First Texas Heavy Artillery were assigned to man the guns. One exception was F Company, commanded by Capt. Frederick Odlum. This company, made up primarily of Irishmen from Houston, was assigned to Sabine Pass. It was there that F Company, known as the Davis Guards, won a place for itself in history, first in helping capture two Union blockade ships and later in defeating a large Union naval-military force that tried to come up Sabine Pass.[7]

The capture of the two Union ships occurred shortly after Odlum's company arrived at Sabine Pass. Local Confederates were determined to break the Union naval blockade of the upper Texas coast. Two river steamers, *Josiah Bell* and *Uncle Ben*, were outfitted as cotton-clad gunboats. Artillerists from Capt. K. D. Keith's Company B of Spaight's Battalion were detailed to man the two guns on *Uncle Ben*, and men from Odlum's company were assigned to handle the 64-pound rifled cannon on *Josiah Bell.* Men from Spaight's Battalion and Pyron's Cavalry Regiment served as sharpshooters on the two vessels.

On the morning of January 21, 1863, the two Confederate vessels crossed the bar at Sabine Pass and set out in pursuit of two Federal blockaders, the sloop *Morning Light* and the schooner *Velocity.* In a running battle the gunners on *Josiah Bell*, under the immediate command of Lt. Richard W. "Dick" Dowling, poured a dozen shots into *Morning Light.* As the ships closed, Texas sharpshooters, protected by bales of cotton, forced the Federal gun crews from the decks. To avoid further casualties the captain of *Morning Light* surrendered his vessel. Meanwhile, Lieutenant Keith's men on *Uncle Ben* forced *Velocity* to strike her colors.

Prize crews brought the two captured ships to Sabine Pass; however, after attempts to float *Morning Light* over the bar failed, she was scuttled and burned when Federal warships approached.[8]

The success of Odlum's (and Keith's) artillerymen in capturing the Union blockaders was overshadowed later by what historian Andrew Forest Muir described as "the most brilliant victory of Confederate forces in Texas," the repulse of a huge Union invasion force at Sabine Pass on September 8, 1863. This victory, achieved later that year by Dick Dowling and the Davis Guards, ranks with the defense of the Alamo and the Battle of San Jacinto in terms of significant military engagements in Texas.[9]

After the capture of the two Union blockaders, the men of Odlum's company spent the next several months in routine duty in and around Sabine Pass. When a new earthen fort was built near the head of the channel several hundred yards above the location of the fort destroyed by the Federals the previous year, the Davis Guards were assigned to man the six cannon that were eventually in place. The fortification, known locally as Fort Griffin for Lt. Col. William H. Griffin, who commanded the post of Sabine Pass, was triangular in shape and about 100 feet long on each side. The fort had a sawtooth front where the cannon were mounted, sloping walls ten feet high, and a parapet twenty feet wide.[10]

The Davis Guards spent the last part of August and the first week of September in daily practice with their guns, two 24-pounder smoothbores, two 32-pounder smoothbores, and two 32-pounder howitzers. Stakes driven in the two channels of the pass helped the gun crews zero in on every inch of the waterway.[11]

On September 8, 1863, the men of F Company, First Texas Heavy Artillery, were called upon to meet their greatest challenge. A large Union invasion force consisting of four gunboats, twenty-two transport vessels, and 5,000 troops commanded by Maj. Gen. William B. Franklin prepared to make a landing on the upper Texas coast. Before attempting a landing, Franklin sent his gunboats to shell Fort Griffin into submission. When the four Union gunboats steamed in the two channels of the pass, the Confederate gunners, commanded by Lieutenant Dowling in the absence of Captain Odlum (who was temporarily in charge of headquarters at the town of Sabine Pass), opened fire. For over half an hour the Confederate guns blazed away. Two Union gunboats, *Sachem* and *Clifton,* suffered heavy damage and were forced to surrender; the other two Union gunboats withdrew from the pass. Union General Franklin, convinced the Rebel defenses were much stronger than they actually were, ordered his task force back to New Orleans.[12]

In this short but decisive encounter, Dick Dowling and the forty-two men under his command captured two Union gunboats, killed or wounded nearly one hundred,

Richard W. "Dick" Dowling, Lieutenant, Davis Guards.
—Courtesy Center for American History, UT-Austin

captured three hundred of the enemy, and turned back a major Union expedition. Amazingly, none of Dowling's men suffered severe wounds, although several had powder burns and burned hands from manning their guns.[13]

Dowling and his men were highly praised for their victory. General Magruder commended the Davis Guards in a special order and conferred upon them the privilege of wearing "Sabine" embroidered in a wreath design upon their hats. The Confederate Congress passed a congratulatory resolution which President Davis signed describing the defense of Sabine Pass as "one of the most brilliant and heroic achievements of the war." A special medal, attached to a green ribbon, was struck for each member of the garrison.[14]

The battle at Sabine Pass was the last engagement in which Company F, the Davis Guards, participated. The company remained at Sabine Pass during the autumn and winter of 1863-1864. Sometime in early 1864 the Guards joined other companies of the regiment back at Galveston.[15]

The other companies of the First Texas Heavy Artillery Regiment remained on garrison duty in Galveston during 1863. Command reports for February 1864 (before the return of F Company) show the regiment with thirty-four officers and 493 men manning thirty-one heavy guns in five different artillery positions on the island. In May five companies of the regiment, including F Company, were ordered to Hempstead, where they remained for several months.[16]

By the first of 1865 all the companies of the regiment were back at Galveston, except for Capt. Charles Mason's Company D, which had been detached the previous fall and sent to Louisiana. The size of the regiment fluctuated due to illness, furloughs, and desertions. At the end of March the regiment reported twenty-eight officers and 430 men present for duty at Galveston, but this dropped to sixteen officers and 208 men by the end of April. The last report for the regiment listed sixteen officers and 190 men present on May 10, 1865.[17]

ARTILLERY BATTALIONS

As pointed out earlier, all artillery units in the Trans Mississippi Department were grouped into battalion organizations in November 1864. This administrative action had little real effect upon operations of the various artillery units as they continued to be assigned as needed, often with little relationship to the battalion. Earlier in the war there were four instances in which Texas batteries were formed into battalions for effective military operation. One of these, the Third Texas Artillery Battalion, was eventually increased to regimental size and became the First Texas Heavy Artillery Regiment (just discussed).

Soon after the Third Artillery Battalion was formed, another battalion, the Fourth Texas Artillery, was organized by bringing together two artillery batteries, Daniel D. Shea's Van Dorn Guards and Joseph M. Reuss' Indianola Artillery Guards. When the Fourth Texas was formed as a battalion of two companies, Shea was promoted to major and commander. John A. Vernon succeeded Shea as commander of the Van Dorn Guards, now Company A. Joseph Ruess, an Indianola physician, continued as commander of the Indianola battery, now Company B of the battalion.[18]

Shea's Battalion, consisting of 180 men and armed initially with four 24-pounder siege guns, two 12-pounder siege guns, and one 6-pounder field gun, occupied Matagorda Island in late 1861. In December the battalion exchanged fire with a Federal patrol ship and claimed several hits. In February 1862, under the direction of a trained artillery officer, Maj. Caleb S. Forshey, the battalion began building Fort Esperanza on the eastern shore of Matagorda Island facing Cavallo Pass, the entry into Matagorda Bay. With the arrival of several additional artillery pieces, Shea was hopeful that any enemy attack could be driven off. However, on October 25, 1862, Union warships *Westfield* and *Clifton* sailed past the fort and into the bay. Fearing that he might be cut off from retreat, Shea abandoned the island and moved to the mainland.[19]

The Union naval commander demanded the surrender of Port Lavaca. When Major Shea, whose troops were now at Lavaca, refused to surrender, the Union ships opened fire. With only two small batteries commanded by Captains Vernon and Reuss, Shea's Battalion returned the fire and drove the enemy warships off. The Confederates then reoccupied Fort Esperanza.[20]

In February 1863 Shea's small battalion was consolidated with the Eighth Texas Infantry Battalion to form the Eighth Texas Infantry Regiment. The regiment, including Shea's artillery, took part in the unsuccessful defense of Fort Esperanza in November 1863 (described in the previous chapter). Men of the old battalion continued to serve with the Eighth Infantry during the last two years of the war.[21]

Several months after Shea's Fourth Artillery Battalion became part of the Eighth Infantry, another artillery battalion was created. The Seventh Texas consisted of two batteries, one commanded by Capt. O. G. Jones and the other by Capt. William G. Moseley. Maj. Sidney T. Fontaine, previously a company commander in Cook's First Texas Heavy Artillery Regiment, was named commander of the new battalion.[22]

Fontaine's command functioned only briefly as a true battalion. The two batteries were together at Galveston in the summer of 1863, at Sabine Pass in October 1863, and in camp at Cedar Lake in January 1864. In spring 1864 Moseley's company was sent to Louisiana; Jones' Battery remained on the Texas coast. The battalion organization was officially ended in November 1864, when Jones' Battery was designated as the Third Texas Field Artillery Battery and Moseley's company became the Seventh Texas Field Artillery Battery.[23]

A fourth Texas artillery battalion, designated on occasion as the Sixth Texas Mounted Artillery Battalion and at other times as Willke's Texas Artillery Battalion, was created in the summer of 1863. Consisting of four batteries commanded by Maj. H. Willke, the battalion is mentioned only briefly in the *Official Records.* In the Confederate reorganization of artillery in November 1864 the batteries became part of the new battalion commanded by Maj. Sidney T. Fontaine.[24]

ARTILLERY BATTERIES

Abat-Dashiell's Battery. The field artillery battery commanded first by Capt. E. Abat and later by Capt. George Dashiell was organized in September 1862. Armed with four 6-pounder smoothbores, the battery was stationed at Galveston after the Confederate reoccupation of the island. The battery was moved to Houston in the autumn of 1863 but transferred to Victoria in mid-November. The battery remained in the Victoria-Port Lavaca area until the spring of 1864, when it was ordered to join the Confederates in Louisiana.[25]

On the way to Louisiana in May 1864, the battery, now commanded by Captain Dashiell, was diverted and assigned to Henry McCulloch's command at Bonham, Texas. In August 1864 the battery, consisting of three officers and sixty-two men, was camped at McKinney, Texas. Later that month Dashiell received orders to join an artillery battalion in Douglas Cooper's Division in Indian Territory. The battery remained there until late 1864, when it was transferred to a new infantry division commanded by Samuel Bell Maxey in Texas. In the organization of Trans Mississippi artillery in November 1865 it was designated as the Fourteenth Texas Field Artillery Battery.[26]

Cayce-Allen's Battery. According to Stewart Sifakis, in *Compendium of the Confederate Armies: Texas,* Cayce's Battery was created in May 1862. The battery was first commanded by Lt. Henry P. Cayce and later by Lt. W. H. Allen. No reference to the battery has been found in the *Official Records*.[27]

Christmas' Battery. Organization of Capt. H. H. Christmas' Battery began at San Antonio in November 1863. Designed as a four-gun battery, the unit apparently failed to complete its organization and was merged with Jones' Artillery Battery in the autumn of 1864.[28]

Creuzbaur-Welhausen's Battery. Edmund Creuzbaur's Artillery Battery was organized in Fayette County on October 12, 1861. Composed of German immigrants, the battery was assigned duty with John Ford's command along the lower Rio Grande. The battery remained there until the fall of 1861, when it was ordered back to Central Texas for refitting. According to Confederate authorities the battery was without horses and "in a wretched state of inefficiency" at the time.[29]

The battery was assigned to Galveston in March 1863 but was ordered to Sabine Pass in March 1864. In early May the battery was part of the Confederate force commanded by Lt. Col. William H. Griffin that attacked the two Union warships at Calcasieu Pass, Louisiana. In the battle Lt. Charles Welhausen's section of two 12-pounders hit the Union gunboat *Granite City* with one of its first rounds. Lt. John E. Micksh's section of two 6-pounders concentrated its fire on the Union vessel *Wave.* The warships returned the fire, killing one of the Texans and wounding six others. Creuzbaur's gunners continued their fire while Confederate infantry sharpshooters directed rifle fire on the warship gunners. After ninety minutes of fighting, the Union commanders surrendered their ships to the Confederates.[30]

After the victory at Calcasieu Pass, Griffin's troops, including Cruezbaur's Battery, returned to southeast Texas. In August 1864 the battery was stationed at Liberty; in September it was at Bellville. By this time Welhausen had replaced Creuzbaur as commander. In the reorganization of Confederate artillery in November 1864 the unit was officially designated as the Fifth Texas Field Artillery Battery.[31]

Welhausen's Battery remained in Central Texas until May 1865, when it was transferred to Virginia Point. During the last months of the war the number of men present for duty was fairly constant: three officers and from forty-four to fifty-three men.[32]

Daniel's Battery. James M. Daniel's Field Artillery Battery, known also as the Lamar Artillery, was organized at Paris, Texas, in June 1861. The battery was ordered to join Confederate forces at Little Rock, Arkansas, in late summer 1862. After brief service with Allison Nelson's Division, the battery was assigned to Henry E. McCulloch's Division. The battery was attached to Horace Randal's Brigade, when the division, now commanded by John G. Walker, was ordered to northern Louisiana in early 1863. During the summer and fall the battery participated in Confederate operations along the Mississippi River aimed at disrupting Union shipping. One section of the battery took part in the successful Confederate attack against William B. Franklin's army at Bayou Bourbeau on November 3, 1863.[33]

Daniel's Battery was with Walker's Texas Division in the Red River campaign of 1864. In the battle at Mansfield the battery was on the Confederate right between Waul's and Scurry's brigades. At Pleasant Hill the next day the battery supported the advance of Churchill's Division on the Confederate right. When the Union counterattack rolled back the Confederate line, the battery lost two of its four guns.[34]

Daniel's Battery accompanied Walker's Division when it marched north to assist Sterling Price in turning back Frederick Steele's army in southern Arkansas, but apparently did not take part in the Battle of Jenkins' Ferry. Following this battle, the division returned to Louisiana and remained there for most of the year. When the Confederate artillery was reorganized in November 1864, Daniel's Battery was designated as the Ninth Texas Field Artillery Battery in Maj. C. W. Squires' Fourth Battalion. The battery officially surrendered on May 3, 1865, at Natchitoches, Louisiana. At the close of the war the battery had two 3-inch rifled guns and two 12-pounder howitzers.[35]

Duke's Battery. A small, independent artillery company known as the Jefferson Guards, or Duke's Battery, was organized in East Texas on August 1, 1861, with William H. Duke as captain. The company traveled to Virginia in autumn and was assigned to Brig. Gen. Gabriel J. Rains' Division and later John B. Magruder's Division on the York Peninsula. In early 1862 the Confederate War Department ordered the company disbanded and the men transferred to companies of Hood's Texas Brigade.[36]

Edgar-Ransom's Battery. This battery, known locally as the Alamo City Guards, was the first Texas field artillery battery accepted for Confederate service. When Confederate artillery in the Trans Mississippi was reorganized in November 1864, the Guards, by then known as Edgar's Battery, received the honored designation as the First Texas Field Artillery Battery.[37]

Led by Capt. William M. Edgar (and later Capt. James M. Ransom), the Alamo Guards, sixty men strong, served with Ben McCulloch when he obtained the surrender of Federal property in Texas in February 1861. Supplied with cannon from the captured U.S. arsenal, Edgar's men were stationed on Galveston Island during autumn 1861. In spring 1862 the battery was briefly attached to Waul's Legion but then was ordered to join Henry McCulloch's Division in Arkansas. Like Daniel's Battery, Edgar's Battery moved with the division to Louisiana in early 1863. The battery took part in several skirmishes with the enemy in May and June and was praised by Confederate commanders for its effective fire against the enemy at Perkins Landing, twenty-five miles south of Vicksburg.[38]

Edgar's Battery and the Second Louisiana Cavalry were captured by the enemy at Henderson Hill on March 21 in the opening phase of the Red River campaign. The men were later exchanged and the battery reformed. In autumn 1864 the battery was assigned to the Fourth Artillery Battalion. When the war ended, the battery was equipped with four 3.67-inch rifled guns.[39]

Galveston Battery. According to historian Alwyn Barr, the Galveston artillery could claim to be the oldest battery in Texas when the Civil War began. Organized by wealthy Galvestonians in 1840, the battery received its first weapons from a ship of the Texas Revolutionary navy. Commanded by Capt. H. Van Buren, the battery sailed with John S. Ford to Brownsville in February 1861. During April the battery helped in the capture of the Federal warship *Star of the West* at Saluria. When the six-month enlistment period of its men expired in autumn 1861, the battery disbanded and most of its members joined other Confederate units.[40]

Gibson's Battery. In February 1863 Second Company H, Thirteenth Texas Infantry, was converted to a field artillery battery commanded by Capt. William E. Gibson. Armed with four guns, the battery was stationed at Galveston in December 1863 but moved to Velasco in early January 1864. In March the battery was ordered to join Richard Taylor's army in Louisiana. The battery was in the vicinity of Mansfield in early April, but a misunderstanding of verbal orders caused Captain Gibson to withhold the battery from the fighting. The battery took part in the last stages of the Red River campaign. In the reorganization of artillery in November 1864 the battery was designated as the Sixteenth Texas Field Artillery and placed in the Fourth Battalion with Daniel's, Edgar's, and Haldeman's batteries. The battery was armed with two 12-pounder howitzers when the war ended.[41]

Good-Douglas' Battery. The Good-Douglas Battery was the most famous Civil War battery from Texas and the only one to see extensive service east of the Mississippi River. The battery entered Confederate service on July 2, 1861, with the merger of the Dallas Light Artillery commanded by John J. Good of Dallas and recruits from Smith County led by James P. Douglas. Good, chosen captain of the battery, was a graduate of Cumberland University in Tennessee, a former brigadier general in the Alabama militia, and an experienced trial lawyer. Douglas, chosen first lieutenant, was nine years younger than Good. A native of South Carolina, Douglas moved to Texas in 1847. As a young man he had been a schoolteacher, law student, and newspaper editor. When Texas seceded from the Union, Douglas was editor and co-owner of the *Tyler Reporter.*[42]

The Good Battery, consisting of five officers and ninety-two

James Douglas, Major, Douglas' Artillery Battery.
—Courtesy Harold B. Simpson Research Center, Hillsboro, Texas

enlisted men, left Dallas in August 1861 with orders to join Ben McCulloch's army in Arkansas. The battery was equipped with six cannon: four 12-pounder guns and two 12-pounder howitzers. The battery marched north with Elkanah Greer's Third Texas Cavalry but remained at Fort Smith when the Texas horsemen rode north to join McCulloch at the Battle of Wilson's Creek.

The first combat of the battery was at Pea Ridge in March 1862. It saw limited action in the first day of battle but was heavily engaged on the second day, fighting until its ammunition was exhausted. It was one of the last Rebel units to leave the field when Earl Van Dorn ordered the Confederate withdrawal. The battery had one man killed, fourteen wounded, and two missing in the battle.[43]

The Good Battery moved with Van Dorn's army to Corinth, Mississippi, following the Battle of Pea Ridge. In early May Captain Good, who was in poor health, resigned from active duty and returned home. In the reorganization that followed Douglas was elected captain and James N. Boren, J. H. Bingham, and Ben Hardin were chosen lieutenants of what was known thereafter as Douglas' Texas Battery.[44]

The battery was attached to Joseph L. Hogg's Brigade in spring 1862. Following Hogg's death, first W. L. Cabell and then Matthew D. Ector commanded the brigade. As part of the brigade,

Douglas' Texans were assigned to Edmund Kirby Smith's army in eastern Tennessee. At the Battle of Richmond, Kentucky, in late August, the battery supported Pat Cleburne's Division in the attack on the center of the enemy line. In this engagement Lieutenant Boren was killed and Lieutenant Bingham seriously wounded.[45]

The battery continued to serve with Ector's Brigade during the Tennessee campaigns of 1862-1863. At the Battle of Murfreesboro, or Stones River, the battery saw heavy action in the attack on the enemy's right flank. In the Chickamauga-Chattanooga campaign in autumn 1863 the battery was again assigned to Cleburne's Division. According to James Lunsford, a private in Douglas' artillery, the battery was "hotly engaged at Chickamauga," and in "the hottest of the fight at Missionary Ridge."[46]

The battery spent the winter of 1863-1864 at Dalton, Georgia. In January the entire company adopted a series of patriotic resolutions and reenlisted for the duration of the war. These were measures that won approval from Gen. Joseph E. Johnston and the Confederate Congress.[47]

Douglas' Battery served in the Atlanta campaign as one of three batteries in a battalion commanded by Maj. Alfred R. Courtney. The battalion was assigned to the corps commanded first by John B. Hood and later Frank Cheatham and Stephen D. Lee. For nearly one hundred days the Texans were engaged in battle. According to Private Lunsford the battery was "under fire all the time except at times . . . changing position or moving to a new line." In the Battle of Atlanta on July 22 the Confederates captured several enemy cannon; four of them, all 12-pounder Napoleons, were turned over to Douglas in exchange for his old guns, two 12-pounders, and two 6-pounders.[48]

The battery was with Hood's army when it withdrew from Atlanta. Douglas and his men remained with the army when it moved into Alabama and Tennessee. As the army traveled north in November, Douglas' Battery had several sharp exchanges with the enemy. At Franklin, Tennessee, on November 30 the battery supported Granbury's Brigade in the costly but futile assault on the enemy in a battle that Captain Douglas reported as "the bloodiest I have ever seen."[49]

In the Battle of Nashville, fought in mid-December, the

Douglas Battery was under heavy fire. When the Confederates began their retreat, Douglas' Battery was placed in the rear to help cover the withdrawal. South of Franklin, Union cavalry overran Douglas' position. Although Douglas and most of his men escaped, the enemy captured the battery's guns.[50]

The company, without its guns, retreated with Hood's army to Mississippi. In January the battery was assigned to man the siege guns at Fort Sidney Johnston at Mobile. When Douglas and a number of men received furloughs to visit home, Lt. Ben Hardin took command of the battery. At the evacuation of Mobile in early April the company was given a light battery with what Private Lunsford described as "a splendid outfit of horses."[51]

The battery marched to northern Mississippi and was camped at Artesia when the men received news of the Confederate surrender. Some of the men went home immediately, but most waited to take their parole on May 14, before heading to Texas. About fifty of the original company were present at the final surrender. Captain Douglas was on his way back to the battery from Texas when he learned of the surrender, so he returned to his home in Tyler.[52]

Greer's Rocket Battery. This unusual artillery battery was organized in late 1863 by Capt. John S. Greer, a former ordnance sergeant in the U.S. Army, for the purpose of firing rockets to be produced in a San Antonio factory. Unfortunately, the test of the Texas rockets was unsuccessful as several of the rockets exploded prematurely. The battery was assigned regular duty near East Bernard in spring 1864 but apparently was disbanded soon thereafter. The men were then redistributed among other units.[53]

Howe's Battery. A heavy artillery battery was organized in June 1863 with Capt. M. G. Howe as commander. The battery served as part of the Galveston defenses during the last half of the year. According to historian Alwyn Barr, the battery was actually a company of sappers and miners. In April 1864 it became Company E, First Confederate Engineers' Battalion.[54]

Howell's Battery. Capt. Sylvanus Howell's Battery, organized in April 1862, spent most of the Civil War in Indian Territory. Initially a four-gun battery, Howell's company, recruited in North Texas, was ordered across the Red River in early summer 1862. The battery was assigned to Douglas H. Cooper's Brigade and took part in the battle at Newtonia, Missouri, on September 30, 1862. When the enemy attempted to outflank the Confederates on the right, Cooper sent Howell and two of his guns to drive the Union infantry from the field. For this action Howell's gunners won the praise of Cooper for handling "their guns with the greatest of coolness and celerity."[55]

Howell's Battery was with Cooper's Brigade in an ill-conceived expedition to attack Fort Scott, Kansas, in October 1862. Union troops, commanded by Brig. Gen. James G. Blunt, routed Cooper's command at Old Fort Wayne, just inside Indian Territory. In a brief but violent engagement Howell's Battery at first stopped the Union advance but lost its guns when the Federals overran their position. The battery suffered twenty-two casualties in the Confederate defeat.[56]

Although without guns for several months, Howell's company remained assigned to Cooper's Brigade during most of 1863. Conditions in Indian Territory and Arkansas continued to deteriorate for the Confederates, especially after Cooper's defeat at Honey Springs in July. New guns were not received by the battery until the end of summer. To Cooper's dissatisfaction, the battery, finally equipped with two 12-pounder howitzers and two 6-pounder smoothbores, was transferred to a new brigade just up from Texas commanded by Richard Gano. The battery was with Gano's Brigade in the Confederate victories at Poison Spring (April 1864) and Cabin Creek (September 1864). For their part in the capture of a Union wagon train at Cabin Creek, Howell and his officers received special mention by General Gano for their gallantry and efficiency.[57]

In the reorganization of Trans Mississippi artillery in November 1864, Howell's Battery was designated as the Eleventh Texas Field Artillery in Maj. William B. Krumbhaar's Battalion. This battalion returned to Texas in December 1864 and was assigned to Maxey's Division. When the war ended, Howell's Battery had two 12-pounder howitzers and four 6-pounder smoothbores.[58]

O. G. Jones' Battery. Jones' Battery had its origin as First Company A of Cook's Heavy Artillery Regiment. In June 1863 the battery became Company A of the Seventh Texas Artillery Battalion. As part of the battalion the company, commanded by Capt. O. G. Jones, was stationed at Galveston, Houston, and Sabine Pass in the last half of 1863. In early 1864 Jones' Battery was camped at Cedar Lake in Brazoria County. The battery was moved to San Antonio in the summer of 1864. In early September the battery reported three officers, fifty-one men, and six guns available for duty.[59]

Toward the end of September in 1864 Jones' Battery was ordered to Brownsville to help meet the threat from actitivies by Juan Cortina. In the November 1864 reorganization of Trans Mississippi Artillery, Jones' Battery was designated as the Third Texas Field Artillery. The battery had the distinction of firing the last artillery salvo of the Civil War at Palmito Ranch, May 13, 1865. At the close of the war the battery had one 3.67-inch rifle, one 3-inch rifle, one 12-pounder howitzer, and three 6-pounder smoothbore guns.[60]

William R. Jones' Battery. This battery was formed in March 1863 by the conversion of Company F, Thirteenth Texas Infantry, into a heavy artillery battery to protect the port of Velasco. The battery, commanded by Capt. William R. Jones, a West Pointer, remained under the general direction of Col. Joseph Bates, who was responsible for the defense of the lower Brazos.[61]

Keith's Battery. This battery, made up of southeast Texas residents, was originally Company B of James B. Likens' Infantry Battalion. When Likens was promoted and authorized to raise his own regiment, Ashley W. Spaight became commander of the battalion. Kosciuszko D. Keith, a Sabine Pass businessman and native of Georgia, commanded the battery. The battery was assigned to Fort Sabine, but when that fort was abandoned by the Confederates in October 1862 Keith and his men were sent to Grigsby's Bluff to man two 24-pounder guns at Fort Grigsby, a new fortification on the Neches River.[62]

In January 1863 Keith's company was ordered to Orange, where his artillerists were detailed to man two 12-pounder guns on the *Uncle Ben,* one of two river steamers being converted to gunboats. As gunners on *Uncle Ben* Keith and his men helped in the capture of the *Morning Light* and *Velocity* on January 21, 1863.[63]

Keith's men were still serving on the *Uncle Ben* in the summer of 1863. In September, during the battle between Dick Dowling's command at Fort Griffin and Federal gunboats, Keith's gunners were on the *Uncle Ben* as it steamed up the channel to draw enemy fire. However, the *Uncle Ben* withdrew to Sabine Lake when fire from the enemy ships came too close.

Following the successful defense of Sabine Pass in early September, Keith's company was sent to man the additional guns the Confederates placed at Fort Griffin. In March 1864 Keith's troops accompanied Col. W. H. Griffin's Confederate forces in the attack on the two Union gunboats at Calcasieu Pass. The battery then returned to Fort Griffin, where it remained until November 1864 when Keith's company was redesignated Company I of the Thirteenth Infantry Regiment and assigned to Fort Manhasset, a new fort built seven miles west of Fort Griffin. The battery remained there until the end of the war.[64]

Krumbhaar-Stafford's Battery. The Krumbhaar Battery, also known as the Texas Guards, was created in April 1863. The commander of the battery, William Butler Krumbhaar, served as a private in the famed Washington Artillery at the Battle of Shiloh. Promoted to first lieutenant in November 1862, he helped organize his own Texas field artillery battery.[65]

Krumbhaar's Battery was ordered to report to acting Brig. Gen. Smith Bankhead at Bonham almost immediately after its creation. In late August 1863 the battery moved to Boggy Depot in Indian Territory, where it was assigned to Richard Gano's Brigade. The Trans Mississippi Department's inspector general gave the battery high marks on a visit in late October. According to the inspector, the battery was "in very good order, discipline good, drill very good, military appearance fair." He did note that the caissons and carriages for the battery's four guns were not clean but added that the ammunition was well packed and the clothing of the men better than he observed elsewhere.[66]

The battery was with Gano's Brigade when it was sent to reinforce Sterling Price's army in Arkansas. Consisting of only thirty men at the time, the battery took part in the Battle of Poison Spring on April 18, 1864.[67]

In summer 1864 Captain Krumbhaar was placed in command of an artillery battalion consisting of his own battery, now commanded by Lt. W. M. Stafford, and batteries commanded by George Dashiell and Sylvanus Howell. In November the batteries were given numerical designations, and the Krumbhaar-Stafford Battery became the Seventeenth Texas Field Battery. The battalion returned to Texas in late 1864 as part of Sam Maxey's Division. When the war ended, the battery had three 3.40-inch rifles and one 6-pounder howitzer.[68]

Lee-Humphreys' Battery. Lee-Humphreys' Battery was organized in early 1863. The commander of the battery, Capt. Roswell W. Lee, was an 1833 graduate of the U.S. Military Academy. Commissioned in the engineers, Lee served in the Seminole War. After dismissal from the U.S. Army in 1838 for signing false certificates, Lee went to Texas. He soon restored his reputation by serving as an officer in the Army of the Republic, court clerk, surveyor, and colonel of the state militia.[69]

With the outbreak of the Civil War, Lee was appointed captain in the Confederate army and assigned to the staff of Col. Douglas H. Cooper in Indian Territory. Lee took part in operations against the enemy in Indian Territory and Arkansas, winning the praise of both Cooper and Albert Pike, commanding Confederate Indians.[70]

In 1863 Lee was given command of his own artillery battery in Cooper's Brigade. Lee's Battery was the only artillery with Cooper in the battle at Honey Springs in July 1863. Although the Confederates held off the larger Federal force for two hours, Lee's four howitzers were no match for the enemy's twelve guns. The Confederates were forced to retreat after a bitter battle.[71]

Lee left the battery soon afterward. The battery, commanded now by Capt. John T. Humphreys, remained with Cooper's Brigade throughout much of 1864. In operations around Fort Smith in July, Humphreys and his men gained the praise of Cooper for behaving "in the most gallant manner."[72]

The Lee-Humphreys Battery was not among the Trans Mississippi batteries given numercial designations in November 1864. An organizational chart for the artillery of the department for December 1864 shows the battery as part of Krumbhaar's Artillery Battalion. In his *Compendium of Confederate Armies: Texas,* Stewart Sifakis says the battery was "apparently disbanded in early 1865."[73]

Maclin-Fox-Dege's Battery. R. B. Maclin's Battery was organized in Bexar County in November 1861. The battery was stationed on the Rio Grande during 1862 and early 1863. In summer 1863 the battery was ordered to join Confederate defense forces at Galveston. Capt. P. Fox succeeded Maclin as commander of the battery and remained in command until January 1864, when A. E. Dege became commander.

Dege's Battery remained in Galveston until the end of the war. Abstract returns show that the battery had four guns in April 1864 but was armed with eight guns during summer 1864. The number of guns was back at four by September. In November the battery was designated as the Eighth Texas Field Artillery and assigned to an artillery battalion commanded by Sidney T. Fontaine. The battery was fairly large in terms of numbers, listing over two hundred men on its muster rolls with eighty-nine men present for duty at most times. When the war ended, the battery was armed with two 12-pounder howitzers and two 12-pounder smoothbores.[74]

McMahan's Battery. This battery was formed in late 1863 by the detachment of Company E, First Texas Heavy Artillery Regiment. Commanded by Capt. M. V. McMahan, the battery was at Harrisburg, Texas, in November 1863. In late December the battery moved with Xavier Debray's Brigade to the mouth of the Caney River in Brazoria County. In early March 1864 McMahan and several other Texas battery commanders received orders to join Richard Taylor's army in Louisiana.[75]

McMahan's Battery was in both the battles at Mansfield and Pleasant Hill. Historian Alwyn Barr has pointed out that because of the terrain the Confederate batteries were limited in their effectiveness at Mansfield. He noted that "only the batteries of Nettles [the Valverde Battery] and McMahan (Lt. Sam Houston, Jr., commanding one section) were of real service maintaining fire to support the assault from the roadway." In a twenty-minute duel McMahan and his gunners silenced the artillery of the Fifth U.S. Regular Battery.[76]

McMahan's artillery was one of four Texas batteries sent to challenge Union shipping at Blair's Landing. The battery was part of Hamilton P. Bee's command at Monett's Ferry. It engaged in an exchange with Banks' artillery at Mansura and was credited with preventing the enemy from following up its success at Yellow Bayou.[77]

McMahan's Battery remained in Louisiana after the end of the Red River campaign. In September 1864 it was one of the four batteries assigned to an artillery battalion commanded by Maj. Oliver Semmes. In the November reorganization of Trans Mississippi artillery, McMahan's Battery was designated as the Second Texas

Field Artillery Battery. The battery was stationed near Alexandria, Louisiana, when the war ended. In its possession were two 3.67-inch rifled guns and two 12-pounder howitzers at the time.[78]

Marmion's Battery. Marmion's Battery was organized only for a brief time. Formed in Bexar County on September 10, 1861, the battery was commanded by Capt. James R. Marmion. The battery was sent to Fort Brown soon thereafter. According to Col. Augustus Buchel, the experienced professional who took command of the fort in late autumn, Marmion's company was composed partly of Mexican nationals and deserters from the Federal army. "With few exceptions," Buchel reported, "they are a class of men in whom no dependence whatever may be placed." His superiors apparently agreed because the battery was disbanded soon after.[79]

Mechling-Haldeman's Battery. The Mechling Battery was one of three artillery companies formed in San Antonio in autumn 1861. The captain of the battery, William T. Mechling, was born in Pennsylvania. He graduated from the U.S. Military Academy at West Point in 1848 and was commissioned in the infantry. He served with the army on frontier duty from 1848 to 1855, when he was dismissed for unknown reasons. Mechling settled in Bexar County and was farming when Texas seceded. He served as assistant adjutant general with Ben McCulloch's forces when they caused David Twiggs' surrender in February 1861.[80]

Mechling's Battery, also known as the Van Dorn Light Artillery, was stationed at Galveston briefly but ordered to join Henry E. McCulloch's Division in Arkansas in late summer 1862. When Mechling was promoted to major and became an officer on McCulloch's staff, another West Pointer, Horace Haldeman, became battery commander. The battery remained with the division when it (now led by John G. Walker) was ordered to Louisiana in 1863. Attached to Overton Young's First Brigade, the battery served in the Louisiana bayou campaigns during autumn 1863.[81]

The batteries of Captain Haldeman and Capt. James Daniel provided artillery support for Walker's Division in the battles at Mansfield and Pleasant Hill. Both batteries accompanied the division when ordered to Arkansas to support Sterling Price's efforts to block the movement of Union Gen. Frederick Steele. Although Haldeman's Battery was at the Battle of Jenkins' Ferry, it was not heavily engaged.[82]

In the November 1864 reorganization of artillery, Haldeman's Battery was designated as the Fourth Texas Field Artillery. When the war ended, the battery had two 12-pounder howitzers and two 12-pounder smoothbores.[83]

Moseley's Battery. Capt. William G. Moseley, a Brazoria cotton planter, recruited a company to take part in John S. Ford's Rio Grande Valley expedition in February–March 1861. After his seventy-five men, largely from Brazoria County, were released from state service he convinced most of them to enlist in Confederate service. They first served as artillerymen with the Thirteenth Infantry guarding the port of Velasco. In June 1863 the battery was designated as Company B, Seventh Texas Artillery Battalion.[84]

Moseley's Battery was stationed in Galveston during the summer and autumn of 1863. In December the battery moved back to Brazoria County as part of Confederate efforts to prevent Union landings on the Texas coast. The battery remained at Cedar Lake until ordered to Louisiana in March 1864. Moseley and his men joined Richard Taylor's army several days before the Battle of Mansfield and took part in all the major engagements of the Red River campaign. At Pleasant Hill, Moseley's company was one of several Texas batteries that supported Arkansas troops under Thomas Churchill in the assault against the Union left flank. The battery was with Hamilton P. Bee's command at Monett's Ferry in late April. When Bee ordered a withdrawal, Moseley's Battery helped cover the retreat. The battery was assigned to William Steele's Brigade in the closing phases of the Red River campaign. In his report Steele praised Moseley for the manner in which he directed his battery.[85]

The battery remained in Louisiana during 1864 as part of John A. Wharton's Cavalry Corps. In November the battery, with its two officers, fifty-eight men, and four guns, was designated as the Seventh Texas Field Artillery and assigned to the battalion commanded by Maj. Oliver J. Semmes.[86]

Neal-Maltby's Battery. This heavy artillery battery of three guns (12-, 18-, and 24-pounders) and ninety-one men was organized, financed, and originally commanded by Benjamin F. Neal. Neal, a lawyer, newspaper editor, and first mayor of the incorporated city of Corpus Christi, made a small fortune in Arizona through mining. He created the battery to defend Corpus Christi against enemy attack. When Neal was chosen district judge in 1862, William N. Maltby became commander of the battery. Maltby's Battery aided in the successful defense of Aransas Bay in February and July 1862 but was captured by enemy forces on Mustang Island, November 17, 1863.[87]

Nichols' Battery. William H. Nichols' Battery was organized in 1863 by the change of designation of Company D, First Texas Heavy Artillery. The battery was one of several Texas artillery units sent to support Tom Green's cavalry operations in Louisiana. Along with the Valverde Battery, Nichols' Battery took part in the capture of Brashear City in June 1863.[88]

Nichols' Battery was ordered to Sabine Pass several days after Dowling and his gunners repulsed the Union invasion in early September 1863. According to the inspector general's report the battery was filled with new conscripts in October 1863. The report indicated that drill in the battery was imperfect. Horses and guns were in good condition, but carriages and harnesses needed repair.[89]

When the newly constructed Fort Manhasset was fitted with artillery, Nichols' Battery was assigned to man the guns. The battery remained at Sabine Pass until early March 1864, when it was ordered to the Houston area. In May the battery was sent back to Sabine Pass, where it joined Lt. Col. W. H. Griffin's Confederates in the march to Calcasieu Pass. There they captured two Union gunboats. By late summer Nichols and his men were back in Texas, assigned to the defense of the lower Brazos. Abstract returns show the battery with two or three officers and from fifty-two to sixty-two men present for duty throughout autumn and winter 1864-1865.[90]

The battery was designated as the Fifteenth Texas Field Artillery in November 1864. At the end of the war it had one 3-inch rifle, one 12-pounder howitzer, and two 6-pounder smoothbores.[91]

Perry's Battery. Perry's Battery, also known as the Austin Grays, was originally Company B of the Thirteenth Texas Infantry. In June 1863 the company was converted to an artillery battery. Commanded by Capt. James S. Perry, the battery, along with William S. Jones' Battery, manned the heavy guns at the mouth of the Brazos near Velasco.[92]

Pratt-Hynson's Battery. The men of Pratt's artillery battery, which saw extensive service in Arkansas and Missouri, were recruited in Harrison, Marion, and Cass counties during the spring of

1861. Joseph H. Pratt, an East Texas railroad builder, was the first captain of the battery. When he was promoted to major, commanding an artillery battalion, H. C. Hynson, a young man from Marshall, became battery commander.[93]

Pratt's Battery, consisting initially of seventy-two men, was ordered to join Confederate forces near Little Rock in spring 1862. The battery was assigned to Col. William H. Parsons' Brigade and served with that brigade in patrolling and skirmishing along the lower Arkansas River in summer and autumn. In April 1863 the battery participated in John S. Marmaduke's Cape Giradeau raid.[94]

In September 1863 Pratt's Battery assisted in the defense of Little Rock. Stationed several miles below the town, Pratt's gunners delayed the enemy crossing of the Arkansas River until superior Union firepower forced the Texans to withdraw to Bayou Fourche, a tributary of the Arkansas. Here again Pratt's men delayed the enemy until forced to give ground and withdraw.[95]

In late October Pratt's Battery was heavily engaged in the unsuccessful assault on the enemy position at Pine Bluff. In this campaign John S. Marmaduke, the Confederate commander, attempted to overwhelm the enemy with superior numbers but failed. In the fighting Pratt and his gunners "behaved with their accustomed bravery and steadiness" while driving the enemy back into the center of town. However, the Confederates were unable to dislodge the enemy and eventually retreated.[96]

The battery was attached to George W. Carter's Cavalry Brigade during autumn and winter. Morale was low following the loss of Little Rock and the failure at Pine Bluff. Historian Anne Bailey noted that "lethargy prevailed everywhere," but that Pratt's Battery was a source of pride. In an autumn report the inspector general observed that Pratt's Battery was "in very fine order, and a model command. Their discipline is very good. The men are well drilled, and care is taken of the horses and everything about the battery."[97]

Pratt's Battery continued to support cavalry operations in eastern Arkansas during spring and summer 1864. In late May the battery opened fire on enemy ships on the Mississippi, forcing the surrender of a Federal transport. In early June the battery supported Marmaduke's cavalry operations around Lake Chicot. For his achievements Pratt was promoted to major in late summer and placed in command of an artillery battalion in Marmaduke's Division, consisting of the Texas battery, now commanded by Captain Hynson, two Missouri batteries, and an Arkansas battery.[98]

Pratt's Battalion accompanied Sterling Price in his raid into Missouri in September-October 1864. The raid accomplished little and proved disastrous for the Confederates. In the course of the retreat, Brigadier General Marmaduke was captured, Major Pratt seriously wounded, and the guns of Hynson's Battery lost to the enemy.[99]

Price's army, including what was left of Hynson's Battery, eventually made its way back to southern Arkansas. In November 1864 Hynson's Battery, still without guns, officially became the Tenth Texas Field Artillery. The battery was serving in the Trans Mississippi Department's Reserve Artillery Battalion when the war ended in May 1865.[100]

Reily's Battery. This battery was one of a couple of four-gun batteries of 12-pounder mountain howitzers created by order of Brig. Gen. Henry H. Sibley to accompany his regiments in the New Mexico campaign. In his book *Blood & Treasure,* Donald S. Frazier pointed out that the weapons were light and easily disassembled for transportation aboard pack mules. The disadvantage of the guns was the limited range of only 1,000 yards with shell, and only 800 yards with spherical case. None could fire solid shot.[101]

Lt. John Reily, son of Col. James Reily, commander of the Fourth Texas Cavalry, was appointed commander of the battery. The thirty-six men who crewed the guns were drawn from different companies of the Fourth Cavalry. The battery accompanied the Fourth Cavalry in the march to New Mexico and saw action in the Battle of Valverde on February 21, 1862. Reily's Battery was on the Confederate left in the early morning fighting for control of the fords. The battery fired one of the opening salvos of the battle but due to the longer range of enemy guns on the western shore, Lieutenant Colonel Scurry, commanding Rebel troops in that sector, ordered all but one of Reily's guns pulled back to high ground. The remaining gun continued to exchange fire with the enemy while some of Reily's other gunners were dispatched to man other Confederate guns when their crews were wounded.[102]

Reily's Battery moved north with Sibley's army after the Battle of Valverde. The battery remained in Albuquerque with detachments of the Second and Fourth regiments while Sibley himself pushed on to Santa Fe. When Union forces attacked the city in early April, fire from Reily's guns helped convince the Federals to call off their attacks. General Sibley meanwhile decided to withdraw his troops from New Mexico to avoid encirclement. When the Confederates began their retreat they buried several of their cannon, including Reily's guns, near Albuquerque plaza to keep them out of Federal hands.[103]

The burial of its guns meant the effective end of Reily's Battery. Reily and a few of the men helped in the withdrawal of several guns left under the command of Maj. Trevanion T. Teel, while the others returned to the Fourth Cavalry on the long retreat back to Texas.

Reuss' Battery. Joseph Reuss' Battery, known also as the Indianola Artillery Guards, was organized in Calhoun County in 1861. The battery became part of the Fourth Texas Artillery Battalion later in the year and took part in the successful defense of Port Lavaca in late October 1862. The Fourth Artillery Battalion was later incorporated with the Eighth Texas Infantry Battalion to form the Eighth Texas Infantry Regiment.[104]

Shea-Vernon's Battery. Daniel Shea's Battery, the Van Dorn Guards, was organized in July 1861. The battery became Company A of the Fourth Texas Artillery Battalion in December. When Shea was promoted to battalion commander, John A. Vernon became battery commander. Along with Reuss' Battery, Vernon's Battery helped defend Port Lavaca in October 1862 and later became part of the Eighth Texas Infantry Regiment.[105]

Teel's Battery. Trevanion T. Teel, Mexican War veteran, successful criminal attorney from San Antonio, and active Knight of the Golden Circle, organized a company that served with Ben McCulloch when David Twiggs surrendered Federal property in Texas. His company was later mustered into Confederate service as Light Company B, First Artillery. The company was part of the forces that secured the surrender of Federal forces at San Lucas Springs in May 1861.[106]

Teel's Battery accompanied Lt. Col. John R. Baylor's troops in the march to El Paso and the occupation of the Mesilla Valley in the summer of 1861. When Henry H. Sibley took command of all Confederate forces in New Mexico, he promoted Teel to major and chief of his artillery. At that time the artillery consisted of howitzer batteries commanded by Lt. John Reily and Lt. William Wood, as well as his own battery consisting of four 6-pounder field guns.[107]

In the battle at Valverde, Teel's Battery was in the center of the Confederate line. One section (two guns) under Lt. James Bradford was at the front of the column with Scurry's Regiment. Teel himself was near the rear of the column with his other section. In the course of the fighting the battery was moved to the extreme right of the Confederate line. Although Teel's guns lacked the range of the Union artillery his men kept up a steady fire during the afternoon Confederate attack that swept the enemy from the field.[108]

Teel's Battery was engaged in the other major fighting in New Mexico at Apache Canyon and Glorieta Pass. Two of Teel's guns were with Maj. Charles Pyron in the battle at Apache Canyon and helped keep the enemy at bay for much of the day. The other two guns were brought up with Lt. Col. William R. Scurry the next day and used in the Battle of Glorieta Pass on March 28.[109]

When the Confederates retreated from New Mexico in early summer 1862, the Teel Battery, now commanded by Capt. Jordan Bennett, helped cover the withdrawal.

The fate of the Teel Battery after the end of the New Mexico campaign is something of a mystery. Historian Tom Cutrer, writing in the *New Handbook of Texas,* declared that the battery was assigned to Van Dorn's Army of the West and saw service in Arkansas, Missouri, and Mississippi. Alwyn Barr, in his study of Confederate artillery, stated that the battery was disbanded in 1863 and some of the officers transferred to Christmas' Battery. The *Official Records* are silent on the matter, although Teel's Battery is listed with the Army of the West [Van Dorn's army] on March 17, 1862, nine days before the battery took part in the Battle of Glorieta Pass in New Mexico Territory.[110]

Valverde Battery. One of the most celebrated of all Texas artillery units, the Valverde Battery was officially organized in summer of 1862 using artillery pieces captured from the enemy by the Confederates at the Battle of Valverde, New Mexico, in February 1862. In the battle the Confederates overran the six-gun Union battery commanded by Capt. Alexander McRae. These enemy weapons, three 6-pounders and three 12-pounder howitzers, were used by the Confederates during later fighting in New Mexico and brought back to Texas when Sibley's army retreated.[111]

The battery, made up of volunteers from the regiments in Sibley's Brigade, was commanded by Capt. Joseph Sayers, who later became governor of Texas. Sayers' Battery accompanied Sibley's Brigade when it was assigned to Richard Taylor's army in the Louisiana bayou country. The battery was responsible for the capture of the enemy gunboat *Dianna* in March 1863 and took part in the fighting at Bisland, Vermilion Bayou, and Bayou Bourbeau. When Captain Sayers was wounded at Bisland, Timothy D. Nettles took command of the battery, a position he held for the remainder of the war.[112]

The Valverde, or Nettles, Battery participated in the battles at Mansfield and Pleasant Hill as well as various skirmishes with the enemy as Federal forces retreated back down the Red River in late spring 1864. In the reorganization of Trans Mississippi artillery in November, the unit was designated as the Twelfth Texas Field Artillery and assigned to Oliver J. Semmes' Battalion. The battery was armed with two 3-inch rifles and two 12-pounder howitzers when the war ended in 1865.[113]

Willke's Battery. Willke's Battery, or the Austin Light Artillery, was organized in June 1861 and mustered into Confederate service in October. Commanded initially by Capt. H. Willke, the battery was assigned to Fort Brown in November 1861.[114]

With 87 men, four 12-pounder Napoleons, and two 24-pounder howitzers, the battery was ordered to Corpus Christi in late August 1862, after Maj. A. M. Hobby's Infantry Battalion had driven off Union forces that attempted to capture Corpus. One of the battery's guns was used by Capt. John Ireland in the capture of a small Union landing party at Flour Bluff on September 14.[115]

Willke's Battery remained in the Corpus Christi vicinity until autumn 1863, when it was assigned to Xavier Debray's command near Houston. The battery was ordered to McNeel's plantation in Brazoria County in December to meet an expected Union invasion. When this threat passed, the battery was ordered back to Galveston and remained there for the rest of the war. When Willke was promoted to major in command of an artillery battalion, Capt. R. W. Yates succeeded him as battery commander. Yates in turn was succeeded by Capt. Samuel W. Allen in November 1864.[116]

In the reorganization of Confederate artillery, Willke's Battery became the Sixth Texas Field Artillery. The battery was armed with two 24-pounder howitzers and two 12-pounder smoothbores in May 1865.[117]

Wilson-Gonzales-Hughes' Battery. Capt. George R. Wilson's Battery was organized in Galveston in the summer of 1862. The battery was first assigned to Xavier Debray's command at Houston. When Union raiders came ashore at Sabine Pass in September 1862, the battery accompanied Debray as he rushed reinforcements to the area.[118]

The battery returned to the Houston area after the threat to Sabine Pass eased. When Captain Wilson was promoted to major, Lt. Thomas Gonzales, a cotton factor and wholesale grocer from Galveston, was promoted to captain and battery commander. Under Gonzales' command the battery played a signficant role in the Confederate recapture of Galveston on January 1, 1863.[119]

Gonzales' Battery was ordered to Louisiana in spring 1863. Assigned to support the operations of Tom Green's cavalry, the battery took part in operations near Cox's plantation in the bayou country. It returned to Texas in late summer and, after a brief stop at Sabine Pass, continued on to the lower Brazos to meet an expected Union invasion of the upper Texas coast.[120]

Captain Gonzales retired from service in September 1863 due to poor health. He was succeeded as battery commander by Capt. Robert J. Hughes. Although the battery was alerted to move back to Louisiana in spring 1864, it remained on the Texas coast for the rest of the war. In November 1864 it was designated as the Thirteenth Texas Field Artillery. Morning reports show the battery with three officers and forty to fifty men during most of 1864. When the war ended the battery had one 3-inch rifle, one 12-pounder howitzer, and two 6-pounder guns.[121]

Wood's Battery. This battery, commanded by Lt. William S. Wood of the Fifth Texas Cavalry, was the companion to John Reily's Battery. Both were created by Brigadier General Sibley in the New Mexico campaign. Like Reily's Battery, Wood's Battery was armed with four 12-pounder howitzers. It was located on the Confederate right when the Battle of Valverde began but was moved several times during the course of the battle. Like Reily's Battery, Wood and his men buried their guns at Albuquerque when Sibley's army began its retreat from New Mexico. The burial of the guns meant the effective end of the battery.[122]

Appendix

AFTER THE WAR

Listed in this appendix are brief sketches of the postwar career and activities of various individuals mentioned in the text.

Abercrombie, Leonard, Lt. Col. Twentieth Texas Infantry. Resumed legal practice, Huntsville. Served in Texas State Senate, 1887-1889. Died Philadelphia, December 23, 1891. Body returned to Huntsville for burial.

Affleck, Isaac Dunbar, Private, Co. B, Terry's Rangers. Returned to Washington County. Following father's death he managed the family plantation. Studied Texas history, science, politics. Conducted intensive research on the Texas ant. Contributed frequently to newspapers. Edited August Santleben's *A Texas Pioneer* (1910). Died at Confederate Veterans' Home, April 18, 1919. Buried in Brenham.

Allen, Robert T. P., Commander, Seventeenth Texas Infantry. Superintendent of Kentucky Military Institute. Died July 9, 1888, while swimming in Kissimmee River, Florida.

Alexander, Almerine M., Commander, Thirty-fourth Texas Cavalry. Due to poor health forced to resign his commission in May 1863. Died New Orleans, summer 1865.

Anderson, Thomas Scott, Commander, Anderson's Cavalry Regiment. Moved to Eagle Pass. Died at home, September 25, 1868. Buried near graves of Confederate soldiers who had died while camped there.

Archer, James J., First Commander, Fifth Texas Infantry. A Marylander, given his own brigade in June 1862. Captured at Gettysburg; health shattered by imprisonment. Died Richmond, Virginia, on October 24, 1864. Buried Hollywood Cemetery, Richmond.

Bagby, Arthur P., Commander, Seventh Texas Cavalry, later Brigade Commander. Resumed law practice, worked as assistant editor, *Victoria Advocate*. Died Hallettsville, February 21, 1921, one of last surviving Confederate generals. Buried Hallettsville City Cemetery.

Baird, Spruce M., Commander, Fourth Texas Cavalry, Arizona Brigade. Moved to Trinidad, Colorado, opened law office. Died Cimarron, New Mexico, June 5, 1872.

Barron, Sam, Private, Third Texas Cavalry. Returned to Rusk, Cherokee County; married; studied law. Clerk, Cherokee County, 1886-1892; judge, 1896. His memoirs *The Lone Star Defenders* published 1908. Died Palestine, February 2, 1912.

Barry, James B. "Buck," Lieutenant Colonel, Frontier Regiment. Active in the Grange, served in Twelfth Texas Legislature. People's Party candidate for state treasurer, 1898. Retired to ranch near Walnut Springs. Blind near end of life. Died, December 16, 1906.

Bass, Frederick S., Colonel, First Texas Infantry. Returned to Marshall. Became president of Marshall University. Died in Confederate Home, Austin, July 1897.

Bass, Thomas C., Colonel, Twentieth Texas Cavalry. Published Sherman *Courier*, practiced law. Purchased twenty-five-year-old Grayson County Courthouse, had it leveled and sold bricks for chimneys. Went to Memphis to aid in combating yellow fever, contracted the disease, and died September 22, 1878.

Bates, Joseph, Colonel, Thirteenth Texas Infantry. Remained in Brazoria County, active in civic and political affairs. Died February 18, 1888, buried Episcopal Cemetery, Galveston.

Baylor, George W., Colonel, Second Texas Cavalry, Arizona Brigade. Eventually acquitted of John A. Wharton's death. Became Texas Ranger; took part in campaigns against Victorio and Apaches. Lived in Guadalajara, Mexico. Represented El Paso district in Twentieth Legislature, 1887-1888. Died San Antonio, March 27, 1916. Buried Confederate Cemetery there.

Baylor, John R., Lieutenant Colonel, Second Texas Cavalry and Governor of Confederate Territory of Arizona. Settled in San Antonio. Candidate for Democratic gubernatorial nomination in 1873 but defeated by Richard Coke. In 1878 moved to ranch on Nueces River at Montell. Died there on February 6, 1894.

Bee, Hamilton P., Brigade and Division Commander in Texas and Louisiana. He and family moved to Mexico after the war. Lived there until 1876, when he returned to San Antonio. Died from heart disease, October 2, 1897. Buried in San Antonio Confederate Cemetery.

Benavides, Cristobal, Captain, Benavides Regiment. After war married Hamilton P. Bee's daughter; had six daughters and four sons. Wealthy rancher and merchant. Died September 2, 1904; buried in Laredo.

Benavides, Refugio, Captain, Benavides Regiment. Brother of Santos, half-brother Cristobal. Elected mayor of Laredo, 1873. Raised company of Rangers to fight bandits and Kickapoos. Died from chronic diarrhea, Laredo, June 19, 1899, buried in Laredo.

Benavides, Santos, Commander, Benavides Regiment. Continued mercantile and ranching activities, served three terms in state legislature, active in Democratic party. Texas delegate World Cotton Exposition, 1880. Died Laredo, November 9, 1891; buried there.

Blackburn, J. K. P., Captain, Company F, Terry's Rangers. Settled in Giles County, Tennessee. Served in Tennessee legislature. Finished his "Reminiscences of Terry Rangers" in 1916, published in *Southwestern Historical Quarterly,* 1918. Died in Tennessee on July 6, 1923.

Blessington, Joseph Palmer, Private, Seventeenth Texas Infantry. After receiving parole settled in Austin, became salesman. Married, four sons and daughter. Moved to Waco, became city sanitary inspector. Wrote "The Campaigns of Walker's Texas Division," published at own expense, 1875. Three reprints, 1893, 1968, 1994. Died in Waco, December 19, 1898; buried in Waco's Catholic Cemetery.

Bonner, Thomas R., Commander, Eighteenth Texas Infantry. Returned to Rusk County, farmed, admitted to bar. Moved to Tyler, became banker, financier, railroad director. Elected to Texas legislature, 1866 and 1876. Speaker of Texas House, 1876. Died 1891.

Border, John P., Commander, Border's Cavalry Regiment. He and family settled in New Iberia, Louisiana. Died there on June 12, 1873; buried Protestant Cemetery. Widow married former Texas governor O. M. Roberts.

Bourland, James G., Commander, Frontier Regiment. Indicted by grand jury for role in Gainesville hangings; not convicted. Returned to home on Red River, resided there as heavily armed recluse until death on August 20, 1879.

Brown, Reuben R., Commander, Thirty-fifth Texas Cavalry. According to *New Handbook of Texas,* 1:767, Texas Veterans' Board approved his application for pension; nothing more given on postwar activities.

Bryan, Kindallas ("King"), Lieutenant Colonel, Fifth Texas Infantry. Returned home to Liberty. Delegate, constitutional convention of 1866. Died Liberty, October 8, 1866, buried Bryan-Neyland Cemetery.

Bunting, Robert F., Chaplain, Terry's Rangers. Pastor of First Presbyterian Church, Nashville. Returned to Texas, 1869, pastor in Galveston until 1882. Founder and editor *Texas Republican,* synod weekly newspaper. Pastor at Rome, Georgia, and Gallatin, Tennessee. Died Gallatin, September 19, 1891; buried there.

Burford, Nathaniel M., Commander, Nineteenth Texas Cavalry. Returned to Dallas, elected Speaker of House of Representatives in 1866 but removed by General Sheridan. Served as county and district judge. Died, Dallas, May 20, 1898; buried Greenwood Cemetery.

Burleson, Edward ("Bell"), Jr., Major, First Texas Cavalry. Delegate, constitutional convention of 1875; commissioner to locate penitentiary in East Texas. Married; father of ten children. Died, home of sister in Austin, May 12, 1877. Buried family cemetery near Kyle.

Burnett, John H., Commander, Thirteenth Texas Cavalry. Forced to resign commission in November 1863 due to ill health. Returned to Crockett. Moved to Galveston in 1866, became partner in commission business, financed hotel and railroad building. Became president Galveston National Bank. Moved to Houston in 1899; president of Planters and Merchants Bank. Died, Houston, June 24, 1901; buried Greenwood Cemetery. Estate valued at over one million dollars.

Camp, John L., Commander, Fourteenth Texas Cavalry. Elected to U.S. House of Representatives, 1866, but not allowed to take seat. Delegate, constitutional convention, 1866; Texas Senate, 1874; district judge, 1878. Appointed register of land officer in Arizona, 1884. Returned to Texas, died San Antonio, July 16, 1891. Camp County named for him.

Carter, George W., Commander, Twenty-first Texas Cavalry. Member Louisiana legislature, Speaker of the House. U.S. ambassador, Venezuela, 1881. Died Confederate Soldiers Home, Pikesville, Maryland, May 11, 190l. Buried Louden Park, Baltimore.

Cayne, Henry Petty, Lieutenant Colonel, Thirteenth Texas Infantry. Returned to Wharton County, practiced law. Set out for Coryell County, but died from cold and exposure, November 26, 1875. Buried Davilla, Milam County.

Chilton, George W., Major, Third Texas Cavalry. Elected to U.S. House of Representatives, 1866, but not seated. Presidential elector, 1876. Died 1883; buried Oakwood Cemetery, Tyler. Son, Horace, became U.S. senator.

Clark, Edward, Governor and Commander, Fourteenth Texas Infantry. Went to Mexico with a group of Confederate generals and political leaders, returned home soon after. Resumed law practice, Marshall. Died May 4, 1880; buried Marshall.

Coke, Richard, Captain, Company K, Fifteenth Texas Infantry. Elected governor, 1873, U.S. senator, 1877-1895. Died, Waco, May 14, 1897, after becoming ill from exposure while caring for flooded Brazos Valley farm. Buried Oakwood Cemetery, Waco.

Cook, Gustave, last Commander, Terry's Rangers. Moved to Houston; practiced law. Elected to Texas legislature, 1872; district judge, Houston-Galveston area, 1874-1888. Anti-prohibitionist. Opposed James S. Hogg for Democratic gubernatorial nomination, 1890. Moved to San Marcos; died there in 1897.

Cooper, Douglas H., Commander, Indian Division, Indian Territory. Continued to live in Indian Territory after the war. Assisted Choctaws and Chickasaws in suing U.S. government for failed promises. Died Old Fort Washita, Indian Territory, April 19, 1879. Buried there in unmarked grave.

Crump, Phillip, Lieutenant Colonel, First Texas Partisan Rangers. Arrested for execution of Martin Hart, escaped from prison, no further attempt to arrest. Returned to business in Jefferson. Later involved with "Knights of the Rising Sun," arrested for death of former Union officer. Tried by military court but found not guilty. Became ill while in prison; died in October 1869. Buried in Jefferson.

Culberson, David B., Colonel, Eighteenth Texas Infantry. After Vicksburg campaign returned home. Elected to Texas legislature, 1864; to Texas Senate, 1873. Served twelve terms, U.S. House of Representatives, 1875-1897. Died in Jefferson, May 7, 1900; buried in Oakwood Cemetery. Son, Charles, governor (1895-1899) and U.S. senator (1890-1923).

Davis, Nicholas A., Chaplain, Historian, Fourth Texas Infantry. Married wealthy widow, 1865. Continued to preach in East Texas. Diverse business activities; established first commercial orchard in Jacksonville. Board of Trustees, Trinity University. Died San Antonio, November 19, 1894.

Debray, Xavier B., Commander, Twenty-sixth Texas Cavalry. Remained in Houston for two years. In 1867 moved to Galveston, became accountant for Produce Exchange. Member, Galveston City Council. In 1877 moved to Austin, resumed job as Spanish translator for General Land Office. Died, January 6, 1895; buried Texas State Cemetery.

DeMorse, Charles, Commander, Twenty-ninth Texas Cavalry. Returned to edit *Clarksville Standard.* Active in Democratic party and the Grange. Director of Texas A&M College; delegate to constitutional convention of 1875. In 1873 Texas Press and Electoral Commission named him "Father of Texas Journalism." Died October 15, 1887.

Diamond, James J., Colonel, Eleventh Texas Cavalry. Returned to North Texas when not chosen colonel in 1862 election. Involved in Gainesville hangings. Died in 1867 during Houston yellow fever epidemic.

Douglas, James P., Commander, Douglas' Artillery Battery. Returned to Tyler, married wartime sweetheart. Elected to Texas Senate in 1869 representing Smith and Upshur counties. Organized Texas branch,

Cotton Belt Railroad. Planter; developed first peach orchards in East Texas. Owned canning plants. After death of first wife remarried. Ten children. Died November 27, 1901; buried Tyler Oakwood Cemetery.

Dowling, Richard, Commanded Confederate defenders at Sabine Pass. After war returned to Houston; opened coffee amusement house. Various business investments including gas company, warehouse, steamboat, streetcars, railroads, and oil leases. Died yellow fever epidemic, Houston, September 23, 1867. Buried St. Vincent's Cemetery, Houston.

Ector, Matthew, Brigade Commander. Returned to Henderson, practiced law. Elected district judge but removed by Brig. Gen. J. J. Reynolds. Moved to Marshall in 1875; elected to Court of Appeals. Presiding judge, 1876, until death, October 29, 1879. Buried Marshall. Ector County named for him.

Elmore, Henry, Commander, Twentieth Texas Infantry. President of Board of Trustees, Waverly Male and Female Institute. Active in Waverly Methodist Church, donated land on which church was built. Died January 17, 1879. Buried in Waverly Cemetery.

Erath, George B., Captain, Fifteenth Texas Infantry, later commander Frontier District. Returned to Waco, elected to Texas Senate, 1873. Wrote memoirs, later published by Texas State Historical Association. Died May 13, 1891. Buried Oakwood Cemetery, Waco. Erath County named for him.

Field, Charles W., succeeded Hood as Division Commander. Served with Khedive of Egypt after the war. Later doorkeeper, U.S. House of Representatives; superintendent, Hot Springs, Arkansas, Indian Reservation. Died April 9, 1892, in Washington, D.C. Buried Loudon Park Cemetery, Baltimore, Maryland.

Fitzhugh, William F., Commander, Sixteenth Texas Cavalry. Returned to farming at Melissa. Doorkeeper, 1875 constitutional convention and Fifteenth through Eighteenth legislatures. Killed October 23, 1883, when thrown from a wagon. First buried in McKinney but later reinterred in Fairview Cemetery, Denison. Survived by seven children.

Fletcher, William A., Private, Fifth Texas Infantry. After being wounded, joined Terry's Rangers; captured by enemy but escaped. After war returned to Beaumont. Became highly successful in lumber industry. Recounted experiences in *Rebel Private Front and Rear,* published in limited edition, 1908; republished three times. Died January 5, 1915, buried in Beaumont.

Flournoy, George M., Commander, Sixteenth Texas Infantry. Fled to Mexico, served briefly with Maximilian. Returned to Texas, practiced law in Galveston. Delegate, constitutional convention of 1875. Moved to San Francisco, 1876. Died in San Francisco, September 18, 1889.

Fly, George W. L., Major, Second Texas Infantry. Returned to family in Gonzales County. Practiced law; president, Gonzales College. Moved to Victoria. Elected to state legislature in 1880. Active in veterans' affairs and Methodist church. Died at his law office in Victoria, January 17, 1905. Buried in Masonic Cemetery, Victoria. His grandson, Dr. W. Lamar Fly, was later president of Hill Junior College in Hillsboro, Texas.

Foard, Robert L., Major, Thirteenth Texas Texas Infantry. Practiced law and raised stock at Columbus. Died at Columbus, November 8, 1898. Foard County named in his honor.

Ford, John S. ("Rip"), Commander, Second Texas Cavalry and Cavalry of the West. Crossed Rio Grande but returned soon to help Confederates receive paroles. Helped old friend Jose Carbajal drive French troops from Matamoros. Wrote and edited for several Brownsville newspapers. Delegate Democratic National Convention in Baltimore, 1872. Assisted Richard Coke in becoming governor. Mayor of Brownsville, 1874; Texas State Senate, 1876-79; superintendent, Texas Deaf and Dumb School. Wrote reminiscences. Charter member, Texas State Historical Association. Died, San Antonio, November 3, 1897. Buried in San Antonio.

Forney, John, succeeded John G. Walker as Commander of Texas Division. Returned to Alabama, became planter in Marengo and Calhoun counties. Worked as civil engineer for a time. Died September 13, 1902, in Jacksonville, Alabama. Buried there.

Fowler, Andrew Jackson, Lieutenant Colonel, Twentieth Texas Cavalry. Returned home to Lamar County, became tax collector. Appointed district judge by Edmund J. Davis, replaced in 1876. Died Lindale, Smith County, March 31, 1865.

Frost, Thomas C., Lieutenant Colonel, First Texas Cavalry. Refused to take oath of allegiance and therefore could not practice law. Established freight and mercantile business. Became banker, established Frost National Bank of San Antonio. Died in San Antonio, November 21, 1903.

Gano, Richard Montgomery, Brigade Commander, Indian Territory. Moved back to Kentucky for one year. Returned to Texas, became minister in Christian Church, served forty-five years. Active in United Confederate Veterans and prohibition movement. Died from uremic poisoning, March 27, 1910. Buried Oakland Cemetery, Dallas.

Giddings, DeWitt C., Lieutenant Colonel, Twenty-first Texas Cavalry. Returned to Brenham. Member, constitutional convention of 1866. Served in U.S. House of Representatives, 1871-1875, 1877-1879. Engaged in banking, insurance, and railroad development. Died Brenham, August 19, 1903. Buried Prairie Lea Cemetery.

Giddings, George H., Lieutenant Colonel, Giddings Cavalry Battalion (older brother of Dewitt C. Giddings). Lived in Brownsville after the war. Engaged in mining and colonization projects in Mexico. Returned to San Antonio, practiced law and engaged in real estate business. Married twice, eight children. Died at home of daughter in Mexico City, December 12, 1902. Buried in public cemetery in Mexico City.

Giles, L. B., Private, Company D, Terry's Rangers. Returned to farm in Travis County. Inspector of immigrants at Laredo. Memoirs published in Austin, 1911. In 1912 purchased 200 acres of land near Cotulla in LaSalle County, where he farmed until his death June 12, 1922.

Giles, Valerius, Sergeant, Company B, Fourth Texas Infantry. Captured after Battle of Chickamauga; sent to Camp Morton, Indiana. Returned to Texas after the war, lived in Austin, wrote series of articles, planned to complete his writings as a memoir but work was incomplete when he died on January 31, 1915. Mary Lasswell compiled and edited his writings, entitled *Rags and Hopes: The Recollections of Val C. Giles* (1961).

Gonzales, Thomas, Commander, Thirteenth Texas Field Artillery. Forced to resign from service in September 1863 due to ill health. Returned to Galveston, opened cotton firm, became major cotton shipper, extensive real estate holdings, vice president Galveston Cotton Exchange. Died December 2, 1896, while visiting daughter in Boston. Buried Galveston Episcopal Cemetery.

Good, John J., Commander, Good's Field Artillery Battery. Elected judge, 1866; removed as impediment to Reconstruction in 1868. Resumed law practice. Mayor, City of Dallas, 1880. Died in El Paso, September 17, 1882, on trip to California to improve health. Buried Masonic section, Odd Fellows Cemetery, Dallas.

Gould, Robert S., Commander, Gould's Battalion, Randal's Brigade. Wounded Jenkins' Ferry, returned to Centerville. Elected judge, removed as impediment to Reconstruction. Moved to Galveston, 1870. Served on Texas Supreme Court; later law professor, University of Texas. Died Austin, June 30, 1904.

Greer, Elkanah B., Commander, Third Texas Cavalry. Returned home to Marshall. Died while visiting sister at DeVall's Bluff, Arkansas, March 27, 1877. Buried next to parents, Elmwood Cemetery, Memphis, Tennessee.

Griffith, John S., Lieutenant Colonel, Sixth Texas Cavalry. Moved to Terrell, engaged in livestock and mercantile business. Sold bois d'arc seeds to northern buyers to use as windbreaks. Member, Fifteenth Texas Legislature; helped get psychiatric hospital in Terrell. Died in Terrell, August 6, 1901.

Guess, George, Lieutenant Colonel, Thirty-first Texas Cavalry. Returned to law practice in Austin. Elected mayor to fill unexpired term. Died from sunstroke July 10, 1868, on steamer returning from Memphis, Tennessee.

Gurley, Edward J., Commander, Thirtieth Texas Cavalry. Resumed law practice, Waco. Delegate, 1866 constitutional convention; elected to legislature 1867. Owned several plantations along the Brazos. Died July 4, 1914.

Hardeman, Peter, Commander, First Texas Cavalry, Arizona Brigade. Went to Brazil, built sawmill. Died Cillo, Sao Paulo, 1882. In 1977 descendants still lived in Brazil.

Hardeman, William P. ("Gotch"), Commander, Fourth Texas Cavalry Regiment and old Sibley Brigade. Went to Mexico with several others. Returned to Texas in 1866. Farmer; assistant sergeant-at-arms, Texas House of Representatives; superintendent of public buildings and grounds in Austin. Died in Austin, April 8, 1898. Buried in Texas State Cemetery.

Hawpe, Trezevant, Commander, Thirty-first Texas Cavalry. Returned home during war. Hauled supplies to Confederate forces in Arkansas and Indian Territory. Killed Dallas, August 14, 1863, as result of quarrel. Buried Masonic Cemetery in Dallas.

Harrison, James, Commander, Fifteenth Texas Infantry. Returned to Waco. Businessman and Baptist layman; trustee, Baylor University. Paralyzed, 1873. Died, February 23, 1875. Buried First Street Cemetery, Waco. The community of Harrison in McLennan County named for him.

Harrison, Thomas, Commander, Terry's Rangers (younger brother of James Harrison). Resumed law practice in Waco. District judge, 1866-1877, Democratic presidential elector, 1872. Died Waco, July 14, 1891. Buried beside brother, First Street Cemetery, Waco.

Heartsill, William W., Sergeant, Second Texas Cavalry. Returned to Marshall, opened mercantile business. Helped organize a Ku Klux Klan chapter in Marshall. Using small Octavo Novelty Press printed his Civil War journal *Fourteen Hundred and 91 Days in the Confederate Army* page by page. Active in veterans' groups; served as mayor of Marshall. Died July 28, 1916; buried in Marshall.

Hebert, Paul Octave, Commander, District of Texas. Returned to plantation in Louisiana. State and federal engineer, Louisiana. Paralysis, 1879. Died from cancer, August 29, 1880, in New Orleans. Buried Catholic Cemetery, Bayou Gaule.

Hendricks, Sterling B., Lieutenant Colonel, Seventeenth Texas Cavalry. Merchant and farmer, Harrison County. Account of his experiences in the Somervell expedition published in *Southwestern Historical Quarterly* (October 1919) after his death. Died December 11, 1909.

Hobby, Alfred M., Commander, Eighth Texas Infantry. Settled in Galveston. Wrote poetry and nonfiction, including *Life of David G. Burnet* (1871). Last years in Silver City, New Mexico. Died there February 5, 1881.

Hobby, Edwin E., Captain, Company E, Eighth Texas Infantry (younger brother of Alfred M. Hobby). Settled in southeast Texas, admitted to the bar. Served three terms in Texas Senate. District judge, 1879-1888. Lived in Woodville, Moscow, and Livingston. Worked with John Henry Kirby. Died in Houston on November 1, 1899. Buried Glenwood Cemetery, Houston. Son, William, later governor of Texas.

Hood, John Bell, Army Commander. Moved to New Orleans, engaged in merchandising, real estate, insurance. Married 1868; eleven children. Hood, wife, and oldest daughter died in yellow fever epidemic, August 1879. Buried New Orleans Cemetery. Memoir *Advance and Retreat* published in 1880 for Hood Orphan Memorial Fund by former departmental chief P. G. T. Beauregard.

Houston, Sam, Jr., Private, Second Texas Infantry. Studied at Baylor University, Independence; later at medical school, University of Pennsylvania. Practiced medicine briefly, then abandoned medicine for writing. After death of wife in 1886 went to live with sister Margaret at Independence. Died there May 20, 1894. Buried near mother at Independence Cemetery.

Hubbard, Richard B., Commander, Twenty-second Texas Infantry. Resumed law practice. Elected lieutenant governor 1873; became governor when Richard Coke resigned, 1876; served until January 21, 1879. U.S. minister to Japan. Died July 12, 1901, buried Oakwood Cemetery, Tyler.

Ireland, John, Lieutenant Colonel, Eighth Texas Infantry. Delegate, 1866 constitutional convention, district judge, state legislator. Elected governor 1882 and 1884. Resumed law practice, Seguin. Died March 15, 1896.

Johnson, Middleton, Commander, Fourteenth Texas Infantry. Delegate, 1866 constitutional convention. Died on May 15, 1866, from stroke. Buried Texas State Cemetery, then reinterred near his sons in family cemetery, Arlington. Johnson County named for him.

Jones, Dudley, Commander, Ninth Texas Cavalry. Returned home to Titus County. Studied law, moved to Houston to practice law. Edited *Vidette,* a Houston daily. Delegate, 1875 constitutional convention. Died soon after, at age thirty-five.

Jones, George W., Commander, Seventeenth Texas Infantry. Resumed law practice in Bastrop. Delegate, constitutional convention of 1866. Elected lieutenant governor; removed as impediment to Reconstruction. Elected to Congress as independent in 1878; reelected as

Greenbacker in 1880. Ran unsuccessfully for governor in 1882 and 1884. Died in Bastrop, July 11, 1893; buried there.

Keith, Kosciuszko D., Commander, Keith Artillery Battery. Purchased steamboat; lost boat in hurricane. Moved to Galveston and then Luling. Prosperous lumber and hardware dealer. Died 1911; buried in Luling City Cemetery.

Key, John C. G., Commander, Fourth Texas Infantry. Retired from army due to poor health, April 1864. Died in Gonzales, 1866; buried there.

King, Wilburn H., Commander, Polignac's Brigade. Established sugar plantation in Central America. After death of wife and infant child returned to Texas, 1868. Lived briefly in Jefferson, then moved to Sulphur Springs. Mayor, state representative two terms, adjutant general of state, 1881-1891. Died Sulphur Springs, October 12, 1910. Buried Oakwood Cemetery, Corsicana.

Lane, Walter Paye, Commander, First Texas Partisan Rangers. Reestablished mercantile business, Marshall. Became deputy federal marshal and treasurer/tax collector for Harrison County. Never married. Memoirs *Adventures and Recollections of Walter P. Lane* published in 1887. Died at Marshall, January 18, 1892. Buried in the old Marshall Cemetery.

Likens, James B., Commander, Likens' Thirty-fifth Texas Cavalry. After the war practiced law at Beaumont and Sabine Pass in Jefferson County. His law partner during this period was George W. O'Brien, a former captain in Spaight's Battalion. Likens moved to Houston in early 1870s. Died in Houston on September 18, 1878, and buried in Glenwood Cemetery.

Littlefield, George W., Major, Terry's Rangers. Successful cattleman and banker. Board of Regents, University of Texas. Established Littlefield Fund for Southern History. Died at home in Austin, November 10, 1920. Buried in Oakwood Cemetery, Austin.

Luckett, Philip N., Commander, Third Texas Infantry. Went to Mexico with Maj. Gen. John G. Walker and others. Returned to Texas, November 1865. Imprisoned by Federal officials, Fort Jackson, Louisiana. Health impaired, stayed in New Orleans. Later joined relatives in Cincinnati. Died there, May 21, 1869. Buried Spring Grove Cemetery.

McCord, James E., Commander, Frontier Regiment. Returned to Rusk County, moved to Caldwell County, and finally to Coleman. Engaged in real estate and banking. Died at Coleman, December 23, 1914.

McCulloch, Henry E., Division and Brigade Commander. Returned to Seguin, where he resumed business and farming interests. Active in Democratic politics. Superintendent of Texas Deaf and Dumb Asylum. Died Seguin, March 12, 1895; buried in San Geronimo Cemetery.

Mabry, Hinche, Commander, Third Texas Cavalry. Resumed legal practice, Jefferson. Delegate, 1866 constitutional convention. Judge of district court, removed as impediment to Reconstruction. Moved to Fort Worth, 1879. Died at Sherman, March 21, 1884. Buried Oakwood Cemetery, Jefferson.

Magruder, John B., Commander, District of Texas. Went to Mexico after the war. After collapse of Maximilian regime returned to Houston. Lived last years in humble circumstances. Died in Houston, February 18, 1871. Buried in Houston, but later reinterred in Episcopal Cemetery at Galveston, city of his greatest military triumph.

Major, James P., Commander, Major's Regiment and Brigade. Returned to family in Austin. When wife died in 1868, he moved to southeast Louisiana. Became planter and remarried. Died while visiting in Austin on May 7, 1877. Buried Ascension Catholic Cemetery at Donaldsonville, near Fort Butler.

Malone, Frederick J., Commander, Thirty-first Texas Cavalry. Raised cattle at Rockport, then moved to Bee County. Member of commissioners court. Died 1891.

Marmaduke, John S., Commander, Cavalry Brigade. Merchant, newspaper editor. Elected governor of Missouri, but died on December 28, 1877, before completing his term. Lifelong bachelor.

Martin, William H. ("Howdy"), Major, Hood's Brigade. After leading Hood's troops home returned to law practice, Henderson County. Served two terms, U.S. House of Representatives, 1887-1891. President, Hood's Texas Brigade Association, 1883-1885. Died Hill County, February 5, 1898. Buried Hillsboro City Cemetery.

Maxey, Samuel Bell, Commander, Ninth Texas Infantry and Department of Indian Territory. Resumed law practice in Paris, Texas. U.S. senator, 1875-1887. Died Eureka Springs, Arkansas, August 16, 1895. Buried Evergreen Cemetery, Paris. His home in Paris, built in 1868, has been restored and furnished as a state historic site.

Mechling, William T., Battery Commander and Staff Officer. Severely wounded at Monett's Ferry. Returned to Bexar County and resumed farming. Died October 10, 1898.

Medford, Henry C., Private, Lane's Cavalry. Went to Tupelo, Mississippi, following the war. Admitted to bar and practiced law. Mayor of Tupelo and two terms in Mississippi legislature. Died Tupelo, October 17, 1902.

Miller, Crill, Lieutenant Colonel, Second Texas Cavalry, Arizona Brigade. Obtained land in Indian Territory, claiming Indian heritage. Moved family there and established ranch. Later returned to Dallas to raise cattle and establish horse breeding farm. Died, June 4, 1892. Buried family cemetery, Dallas.

Mills, Roger Q., Commander, Tenth Texas Infantry. Resumed law practice. Elected to U.S. Congress; became chairman of House Ways and Means Committee. U.S. Senate, 1893-1899. Died Corsicana, September 2, 1911. Buried Oakwood Cemetery, Austin.

Moody, William L., Commander, Seventh Texas Infantry. Returned to Fairfield. Moved to Galveston, 1866, created cotton factorage firm. Participated in founding Galveston Cotton Exchange. Extensive banking, railroad, cotton compress interests. Active in Democratic party affairs; advisor for governors and William Jennings Bryan. Died July 17, 1920. Buried in family cemetery, Chesterfield County, Virginia.

Moore, John Creed, Commander, Second Texas Infantry. Returned to Texas following the war. Spent most of his career as a teacher and school administrator. Died December 31, 1910, at Osage, Texas. Buried in city cemetery there.

Morgan, Charles, Commander, Morgan's Cavalry Battalion. Married Mary A. Duvall; six daughters and one son. Merchandising business. Active in Parsons' Brigade Association. Died, March 11, 1924, Runnels County.

Nance, David, Private, Twelfth Texas Cavalry. Purchased farm in Fannin County. Farmer, teacher, carpenter, and real estate. Moved to Dallas County; operated gristmill at Duncanville. Crippled by rheumatoid arthritis. Died summer 1925, aged eighty-two. Buried Rawlings' Cemetery near Lancaster. B. P. Gallaway described his experiences in *The Rugged Rebel: A Common Soldier in W. H. Parsons' Texas Cavalry, 1861-1865* (Austin: University of Texas Press, 1988).

Neal, Benjamin, Commander, Neal's Artillery Battery. District judge, removed by Federal authorities 1867. Promoter of deep port and rail for Corpus Christi. Died Corpus Christi, July 18, 1873. Monument of him in Corpus Christi.

Nichols, Ebenezer B., Commander, Nichols' Ninth Texas Infantry. Organized Bank of Galveston, later merged to form National Bank of Texas with himself as president. In 1870 was still one of the richest men in Texas with $100,000 in property. Grand Master of Masonic Order of Texas. Died at home, November 30, 1873.

Norris, James M., Commander, Frontier Regiment. After removal as commander of regiment practiced law in Burleson, Coryell, and McLennan counties. Died, stroke at home, McLennan County, April 21, 1874.

O'Brien, George W., Captain, Spaight's Battalion. After the war active in Democratic party affairs in Beaumont. Practiced law; district attorney for Jefferson County, 1874-1875. Published *Neches Valley News* and later Beaumont *New Beacon.* Vice president, Gladys City Oil Company. Died in Beaumont on June 30, 1909, buried in Magnolia Cemetery, Beaumont.

Ochiltree, William Beck, Commander, Eighteenth Texas Infantry. Ill health, forced to resign command, 1863. Lived in Jefferson until death, December 17, 1867. Ochiltree County is named for him.

Parsons, William H., Commander, Parsons' Cavalry Brigade and Twelfth Texas Cavalry. Went to British Honduras, soon returned to Texas. State Senate, 1869-1871. Appointed U.S. Centennial Commission by President Grant. Brother Albert executed for involvement in Haymarket riot. Died October 2, 1907, in Chicago. Buried Mount Hope Cemetery, Hastings, New York.

Polignac, Prince de, Brigade Commander. Left command in March 1865 to make pleas to Napoleon III to aid CSA. In Spain when war ended. Returned to France. Major general in Franco-Prussian War, awarded Legion of Honor. Studied math and political economy. Died November 15, 1913, from cerebral edema while working on a math problem. Last Confederate major general to die. Buried Frankfurt on Main, Germany.

Powell, Robert M., Last Commander, Hood's Texas Brigade. Returned to Texas, practiced law. Moved to St. Louis, 1882. Died, pneumonia, St. Louis, January 15, 1916, aged ninety years.

Pratt, Joseph, Commander of Pratt's Artillery Battalion. Wounded while commanding artillery in Sterling Price's Missouri raid. Died from effects of the wound and buried in Oakwood Cemetery, Jefferson, Texas.

Price, Frank, Private, First Texas Partisan Rangers. Returned to San Augustine. Drove herd to New Orleans; contracted yellow fever and died. Body returned to San Augustine.

Price, Sterling, Army Commander. Went to Mexico with group of fellow Confederates. Leader in Carlota colony. Returned to Missouri in early 1867. Established commisssion business in St. Louis. Died from cholera there on September 19, 1867.

Pyron, Charles L., Commander, Second Texas Cavalry. Returned to San Antonio, amassed small fortune in ranching. Died at ranch in 1868.

Rainey, Alexis T., Commander, First Texas Infantry. Wounded at Gaines' Mill, returned to Texas. Practiced law and farmed at Palestine. Served in Texas legislature; presidential elector for Greeley in 1872. Died May 1891, at Elkart, Anderson County.

Reeves, George R., Commander, Eleventh Texas Cavalry. Elected to legislature 1870, 1875, 1879, 1881-1882; Speaker last term. Died from hydrophobia, September 5, 1882, after bitten by mad dog. Buried Georgetown Cemetery.

Ridley, Alonzo, Major, Third Texas Cavalry, Arizona Brigade. Joined Maximilian's army. Employed by British railroad company to supervise construction between Vera Cruz and Mexico City. Moved to Arizona Territory, engaged in mining. Served with army as interpreter in Geronimo campaign and war with Spain. Died peacefully, aged ninety-one years, March 25, 1909.

Roberts, Oran M., Commander, Eleventh Texas Infantry. Delegate, 1866 constitutional convention. Unrecognized as U.S. senator. Chief justice, Texas Supreme Court. Elected governor, 1878 and 1880. University of Texas law professor. Author of Texas volume in *Confederate Military History*. First president, Texas State Historical Association. Died, Austin, May 19, 1898; buried Texas State Cemetery.

Robertson, Jerome B. ("Aunt Polly"), Commander of Hood's Texas Brigade. Returned to Independence, resumed medical practice. In 1874 appointed superintendent state bureau of immigration. Active in railroad promotion. Organizer and several times president, Hood's Texas Brigade Association. Died on January 7, 1890; buried Oakwood Cemetery, Waco.

Rose, Victor M., Sergeant, Company A, Third Texas Cavalry. Returned to Victoria County. Married; wife died in yellow fever epidemic which nearly killed Rose. Admitted to bar but devoted energy to *Victoria Advocate*, of which he was co-editor and publisher, 1869-1873. Moved to Laredo, edited *Laredo Times*, wrote poetry and historical works including *Ross' Texas Brigade* (1881) and *Life and Services of Gen. Ben McCulloch* (1888). Died from pneumonia, February 5, 1893.

Ross, Lawrence Sullivan ("Sul"), Brigade and Regimental Commander. Returned to home in Waco. Sheriff, McLennan County, 1873; delegate 1875 constitutional convention; state senate, 1880. Elected governor, 1886 and 1888. President of Texas A&M College until death January 3, 1898. Buried in Waco. Sul Ross State College (now University) named for him.

Sayers, Joseph, Commander, Valverde Battery. Returned to Bastrop; taught and practiced law. State senate, 1873-1879; lieutenant governor, 1879-1881; U.S. Congress, 1885-1889; governor, 1899-1903. After governorship practiced law, Austin and San Antonio. Served on various state boards. Died May 15, 1929. Buried Fairview Cemetery, Bastrop.

Slaughter, James E., Commander, Brigade and Western Subdistrict of Texas. Went to Mexico, operated sawmill in Carlota colony. Returned to United States, 1867, engaged in civil engineering. Died Mexico City while visiting, January 1, 1901. Buried in Mexico. Only one of two American-born Confederate generals buried on foreign soil (Mosby M. Parsons the other).

Smith, Ashbel, Commander, Second Texas Infantry. Returned to plantation Evergreen on Galveston Bay. Texas legislature, 1866, 1879. Delegate to Democratic National Convention, 1868, 1872, 1876. Continued interest in medicine, agriculture, and science. Numerous honors; first president University of Texas Board of Regents. Died on January 21, 1886 at Evergreen; buried in Texas State Cemetery.

Steele, William, Commander, Seventh Texas Cavalry, Indian Territory, and Brigade. Returned to San Antonio. Moved to Austin in 1874, became state adjutant general. Reorganized Texas Rangers. Died from stroke, San Antonio, January 12, 1885. Buried Oakwood Cemetery, Austin.

Stone, W. Barton, Commander, Sixth Texas Cavalry and Second Partisan Rangers. Moved to Missouri, farmed and practiced law. Returned to Dallas, 1879. Died from heart attack, February 26, 1881.

Sweet, James, Lieutenant Colonel, Thirty-third Texas Cavalry. Went to Mexico with Jo Shelby, returned after several years. Purchased interest in *San Antonio Herald*, 1873. His son, Alexander, who was also in Thirty-third Cavalry, later gained fame as a journalist. Died, San Antonio, December 12, 1880. Buried in city cemetery.

Spaight, Ashley W., Commander, Twenty-first Texas Infantry. Delegate, 1866 constitutional convention. Moved to Galveston, 1869. State commissioner of insurance, statistics and history, 1881-1883. Died, Galveston, December 23, 1916. Buried Lakeview Cemetery, Galveston.

Speight, Joseph W., Commander, Fifteenth Texas Infantry. After resigning from command in 1864 due to poor health returned to Waco. Withdrew from legal practice, engaged in agricultural pursuits. One of organizers of move to construct suspension bridge across Brazos. Died April 26, 1888. Buried Oakwood Cemetery, Waco.

Stevens, James G., Commander, Twenty-second Texas Cavalry. Returned to Hunt County; moved to Dallas, 1867. Superintendent, Dallas schools, in 1880s. Vice president, Confederate Veterans of Polignac's Brigade. Died, Dallas, May 24, 1889.

Taylor, Robert H., Commander, Twenty-second Texas Cavalry. Supported Republican party. Appointed district judge by E. J. Davis. Unsuccesful Republican candidate for lieutenant governor, 1873. Represented Fannin County in Sixteenth Legislature. Married three times. Died Bonham, May 10, 1899. Buried Willow Wild Cemetery, Bonham.

Teel, Trevanion T., Commander, Artillery Battery and Battalion, Sibley's Brigade. Resumed law practice, gained prominence in criminal defense, claimed to have defended more than 700 clients charged with capital offensive and saved them all from execution. Died, heart attack, El Paso, July 6, 1899. Buried Odd Fellows Cemetery, San Antonio.

Terrell, Alexander W., Commander, Terrell's Texas Cavalry. Joined group who went to Mexico, served in Maximilian's army, returned to Texas when French withdrew. Practiced law, served in Texas House and Senate, authored Terrell election laws. Ambassador to Turkey; University of Texas

Board of Regents; president, Texas State Historical Association. Died September 9, 1912, in Mineral Wells. Buried Texas State Cemetery.

Terry, David S., Commander, Terry's Cavalry Regiment. Went to Mexico. Moved to California, 1868, practiced law. Member California constitutional convention of 1878-1879. Had altercation with U.S. Supreme Court Justice Stephen J. Field; shot to death by judge's bodyguard.

Throckmorton, James W., Major, Second Texas Cavalry, Partisan Rangers and Brigadier General, State Troops. Elected governor, 1866, removed as impediment to Reconstruction. Continued to be active in Democratic politics and in railroad promotion. Attorney for Texas and Pacific Railroad. U.S. Congress, 1875-1879, 1883-1887. Died at home in McKinney, April 12, 1894. Buried Pecan Grove Cemetery.

Upton, William F., Lieutenant Colonel, Bradford's Regiment. Moved to Schulenberg, elected alderman. Represented Fayette County in Texas legislature, 1866, 1879-1885. Died in Schulenberg, 1887. Upton County named for him.

Walker, John George, Commander, Walker's Texas Division. Went to Mexico, wrote manuscript "War of Secession West of the Mississippi River, During the Years, 1863-4-65," never published. Returned to U.S. in late 1860s; made home in Virginia. Appointed U.S. consul-general at Bogota, Colombia, by President Grover Cleveland. Special commission to invite South American Republics to Pan American Conference. Died, Washington, D.C., July 20, 1893. Buried Winchester, Virginia.

Waller, Edwin, Jr., Major, Second Texas Cavalry, Lieutenant Colonel, Waller's Thirteenth Cavalry Battalion. Returned to home in Austin County and resumed role as farmer and businessman. Justice of peace, postmaster. Died at Richmond, July 6, 1878, and buried there.

Walton, William M. ("Buck"), Major, Twenty-first Texas Cavalry. Elected Texas attorney general in 1866; removed as impediment to Reconstruction. Resumed law practice. Chair, State Democratic party executive committee, 1868-1872. Died, Austin, July 1, 1915; buried Oakwood Cemetery. His memoirs, *An Epitome of My Life*, published by Friends of Austin Public Library, 1965.

Waterhouse, Richard M., Commander, Nineteenth Texas Infantry and Third Brigade, Walker's Texas Division. Returned to East Texas, speculated in land in San Augustine and Jefferson. While in Waco dealing with land matters fell down stairs, dislocating shoulder; contracted pneumonia, died two days later, March 20, 1876. Buried Oakwood Cemetery, Jefferson.

Waul, Thomas N., Commander, Waul's Legion. Returned to plantation, Gonzales County. Delegate, 1886 constitutional convention. Moved to Galveston, practiced law. Died on farm near Greenville, Hunt County, on July 18, 1908. Interred Oakwood Cemetery, Fort Worth.

Whitfield, John W., Commander, Whitfield's Legion. Delegate from Lavaca County to 1866 and 1875 constitutional conventions. Farmer; $18,000 in property, 1870. Died October 27, 1879, near Hallettsville; buried in Hallettsville Cemetery.

Wigfall, Louis T., Commander, Texas Brigade and Confederate Senator. Returned to Texas under disguise. In 1866 went to England. Returned to U.S. in 1872. He and wife lived in Baltimore until 1874, when he returned to Texas. Died in Galveston, February 18, 1874; buried in Episcopal Cemetery, Galveston.

Wilkes, Franklin C., Commander, Twenty-fourth Texas Cavalry. Returned to ministry, served in Brenham in 1866 and Austin from 1869 to 1873. General agent for Bayland Orphans' Home for Boys. Chaplain, Texas Senate in 1881. Moved to Lampasas, died there December 8, 1881. Buried in Lampasas.

Woods, Peter C., Commander, Thirty-sixth Texas Cavalry. Returned to San Marcos, resumed medical practice and farming. Delegate, 1866 constitutional convention. Died, San Marcos, January 27, 1898; buried there.

Work, Philip A., Commander, First Texas Infantry. Resumed law practice at Woodville. In October 1865 moved to New Orleans, practiced law and engaged in steamboat business. After 1874 lived in Hardin County. Practiced law; owned steamboat *Tom Parker*, which navigated Neches River. Died March 17, 1911; buried in old Hardin Cemetery near Kountze.

Young, William C., Commander, Eleventh Texas Cavalry. Left Eleventh Texas in April 1862 because of poor health. Returned to Cooke County; killed while tracking down outlaws, October 16, 1862. Son captured and executed murderers.

Young, William H., Commander, Ninth Texas Infantry. Wounded and captured. Imprisoned Johnson's Island. Released July 24, 1865. Moved to San Antonio. Studied law, practiced briefly. Various business ventures. Died San Antonio, November 28, 1901, pulmonary congestion. Interred Confederate Cemetery, San Antonio.

Zuber, William P., Captain, Company H, Twenty-first Texas Cavalry. Disabled by pneumonia, 1864, returned home to Grimes County. Farmed and taught. County commissioner, 1876-1878. Wrote history; charter member, Texas State Historical Association. Honored by legislature in 1909 as last surviving member of the Army of San Jacinto. Died Austin, September 22, 1913. Buried Texas State Cemetery. In 1971 University of Texas Press published his memoirs, *My Eighty Years in Texas.*

Notes

CHAPTER ONE

1. There are various accounts of this incident. See particularly Harold B. Simpson, *Hood's Texas Brigade: Lee's Grenadier Guard* (Waco: Texian Press, 1970), 395-401; Robert K. Krick, "'Lee to the Rear' the Texans Cried," in Gary W. Gallagher, ed., *The Wilderness Campaign* (Chapel Hill: University of North Carolina Press, 1997), 176-180; Gordon S. Rhea, *The Battle of the Wilderness, May 5-6, 1864* (Baton Rouge: Louisiana State Univesity Press, 1994), 299-312; Douglas S. Freeman, *Lee's Lieutenants: A Study in Command,* 3 vols. (New York: Charles Scribner's Sons, 1942-1944), 3: 356-358; Dayton Kelley, *General Lee and Hood's Texas Brigade at the Battle of the Wilderness* (Hillsboro: Hill Junior College Press, 1969), 45-50; R. C., "Gen. Lee at the 'Wilderness'," *Land We Love* 5 (October 1868): 482-485.

2. Simpson, *Hood's Texas Brigade: Lee's Grenadier Guard,* 401.

3. In addition, four cavalry regiments, five cavalry battalions, and five infantry regiments were recruited for state service during the war. Stewart Sifakis, *Compendium of the Confederate Armies: Texas* (New York: Facts on File, 1995); Lester N. Fitzhugh, comp., *Texas Batteries, Battalions, Regiments, Commanders and Field Officers, Confederate States Army, 1861* (Midlothian: Mirror Press, 1950); Marcus J. Wright, *Texas in the War, 1861-1865,* ed. Harold B. Simpson (Waco: Texian Press, 1977), 18-49. The number of cavalry regiments given here varies slightly from Stephen B. Oates, *Confederate Cavalry West of the River* (Austin: University of Texas Press, 1961), 179. Oates includes four state regiments and counts the First Mounted Rifles and First Texas Cavalry as separate regiments. Oates does not include the Seventeenth Consolidated Cavalry, which served in Polignac's Brigade and is discussed in Chapter Six of this book.

CHAPTER TWO

1. Ron Tyler, et al., eds., *The New Handbook of Texas,* 6 vols. (Austin: Texas State Historical Association, 1996), 3: 687. The definitive works on the Texas Brigade are the volumes by Harold B. Simpson, *Hood's Texas Brigade in Poetry and Song* (Waco: Texian Press, 1968), *Hood's Texas Brigade: Lee's Grenadier Guard* (Waco:

Texian Press, 1970), *Hood's Texas Brigade in Reunion and Memory* (Waco: Texian Press, 1974), *Hood's Texas Brigade: A Compendium* (Waco: Texian Press, 1977).

2. The definition of "East Texas" used here is that given in Tyler, ed., *New Handbook of Texas,* 2: 770. It begins in Lamar County, runs southward to Limestone County, and then southeastward to Galveston Bay. Simpson, "East Texas Companies in Hood's Brigade," *East Texas Historical Journal* 3 (March 1965): 5, uses the Trinity River as the dividing line beween East and Central Texas.

3. Simpson, *Hood's Texas Brigade: Lee's Grenadier Guard* (hereinafter cited as *Lee's Grenadier Guard*), 10-13; Wright and Simpson, *Texas in the War, 1861-1865,* 207-214: Harry M. Henderson, *Texas in the Confederacy* (San Antonio: Naylor Co., 1955), 47-48.

4. Quotation, Mary Laswell, comp. and ed., *Rags and Hope: The Recollections of Val C. Giles, Four Years with Hood's Brigade, Fourth Texas Infantry* (New York: Coward-McCann, Inc., 1961), 23; Simpson, *Lee's Grenadier Guard,* 14-21; B. T. Hanks, Reminiscences, MSS, University of Texas Archives, 4-7.

5. Simpson, *Lee's Grenadier Guard,* 25, 43, 48, 72-74; Alvy L. King, *Louis T. Wigfall: Southern Fire-eater* (Baton Rouge: Louisiana State University Press, 1970), 129-134; Robert K. Krick, *Lee's Colonels: A Biographical Register of the Field Officers of the Army of Northern Virginia* (4th ed., Dayton, Ohio: Morningside House, 1992), 255-256, 312-313.

6. Simpson, *Lee's Grenadier Guard,* 41-55. For descriptions of the journey see Giles, *Rags and Hope,* 27-41; Donald E. Everett, ed., *Chaplain Davis and Hood's Texas Brigade* (San Antonio: Principa Press of Trinity University, 1962), 34-43; and William A. Fletcher, *Rebel Private Front and Rear,* ed. Bell I. Wiley (Austin: University of Texas Press, 1954), 7-8.

7. Everett, ed., *Chaplain Davis and Hood's Texas Brigade,* 44. Allen returned to Texas, where he recruited the Seventeenth Texas Infantry and commanded it until November 1863, when he was given charge of Camp Ford, the Confederate prisoner of war camp near Tyler. Tyler, ed., *New Handbook of Texas,* 1:113.

8. Quote, Everett, ed., *Chaplain Davis and Hood's Texas Brigade,* 149. For more on Hood see his own *Advance and Retreat: Personal Experiences in the United States and Confederate States Armies* (New Orleans: G. T. Beauregard, 1880) and biographies by John P. Dyer, *The Gallant Hood* (Indianapolis: Bobbs-Merrill Co., 1950); Richard O'Connor, *Hood: Cavalier General* (New York: Prentice-Hall, 1949); and Richard M. McMurry, *John Bell Hood and the War for Southern Independence* (Lexington: University Press of Kentucky, 1982).

9. Quote, Everett, ed., *Chaplain Davis and Hood's Texas Brigade,* 45. See also Giles, *Rags and Hope,* 43-44.

10. Quote, Giles, *Rags and Hope,* 45; Mrs. A. V. Winkler, *The Confederate Capital and Hood's Texas Brigade* (Austin: Von Boeckmann, 1894), 34-35.

11. The first name of Shaller is not given in Simpson, *Lee's Grenadier Guard* nor in Everett, ed., *Chaplain Davis and Hood's Texas Brigade.* Chaplain Davis, ibid., 46, and Judy and Nath Winfield, eds., *War Letters of Tacitus T. Clay, C.S.A.* (Chappell Hill, TX: priv. printing, 1968), 2, note there was some initial resentment toward Archer. For more on Archer see Jeffry Wert, "James Jay Archer," in William C. Davis, ed., The *Confederate General,* 6 vols. (National Historical Society, 1991), 1: 37-38.

12. Anne Bailey, "Jerome Bonaparte Robertson," in *The Confederate General,* 5: 102-103; Krick, *Lee's Colonels,* 312; Giles, *Rags and Hope,* 47-48.

13. *The War of the Rebellion: A Compilation of the Official Records of the Union and Confederate Armies,* 128 vols. (Washington: Government Printing Office, 1880-1901), Series I, 5: 913-914 [hereinafter cited as *Official Records;* unless indicated all citation are to Series I]; Simpson, *Lee's Grenadier Guard,* 65-70; Paul N. Spellman, *Forgotten Texas Leader: Hugh McLeod and the Santa Fe Expedition* (College Station: Texas A&M University Press, 1999), 179-180.

14. J. B. Polley, *Hood's Texas Brigade: Its Marches, Its Battles, Its Achievements* (New York: Neale Publishing Co., 1910), 15-19; Simpson, *Lee's Grenadier Guard,* 70-74.

15. Simpson, *Hood's Texas Brigade: A Compendium,* viii-ix; Simpson, *Lee's Grenadier Guard,* 75-84. For some of the military activity during this time see Judith N. McArthur, ed., " 'Those Texians are Number One Men': A New Confederate Account of the Affair at Lee's House, Virginia," *Southwestern Historical Quarterly* 95 (April 1992): 488-496.

16. Richard McMurry, *John Bell Hood,* 35, observes that the promotion of Hood over two senior colonels, Archer and William T. Wofford, was probably due to Hood's West Point background. He notes also that Hood's promotion allowed Davis to elevate his old friend, John Marshall, to command the Fourth Texas.

17. *Official Records,* 11, Pt. 1: 614-633; McMurry, *John Bell Hood,* 39-39; Hood, *Advance and Retreat,* 20-22; Stephen W. Sears, *To the Gates of Richmond: The Peninsula Campaign* (New York: Ticknor & Fields, 1992), 85-86; Polley, *Hood's Texas Brigade,* 23-28.

18. Hood, *Advance and Retreat,* 24-26; Everett, ed., *Chaplain Davis and Hood's Texas Brigade,* 22-28.

19. Quote, McMurry, *John Bell Hood,* 49. For a description of the attack by participants see Robert W. Glover, ed., *"Tyler to Sharpsburg": The War Letters of Robert H. and William H. Gaston, Company H, First Texas Infantry Regiment, Hood's Texas Brigade* (Waco: Texian Press, 1960), 18-19; O. T. Hanks, MSS, University of Texas Archives, 28-29. See also Jonathan D. Hood, "A Yellow Rose in the Old Dominion: The Civil War Reminiscences of Orlando T. Hanks" (M.A. thesis, Stephen F. Austin State University, 1997), 71-73.

20. Jerome B. Robertson, comp., *Touched With Valor: The Civil War Papers and Casualty Reports of Hood's Texas Brigade,* ed. Harold B. Simpson (Hillsboro: Hill Junior College Press, 1964), 80-82.

21. *Official Records,* 11, Pt. 2: 773; Everett, ed., *Chaplain Davis and Hood's Texas Brigade,* 91-92; Jack D. Welsh, *Medical Histories of Confederate Generals* (Kent, OH: Kent State University Press, 1995), 187.

22. Sears, *To the Gates of Richmond,* 249.

23. Simpson, *Lee's Grenadier Guard,* 143n, points out that there is some question who commanded the brigade in the Second Manassas campaign. In his memoirs *Advance and Retreat,* 37, Hood states his adjutant, Maj. W. H. Sellers, led the Texas Brigade. However, Col. W. T. Wofford, commander of the Eighteeenth Georgia, was the next ranking officer to Hood, and by military protocol should have headed the brigade. Simpson notes that Lt. Col. N. W. Gary, commander of Hampton's Legion, addressed his reports to Wofford as commander of the

brigade. Wofford sent his own report to Hood. The three Texas regimental commanders, Philip A. Work (who took command of the First Texas when A. T. Rainey was wounded at Gaines' Mill), Benjamin F. Carter (who succeeded Marshall as commander of the Fourth Texas), and Jerome B. Robertson, sent their reports to Major Sellers. *Official Records,* 12, Pt. 2: 608-622.

24. Hood, *Advance and Retreat,* 34-35; John J. Hennessy, *Return to Bull Run: The Campaign and Battle of Second Manassas* (New York: Simon & Schuster, 1993), 294-299.

25. *Official Records,* 12, Pt. 2: 608-622; Fletcher, *Rebel Private Front and Rear,* 37-42; Everett, *Chaplain Davis and the Texas Brigade,* 112-120; Polley, *Hood's Texas Brigade,* 83-111; Simpson, *Lee's Grenadier Guard,* 146-155; Giles, *Rags and Hope,* 123-132; Mamie Yeary, *Reminiscences of the Boys in Gray* (Dallas: Smith & Lamar, 1912), 816-817.

26. Hennessy, *Return to Bull Run,* 381.

27. The death of Upton, "regarded as one of the outstanding outpost officers in Lee's army" (according to Harold Simpson, *Lee's Grenadier Guard,* 142), was a particularly bitter loss to the brigade. See Douglas Southall Freeman, *Lee's Lieutenants: A Study in Command,* 3 vols. (New York: Charles Scribner's Sons, 1943), 2: 142.

28. *Official Records,* 12, Pt. 2: 560-562, 607-608, 609-611, 618-619. These figures, given also in Simpson, *Lee's Grenadier Guard,* 156-157, differ slightly from those found in Simpson, *Hood's Texas Brigade: A Compendium,* 534.

29. Hood, *Advance and Retreat,* 38-39; Everett, ed., *Chaplain Davis and Hood's Texas Brigade,* 124-125; Freeman, *Lee's Lieutenants,* 2:147.

30. Polley, *Hood's Texas Brigade,* 114; McMurry, *John Bell Hood,* 57.

31. Hood, *Advance and Retreat,* 41-43; Simpson, *Lee's Grenadier Guard,* 168-170; *Official Records,* 19, Pt. 1: 268-269.

32. Quote, Stephen W. Sears, *Landscape Turned Red: The Battle of Antietam* (New York: Ticknor and Fields, 1983), 201. See also Jerry W. Holsworth, "Uncommon Valor: Hood's Texas Brigade in the Maryland Campaign," *Blue & Gray Magazine* 13 (August 1996): 17-20; and George E. Otott, "1st Texas in the Cornfield," *Civil War Regiments* 15 (no. 3, 1997): 73-123.

33. Polley, *Hood's Texas Brigade,* 115-133; Everett, *Chaplain Davis and Hood's Texas Brigade,* 126-128; Sears, *Landscape Turned Red,* 180-201; *Official Records,* 19, Pt. 1: 922-937.

34. Simpson, *Lee's Grenadier Guard,* 176-178; Simpson, *Hood's Texas Brigade: A Compendium,* 535. These figures differ slightly from those given in John Michael Priest, *Antietam: The Soldiers' Battle* (New York: Oxford University Press, 1989), 323.

35. Simpson, *Lee's Grenadier Guard,* 183.

36. First quote, Douglas Southall Freeman, *R. E. Lee: A Biography,* 4 vols. (New York: Charles Scribner's Sons, 1936), 2: 420; second quote, Inspector General's Report, *Official Records,* 19, Pt. 2: 718-719. See also Harry M. Henderson, *Texas in the Confederacy* (San Antonio: Naylor Co., 1955), 22. The non-Texans in the brigade were more poorly shod than the Texans. The inspector general reported that one hundred men in the Eighteeenth Georgia and one hundred men in the South Carolina Legion lacked shoes. In the three Texas regiments

combined 180 men were barefoot: sixty in the First Texas, seventy-five in the Fourth Texas, and forty-five in the Fifth Texas.

37. Everett, ed., *Chaplain Davis and Hood's Texas Brigade,* 178.

38. *Ibid.*, 178-179.

39. *Official Records,* 19, Pt. 2: 699, 719; Krick, *Lee's Colonels,* 74, 85, 223, 308, 408; Tyler, ed., *New Handbook of Texas,* 6: 1075; Kevin Ladd, "Lt. Colonel King Bryan: A Forgotten Hero," *Texas Illustrated Magazine* (November 1996): 7-8. Val Giles, *Rags and Hope,* 50, notes "there was not an officer in Hood's Texas Brigade in the Army of Northern Virginia who was more universally loved and admired by the soldiers of the old command than Lieutenant Colonel Ben F. Carter of the Fourth Texas Regiment . . ."

40. Hood, *Advance and Retreat,* 49-50; Everett, ed., *Chaplain Davis and Hood's Texas Brigade,* 142-144; *Official Records,* 21, Pt. 1: 559-560, 621-623. For more on the Battle of Fredericksburg see Victor Brooks, *The Fredericksburg Campaigns, October 1862–January 1863* (Conshohocken, PA: Combined Publishing, 2000); Daniel E. Sutherland, *Fredericksburg & Chancellorsville: The Dare Mark Campaign* (Lincoln: University of Nebraska Press, 1998), 40-60, and Gary E. Gallagher, ed., *The Fredericksburg Campaign: Decision on the Rappahannock* (Chapel Hill, NC: University of North Carolina Press, 1995).

41. Fletcher, *Rebel Private Front and Rear,* 51-52. For another description of the construction of a winter hut see Simpson, *Lee's Grenadier Guard,* 202-203.

42. Giles, *Rags and Hope,* 157.

43. *Ibid.*, 158-161.

44. Fletcher, *Rebel Private Front and Rear*, 53.

45. Hood, *Advance and Retreat*, 51.

46. Simpson, *Lee's Grenadier Guard*, 203-204; Simpson, *Hood's Texas Brigade: A Compendium,* 14, 94-95, 172; Polley, *Hood's Texas Brigade,* 139-140.

47. Quote, Fletcher, *Rebel Private Front and Rear*, 52-53; Giles, *Rags and Hope,* 167-170. Longstreet himself was the occasional target of the snowballs from the Texans. After several days of enduring the snowball barrages he told the Texans to "throw your snowballs, men, if you want to, as much as you please. But if one of them touches me, not a man in this brigade shall have a furlough this winter." According to his biographer Longstreet was untouched thereafter. Jeffry D. Wert, *General James Longstreet: The Confederacy's Most Controversial Soldier: A Biography* (New York: Simon & Schuster, 1993), 225.

48. *Official Records*, 18: 876, 880; Polley, Hood's Texas Brigade, 140-142.

49. Quote, Hood, *Advance and Retreat*, 52; *Official Records*, 18: 324-326, 1010; 57, Pt. 2: 697.

50. Quote, Wert, *General James Longstreet,* 237.

51. *Official Records*, 18: 278, 1032, 1038, 1042, 1052; Wert, *General James Longstreet*, 238-239.

52. McMurry, *John Bell Hood*, 73.

53. Hood, *Advance and Retreat*, 54.

54. *Ibid.*, 54.

55. John West, *A Texan in Search of a Fight* (Waco: J. C. West, 1901), 91; Fletcher, *Rebel Private Front and Rear*, 54; J. B. Polley, *A Soldier's Letters to Charming Nelly* (New York: Neale Publishing Co., 1908), 121; and John W.

Stevens, *Reminiscences of the Civil War* (Hillsboro: Hillsboro *Mirror,* 1902), 105-106, describe the drinking that occurred.

56. Arthur J. L. Fremantle, *The Fremantle Diary, Being the Journal of Lieutenant Colonel Arthur James Lyon Fremantle, Coldstream Guards, and His Three Months in the Southern States,* ed. Walter Lord (Reprint, New York: Capricorn Books, 1960), 191.

57. Polley, *Hood's Texas Brigade,* 147-148.

58. Various accounts including Freeman, *Lee's Lieutenants,* 3: 106-116 and Wert, *General James Longstreet*, 257-263, describe these discussions. For a perceptive, and critical, account of the matter see Robert K. Krick, "'If Longstreet . . . Says So, It is Most Likely Not True,': James Longstreet and the Second Day at Gettysburg," in Gary W. Gallagher, ed., *The Second Day at Gettysburg: Essays on Confederate and Union Leadership* (Kent, OH: Kent State University Press, 1993), 57-86.

59. McMurry, *John Bell Hood*, 75; Simpson, *Lee's Grenadier Guard*, 268; Hood, *Advance and Retreat*, 57-59.

60. *Official Records*, 27, Pt. 2: 405, 411-414; Krick, *Lee's Colonels,* 74, 85, 222-223, 308-309.

61. *Official Records*, 17: 408-414; Simpson, *Lee's Grenadier Guard*, 269-285. For a good description of the battle by a participant see Eddy R. Parker, ed., *Touched By Fire: Letters from Company D, 5th Texas Infantry, Hood's Brigade, Army of Northern Virginia, 1862-1865* (Hillsboro: Hill College Press, 2000), 64-67.

62. Casualty figures vary widely. The ones given here are those in Simpson, *Lee's Grenadier Guard*, 285, and *Official Records*, 27, Pt. 2: 339. These differ from those given in *Hood's Texas Brigade: A Compendium*, 535.

63. Writing to his wife in Washington County, Capt. Tacitus T. Clay of the Fifth Texas reported "our Army is in fine spirits, and is receiving accessions to it every day." Winfield, eds., *Clay Letters,* 12.

64. For more information on the Confederate plan to reinforce Bragg see Peter Cozzens, *This Terrible Sound: The Battle of Chickamauga* (Urbana: University of Illinois Press, 1992), 28-29, 59-60; Steven E. Woodworth, *Jefferson Davis and His Generals: The Failure of Confederate Command in the West* (Lawrence: University of Kansas Press, 1990), 229-230; Steven E. Woodworth, *A Deep Steady Thunder: The Battle of Chickamauga* (Abilene: McWhiney Foundation Press, 1998), 24-25; and Wert, *General James Longstreet*, 300-305.

65. *Official Records*, 30, Pt. 2: 511-516; Hood, *Advance and Retreat*, 61-62; D. H. Hamilton, *History of Company H, First Texas Volunteer Infantry* (Waco: W. M. Morrison, 1962), 31-32.

66. Simpson, *Lee's Grenadier Guard*, 324. Simpson points out that not only were Robertson's troops in front of other Confederates but also that their new uniforms issued at Fredericksburg appeared more blue than gray in color.

67. *Official Records*, 30, Pt. 2: 288; Hood, *Advance and Retreat*, 63-65; Woodworth, *A Deep Steady Thunder,* 50-51, 87.

68. Cozzens, *This Terrible Sound,* 534; *Official Records*, 30, Pt. 2: 25, 35.

69. Simpson, *Lee's Grenadier Guard*, 327; Simpson, *Hood's Texas Brigade: A Compendium,* 535; *Official Records*, 30, Pt. 2: 291, 511, 516, 517.

70. William C. Davis, "John Gregg," in *The Confederate General,* 3: 36-38; Simpson, *Lee's Grenadier Guard*, 320-321.

71. Simpson, *Lee's Grenadier Guard*, 341. For the perspective of members of the Fourth Texas see Giles, *Rags and Hope*, 213-216, and Polley, *Hood's Texas Brigade*, 215-220.

72. *Official Records*, 31, Pt. 1: 455-467; James Longstreet, *From Manassas to Appomattox: Memoirs of the Civil War in America*, ed. James I. Robertson (Bloomington, IN: Indiana University Press, 1960), 502-507; Gary W. Gallagher, ed., *Fighting for the Confederacy: The Personal Recollections of Edward Porter Alexander* (Chapel Hill: University of North Carolina Press, 1989), 324-327.

73. Quote, Hamilton, *History of Company M*, 45; Longstreet, *From Manassas to Appomattox*, 520-521; O. T. Hanks, "History of B. F. Benton's Company, or Account of Civil War Experiences," MSS, University of Texas Archives, 33; West, *Texan in Search of a Fight*, 140-141.

74. Robertson, *Touched with Fire*, 52-53.

75. *Official Records*, 29, Pt. 2: 869-870.

76. Lawrence L. Hewitt, "Evander McIvor Law," in *The Confederate General*, 4: 23-24. For the full particulars of this controversy see Gary R. Swanson and Timothy D. Johnson, "Conflict in East Tennessee: Generals Law, Jenkins, and Longstreet," *Civil War History* 31 (June 1985): 101-110.

77. Simpson, *Lee's Grenadier Guard*, 384-385; *Official Records*, 31, Pt. 1: 466-467; Winkler, *The Confederate Capital and Hood's Texas Brigade*, 151.

78. Miles V. Smith, "Reminiscences of the Civil War," 48, quoted by Simpson, *Lee's Grenadier Guard*, 386. For a more critical view of Robertson by a fellow Texan who was an officer on Longstreet's staff see Langston James Goree, ed., *The Thomas Jewett Goree Letters* (Bryan: Family History Foundation, 1981), 200.

79. William C. Davis, "John Gregg," in *The Confederate General*, 3: 38-39.

80. Polley, Hood's Texas Brigade, 226-227. Longstreet attempted to thwart Davis' decision to appoint Field, leading the Confederate War Department, at Davis' instruction, to reprimand Longstreet. Wert, *General James Longstreet*, 373-374.

81. Winkler, *The Confederate Capital and Hood's Texas Brigade*, 151.

82. Simpson, *Lee's Grenadier Guard*, 401-403.

83. Gordon C. Rhea, *The Battle of the Wilderness, Mary 5-6, 1864* (Baton Rouge: Louisiana State University Press, 1994), 303. In addition to the various accounts cited in Chapter One see also E. M. Law, "From the Wilderness to Cold Harbor," *Battles & Leaders*, 4 vols. (Reprint, New York: Thomas Yoseloff, Inc., 1956), 4: 118-125; Gallager, ed., *Fighting for the Confederacy*, 358; R. C., "Texans Always Move Them," in *The Blue and the Gray*, ed. Henry S. Commager, 2 vols. (Indianopolis: Bobbs-Merrill Company, 1950), 2: 982-985; Dayton Kelley, "The Texas Brigade at the Wilderness, May 6, 1864," Texana 11 (No. 2, 1973): 103-132; Hood, "A Yellow Rose in the Old Dominion," 100-101.

84. Diary, May 10, 1864, Thomas L. McCarty Papers, MSS, University of Texas Archives; *Official Records*, 51, Pt. 2: 911; Law, "From the Wildernss to Cold Harbor," 129; William D. Matter, *If It Takes All Summer: The Battle of Spotsylvania* (Chapel Hill: University of North Carolina Press, 1988), 154-155; Gordon C. Rhea, *The Battles for Spotsylvania Court House and the Road to Yellow Tavern*, May 7-12, 1864 (Baton Rouge: Louisiana State University Press, 1997), 180-181.

85. Quote, Hamilton, *History of Company M*, 60. See also J. J. Cosgrove, "About the Attack at Cold Harbor," *Confederate Veteran* 20 (November 1912):

511; Ernest B. Fergurson, *Not War But Murder: Cold Harbor 1864* (New York: Alfred A. Knopf, 2000).

86. Polley, *Hood's Texas Brigade,* 244-248; Simpson, *Lee's Grenadier Guard,* 422-427.

87. *Official Records*, 42, Pt. 2: 1301, 1304; Richard Sommers, *Richmond Redeemed: The Siege at Petersburg* (Garden City, NY: Doubleday & Co., 1981), 17-18, 28-34, 45-47.

88. Polley, *Hood's Texas Brigade*, 257-259; Simpson, *Lee's Grenadier Guard,* 438-492; Gallagher, ed., *Fighting for the Confederacy,* 483-484.

89. *Official Records*, 42, Pt. 4: 872, 877.

90. *Ibid*., 36, Pt. 3: 894-895.

91. Winkler, *The Confederate Capital and Hood's Brigade,* 206-207.

92. *Ibid*., 208-209, quoted in Simpson, *Lee's Grenadier Guard*, 455-456.

93. Robertson, *Touched With Valor,* 102-104. Simpson, *Lee's Grenadier Guard*, 456n, points out that even in the final days of the Confederacy desertion rates in the Texas Brigade were low. For the ten-day period ending March 8, 1865, the Army of Northern Virginia listed 779 desertions; only three of these were in the Texas Brigade. In the next ten-day period the brigade listed no deserters. For more on the difficulties facing the men in Lee's army see J. Tracy Power, *Lee's Miserables: Life in the Army of Northern Virginia from the Wilderness to Appomattox* (Chapel Hill: University of North Carolina Press, 1998), esp. 245-285.

94. Polley, *Hood's Texas Brigade*, 274-277. Colonel Powell had been wounded and captured while leading the Fifth Texas at Gettysburg. When he was exchanged in February 1865 he replaced Colonel Bass (whom he outranked) as brigade commander. Krick, *Lee's Colonels,* 48, 308-309.

95. These figures are taken from Simpson, *Lee's Grenadier Guard*, 468n, and Henderson, *Texas in the Confederacy,* 48-50. For the surrender ceremony itself see Harold B. Simpson, "Hood's Brigade at Appomattox," *Texana* 3 (Spring 1965): 1-19.

96. For more on the postwar activities of members of the brigade see Simpson, *Hood's Brigade in Reunion and Memory.*

CHAPTER THREE

1. Thomas L. Connelly, *Army of the Heartland: The Army of Tennessee, 1861-1862* (Baton Rouge: Louisiana State University Press, 1967), ix, 3.

2. A complete account of the Rangers is *None But Texians: A History of Terry's Texas Rangers* (Eakin Press, 2001) by Jeffrey D. Murrah. There are numerous accounts of the Rangers written by participants. Three of these have been brought together in the *Terry Texas Ranger Trilogy* (Austin: State House Press, 1996), with an excellent introduction by Thomas W. Cutrer. See also Cutrer's essay on the Rangers in Tyler, ed., *New Handbook of Texas,* 2: 805-806, and Anne J. Bailey's sketch of Terry and other Rangers in *Texans in the Confederate Cavalry* (Fort Worth: Ryan Place Publishers, 1995), 19-33. For more on the personal qualities of the Rangers see C. C. Jeffries, "The Character of Terry's Texas Rangers," *Southwestern Historical Quarterly* 64 (April 1961): 454-462.

3. L. B. Giles, "Terry's Texas Rangers," in *Terry Texas Ranger Triology,* 9; Cutrer, "Eighth Texas Cavalry," in Tyler, *New Handbook of Texas*, 2: 805; Clement

Evans, ed., *Confederate Military History,* 12 vols. (Atlanta: Confederate Publishing Co., 1898), 11: 52.

4. First quote, Fremantle, *Diary,* 58; second quote, Edward Clark to the Legislature, November 7, 1861, in James M. Day, ed., *Senate Journal of the Ninth Legislature of the State of Texas, November 4, 1861-January 14, 1862* (Austin: Texas State Library, 1963), 12-14. See also Stephen B. Oates, "Recruiting Confederate Cavalry in Texas," *Southwestern Historical Quarterly* 64 (April 1961): 473-475.

5. Based upon information from Giles, "Terry's Texas Rangers," 10-11; and Henderson, *Texas in the Confederacy,* 102.

6. Giles, "Terry's Texas Rangers," 11-13; Blackburn, "Reminiscences of Terry Rangers," in *Terry Texas Ranger Trilogy,* 95-104. C. C. Jeffries, *Terry's Rangers* (New York: Vantage Press, 1961), 20-28, points out there is some dispute just when and where the name "Terry's Texas Rangers" came into being. He notes that the number eight was disappointing to some of the men who believed the delay in completing formal organization resulted in the higher number. Most of the Rangers considered they were not "eighth" in anything.

7. Blackburn, "Reminiscences of Terry Rangers," 102; Connelly, *Army of the Heartland,* 70. For problems associated with obtaining horses for the regiment see the exchange between Albert Sidney Johnston and Secretary of War Judah P. Benjamin, *Official Records*, 4: 430, 469, 504. John W. Rabb, a corporal in F Company, reported that his company received its horses on October 21. According to Rabb his was the first company to receive its mounts. See Thomas W. Cutrer, ed., "'We Are Stern and Resolved': The Civil War Letters of John Wesley Rabb, Terry's Texas Rangers," *Southwestern Historical Quarterly* 91 (October 1987): 189-190.

8. *Official Records*, 7: 19-20; Blackburn, "Reminiscences of Terry Rangers," 104-105; Giles, "Terry's Texas Rangers," 15-18; H. J. H. Rugeley, ed., *Batchelor-Turner Letters, 1861-1864, Written by Two of Terry's Texas Rangers* (Austin: Steck Co., 1961), 2-4.

9. Cutrer, "Introduction," *Terry Texas Ranger Trilogy,* xiii. In death Terry became a legendary hero for the Confederate cause. One soldier, Sgt. Robert J. Hodges, Jr., who earlier criticized Terry as "unwise" and "a saphead," now referred to him as "our gallant and beloved leader Col. Terry." Maury Darst, "Robert Hodges, Jr.: Confederate Soldier," *East Texas Historical Journal* 9 (March 1971): 26, 28.

Terry's body was taken by train to Nashville, where it lay in state in the Tennessee capitol. From there it was taken to New Orleans and then on to Houston, where an imposing funeral procession took place. Terry County was later named in his honor. Tyler, ed., *New Handbook of Texas*, 6: 265.

10. *Official Records*, 7: 781, 809; Blackburn, "Reminiscences of Terry Rangers," 106. Frank Batchelor, a member of the Rangers, noted in a letter home that Generals Johnston and William J. Hardee favored a system of promoting the next senior officer but the men insisted on their "right of voting." Rugeley, ed., *Batchelor-Turner Letters,* 11.

11. Giles, "Terry's Texas Rangers," 18. For more on John A. Wharton see Ralph A. Wooster, *Lone Star Generals in Gray* (Austin: Eakin Press, 2000), 65-74. In the same election John G. Walker of Harris County, commander of K Company, was chosen as lieutenant colonel. Walker was one of those wounded at Woodsonville. He is sometimes mistaken for John G. Walker of Missouri, who

later commanded the division of Texas infantry in Louisiana described in Chapter Six.

12. *Official Records*, 7: 911; Blackburn "Reminiscences of Terry Rangers," 107-111; Cutrer, ed., "Civil War Letters of John Wesley Rabb," 198-199.

13. Giles, "Terry's Texas Rangers," 23-24; George W. Baylor, "With Gen. A. S. Johnston at Shiloh," *Confederate Veteran* 5 (1897): 609.

14. *Official Records*, 10, Pt. 1: 569, 626-627; Blackburn, "Reminiscences of Terry Rangers," 113-122; Giles, "Terry's Texas Rangers," 24-26; Henry W. Graber, *The Life of H. W. Graber, A Terry Texas Ranger, 1861-1865* (Dallas: Privately printed, 1916), 57-58.

15. First quote, Robert W. Williams, Jr., and Ralph A. Wooster, eds., "With Terry's Texas Rangers: The Letters of Dunbar Affleck," *Civil War History* 9 (September 1963): 302-305; second quote, Giles, "Terry's Texas Rangers," 26. Affleck was correct in the number of Rangers in camp. On April 28, 1862, the abstract field returns showed 666 Rangers present. The aggregate number for present and absent was 813. *Official Records*, 10, Pt. 2: 459.

16. *Official Records*, 10, Pt. 1: 809-811, 813-900; Pt. 2: 509-510; Giles, "Terry's Texas Rangers," 27-30; Blackburn, "Reminiscences of Terry Rangers," 123-127; David B. Gracy II, "With Danger and Honor: George W. Littlefield, 1861-1864," Texana 1 (Winter 1963): 15-17; Brian Steele Wills, *A Battle from the Start: The Life of Nathan Bedford Forrest* (New York: Harper Collins, 1992), 74-76; Welsh, *Medical Histories of Confederate Generals,* 231. In his report of the fighting at Murfreesboro, Lt. Col. John G. Parkhurst of the Ninth Michigan Infantry noted "there were also quite a few negroes attached to the Texas and Georgia troops, who were armed and equipped, and took part in several engagements with my forces during the day." *Official Records*, 10, Pt. 1: 805.

17. *Official Records*, 16, Pt. 1: 1098, 1109-1110; Cutrer, ed., "Civil War Letters of John Wesley Rabb," 203-204; Graber, *Life Record,* 170-175; Williams and Wooster, eds., "Letters of Dunbar Affleck," 310; James Lee McDonough, *War in Kentucky: From Shiloh to Perryville* (Knoxville: University of Tennessee Press, 1994), 233, 241; Kenneth A. Hafendorf, *Perryville: Battle for Kentucky* (Louisville: K H Press, 1991), 74-75, 141, 191-193.

18. Giles, "Terry's Texas Rangers," 13, 36; Photo caption, *Terry Texas Ranger Trilogy,* 54; Welsh, *Medical Histories of Confederate Generals,* 95; Arthur W. Bergeron, Jr., "Thomas Harrison," in *The Confederate General,* 3: 70-71. Frank Batchelor, a young lieutenant who served as Harrison's adjutant, found no fault with Harrison "except that he is addicted to getting drunk & does it when a battle is pending . . . ." Rugeley, ed., *Batchelor-Turner Letters*, 44-45. Tom Burney, a member of Company C, described Harrison as "a gallant old man who was sometimes mean to his men in camp." Eighth Texas Cavalry Regiment website. Harrison and his older brother James later became brigadier generals in the Confederate army.

19. *Official Records*, 20, Pt. 1: 661, 665, 670, 774, 966-970; Blackburn, "Reminiscences of Terry Rangers," 135-138; Edwin C. Bearss, "Cavalry Operations in the Battle of Stones River," *Tennessee Historical Quarterly,* 19 (June 1960), Pt. 2: 118-120, 136-137. James Lee McDonough, *Stones River—Bloody Winter in Tennessee* (Knoxville: University of Tennessee Press, 1980), 146, believes that had Wharton been given more support in his attack on the morning of

December 31 the Confederates could have cut the Union supply line, forcing Rosecrans to retreat.

20. Steven E. Woodworth, *Jefferson Davis and His Generals: The Failure of Confederate Command in the West* (Lawrence: University of Kansas Press, 1990), 194. Wharton's cavalry entered the Murfreesboro campaign with brigade strength of approximately 1,300 effectives. Effective strength of the Rangers was approximately 400. *Official Records*, 20, Pt. 2: 406. Wharton does not give casualties for the campaign by regiment. He reported 108 killed and wounded and 107 captured for the brigade. *Ibid.*, 20, Pt. 1: 970.

21. Quote, Giles, "Terry's Texas Rangers," 41; Rugeley, ed., *Batchelor-Turner Letters*, 45-47; *Official Records*, 23, Pt. 1: 33-35, 39, 40-41; Wills, *Battle from the Start*, 98-102; Jack Hurd, *Nathan Bedford Forrest: A Biography* (New York: Alfred A. Knopf, 1993), 113-114; John P. Dyer, *"Fightin' Joe" Wheeler* (Baton Rouge: Louisiana State University Press), 91-96.

22. Giles, "Terry's Texas Rangers," 42.

23. "Diary of Ephraim Shelby Dodd," in *Terry Texas Rangers Trilogy* (Austin: State House Press, 1996), 196; Williams and Wooster, eds., "With Terry's Texas Rangers," 318.

24. First quote, Giles, "Terry's Texas Rangers," 43; second quote, Rugeley, ed., *Batchelor-Turner Letters*, 62-63; third quote, "Diary of Ephraim Shelby Dodd," 208. Finding mounts for the regiment was a constant problem. In field returns for January 14, 1863, the Rangers reported 419 officers and men present for duty but only 325 serviceable horses. *Official Reports,* 17, Pt. 2: 835.

25. Larry J. Daniel, *Soldiering in the Army of Tennessee: A Portrait of Life in a Confederate Army* (Chapel Hill: University of North Carolina Press, 1991), 118. For more on Bunting see Paula Mitchell Marks, "The Ranger Reverend," *Civil War Times Illustrated* 21 (December 1958): 40-45.

26. Giles, "Terry's Texas Rangers," 36; Jeffries, *Terry's Rangers,* 136; Tyler, ed., *New Handbook of Texas*, 2: 302-303. There is disagreement over the spelling of the last name of the new commander. The name is spelled "Cook" in the *New Handbook of Texas* and in Giles' account. It is spelled Cooke in the caption to his photo in the *Terry Texas Ranger Trilogy,* 80, in Wright and Simpson, *Texas in the War, 1861-1865,* 112-113, and in *Members of the Texas Legislature, 1846-1962* (Austin, 1963), 72. It is spelled both "Cook" and "Cooke" in O. M. Roberts' essay on Texas in Evans, ed., *Confederate Military History,* 11: 159, 174, 187.

27. Giles, "Terry's Texas Rangers," 46; Blackburn, "Reminiscences of Terry Rangers," 138-140. Wheeler's report of the battle mentions the Eighth Texas Cavalry only once. Neither Wharton's nor Harrison's reports of Chickamauga are in the *Official Records*.

28. Blackburn, "Reminiscences of Terry Rangers," 141-149; Giles, "Terry's Texas Rangers," 52-53; Rugeley, ed., *Batchelor-Turner Letters*, 71.

29. It was during the Knoxville campaign that Ephraim S. Dodd, a private in Company D, was captured by the enemy in Sevier County, Tennessee. Because he was wearing blue trousers and overcoat, Union authorities were convinced he was a spy. He was executed on January 8, 1864. His diary is published in *Terry Texas Ranger Trilogy*, 185-220, and in *Civil War Series No. 1, Diary of E. S. Dodd, Co. D,*

Terry's Texas Rangers: An Account of his Hanging as a Confederate Spy (Austin: Ranger Press, 1979).

30. Connelly, *Autumn of Glory: The Army of Tennessee, 1862-1865* (Baton Rouge: Louisiana State University Press, 1971), 361. For more on the Wharton-Wheeler controvery see Wooster, *Lone Star Generals in Gray*, 71-72.

31. Quote, Jeffries, *Terry's Rangers*, 92. For the Rangers' role in north Georgia see *Official Records*, 38, Pt. 3: 38, 944, 947, 950; Giles, "Terry's Texas Rangers," 61-62.

32. *Ibid*., 63-66.

33. Quote, Connelly, *Autumn of Glory*, 435.

34. Jeffries, *Terry's Rangers*, 95-99; Giles, "Terry's Texas Rangers," 67-69.

35. First quote, Connelly, *Autumn of Glory*, 435; second quote, Graber, *Life Record*, published in Cutrer, "Introduction," *Terry Texas Ranger Trilogy*, xxiii.

36. The "Rome Races" are described by Giles, "Terry's Texas Rangers," 71-73; Cutrer, ed., "Civil War Letters of John Wesley Rabb," 221-223; Graber, *Life Record*, 201-204; and Jeffries, *Terry's Rangers*, 103. The flag was returned to Texas by the governor of Indiana in October 1899 and was in the possession of the Texas Division, United Daughters of the Confederacy. According to Alan K. Sumrall, *Battle Flags of Texans in the Confederacy* (Austin: Eakin Press, 1995), the flag has been reported stolen.

37. *Official Records*, 44: 409-41l; Giles, "Terry's Texas Rangers," 75-76; Blackburn, "Reminiscences of Terry Rangers," 167-170; Fletcher, *Rebel Private Front and Rear*, 139-144.

38. Quote, Blackburn, "Reminiscences of Terry Rangers," 170. See also *Official Records*, 47, Pt. 1: 1057, 1092; Giles, "Terry's Texas Rangers," 76-77; Graber, *Life Record*, 226-227; Nathaniel C. Hughes, Jr., *Bentonville: The Final Battle of Sherman and Johnston* (Chapel Hill: University of North Carolina Press, 1996), 204-207; Mark L. Bradley, *The Battle of Bentonville: Last Stand in the Carolinas* (Campbell, CA: Savas Woodbury Publishers, 1996), 382-390; M. J. Davis, "Eighth Texas Cavalry at Bentonville," *Confederate Veteran* 24 (April 1916): 184; A. P. Harcourt, "Terry's Texas Rangers," *The Southern Bivoauc*, 1 (No. 8, Old Series, November 1882): 89-97.

39. *Official Records*, 47, Pt. 1: 1057; Hughes, *Bentonville*, 204-207; Bradley, *Battle of Bentonville*, 394-395.

40. Quote, Giles, "Terry's Texas Rangers," 78-79.

41. Quote, Harold B. Simpson, ed., *Texas in the War, 1861-1865*, 114. As an example of the greater attention given to the Rangers, the index to Larry J. Daniel's *Soldiering in the Army of Tennessee* has ten entries for the Eighth Texas and none for the Eleventh. Anne J. Bailey, *Texans in the Confederate Cavalry*, has eleven entries for the Rangers and one for the Eleventh Texas.

42. Richard B. McCaslin, "Conditional Confederates: The Eleventh Texas Cavalry West of the Mississippi River," *Military History of the Southwest* 21 (Spring 1991): 87-99. For more on opposition to secession in the area see Richard B. McCaslin, *Tainted Breeze: The Great Hanging at Gainesville, Texas, 1862* (Baton Rouge: Louisiana State University Press, 1994), 9-37.

43. Neither Throckmorton nor Hugh Young remained with the Eleventh Cavalry for long. Throckmorton left to become an officer in the Sixth Cavalry and

Young, who was fifty-three years old, became a brigadier general in state reserve troops. McCaslin, "Conditional Confederates," 90-91; Oates, "Recruiting Confederate Cavalry in Texas," 468; Tyler, ed., *New Handbook of Texas*, 6: 486, 1126, 1129.

44. David Paul Smith, *Frontier Defense in the Civil War: Texas Rangers and Rebels* (College Station: Texas A&M University Press, 1992),58; Lary C. Rampp and Donald L. Rampp, *The Civil War in Indian Territory* (Austin: Presidial Press, 1975), 3-6.

45. *Official Records*, 4: 95, 98; McCaslin, "Conditional Confederates," 42.

46. *Official Records*, 4: 113-114; McCaslin, *Tainted Breeze*, 44-46.

47. *Official Records*, 8: 26-27; McCaslin, *Tainted Breeze*, 46-47; Rampp and Rampp, *Civil War in Indian Territory*, 6-8; Kenny A. Franks, "Operations Against Opothleyahola, 1861," *Military History of Texas and the Southwest* 10 (No. 3, 1972): 187-196.

48. *Official Records*, 8: 746; Thomas W. Cutrer, *Ben McCulloch and the Frontier Military Tradition* (Chapel Hill: University of North Carolina Press, 1993), 271-281.

49. *Official Records*, 8: 193-194; William L. Shea and Earl J. Hess, *Pea Ridge: Campaign in the West* (Chapel Hill: University of North Carolina Press, 1992), 97-99, 109-119, 143-147, 210-222; Cutrer, *Ben McCulloch*, 290-309.

50. Tom Coleman quoted in William L. Shea, *War in the West: Pea Ridge and Prairie Grove* (Abilene: McWhiney Foundation Press, 1998), 69; Shea and Hess, *Pea Ridge*, 47.

51. Shea and Hess, *Pea Ridge*, 267-268, 286-289.

52. *Official Records*, 10, Pt. 2: 490; McCaslin, *Tainted Breeze*, 47-48. William C. Young and James Diamond were both involved in the affairs in Cooke County that led to the "great hanging" of October 1862. Young was later killed while tracking down a murderer.

53. Tyler, ed., *New Handbook of Texas*, 1: 835; *Official Records*, 10: 462-463; 16, Pt. 1: 941-942, Pt. 2: 634.

54. *Official Records*, 16, Pt. 1: 933-935, 940-941; McDonough, *War in Kentucky*, 134-139.

55. Quote, John C. Burks, reported by Matthew D. Ector, *Official Records*, 20, Pt. 1: 929. See also *ibid.*, 680, 914, 927, 932-933; McDonough, Stones River, 90-101.

56. Quote, Matthew D. Ector, in *Official Records*, 20, Pt. 1: 929.

57. *Official Records*, 20, Pt. 1: 932-933; Tyler, *New Handbook of Texas*, 1: 662.

58. *Official Records*, 23, Pt. 2: 613.

59. *Ibid.*, 31, Pt. 1: 541; Pt. 2: 662.

60. For more on the affair see Steve Peters, "The Murder of Joseph M. Bounds, Eleventh Texas Cavalry, Young's Regiment, C.S.A.," *Texana* 12 (No. 1, 1974): 56-60.

61. Wright and Simpson, *Texas in the War, 1861-1865,* 115; Tyler, ed., *New Handbook of Texas*, 5: 507-508.

62. *Official Records*, 44: 409-410; Evans, *Confederate Military History*, 11: 187-188; Lee Kennett, *Marching Through Georgia* (New York: Harper Collins, 1995), 246-247, 263-264, 297-298.

63. *Official Records*, 47, Pt. 1: 1057, 1065; Bradley, *Battle of Bentonville,* 382-383.

64. Sifakis, *Compendium of Confederate Armies: Texas,* 47-48, 50, 55-56, 61-62; Tyler, ed., *New Handbook of Texas*, 5: 692; Shea and Hess, *Pea Ridge*, 335.

65. Douglas Hale, *The Third Texas Cavalry in the Civil War* (Norman: University of Oklahoma Press, 1993), 25-27; S. B. Barron, *The Lone Star Defenders: A Chronicle of the Third Texas Cavalry, Ross' Brigade* (New York: Neale Publishing Co., 1908), 23-27; A. W. Sparks, *The War Between the States, As I Saw It* (Tyler: Lee & Burnett, 1900), 130-131. For more on Greer see Ralph A. Wooster, *Lone Star Generals in Gray* (Austin: Eakin Press, 2000), 126-131.

66. Hale, *Third Texas Cavalry,* 33, 37, 41-45.

67. *Ibid*., 28-29, 47: Victor M. Rose, *Ross' Texas Brigade* (Reprint, Kennesaw, GA: Continental Book Co., 1906), 16.

68. Hale, *Third Texas Cavalry,* 50-69; *Official Records*, 3: 74, 87-88, 119; Rose, *Ross' Texas Brigade,* 18-31; Barron, *Lone Star Defenders,* 28-46; Douglas J. Cater, *As It Was: Reminscences of a Soldier of the Third Texas Cavalry and the Nineteenth Louisiana Infantry* (Austin: State House Press, 1990), 75-90; Sparks, *As I Saw It,* 136-149; William Garrett Piston and Richard W. Hatcher III, *Wilson's Creek: The Second Battle of the Civil War and the Men Who Fought It* (Chapel Hill: University of North Carolina Press, 2000), 223-236, 260, 270-272. Piston and Hatcher are critical of Greer's leadership in the battle. They believe Greer "bungled the attack" in the second charge. *Ibid*., 272.

69. Cutrer, *Ben McCulloch,* 245-265; Cater, *As It Was,* 91-100.

70. Tyler, *New Handbook of Texas*. 6: 945.

71. *Ibid*., 3: 339, 5: 688, 6: 110; Rose, *Ross' Texas Brigade.* 36-37; Max Lale, ed., *The Civil War Letters of David R. Garrett* (Marshall: Port Caddo Press, n.d.),1-6, 25-30. Barton Warren Stone, usually referred to as B. Warren Stone, was the ninth child of the noted evangelist Barton W. Stone. The younger Stone was himself an evangelist at one time. According to Lester N. Fitzhugh, ed., *Cannon Smoke: The Letters of Captain John J. Good, Good-Douglas Battery, CSA* (Hillsboro: Hill Junior College Press, 1971), 29n, Stone was acquainted with Jefferson Davis, who commissioned him to raise a cavalry regiment. Stone later commanded the Second Texas Partisan Rangers in Major's Cavalry Brigade. See Chapter Five for his role in this regiment.

72. Martha L. Crabb, *All Afire to Fight: The Untold Tale of the Civil War's Ninth Texas Cavalry* (New York: Avon Books, 2000), 3-14; Rose, *Ross' Texas Brigade,* 49; Sparks, *The War Between the States,* 16-17; Homer L. Kerr, ed., *Fighting With Ross' Texas Cavalry Brigade, C.S.A.: The Diary of George L. Griscom, Adjutant, 9th Texas Cavalry Regiment* (Hillsboro: Hill Junior College Press, 1976), 1-2; Sid S. Johnson, *Texans Who Wore the Gray* (Tyler: priv. printed, 1907), 117.

73. Richard Lowe, ed., *A Texas Cavalry Officer's Civil War: The Diary and Letters of James C. Bates* (Baton Rouge: Louisiana State University Press, 1999), 18-61; Crabb, *All Afire to Fight,* 17-38; Rose, *Ross' Texas Brigade,* 49-51; Kerr, ed., *Griscom Diary,* 3-11.

74. Quote, Shea and Hess, *Pea Ridge*, 99; Lale, ed., *Civil War Letters of David R. Garrett,* 49-50; Kerr, ed., Griscom Diary, 14-15; Lowe, ed., *Texas Cavalry Officer's Civil War,* 78-83; Crabb, *All Afire to Fight,* 74-80.

75. Shea and Hess, *Pea Ridge*, 113-115, 143, 210-211; Rose, *Ross' Texas Brigade,* 53-62; Hale, *Third Texas Cavalry,* 93-96; Cutrer, *Ben McCulloch,* 297-306.

76. First quote, William C. Billingsley, ed., "'Such Is War': The Confederate Memoirs of Newton Asbury Keen," *Texas Military History* 6 (Winter 1967): 251;

second quote, Cater, *As It Was*, 119; third quote, Walter P. Lane, *The Adventures and Recollections of General Walter P. Lane, A San Jacinto Veteran, Containing Sketches of the Texan, Mexican, and Late Wars, with Several Indian Fights Thrown In* (Reprint, Austin: Pemberton Press, 1970), 92; fourth quote, Shelly Morrison, ed., *Personal Civil War Letters of General Lawrence Sullivan Ross* (Austin: priv. publ., 1994), 22; fifth quote, Shea and Hess, *Pea Ridge*, 311.

77. Hale, *Third Texas Cavalry*, 115-116; Rose, *Ross' Texas Brigade*, 65; Cater, *As It Was*, 132.

78. Kerr, ed., *Griscom Diary*, 38, 200, 212-237; Rose, *Ross' Texas Brigade*, 95, 129-130; Crabb, *All Afire to Fight*, 93-97; Lowe, ed., *Texas Cavalry Officer's Civil War*, 94-97; Tyler, ed., *New Handbook of Texas*, 6: 445. Because it had twelve, rather than the ten companies normally in a regiment, the Twenty-seventh Texas was often referred to as the First Texas Legion or Whitfield's Legion; see for example, Earl J. Hess, *Banners to the Breeze: The Kentucky Campaign, Corinth, and Stones River* (Lincoln: University of Nebraska Press, 2000), 143, 168-169.

79. *Official Records*, 17, Pt. 1: 123, 128-129; Morrison, ed., *Personal Civil War Letters of Ross*, 46-47; Barron, *Lone Star Defenders*, 106-108; Rose, *Ross's Texas Brigade*, 95-96; Hale, *Third Texas Cavalry*, 127; Peter Cozzens, *The Darkest Days of the War: The Battles of Iuka & Corinth* (Chapel Hill: University of North Carolina Press, 1997), 91-92, 95-96, 99, 101-102, 106; Hess, *Banners to the Breeze*, 133-136; Bruce S. Allardice, *More Generals in Gray* (Baton Rouge: Louisiana State Univesity Press, 1995), 146, 181.

80. Hale, *Third Texas Cavalry*, 130-132; Cozzens, *Darkest Days of the War*, 105-106.

81. *Official Records*, 17, Pt. 1: 382-383; Lowe, ed., *Texas Cavalry Officer's Civil War*, 185-190; Cozzens, *Darkest Days of the War*, 266-268; Sparks, *War Between the States*, 192-195.

82. Rose, *Ross' Texas Brigade*, 73-75; Crabb, *All Afire to Fight*, 118-120; Hess, *Banners to the Breeze*, 168-169.

83. *Official Records*, 17, Pt. 1: 539, Pt. 2: 716, 718, 728, 733, 787, 844, 847; Kerr, ed., *Griscom Diary*, 48-49; Rose, *Ross' Texas Brigade*, 78-80; Johnson, *Texans Who Wore the Gray*, 268-271. Kerr, ed., *Griscom Diary*, 98n, points out that the Third, Sixth, and Twenty-seventh regiments received their horses by early November 1862, but the Ninth Texas did not get its mounts until December 8.

84. Barron, *Lone Star Defenders*, 127-131; Rose, *Ross' Texas Brigade*, 130; Hale, *Third Texas Cavalry*, 140-142.

85. Crabb, *All Afire to Fight*, 129-130; Rose, *Ross' Texas Brigade*, 133-134, provides a copy of Griffith's letter.

86. Barron, *Lone Star Defenders*, 133-136; Lowe, ed., *Texas Cavalry Officer's Civil War*, 219-222; Rose, *Ross' Texas Brigade*, 84-90; *Official Records*, 17, Pt. 1: 503, Pt. 2: 463; Billingsley, ed., "'Such Is War,'" 7 (Spring 1968): 57-58; Robert G. Hartje, *Van Dorn: The Life and Times of a Confederate General* (Nashville: Vanderbilt University Press, 1967), 255-270; J. G. Deupree, "The Capture of Holly Springs, Mississippi, Dec. 20, 1862," *Publications of the Mississippi Historical Society*, 4 (1900): 49-61.

87. Kerr, ed., *Griscom Diary*, 59-60; Ross, *Ross' Texas Brigade*, 92-94; *Official Records*, 23, Pt. 1: 116-118, 123-125.

88. *Official Records*, 24, Pt. 3: 941, 959; 30, Pt. 2: 815; 52, Pt. 2: 490, 497, 577. For more on the Whitfield-Ross controversy see Wooster, *Lone Star Generals in Gray*, 214-215.

89. Hale, *Third Texas Cavalry*, 196. The standard biography of Ross is Judith Ann Benner, *Sul Ross: Soldier, Statesman, Educator* (College Station: Texas A&M University Press, 1983). For an excellent short biography see T. Michael Parrish's introduction to *Personal Civil War Letters of Ross*, ix-xii.

90. *Official Records*, 22, Pt. 1: 326-328, 357, 365-369, 385; Barron, *Lone Star Defenders*, 182-184.

91. Kerr, ed., *Griscom Diary*, 138-140; Barron, *Lone Star Defenders*, 186-189; Lowe, ed., *Texas Cavalry Officer's Civil War*, 287-288.

92. Quote, Billingsley, ed., "'Such Is War,'" 7 (Summer 1968): 107; also quoted in Hale, *Third Texas Cavalry*, 222.

93. See Wooster, *Texas and Texans in the Civil War*, 161, 246-247.

94. *Official Records*, 38, Pt. 3: 955, 963-965; Barron, *Lone Star Defenders*, 200-204; Crabbe, *All Afire to Fight*, 231-239.

95. Barron, *Lone Star Defenders*, 205-206; Crabbe, *All Afire to Fight*, 243-250; Hale, *Third Texas Cavalry*, 234-241.

96. Kerr, ed., *Griscom Diary*; Hale, *Third Texas Cavalry*, 248-266. The brigade lost eighty-seven men in the Tennessee campaign. Lowe, ed., *Texas Cavalry Officer's Civil War*, 329.

97. Quote, Barron, *Lone Star Defenders*, 268-269; Crabbe, *All Afire to Fight*, 291-293; Hale, *Third Texas Cavalry*, 267-273; Benner, *Sul Ross*, 112-113. James C. Bates, recently promoted to lieutenant colonel, took command of the Ninth Texas while Jones directed the brigade. Lowe, ed., *Texas Cavalry Officer's Civil War*, 329-330.

CHAPTER FOUR

1. For more on John C. Moore see Wooster, *Lone Star Generals in Gray*, 198-203; Wright and Simpson, *Texas in the War, 1861-1865*, 88-89; Arthur W. Bergeron, "John Creed Moore," in *The Confederate General*, 4: 180-181.

2. Joseph E. Chance, *The Second Texas Infantry: From Shiloh to Vicksburg* (Austin: Eakin Press, 1984), 2.

3. Based upon Chance, *Second Texas Infantry*, 3-9; Charles I. Evans, "Second Texas Infantry," in Dudley G. Wooten, *A Comprehensive History of Texas, 1685 to 1897*, 2 vols. (Dallas: William G. Scarff, 1898), 1: 575-576; Henderson, *Texas in the Confederacy*, 113.

4. Evans, "Second Texas Infantry," 575.

5. Tyler, ed., *New Handbook of Texas*, 5: 665.

6. Ralph J. Smith, *Reminiscences of the Civil War and Other Sketches* (Reprint, Waco: W. M. Morrison Co., 1962), 2.

7. Henderson, *Texas in the Confederacy*, 113; Evans, "Second Texas Infantry," 577-578.

8. *Official Records*, 4: 155, 166, 169; 10, Pt. 1: 560-561; Kevin R. Young, *To the Tyrants Never Yield: A Civil War Sampler* (Plano: Wordware Publishing Co., 1992), 113-114.

9. Chance, *Second Texas Infantry*, 26-33; Evans, "Second Texas Infantry," 579-590; Sam Houston, Jr., "Shiloh Shadows," *Southwestern Historical Quarterly* (April

1931) 34: 329-333; Elizabeth Silverthorne, *Ashbel Smith of Texas* (College Station: Texas A&M University Press, 1982), 149-150; Larry J. Daniel, *Shiloh: The Battle That Changed the Civil War* (New York: Simon & Schuster, 1997), 199-200, 235-236.

10. Quote, Hardee's report, *Official Records*, 10, Pt. 1: 572.

11. Quote, Hardee's report, *Official Records*, 10, Pt. 1: 572; Daniel, *Shiloh*, 273.

12. Moore's report, *Official Records*, 10, Pt. 1: 563-564; first quote, Chance, *Second Texas Infantry*, 37; second quote, Young, *To the Tyrants Never Yield*, 116.

13. Chance, *Second Texas Infantry*, 37-41; Silverthorne, *Ashbel Smith*, 150-151; John Hoyt Williams, *Sam Houston: A Biography of the Father of Texas* (New York: Simon & Schuster, 1993), 354-355.

14. *Official Records*, 10, Pt. 1: 503, 789, Pt. 2: 549; Chance, *Second Texas Infantry*, 48-49.

15. Quote, Chance, *Second Texas Infantry*, 49; Eleanor D. Pace, ed., "The Diary and Letters of William P. Rogers, 1846-1862," *Southwestern Historical Quarterly* 32 (April 1929): 289-290.

16. Chance, *Second Texas Infantry*, 99-103; Cozzens, *Darkest Days of the War*, 74-126.

17. *Official Records*, 17, Pt. 1: 136-137; Cozzens, *Darkest Days of the War*, 131.

18. Albert Castel, *General Sterling Price and the Civil War in the West* (Baton Rouge: Louisiana State University Press, 1968), 106-107; Hess, *Banners to the Breeze*, 141-142.

19. Robert G. Hartje, *Van Dorn: The Life and Times of a Confederate General* (Nashville: Vanderbilt University Press, 1967), 214-226; Cozzens, *Darkest Days*, 135-159; Hess, *Banners to the Breeze*, 142-143.

20. Chance, *Second Texas Infantry*, 66-71; Cozzens, *Darkest Days*, 160-193.

21. *Official Records*, 17, Pt. 1: 393-400; Evans, "Second Texas Infantry," 588, 608; Pace, ed., "Diary and Letters of William P. Rogers," 198-299; Young, *To the Tyrants Never Yield*, 73-76; Hess, *Banners to the Breeze*, 154-166. Cozzens, *Darkest Days*, 355n, points out there are numerous versions of Rogers' death. Some sources say he was on horseback carrying the flag when hit; others say he was on the parapet of Battery Robinett on foot, waving his handkerchief, sword, or pistol; while some describe him as dismounted in the ditch. For Cozzens' view see *Darkest Days*, 260-265.

22. *Official Records*, 17, Pt. 1: 382-385, 395-397; Cozzens, *Darkest Days*, 305-306; Chance, *Second Texas Infantry*, 76-77.

23. Chance, *Second Texas Infantry*, 85-86; Silverthorne, *Ashbel Smith*, 152.

24. Quote, Lee, *Official Records*, 17, Pt. 1: 684-685; Herman Hattaway, *General Stephen D. Lee* (Jackson: University Press of Mississippi, 1976), 75.

25. *Official Records*, 24, Pt. 1: 415-417; Silverthorne, *Ashbel Smith*, 153.

26. Silverthorne, *Ashbel Smith*, 155-156; Chance, *Second Texas Infantry*, 102-112; *Official Records*, 24, Pt. 2: 384-394; James R. Arnold, *Grant Wins the War: Decision at Vicksburg* (New York: John Wiley & Sons, 1997), 246-255.

27. In his report Ashbel Smith listed thirty-eight killed, seventy-three wounded, and fifteen missing in the Vicksburg campaign. *Official Records*, 24, Pt. 2: 394; Silverthorne, *Ashbel Smith*, 157-159. For a description of the siege by a lieutenant in the Second Texas Infantry see Walter H. Mays, ed., "The Vicksburg Diary of M. K. Simons, 1863," *Texas Military History* 5 (Spring 1965): 30-35.

28. Quote, Ralph Smith, *Reminiscences of the Civil War,* 30.

29. *Official Records*, 34, Pt. 2: 904, 932, 1040, Pt. 3: 753, 800, 834, Pt. 4: 638, 701; 48, Pt. 1: 1355, 1408, Pt. 3: 438.

30. Silverthorne, *Ashbel Smith,* 162-163; Ralph Smith, *Reminiscences of the Civil War,* 32-37; Edward T. Cotham, Jr., *Battle on the Bay: The Civil War Struggle for Galveston* (Austin: University of Texas Press, 1988), 177-178.

31. Tyler, ed., *New Handbook of Texas*, 6: 852; Lester N. Fitzhugh, *Texas Batteries, Battalions, Regiments, Commanders and Field Officers, Confederate States Army, 1861-1865* (Midlothian, TX: Mirror Press, 1958), 33.

32. Tyler, ed., *New Handbook of Texas*, 6: 852; Laura Simmons, "Waul's Legion from Texas to Mississippi," *Texana* 7 (Spring 1969): 2-3.

33. Based upon examination of data included in the roster of Waul's Legion in Robert A. Hasskarl and Leif R. Hasskarl, *Waul's Texas Legion, 1862-1865* (Ada, OK: priv. publ., 1985), 119-189. This roster provides rank, name, organization, and residence for 1,350 members of the Legion. Birthplace, age, and marital status is provided for many of those listed.

34. Hasskarl and Hasskarl, *Waul's Texas Legion,* 2-5; Simmons, "Waul's Legion from Texas to Mississippi," 4-5.

35. *Official Records*, 15: 794-795; 17, Pt. 2: 711-712, 52, pt. 2: 334; Tyler, ed., *New Handbook of Texas*, 6: 852; Simmons, "Waul's Legion from Texas to Mississippi," 5-12. A diary kept (in German) by one of Waul's soldiers, Siebert Behrens, chronciled the journey from Central Texas to Holly Springs and Grenada. According to Behrens' diary the Legion marched through Fairfield, Palestine, Rusk, and Shreveport. From Shreveport they traveled across northern Louisiana and western Mississippi by train and foot, reaching Holly Springs on October 10. They were in the Grenada area from December 9-January 5. Translated transcript of MSS Diary of Siebert Behrens, 1862-1863, pp. 1-9, in possession of Behrens' great-grandson, Dr. Kevin Smith, Beaumont, Texas.

36. *Official Records*, 24, Pt. 1: 416, Pt. 3: 602, 640, 682; Hasskarl and Hasskarl, *Waul's Texas Legion,* 16-21; Behrens Diary, 10-12.

37. *Official Records*, 24, Pt. 2: 365, Pt. 3: 774, 830, 852; Behrens Diary, 17-18; Hattaway, *General Stephen D. Lee,* 86-88; Arnold, *Grant Wins the War,* 154-158, 170-183.

38. *Official Records*, 24, Pt. 1: 271-273, Pt. 2: 350-351, 367; Behrens Diary, 20-22.

39. *Official Records*, 24, Pt. 2: 357-358; Hasskarl and Hasskarl, *Waul's Texas Legion,* 23-29; Hattaway, *General Stephen D. Lee*, 93-94; Arnold *Grant Wins the War,* 250-258; Simmons, "Waul's Legion from Texas to Mississippi," 14-15; Wayne Flynt, "The Texas Legion at Vicksburg," *East Texas Historical Journal* 17 (Spring 1979): 60-67.

40. Arnold, *Grant Wins the War,* 272-273.

41. Hattaway, *General Stephen D. Lee,* 94-98; *Official Records*, 24, Pt. 3: 979.

42. The Milliken's Bend expedition will be discussed in Chapter Six. See also Terrence J. Winschel, "To Rescue Gibraltrar: John Walker's Texas Division and Its Expedition to Relieve Vicksburg," *Civil War Regiments* 3 (No. 3, 1994): 33-51; James M. McPherson, *Battle Cry for Freedom: The Civil War Era* (New York: Oxford University Press, 1988), 634-635; J. P. Blessington, *The Campaigns of Walker's Texas Division* (Reprint, Austin: State House Press, 1994), 95-109.

43. Quote, Stephen D. Lee report, *Official Records*, 24, Pt. 2: 357. See also 325-329, 350-351, 358.

44. The cavalry battalion was still referred to as "Waul's Legion" in the *Official Records* on occasion but more often it was listed under "Willis's (Texas) Battalion." *Official Records*, 24, Pt. 3: 934; 31, Pt. 3: 590, 728, 865; 32, Pt. 3: 594, 605; 39, Pt. 1: 325, Pt. 2: 631, 648, 717, 805. Robert A. Hasskarl and Leif R. Hasskarl, *Waul's Texas Legion,* 101-115, list all the campaigns and battles of Willis' cavalry.

45. In their accounts of the affair Lt. Col. Creasman and naval Capt. Isaac N. Brown were highly critical of Voight. *Official Records*, 24, Pt. 2: 671-672. Information on the whole episode is sketchy. In his report, *Official Records*, 24, Pt. 2: 668-669, Maj. Gen. Herron stated that 300 enlisted men and eight commissioned officers were taken prisoner, but in their study of the Legion the Hasskarls state that "a total of 46 men who belonged to infantry Co. C of Waul's Legion were captured in the engagement." *Waul's Texas Legion,* 34. They believe no other Confederates were captured at Yazoo City.

46. *Official Records*, 24, Pt. 2: 249-250, 407, 425; Series II, 6: 280, 296; Hasskarl and Hasskarl, *Waul's Texas Legion,* 30-31, 53-55.

47. *Official Records*, 30, Pt. 3: 753, 796; 34, Pt. 3: 806, 807, 812.

48. *Ibid*., 34, Pt. 4: 638; 41, Pt. 3: 965; 48, Pt. 1: 1408, Pt. 2: 1288.

49. *Ibid*., 48, Pt. 2: 1288; Hasskarl and Hasskarl, *Waul's Texas Legion,* 59.

50. *Official Records*, 16, Pt. 2: 984; 20, Pt. 1: 660, Pt. 2: 413; 23: 655; 30, Pt. 2: 14.

51. *Ibid*., 4: 85; Jon H. Harrison, "Tenth Texas Cavalry, C.S.A.," *Military History of Texas and the Southwest* 12 (No. 2): 93-96.

52. Back in Texas, Johnson helped supervise blockade runners bringing vital supplies to Texas. Tyler, ed., *New Handbook of Texas*, 3: 959-960; Oates, *Confederate Cavalry West of the River,* 37.

53. To add to the confusion, the Fifteenth Texas Cavalry (commanded by George H. Sweet) was sometimes called the Thirty-second Cavalry. Another regiment, Peter Woods' Thirty-sixth Texas Cavalry, was also sometimes called the Thirty-second Cavalry. Sifakis, *Compendium of Confederate Armies: Texas,* 72-73, 88-90; Wright and Simpson, *Texas in the War*, 121.

54. Quote, Kirby Smith, *Official Records*, 16, Pt. 1: 934; McDonough, *War in Kentucky,* 134-145; Hess, *Banners to the Breeze,* 39-41; Harrison, "Tenth Texas Cavalry, C.S.A.," 99-102.

55. *The Confederate General,* 2: 95; Tyler, ed., *New Handbook of Texas*, 3: 922.

56. *The Confederate General,* 2: 94-95; Tyler, ed., *New Handbook of Texas*, 2: 120; 8: 29, 299; 16: 934, 942.

57. *Official Records*, 20, Pt. 1: 680-681, 926-930; Harrison, "Tenth Texas Cavalry, C.S.A.," 103-107; McDonough, *Stones River*, 86-91; Hess, *Banners to the Breeze,* 199-200, 202-203, 208.

58. *Official Records*, 23, Pt. 2: 613; Harrison, "Tenth Texas Cavalry, C.S.A.," 172.

59. Louise Horton, *Samuel Bell Maxey: A Biography* (Austin: University of Texas Press, 1974), 19-23; *Official Records*, 52, Pt. 2: 237. The most complete history of the Ninth Texas Infantry is that by Tim Bell on the 9th Texas Infantry website.

60. Horton, *Samuel Bell Maxey*, 27.

61. *Official Records*, 52, Pt. 1: 37.

62. *Official Records*, 10, Pt. 1: 508-509; Wiley Sword, *Shiloh: Bloody April* (New York: William Morrow & Co., 1974), 184-185, 292-293, 320-321. The location of the Ninth Infantry is shown on the excellent maps on pages 165, 181, 187, 205, 234, 247, in Larry J. Daniel's *Shiloh: The Battle That Changed the War.*

63. *Official Records*, 10, Pt. 1: 510-511.

64. *The Confederate General,* 6: 172.

65. *Official Records*, 17, Pt. 1: 934, 1108-1109, Pt. 2: 603, 643; Horton, *Samuel Bell Maxey,* 30-31. The Ninth Texas lost only one man (Capt. John Lane of Company F) in the battle of Perryville. The most complete account of Perryville, Kenneth A. Hafendorfer, *Perryville: Battle for Kentucky* (Louisville: K H Press, 1991), fails to mention the Ninth Texas in the 443-page text. The regiment is listed in the Appendix showing units involved in the battle.

66. *Official Records*, 20, Pt. 1: 677, 706, 709, 744-749, 749-750; McDonough, *Stones River,* 88-106; Hess, *Banners to the Breeze,* 204-205; Welsh, *Medical Histories of Confederate Generals,* 242. In his report Col. Alfred J. Vaughan, Jr., who commanded Smith's Brigade in the battle, praised Young for leading the attack "in most gallant style" and seizing "the colors of his regiment in one of its gallant charges . . ." *Official Records*, 20, Pt. 1: 745.

67. *Official Records*, 24, Pt. 1: 222; Pt. 3: 889, 925, 1041.

68. Sifakis, *Compendium of Confederate Armies: North Carolina,* 127; Warner, *Generals in Gray,* 313-314.

69. *Official Records*, 30, Pt. 2: 239-243, 247-250, 524; Steven E. Woodworth, *A Deep Steady Thunder: The Battle of Chickamauga* (Abilene: McWhiney Foundation Press, 1998), 33-44; Cozzens, *This Terrible Sound: The Battle of Chickamauga* (Urbana: University of Illinois Press, 1992), 128-138; Willis, *A Battle from the Start,* 116; Robert Selph Henry, *"First With the Most" Forrest* (Indianapolis: Bobbs-Merrill, 1941), 332; Mark W. Johnson, "Holding the Left of the Line: The Brigade of United States Regulars at Chickamauga," *Civil War Regiments* 7 (No. 1, 2000): 48-49.

70. *Official Records*, 30, Pt. 2: 239-240, 243, 244-247; Woodworth, *A Deep Steady Thunder,* 97-98; Welsh, *Medical History of Confederate Generals,* 60.

71. *Official Records*, 30, Pt. 4: 648; 31, Pt. 3: 228, 573, 726; 32, Pt. 2: 534, 701, 721, 724, 730; Andrew J. Fogle to Miss [Lou], March 7, 1864, in Andrew J. Fogle Papers, University of Texas Archives. The inspector general's report on May 2 indicated Ector's Brigade "was poorly armed and not well clothed, but still presented a most soldierly appearance." *Official Records*, 34, Pt. 2: 569.

72. Sifakis, *Compendium of Confederate Armies: North Carolina,* 139-140.

73. *Official Records*, 38, Pt. 3: 908; Albert Castel, *Decision in the West: The Atlanta Campaign of 1864* (Lawrence: University Press of Kansas, 1992), 221-226, 285-287; William R. Scaife, *The Campaign for Atlanta* (Atlanta: priv. publ., 1990), 38-42.

74. Scaife, *Campaign for Atlanta,* 48; *Official Records*, 38, Pt. 3: 908.

75. *Official Records*, 38, Pt. 3: 904, 909-910; Judy Watson McClure, *Confederate From East Texas: The Civil War Letters of James Monroe Watson* (Quannah, TX: Nortex Press, 1976), 299.

76. Scaife, *Campaign for Atlanta,* 97-103; Evans, ed., *Confederate Military History,* 11: 188-189; *Official Records*, 39, Pt. 1: 760-766, 816-819, 822-823;

Harrison, "Tenth Texas Cavalry, C.S.A.," 173-178; Fred L. Brown, "The Battle of Allatoona," *Civil War History* 6 (September 1960): 277-297; Sam Davis Elliott, *Soldier of Tennessee: General Alexander P. Stewart and the Civil War in the West* (Baton Rouge: Louisiana State University Press, 1999), 219-222.

77. Welsh, *Medical Histories of Confederate Generals,* 243; Hugh H. Young, "Two Texas Patriots," *Southwestern Historical Quarterly* 44 (July 1940): 24-25. Johnson's Island Military Prison was in Lake Erie near Sandusky, Ohio. According to Lonnie R. Speer, *Portrals to Hell: Military Prisons of the Civil War* (Chambersburg, PA: Stackpole Books, 1997), 77-78, the prison held between 600 and 2,000 inmates. For more on the prison see Edward T. Downer, "Johnson's Island," *Civil War History* 8 (June 1962): 202-217.

78. Evans, *Confederate Military History,* 11: 188-189; *Official Records*, 39, Pt. 1: 815-820, 821-824.

79. *Official Records*, 45, Pt. 1: 666, 687.

80. *Ibid.*, 45, Pt. 1: 708; Elliott, *Soldier of Tennessee,* 242-243. Several sources incorrectly indicate the brigade was in the battle at Franklin. Stanley F. Horn in his excellent *The Decisive Battle of Nashville* (Baton Rouge: Louisiana State University Press, 1956), 40, in describing Ector's Brigade on the eve of the battle of Nashville, states "the brigade had suffered severely at Franklin, being now reduced to 700 men. . . ."

81. Colonel Coleman, quoted in Horn, *Decisive Battle of Nashville,* 105, and Wiley Sword, *The Confederacy's Last Hurrah: Spring Hill, Franklin, and Nashville* (Lawrence: University Press of Kansas, 1993), 341-343.

82. McMurry, *John Bell Hood and the War for Southern Independence,* 179; *Official Records*, 45, Pt. 1: 709-712; Sword, *Confederacy's Last Hurrah,* 324-325, 369-374; Horn, *Decisive Battle of Nashville,* 108-153; Elliott, *Soldier of Tennessee,* 248-252.

83. *Official Records*, 45, Pt. 1: 730, 771-772; Sword, *Confederacy's Last Hurrah*, 407-421.

84. Chester G. Hearn, *Mobile Bay and the Mobile Campaign: The Last Great Battles of the Civil War* (Jefferson, NC: McFarland & Co., 1993), 158-177; Noah Andre Trudeau, *Out of the Storm: The End of the Civil War, April-June 1865* (Boston: Little, Brown and Co., 1994), 175-178; *Official Records*, 49, Pt. 1: 313-318, Pt. 2: 1184-1187, 1218.

85. Hearn, *Mobile Bay and the Mobile Campaign,* 107-208.

86. James M. McCaffrey, *This Band of Heroes: Granbury's Texas Brigade,* C.S.A. (Originally published, Austin: Eakin Press, 1985; Reprint, College Station: Texas A&M University Press, 1996), 1.

87. *Ibid.*, 4; Sifakis, *Compendium of Confederate Armies: Texas,* 72, 74-76, 80-82.

88. Charles D. Spurlin, ed., *The Civil War Diary of Charles A. Leuschner* (Austin: Eakin Press, 1992), 2-3.

89. First quote, Jim Turner, "Jim Turner, Co. G, 6th Texas Infantry, C.S.A., From 1861-1865," *Texana* 12 (No. 2, 1974): 152; second quote, "Recollections of William J. Oliphant," manuscript, Austin Public Library, 32-33, published in Spurlin, ed., *Diary of Charles A. Leuschner,* 6. Training was briefly interrupted in December 1861 when four companies were dispatched to Matagorda Island to support Confederate forces there against a possible Union attack.

90. Spurlin, ed., *Diary of Charles A. Leuschner,* 7-8.

91. According to the roster of personnel in McCaffrey, *This Band of Heroes,* 224, nineteen members of Company G, Twenty-fourth Texas Cavalry, were Indians. See also Anne J. Bailey, *Between the Enemy and Texas: Parsons's Texs Cavalry in the Civil War* (Fort Worth: Texas Christian University Press, 1989), 18-25; Norman D. Brown, ed., *One of Cleburne's Command: The Civil War Reminiscences and Diary of Capt. Samuel T. Foster, Granbury's Texas Brigade* (Austin: University of Texas Press, 1980), xxxviii-xlv.

92. There is no mention of the lances after reaching Arkansas. Norman Brown, ed., *One of Cleburne's Command,* xlii, notes "no more was heard of the lances, so presumably they were left behind [in Texas]."

93. Spurlin, ed., *Diary of Charles Leuschner,* 8-9; McCaffrey, *This Band of Heroes,* 9-10.

94. McCaffrey, *This Band of Heroes,* 28-30; Spurlin, ed., *Diary of Charles Leuschner,* 8-10.

95. Wooster, *Lone Star Generals in Gray*, 120.

96. McCaffrey, *This Band of Heroes,* 10-11; Harold B. Simpson, ed., *The Bugle Softly Blows: The Confederate Diary of Benjamin M. Seaton* (Waco: Texian Press, 1965), ix. Muster rolls for the Tenth Texas are in McCaffrey, *This Band of Heroes,* 189-196. There is an excellent website for the Tenth Texas Infantry prepared by Scott McKay.

97. *Official Records*, 13: 36.

98. McCaffrey, *This Band of Heroes,* 12-14.

99. *Ibid*., 14-18; Tyler, ed., *New Handbook of Texas*, 2: 512; 3: 561; 4: 819; 6: 171. Colonel Moore of the Seventeenth Texas resigned his commission in 1862 when appointed to the Texas Supreme Court. Capt. James Taylor was elected to succeed him as regimental commander.

100. Quote, McCaffrey, *This Band of Heroes*, 24. For more on the battle at Cotton Plant see Bailey, *Between the Enemy and Texas*, 67-73, and William L. Shea, "The Confederate Defeat at Cache River," *Arkansas Historical Quarterly* 52 (Summer 1993): 129-155.

101. Brown, ed., *One of Cleburne's Command,* xxxv.

102. First quote, Austin *Weekly Texas Gazette,* October 22, 1862, published in Brown, ed., *One of Cleburne's Command,* xxxvi; second quote, *Official Records*, 13: 887.

103. *The Confederate General,* 2: 66-67; Simpson, ed., *The Bugle Slowly Blows,* 27-28; Charleen Plumly Pollard, ed., "Civil War Letters of George W. Allen," *Southwestern Historical Quarterly* 83 (July 1979): 51-52.

104. First quote, Jim Turner, "Jim Turner, Co. G, 6th Texas Infantry," 144; second quote, Joe R. Wise, ed., "Letters of Lt. Flavius W. Perry, 17th Cavalry — 1862-1863," *Military History of Texas and the Southwest* 13 (No. 2, 1976): 27. See also Maury Darst, "Robert Hodges, Jr.: Confederate Soldier," *East Texas Historical Journal* 9 (March 1971): 33-34.

105. *Official Records*, 17, Pt. 1: 781-785; Brown, ed., *One of Cleburne's Command,* 14-22; Gilbert Cuthberston, "Coller of the Sixth Texas: Correspondence of a Texas Infantry Man, 1861-64," *Military History of Texas and the Southwest* 9 (No. 2, 1972): 133-135; Norman C. Delaney, "Diary and Memoirs of

Marshall Samuel Pierson, Company C, 17th Regt., Texas Cavalry, 1862-1865," *Military History of Texas and the Southwest* 13 (No. 3, 1976): 27-28; W. W. Heartsill, *Fourteen Hundred and 91 Days in the Confederate Army,* ed. Bell I. Wiley (reprint, Jackson, TN: McCowat-Mercer Press, 1953), 89-97; Arthur Marvin Shaw, ed., "A Texas Ranger Company at Arkansas Post," *Arkansas Historical Quarterly* 9 (Winter 1951): 289-294; Thomas A. DeBlack, "1863: 'We Must Stand or Fall Alone,'" in Mark E. Christ, ed., *Rugged and Sublime: The Civil War in Arkansas* (Fayetteville: University of Arkansas Press, 1994), 59-65. A detailed account of the struggle for Arkansas Post is Edwin C. Bearrs, "The Battle of the Post of Arkansas," *Arkansas Historical Quarterly* 18 (Autumn 1959): 237-279. For the unsuccessful efforts to reinforce the garrison see Anne J. Bailey, "The Texas Cavalry's Race to Reinforce Arkansas Post, 1863," *East Texas Historical Journal* 28 (Spring 1990): 45-56.

106. *Official Records*, 17, Pt. 1: 781-785, 790-796; Delaney, ed., "Diary and Memoirs of Marshall Samuel Pierson," 28-29. McCaffrey, *This Band of Heroes*, 175, notes that not all the Texans assigned to Arkansas Post were taken prisoner. Some were on sick leave, some were detailed elsewhere, and some escaped during the confusion. These men were later brought together in the Seventeenth Consolidated Regiment. This regiment is discussed in Chapter Six.

107. Spurlin, ed., *Civil War Diary of Charles A. Leuschner,* 12. For Garland's appeals see *Official Records*, 17, Pt. 1: 786-790. See also Steven E. Woodworth, "The Scapegoat of Arkansas Post," *The Quarterly Journal of Military History* 13 (Spring 2001): 58-67.

108. Quote, Brown, ed., *One of Cleburne's Command,* 20; Turner, "Jim Turner, Co. G, 6th Texas Infantry," 159; Wise, ed., "Letters of Lt. Falvius W. Perry," 31-33; Cuthberston, "Coller of the Sixth," 135; Simpson, ed., *The Bugle Softly Blows,* 32.

109. *Official Records*, 23, Pt. 2: 442; McCaffrey, *This Band of Heroes*, 60-62.

110. Quote, Brown, ed., *One of Cleburne's Command,* 43. See also Daniel, *Soldiering in the Army of Tennessee,* 3-4, and Craig L. Symonds, *Stonewall of the West: Patrick Cleburne & the Civil War* (Lawrence: University Press of Kansas, 1997), 128.

111. Turner, "Jim Turner, Co. G, 6th Texas Infantry," 162.

112. McCaffrey, *This Band of Heroes*, 70-71; Spurlin, ed., *Diary of Charles A. Leuschner,* 120.

113. *Official Records*, 30, Pt. 2: 187-195; Symonds, *Stonewall of the West,* 147-151.

114. *Official Records*, 30, Pt. 2: 189, 194-195; McCaffrey, *This Band of Heroes*, 79.

115. James Argyle Smith was a native Tennessean whose family moved to Mississippi. He graduated from West Point in 1853 and served on the frontier in the 1850s. He was a veteran of Shiloh, Perryville, and Chickamauga. *The Confederate General,* 5: 176-177.

116. The fifteen counties from which troops were drawn were Anderson, Cass, Cherokee, Freestone, Harrison, Henderson, Kaufman, Limestone, McLennan, Panola, Rusk, Smith, Titus, Upshur, and Wood. Data concerning characteristics of the members of the Seventh Texas is taken from James Lynn Newsom, "Intrepid Gray Warriors: The 7th Texas Infantry, 1861-1865" (Ph.D. dissertation, Texas Christian University, 1995), 5-12.

117. *Ibid.*, 16-29.

118. *Ibid.*, 31-38. There is still some debate over the exact number of Confederates surrendered. The figure given above is taken from Benjamin Franklin Cooling, *Forts Henry and Donelson: The Key to the Confederate Heartland* (Knoxville: University of Tennessee Press, 1987), 216. General Buckner estimated the number between 12,000 and 15,000.

119. Newsom, "Intrepid Gray Warriors," 48-63.

120. *Official Records*, 24, Pt. 3: 800-801; Lawrence L. Hewitt, *Port Hudson: Confederate Bastion on the Mississippi* (Baton Rouge: Louisiana State University Press, 1987), 62; Newsom, "Intrepid Gray Warriors," 59-65, 75-78; Stephen E. Ambrose, "Struggle for Vicksburg," in *Americans at War* (Jackson: University Press of Mississippi, 1997), 18-45.

121. *Official Records*, 24, Pt. 1: 737-739, 747-748; Newsom, "Intrepid Gray Warriors," 78-79.

122. *Official Records*, 30, Pt. 2: 456-458; Heartsill, *Fourteen Hundred and 91 Days,* 151-155; Newsom, "Intrepid Gray Warriors," 108-117; Cozzens, *This Terrible Sound,* 199-201, 233, 259-262. Lt. Col W. L. Moody of the Seventh Texas was seriously wounded in fighting in Mississippi and was no longer with the regiment. Tyler, ed., *New Handbook of Texas*, 4: 813.

123. *Official Records*, 31, Pt. 2: 748-753; Spurlin, ed., *Civil War Diary of Charles A. Leuschner,* 23-26; Pvt. Isaiah Hughes to mother, March 23, 1864, on Tenth Infantry website; Steven E. Woodworth, *Six Armies in Tennessee: The Chickamauga and Chattanooga Campaigns* (Lincoln: University of Nebraska Press, 1998), 184-185, 191-193; Symonds, *Stonewall of the West*, 166-169; Wiley Sword, *Mountains Touched with Fire: Chattanooga Besieged, 1863* (New York: St. Martin's Press, 1995), 243-244, 246-247; Michael A. Hughes, "The Battle for Missionary Ridge, November 25, 1863," *Civil War Regiments* 7 (No. 1, 2000): 6-8; Craig Symonds, "'Stonewall' of the West: Pat Cleburne and the Defense of Tunnel Hill," *ibid.*, 75-88.

124. *Official Records*, 31, Pt. 2: 773-775.

125. *Ibid.*, 32, Pt. 2: 867. McCaffrey, *This Band of Heroes*, 99. James L. Newsom, "Intrepid Gray Warriors," 131-132, notes that Maj. K. M. Van Zandt, who should have succeeded Granbury as commander of the Seventh Texas, had returned to Texas because of illness and remained in the Trans Mississippi Department.

126. Quote, *Official Records*, 38, Pt. 3: 746. Castel, *Decision in the West*, 134-135, 229-241; McCaffrey, *This Band of Heroes*, 106-110.

127. First quote, Brown, ed., *One of Cleburne's Command,* 159; second quote, Bill O'Neal, ed., "The Civil War Memoirs of Samuel Alonza Cooke," *Southwestern Historical Quarterly* 74 (April 1971): 543. Hosea Garrett, color bearer, Co. G, Tenth Infantry, agreed "the men had utmost confidence in Genl. Johnston." Tenth Infantry website.

128. Quote, Brig. Gen. James Smith, *Official Records*, 38, Pt. 3: 746; Turner, "Jim Turner, Co. G, 6th Texas Infantry," 172-179; McCaffrey, *This Band of Heroes*, 114-120; Brown, ed., *One of Cleburne's Command,* 109-110; Irving Buck, *Cleburne and His Command* (1908, reprint; Jackson, TN: McCowat-Mercer Press, 1959), 213-214.

129. *Official Records*, 38, Pt. 3: 545-546, 564-569, 731-732, 747-754; Spurlin, ed., *Civil War Diary of Charles A. Leuschner,* 48; Castel, *Decision in the West,* 385-414; Brown, ed., *One of Cleburne's Command,* 110-112.

130. Granbury quote, Symonds, *Stonewall of the West,* 237.

131. *Official Records*, 45, Pt. 1: 684-685, 707-708; Brown, ed., *One of Cleburne's Command,* 147-151; James Lee McDonough and Thomas L. Connelly, *Five Tragic Hours: The Battle of Franklin* (Knoxville: University of Tennessee Press, 1983), 92-168.

132. *Official Records*, 45, Pt. 1: 709-710; Horn, *Decisive Battle of Nashville,* 92-96; Newsom, "Intrepid Gray Warriors," 157-158.

133. McCaffrey, *This Band of Heroes*, 148-153; Brown, ed., *One of Cleburne's Command,* 163.

134. McCaffrey, *This Band of Heroes*, 154-156. In Appendix C, 177-235, McCaffrey provides a roster of all the men who served in the regiments that made up the brigade. In this roster he has an asterisk (*) by the name of each soldier who was present with his command at the time of the surrender on April 26, 1865. A hand count enumerates 387 such individuals. The Tenth Infantry with seventy-eight individuals had the highest number; the Twenty-fifth Cavalry with thirty individuals had the lowest number. Four companies had no individuals at the time of the surrender. Company G, Tenth Infantry, and Company D, Sixth Infantry, had the highest number of men still present, fourteen in each company.

135. First quote, Brown, ed., *One of Cleburne's Command,* 169; second quote, 173.

Chapter Five

1. For Sibley's biography see Jerry Thompson, *Confederate General of the West: Henry Hopkins Sibley* (Natchitoches: Northwestern State University Press, 1987; republished, College Station: Texas A&M University Press, 1996).

2. There has been much speculation about Sibley's plans and motives. Capt. Trevanion T. Teel, an artillery officer who served with Sibley, later wrote that Sibley had told him his ultimate goal was the conquest of California and the annexation of northern Mexico. T. T. Teel, "Sibley's New Mexico Campaign—Its Objects and Cause of Its Failure," *Battles & Leaders,* 2:700. Jerry Thompson, *Confederate General of the West,* 219, points out that while the seizure of California was not specifically mentioned in Sibley's orders "there was little doubt that it was the eventual objective of the impending campaign." Martin Hall, *Sibley's New Mexico Campaign* (Austin: University of Texas Press, 1960), 32, states that while Sibley may have planned to move into California there is no record of it. For other views see Donald S. Frazier, *Blood & Treasure: Confederate Empire in the Southwest* (College Station: Texas A&M University Press, 1995), 3-4, 75; Don E. Alberts, *The Battle of Glorieta: Union Victory in the West* (College Station: Texas A&M University Press, 1998), 7-8; W. H. Watford, "Confederate Western Ambitions," *Southwestern Historical Quarterly* 44 (October 1940): 161-187; and Jason H. Silverman, "Confederate Ambitions for the Southwest: A New Perspective," *Red River Valley Historical Review* 4 (Winter 1979): 62-71.

3. *Official Records*, 4: 5-20; Jerry Don Thompson, *Colonel John Robert Baylor: Texas Indian Fighter and Confederate Soldier* (Hillsboro, TX: Hill Junior

College Press, 1971), 45-46. The role of the Second Mounted Rifles, or Second Cavalry, will be discussed more fully later in this chapter.

4. Biographical data for these and other regimental officers of Sibley's Brigade has been taken from Frazier, *Blood & Treasure,* 78-83, 97-99; Martin H. Hall, *The Confederate Army of New Mexico* (Austin: Presidial Press, 1978), 53-54, 133-134, 217-218; Hall, *Sibley's New Mexico Campaign,* 35-36; Warner, *Generals in Gray,* 117-118, 270-271, 289-290; Tyler, ed., *New Handbook of Texas*, 1: 332; 3: 316-317; 5: 520-521, 946; 6: 79, 159; and Wooster, *Lone Star Generals in Gray*, 95-113, 158-166.

5. Frazier, *Blood & Treasure,* 80.

6. *Ibid.*, 86. Muster rolls of the three regiments may be found in Hall, *Sibley's New Mexico Campaign,* 235-304.

7. Thompson, *Confederate General of the West,* 226-230; Don E. Alberts, ed., *Rebels on the Rio Grande: The Civil War Journal of A. B. Peticolas* (Albuquerque, NM: Merit Press, 1993), 20-22; Hall, *Sibley's New Mexico Campaign,* 39-44; Theophilus Noel, *A Campaign From Santa Fe to the Mississippi* (Shreveport, LA: Shreveport News, 1865), 7-9.

8. *Official Records*, 4: 90, Noel, *Campaign From Santa Fe to the Mississippi,* 9-11; Frazier, *Blood & Treasure,* 121-131; Hall, *Sibley's New Mexico Campaign,* 45-47; Martin H. Hall, "The Formation of Sibley's Brigade and the March to New Mexico," *Southwestern Historical Quarterly* 61 (January 1958): 401-403; Oscar Haas (trans.), "The Diary of Julius Giesecke, 1861-1862," *Texas Military History* 3 (Winter 1963): 229-232; Michael L. Tate, ed., "A Johnny Reb in Sibley's New Mexico Campaign: Reminiscences of Pvt. Henry C. Wright, 1861-1862," *East Texas Historical Journal* 25 (Fall 1987): 23-24.

9. Frazier, *Blood & Treasure,* 135-149. For more on Canby see Max C. Heyman, Jr., *Prudent Soldier: A Biography of Major General E. R. S. Canby, 1817-1873* (Glendale, CA: The Arthur H. Clark Company, 1959).

10. The most complete account of the battle is John Taylor, *Bloody Valverde: A Civil War Battle on the Rio Grande, February 21, 1862* (Albuquerque: University of New Mexico Press, 1995). See also Alberts, ed., *Rebels on the Rio Grande,* 41-49; George H. Pettis, "The Confederate Invasion of New Mexico and Arizona," *Battles & Leaders* 2: 106-108; David P. Perrine, "The Battle of Valverde, New Mexico Territory, February 21, 1862," *Journal of the West* 19 (October 1980): 26-38; Alwyn Barr, ed., *Charles Porter's Account of the Confederate Attempt to Seize Arizona and New Mexico* (Austin: Pemberton Press, 1968), 14-16; David Gracy, II, ed., "New Mexico Campaign Letters of Frank Starr, 1861-1862," *Texas Military History* 4 (Fall 1964): 172-175.

11. Quote, Frazier, *Blood & Treasure,* 178.

12. Jerry D. Thompson, ed., *Westward the Texans: The Civil War Journal of Private William Randolph Howell* (El Paso: Texas Western Press, 1990), 5.

13. Alberts, *Battle of Glorieta,* 14-22, 48-68; Thomas E. Edrington and John Taylor, *The Battle of Glorieta Pass: A Gettysburg in the West, March 26-28, 1862* (Albuquerque, NM: University of New Mexico Press, 1998), 41-55.

14. *Official Records*, 9: 530-545; Alberts, *Battle of Glorieta,* 74-150; Edrington and Taylor, *Battle of Glorieta Pass,* 57-100; J. F. Santee, "The Battle of La Glorieta Pass," *New Mexico Historical Review* 6 (January 1931): 66-75; David

Westphall, "The Battle of Glorieta Pass: Its Importance in the Civil War," *ibid.*, 44 (April 1969): 144-150; Gracy, ed., "New Mexico Campaign Letters of Frank Starr," 177-178; Terry L. Jordan-Bychkov, et al., "The Boesel Letters: Two Texas Germans in Sibley's Brigade," *Southwestern Historical Quarterly* 102 (April 1999): 467.

15. Frazier, *Blood & Treasure,* 239-240; Thompson, *Confederate General of the West,* 292-293.

16. Quote, Thompson, *Confederate General of the West,* 304. Frazier, *Blood & Treasure,* 292-293, points out some Southerners, including John R. Baylor, would continue to dream about a Confederate conquest of the western territories. *Official Records*, 9: 509-512; Alberts, ed., *Rebels on the Rio Grande,* 97-152; Haas, "Diary of Julius Giesecke," 234-242; Gracy, "New Mexico Campaign Letters of Frank Starr," 181-185; Noel, *Campaign From Santa Fe to the Mississippi,* 25-32.

17. Hall, *Sibley's New Mexico Campaign,* 202-203.

18. Thompson, *Confederate General of the West,* 309-314.

19. *Ibid*., 320-321; Edward T. Cotham, *The Battle on the Bay: The Civil War Struggle for Galveston* (Austin: University of Texas Press, 1998), 103.

20. Donald S. Frazier, *Cottonclads! The Battle of Galveston and the Defense of the Texas Coast* (Fort Worth: Ryan Place Publishers, 1996), 56-57; Donald S. Frazier, "Sibley's Texans and the Battle of Galveston," *Southwestern Historical Quarterly* 99 (October 1995): 176-178; Paul D. Casdorph, *Prince John Magruder: His Life and Campaigns* (New York: John Wiley & Sons, Inc., 1996), 225-227; Cotham, *Battle on the Bay,* 111-112; Odie Faulk, *General Tom Green: Fightin' Texan* (Waco: Texian Press, 1963), 49.

21. *Official Records*, 15: 211-220, 884-886; *Official Records of the Union and Confederate Navies in the War of Rebellion* (30 vols., Washington: Government Printing Office, 1984-1922); hereinafter cited as *Official Records, Navies,* 19: 471-472; Cotham, *Battle on the Bay,* 114-115; Frazier, *Cottonclads!,* 57-61.

22. *Official Records*, *Navies,* 19: 473-474; Cotham, *Battle on the Bay,* 116-221; Frazier, "Sibley's Texans and the Battle of Galveston," 184-187.

23. Charles C. Cumberland, "The Confederate Loss and Recapture of Galveston, 1862-1863," *Southwestern Historical Quarterly* 51 (October 1947): 123-126; Frazier, "Sibley's Texans and the Battle of Galveston," 187-191; *Official Records*, *Navies*, 19: 474-475.

24. Frazier, "Sibley's Texans and the Battle of Galveston," 196-197. Frazier points out that a drinking spree of some of the officers of the brigade a week after the battle contributed to the "loose-disciplined reputation of the unit."

25. T. Michael Parrish, *Richard Taylor: Soldier Prince of Dixie* (Chapel Hill: University of North Carolina Press, 1992), 267-279; Donald S. Frazier, "Texans on the Teche: The Texas Brigade at the Battles of Bisland and Irish Bend, April 12-14, 1863," *Louisiana History* 32 (Fall 1991): 417-435; Stephen S. Michot, "In Relief of Port Hudson: Richard Taylor's 1863 Lafourche Offensive," *Military History of the West* 23 (Fall 1993): 103-117; Morris Raphael, *The Battle in the Bayou Country* (Detroit: Harlo Press, 1975), 86-120; Barnes F. Lathrop, "The Lafourche District in 1862: Revival," *Louisiana History* 1 (Fall 1960): 301-391; Lathrop, "The Lafourche District in 1862: Invasion," *ibid*. 2 (Spring 1961): 178-201.

26. L. Boyd Finch, "Surprise at Brashear City: Sherod Hunter's Sugar Cooler Cavalry," *Louisiana History,* 26 (Fall 1984): 430-434; James T. Matthews,

"A Time for Desperate Valor: The Confederate Attack on Fort Butler, Louisiana, 1863," *Military History of the West* 26 (Spring 1996): 23-34; Michot, "In Relief of Port Hudson," 109-122; Charles Spurlin, ed., *West of the Mississippi with Waller's 13th Texas Cavalry Battalion, CSA* (Hillsboro: Hill Junior College Press, 1971), 5-6; J. H. McLeary, "History of Green's Brigade," in Wooten, ed., *Comprehensive History of Texas,* 1: 714-717; Donald S. Frazier, "'The Battles of Texas Will Be Fought in Louisiana': The Assault on Fort Butler, June 28, 1863," *Southwestern Historical Quarterly* 104 (January 2001): 334-362.

27. Richard Taylor, *Destruction and Reconstruction: Personal Experiences of the Late War,* ed. Richard Harwell (New York: Longman, Green and Co., 1955), 173-176; Curtis M. Milburn, "Brigadier General Tom Green of Texas," *East Texas Historical Journal* 32 (Spring 1994): 7; Michot, "In Relief of Port Hudson," 130-133; John D. Winters, *The Civil War in Louisiana* (Baton Rouge: Louisiana State University Press, 1963), 292-293.

28. Ethel Taylor, "Discontent in Confederate Louisiana," *Louisiana History* 2 (Fall 1961): 421-422.

29. Banks' plans are covered fully by Richard Lowe, *The Texas Overland Expedition of 1863* (Abilene: McWhiney Foundation Press, 1998), 25-35.

30. *Ibid*., 29-30.

31. Parrish, *Richard Taylor,* 309; Winters, *Civil War in Louisiana,* 296-297; Lowe, *Texas Overland Expedition,* 49-56.

32. *Official Records*, 26, Pt. 1: 354-359, 393-395; Alwyn Barr, ed., "The Battle of Bayou Bourbeau, November 3, 1863: Colonel Oran Roberts' Report," *Louisiana History* 6 (Winter 1965): 83-91; Lowe, *Texas Overland Expedition,* 80-100.

33. *Official Records*, 34, Pt. 2: 932, 1010.

34. *Official Records*, 34, Pt. 1: 562-563; William R. Brooksher, *War Along the Bayous: The 1864 Red River Campaign in Louisiana* (Washington: Brassy's, 1998), 69-72.

35. *Official Records*, 34, Pt. 1: 564-568; Ludwell H. Johnson, *Red River Campaign: Politics and Cotton in the Civil War* (Org. publ. 1958; Kent, OH: Kent State University Press, 1993), 134-139; Parrish, *Richard Taylor,* 342-354; Brooksher, *War Along the Bayous,* 95-103; Curt Anders, *Disaster in Damp Sand: The Red River Expedition* (Indianapolis: Guild Press of Indiana, 1997), 59-62.

36. *Official Records*, 34, Pt. 1: 569. Brigade casualties are based upon Noel, *From Santa Fe to the Mississippi,* 131-146. According to Noel the Fourth Texas, with six men killed and sixteen wounded, had the highest casualties in the brigade.

37. *Official Records*, 34, Pt. 1: 567; Johnson, *Red River Campaign,* 155-162; Brooksher, *War Along the Bayous,* 109-114. Noel, *From Santa Fe to the Mississippi,* 134-146, records only one member of the brigade killed and twelve wounded at Pleasant Hill.

38. Quote, *Official Records*, 34, Pt. 1: 570. For Banks' decision to withdraw see James G. Hollandsworth, Jr., *Pretense of Glory: The Life of Nathaniel P. Banks* (Baton Rouge: Louisiana State University Press, 1998), 193-194.

39. Alwyn Barr, "The Battle of Blair's Landing," *Louisiana Studies* 2 (Winter 1963): 203-212; Winters, *Civil War in Louisiana,* 358-359; Brooksher, *War Along the Bayous*, 155-157.

40. For more on Monett's Ferry see Fredericka Meiners, "Hamilton P. Bee

in the Red River Campaign," *Southwestern Historical Quarterly* 78 (July 1974): 33-38.

41. Brooksher, *War Along the Bayous,* 181-182; *Official Records*, 34, Pt. 1: 589-591, Pt. 3: 764: *Official Records, Supplement,* 6: 342-343. In a letter to Bee written on June 30, John A. Wharton, who succeeded Green as commander of all Confederate cavalry in Louisiana, stated that he, Bagby, and Major all supported Bee in his decision at Monett's Ferry.

42. These brigade losses are based upon information given by Noel, *From Santa Fe to the Mississippi,* 131-142. For more on Yellow Bayou see *Official Records*, 34, Pt. 1: 594-595; *Official Records, Supplement,* 6: 349; Anne J. Bailey, *Texans in the Confederate Cavalry* (Fort Worth: Ryan Place Publishers, 1995), 63-75; Brooksher, *War Along the Bayous,* 220-225; Johnson, *Red River Campaign,* 275-276. Julius Giesecke, a captain in the Fourth Texas Cavalry, said of Wharton's decision to attack at Yellow Bayou "our general made a great mistake to attack there." Haas, ed., "Diary of Julius Giesecke," *Texas Military History* 4 (Spring 1964) 52.

43. Noel, *From Santa Fe to the Mississippi,* 94-96; *Official Records*, 41, Pt. 2: 728.

44. Noel, *From Santa Fe to the Mississippi,* xvii; *Official Records*, 48, Pt. 1: 1390, 1392-93, 1458.

45. See *Official Records*, 34, Pt. 1: 524; Carl L. Duaine, *The Dead Men Wore Boots: An Account of the 32nd Texas Volunteer Cavalry, CSA, 1862-1865* (Austin: San Felipe Press, 1966), 54-55, 85; Sifakis, *Compendium of the Confederate Armies: Texas,* 38-39, 80, 83, 92-93, 101.

46. Stanley S. McGowen, *Horse Sweat and Powder Smoke: The First Texas Cavalry in the Civil War* (College Station: Texas A&M University Press, 1999), 10-12, 20-37; David Paul Smith, *Frontier Defense in the Civil War: Texas' Rangers and Rebels* (College Station: Texas A&M University Press, 1992), 21-40; James K. Greer, ed., *Buck Barry, Texas Ranger and Frontiersman* (Reprint, Lincoln: University of Nebraska Press, 1978), 126-127.

47. McGowen, *Horse Sweat and Powder Smoke,* 39-95; Tyler, ed., *New Handbook of Texas*, 3: 16. A detachment of Taylor's Battalion participated in the attack on German Unionists fleeing the state in early August 1862. See Robert W. Shook, "The Battle of the Nueces, August 10, 1862," *Southwestern Historical Quarterly* 66 (July 1962): 31-42, and Stanley L. McGowen, "Battle or Massacre? The Incident on the Nueces, August 10, 1862," *ibid*., 104 (July 2000): 71-73.

48. McGowen, *Horse Sweat and Powder Smoke,* 96.

49. Stanley S. McGowen, "Augustus Buchel: A Forgotten Texas Patriot," *Military History of the West* 25 (Spring 1995) 1-8; *Official Records*, 4: 149-151, 166.

50. McGowen, *Horse Sweat and Powder Smoke,* 102-110; *Official Records*, 26, Pt. 2: 99, 281.

51. *Official Records*, 26, Pt. 2: 509, 564; McGowen, *Horse Sweat and Powder Smoke,* 115-117.

52. McGowen, *Horse Sweat and Powder Smoke,* 121-122; *Official Records*, 26, Pt. 1: 485-586.

53. Xavier B. Debray, *A Sketch of the History of Debray's 26th Regiment of Texas Cavalry* (Austin, 1884; reprint, Waco: Village Press, 1961), 3-4. The earlier printing capitalized the B in Debray's name; most modern publications do not. A

more recent edition (including a regimental roster) has been published by Joseph V. Patterson, Camas, Washington, 1998). For more on Debray's background see Alwyn Barr, "Xavier Blanchard Debray," in *The Confederate General* 6: 180-181; Bruce S. Allardice, *More Generals in Gray* (Baton Rouge: Louisiana State University Press, 1995), 74-75; and Wooster, *Lone Star Generals in Gray*, 119-122.

54. Debray, *History of Debray's 26th Regiment*, 6.

55. *Official Records*, 9: 721; Debray, *History of Debray's 26th Regiment*, 6-7; Frazier, *Cottonclads!*, 52; Casdorph, *Prince John Magruder*, 225.

56. *Official Records*, 15: 836-837, 855, 856-857; Cotham, *Battle on the Bay*, 67.

57. *Official Records*, 15: 148-149, 217; Frazier, *Cottonclads!*, 69.

58. *Official Records*, 26, Pt. 2: 25, 65, 99, 184, 242, 244, 281; Cotham, *Battle on the Bay*, 156-157.

59. *Official Records*, 26, Pt. 2: 472-473, 509, 564. The morning report for December 31, 1863 showed sixty-nine officers and 1,016 men present for duty. A similar report a week later listed ninety-three officers and 1,436 men present for duty. *Ibid.*, 34, Pt. 2: 837. Bill Winsor, *Texas in the Confederacy: Military Installations, Economy and People* (Hillsboro: Hill Junior College Press, 1978), 37, points out there were four different camps in the area known as Camp Wharton. The name of Camp Wharton No. 1, where Debray made his headquarters, was changed to Camp Dixie in February 1864.

60. For Gould's role with Forrest see John A. Wyeth, *The Devil Forrest: The Life of General Nathan Bedford Forrest* (1899; reprint, New York: Harper and Row, 1959), 24-28; William J. Stier, "Fury Takes the Field," *Civil War Times Illustrated* 38 (December 1999): 44; William J. Davis, ed., *The Partisan Rangers of the Confederate States Army: Memoirs of General Adam R. Johnson* (1904; reprint, Austin: State House Press, 1995), 39, 42.

61. Fitzhugh, *Texas Batteries, Battalions, Regiments*, 18; *Official Records*, 15: 886, 1054, 1057; 26, Pt. 2: 84, 99. A paper by Elizabeth R. Spencer, "Changing History," in the Regimental File, Simpson Confederate Research Center, Hillsboro, Texas, shows that the Twenty-third Cavalry was divided into smaller sub-regimental units patrolling the Indian frontier from Montague to Fort Clark in autumn, 1862.

62. Quote, McCulloch, *Official Records*, 26, Pt. 2: 345.

63. *Official Records*, 26, Pt. 2: 183, 281; 34, Pt. 2: 837. Wooten, ed., *Comprehensive History of Texas*, 2: 636, states that the Twenty-third saw service in Indian Territory; this is repeated in Henderson, *Texas in the Confederacy*, 130, and David Pickering and Judy Falls, *Brush Men & Vigilantes: Civil War Discontent in Texas* (College Station: Texas A&M University Press, 2000), 48. This may have occurred when the regiment was in the Red River country or Wooten may have confused Nicholas Gould's Regiment with Robert S. Gould's Sixth Texas Cavalry Battalion, which did see action in Indian Territory.

64. John W. Spencer, *Terrell's Texas Cavalry* (Burnet, TX: Eakin Press, 1982), v-vi. The Thirty-fourth Texas Cavalry (dismounted) will be discussed in the next chapter. Some sources show Terrell's Regiment as the "Thirty-seventh Texas Cavalry," but the men of the regiment always referred to their organization as the "Thirty-fourth Texas," or "Terrell's Texas Cavalry."

65. Charles K. Chamberlain, "Alexander Watkins Terrell: Citizen,

Statesman" (Ph.D. dissertation, University of Texas, 1957), 6-60; Spencer, *Terrell's Texas Cavalry*, 93-95.

66. Tyler, ed., *New Handbook of Texas*, 5: 618; Spencer, *Terrell's Texas Cavalry*, 101-107.

67. *Official Records*, 26, Pt. 2: 237-239, 469-471, 536; Spencer, *Terrell's Texas Cavalry*, 3-7.

68. *Official Records*, 34, Pt. 2: 437. The aggregate number present and absent was 701; this included Company B, which was on duty in the Waco area rounding up deserters.

69. Spencer, *Terrell's Texas Cavalry*, 8; *Official Records*, 34, Pt. 2: 988.

70. As if this is not confusing enough, Andrews' Thirty-second Regiment (discussed in Chapter Four as part of Ector's Brigade) was also known as the Fifteenth Texas Cavalry. See Sifakis, *Compendium of Confederate Armies: Texas,* 73, 88-89, 93.

71. Duaine, *Dead Men Wore Boots,* 21-26; Tyler, ed., *New Handbook of Texas*, 6: 1067.

72. *Official Records*, 26, Pt. 2: 99, 281; 34, Pt. 2: 932; Tyler, ed., *New Handbook of Texas*, 6: 1067.

73. *Official Records*, 4: 135-136, 158; W. T. Block, *A History of Jefferson County, Texas From Wilderness to Reconstruction* (Nederland, TX: Nederland Printing Company, 1976), 99-100; Charles D. Walker, "Spaight's Battalion, C.S.A.," *Texas Gulf Historical and Biographical Record* 8 (November 1972), 22-23; Spencer, *Terrell's Texas Cavalry*, 158. The muster rolls for the Thirty-fifth Texas are printed in Janet B. Hewett, ed., *Texas Confederate Soldiers, 1861-1865,* 2 vols. (Wilmington, NC: Broadfoot Publishing Company, 1997), 2: 235-236.

74. *Official Records*, 26, Pt. 2: 472, 485, 488, 34, Pt. 2: 906; Spencer, *Terrell's Texas Rangers,* 159.

75. *Official Records*, 34, Pt. 1: 524, 606; 34, Pt. 2: 1037-1038; Pt. 3: 725; Meiners, "Hamilton P. Bee in the Red River Campaign of 1864," 23-24.

76. *Official Records*, 34, Pt. 1: 520, 563, 606-607; Debray, *History of Debray's 26th Regiment,* 16-17; Meiners, "Hamilton P. Bee in the Red River Campaign of 1864," 24-25; McGown, *Horse Sweat and Powder Smoke,* 127-129.

77. *Official Records*, 34, Pt. 1: 563-564, 607; Spencer, *Terrell's Texas Cavalry*, 16-20; Debray, *History of Debray's Twenty-sixth Regiment,* 17; McGowen, *Horse Sweat and Powder Smoke,* 127-129.

78. *Official Records*, 34, Pt. 1: 607-608; Meiners, "Hamilton P. Bee in the Red River Campaign of 1864," 28.

79. Spencer, *Terrell's Texas Cavalry*, 37-38.

80. McGowen, "Augustus Buchel," 18-19; Brooksher, *War Along the Bayous,* 127-128.

81. Taylor quote, *Official Records*, 34, Pt. 1: 567; Debray, *History of Debray's 26th Regiment,* 18-19; Brooksher, *War Along the Bayous,* 128-134.

82. *Official Records*, 34, Pt. 1: 571; Alwyn Barr, "The Battle of Blair's Landing," *Louisiana Studies* 2 (Winter 1963): 203-212; Duaine, *Dead Men Wore Boots,* 57-64; Bailey, *Texans in the Confederate Cavalry,* 55-57.

83. *Official Records*, 34, Pt. 1: 580-581; Debray, *History of Debray's 26th Regiment,* 19-21; Meiners, "Hamilton P. Bee in the Red River Campaign of 1864," 22-43.

84. *Official Records, Supplement,* 6: 343; McGowen, *Horse Sweat and Powder Smoke,* 154-155.

85. *Official Records*, 34, Pt. 1: 583, 594-595; *Official Records, Supplement,* 6: 346-350; Spencer, *Terrell's Texas Cavalry*, 50; Duaine, *Dead Men Wore Boots*, 80-83; Bailey, *Texans in the Confederate Cavalry,* 65-73.

86. *Official Records*, 41, Pt. 1: 810; Spencer, *Terrell's Texas Cavalry*, 52-54; McGowen, *Horse Sweat and Powder Smoke,* 162-163.

87. Quote, Debray, *History of Debray's 26th Regiment,* 24; *Official Records*, 41, Pt. 3: 854, Pt. 4: 896, 955.

88. Debray, *History of Debray's 26th Regiment,* 24-26; *Official Records*, 48, Pt. 1: 1459; Pt. 2: 1281.

89. *Official Records*, 48, Pt. 2: 1266, 1291; McGowen, *Horse Sweat and Powder Smoke,* 165-166; Spencer, *Terrell's Texas Cavalry*, 62.

90. Debray, *History of Debray's 26th Regiment,* 25; Duaine, *Dead Men Wore Boots*, 94-95; *Official Records*, 48, Pt. 2: 1297.

91. Anne Bailey, "James Patrick Major," *The Confederate General* 4: 148; *Official Records*, 3: 100; 15: 19; 17, Pt. 1: 448-449.

92. *Official Records*, 8: 1049; Sifakis, *Compendium of Confederate Armies: Texas,* 40, 42, 44-46; Bailey, "James Patrick Major," 148-149.

93. James T. Matthews, "Major's Confederate Cavalry Brigade" (M. A. thesis, Texas Tech University, 1991), 9-10; Bell I. Wiley, *The Life of Johnny Reb: The Common Soldier of the Confederacy* (Baton Rouge: Louisiana State University Press, 1943), 45-46.

94. Quote, Douglas Hale, *Third Texas Cavalry in the Civil War,* 47. For more on W. P. Lane see Wooster, *Lone Star Generals in Gray*, 142-145; Jimmy L. Bryan, Jr., "Walter P. Lane: The Romantic Adventurer or Agent of U.S. Expansionism" (M.A. thesis, University of Texas at Arlington, 1999); and Lane's own *The Adventures and Recollections of General Walter P. Lane . . .* (Marshall, TX, 1887; reprint, Austin: Pemberton Press, 1970).

95. *Official Records*, 3: 120, 297-301; 8: 22-23, 28-29; Lane, *Adventures and Recollections,* 98; Hale, *Third Texas Cavalry*, 62-63, 68, 79-81, 91-92, 95-97.

96. Sifakis, *Compendium of Confederate Armies: Texas,* 37; T. C. Chaddick, "Jefferson's Indomitable Richard Phillip Crump," *East Texas Historical Journal* 8 (October 1970): 163-166.

97. Matthews, "Major's Confederate Cavalry Brigade," 14-17. Matthews points out that muster rolls for the Partisan Rangers no longer exist. He recreated the general company structure from casualty reports, Adjutant General of Texas records, and county histories. *Ibid*., 40, 30fn.

98. Lane, *Adventures and Recollections,* 105; William Shea, *War in the West*, 94-103; Oates, *Confederate Cavalry West of the River,* 105-112.

99. For more on Hart see William E. Sawyer, "Martin Hart, Civil War Guerrilla," *Texas Military History* 3 (Fall 1963): 146-153; Sawyer, "The Martin Hart Conspiracy," *Arkansas Historical Quarterly* 23 (Summer 1964): 154-165; J. S. Duncan, "Martin Hart, Civil War Guerrilla: Addenda," *Military History of Texas and the Southwest* 11 (No. 2, 1973): 137-142; Pickering and Falls, *Brush Men and Vigilantes*, 68-80.

100. Quote, Matthews, "Major's Confederate Cavalry Brigade," 25; *Official Records*, 22, Pt. 1: 29-29.

101. *Official Records*, 22, Pt. 2: 827, 830, 834; 26, Pt. 1: 218-219. Lane does not mention this matter in his memoirs.

102. Tyler, ed., *New Handbook of Texas*, 6: 110, 486. Chisum and Throckmorton had served in the secession convention; Chisum supporting secession and Throckmorton opposing.

103. Matthews, "Major's Confederate Cavalry Brigade," 30-35; Regimental File, Second Partisan Rangers, Simpson Confederate Research Center.

104. *Ibid.*, 36; *Official Records*, 15: 902, 1054-1055.

105. Matthews, "Major's Confederate Cavalry Brigade, 46-63, discusses the early Confederate efforts in Arizona and New Mexico. For more on the controversial John R. Baylor, see Thompson, *Colonel John Robert Baylor,* esp. 82-84, and George W. Baylor, *John Robert Baylor: Confederate Governor of Arizona,* ed. Odie B. Faulk (Tucson: Arizona Pioneer's Historical Society, 1966).

106. Matthews, "Major's Confederate Cavalry Brigade," 72-76; *Official Records*, 50, Pt. 2: 332-333. Spruce M. Baird and the Fourth Texas Cavalry (Arizona Brigade) are discussed later in this chapter. See Slaughter's Brigade.

107. For more on George W. Baylor, see Jerry D. Thompson, "Introduction," to George Wythe Baylor, *Into the Far, Wild Country: True Tales of the Old Southwest* (El Paso: Texas Western Press, 1996), 1-44; Kenneth A. Goldblatt, "George Wythe Baylor, Frontier Hero" (M.A. thesis, University of Texas at El Paso, 1969); and John L. Waller, "Colonel George Wythe Baylor," *Southwestern Social Science Quarterly* 24 (June 1943): 23-35.

108. Matthews, "Major's Confederate Cavalry Brigade," 50-51, 68-77. For more on Hunter see L. Boyd Finch, "Sherod Hunter and the Confederates in Arizona," *Journal of Arizona History* 10 (Autumn 1969): 137-206.

109. Matthews, "Major's Confederate Cavalry Brigade," 51-52, 59-60, 78-81.

110. *Official Records*, 26, Pt. 1: 226-227.

111. *Ibid.*, 26, Pt. 1: 191-192, 217-219, 225; L. Boyd Finch, "Surprise at Brashear City: Sherod Hunter's Sugar Cooler Cavalry," *Louisiana History* 25 (Fall 1984): 403-434; Stephen S. Michot, "In Relief of Port Hudson: Richard Taylor's 1863 Lafourche Offensive," *Military History of the West* 23 (Fall 1993): 109-117.

112. *Official Records*, 26, Pt. 1: 227-229; James T. Matthews, "A Time for Desperate Valor: The Confederate Attack on Fort Butler, Louisiana, 1863," *Military History of the West* 26 (Spring 1996): 28-32; Michot, "In Relief of Port Hudson," 118-122; Frazier, "'The Battle of Texas will be Fought in Louisiana'," 350-358.

113. Matthews, "A Time for Desperate Valor," 32.

114. Taylor, *Destruction and Reconstruction,* 173-174; Winters, *Civil War in Louisiana,* 292-293.

115. *Official Records*, 22, Pt. 2: 988, 999, 1014.

116. Quote, Green, *ibid.*, 26, Pt. 1: 329-333, 394-395; David C. Edmonds, "Surrender on the Bourbeux: Honorable Defeat or Incompetency Under Fire," *Louisiana History* 18 (Winter 1977): 63-86.

117. *Official Records*, 26, Pt. 2: 527-528; 34, Pt. 2: 4-5. For an excellent description of camp life at Virginia Point by a private in Lane's cavalry see Rebecca

W. Smith and Marion D. Mullins, eds., "Diary of H. C. Medford, Confederate Soldier, 1864," *Southwestern Historical Quarterly* 34 (October 1930): 115-127.

118. *Official Records*, 34, Pt. 1: 563; Matthews, "Major's Confederate Cavalry Brigade," 141-142.

119. *Official Records*, 34, Pt. 1: 563-564, 616-618; Smith and Mullins, ed., "Diary of H. C. Medford," 215-220; Welsh, *Medical Histories of Confederate Generals*, 129.

120. *Official Records*, 34, Pt. 1: 567, 617-618; Smith and Mullins, ed., "Diary of H. C. Medford," 220-222.

121. *Official Records*, 34, Pt. 1: 618-619. Although Bee was eventually removed from command for his failure to make a more determined stand, both Generals Major and Bagby supported his decision. Meiners, "Hamilton P. Bee in the Red River Campaign," 39-44. For a critical view of Bee's action by a private in Lane's Regiment see Jimmy L. Bryan, ed., "'Whip Them Like the Mischief': The Civil War Letters of Frank and Mintie Price," *East Texas Historical Journal* 26 (Fall 1998): 77.

122. Matthews, "Major's Confederate Cavalry," 148-157; Bailey, *Texans in the Confederate Cavalry*, 66-75; *Official Records*, *Supplement*, 6: 346.

123. Alwyn Barr, "Texan Losses in the Red River Campaign, 1864," *Texas Military History* 3 (Summer 1963): 110.

124. Matthews, "Major's Confederate Cavalry Brigade," 162-165.

125. *Official Records*, 41, Pt. 3: 996, 998-999. Colonel Chisum had been arrested and court-martialed at Camden on September 16, 1864. See Carey Bracewell to Dr. P. D. Patterson, November 17, 2000, Regimental File, Simpson Confederate Research Center.

126. *Ibid.*, 48, Pt. 1: 1351-1352, 1392-1393, 1458.

127. For Baylor's version of the affair see his "My Troubles With General John A. Wharton," Thompson, ed., *Into the Far, Wild Country*, 232-246.

128. Matthews, "Major's Confederate Cavalry Brigade," 205.

129. Anne J. Bailey, *Between the Enemy and Texas: Parsons's Texas Cavalry in the Civil War* (Fort Worth: Texas Christian University Press, 1989), 5-9; Tyler, ed., *New Handbook of Texas*, 5: 74-75; *Official Records*, 4: 95.

130. Sifakis, *Compendium of Confederate Armies: Texas*, 44, 67, 100; Bailey, *Between the Enemy and Texas*, 9-10. Mullen later formed his own infantry battalion and was lieutenant colonel of the Fourth Texas Cavalry, Arizona Brigade. Bailey, *ibid.*, 10, notes that Burleson had a drinking problem and often was in trouble with his superiors for insubordination.

The companies of the regiment had individual names before they received their letter designation. These were Hill County Volunteers (A), Freestone County Volunteers (B), Johnson County Slashers (C), Bastrop County Rawhides (D), Ellis County Grays (E), Ellis County Rangers (F), Kaufman County Guards (G), Eutaw Blues (H), William County Bowies (I), and Limestone County Mounted Rifles (K). B. P. Gallaway, *The Rugged Rebel: A Common Soldier in W. H. Parsons' Texas Cavalry, 1861-1865* (Austin: University of Texas Press, 1998), 18.

131. John Q. Anderson, ed., *Campaigning with Parsons' Texas Cavalry Brigade, CSA: The War Journals and Letters of the Four Orr Brothers, 12th Texas Cavalry Regiment* (Hillsboro: Hill Junior College Press, 1967), 4-31; Gallaway, *The*

Rugged Rebel, 15-22; Henry L. Ingram, comp., *Civil War Letters of George W. and Martha F. Ingram, 1861-1865* (College Station: Texas A&M University Press, 1973), 10-19.

132. Anderson, *Campaigning with Parsons' Texas Cavalry Brigade,* 31-47; Gallaway, *The Ragged Rebel,* 32-35; Bailey, *Between the Enemy and Texas,* 47-50.

133. *Official Records*, 13: 37-38, 204; Bailey, *Between the Enemy and Texas,* 53-81; William L. Shea, "The Confederate Defeat at Cache River," *Arkansas Historical Quarterly* 52 (Summer 1993): 129-155; Shea, "1862: A Continual Thunder," in Mark K. Christ, ed., *Ragged and Sublime: The Civil War in Arkansas* (Fayetteville: University of Arkansas Press, 1994), 42-44; Anderson, ed., *Campaigning with Parsons' Texas Cavalry Brigade,* 47-67.

134. *Official Records*, 13: 884.

135. Bailey, *Between the Enemy and Texas,* 17-29; Wright and Simpson, *Texas In the War,* 1861-1865, 118.

136. Anne Bailey, *Between the Enemy and Texas,* 251 fn, points out that the only account explaining the circumstances for the formation of the brigade is by William P. Zuber, a member of the Twenty-first Texas, in his *My Eighty Years in Texas,* ed. Janis B. Mayfield (Austin: University of Texas Press, 1971), 141-142.

137. Bailey, *Between the Enemy and Texas,* 37-41.

138. Quote, Bailey, *Between the Enemy and Texas,* xv. See also her comments, *ibid*., 43-44. Fitzhugh, *Texas Batteries, Battalions, Regiments,* 9, points out that although Morgan's cavalry had ten companies in late 1864 it was never formally organized nor its field officers promoted or commissioned. Sifakis, *Compendium of Confederate Armies: Texas,* 99-100, states that Morgan's cavalry was not recognized as a regiment by the Confederate War Department.

Sam Richardson's cavalry, better known as "W. P. Lane Rangers," was one of the companies that served under Morgan. One of Richardson's non-commissioned officers, W. W. Heartsill, wrote one of the better known Civil War reminiscences, *Fourteen Hundred and 91 Days in the Confederate Army* (Reprint, Jackson, TN: McCowat-Mercer Press, 1953).

139. Zuber, *My Eighty Years in Texas,* 150-153; Anderson, *Campaigning with Parsons' Texas Cavalry Brigade,* 74-81; Buck Walton, *An Epitome of My Life: Civil War Reminiscences* (Austin: Waterloo Press, 1965), 27-41.

140. Anderson, ed., *Campaigning with Parsons' Texas Cavalry Brigade,* 80-87; Ingram, ed., *Civil War Letters of George W. and Martha F. Ingram,* 39-42; Bailey, *Between the Enemy and Texas,* 95-97; *Official Records*, 22, Pt. 1: 904; Bailey, "Texas Cavalry's Race to Reinforce Arkansas," 45-56.

141. Bailey, *Between the Enemy and Texas,* 110-111, 116. According to Jack D. Welsh, *Medical Histories of Confederate Generals,* 95, Hawes suffered from rheumatism. Henry Orr, a soldier in the Twelfth Texas, wrote his parents on February 18 that Carter was in command of the brigade, "Gen. Hawes having got sick and gone to Hot Springs." Anderson, ed., *Campaigning with Parsons' Texas Cavalry Brigade,* 91.

142. Oates, *Confederate Cavalry West of the River,* 123-126; Zuber, *My Eighty Years in Texas,* 166-168.

143. Quote, Oates, *Confederate Cavalry West of the River,* 130. For more on the raid see Zuber, *My Eighty Years in Texas,* 168-174; Walton, *An Epitome of My*

Life, 42-53; John N. Edwards, *Shelby and His Men; or the War in the West* (1867, reprint; Kansas City, MO: Hudson-Kimberly Publishing Co., 1897), 126-133; *Official Records*, 22, Pt. 1: 285-288, 300-301. The brigade had seven men killed, thirty-seven wounded, and ten captured in the raid.

144. Anderson, ed., *Campaigning with Parsons' Texas Cavalry Brigade,* 109-115; Ingram, *Civil War Letters of George F. and Martha Ingram,* 55-56; Bailey, *Between the Enemy and Texas,* 138-146.

145. Walton, *An Epitome of My Life,* 67-68; Zuber, *My Eighty Years in Texas,* 190-196; Edwin C. Bearss, "Marmaduke Attacks Pine Bluff," *Arkansas Historical Quarterly* 23 (Winter 1964): 291-313; *Official Records*, 22, Pt. 1: 541-542, 738-739.

146. Ingram, ed., *Civil War Letters of George F. and Martha Ingram,* 65-67; Zuber, *My Eighty Years in Texas,* 197; *The Confederate General,* 1: 187. Churchill, who had been Confederate commander at Arkansas Post, blamed Texans for the surrender. As a result he was never popular with troops from the state. In the previous chapter it was pointed out that Granbury's men were pleased when Churchill was transferred from command of their brigade.

147. *Official Records*, 34, Pt. 2: 868, 885, 1061; Anderson, ed., *Campaigning with Parsons' Texas Cavalry Brigade,* 129-130; Gallaway, *The Ragged Rebel,* 75-78; Zuber, *My Eighty Years in Texas,* 198-199. Burleson's Battalion was assigned to Henry E. McCulloch's Northern Sub-district during the winter of 1863-1864. In a report on efforts to round-up deserters, McCulloch praised Burleson's company as "the most efficient men that ever have been in the district." At the same time he admitted they "drank too much whisky and committed some other indiscretions." *Official Records*, 34, Pt. 3: 742.

148. Gallaway, *The Ragged Rebel,* 90-101; Barr, "Battle of Blair's Landing," 204-212; Bailey, *Texans in the Confederate Cavalry,* 54-56.

149. *Official Records*, 34, Pt. 1: 625-628.

150. Brooksher, *War Along the Bayous,* 219-220.

151. Anderson, ed., *Campaigning with Parsons' Texas Cavalry Brigade,* 139-140; Gallaway, *The Ragged Rebel,* 114-121; Brooksher, *War Along the Bayous,* 221-223.

152. *Official Records*, 34, Pt. 1: 594-595, 637.

153. Anderson, ed., *Campaigning with Parsons' Texas Cavalry Brigade,* 145.

154. *Ibid*., 149-151; *Official Records*, 41, Pt. 3: 920, 968-969; Pt. 4: 1144.

155. Gallaway, *The Ragged Rebel,* 125-126; Heartsill, *Fourteen Hundred and 91 Days,* 217-233; *Official Records*, 48, Pt. 1: 1351-1352.

156. *Official Records*, 48, Pt. 1: 1392-1393, 1458.

157. Hearstill, *Fourteen Hundred and 91 Days,* 241-246. Parsons went to Central America. He returned shortly thereafter and later held several positions with the federal government. Bailey, *Between the Enemy and Texas,* 202-203, 206.

158. Sifakis, *Compendium of Confederate Armies: Texas,* 39-40, 54, 86-87; Fitzhugh, *Texas Batteries, Battalions, Regiments,* 11, 13-14, 19-20.

159. Ernest Wallace, *Charles DeMorse: Pioneer Editor and Statesman* (Lubbock: Texas Tech Press, 1943), 1-144.

160. Bradford K. Felmly and John C. Grady, *Suffering to Silence: 29th Texas Cavalry, CSA, Regimental History* (Quanah, TX: Nortex Press, 1975), 31-35, 200-209; William L. Shea and Earl J. Hess, *Pea Ridge: Civil War Campaign in the West* (Chapel Hill: University of North Carolina Press, 1992), 101, 336.

161. Felmly and Grady, *Suffering to Silence,* 9-30; Wallace, *Charles DeMorse,* 144-145. Felmly and Grady, *Suffering to Silence,* 49-57, point out that in October Company B was assigned to duty in Gainesville, where a threat of a Unionist plot eventually led to the "great hanging." See also Richard B. McCaslin, *Tainted Breeze: The Great Hanging at Gainesville, Texas,* 1862 (Baton Rouge: Louisiana State University Press, 1994), 73.

162. Felmly and Grady, *Suffering to Silence,* 59-73; Wallace, *Charles DeMorse,* 145-146.

163. Quote, Alvin M. Josephy, Jr., *The Civil War in the American West* (New York: Alfred A. Knopf, 1991), 372; *Official Records*, 22, Pt. 1: 461-462.

164. Felmly and Grady, *Suffering to Silence,* 82-95; Rampp and Rampp, *Civil War in Indian Territory,* 21-29.

165. *Official Records*, 22, Pt. 1: 461.

166. *Ibid*., 461.

167. Sifakis, *Compendium of Confederate Armies: Texas,* 54; Fitzhugh, *Texas Batteries, Battalions, Regiments,* 6, 13-14.

168. Felmly and Grady, *Suffering to Silence,* 96-100; Wallace, *Charles DeMorse,* 148. Some of DeMorse's fellow officers were rather critical of the Clarksville editor-colonel. In February 1864 William L. Cabell, a West Point professional who commanded a brigade under Sterling Price, observed that DeMorse was "a terribly incompetent man." *Official Records*, 34, Pt. 2: 905.

169. *Official Records*, 22, Pt. 2: 1037; Smith, *Frontier Defense in the Civil War,* 106-111; Edward E. Leslie, *The Devil Knows How to Ride: The Story of William Clarke Quantrill and His Confederate Raiders* (New York: DaCapo Press, 1998), 298-299.

170. *Official Records*, 22, Pt. 2: 113; 32, Pt. 3: 728-730; 34, Pt. 2: 1050, 1067-1068; 53: 964.

171. *Ibid*., 22, Pt. 2: 1048, 1062, 1067, 1112; Allardice, *More Generals in Gray,* 26.

172. *Official Records*, 22, Pt. 2: 1052. The same inspector found DeMorse's Twenty-ninth Texas "poorly drilled, armed, and disciplined." For more on Richard Gano see Wooster, *Lone Star Generals in Gray*, 123-126.

173. The First Cavalry, Arizona Brigade, was sometimes referred to as the Thirty-first Texas Cavalry. Sifakis, *Compendium of Confederate Armies: Texas,* 39; Tyler, ed., *New Handbook of Texas*, 3: 448-450. For more on the Hardemans see Nicholas P. Hardeman, *Wilderness Calling: The Hardeman Family in the Western Movement, 1730-1930* (Knoxville: University of Tennessee Press, 1977).

174. Bailey, *Between the Enemy and Texas,* 236-238; Tyler, ed., *New Handbook of Texas*, 1: 418; 3: 390. Edward J. Gurley, who had served as legal counsel for Brazos Reserve Indians in the late 1850s, had been highly critical of Texas Ranger Captain John S. "Rip" Ford for his failure to arrest Peter Gerland for the massacre of seven Indians in 1858. See Stephen B. Oates, ed., *Rip Ford's Texas* (Austin: University of Texas Press, 1963), xxxiv, 250-252.

175. *Official Records*, 15: 903-904, 936-937, 1055; 22, Pt. 2: 922, 963, 977.

176. *Ibid*., 22, Pt. 2: 1064, 1085; 34, Pt. 2: 1007; Felmly and Grady, *Suffering to Silence,* 112; John C. Waugh, *Samuel Bell Maxey and the Confederate Indians* (Fort Worth: Ryan Place Publishers, 1995), 42-45.

177. Waugh, *Maxey and the Confederate Indians,* 52-56; David B. Gracy, II, ed., *Maxey's Texas* (Austin: Pemberton Press, 1965), 16-17.

178. *Official Records*, 34, Pt. 1: 779, 783; Waugh, *Maxey and the Confederate Indians,* 56; Felmly and Grady, *Suffering to Silence,* 114-115.

179. Horton, *Samuel Bell Maxey,* 37; *Official Records*, 34, Pt. 1: 841-842.

180. Waugh, *Maxey and the Confederate Indians,* 59-60; Horton, *Samuel Bell Maxey,* 37-38.

181. For more on the controversy over the killing of black soldiers at Poison Spring see Gregory J. W. Urwin, "'We Cannot Treat Negroes . . . As Prisoners of War': Racial Atrocities and Reprisals in Civil War Arkansas," *Civil War History* 42 (September 1996): 197-204; Anne J. Bailey, "Was There a Massacre at Poison Spring?" *Military History of the Southwest* 20 (Fall 1990): 162.

182. Edwin C. Bearss, *Steele's Retreat from Camden and the Battle of Jenkins Ferry* (Little Rock: Arkansas Civil War Centennial Commission, 1967), 40-41. Gano's Brigade took 635 men into battle. These were as follows: First Texas (reported as the Thirty-first) 175; Twenty-ninth Texas, 211; Thirtieth Texas, 175; Welch's independent company, 44; and Krumbhaar's artillery battery, 30. *Official Records*, 34, Pt. 1: 848.

It is difficult to determine the number of troops involved at Poison Spring. Maxey reported the Confederates, with fewer than 1,800 men, defeated 2,500 enemy troops. Don Richards, "The Battle of Poison Spring," *Arkansas Historical Quarterly* 18 (Winter 1959): 342-344, estimated 1,170 Federals and 3,335 Confederates.

183. Felmly and Grady, *Suffering to Silence,* 143-145.

184. *Official Records*, 41, Pt. 1: 32; Felmly and Grady, *Suffering to Silence,* 142-149. Gano was not a general at the time. He had been recommended for promotion but approval did not come until March 18, 1865. Wooster, *Lone Star Generals in Gray*, 126.

185. Once again Gurley's Thirtieth Texas, with nineteen casualties, had the highest losses in the brigade. *Official Records*, 41, Pt. 1: 788-792; Marvin J. Hancock, "The Second Battle of Cabin Creek, 1864," *Chronicles of Oklahoma* 39 (Winter 1963): 414-426; Phillip W. Steele and Steve Cottrell, *Civil War in the Ozarks* (Gretna, LA: Pelican Publishing Co., 1998), 90-92; Laurence M Hauptman, *Between Two Fires: American Indians in the Civil War* (New York: Free Press, 1995), 54-57; Waugh, *Maxey and the Confederate Indians,* 73-78; Rampp and Rampp, *Civil War in Indian Territory,* 105-113.

186. Felmly and Grady, *Suffering to Silence,* 181; *Official Records*, 52, 1029-1030.

187. Sifakis, *Compendium of Confederate Armies: Texas,* 70, 90; Claude Elliott, "Union Sentiment in Texas, 1861-1865," *Southwestern Historical Quarterly* 50 (April 1947): 464-466; Shook, "The Battle of the Nueces," 32-37, 42. For a defense of Duff's role in the Texas Hill Country see McGowen, "Battle or Massacre: The Incident on the Nueces, August 10, 1862," 73-75, and Richard Selcer and William Paul Barrier, "What Really Happened on the Nueces: James Duff, a Good Soldier or 'The Butcher of Fredericksburg,'" *North and South* 2 (January 1998): 57-60.

188. *Official Records*, 15: 1077; 26, Pt. 2: 84, 443, 565; 32, Pt. 2: 926, 932, Pt. 3: 800, 816; 41, Pt. 3: 967.

189. Quote, Maxey, *ibid.*, 53: 1029.

190. Quote, DeMorse, *ibid.*, 34, Pt. 4: 699-700, published by Felmly and Grady, *Suffering to Silence,* 182-183.

191. Felmly and Grady, *Suffering to Silence,* 185-186.

192. *Official Records*, 48, Pt. 1: 1390-1392, 1459; Tyler, ed., *New Handbook of Texas*, 3: 450; 6: 172.

193. Albert Castel, "James Edwin Slaughter," in *The Confederate General,* 5: 160-161. The Western Sub-district was a vast area that included all of Texas west of a line running from Burkburnett on the Red River to Indianola on the Gulf.

194. Oates, *Confederate Cavalry West of the River,* 5; Wooten, *Comprehensive History of Texas,* 2: 573-574.

195. Oates, ed., *Rip Ford's Texas,* 318-324; J. J. Bowden, *The Exodus of Federal Forces from Texas, 1861* (Austin: Eakin Press, 1986), 83-91; *Official Records*, 8: 651-652; Frazier, *Blood & Treasure,* 30-31.

196. For more on John R. Baylor see Thompson, *Colonel John R. Baylor,* and Baylor, *John Robert Baylor.*

197. Frazier, *Blood & Treasure,* 40-43; Thompson, *Colonel John R. Baylor,* 24-28; Hall, *Sibley's New Mexico Campaign,* 25-26. Company F of the Second Cavalry, recruited in Harrison County, known as the "W. P. Lane Rangers," was later part of Morgan's Cavalry Battalion described earlier in the chapter.

198. *Official Records*, 4: 5-20; Martin Hardwick Hall, "The Skirmish at Mesilla," *Arizona and the West* 1 (Winter 1959): 343-351; Frazier, *Blood & Treasure,* 56-61.

199. Frazier, *Blood & Treasure,* 104-110.

200. Capt. Peter Hardeman of Company A was promoted to lieutenant colonel and was now senior officer of the Second Cavalry in New Mexico, but Hardeman apparently remained in the Mesilla Valley with Company A during the campaign. Pyron led the Second Cavalry in all the major action. Hall, *Confederate Army of New Mexico,* 295-301.

201. Taylor, *Bloody Valverde,* 157; *Official Records*, 9: 512-513.

202. Alberts, *Battle of Glorieta,* 14-15; Alberts, ed., *Rebels on the Rio Grande,* 63fn; Hall, *Sibley's New Mexico Campaign,* 115-116.

203. Hall, *Sibley's New Mexico Campaign,* 131; Edrington and Taylor, *Battle of Glorieta Pass,* 34.

204. Alberts, *Battle of Glorieta,* 44-66; Edrington and Taylor, *Battle of Glorieta Pass,* 41-55.

205. Quote, Alberts, *Battle of Glorieta,* 66. These figures, taken from Alberts, vary slightly from those given in Edrington and Taylor, *Battle of Glorieta Pass,* 125, 128, Frazier, *Blood & Treasure,* 21, and Hall, *Sibley's New Mexico Campaign,* 139-140; all of whom differ from each other.

206. *Official Records*, 9: 541-545; Alberts, *Battle of Glorieta,* 85-138. The Second Texas had one man killed, two wounded, and two captured in the fighting on the 28th.

207. Hall, *Sibley's New Mexico Campaign,* 209-214.

208. Oates, ed., *Rip Ford's Texas,* 331-332; Sifakis, *Compendium of Confederate Armies: Texas,* 42.

209. Cotham, *Battle on the Bay,* 116; Frazier, *Cottonclads!,* 61; Frazier, "Sibley's Texans and the Battle of Galveston," 182.

210. Quote, Major, *Official Records*, 26, Pt. 1: 218. Apparently, Major had intended Pyron only to make a demonstration to divert attention from his move against Brashear City. "Had I known his intention to assault the works," wrote Major, "I could have sent him such re-enforcements as would have insured success." *Ibid.*, 218.

211. The Union commander estimated Texas losses at fifty-three killed, nearly sixty wounded, and sixteen captured. Richard Taylor reported only thirty-one Texans killed and eighteen wounded. *Official Records*, 26, Pt. 1: 187, 196.

212. *Official Records*, 26, Pt. 1: 199.

213. *Ibid.*, 26, Pt. 2: 563-564; 34, Pt. 2: 932.

214. *Ibid.*, 34, Pt. 4: 675; 41, Pt. 2: 1035.

215. Tyler, ed., *New Handbook of Texas*, 1: 341; Frazier, *Blood & Treasure,* 195-196, 241, 293.

216. *Official Records*, 26, Pt. 1: 93, Pt. 2: 378-379. The Regimental File, Simpson Confederate Research Center, indicates that a number of Confederate sympathizers from California served in the Fourth Cavalry, Arizona Brigade.

217. Oates, ed., *Rip Ford's Texas,* 346. Oates notes there was a question of Ford's rank. He held the rank of colonel of state forces but refused to hold elections that would have made him colonel of Confederate troops. Later Govenor Murrah appointed him brigadier general of a state corps. Ford himself claimed the rank of colonel of cavalry throughout the war and was so recognized by successive Confederate district commanders of Texas.

218. *Official Records*, 34, Pt. 1: 647-649; Oates, ed., *Rip Ford's Texas,* 355-357; Jerry Don Thompson, "A Stand Along the Border: Santos Benavides and the Battle for Laredo," *Civil War Times Illustrated* 19 (August 1980): 26-33; Thompson, *Sabers on the Rio Grande* (Austin: Presidial Press, 1974), 211-213.

219. Tyler, ed., *New Handbook of Texas* 1: 485; Jerry D. Thompson, *Vaqueros in Blue & Gray* (Austin: Presidial Press, 1976), 98-99; Allardice, *More Generals in Gray,* 36-37. For more on Santos Benavides see John Denny Riley, "Santos Benavides: His Influence on the Lower Rio Grande, 1823-1891" (Ph.D. dissertation, Texas Christian University, 1976).

220. *Official Records*, 34: 1054-1056; Oates, ed., *Rip Ford's Texas*, 359-363; Thompson, *Vaqueros in Blue & Gray,* 110-115.

221. Oates, ed., *Rip Ford's Texas,* 363-364; Thompson, *Vaqueros in Blue & Gray,* 118. Ford blamed Showalter's failing due to excessive drinking; of Showalter Ford wrote: "when not under the influence of liquor, he was as chivalrous a man as ever drew a sword." *Rip Ford's Texas,* 366.

222. Stephen B. Oates, "John S. 'Rip' Ford: Prudent Cavalryman, C.S.A.," *Southwestern Historical Quarterly* 64 (January 1961): 306-307. In his memoirs Ford stated "unfortunately Colonel Showalter had recourse to the bottle" before the attack on the 6th. "He came to town in a maudlin condition," noted Ford. Brig. Gen. Thomas Drayton, the Confederate Sub-district commander, had Showalter arrested because of conduct on the 6th. Showalter was subsequently acquitted by

a court-martial and restored to command of the Fourth Texas (Arizona Brigade). Oates, ed., *Rip Ford's Texas*, 375-376.

223. *Official Records*, 41, Pt. 3: 969, Pt. 4: 1014.

224. *Ibid.*, 41, Pt. 3: 922, 966, Pt. 4: 1064; Tyler, ed., *New Handbook of Texas*, 1: 168-169, 648; F. Lee Lawrence and Robert W. Glover, *Camp Ford, C.S.A.: The Story of Union Prisoners in Texas* (Austin: Texas Civil War Centennial Commission, 1964), 25, 43-45, 66-67; Leon Mitchell, Jr., "Camp Ford: Confederate Military Prison," *Southwestern Historical Quarterly*, 66 (July 1962): 13.

225. *Official Records*, 41, Pt. 4: 1738.

226. Quote, Magruder, *Official Records*, 48, Pt. 2: 1271; see also 48, Pt. 1: 1190, 1353, 1456-57, Pt. 2: 1281.

227. W. J. Hughes, *Rebellious Ranger: Rip Ford and the Old Southwest* (Norman: University of Oklahoma Press, 1964), 245-271; *The Confederate General*, 5: 161.

228. Readers are reminded there was another Thirty-fifth Texas Regiment commanded by James B. Likens. Likens' Regiment, which served in Hamilton P. Bee's Cavalry Division during the Red River campaign, is described earlier in the chapter.

229. Tyler, ed., *New Handbook of Texas*, 1: 767.

230. *Official Records*, 26: Pt. 2: 99, 281, 409, 484, 563.

231. *Ibid.*, 26, Pt. 2: 468; 34, Pt. 1: 1034, 1040.

232. *Ibid.*, 41, Pt. 3: 966, Pt. 4: 1138.

233. Tyler, ed., *New Handbook of Texas*, 1: 693; Arthur W. Bergeron, Jr., *Guide to Louisiana Confederate Military Units, 1861-1865* (Baton Rouge: Louisiana State University Press, 1989), 155.

234. Hewett, ed., *Texas Confederate Soldiers, 1861-1865*, 2: 283-287; *Official Records*, 41, Pt. 3: 965, Pt. 4: 1084, 1138; 48, Pt. 1: 1408, 1459, Pt. 2: 1288, 1297.

235. David Paul Smith, *Frontier Defense in the Civil War: Texas' Rangers and Rebels* (College Station: Texas A&M University Press, 1992). See also Jeffry M. Roth, "Civil War Frontier Defense Challenges in Northwest Texas," *Military History of the West* 30 (Spring 2000): 21-44.

236. Smith, *Frontier Defense in the Civil War,* 42-43.

237. Tyler, ed., *New Handbook of Texas*, 4: 379, 1036; Ralph A. Wooster, "Analysis of Membership of the Texas Secession Convention," *Southwestern Historical Quarterly* 62 (January 1959): 330-333.

238. Smith, *Frontier Defense in the Civil War,* 48; Tyler, ed., *New Handbook of Texas*, 1: 396-397.

239. Smith, *Frontier Defense in the Civil War,* 50-51.

240. *Ibid.*, 53; Greer, ed., *Buck Barry,* 146-151.

241. Richard B. McCaslin, "Dark Corner of the Confederacy: James G. Bourland and the Border Regiment," *Military History of the West* 24 (Spring 1994): 57-70; Smith, *Frontier Defense in the Civil War,* 64-65. Much information on Bourland, Diamond, and Roff may be found in McCaslin, *Tainted Breeze: The Great Hanging at Gainesville, Texas, 1862.*

242. Smith, *Frontier Defense in the Civil War,* 64-65; *Official Records*, 34, Pt. 2: 1102; Hewett, ed., *Texas Confederate Soldiers,* 2: 264-267; Roth, "Civil War

Frontier Defense," 36-37. Bourland's companies were uneven in size, ranging from 130 men in Company H to only forty in Company F.

243. *Official Records*, 41, Pt. 1: 884-886; Daniel Paul Smith, "The Elm Creek Raid, 1864: State and Confederate Defense and Response," *Military History of the Southwest* 19 (Fall 1989): 121-136; Kenneth Neighbours, "Elm Creek Raid in Young County, 1864," *West Texas Historical Association Year Book* 40 (October 1964): 83-89; J. Marvin Hunter, "The Battle of Dove Creek," *ibid.* 18 (October 1942): 74-87; William C. Pool, "The Battle of Dove Creek," *Southwestern Historical Quarterly* 53 (April 1950): 367-385; Phillip Rutherford, "The Other Civil War: Disaster at Dove Creek," *Civil War Times Illustrated* 22 (April 1983): 20-25.

244. Quote, Smith, *Frontier Defense in the Civil War,* 173.

245. Tyler, ed., *New Handbook of Texas*, 6: 265-266; Albert Russell Buchanan, *David S. Terry of California: Dueling Judge* (San Marino, CA: Huntington Library, 1956); Charles S. Potts, "David S. Terry: The Romantic Story of a Great Texan," *Southwest Review* 19 (April 1934): 295-334.

246. *Official Records*, 42, Pt. 3: 917, 925, 938, 950; 48, Pt. 2: 1266, 1315; Muster rolls, Hewett, ed., *Texas Confederate Soldiers, 1861-1865,* 2: 308-311.

247. Muster rolls, Hewett, ed., *Texas Confederate Soldiers, 1861-1865,* 2: 317-319; *Official Records*, 34, Pt. 2: 1050, 41, Pt. 1: 29, 30, 31-36, Pt. 3: 882, 967, 983.

248. *Official Records*, 40, Pt. 1: 1392, 1405, 1426; Blessington, *The Campaigns of Walker's Texas Division,* 291-303; Arthur W. Bergeron, Jr., "John Horace Forney," in *The Confederate General,* 2: 135.

249. Sifakis, *Compendium of Confederate Armies: Texas,* 37-100; Tyler, ed., *New Handbook of Texas*, 3: 153-154.

250. Oates, ed., *Rip Ford's Texas,* 358-359, 374-375, 389-393.

251. Muster rolls, Hewett, ed., *Texas Confederate Soldiers, 1861-1865,* 2: 302-306.

252. *Official Records*, 34, Pt. 1: 902-903, Pt. 2: 850, 932, Pt. 3: 800; Alwyn Barr, "The Battle of Calcasieu Pass," *Southwestern Historical Quarterly* 66 (July 1962): 58-67; W. T. Block, "Calcasieu Pass, Victory, Heroism 'Equal of Dowling's'," *East Texas Historical Journal* 9 (Fall 1971): 139-144.

253. *Official Records*, 41, Pt. 3: 970, Pt. 4: 1144; 48, Pt. 1: 1356, Pt. 2: 1284, 1298; Block, *History of Jefferson County,* 119-120.

CHAPTER SIX

1. *Official Records*, 9: 718, 730, 731; 13: 883-884; Anne J. Bailey, "Henry McCulloch's Texans and the Defense of Arkansas in 1862," *Arkansas Historical Quarterly* 46 (Spring 1987): 49-52; Tyler, ed., *New Handbook of Texas*, 6: 802-803, 1127; Wooster, *Lone Star Generals in Gray*, 156-157.

2. Blessington, *Walker's Texas Division*, 45-58; Bailey, "Henry McCulloch's Texans," 52-55. The men of Deshler's Brigade were captured at Arkansas Post in early 1863. After some months of imprisonment they were exchanged and returned to Confederate service. They formed part of Granbury's Brigade described in Chapter Four.

3. Tyler, ed., *New Handbook of Texas*, 1: 853; 3: 757; 4:1103. The Twelfth Texas is incorrectly referred to as the Eighth Texas in several accounts including

the *Official Records*. James Henry Davis, ed., *Texans in Gray: A Regimental History of the Eighteenth Texas Infantry, Walker's Texas Division in the Civil War* (Tulsa: Heritage Oak Press, n.d.), 10, provides a roster of the men who served in the Eighteenth Infantry as well as names of the town and the initial captains of the eleven companies of the regiment.

4. Muster rolls, Hewett, ed., *Texas Confederate Soldiers, 1861-1865,* 2: 100-107, 448-455, 492-498, 518, 525.

5. M. Jane Johansson, *Peculiar Honor: A History of the 28th Texas Cavalry, 1862-1865* (Fayetteville: University of Arkansas Press, 1998), 13-14, 32.

6. Quote, Johansson, *Peculiar Honor,* 26.

7. Lelia Bailey, "The Life and Public Career of O. M. Roberts, 1815-1863" (Ph.D. dissertation, University of Texas, 1932), 133-137.

8. W. Buck Yearns, *The Confederate Governors* (Athens: University of Georgia Press, 1985), 195-199. In his master's thesis "'The Best Stuff Which the State Affords': A Portrait of the Fourteenth Texas Infantry in the Civil War, 1862-1865" (M.A. thesis, University of North Texas, 1998), Scott Dennis Parker provides a detailed examination of the men who made up the Fourteenth Texas Infantry. He points out that two-thirds of the volunteers came from Harrison and Smith counties; the other third from Rusk, Upshur, and Polk. Three-fourths of the men were engaged in agriculture prior to the war. Ninety-five percent of them were born in the South; 64.7 percent in the lower South and 30.2 percent in the upper South. Thirty-four percent of the men were slaveholders.

9. A typescript copy of "Biography and Diaries of Robert Simonton Gould" is in the University of Texas Archives, Austin, Texas. *Official Records*, 13: 884, 22, Pt. 1: 904; Tyler, ed., *New Handbook of Texas*, 3: 258; Oates, *Confederate Cavalry West of the River,* 182. A fourth regiment, Col. Joseph W. Speight's Fifteenth Texas Infantry, was in Randal's Brigade from September 1862 until early January 1863 when it was transferred to Indian Territory. The Fifteenth Infantry served with Polignac's Brigade during the Red River campaign and will be discussed as a part of that brigade later in this chapter.

10. The first edition of Blessington's *Campaigns of Walker's Texas Division* was published in New York City at the author's expense in 1875 by Lange, Little & Company. The work was reprinted in 1968, 1983, and 1994. I have used the 1994 edition published by State House Press of Austin.

11. An incisive sketch of R. T. P. Allen may be found in Norman D. Brown, ed., *Journey to Pleasant Hill: The Civil War Letters of Captain Elijah P. Petty, Walker's Texas Division, C.S.A.* (San Antonio: Institute of Texan Cultures, 1982), 68-69n.

12. Tyler, ed., *New Handbook of Texas*, 3: 982.

13. Brown, ed., *Journey to Pleasant Hill,* ix-xv, provides information about Petty and his letters.

14. Wooster, *Lone Star Generals in Gray*, 170-171; Wright and Simpson, *Texas in the War, 1861-1865,* 21.

15. *Official Records*, 13: 884, 22, Pt. 1: 904; Tyler, ed., *New Handbook of Texas*, 2: 1017; Oates, *Confederate Cavalry West of the River,* 37, 48.

16. Quote, Brown, ed., *Journey to Pleasant Hill,* 98; Johansson, *Peculiar Honor,* 32-34; Robert W. Glover, ed., "The War Letters of a Texas Conscript in

Arkansas," *Arkansas Historical Quarterly* 20 (Winter 1961): 368-375; Thomas W. Cutrer, ed., "'An Experience in Soldier's Life': The Civil War Letters of Volney Ellis, Adjutant, Twelfth Texas Infantry, Walker's Texas Division, C.S.A.," *Military History of the Southwest* 22 (Fall 1992): 117-121; Cutrer, ed., "'Bully for Flournoy's Regiment, We Are Some Punkins, You'll Bet': The Civil War Letters of Virgil Sullivan Rabb, Captain, Company 'I', Sixteenth Texas Infantry, C.S.A.," *ibid.* 19 (Fall 1989): 171-172; Thomas Reid, *Captain Jack and the Tyler County Boys: A History of Company K, Thirteenth Texas Cavalry Regiment, CSA* (Woodville, TX: privately printed, 2000), 21-23.

17. Blessington, *Walker's Texas Division,* 65.

18. *Ibid.*, 71-74; Norman D. Brown, "John George Walker," in *The Confederate General,* 6: 88-89; Terrence J. Winschel, *Triumph & Defeat: The Vicksburg Campaign* (Mason City, IA: Savas Publishing Co., 1999), 159.

19. Blessington, *Walker's Texas Division,* 66-71; L. David Norris, ed., *With the 18th Texas Infantry: The Autobiography of Wilburn Hill King* (Hillsboro: Hill Junior College Press, 1996), 45-47; Winschel, *Triumph and Defeat,* 162.

20. William C. Davis, "James Morrison Hawes," in *The Confederate General,* 3: 74-75.

21. Johansson, *Peculiar Honor*, 46-53; Blessington, *Walker's Texas Division*, 79-94; Norris, ed., *With the 18th Texas Infantry*, 49-50; Winschel, *Triumph and Defeat,* 165-167.

22. Johansson, *Peculiar Honor*, 54-55; Blessington, *Walker's Texas Division*, 94. For more on the attack and the controversy over the killing of black troops see Joseph T. Glatthar, *Forged in Battle: The Civil War Alliance of Black Soldiers and White Officers* (New York: Free Press, 1990), 132-135; and Winschel, *Triumph & Defeat*, 167-174.

23. Brown, ed., *Journey to Pleasant Hill,* 235-236.

24. *Official Records*, 24, Pt. 2: 448, 470.

25. *Ibid.*, 24, Pt. 2: 459-460, 462-465, 467-470.

26. *Ibid.*, 24, Pt. 2: 459-460, 471-472; Brown, ed., *Journey to Pleasant Hill,* 235-237; Davis, ed., *Texans in Gray,* 39-41; Reid, *Captain Jack*, 32-33. Hawes' failure to carry out the attack at Young's Point led the Confederate secretary of war to ask if Hawes should not be court-martialed or replaced. The decision was left to Kirby Smith, who eventually transferred Hawes to Texas. *Official Records*, 24, Pt. 2: 465.

27. T. Michael Parrish, *Richard Taylor: Soldier Prince of Dixie* (Chapel Hill: University of North Carolina Press, 1992), 295-296; Anne J. Bailey, "A Texas Cavalry Raid: Reaction to Black Soldiers and Contrabands," *Civil War History* 35 (June 1989): 143-145.

28. First quote, Blessington, *Walker's Texas Division*, 116-117; second quote, John Q. Anderson, ed., *A Texas Surgeon in the C.S.A.* (Tuscaloosa: Confederate Publishing, 1957), 67-69.

29. *Official Records*, 26, Pt. 2: 120, 188.

30. Blessington, *Walker's Texas Division*, 131-132. Randal was ordered to Harrisonburg, Louisiana, to support a small Confederate garrison under attack by a large raiding party from Natchez. Except for a brief skirmish with the enemy

there was little fighting as Randal withdrew in face of a much larger foe. *Official Records*, 26, Pt. 2: 279-289.

31. Brown, ed., *Journey to Pleasant Hill,* 260-268; Johansson, *Peculiar Honor*, 81-82.

32. Blessington, *Walker's Texas Division*, 135-136.

33. First quote, Blessington, *ibid.*, 136; second quote, Brown, ed., *Journey to Pleasant Hill,* 271.

34. Richard Lowe, *The Texas Overland Expedition of 1863* (Abilene: McWhiney Foundation Press, 1998), 80-104; Alwyn Barr, ed., "The Battle of Bayou Bourbeau, November 3, 1863: Colonel Oran M. Roberts' Report," *Louisiana History* 6 (Winter 1963): 83-91; Norris, ed., *With the 18th Texas Infantry,* 52-53, 64-65; Davis, ed., *Texans in Gray,* 57-62.

35. *Official Records*, 26, Pt. 2: 465; Brown, ed., *Journey to Pleasant Hill,* 280-293; Blessington, *Walker's Texas Division*, 150-164.

36. Quote, Blessington, *ibid.*, 165. Norman Brown, ed., *Journey to Pleasant Hill,* 368n, points out that General Taylor tried to keep Hawes but Kirby Smith, who had not forgotten the inquiries earlier by the Confederate War Department, refused to rescind the order. The Thirteenth Cavalry (dismounted) also had a new commander; because of ill health, Colonel Burnett relinquished command to his good friend Lt. Col. Anderson F. Crawford of Jasper (Reid, *Captain Jack*, 34-35).

37. For more on Waul see Wooster, *Confederate Generals in Gray,* 172-175, 235-236.

38. Brown, ed., *Journey to Pleasant Hill,* 291.

39. Johansson, *Peculiar Honor*, 88-89. Johansson points out that little information on the mutiny of the Twenty-eighth Texas exists. She concludes that "questions pertaining to what sparked the mutiny or the final disposition of the inciters are unanswerable at this time." *Ibid.*, 166n.

40. *Official Records*, 34, Pt. 1: 479, Pt. 2: 1062-1063; Johnson, *Red River Campaign,* 87, 120.

41. Blessington, *Walker's Texas Division*, 167-181; Taylor, *Destruction and Reconstruction,* 186-191; Brown, ed., *Journey to Pleasant Hill,* 377-387.

42. Taylor, *Destruction and Reconstruction,* 190-194; Parrish, *Richard Taylor,* 338-339.

43. *Official Records*, 34, Pt. 1: 563-564; Brown, ed., *Journey to Pleasant Hill,* 342-343.

44. James G. Hollandsworth, Jr., *Pretense of Glory: The Life of General Nathaniel P. Banks* (Baton Rouge: Louisiana State University Press, 1998), 186-187.

45. Quote, Blessington, *Walker's Texas Division*, 189; Taylor, *Destruction and Reconstruction,* 196-197; *Official Records*, 34, Pt. 1: 421-422, 564-565; Smith and Mullins, eds., "The Diary of H. C. Medford," 216-219; Max S. Lale, "New Light on the Battle of Mansfield," *East Texas Historical Journal* 25 (Fall 1987): 34-41; Parker, "'The Best Stuff Which the State Affords'," 54-59.

46. Taylor, *Destruction and Reconstruction,* 199-200.

47. Blessington, *Walker's Texas Division*, 193-200; Alwyn Barr, ed., "The Civil War Diary of James Allen Hamilton, 1861-1864," *Texana* 2 (Summer 1964): 142.

48. Taylor, *Destruction and Reconstruction,* 196-198, 206; Brown, ed., *Journey to Pleasant Hill,* 411-413.

49. For comparative purposes I have used the numbers given by Barr, "Texan Losses in the Red River Campaign, 1864," 104-105. The figures for Randal's Brigade given here differ slightly from those in Jane Harris Johansson and David H. Johansson, "Two 'Lost' Battle Reports: Horance Randal's and Joseph L. Brent's Reports of the Battles of Mansfield and Pleasant Hill, 8 and 9 April 1864," *Military History of the West* 23 (Fall 1993): 169-180.

50. Taylor, *Destruction and Reconstruction,* 213-214; Joseph Howard Parks, *General Edmund Kirby Smith, C.S.A.* (Baton Rouge: Louisiana State University Press, 1954), 391-396.

51. Blessington, *Walker's Texas Division*, 241-242.

52. *Official Records*, 34, Pt. 1: 816-818; Bearss, *Steele's Retreat from Camden,* 148-162; David E. Sutherland, "1864: 'A Strange and Wild Time'," in Christ, ed., *Ragged and Sublime,* 120-123.

53. Welsh, *Medical Histories of Confederate Generals,* 193, 230; *The Confederate General,* 5: 135, 6: 193.

54. Barr, "Texan Losses in the Red River Campaign, 1864," 114-115.

55. Allardice, *More Generals in Gray,* 148-149; *The Confederate General,* 6: 190; Johansson, *Peculiar Honor*, 125-126.

56. Quote, Johansson, *ibid.*, 125. Command of the First Brigade remained technically in Waul's hands. After Maclay had been appointed commander of the Second Brigade, Brig. Gen. Wilburn Hill King was named temporary commander; however, because of injuries received at Mansfield he apparently never actually assumed command. Waul returned to the brigade in autumn but went back to Texas soon thereafter because his injuries had not healed properly. *Official Records*, 41, Pt. 3: 966-967, 1141-1142.

57. Quote, Blessington, *Walker's Texas Division*, 262.

58. Quote, *ibid.*, 276; Brown, ed., *Journey to Pleasant Hill,* 436-437; Norris, ed., *With the 18th Texas Infantry,* 76.

59. Robert L. Kerby, *Kirby Smith's Confederacy: The Trans-Mississippi South, 1863-1865* (New York: Columbia University Press, 1972), 324-329; Parks, *General Edmund Kirby Smith,* 420-428; Arthur W. Bergeron, ed., *Reminiscences of Major Silas T. Grisamore, C.S.A.* (Baton Rouge: Louisiana State University Press, 1993), 164-165; Edwin C. Bearss, ed., *A Louisiana Confederate: Diary of Felix Pierre Porche* (Natchitoches: Northwestern State University, 1972), 156.

60. Brown, ed., *Journey to Pleasant Hill,* 438; Kerby, *Kirby Smith's Confederacy,* 331-334.

61. Blessington, *Walker's Texas Division*, 276-278; Johansson, *Peculiar Honor*, 131-133; Parker, "'The Best Stuff Which the State Affords'," 81-83.

62. Brown, ed., *Journey to Pleasant Hill,* 439-440; Seymour V. Connor, ed., *Dear America: Some Letters of Orange Cicero and Mary America (Aiken) Connor* (Austin: Jenkins Publishing Co., 1971), 102-110.

63. The Second Partisan Rangers replaced the Sixteenth Infantry in Waterhouse's Brigade and the Twenty-ninth Cavalry replaced the Eighteenth Infantry in Waul's Brigade. *Official Records*, 48, Pt. 1: 1405-1406.

64. Blessington, *Walker's Texas Division*, 292-307; Brown, ed., *Journey to Pleasant Hill*, 443-448.

65. Alwyn Barr, *Polignac's Texas Brigade* (2nd ed., College Station: Texas A&M University Press, 1998), xv.

66. Wright and Simpson, *Texas in the War, 1861-1865*, 118-119; Tyler, ed., *New Handbook of Texas*, 6: 220-221.

67. Tyler, ed., *New Handbook of Texas*, 3: 963-964, 6: 95; Wooster, "Analysis of the Membership of the Texas Secession Convention," 322-335.

68. Tyler, ed., *New Handbook of Texas*, 1: 99; John Calvin Williams, "A Rebel Remembers the Red River Campaign," *Civil War Times Illustrated* 17 (January 1979): 24-25; Hewett, ed., *Texas Confederate Soldiers, 1861-1865*, 2: 225-229. There are 1,135 men listed on the muster rolls for the Twenty-seventh Texas. *Ibid.*, 154-159.

69. Douglas V. Meed, *Texas Wanderlust: The Adventures of Dutch Wurzbach* (College Station: Texas A&M University Press, 1997), 100-101; Tyler, ed., *New Handbook of Texas*, 3: 513-514; 4: 476; Barr, *Polignac's Texas Brigade*, 4-50; Wooten, *A Comprehensive History of Texas*, 2: 637-638. Eventually the Thirty-first Cavalry listed 932 men on its muster rolls. Hewett, ed., *Texas Confederate Soldiers, 1861-1865*, 2: 210-214.

70. *Official Records*, 13: 296-300, 305-307; Meed, *Texas Wanderlust*, 115-117; Josephy, *Civil War in the American West*, 361; Williams, "A Rebel Remembers the Civil War," 25; Robert S. Weddle, *Plow-Horse Cavalry: The Caney Creek Boys of the Thirty-fourth Texas* (Austin: Madrona Press, 1974), 56-64.

71. Barr, *Polignac's Texas Brigade*, 8-9: Weddle, *Plow-Horse Cavalry*, 64-67.

72. Quote, Hindman, *Official Records*, 13: 47-48; Weddle, *Plow-Horse Cavalry*, 66-67; Meed, *Texas Wanderlust*, 119-128.

73. Total Confederate losses at Prairie Grove were reported as 1,317; Union casualties were 1,251. Casualties in the Texas Brigade alone were not given in the official reports. One member of the Thirty-fourth Texas, Alexander Cameron, stated only three men were killed and eleven wounded in his regiment. J. S. Duncan, ed., "A Soldier's Fare is Rough: Letters from A. Cameron in Indian Territory, Arkansas Campaign, 1862-1864," *Military History of Texas and the Southwest* 12 (No. 1 1975): 51-52. See also Stephen B. Oates, "The Prairie Grove Campaign, 1862," *Arkansas Historical Quarterly* 19 (Summer 1960): 119-141; Ival L. Gregory, "The Battle of Prairie Grove, Arkansas, December 7, 1862," *Journal of the West* 19 (October 1980): 63-75; Shea, *War in the West: Pea Ridge and Prairie Grove*, 94-103; Weddle, *Plow-Horse Cavalry*, 77-85; Peter Cozzens, "Hindman's Grand Delusion," *Civil War Times Illustrated* 39 (October 2000): 29-35, 66-69.

74. Barr, *Polignac's Texas Brigade*, 11; Tyler, ed., *New Handbook of Texas*, 6: 25.

75. Barr, *Polignac's Texas Brigade*, 11-12; Merle Mears Duncan, "David Richard Wallace: Pioneer in Psychiatry," *Texana* 1 (Fall 1963): 348-362; Tyler, ed., *New Handbook of Texas*, 2: 193, 880; 3: 986; 6: 805.

76. *Official Records*, 22, Pt. 2: 909; Weddle, *Plow-Horse Cavalry*, 87-88.

77. *Official Records*, 22, Pt. 2: 804-805, 809-810, 815, 823; Meed, *Texas Wanderlust*, 125-129.

78. Weddle, *Plow-Horse Cavalry,* 89-90; Wooten, ed., *Comprehensive History,* 2: 640.

79. Barr, *Polignac's Texas Brigade,* 20-21.

80. Delaney, "Diary and Memoirs of Marshall Samuel Pierson," 27-29. McCaffrey, *This Band of Heroes*, 175, points out that among the Texas regiments that surrendered at Arkansas Post there were many men absent on furlough, detached on temporary duty elsewhere, or who escaped during the confusion. Those Texans who had been captured were later exchanged. Their regiments later served in Granbury's Brigade, discussed in Chapter Four of this book.

Apparently, however, some of those who had been exchanged served in the Seventeenth Consolidated Regiment. See Douglas Hale, "One Man's War: Captain Joseph Burton, 1861-1865," *East Texas Historical Journal* 20 (February 1982): 35.

81. Terry L. Jones, "Camille Armand Jules Marie, Prince de Polignac," in *The Confederate General,* 5: 41. For more background information on Polignac see Jeff Kinard, *Lafayette of the South: Prince Camille de Polignac and the American Civil War* (College Station: Texas A&M University Press, 2001).

82. *Official Records*, 24, Pt. 2: 109, 111, 113.

83. W. T. Block, "The Swamp Angels: A History of Spaight's 11th Battalion, Texas Volunteers, Confederate States Army," *East Texas Historical Journal* 30 (Spring 1992): 44-51; Cooper K. Ragan, ed., "The Diary of George W. O'Brien, 1863," *Southwestern Historical Quarterly*, 67 (July 1963): 30-33, 45-48. Block, "Swamp Angels," 50, points out that historians often confuse the names of Col. J. W. Speight and Lt. Col. Ashley W. Spaight; both were pronounced "spate." Muster rolls for the battalion are printed in Charles R. Walker, "Spaight's Battalion," *Texas Gulf Historical and Biographical Record* 8 (November 1972): 22-38.

84. *Official Records*, 26, Pt. 1: 320-326, 329-332; Ragan, ed., "Diary of George W. O'Brien," 235-246; J. S. Duncan, "Alexander Cameron in the Louisiana Campaign, 1863-1865," *Military History of Texas and the Southwest* 12 (No. 4, 1975): 34-41. Meed, *Texas Wanderlust,* 141-142, points out that Lieutenant Colonel Guess had been charged with trading with the enemy and placed under arrest before the battle. Colonel Speight alleged that Guess had been paid by the enemy to buy cotton for Federal speculators. Meed notes that since Guess was captured during a truce he may have been happy to surrender to the enemy.

85. Ragan, ed., "Diary of George W. O'Brien," 413-417.

86. Barr, *Polignac's Texas Brigade,* 29n, points out that Kirby Smith recommended Speight for promotion but Speight resigned his commission in spring 1864, apparently never having returned to active duty.

87. Quote, Taylor, *Destruction and Reconstruction,* 184; Parrish, *Richard Taylor,* 326-329.

88. Tyler, ed., *New Handbook of Texas*, 1: 1044, 4: 476, 6: 95; Ragan, ed., "Diary of George W. O'Brien," 418-423.

89. *Official Records*, 26, Pt. 1: 392-395; Lowe, *Texas Overland Expedition of 1863,* 80-100.

90. Ragan, ed., "Diary of George W. O'Brien," 425-433; Block, "Swamp Angels," 52.

91. *Official Records*, 34, Pt. 2: 934-935, 952-953; William Clark Griggs, *Parson Henry Renfro: Free Thinker on the Texas Frontier* (Austin: University of

Texas Press, 1994), 78; Delaney, ed., "Diary and Memoirs of Marshall Samuel Pierson," 29-31; Kinard, *Lafayette of the South*, 122-128.

92. Taylor, *Destruction and Reconstruction*, 187-190; Johnson, *Red River Campaign*, 87-89, 96-97, 120-122.

93. Taylor, *Destruction and Reconstruction*, 194-195; *Official Records*, 34, Pt. 1: 563; Kinard, *Lafayette of the South*, 139-140.

94. Brown, ed., *Journey to Pleasant Hill*, 394-398; Weddle, *Plow-Horse Cavalry*, 115-119; William Arcenaux, *Acadian General: Alfred Mouton and the Civil War* (Lafayette, LA: Center for Lousiana Studies, University of Southwest Louisiana, 1981), 130-133; Smith and Mullins, eds., "The Diary of H. C. Medford," 215-220.

95. Taylor, *Destruction and Reconstruction*, 200-206; Blessington, *Walker's Texas Division*, 193-197; Barr, ed., "Civil War Diary of James Allen Hamilton," 142; Delaney, ed., "Diary and Memoirs of Marshall Samuel Pierson," 35-36; Kinard, *Lafayette of the South*, 150-151.

96. Taylor reported total Confederate losses as 2,200 in the two days. Of these, 1,274 were Texans. Barr, "Texan Losses in the Red River Campaign," 105.

97. Harrison had been home on leave in Texas when his horse ran away. By the time he obtained a mount the battles at Mansfield and Pleasant Hill had been fought. Barr, *Polignac's Texas Brigade*, 39.

98. Johnson, *Red River Campaign*, 236-241; Parrish, *Richard Taylor*, 383-384; Barr, *Polignac's Texas Brigade*, 41-43.

99. This is discussed in the section on Bee's Cavalry Division in the preceding chapter.

100. Barr, *Polignac's Texas Brigade*, 44-46; Bergeron, ed., *Reminiscences of Major Silas T. Gilmore*, 158-158; Bearrs, ed., *A Louisiana Confederate*, 122-124; Bailey, *Texans in the Confederate Cavalry*, 63-74.

101. Barr, "Texan Losses in the Red River Campaign," 107.

102. Barr, *Polignac's Texas Brigade*, 47-48; Parks, *Kirby Smith*, 419.

103. Parks, *Kirby Smith*, 420-428; Blessington, *Walker's Texas Division*, 273-275.

104. For more on this issue see Wooster, *Lone Star Generals in Gray*, 137, and Barr, *Polignac's Texas Brigade*, 50-55.

105. Barr, *Polignac's Texas Brigade*, 51-52.

106. *Official Records*, 48, Pt. 1: 1371-1372, 1390, Pt. 2: 1266, 1281. In mid-April 1865 the Twentieth Texas Infantry replaced the Thirty-fifth Texas Cavalry in Harrison's Brigade.

107. *Official Records*, 48, Pt. 2: 1286, 1303; Weddle, *Plow-Horse Cavalry*, 158-162; Barr, *Polignac's Texas Brigade*, 55-57.

108. Sifakis, *Compendium of Confederate Armies: Texas*, 111, indicates the Third Texas took part in the battles at Mansfield and Pleasant Hill. Blessington, *Walker's Texas Division*, 242, correctly notes the Third Infantry joined Walker's Division on April 15 after just arriving from Texas.

109. Hewett, ed., *Texas Confederate Soldiers, 1861-1865*, 2: 376-382; *Official Records*, 15: 851.

110. *Official Records*, 4: 97; Allardice, *More Generals in Gray*, 144-145; Tyler, ed., *New Handbook of Texas*, 4: 329-330. Tom Cutrer, writing in the *Handbook*,

states that Luckett never enrolled at West Point; Allardice says he attended but did not graduate. Earl Van Dorn, while commander of the Texas District, referred to Luckett as "a West Pointer" in his recommendation that Luckett be appointed colonel. Luckett is described by British visitor Lt. Col. Arthur Fremantle as "a handsome man, a doctor by profession, well informed and agreeable, but most bitter against the Yankees." Lord, ed., *Fremantle Diary*, 13.

111. Oates, ed., *Rip Ford's Texas*, 329; *Official Records*, 4: 169; 5: 851.

112. *Official Records*, 26, Pt. 2: 132.

113. Cotham, *Battle on the Bay*, 156; *Official Records*, 26, Pt. 1: 241; Casdorph, *Prince John Magruder*, 250-251.

114. *Official Records*, 26, Pt. 1: 242.

115. Quote, Cotham, *Battle on the Bay*, 156; *Official Records*, 26, Pt. 1: 245-246.

116. *Official Records*, 26, Pt. 2: 183.

117. *Ibid.*, 26, Pt. 2: 247, 280; Block, *History of Jefferson County*, 115.

118. Quote, Assistant Inspector General's Report, *Official Records*, 26, Pt. 2: 318.

119. *Ibid.*, 22, Pt. 2: 456, 496, 564, 1132.

120. *Ibid.*, 34, Pt. 2: 1040; Blessington, *Walker's Texas Division*, 241-242.

121. Barr, "Texan Losses in the Red River Campaign," 115. The memoirs of Adam Quincy Clements, compiled by Anice Vance, in the Regimental File, Third Texas Infantry, Simpson Confederate Research Center, describe the battle.

122. Allardice, *More Confederate Generals in Gray*, 144.

123. Hobby's Eighth Texas is often confused with Overton Young's Twelfth Infantry, which is frequently referred to in the *Official Records* and Blessington's *Walker's Texas Division* as the Eighth Texas Infantry.

124. Barr, "Texas Coastal Defense," 11-12; Norman Delaney, "Corpus Christi—The Vicksburg of Texas," *Civil War Times Illustrated* 16 (July 1977): 4-9, 44-48.

125. Barr, "Texas Coastal Defense," 12; *Official Records*, 15: 851; Young, *To the Tyrants Never Yield*, 124-127.

126. *Official Records*, 9: 626; Tyler, ed., *New Handbook of Texas*, 3: 867.

127. Hewett, ed., *Texas Confederate Soldiers, 1861-1865*, 2: 412-419.

128. *Official Records*, 15: 404-405; Tyler, ed., *New Handbook of Texas*, 2: 1100; Lester N. Fitzhugh, "Saluria, Fort Esperanza, and Military Operations on the Texas Coast, 1861-1864," *Southwestern Historical Quarterly* 61 (July 1957): 95-97.

129. *Official Records*, 26, Pt. 2: 489, 492, 522; 53: 919.

130. *Ibid.*, 34, Pt. 3: 805, Pt. 4: 638, 701; 41, Pt. 2: 1035, Pt. 3: 965, Pt. 4: 1084, 1139.

131. Cotham, *Battle on the Bay*, 164-166.

132. *Official Records*, 48, Pt. 1: 1408; Cotham, *Battle on the Bay*, 176-183.

133. Sifakis, *Compendium of Confederate Armies: Texas*, 121-122.

134. *Official Records*, 53: 647-659, 657-661, 664-666; Tyler, ed., *New Handbook of Texas*, 4: 1010; Cotham, *Battle on the Bay*, 8-12; Allardice, *More Generals in Gray*, 52; Earl W. Fornell, *The Galveston Era: The Texas Crescent on the Eve of Secession* (Austin: University of Texas Press, 1961), 16-18, 291, 293; Ralph

A. Wooster, "Wealthy Texans, 1860," *Southwestern Historical Quarterly* 71 (October 1967): 163-180.

135. Hewett, ed., *Texas Confederate Soldiers, 1861-1865,* 2: 419-424; *Official Records*, 9: 701.

136. Under this act twelve-month volunteers, such as those in Nichols' Regiment, were entitled to a sixty-day furlough and then were given the privilege of choosing their own company-level officers. See Emory Thomas, *The Confederate Nation, 1861-1865* (New York: Harper & Row, 1979), 152-153.

137. Fitzhugh, *Texas Batteries, Battalions, Regiments,* 28, notes "a large percentage of its [Ninth Infantry] personnel appears to have entered Waul's Legion."

138. *Official Records*, 4: 111.

139. Tyler, ed., *New Handbook of Texas*, 1: 414; Wooster, "Wealthy Texans, 1860," 172.

140. *Official Records*, 9: 545-546, 609-610. This incident is described in a manuscript "Civil War Reminiscence" (author unknown), in the Thirteenth Texas File, Simpson Confederate Research Center, Hillsboro, Texas.

141. Sifakis, *Compendium of Confederate Armies: Texas,* 124-125. Reuben R. Brown's Twelfth Texas Cavalry Battalion later consolidated with Rountree's Battalion to form the Thirty-fifth Texas (Brown's) Cavalry Regiment, which is described in Chapter Five.

142. *Official Records*, 15: 148, 838, 854; Tyler, ed., *New Handbook of Texas*, 1: 1050, 2: 1047.

143. Winters, *Civil War in Louisiana,* 202; Henderson, *Texas in the Confederacy,* 121; *Official Records*, 24, Pt. 1: 329-330. On September 15, 1863, Bates wrote a letter from Velasco stating that he had just returned from Louisiana and indicating he had earlier marched to Opelousas. *Ibid.*, 24, Pt. 2: 230.

144. *Official Records*, 34, Pt. 3: 800, Pt. 4: 701, 1023.

145. *Ibid.*, 34, Pt. 4: 1139.

146. *Ibid.*, 48, Pt. 2: 1284, 1292, 1298.

147. Hewett, ed., *Texas Confederate Soldiers, 1861-1865,* 2: 504-513; *Official Records*, 41, Pt. 4: 870, 1137, 48, Pt. 1: 1355; Henderson, *Texas in the Confederacy,* 121; Walker County Genealogical Society and Walker County Historical Society, *Walker County, Texas: A History* (Dallas: Media Corporation, 1986), 324.

148. Tyler, ed., *New Handbook of Texas*, 1: 6; *Members of the Texas Legislature, 1846-1962* (Austin: n. p., 1962), 41; *Walker County, Texas,* 334.

149. *Official Records*, 9: 723, 15: 143-144.

150. Quote, Debray to Hebert, *Official Records*, 15: 816. Block, *History of Jefferson County,* 102, notes that the threat of yellow fever at Sabine Pass was real. Fifty deaths in the seaport led to the evacuation of most of the town's residents. The epidemic was abating somewhat by the first of October although there were afflicted residents as late as October 20.

151. Cotham, *Battle on the Bay,* 116; Frazier, *Cottonclads!,* 52, 61, 69, 82; Frazier, "Sibley's Texans and the Battle of Galveston," 185-186; *Official Records*, 15: 217.

152. *Official Records*, 26, Pt. 2: 218, 319.

153. *Ibid.*, 22, Pt. 2: 1132.

154. *Ibid.*, 41, Pt. 3: 941.

155. *Ibid.*, 34, Pt. 2: 932, Pt. 4, 638; 41, Pt. 3: 965, 969; 48, Pt. 1: 1370, 1408, 1459, Pt. 2: 1281.

156. *Ibid.*, 48, Pt. 2: 1287, 1288, 1315, 1318-1319.

157. Sifakis, *Compendium of Confederate Armies: Texas,* 131; Block, "Swamp Angels," 44.

158. Cotham, *Battle on the Bay,* 116-134; Frazier, *Cottonclads!,* 52, 61, 69.

159. Sifakis, *Compendium of Confederate Armies: Texas,* 65; Block, "Swamp Angels," 45-46.

160. Block, *History of Jefferson County,* 104-105; K. D. Keith, "The Memoirs of Captain Kosciuszko D. Keith," *Texas Gulf Historical and Biographical Record* 9 (November 1974): 58-59.

161. Quote, Block, "Swamp Angels," 49. W. D. "Bill" Quick of Nederland has pointed out that the *Official Records of the Union* and *Records of the Union and Confederate Armies in the War of Rebellion*, 30 vols. (Washington: Government Printing Office, 1899-1922), Series II, 1:71, indicate the *Dan* sank the following year in the Mississippi River.

162. Keith, "Memoirs," 62; Block, *History of Jefferson County,* 106-107.

163. Block, "Swamp Angels," 50-52; Barr, *Polignac's Texas Brigade,* 23, 25, 27-28, 33-34; Ragan, ed., "Diary of Captain George W. O'Brien," 241-243, 417-428.

164. Block, "Swamp Angels," 52-53; Block, *History of Jefferson County,* 115-116. In April 1863 a detachment from Griffin's Battalion captured eight prisoners when a Union landing party came ashore on the Louisiana side of Sabine Pass. *Official Records*, 15: 402-404.

165. Block, "Swamp Angels," 52-53; Barr, "The Battle of Calcasieu Pass," 58-67.

166. *Official Records*, 41, Pt. 4: 1139, 48, Pt. 2: 1287; Block, "Swamp Angels," 53-54.

167. Sifakis, *Compendium of Confederate Armies: Texas,* 77-78.

168. Tyler, ed., *New Handbook of Texas*, 1: 408-409, 2: 1143.

169. *Official Records*, 13: 47-48.

170. Shea, *War in the West: Pea Ridge and Prairie Grove,* 94-103.

171. *Ibid.*, 22, Pt. 2: 909. According to General Steele the regiment "was found to be greatly demoralized and in a very short time after being put on duty exhibited an effective strength of less than 100 men, the depletion arising, in the main, from desertion." *Ibid.*, 29.

172. Quote, Cooper's report, *Official Records*, 22, Pt. 1: 460-461, Pt. 2: 833, 895; Josephy, *Civil War in the West,* 461-462.

173. Inspector General's report, October 26, 1863, *Official Records*, 22, Pt. 2: 1051.

174. *Ibid.*, 1052.

175. *Ibid.*, 34, Pt. 2: 876, 1012, 1050.

176. *Ibid.*, 48, Pt. 2: 1286, 1291, 1365.

CHAPTER SEVEN

1. *Official Records*, 41, Pt. 4: 1064. The most thorough account of artillery

in the Trans Mississippi is Chester Alwyn Barr, Jr., "Confederate Artillery in the Trans-Mississippi" (M. A. thesis, University of Texas, 1961). A shortened version, describing Texas field artillery, by Barr is "Texas' Confederate Field Artillery," *Texas Military History* 1 (August 1961): 1-8.

2. Sifakis, *Compendium of Confederate Armies: Texas,* 6, 12; Wright and Simpson, *Texas in the War, 1861-1865,* 130; Barr, "Texas Coastal Defense, 1861-1865," 5.

3. Barr, "Texas Coastal Defense, 1861-1865," 10; Tyler, ed., *New Handbook of Texas*, 4: 485.

4. Based on data taken from Hewett, ed., *Texas Confederate Soldiers,* 1861-1865, 2: 321-330; Sifakis, *Compendium of Confederate Armies: Texas,* 6-14; Barr, "Confederate Artillery in the Trans-Mississippi," 107-108.

5. Cotham, *Battle on the Bay,* 36-39, 50-63; Frazier, *Cottonclads!,* 27-30.

6. Cotham, *Battle on the Bay,* 106-123; Frazier, *Cottonclads!,* 53, 66.

7. For the early history of the Davis Guards in assisting John S. Ford in South Texas and as part of Magruder's forces that recaptured Galveston see Andrew Forest Muir, "Dick Dowling and the Battle of Sabine Pass," *Civil War History* 4 (December 1958): 400-408.

8. Keith, "Memoirs," 60-62; *Official Records*, 19: 553-573; Muir, "Dick Dowling and the Battle of Sabine Pass," 408-410.

9. Quote, Muir, "Dick Dowling and the Battle of Sabine Pass," 412.

10. W. T. Block, "Sabine Pass in the Civil War," *East Texas Historical Journal* 9 (October 1971): 132; Block, "Fort Griffin Myths Explored," *ibid.*, 137-138; Block, *History of Jefferson County,* 108; Harold B. Simpson, "The Battle of Sabine Pass," in Seymour Connor, et al., *Battles of Texas* (Waco: Texian Press, 1967), 139-140, 145-149.

11. Barr, "Texas Coastal Defense, 1861-1865," 24.

12. For a more detailed description of the battle see Muir, "Dick Dowling and the Battle of Sabine Pass," 417-419; Ernest Jones, "The Battle of Sabine Pass, September 8, 1863," *Blue & Gray Magazine* 4 (September 1986): 19-24, 47-48, 50-53; Frank X. Tolbert, *Dick Dowling at Sabine Pass* (New York: McGraw-Hill, 1962); Alwyn Barr, "Sabine Pass, September 1863," *Texas Military History* 2 (February 1962): 17-22; H. L. Sandefer and Archie P. McDonald, "Sabine Pass: David and Goliath," *Texana* 7 (Fall 1969): 177-188; Simpson, "The Battle of Sabine Pass," 137-169.

13. It is difficult to determine the exact number of men involved in the Confederate defense. Andrew Forest Muir, "Dick Dowling and the Battle of Sabine Pass," 417n, points out in his report Dowling referred to forty-seven men among the defenders, but he included several individuals (such as Captain Odlum and Capt. Leon Smith) who were there only briefly. It appears that three officers (including Dowling) and forty enlisted men were present for duty at Fort Griffin that day.

14. Muir, "Dick Dowling and the Battle of Sabine Pass," 421-422; *Official Records*, 26, Pt. 1: 302-306.

15. *Official Records*, 26, Pt. 2: 281, 320, 563; *Official Records, Supplement,* 68: 460-461. The author wishes to thank W. D. "Bill" Quick of Nederland for his assistance in matters relating to the Davis Guards. Company A of the First Texas

Heavy Artillery was sent to Sabine Pass in late September 1863, but when the threat of another invasion passed they returned to Galveston.

16. *Official Records*, 34, Pt. 2: 1010, Pt. 3: 813.

17. *Ibid.*, 48, Pt. 2: 92, 116, 1292, 1297.

18. Sifakis, *Compendium of Confederate Armies: Texas*, 14-15; Barr, "Confederate Artillery in the Trans-Mississippi," 110. Apparently there were no First, Second, or Fifth Texas Artillery Battalions. Sifakis, *Compendium of Confederate Armies: Texas* lists only the Third, Fourth, Sixth, and Seventh Battalions.

19. *Official Records*, 4: 117, 129-133, 153; Fitzhugh, "Saluria, Fort Esperanza, and Military Operations on the Texas Coast," 68-73; Tyler, ed., *New Handbook of Texas*, 2: 1100.

20. Fitzhugh, "Saluria, Fort Esperanza, and Military Operations on the Texas Coast," 80; Barr, "Texas Coastal Defense, 1861-1865," 14; Young, *To the Tyrants Never Yield*, 124-127; Brownson Malsch, *Indianola: The Mother of Western Texas* (Austin: State House Press, 1988), 169.

21. Sifakis, *Compendium of Confederate Armies: Texas*, 14. Fitzhugh, "Saluria, Fort Esperanza, and Military Operations on the Texas Coast," 97, points out that the record provides no clue as to the whereabouts of Lt. Col. Shea during the defense of Fort Esperanza. Fitzhugh speculates that he may have been ill during the time.

22. Sifakis, *Compendium of Confederate Armies: Texas*, 17-18; Wright and Simpson, *Texas in the War, 1861-1865*, 41, 42, 134, 136.

23. *Official Records*, 26, Pt. 1: 347, Pt. 2: 281, 319; 34, Pt. 2: 932; Sifakis, *Compendium of Confederate Armies: Texas*, 17-18.

24. Sifakis, *Compendium of Confederate Armies: Texas*, 35; Wright and Simpson, *Texas in the War, 1861-1865*, 36, 130; *Official Records*, 26, Pt. 2: 194; 41, Pt. 3: 969, Pt. 4: 1064. Information on the organization of Willke's Battalion is sketchy. It is not mentioned by Henderson, *Texas in the Confederacy*, Barr, "Confederate Artillery in the Trans-Mississippi," or Fitzhugh, *Texas Batteries, Battalions, Regiments*.

25. Wright and Simpson, *Texas in the War, 1861-1865*, 36; *Official Records*, 26, Pt. 1: 347, Pt. 2: 84, 99, 407, 512; 34, Pt. 2: 932, 1042, 1052, 1100.

26. *Official Records*, 34, Pt. 3: 800, 809, 816, Pt. 4: 630; 41, Pt. 2: 1097, 1098, Pt. 4: 1064, 1146; 48, Pt. 2: 963.

27. Sifakis, *Compendium of Confederate Armies: Texas*, 26. The battery is also listed in Wright and Simpson, *Texas in the War, 1861-1865*, 36. It is not listed in Fitzhugh, *Texas Batteries, Battalions, Regiments*, Henderson, *Texas in the Confederacy*, or Barr, "Confederate Artillery in the Trans-Mississippi."

28. *Official Records*, 26, Pt. 2: 510; 34, Pt. 2: 932, 1100; Henderson, *Texas in the Confederacy*, 145-146; Wright and Simpson, *Texas in the War, 1861-1865*, 36-37, 130; Barr, "Texas' Confederate Field Artillery," 5-6.

29. John B. Magruder to Hamilton P. Bee, November 17, 1863, *Official Records*, 26, Pt. 2: 424. See also *ibid.*, 436, 443.

30. *Ibid.*, 26, Pt. 2: 565; 34, Pt. 1: 912-914, Pt. 2: 1040, 1099, Pt. 3: 800; Barr, "The Battle of Calcasieu Pass," 60-67; Block, "Calcasieu Pass," 139-144. For more

on Creuzbaur's Battery see Paul Boethal, *The Big Guns of Fayette* (Austin: Von Boeckmann-Jones, 1965).

31. *Official Records*, 41, Pt. 2: 1097, Pt. 3: 966, Pt. 4: 1065.

32. *Ibid.*, 41, Pt. 4: 1066, 117, 1137; 48, Pt. 1: 1357, Pt. 2: 1316.

33. *Ibid.*, 13: 978; 22, Pt. 1: 963; 26, Pt. 1: 394, 395, 454; John D. Perkins, *Daniel's Battery: The Ninth Texas Field Battery* (Hillsboro: Hill College Press), 5-18; Alwyn Barr, "Confederate Artillery in Arkansas," *Arkansas Historical Quarterly* 22 (Autumn 1963): 253; Blessington, *Walker's Texas Division*, 54, 133, 150-154.

34. *Official Records*, 34, Pt. 1: 536, 566; Perkins, *Daniel's Battery*, 21-22; Alwyn Barr, "Confederate Artillery in Western Louisiana, 1864," *Louisiana History* 5 (Winter 1964): 53, 59, 61.

35. Bearss, *Steele's Retreat from Camden*, 166; *Official Records*, 41, Pt. 4: 1069; 48, Pt. 2: 963; Perkins, *Daniel's Battery*, 28-53, provides analysis of membership in the battery.

36. *Official Records*, 9: 37; 51, Pt. 2: 570; Sifakis, *Compendium of Confederate Armies: Texas*, 31; Wright and Simpson, *Texas in the War, 1861-1865*, 38. The battery is not included in Henderson, *Texas in the Confederacy*, Fitzhugh, *Texas Batteries, Battalions, Regiments*, nor Jenning C. Wise, *The Long Arm of Lee: The History of the Artillery of the Army of Northern Virginia* (Reprint; New York: Oxford University Press, 1959).

37. Barr, "Texas' Confederate Field Artillery," 1.

38. Barr, "Confederate Artillery in Arkansas," 253; Blessington, *Walker's Texas Division*, 43, 54, 88, 90-91; *Official Records*, 9: 701.

39. *Official Records*, 34, Pt. 1: 179, 225, 307, 561-562; 41, Pt. 4: 1064; 48, Pt. 2: 963; Barr, "Confederate Artillery in Western Louisiana, 1864," 58; Wright and Simpson, *Texas in the War, 1861-1865*, 172.

40. Barr, "Texas' Confederate Field Artillery," 1; Barr, "Confederate Artillery in the Trans-Mississippi," 212. According to Barr the Galveston Battery had four 6-pounder smoothbores and two 4-pounder smoothbores in 1861.

41. Sifakis, *Compendium of Confederate Armies: Texas*, 25; Barr, "Confederate Artillery in Western Louisiana, 1864," 71-72; *Official Records*, 26, Pt. 2: 509; 34, Pt. 2: 915, 932, 1040, 1106; 41, Pt. 4: 1064; 48, Pt. 2: 963.

42. Biographical data taken from Barr, "Texas' Confederate Field Artillery," 2; Lucia Rutherford Douglas, editor, *Douglas's Texas Battery, CSA* (Waco: Texian Press, 1966), vii-viii; Lester N. Fitzhugh, editor, *Cannon Smoke: The Letters of Captain John J. Good, Good-Douglas Texas Battery, CSA* (Hillsboro: Hill Junior College Press, 1971), v-viii.

43. Piston and Hatcher, *Wilson's Creek*, 123-124; Shea and Hess, *Pea Ridge*, 97, 109, 128, 231-233, 246, 252; Fitzhugh, ed., *Cannon Smoke*, 162-167; James Lunsford, "Brief Sketch of Douglas's First Texas Battery," in Douglas, ed., *Douglas's Texas Battery*, 161-164; *Official Records*, 3: 730.

44. Lester N. Fitzhugh, editor of Good's letters, noted that the exact nature of Good's disability is obscure. He believed it probable that Good was suffering from the pulmonary condition which caused his death at age fifty-five in 1882. *Cannon Smoke*, 191n.

45. *Official Records*, 10, Pt. 1: 463, 450, 551, 789; 16, Pt. 1: 936, 941, 945; Lunsford, "Brief Sketch of Douglas's First Texas Battery," 164-165.

46. Quote, Lunsford, "Brief Sketch of Douglas's First Texas Battery," 165. See also Douglas, ed., *Douglas's Texas Battery*, 56-57; *Official Records*, 20, Pt. 1: 660, 681, 936-937; 31, Pt. 1: 749-750. For more on Douglas' Battery in the Tennessee campaigns see Larry J. Daniel, *Cannoneers in Gray: The Field Artillery of the Army of Tennessee, 1861-1865* (University, AL: University of Alabama Press, 1984), 60-61, 96-98, 113.

47. Lunsford, "Brief Sketch of Douglas's First Texas Battery," 166; *Official Records*, 32, Pt. 2: 754.

48. Quote, Lunsford, "Brief Sketch of Douglas's First Texas Battery," 166; Douglas, ed., *Douglas's Texas Battery*, 161; *Official Records*, 38, Pt. 3: 651, 658, 667.

49. Douglas quote, *Douglas's Texas Battery*, 150. See also Daniel, *Cannoneers in Gray*, 173.

50. Douglas, ed., *Douglas's Texas Battery*, 151-152; Lunsford, "Brief Sketch of Douglas's First Texas Battery," 167.

51. Quote, Lunsford, "Brief Sketch of Douglas's First Texas Battery," 168.

52. Douglas, ed., *Douglas's Texas Battery*, 157n.

53. *Official Records*, 26, Pt. 2: 500; 34, Pt. 2: 930, 1100, Pt. 3: 779; Wright and Simpson, *Texas in the War, 1861-1865*, 133n; Barr, "Confederate Artillery in the Trans-Mississippi," 213.

54. *Official Records*, 26, Pt. 2: 500; 34, Pt. 2: 930, 1100, Pt. 3: 779; Wright and Simpson, *Texas in the War, 1861-1865*, 133n; Barr, "Confederate Artillery in the Trans-Mississippi," 213.

54. Barr, "Confederate Artillery in the Trans-Misssissippi," 218; Sifakis, *Compendium of Confederate Armies: Texas*, 30; *Official Records*, 26, Pt. 2: 84, 99, 281.

55. Quote, Cooper, *Official Records*, 13: 298. See also *Ibid.*, 299-300, 304; Barr, "Confederate Artillery in Arkansas," 251.

56. *Official Records*, 13: 335-336; Barr, "Confederate Artillery in Arkansas," 251-252; Josephy, *Civil War in the American West*, 362.

57. *Official Records*, 22, Pt. 1: 903, Pt. 2: 998, 1064; 41, Pt. 1: 789-792; Rampp and Rampp, *Civil War in Indian Territory*, 105-113.

58. *Official Records*, 41, Pt. 4: 1064, 1146; 48, Pt. 2: 963.

59. *Ibid.* 26, Pt. 1: 319, 347, Pt. 2: 281, 319, 407, 914; 34, Pt. 2: 932, 1099, Pt. 3: 800; 41, Pt. 3: 966.

60. Wright and Simpson, *Texas in the War, 1861-1865*, 134n; Barr, "Confederate Artillery in the Trans-Mississippi," 213-214; Sifakis, *Compendium of Confederate Armies: Texas*, 13-14, 17-18; *Official Records*, 41, Pt. 3: 955-956; 48, Pt. 1: 1457, Pt. 2: 963.

61. Barr, "Confederate Artillery in the Trans-Mississippi," 219; Wright and Simpson, *Texas in the War, 1861-1865*, 41; *Official Records*, 26, Pt. 1: 66. This battery is not listed in Sifakis, Henderson, or Fitzhugh.

62. Wright and Simpson, *Texas in the War, 1861-1865*, 36, 41, 130n; Block, *History of Jefferson County*, 99, 104; Keith, "Memoirs," 44-59.

63. Block, *History of Jefferson County*, 106-107; Keith, "Memoirs," 60-62.

64. Block, *History of Jefferson County*, 112, 116, 119-120; W. T. Block,

"Versatility Was Proud Boast of Area Civil War Outfit," *East Texas Historical Journal* 9 (October 1971): 150-151.

65. Nathaniel C. Hughes, Jr., *The Pride of the Confederate Artillery: The Washington Artillery in the Army of Tennessee* (Baton Rouge: Louisiana State University Press, 1997), 320; William M. Owen, *In Camp and Battle with the Washington Artillery of New Orleans* (2nd. ed., Boston: Ticknor and Co., 1885), 404.

66. Inspector General's Report, October 26, 1863, *Official Records*, 22, Pt. 2: 1052.

67. *Official Records*, 34, Pt. 1: 786, 841-848; Bearss, *Steele's Retreat from Camden*, 19-20, 23-25, 27, 38, 40; Barr, "Confederate Artillery in Arkansas," 265, 267-268.

68. *Official Records*, 41, Pt. 3: 471, Pt. 4: 164; 48, Pt. 2: 963.

69. Barr, "Texas' Confederate Field Artillery," 5; Wright and Simpson, *Texas in the War, 1861-1865*, 135n.

70. *Official Records*, 8: 6, 8, 10, 288.

71. *Ibid.*, 22: Pt. 1: 459-460, 462; Josephy, *Civil War in the American West*, 371.

72. Quote, Cooper, *Official Records*, 41, Pt. 1: 36.

73. Sifakis, *Compendium of Confederate Armies: Texas*, 31; *Official Records*, 41, Pt. 4: 1064, 1146.

74. Sifakis, *Compendium of Confederate Armies: Texas*, 19; *Official Records*, 15: 851; 26, Pt. 2: 407, 563; 34, Pt. 2: 932, 3: 800; 41, Pt. 2: 1097, Pt. 3: 966; 48, Pt. 1: 1355, 1408, Pt. 2: 963, 1292, 1297; Hewett, ed., *Texas Confederate Soldiers, 1861-1865*, 2: 339.

75. *Official Records*, 26, Pt. 2: 407, 564, 849, 1040; Sifakis, *Compendium of Confederate Armies: Texas*, 12.

76. Quote, Barr, "Confederate Artillery in Western Louisiana, 1864," 60.

77. *Ibid.*, 63-64, 67, 69-70, 71; *Official Records*, 34, Pt. 1: 562, 563, 571, 588, 594.

78. *Official Records*, 41, Pt. 3: 967, Pt. 4: 1064; 48, Pt. 2: 1310.

79. Quote, Augustus Buchel, *Official Records*, 4: 152; Barr, "Confederate Artillery in the Trans-Mississippi," 215; Thompson, *Vaqueros in Blue & Gray*, 48.

80. *Official Records*, Series II, 1: 35; Wright and Simpson, *Texas in the War, 1861-1865*, 137n; Barr, "Texas' Confederate Field Artillery," 3.

81. *Official Records*, 4: 108; 12: 978; Barr, "Confederate Artillery in Arkansas," 253; Blessington, *Walker's Texas Division*, 50, 135; Wright and Simpson, *Texas in the War, 1861-1865*, 133-134n.

82. *Official Records*, 34, Pt. 1: 536; Bearss, *Steele's Retreat from Camden*, 166. For Mechling's account of the Red River campaign see Alwyn Barr, ed., "William T. Mechling Journal of the Red River Campaign, April 7 - May 10, 1864," *Texana* 1 (Fall 1963): 363-379.

83. *Official Records*, 41, Pt. 4: 1064; 48, Pt. 2: 963.

84. Barr, "Texas' Confederate Field Artillery," 3; Sifakis, *Compendium of Confederate Armies: Texas*, 18, 32.

85. Barr, "Confederate Artillery in Western Louisiana, 1864," 59-70; *Official Records*, 26, Pt. 2: 84, 99, 281, 509, 563; 34, Pt. 1: 562, 567, 628, 787, Pt. 2: 932, 1040.

86. *Official Records*, 41, Pt. 4: 1064; 48, Pt. 1: 1457.

87. *Ibid.*, 9: 483-484, 526, 613-614, 720-721; Tyler, ed., *New Handbook of Texas*, 4: 962; Sifakis, *Compendium of Confederate Armies: Texas*, 32-33; Wright and Simpson, *Texas in the War, 1861-1865*, 135n, 136n. For an extremely critical view of the conduct of both Neal and Maltby see the report by Maj. C. G. Forshey, February 19, 1862, *Official Records*, 53: 787.

88. Sifakis, *Compendium of Confederate Armies: Texas*, 24; Alwyn Barr, "Confederate Artillery in Western Louisiana, 1862-1863," *Civil War History* 9 (March 1963): 83; *Official Records*, 26, 2: 565n.

89. *Official Records*, 26, Pt. 2: 319. The inspector general concluded that Captain Nichols "appears to be a young officer of merit."

90. Block, *History of Jefferson County*, 115-116; *Official Records*, 26, Pt. 2: 565; 34, Pt. 2: 1040, 1100, Pt. 3: 806; 41, Pt. 2: 1097, Pt. 3: 1966.

91. *Official Records*, 41, Pt. 4: 1064; 48, Pt. 2: 963.

92. Barr, "Confederate Artillery in the Trans-Mississippi," 218; Wright and Simpson, *Texas in the War, 1861-1865*, 136n. Sifakis, *Compendium of Confederate Armies: Texas*, 26, points out that the battery does not appear as a separate entry in the *Official Records*.

93. Bailey, *Between the Enemy and Texas*, 45-46, 256n.

94. *Official Records*, 22, Pt. 1: 286, 300-303; Oates, *Confederate Cavalry West of the River*, 124-131.

95. Bailey, *Between the Enemy and Texas*, 152-153; *Official Records*, 22, Pt. 1: 539, 542-543.

96. Quote, Col. Robert C. Newton, Fifth Arkansas Cavalry, *Official Records*, 22, Pt. 1: 736.

97. First quote, Bailey, *Between the Enemy and Texas*, 158; second quote, Inspector General's report, *Official Records*, 22, Pt. 2: 1051.

98. *Official Records*, 34, Pt. 1: 947, 950, 958; 41, Pt. 3: 969.

99. Bailey, *Between the Enemy and Texas*, 195-196; Barr, "Confederate Artillery in the Trans-Mississippi," 266; Oates, *Confederate Cavalry West of the River*, 140-154.

100. Sifakis, *Compendium of Confederate Armies: Texas*, 20; *Official Records*, 41, Pt. 4: 1064; 48, Pt. 2: 963. Bailey, *Between the Enemy and Texas*, 311n, notes that Pratt's tombstone in Jefferson, Texas, states that he died of effects of the gunshot wound received while on the Missouri raid. According to R. J. Oliphant, a member of Pratt's battery, there were only seventeen of the original members of the battery when the men were discharged near Crockett following Lee's surrender. Yeary, Comp., *Reminiscences of the Boys in Gray*, 575.

101. Frazier, *Blood & Treasure*, 94-95. See Alberts, *Battle of Glorieta*, 187n, for an excellent discussion of various types of artillery used in the New Mexico campaign.

102. *Official Records*, 9: 508, 514, 518-520, 524; Hall, *Sibley's New Mexico Campaign*, 84, 86-87, 89-90, 93; Taylor, *Bloody Valverde*, 53, 57, 61, 80, 155-156n.

103. Hall, *Sibley's New Mexico Campaign*, 169, 172-173; Alberts, ed., *Rebels on the Rio Grande*, 101n; Howard Bryan, "The Man Who Buried the Cannons," *New Mexico Magazine* 40 (January 1962): 13-15, 35.

104. Sifakis, *Compendium of Confederate Armies: Texas*, 14-15, 30; Young, *To the Tyrants Never Yield*, 126-127.

105. Sifakis, *Compendium of Confederate Armies: Texas*, 14; Wright and Simpson, *Texas in the War, 1861-1865*, 341n.

106. Tyler, ed., *New Handbook of Texas*, 6: 234; Frazier, *Blood & Treasure*, 23, 36.

107. Frazier, *Blood & Treasure*, 139; Hall, *Sibley's New Mexico Campaign*, 45, 76.

108. *Official Records*, 9: 523-525, 543; Taylor, *Bloody Valverde*, 35, 44, 51, 70, 102.

109. See Don Alberts, *The Battle of Glorieta*, 50, 58-61, 73-76, 100-102.

110. Thomas W. Cutrer, "Trevanion Theodore Teel," in Tyler, ed., *New Handbook of Texas*, 6: 234; Barr, "Confederate Artillery in the Trans-Mississippi," 216; *Official Records*, 8: 788; 10, Pt. 2: 495. In his report of the Battle of *Pea Ridge* Col. Henry Little of the Missouri Volunteers mentions Teel's Battery as occupying a position between Rives' Regiment and Martin E. Green's command. *Official Records*, 8: 309. Harry M. Henderson, *Texas in the Confederacy*, 146, states there were two Teel batteries, one of which served in Missouri and Arkansas. Wright and Simpson, *Texas in the War, 1861-1865*, 137n, believe there was only one Teel Battery but that it later fought in Missouri and Arkansas and went to Mississippi with Van Dorn's army. However, they fail to give any dates. I have found no reference to Teel's Battery in Van Dorn's Army of the West other than the March 17, 1862, organization chart mentioned in the text.

111. Frazier, *Blood & Treasure*, 174-177, 180, 261; Hall, *Sibley's New Mexico Campaign*, 169, 182, 191, 213; Taylor, *Bloody Valverde*, 85-90. Don Alberts, ed., *Rebels on the Rio Grande*, 111n, points out that it cannot be positively determined whether the six original guns were still together or whether only five were retained. Frazier, *Blood & Treasure*, 180, says six guns were captured but later (p. 261) states the Valverde Battery had only two 12-pounders and three 6-pounders.

112. Nettles had been one of the privates who manned Confederate artillery at the Battle of Glorieta Pass. P. D. Browne, "Captain T. D. Nettles and the Valverde Battery," *Texana* 2 (Spring 1964): 6-14; *Official Records*, 15: 389-390, 395, 1092; 26, Pt. 1: 225, 374, 394; Winters, *Civil War in Louisiana*, 221-222, 225, 232.

113. *Official Records*, 34, Pt. 1: 520, 563, 583-584, 628; Browne, "Captain Nettles and the Valverde Battery," 14-20; Barr, "Confederate Artillery in Western Louisiana," 59-61, 63-67; Barr, "Confederate Artillery in the Trans-Mississippi, 1864" 183; Tyler, ed., *New Handbook of Texas*, 6: 694.

114. *Official Records*, 4: 137; 9: 731.

115. *Ibid.*, 9: 620, 626.

116. *Ibid.*, 26, Pt. 2: 407, 563; 34, Pt. 1: 932, 1099, Pt. 3: 800; 41, Pt. 3: 969, 1097, Pt. 4: 969, 1064, 1117, 1146.

117. *Ibid.*, 41, Pt. 4: 1064; 48, Pt. 2: 963.

118. *Ibid.*, 15: 143, 145, 813-815; Block, *History of Jefferson County*, 103-104.

119. Frazier, *Cottonclads!*, 69; Cotham, *Battle on the Bay*, 115. Edward Simmen, writing in the *New Handbook of Texas*, 3: 228, states that Gonzales organized, trained, and outfitted the battery with his own money.

120. *Official Records*, 26, Pt. 1: 222, 230, 303, Pt. 2: 473; Barr, "Confederate Artillery in Western Louisiana, 1862-1863," 83-84.

121. *Official Records*, 34, Pt. 2: 932, 1040, 1052, 1099, Pt. 3: 800; 41, Pt. 2: 1097, Pt. 4: 1064; 48, Pt. 2: 964.

122. *Ibid.*, 9: 524; Hall, *Sibley's New Mexico Campaign*, 89, 93, 100; Taylor, *Bloody Valverde*, 95-96, 126; Frazier, *Blood & Treasure*, 229.

Bibliography

The basic source of information for any Civil War study is the venerable 128-volume *The War of the Rebellion: A Compilation of the Official Records of the Union and Confederate Armies* (Washington: Government Printing Office, 1880-1901). These volumes, frequently cited simply as *Official Records* or *OR*, are indispensable as they contain the correspondence and reports for all Civil War military operations that were available at the time of publication. In recent years additional materials have been located and published as *Supplement to the Official Records of the Union and Confederate Armies,* ed. by Janet B. Hewett, Noah Andre Trudeau, and Bryce A. Suderow, 100 vols. (Wilmington, NC: Broadfoot Publishing Company, 1994-2001). Additional accounts by participants, first published by *Century Magazine* two decades after the war and then printed in book form, are found in Robert U. Johnson and Clarence C. Buels, eds., *Battles & Leaders of the Civil War,* 4 vols. (New York, 1888; reprint, New York: Thomas Yoseloff, 1956).

In addition *The Official Records of the Union and Confederate Navies in the War of Rebellion*, 30 vols. (Washington: Government Printing Office, 1892-1922), provides valuable information on naval operations along the Texas coast.

Several sources are helpful for determining the basic organization and senior officers for Texas brigades, regiments, battalions, and batteries. Among these the most important are Stewart Sifakis, *Compendium of Confederate Armies: Texas* (New York: Facts on File, 1995); Marcus J. Wright, comp., *Texas in the War, 1861-1865*, ed. Harold B. Simpson (Hillsboro: Hill Junior College Press, 1965); and the Regimental File for Texas Confederate military units in the Harold B. Simpson Confederate Research Center, Hillsboro, Texas. Less valuable but useful are Lester N. Fitzhugh, comp., *Texas Batteries, Battalions, Regiments, Commanders and Field Officers, Confederate States Army, 1861-1865* (Midlothian: Mirror Press, 1959) and Harry M. Henderson, *Texas in the Confederacy* (San Antonio: Naylor Company, 1955).

The six-volume *New Handbook of Texas* (Austin: Texas State Historical Association, 1996), ed. Ron Tyler, et al., is an indispensable source of information not only for biographical sketches of many of the officers of Texas brigades and regiments but also for descriptions of some of the better known Texas military units such as Hood's Brigade, Terry's Rangers, and Ross' Cavalry Brigade.

Also valuable for information on Texans who commanded brigades and regiments are the six volumes edited by William C. Davis, *The Confederate General* (National Historical Society, 1991); Ezra J. Warner, *Generals in Gray: Lives of Confederate Commanders* (Baton Rouge: Louisiana State University Press, 1959); Jack D. Welsh, M.D., *Medical Histories of Confederate Generals* (Kent, OH: Kent State University Press, 1995); Bruce S. Allardice, *More Generals in Gray* (Baton Rouge: Louisiana State University Press, 1995).

Muster rolls for Texas regiments are located in various research depositories. Fortunately, a recent publication entitled *The Roster of Confederate Soldiers, 1861-1865*, 16 vols. (Wilmington: Broadfoot Publishing Company, 1997) contains the names from the 535 microfilm reels of the National Archives M253, Consolidated Index to the Compiled Service Records of Confederate Soldiers. In a two-volume set, extracted from the Index, edited by Janet B. Hewett and arranged by Joyce Lawrence, entitled *Texas Confederate Soldiers, 1861-1865* (Wilmington: Broadfoot Publishing Company, 1997), the names and units of Texas Confederates are given. In Volume One the names of all Texas Confederate soldiers are arranged alphabetically with the regiment and company or battery identification and highest rank provided. Volume Two, which was more valuable for this study, provides consolidated muster rolls for most Texas cavalry and infantry regiments and artillery regiments and batteries.

Some of the Texas military units have been the subject of division, brigade, and regimental histories. Notable in this respect is Harold B. Simpson's four-volume account of *Hood's Texas Brigade*, published by Texian Press in Waco: *Hood's Texas Brigade in Poetry and Song* (1968), *Hood's Texas Brigade*: *Lee's Grenadier Guard* (1970), *Hood's Texas Brigade in Reunion and Memory* (1974), and *Hood's Texas Brigade: A Compendium* (1977). These should be supplemented by Simpson's *Gaines Mill to Appomattox: Waco and McLennan County in Hood's Texas Brigade* (Waco: Texian Press, 1968); *The Marshall Guards: Harrison County's Contribution to Hood's Texas Brigade* (Marshall: Port Caddo Press, 1967); *Touched with Valor: The Civil War Papers and Casualty Reports of Hood's Texas Brigade* (Hillsboro: Hill Junior College Press, 1964); "East Texas Companies in Hood's Brigade," *East Texas Historical Journal* 3 (March 1965): 5-17; "Foraging with *Hood's Texas Brigade* From Texas to Pennsylvania," *Texana* 1 (Summer 1963): 258-276; "Hood's Brigade at Appomattox," *Texana* 3 (Spring 1965): 1-19; and "The Recruiting, Training, and Camp Life of a Company of Hood's Brigade in Texas," *Texas Military History* 2 (August 1962): 171-192.

Several of the officers and men of Hood's Brigade wrote of their experiences in that famous Texas unit. Among these the most helpful are Chaplain Nicholas Davis, *The Campaign from Texas to Maryland, with the Battle of Sharpsburg* (Richmond, 1863), which has been edited by Donald E. Everett, Chaplain Davis and *Hood's Texas Brigade* (San Antonio: Principia Press of Trinity University, 1962; new edition, Louisiana State University Press, 1999); Val C. Giles, *Rags and Hope: The Recollections of Val C. Giles, Four Years with Hood's Brigade, Fourth Texas Infantry*, ed. Mary Lasswell (New York: Coward-McCann, Inc., 1961); John B. Hood, *Advance and Retreat*: *Personal Experiences in the United States and*

Confederate Armies (New Orleans: P.G.T. Beauregard, 1880); Judy and Nath Winfield, eds., *War Letters of Tacitus T. Clay, CSA* (Chappell Hill, TX: privately printed, 1968); Robert W. Glover, ed., *"Tyler to Sharpsburg": The War Letters of Robert H. and William H. Gaston, Company H, First Texas Infantry Regiment, Hood's Texas Brigade* (Waco: Texian Press, 1960); Eric Fleming, ed., "Some Hard Fighting: Letters of Private Robert T. Wilson, 5th Infantry, Hood's Brigade, 1862-1865," *Military History of Texas and the Southwest* 9 (No. 4, 1971): 289-302; William A. Fletcher, *Rebel Private Front and Rear*, ed. Bell I. Wiley (Austin: University of Texas Press, 1954); Langston James Goree, ed., *The Thomas Goree Letters*, Vol. 1 (Bryan: Family History Foundation, 1981); Eddy R. Parker, ed., *Touched By Fire: Letters from Company D, 5th Texas Infantry, Hood's Brigade, Army of Northern Virginia, 1862-1865* (Hillsboro: Hill College Press, 2000); J. B. Polley, *A Soldier's Letters to Charming Nellie* (New York: Neale Publishing Company, 1908), 121; John W. Stevens, *Reminiscences of the Civil War* (Hillsboro: Hillsboro Mirror, 1902); O. T. Hanks, "History of B. F. Benton's Company, or Account of Civil War Experiences," Manuscript, Archives Division, University of Texas; and Thomas L. McCarthy Papers, 1864-1865, Manuscript, Archives Division, University of Texas; Robert Campbell, "A Lone Star in Virginia," *Civil War Times Illustrated* 39 (December 2000): 34-40, 86-00.

Much additional information on the Texas regiments that made up Hood's Brigade may be found in two early works by Mrs. A. V. Winkler, *The Confederate Capital and Hood's Texas Brigade* (Austin: Von Boeckmann, 1894), and J. B. Polley, *Hood's Texas Brigade: Its Marches, Its Battles, Its Achievements* (New York: Neale Publishing Company, 1910). Richard M. McMurry's *John Bell Hood and the War for Southern Independence* (Lexington: University Press of Kentucky, 1982) contains material on the brigade and its leader. Information on the regimental commanders may be found in Robert K. Krick, *Lee's Colonels: A Biographical Register of the Field Officers of the Army of Northern Virginia* (9th ed., Dayton, OH: Morningside House, 1992). J. Tracy Power, *Lee's Miserables: Life in the Army of Northern Virginia from the Wilderness to Appomattox* (Chapel Hill: University of North Carolina Press, 1998), provides a thorough description of the hardships endured by men of Hood's Brigade and other units in the Army of Northern Virginia.

The major battles in which Hood's Brigade fought provide much information pertaining to the three Texas regiments. Especially helpful are Stephen W. Sears, *To the Gates of Richmond: The Peninsula Campaign* (New York: Ticknor & Fields, 1992); Steven H. Newton, *Joseph E. Johnston and the Defense of Richmond* (Lawrence: University Press of Kansas, 1998); John J. Hennessy, *Return to Bull Run: The Campaign and Battle of Second Manassas* (New York: Simon & Schuster, 1993); Stephen W. Sears, *Landscape Turned Red: The Battle of Antietam* (New Haven: Ticknor and Fields, 1983); Gary E. Gallagher, ed., *The Antietam Campaign* (Chapel Hill: University of North Carolina Press, 1999); George E. Otott, "1st Texas in the Cornfield," *Civil War Regiments* 15 (No. 3, 1997): 73-123; Daniel E. Sutherland, *Fredericksburg and Chancellorsville: The Dare Mark Campaign* (Lincoln: University of Nebraska Press, 1998); Gary W. Gallagher, ed., *The Fredericksburg Campaign: Decision on the Rappahannock* (Chapel Hill: University of North Carolina Press, 1995); Gallagher, ed., *The Second Day at Gettysburg:*

Essays on Confederate and Union Leadership (Kent, OH: Kent State University Press, 1993); Peter Cozzens, *This Terrible Sound: The Battle of Chickamauga* (Urbana, IL: University of Illinois Press, 1992); Gordon C. Rhea, *The Battle of the Wilderness, May 5-6, 1864* (Baton Rouge: Louisiana State University Press, 1994); Rhea, *The Battles for Spotsylvania Court House and the Road to Yellow Tavern, May 7-12, 1864* (Baton Rouge: Louisiana State University Press, 1997); Gary W. Gallagher, ed., *The Wilderness Campaign* (Chapel Hill: University of North Carolina Press, 1997); Ernest B. Fergurson, *Not War But Murder: Cold Harbor 1864* (New York: Alfred A. Knopf, 2000); and Richard Sommers, *Richmond Redeemed: The Siege at Petersburg* (Garden City, NY: Doubleday & Company, 1981).

Hood's Brigade was the best known of all the infantry units from Texas. The Eighth Texas Cavalry, or Terry's Texas Rangers, was the best-known mounted unit from the Lone Star State. A complete account of the Rangers is in the recently published *None But Texians: A History of Terry's Texas Rangers* (Austin: Eakin Press, 2001) by Jeffrey D. Murrah. Excellent short accounts of the Rangers may be found in Thomas W. Cutrer's "Eighth Texas Cavalry" in the *New Handbook of Texas*, 1: 805-806 and in his introduction to *Terry Texas Ranger Trilogy* (Austin: State House Press, 1966), vii-xxxii. In this latter work Cutrer has brought together firsthand accounts by Rangers L. B. Giles, J. K. P. Blackburn, and Ephraim Shelby Dodd (all of which had previously been published). Cutrer has also edited the letters of another Ranger, "'We Are Stern and Resolved': The Civil War Letters of John Wesley Rabb, Terry's Texas Rangers," *Southwestern Historical Quarterly* 91 (October 1987): 185-226. Other accounts by Terry's men may be found in Henry W. Graber, *The Life Record of H. W. Graber: A Terry Texas Ranger, 1861-1865* (Dallas, privately printed, 1916); H. J. Rugeley, ed., *Batchelor-Turner Letters, 1861-1864, Written by Two of Terry's Texas Rangers* (Austin: Steck Company, 1961); and Robert W. Williams, Jr., and Ralph A. Wooster, eds., "With Terry's Texas Rangers: The Letters of Dunbar Affleck," *Civil War History* 9 (September 1963): 299-319. See also C. C. Jeffries, *Terry's Rangers* (New York: Vantage Press, 1961); Jeffries, "The Character of Terry's Texas Rangers," *Southwestern Historical Quarterly* 64 (April 1961): 454-462; Lester N. Fitzhugh, "Terry's Texas Rangers," in James M. Day, et al., *Soldiers of Texas* (Waco: Texian Press, 1973), 75-93; Maury Darst, "Robert Hodges, Jr.: Confederate Soldier," *East Texas Historical Journal* 9 (March 1971): 20-49; David Gracy II, "With Danger and Honor: George W. Littlefield, 1861-1864," *Texana* 1 (Winter 1963): 1-19, (Spring 1964): 120-152; Paula Mitchell Marks, "The Ranger Reverend," *Civil War Times Illustrated* 24 (December 1985): 40-45; and Ralph A. Wooster, "With the Confederate Cavalry in the West: The Civil War Experiences of Isaac Dunbar Affleck," *Southwestern Historical Quarterly* 83 (July 1979): 1-28.

As was true of Hood's Brigade, considerable information about the Rangers may be found in accounts of battles in which they participated. See especially Larry Daniel, *Shiloh: The Battle That Changed the Civil War* (New York: Simon & Schuster, 1997); Wiley Sword, *Shiloh: Bloody April* (New York: William Morrow & Company, 1974); James Lee McDonough, *Shiloh—in Hell Before Night* (Knoxville: University of Tennessee Press, 1977); James Lee McDonough, *War in Kentucky: From Shiloh to Perryville* (Knoxville: University of Tennessee Press, 1994);

Kenneth A. Hafendorf, *Perryville: Battle for Kentucky* (Louisville: K H Press, 1991); James Lee McDonough, *Stones River—Bloody Winter in Tennessee* (Knoxville: University of Tennessee Press, 1980); Nathaniel C. Hughes, Jr., *Bentonville: The Final Battle of Sherman and Johnston* (Chapel Hill: University of North Carolina Press, 1996); and Mark L. Bradley, *The Battle of Bentonville: Last Stand in the Carolinas* (Campbell, CA: Savas Woodbury Publishers, 1996).

The Eleventh Texas Cavalry, which fought in many of the same campaigns as *Terry's Rangers*, has received scant attention from historians. With the exception of Richard B. McCaslin's "Conditional Confederates: The Eleventh Texas Cavalry West of the Mississippi River," *Military History of the Southwest* 21 (Spring 1991): 87-99, little has been published about this Northeast Texas regiment. The regiment is mentioned several times in William L. Shea and Earl J. Hess, *Pea Ridge: Campaign in the West* (Chapel Hill: University of North Carolina Press, 1992). Larry J. Daniel's *Soldiering in the Army of Tennessee: A Portrait of Life in a Confederate Army* (Chapel Hill: University of North Carolina Press, 1991) has ten entries for *Terry's Rangers* but none for the Eleventh Texas. Anne J. Bailey in her *Texans in the Confederate Cavalry* (Fort Worth: Ryan Publishers, 1995) has eleven entries for the Rangers but only one for the Eleventh Texas. The death of one of the commanders of the Eleventh Texas is discussed by Steve Peters, "The Murder of Col. Joseph M. Bounds, Eleventh Texas Cavalry, Young's Regiment, C.S.A.," *Texana* 12 (No. 1, 1974): 56-73. The Eleventh Cavalry website by Michael Cobb, Jr., provides valuable socio-economic data on the men of Company B.

Numerous works describe the four regiments in Ross' Cavalry Brigade. Among these are letters, memoirs, and diaries: Samuel B. Barron, *The Lone Star Defenders: A Chronicle of the Third Texas Cavalry, Ross' Brigade* (New York: Neale Publishing Company, 1908); William C. Billingsley, ed., "'Such It Was': The Confederate Memoirs of Newton Asbury Keen," *Texas Military History* 6 (Winter 1967): 239-253, 7 (Spring-Fall 1968): 44-70, 103-119, 176-194; Douglas J. Cater, *As It Was: Reminiscences of a Soldier of the Third Texas Cavalry and the Nineteenth Louisiana Infantry* (Reprint, Austin: State House Press, 1990); Homer L. Kerr, ed., *Fighting With Ross' Texas Cavalry Brigade, C.S.A.: The Diary of George L. Griscom, Adjutant, 9th Texas Cavalry Regiment* (Hillsboro: Hill Junior College Press, 1976); Richard Lowe, ed., *A Texas Cavalry Officer's Civil War: The Diary and Letters of James C. Bates* (Baton Rouge: Louisiana State University Press, 1999); Max S. Lale, ed., *The Civil War Letters of David R. Garrett* (Marshall: Port Caddo Press, n.d.); Max S. Lale, "The Boy-Bugler of the *Third Texas Cavalry*: The A. B. Blocker Narrative," *Military History of Texas and the Southwest* 14 (No. 2-4, 1976): 71-92, 147-168, 215-228; 15 (No. 1. 1977): 21-34; Walter P. Lane, *The Adventures and Recollections of Walter P. Lane . . .* (Reprint, Austin: Pemberton Press, 1970); and Shelly Morrison, ed., *Personal Civil War Letters of General Lawrence Sullivan Ross* (Austin: privately published, 1994); A. W. Sparks, *The War Between the States As I Saw It* (Tyler: Lee & Burnett, 1900). William Garrett Piston and Richard W. Hatcher III, *Wilson's Creek: The Second Battle of the Civil War and the Men Who Fought It* (Chapel Hill: University of North Carolina Press, 2000), provide much information on the role of the *Third Texas Cavalry* (then known as the South Kansas-Texas Cavalry) in that battle. Similarly, the work of William L. Shea and Earl J. Hess on the battle of Pea Ridge (mentioned in reference to the Eleventh

Texas Cavalry) discusses the role of the Third Texas Cavalry and other Texas cavalry in that battle.

Douglas Hale's *The Third Texas Cavalry in the Civil War* (Norman: University of Oklahoma Press, 1993) is one of the finest regimental histories available. Martha L. Crabb, *All Afire to Fight: The Untold Tale of the Civil War's Ninth Texas Cavalry* (New York: Avon Books, 2000) is an equally well-researched volume on another regiment in Ross' Brigade. Similar in-depth regimental histories have not been published for either of the other two regiments in the brigade, Sul Ross' Sixth Cavalry and John W. Whitfield's Twenty-seventh Cavalry.

Texas infantry and dismounted cavalry units operating in the Confederate Heartland have received only limited attention from historians. Joseph E. Chance, *The Second Texas Infantry: From Shiloh to Vicksburg* (Austin: Eakin Press, 1984) is most helpful in describing that regiment through its most important campaigns. This should be supplemented by Ralph J. Smith, *Reminiscences of the Civil War and Other Sketches* (Reprint, Waco: W. M. Morrison Company, 1962), and Eleanor D. Pace, ed., "The Diary and Letters of William P. Rogers, 1846-1862," *Southwestern Historical Quarterly* 32 (April 1929): 259-299. Kevin R. Young, *To the Tyrants Never Yield: A Civil War Sampler* (Plano: Wordware Publishing Company, 1992) and Peter Cozzens, *The Darkest Days of the War: The Battles of Iuka and Corinth* (Chapel Hill: University of North Carolina Press, 1997) provide valuable information on the Second Texas and other Texas units in the Corinth campaign.

The role of the Second Texas and Waul's Legion at Vicksburg is described in various accounts of that campaign, especially James R. Arnold, *Grant Wins the War: Decision at Vicksburg* (New York: John Wiley & Sons, 1997). For Waul's Legion in particular see Robert A. Hasskarl and Leif R. Hasskarl, *Waul's Texas Legion* (Ada, OK: privately published, 1985), which provides a roster of the Legion, and birthplace, age, and marital status for many members. See also Laura Simmons, "Waul's Legion from Texas to Mississippi," *Texana* 7 (Spring 1969): 1-16; Wayne Flynt, "The Texas Legion at Vicksburg," *East Texas Historical Journal* 17 (Spring 1979): 60-67; and Walter H. Mays, ed., "The Vicksburg Diary of M. K. Simons, 1863," *Texas Military History* 5 (Spring 1965): 21-38. The Simons diary has recently been reprinted in Douglas Lee Braudaway, ed., "A Texan Records the Civil War Siege of Vicksburg, Mississippi: The Journal of Maj. Maurice Kavanaugh Simons, 1863," *Southwestern Historical Quarterly* 105 (July 2001): 93-131. A brief account of the march of Waul's Legion to Vicksburg and the campaign itself is in the manuscript diary of Siebert Behrens, a member of the Legion. A translated copy of the diary is in the possession of Behrens' great-grandson, Dr. Kevin Smith, Beaumont, Texas.

For the four Texas regiments that were part of Matthew D. Ector's Brigade, one must rely heavily upon the *Official Records* and various monographs describing battles in which the regiments took part. Particularly useful are Larry Daniel's Shiloh and Peter Cozzens' *This Terrible Sound: The Battle of Chickamauga* cited earlier; and Steven E. Woodworth, *A Deep Steady Thunder: The Battle of Chickamauga* (Abilene: McWhiney Foundation, 1998); Albert Castel, *Decision in the West: The Atlanta Campaign of 1864* (Lawrence: University Press of Kansas, 1992); Richard M. McMurry, *Atlanta 1864: Last Chance for the Confederacy* (Lincoln: University of Nebraska Press, 2000); William R. Scaife, *The Campaign for Atlanta* (Atlanta: privately published, 1990); Anne J. Bailey, *The Chessboard of War: Sherman and Hood in the Autumn Campaigns of 1864* (Lincoln: University of Nebraska Press, 2000); Wiley Sword, *The Confederacy's Last Hurrah: Spring Hill, Franklin, and Nashville* (Lawrence: University Press of Kansas, 1993); Charles G. Hearn, *Mobile Bay and the Mobile Campaign: The Last Great Battles of the Civil War* (Jefferson, NC: McFarland & Company, 1993).

Joseph Stroud of Kilgore College has an excellent brief account of Ector in the *New Handbook of Texas* and has presented several papers describing the brigade at meetings of the East Texas Historical Association. The website for the Ninth Texas Infantry by Tim Bell provides good coverage of this North Texas regiment which served in Ector's Brigade. Jon H. Harrison, "Tenth Texas Cavalry, C.S.A.," *Military History of Texas and the Southwest* 12 (no. 2-3. 1975): 93-107, 171-184, provides much information on the Tenth Texas. Judy Watson McClure, *Confederate From East Texas: The Civil War Letters of James Monroe Watson* (Quanah, TX: Nortex Press, 1976), contains letters from a captain in the Tenth Texas Cavalry.

Granbury's Texas Brigade, which participated in many of the same battles as Ector's Brigade, has been the focal point of several studies. James M. McCaffrey, *This Band of Heroes: Granbury's Texas Brigade, C.S.A.* (Austin: Eakin Press, 1985; reprinted by Texas A&M University Press, 1996) provides a good overview of the Texas regiments that made up the brigade. This is supplemented by the reminiscences and diary of Capt. Samuel T. Foster of the Twenty-fourth Cavalry, edited by Norman D. Brown and published as *One of Cleburne's Command* (Austin: University of Texas Press, 1980); Charles D. Spurlin, ed., *The Civil War Diary of Charles A. Leuschner* (Austin: Eakin Press, 1962); Jim Turner, "Jim Turner, Co. G, 6th Texas Infantry, C. S. A. From 1861-1865," *Texana* 12 (No. 2, 1974): 149-178; Harold B. Simpson, ed., *The Bugle Softly Blows: The Confederate Diary of Benjamin M. Seaton* (Waco: Texian Press, 1965); Charleen Plumly Pollard, ed., "Civil War Letters of George W. Allen," *Southwestern Historical Quarterly* 83 (July 1979): 46-52; Joe R. Wise, ed., "Letters of Lt. Flavius W. Perry, 17th Texas Cavalry, 1862-1863," *Military History of Texas and the Southwest* 13 (No. 2, 1976): 11-37; Gilbert Cuthberston, "Coller of the Sixth Texas: Correspondence of a Texas Infantry Man, 1861-1864," *ibid.* 9 (No. 2, 1971): 129-136; Norman C. Delaney, "Diary and Memoirs of Marshall Samuel Pierson, Company C, 17th Regt., Texas Cavalry," *ibid.* 13 (No. 3, 1976): 23-38; Bill O'Neal, ed., "The Civil War Memoirs of Samuel Alonza Cooke," *Southwestern Historical Quarterly* 74 (April 1971): 535-548. For additional information on Granbury's own regiment, the Seventh Texas Infantry, see James Lynn Newsom, "Intrepid Gray Warriors: The 7th Texas Infantry, 1861-1865" (Ph.D. dissertation, Texas Christian University, 1995). See also the Tenth Infantry website produced by Scott McKay for informative letters by members of the regiment.

The Texas cavalry regiments that made up the old Sibley Brigade have been described in numerous accounts. The late Martin Hardwick Hall discussed the brigade's formation and march into New Mexico in Sibley's *New Mexico Campaign* (Austin: University of Texas Press, 1960) and provided more biographical and organizational information in *The Confederate Army of New Mexico* (Austin: Presidial Press, 1978). Donald S. Frazier, *Blood & Treasure: Confederate*

Empire in the Southwest (College Station: Texas A&M University Press, 1995) has added much additional information about the composition of the brigade's regiments. Don E. Alberts, ed., *Rebels on the Rio Grande: The Civil War Journal of A. B. Peticolas* (Albuquerque: Merit Press, 1993) is an unusually fine description of the New Mexico campaign by a young lawyer who served in the Fourth Regiment of Texas Mounted Volunteers. Other firsthand accounts of the campaign are Theophilus Noel, *A Campaign From Santa Fe to the Mississippi: Being a History of the Old Sibley Brigade* (Shreveport: News Printing Establishment, 1865); Alwyn Barr, ed., *Charles Porter's Account of the Confederate Attempt to Seize Arizona and New Mexico* (Austin: Pemberton Press, 1964); Oscar Haas, trans., "The Diary of Julius Giesecke, 1861-1862," *Texas Military History* 3 (Winter 1963): 228-242; David Gracy II, ed., "New Mexico Campaign Letters of Frank Starr, 1861-1862," *ibid.* 4 (Fall 1964): 169-188; Michael L. Tate, "A Johnny Reb in Sibley's New Mexico Campaign: Reminiscences of Pvt. Henry C. Wright, 1861-1862," *East Texas Historical Journal* 25 (Fall 1987): 20-33; 26 (Spring-Fall 1988): 23-35, 48-60; T. T. Teel, "Sibley's New Mexico Campaign—Its Objects and the Cause of Its Failure," in *Battles & Leaders* 2: 700; Jerry D. Thompson, ed., *Westward the Texans: The Civil War Journal of Private William Randolph Howell* (El Paso: Texas Western Press, 1990); Terry L. Jordan-Bychkov, et al., "The Boesel Letters: Two Texas Germans in Sibley's Brigade," *Southwestern Historical Quarterly* 102 (April 1999): 457-484.

The major battles of the New Mexico campaign are described in John Taylor, *Bloody Valverde: A Civil War Battle on the Rio Grande*, February 21, 1862 (Albuquerque: University of New Mexico Press, 1995); Thomas E. Edrington and John Taylor, *The Battle of Glorieta Pass: A Gettysburg in the West, March 26-28, 1862* (Albuquerque: University of New Mexico Press, 1998); Don E. Alberts, *The Battle of Glorieta: Union Victory in the West* (College Station: Texas A&M University Press, 1998); David P. Perrine, "The Battle of Valverde, New Mexico Territory, February 21, 1862," *Journal of the West* 19 (October 1980): 26-38; J. F. Santee, "The Battle of Glorieta Pass," *New Mexico Historical Review* 6 (January 1931): 66-75; David Westphall, "The Battle of Glorieta Pass: Its Importance in the Civil War," *ibid.* 44 (April 1969): 137-154.

Jerry Thompson's biographies of the two leading figures in the New Mexico campaign provide much information on the Texas regiments involved: *Confederate General of the West: Henry Hopkins Sibley* (Org. publ. Natchitoches, LA: Northwestern State University Press, 1957; new ed., College Station: Texas A&M University Press, 1996), and *Colonel John Robert Baylor: Texas Indian Fighter and Confederate Soldier* (Hillsboro: Hill Junior College Press, 1971). Odie Faulk, *General Tom Green: Fightin' Texan* (Waco: Texian Press, 1963) is a brief biography of the Texas cavalry commander who replaced Sibley as brigade commander.

Many of the men in the Sibley Brigade were also in the Confederate recapture of Galveston on January 1, 1863. For their role in the battle see Donald S. Frazier, "Sibley's Texans and the Battle of Galveston," *Southwestern Historical Quarterly* 99 (October 1995): 174-198. Edward T. Cotham, Jr., *Battle on the Bay: The Civil War Struggle for Galveston* (Austin: University of Texas Press, 1998) provides additional information on Sibley's troops as well as other Texans involved in the battle. See also Donald S. Frazier, *Cottonclads! The Battle of Galveston and the*

Defense of the Texas Coast (Fort Worth: Ryan Publishers, 1996); Charles C. Cumberland, "The Confederate Loss and Recapture of Galveston, 1862-1863," *Southwestern Historical Quarterly* 51 (October 1947): 109-130; Alwyn Barr, "Texas Coastal Defense, 1861-1865," *ibid.* 65 (July 1961): 1-31; Paul D. Casdorph, *Prince John Magruder: His Life and Campaigns* (New York: John Wiley & Sons, 1996); and Thomas M. Settles, "The Military Career of John Bankhead Magruder" (Ph.D. dissertation, Texas Christian University, 1972).

Texas cavalry and infantry regiments took part in campaigning in Arkansas and Louisiana. In addition to the books cited above for regiments in Ross' Cavalry Brigade which fought in Arkansas, see also Joseph P. Blessington, *The Campaigns of Walker's Texas Division* (Reprint, Austin: State House Press, 1994); Alwyn Barr, *Polignac's Texas Brigade* (2nd ed., College Station: Texas A&M University Press, 1998); Carl L. Duaine, *The Dead Men Wore Boots: An Account of the 32nd Texas Volunteer Cavalry, CSA, 1862-1865* (Austin: San Felipe Press, 1966); Stanley S. McGowen, *Horse Sweat and Powder Smoke: The First Texas Cavalry in the Civil War* (College Station: Texas A&M University Press, 1999); Xavier B. Debray, *A Sketch of the History of Debray's (26th) Regiment of Texas Cavalry* (Austin: Von Boeckmann, 1884; expanded version published by Joseph V. Patterson, Camas, WA, 1998); John W. Spencer, *Terrell's Texas Cavalry* (Burnet: Eakin Press, 1982); James T. Matthews, "Major's Confederate Cavalry Brigade" (M.A. thesis, Texas Tech University, 1991); Anne J. Bailey, *Between the Enemy and Texas: Parsons's Texas Cavalry in the Civil War* (Fort Worth: Texas Christian University Press, 1989); Bradford K. Felmly and John C. Grady, *Suffering to Silence: 29th Texas Cavalry, CSA, Regimental History* (Quanah: Nortex Press, 1975); M. Jane Johansson, *Peculiar Honor: A History of the 28th Texas Cavalry, 1862-1865* (Fayetteville: University of Arkansas Press, 1998); W. T. Block, "The Swamp Angels: A History of Spaight's 11th Battalion, Texas Volunteers, Confederate States Army," *East Texas Historical Journal* 30 (Spring 1992): 44-57.

Letters, diaries, and memoirs of Texas cavalrymen in the Trans Misssissippi provide additional information on their regiments. Particularly helpful are Charles Spurlin, ed., *West of the Mississippi With Waller's 13th Texas Cavalry Battalion, CSA* (Hillsboro: Hill Junior College, 1971); Oscar Haas, ed., "Diary of Julius Giesecke, 1863-1865," *Texas Military History* 4 (Spring 1964): 27-54; Minetta Altgeld, ed., *Lone Star and Double Eagle: Civil War Letters of a German-Texas Family* (Fort Worth: Texas Christian University Press, 1982); Rebecca W. Smith and Marion Mullins, eds., "The Diary of H. C. Medford, Confederate Soldier," *Southwestern Historical Quarterly* 34 (October 1930-January 1931): 106-140, 203-230; Jimmy L. Bryan, ed., "'Whip Them Life the Mischief': The Civil War Letters of Frank and Mintie Price," *East Texas Historical Journal* 36 (Fall 1998): 68-84; William P. Zuber, *My Eighty Years in Texas*, ed. Janis B. Mayfield (Austin: University of Texas Press, 1971); Buck Walton, *An Epitome of My Life: Civil War Reminiscences* (Austin: Waterloo Press, 1965); John Q. Anderson, ed., *Campaigning with Parsons' Texas Cavalry CSA: The War Journals and Letters of the Four Orr Brothers, 12th Texas Cavalry Regiment* (Hillsboro: Hill Junior College Press, 1967); Henry L. Ingram, comp., *Civil War Letters of George W. and Martha F. Ingram, 1861-1865* (College Station: Texas A&M University Press, 1973); and W. W. Heartsill,

Fourteen Hundred and 91 Days in the Confederate Army, the Journal of W. W. Heartsill (Reprint, Jackson TN: McCowat-Mercer Press, 1953).

Primary accounts of the war by men in Texas infantry and dismounted cavalry units also help understand the nature of campaigning in Arkansas and Louisiana. The letters of Capt. Elijah P. Petty of Walker's Texas Division, ed. by Norman D. Brown, *Journey to Pleasant Hill* (San Antonio: Institute of Texan Cultures, 1982) are especially valuable. Petty's letters, accompanied by Professor Brown's full anotations, provide one of the best accounts of the Louisiana campaigns. Other letters and diaries include J. S. Duncan, ed., "A Soldier's Fare is Rough: Letters from A. Cameron in Indian Territory, Arkansas Campaign, 1862-1864," *Military History of Texas and the Southwest* 12 (No. 1, 1975): 39-61; Duncan, ed., "Alexander Cameron in the Louisiana Campaign, 1863-1865," *ibid.* 12 (No. 4, 1975): 245-271, and 13 (No. 1, 1976): 37-57; Robert W. Glover, ed., "The War Letters of a Texas Conscript in Arkansas," *Arkansas Historical Quarterly* 20 (Winter 1961): 355-387; Thomas W. Cutrer, ed., "'An Experience in Soldier's Life': The Civil War Letters of Volney Ellis, Adjutant, Twelfth Texas Infantry, Walker's Division, C. S. A.," *Military History of the Southwest* 22 (Fall 1992): 109-172; Cutrer, ed., "'Bully for Flournoy's Regiment, We Are Some Punkins, You'll Bet': The Civil War Letters of Virgil Sullivan Rabb, Captain, Company 'I,' Sixteenth Texas Infantry," *ibid.* 19 (Fall 1989): 161-190, and 20 (Spring 1990): 61-96; L. David Norris, ed., *With the 18th Texas Infantry: The Autobiography of Wilburn Hill King* (Hillsboro: Hill Junior College Press, 1996); Alwyn Barr, ed., "The Civil War Diary of James Allen Hamilton, 1861-1864," *Texana* 2 (Summer 1964): 132-145; Alwyn Barr, ed., "William T. Mechling Journal of the Red River Campaign, April 7 - May 10, 1864," *Texana* 1 (Fall 1963): 363-379; Douglas V. Meed, *Texas Wanderlust: The Adventures of Dutch Wurzbach* (College Station: Texas A&M University Press, 1997); John Calvin Williams, "A Rebel Remembers the Red River Campaign," *Civil War Times Illustrated* 17 (January 1979): 24-25; Robert S. Weddle, *Plow-Horse Cavalry: The Caney Creek Boys of the Thirty-fourth Texas* (Austin: Madrona Press, 1974); Cooper K. Ragan, ed., "The Diary of Captain George W. O'Brien," *Southwestern Historical Quarterly* 67 (July 1963-January 1964): 28-54, 235-246, 413-433; Johnette Highsmith Ray, ed., "Civil War Letters from Parsons' Cavalry Brigade," *ibid.* 69 (October 1965): 210-223; Robert W. Williams and Ralph A. Wooster, eds., "With Wharton's Cavalry in Arkansas: The Civil War Letters of Private Isaac Dunbar Affleck," *Arkansas Historical Quarterly* 21 (Autumn 1962): 247-268. Firsthand accounts of service in the Eighteenth Texas Infantry by Sgt. John C. Porter and Colonels William B. Ochiltree and Thomas G. Bonner are published in James Henry Davis, ed., *Texans in Gray: A Regimental History of the Eighteenth Texas Infantry, Walker's Texas Division in the Civil War* (Tulsa: Heritage Oak Press, n.d.)

In addition to the works listed above, several general studies and biographies provide much information on Texas regiments in Arkansas, Louisiana, and Missouri. Among these are Richard Lowe, *The Texas Overland Expedition of 1863* (Abilene: McWhiney Foundation Press, 1998); Lowell H. Johnson, *The Red River Campaign: Politics and Cotton in the Civil War* (Baltimore: Johns Hopkins Press, 1958); Edwin C. Bearss, *Steele's Retreat from Camden and the Battle of Jenkins' Ferry* (Little Rock: Arkansas Civil War Centennial Commission, 1967); Mark K.

Christ, ed., *Rugged and Sublime: The Civil War in Arkansas* (Fayetteville: University of Arkansas Press, 1994); Bobby Roberts and Carl Moneyhon, *Portraits of Conflict: A Photographic History of Arkansas in the Civil War* (Fayetteville: University of Arkansas Press, 1987); B. P. Gallaway, *The Rugged Rebel: A Common Soldier in W. H. Parsons' Texas Cavalry, 1861-1865* (Austin: University of Texas Press, 1988); Joseph H. Parks, *General Edmund Kirby Smith, C.S.A.* (Baton Rouge: Louisiana State University Press, 1954); T. Michael Parrish, *Richard Taylor: Prince of Dixie* (Chapel Hill: University of North Carolina Press, 1992); Jeff Kinard, *Lafayette of the South: Prince Camille de Polignac and the American Civil War* (College Station: Texas A&M University Press, 2001); John D. Winters, *The Civil War in Louisiana* (Baton Rouge: Louisiana State University Press, 1963); Stephen B. Oates, *Confederate Cavalry West of the River* (Austin: University of Texas Press, 1961); William R. Brooksher, *War Along the Bayous: The 1864 Red River Campaign in Louisiana* (Washington, DC: Brassey's, 1998); Curt Anders, *Disaster in Deep Sand: The Red River Expedition* (Indianapolis: Guild Press of Indiana, 1997); William L. Shea and Earl J. Hess, *Pea Ridge: Civil War Campaign in the West* (mentioned earlier); William Garrett Piston and Richard Hatcher III, *Wilson's Creek: The Second Battle of the Civil War and the Men Who Fought It* (also cited earlier); William L. Shea, *War in the West: Pea Ridge and Prairie Grove* (Abilene, TX: McWhiney Foundation Press, 1998); and Robert L. Kerby, *Kirby Smith's Confederacy: The Trans-Mississippi South, 1863-1865* (New York: Columbia University Press, 1972).

Numerous works have been written about Arkansas battles and campaigns in which Texas regiments participated. Particularly important is Anne Bailey's *Between the Enemy and Texas* cited above and a series of articles written by her: "A Texas Cavalry Raid: Reaction to Black Soldiers and Contrabands," *Civil War History* 35 (June 1989): 138-152; "Henry McCulloch's Texans and the Defense of Arkansas in 1862," *Arkansas Historical Quarterly* 46 (Spring 1987): 46-59; "Texans Invade Missouri: The Cape Giradeau Raid, 1863," *Missouri Historical Review* 84 (January 1990): 166-187; "The Texas Cavalry's Race to Reinforce Arkansas Post, January 1863," *East Texas Historical Journal* 28 (Spring 1990): 45-56; and "Was There a Massacre at Poison Spring?" *Military History of the Southwest* 20 (Fall 1990): 157-168.

For more on activities by Texans in Arkansas see also William L. Shea, "The Confederate Defeat at Cache River," *Arkansas Historical Quarterly* 52 (Summer 1992): 129-155; Stephen B. Oates, "The Prairie Grove Campaign, 1862," *Arkansas Historical Quarterly* 19 (Summer 1960): 119-141; and Peter Cozzens, "Hindman's Grand Delusion," *Civil War Times Illustrated* 34 (October 2000), 28-35, 66-69.

Articles by Alwyn Barr are most instructive on cavalry and infantry operations in Louisiana. See "Texan Losses in the Red River Campaign, 1864," *Texas Military History* 3 (Summer 1963): 103-110; "The Battle of Blair's Landing," *Louisiana Studies* 2 (Winter 1963): 204-212; "The Battle of Calcasieu Pass," *Southwestern Historical Quarterly* 66 (July 1962): 58-67; and "The Battle of Bayou Bourbeau, November 3, 1863: Colonel Oran M. Roberts' Report," *Louisiana History* 6 (Winter 1965), 83-91.

Additional insights into Texan campaigns in the Bayou Country are offered by Donald S. Frazier, "Texans on the Teche: The Texas Brigade at the Battles of

Bisland and Irish Bend, April 12-14, 1863," *Louisiana History* 32 (Fall 1991): 417-435; Frazier, "The Battle of Texas will be Fought in Louisiana: The Assault on Fort Butler, June 28, 1863," *Southwestern Historical Quarterly* 104 (January 2001): 334-362; Stephen S. Michot, "In Relief of Port Hudson: Richard Taylor's 1863 Lafourche Offensive," *Military History of the West* 23 (Fall 1993): 103-117; L. Boyd Finch, "Surprise at Brashear City: Sherod Hunter's Sugar Cooler Cavalry," *Louisiana History* 26 (Fall 1974): 413-434; James T. Matthews, "A Time for Desperate Valor: The Confederate Attack on Fort Butler, Louisiana, 1863," *Military History of the West* 26 (Spring 1996), 23-34; and David C. Edmonds, "Surrender on the Bourbeau: Honorable Defeat or Incompetency Under Fire," *Louisiana History* 18 (Winter 1977): 63-86.

Max S. Lale adds information on the Red River campaign in his articles "New Light on the Battle of Mansfield," *East Texas Historical Journal* 25 (Fall 1987): 34-41, and "For Lack of A Nail . . ." *ibid.* 30 (Spring 1992): 34-43. Fredericka Ann Meiners, "Hamilton P. Bee in the Red River Campaign," *Southwestern Historical Quarterly* 78 (July 1974): 21-44 defends Bee's decision to withdraw his Texas cavalry from Monett's Ferry in 1864.

Thomas Reid, *Captain Jack and the Tyler County Boys: A History of Company K, 13th Texas Cavalry Regiment, CSA* (Woodville, TX: priv. printed, 2000), provides much information on the role of the Thirteenth Texas Cavalry in the Louisiana campaigns. Reid's master's thesis on the Thirteenth Cavalry, being completed at Lamar University, will provide a full account of this regiment.

Some Texas cavalry and infantry spent most of the war either in Indian Territory or in Texas itself. Unfortunately there has been comparatively little published about these units. Bill Winsor, *Texas in the Confederacy: Military Installlations, Economy, and People* (Hillsboro: Hill Junior College Press, 1978) is helpful in locating various camps where Texas regiments were trained or stationed. David Paul Smith, *Frontier Defense in the Civil War: Texas' Rangers and Rebels* (College Station: Texas A&M University Press, 1992), provides a good description of the complex organizational structure in which Confederate and state troops worked in dealing with Union invaders, jayhawkers, deserters, and dissenters. John C. Waugh, *Sam Bell Maxey and the Confederate Indians* (Fort Worth: Ryan Place Publishers, 1995) and Louise Horton, *Samuel Bell Maxey: A Biography* (Austin: University of Texas Press, 1974) describe the efforts of Sam Maxey to bring a measure of stability and order to Indian Territory. Lary C. and Donald L. Rampp, *The Civil War in Indian Territory* (Austin: Presidial Press, 1995) is the most satisfactory overview of Confederate operations in Indian Territory. Considerable information on Texas cavalry is also found in Alvin M. Josephy, Jr., *The Civil War in the American West* (New York: Alfred A. Knopf, 1991).

Marvin J. Hancock, "The Second Battle of Cabin Creek: 1864," *Chronicles of Oklahoma* 39 (Winter 1963): 414-426, describes one of the most important victories won by Stand Watie's Indians and Richard Gano's Texans. Several articles are devoted to Confederate and state efforts to deal with Indian raiders, both real and imagined. See David Paul Smith, "The Elm Creek Raid, 1864: State and Confederate Defense and Response," *Military History of the Southwest* 19 (Fall 1989): 121-136; Kenneth Neighbours, "Elm Creek Raid in Young County, 1864," *West Texas Historical Association Year Book* 40 (October 1964): 80-89; J. Marvin

Hunter, "The Battle of Dove Creek," *ibid.* 18 (October 1942): 74-87; William C. Pool, "The Battle of Dove Creek," *Southwestern Historical Quarterly* 53 (April 1950): 367-385; Jerry M. Roth, "Civil War Defense Challenges in Northwest Texas," *Military History of the West* 30 (Spring 2000): 21-44.

The efforts of a controversial but effective regimental commander to deal with frontier problems are described by Richard B. McCaslin, "Dark Corner of the Confederacy: James G. Bourland and the Border Regiment," *Military History of the West* 24 (Spring 1994): 57-70. McCaslin, *Tainted Breeze: The Great Hanging at Gainesville, Texas* (Baton Rouge: Louisiana State University Press, 1994) and David Pickering and Judy Falls, *Brush Men & Vigilantes: Civil War Dissent in Texas* (College Station: Texas A&M University Press, 2000) provide additional glimpses of the Border Regiment.

Defense of the Texas coast involved many of the cavalry and infantry regiments that fought in Louisiana. The best overall description of these efforts is Alwyn Barr, "Texas Coastal Defense, 1861-1865," *Southwestern Historical Quarterly* 65 (July 1961): 1-31. See also Norman Delaney, "Corpus Christi —The Vicksburg of Texas," *Civil War Times Illustrated* 16 (July 1977): 4-9, 44-48; Lester N. Fitzhugh, "Saluria, Fort Esperanza, and Military Operations on the Texas Coast, 1861-1864," *Southwestern Historical Quarterly* 61 (July 1957): 66-100. W. T. Block in his book *A History of Jefferson County, Texas From Wilderness to Reconstruction* (Nederland: Nederland Printing Company, 1976) and a series of articles in the October 1971 issue of the *East Texas Historical Journal* provide insights relating to the defense of the upper Texas coast.

Rip Ford's Texas, ed. Stephen B. Oates (Austin: University of Texas Press, 1963) contains much information on Texas regiments operating in South Texas. See also Oates, "John S. 'Rip' Ford: Prudent Cavalryman, C. S. A.," *Southwestern Historical Quarterly* 64 (January 1961): 289-314; Oates, "Texas Under the Secessionists," *ibid.* 67 (October 1963): 167-212; and W. J. Hughes, *Rebellious Ranger: Rip Ford and the Old Southwest* (Norman: University of Oklahoma Press, 1964).

Jerry Don Thompson, the premier authority on fighting along the Rio Grande, has written several works (in addition to his biographies of Sibley and Baylor cited earlier) which detail operations of Texas regiments in South Texas. See his *Vaqueros in Blue & Gray* (Austin: Presidial Press, 1976); *Sabers on the Rio Grande* (Austin: Presidial Press, 1974); "A Stand Along the Border: Santos Benavides and the Battle for Laredo," *Civil War Times Illustrated* 19 (August 1980): 26-33; and *A Wild and Vivid Land: An Illustrated History of the South Texas Border* (Austin: Texas State Historical Association, 1998).

Alwyn Barr's "Confederate Artillery in the Trans-Mississippi" (M. A. thesis, University of Texas, 1961) is the best single source for Texas artillery operations. Barr also has written a series of articles that contain much material on Texas batteries. See his "Texas' Confederate Field Artillery," *Texas Military History* 1 (August 1961): 1-8; "Confederate Field Artillery in Arkansas," *Arkansas Historical Quarterly* 22 (Autumn 1963): 238-272; "Confederate Artillery in Western Louisiana, 1862-1863," *Civil War History* 9 (March 1963): 74-85; and "Confederate Artillery in Western Louisiana, 1864," *Louisiana History* 5 (Winter 1964): 53-74.

The Battle of Sabine Pass, September 1863, was essentially an artillery duel. Works describing the battle contain considerable information relating to Company F, First Texas Heavy Artillery Regiment, known locally as the Davis Guards.

In addition to the works by W. T. Block cited above, see Andrew Forest Muir, "Dick Dowling and the Battle of Sabine Pass," *Civil War History* 4 (December 1958): 399-428; Ernest Jones, "The Battle of Sabine Pass, September 8, 1863," *Blue & Gray Magazine* 4 (September 1986), 19-24, 47-48, 50-53; Alwyn Barr, "Sabine Pass, September 1863," *Texas Military History* 2 (February 1962): 17-22; H. L. Sandefer and Archie P. McDonald, "Sabine Pass: David and Goliath," *Texana* 7 (Fall 1969): 177-188; Frank X. Tolbert, *Dick Dowling at Sabine Pass* (New York: McGraw-Hill, 1962).

W. T. Block, ed., "The Memoirs of Captain Kosciuszko D. Keith," *Texas Gulf Historical and Biographical Records* 10 (November 1974): 41-64, provides information on Company B of Spaight's Battalion, an artillery battery that served at Sabine Pass. Lester N. Fitzhugh's article "Saluria, Fort Esperanza, and Military Operations on the Texas Coast, 1861-1864," cited earlier, contains insights on artillery operations along the middle Texas coast.

The Good-Douglas Battery, which saw extensive service on both sides of the Mississippi, is described by Lucia Rutherford Douglas, compiler and editor, *Douglas's Texas Battery, CSA* (Waco: Texian Press, 1966), and Lester N. Fitzhugh, compiler and editor, *Cannon Smoke: The Letters of Captain John J. Good, Good-Douglas Battery, CSA* (Hillsboro: Hill Junior College Press, 1971).

The Valverde Battery, which was formed by using Union cannon captured at the Battle of Valverde, is described by P. D. Browne, "Captain T. D. Nettles and the Valverde Battery," *Texana* 2 (Spring 1964): 1-23. General artillery operations in the New Mexico campaign are discussed in works by Don Alberts, Martin H. Hall, and John Taylor cited earlier in reference to Sibley's Brigade. Alberts, *Battle of Glorieta*, 187n, provides a particularly incisive description of the various types of artillery used in that campaign.

John D. Perkins, *Daniel's Battery: The Ninth Texas Field Battery* (Hillsboro: Hill College Press, 1998) is a model study which utilizes socio-economic data to provide an in-depth look at an important Texas military unit. Studies such as this are most helpful in understanding the role played in the war by Texas regiments and batteries.

Index

—C—

—H—

—M—

—P—

—Q—

—R—

—S—

—U—